How to Prepare for SAT II:

Literature

Christina Myers-Shaffer, M. Ed.

Second Edition

BARRON'S

All inquiries should be addressed to:
Barron's Educational Series, Inc.
250 Wireless Boulevard
Hauppauge, NY 11788-3917
http://www.barronseduc.com

Library of Congress Catalog Card No. 99-31976

International Standard Book No. 0-7641-0769-0

Library of Congress Cataloging-in-Publication Data

Myers-Shaffer, Christina.
  How to prepare for SAT II. Literature / by Christina
Myers-Shaffer. — 2nd ed.
    p. cm.
  Includes index.
  ISBN 0-7641-0769-0
  1. Literature—Examinations—Study guides.
2. Scholastic Assessment Test—Study guides.
I. Title.   II. Title: Literature.
PN62.M94 2000
820'.76—dc21   99-31976
                                                    CIP

PRINTED IN THE UNITED STATES OF AMERICA
9 8 7 6 5 4 3

ACKNOWLEDGMENTS

The author gratefully acknowledges the following copyright holders for permission to reprint material used in this publication:

Pages 22–23 and 27: From *The Life of Samuel Johnson, LL.D.* (1964) by J. Boswell. Reprinted by permission of McGraw-Hill, Inc.

Page 33: Excerpt from *Babbitt* by Sinclair Lewis. © 1922 by Harcourt Brace & Company and renewed 1950 by Sinclair Lewis, reprinted by permission of the publisher.

Pages 38–39: From "The Use of Force" from *William Carlos Williams: Doctor Stories.* © 1938 William Carlos Williams. Reprinted by permission of New Directions Publishing Corp.

Pages 58–59: From *Nobody Ever Died of Old Age* by Sharon R. Curtain. © 1972 by Sharon R. Curtain. By permission of Little, Brown and Company.

Page 62: Reprinted by permission of Diana Townsend-Butterworth, author of *Your Child's First School* (Walker, 1992). Excerpted from "Are You a Good Role Model?" *Family Circle* magazine, February, 1995.

Page 62: From "Surviving a Disaster—Together" by Loraine Stern, M.D. © 1995. As published in *Woman's Day* magazine January 10, 1995.

Page 62: From "It's Not Just the Thought" by Shirley Redmond as published in *Woman's Day* magazine January 10, 1995.

Page 66: Preface from *I Love Paul Revere, Whether He Rode Or Not* by Richard Shenkman. © 1991 by Richard Shenkman. Reprinted by permission of HarperCollins Publishers, Inc.

Page 108: From "Pied Beauty" from *Poems of Gerard Manley Hopkins* by Gerard Manley Hopkins. Reprinted with permission of Oxford University Press.

Page 111: Reprinted with permission of Simon & Schuster from *The Steel Albatross* by Scott Carpenter. © 1990 by Scott Carpenter.

Page 112: From "Barn Burning," *Collected Stories of William Faulkner* © 1939 by William Faulkner. Reprinted by permission of Random House, Inc.

Page 119: From *Twenty-Five Years: Reminiscences* (1913) by Katharine Tynan. Reprinted by permission of John Murray Ltd.

Page 139: Reprinted with permission of Simon & Schuster, Inc. from *The Autobiography of William Butler Yeats.* Copyright 1936 by Macmillan Publishing Company; copyright renewed 1964 by Bertha Georgie Yeats.

Page 145: This material is taken from *Our Daily Times With God,* © 1988 by Radio Bible Class. Used by permission of Discovery House Publishers, Box 3566, Grand Rapids, MI 49501. All rights reserved.

Pages 159–160 and 193: Reprinted by permission of The Putnam Publishing Group from *Dead Man's Folly* by Agatha Christie. © 1956 by Agatha Christie Limited.

Page 173: Excerpt from *The Great Code* © 1982, 1981 by Northrop Frye. Reprinted with permission of Harcourt Brace & Company.

Page 172: Excerpt from *Words With Power* © 1990 by Northrop Frye. Reprinted with permission of Harcourt Brace & Company.

Page 179: From "Virga Vay & Allan Cedar" from *Cass Timberlane,* copyright 1945 by Sinclair Lewis. Reprinted by permission of Random House, Inc.

Page 182: Excerpt from *Silent Spring* by Rachel Carson. Copyright © 1962 by Rachel L. Carson. Copyright renewed 1990 by Roger Christie. Reprinted by permission of Houghton Mifflin Co. All rights reserved.

Page 193: By permission. From *The Merriam-Webster Dictionary* © 1997 by Merriam-Webster Inc.

Page 203: Reprinted with the permission of Scribner, a division of Simon & Schuster, from "Liberty Hall" in *Round Up* by Ring Lardner. Copyright 1928 Ellis A. Lardner; copyright renewed 1956 Ellis A. Lardner.

Page 232: Excerpt from a letter from the Lady Mary Wortley Montagu to her daughter. *Montagu's Complete Letters,* edited by Robert Halsbend (Oxford University, 1965–1967).

Page 249: Excerpt from "Coster-Lads" by Henry Mayhew, from *Triumph of Style* by John R. Knott, Jr., and Reeve Parker, © 1969 by Houghton Mifflin Company.

Page 252: "An Encounter with Honey Bees" by Lillian E. Myers © 1999 by Lillian E. Myers. Reprinted by permission of Lillian E. Myers. All rights reserved.

Page 264: "The Introduction," by Anne Finch. From *The Norton Anthology of Literature by Women: The Tradition* in English by Sandra M. Gilbert and Susan Guber. Copyright © 1985 by Sandra M. Gilbert and Susan Guber. Reprint courtesy of W. W. Norton & Company, Inc.

Page 361: Excerpt from "The Sojourner," *The Ballad of the Sad Cafe and Collected Short Stories* by Carson McCullers. Copyright 1936, 1941, 1942, 1950, © 1955 by Carson McCullers. Copyright © renewed 1979 by Floria V. Lasky. Reprinted by permission of Houghton Mifflin Co. All rights reserved.

Excerpts from *Clerihew* (page 92) and *Triolet* (page 95) from *The New Princeton Encyclopedia of Poetry and Poetics* © 1993, Alex Preminger and T.V.F. Brogan co-editors. Reprinted by permission of Princeton University Press.

"Bell-tones" (page 58), "Pity the Poor Raccoon" (page 82), "Know Yourself" (page 84), "Alphabet Soup" (page 93), "Stressed and Unstressed" (pages 77–78), "Is It Euphemism or Euphony?" (page 192), and "That Sound" (page 93) by Lillian E. Myers © 1996 by Lillian E. Myers. Reprinted by permission of Lillian E. Myers. All rights reserved.

Excerpt from *The Wordsworth Companion to Literature in English,* edited by Ian Ousby (Cambridge University Press, 1994). Reprinted with the permission of Cambridge University Press.

Every effort has been made to trace the copyright holders and we apologize in advance for any unintentional omissions. We would be pleased to insert the appropriate acknowledgment in any subsequent edition of this publication.

In preparing to take the SAT II: Literature Subject Test, use this book for...

Review

This book reviews:

- Developing a study plan for taking the test
- The basics of literary analysis
- Basic literary terminology (definitions, uses, and effects)
- Vocabulary

Practice

This book contains:

- Two complete diagnostic tests (60 multiple-choice questions each) with an analysis of each correct answer choice
- Sample questions that cover each of the seven literary elements
- Three interpretive skill practice sets that cover each of the seven literary elements
- Seven complete practice tests (60 multiple-choice questions each)
- A Plan for Writing to Learn the Literary Elements

Reference

This book is a resource for definitions and examples of literary terminology (ranging from basic to advanced) to use in:

- High school literature classes
- College literature classes
- Independent reading and study
- Study groups
- Papers analyzing prose, poetry, and drama

Advancement

This book aims to increase:

- Your skills for taking the test
- Your pleasure in reading
- Your range of reading materials
- Your reading comprehension
- Your analysis skills
- Your writing skills

CONTENTS

PART IV INTERPRETIVE SKILL PRACTICE

PART V PRACTICE TESTS

INTRODUCTION

How to Prepare for SAT II: Literature gives you information you need to develop and improve your reading skills in preparing to take the SAT II: Literature test. The book is a study, reference, and test-prep guide that can be used in many individualized ways, depending upon your available time and personal levels of interest. It is a functional book with different purposes for different sections. Consequently, you will want to decide on a way to use the book that suits your individual needs.

Following are three different ways to use *How to Prepare for SAT II: Literature* to help you find and realize your study goals. "Basic Preparation" is an easy and quick step-by-step reference guide. This guide is followed by a brief discussion of using the book for personal achievement in relation to the SAT II: Literature test and a list of suggested ways the book can be used in your literature classes.

BASIC PREPARATION

In addition to the basic preparation given above,

PERSONAL ACHIEVEMENT (IN RELATION TO THE SAT II: LITERATURE TEST)

Do you enjoy reading? Do you feel a little rush of excitement when you read a poem or story and your mind races with the ideas presented because you *really* understand what the writer is trying to say? Then use the insights and information given throughout the book to help you gain even greater reading comprehension.

Do you enjoy writing? Do you feel a little rush of excitement when you read a poem or story because your mind races with ideas of the poem *you* would like to express or the story *you* would like to tell? Would you like to improve your reading comprehension for the SAT II: Literature test and, at the same time, learn how to use the literary elements from a writer's perspective? If you would, turn to the "Writing to Learn" section and read pages 228–233.

Select an exercise to accomplish, and turn to the appropriate section within pages 234–266 for help in developing your reading/writing exercise.

You will find a review of "The Seven Major Steps of a Writing to Learn Activity" on pages 267–268.

YOUR LITERATURE CLASSES

The College Board recommends that, to prepare to take the SAT II: Literature test, you should engage in a study of English and American literature that involves several genres (poetry, prose, and drama) and literary periods (Renaissance through the twentieth century). Your reading should be from a critical perspective and your study program may take from one to several years.

Literature classes are a logical place for you to gain experience studying literature of different genres and periods and to engage in analyzing literature to increase your reading skills.

You will find background information (given throughout the book) that is helpful to the study of literature. For example, the discussion of historical references and cultural influences in literature (pages 20–28), the analysis of rhythm, rhyme, and physical form as a means of expression in poetry (pages 76–96), and the examination of early dramatic stage productions (pages 99–106) can help

you gain new perspectives as you read literature. Viewing literature in the context in which it was written will give you insight into the cause-and-effect relationships that exist in literary works and how these relationships influence what they mean. Also, you can use the background information to gain better understanding of what you read *about* works of literature.

Perhaps you are writing an analysis of a poem for your literature class. You may discover in the library a book that contains an analysis in which the critic examines the poet's use of language. You can use pages 165–192 of *How to Prepare for SAT II: Literature* to help you understand the analysis and to develop your own analysis. Also, take note of the details included in the background information. You might find, as an example, that the writer analyzing the poem you are reading refers to the poet's use of simile as a "figure of thought." If you read the discussion of figurative language on page 167 in *How to Prepare for SAT II: Literature,* you will discover that a simile is considered a "figure of speech" today.

This book can be used in the following ways as a valuable resource for use in your literature classes.

1. The Literary Elements Chapters ("Interpretive Skills and Critical Reading," pages 55–206) should be used as a literary reference source for anything requiring you to analyze, discuss, or understand literary terms or concepts, such as writing literary analysis papers, preparing literary presentations, and developing special literary projects. Also, you can use the index to locate discussions and illustrations of specific literary terms given throughout the book.
2. "Putting the Seven Literary Elements to Work" (pages 207–227) is a step-by-step guide that gives you a variety of approaches to use to analyze a work of literature, to understand your reading assignments better, and to write literary analysis papers.
3. "A Quick Reference Guide to the Seven Literary Elements" (pages 225–227) can be used to help you keep the literary elements in mind during class discussions and as you write about or read literary selections.
4. "Writing to Learn" (pages 228–268) can be used to develop an independent project or perhaps a semester project in conjunction with your literature or writing classes.

PART I

THE SAT PROGRAM

College Entrance
Examinations

SAT II: Literature
Subject Test

Developing an
Individualized
Study Program

COLLEGE ENTRANCE EXAMINATIONS

The College Board, headquartered in Princeton, New Jersey, administers the SAT Program. The two main categories of tests that comprise the SAT Program are the SAT I: Reasoning Test and the SAT II: Subject Tests. The results of these tests are used by educational counselors, student-placement personnel, and scholarship committees, among others, to assist students in their postsecondary academic careers.

SAT I: REASONING TEST

As its name implies, the SAT I measures your mathematical and verbal reasoning abilities. It consists of three verbal sections, three mathematical sections, and one noncounted section that can be either verbal or mathematical, for a total of seven sections. The results of the SAT I: Reasoning Test provide a comparative measure of your preparation and abilities to those of other students. Your score is used in conjunction with your high school grades, activities, class rank, and other factors (depending upon the require-

ments of the particular institution) to provide you and a wide range of academic professionals with a picture of how you have done, an idea of how you are doing, and most significantly a basis for projection of how you are likely to do in a postsecondary setting.

SAT II: SUBJECT TESTS

The Subject Tests that you need to take will be determined by such factors as the requirements of the postsecondary institution to which you are planning to apply and what subject areas are likely to be significant to your personal academic plan. Your academic counselor should be able to assist you in these areas. As with the SAT I, the Subject Tests of SAT II are used in conjunction with many other factors for admission (both to postsecondary institutions and to programs within those schools), for predicting future performance, for placing students within programs, and for guiding them in their academic choices.

SAT II: LITERATURE SUBJECT TEST

The SAT II: Literature Subject Test is one of the Subject Tests (Achievement Tests) administered by the College Board.

THE COLLEGE BOARD

Students can ask questions and request materials concerning the SAT Program by writing to:

College Board SAT Program
P.O. Box 6200
Princeton, NJ 08541-6200
or by calling: 609-771-7600 (8 A.M. to 9:45 P.M. Eastern Time) Monday–Friday.

You may, however, find one of the College Board's regional offices more convenient. Use the following chart to find the address and phone number for your region.

Your State	*College Board Regional Office*
New England: Maine, Vermont, New Hampshire, Massachusetts, Connecticut, Rhode Island	470 Totten Pond Road Waltham, MA 02154-1982 (781) 890-9150
Middle States: New York, Pennsylvania, New Jersey, Delaware, Maryland, District of Columbia	Suite 410, 3440 Market Street Philadelphia, PA 19104-3338 (215) 387-7600
Midwest: North Dakota, South Dakota, Nebraska, Kansas, Minnesota, Missouri, Iowa, Wisconsin, Illinois, Michigan, West Virginia, Ohio, Indiana	One Rotary Center Suite 1001, 1560 Sherman Avenue Evanston, IL 60201-4805 (708) 866-1700
South: Kentucky, Tennessee, Virginia, North Carolina, South Carolina, Georgia, Alabama, Mississippi, Louisiana, Florida	100 Crescent Centre Parkway, Suite 340 Tucker, GA 30084 (770) 908-9737
West: Washington, Idaho, Oregon, Montana, Wyoming, California, Nevada, Utah, Colorado, Arizona, (Hawaii and Alaska use California address)	Suite 480, 2099 Gateway Place San Jose, CA 95110-1017 (408) 452-1400

Your State	*College Board Regional Office*
Southwest: New Mexico, Oklahoma, Texas, Arkansas	Suite 200, 4330 South MoPac Expressway Austin, TX 78735 (512) 891-8400
Puerto Rico	Suite 1501, Popular Center Building Hato Rey, Puerto Rico 00918 (787) 759-8625
Mailing address:	P.O. Box 71101 San Juan, Puerto Rico 00936-8001

FEES AND REGISTRATION

To obtain a registration form and information concerning how to register for the SAT II: Literature Subject Test, contact the College Board and request the *Registration Bulletin;* or you may be able to get a copy from the guidance or counseling offices of your local high school.

The Literature Subject Test is generally administered several times each year, and you may take up to three different Subject Tests on a test day. Although you are expected to preregister for specific Subject Tests, you may, on the day of the test, add or delete from the Subject Tests being given on that day.

Fees include both a Basic Registration/Reporting Fee (the fee is for your scores to be reported to colleges or scholarship programs, if you have specified these places by the test day) and a per test fee that is charged for each Subject Test you choose to take on that day.

Again, contact the College Board and obtain the most current issue of the *Registration Bulletin* for the latest information concerning test dates, preregistration, the fee structure, and other such details.

THE LITERATURE TEST FORMAT

As with most of the SAT II: Subject Tests, the Literature Subject Test is entirely multiple-choice, expected to take about one hour to administer.

Here are some of the key features concerning the structure and content of the Literature Subject Test.

The Literature Test does:

- Attempt to measure your skills in reading literature
- Contain from six to eight reading selections
- Ask about 60 multiple-choice questions based on those reading selections
- Require extended verbal abilities, particularly in reading comprehension and figurative language
- Contain selections from English and American prose, poetry, and drama written during the Renaissance through the twentieth century (Some selections other than English or American but written in English and some selections other than prose, poetry, or drama might be included.)
- Ask from four to twelve questions per selection
- Ask questions about MEANING, FORM, NARRATIVE VOICE, TONE, CHARACTER, USE OF LANGUAGE, AND MEANING(S) IN CONTEXT
- Require a knowledge of basic literary terminology
- Include selections that are complete short works or excerpts from longer works

THE SELECTIONS ON THE LITERATURE TEST

Source:	0	10	20	30	40	50	60	70	80	90	100 %

English	|||||||||||||||||||||////
American	|||||||||||||||||||||////
Other	////

Century:	0	10	20	30	40	50	60	70	80	90	100 %

16th–17th	||||||||||||
18th–19th	||||||||||||
20th	|||||||||||||||

Genre:	0	10	20	30	40	50	60	70	80	90	100 %

Prose	|||||||||||||||||||||||//
Poetry	|||||||||||||||||||||||//
Drama	////

The individual selections might be, for example, taken from nineteenth-century American prose, sixteenth-century English drama, twentieth-century poetry written in English by a South African, and so forth. The percentage distributions shown in these graphs, however, represent averages and may—or may not—be reflected in any given test. (The slanted lines represent variable numbers. For example, a test may contain 40 to 50 percent selections from English literature.)

The Literature Test does *not*:

- Include test questions about literary periods, authors' biographies, or literary criticism
- Require preknowledge of selections on the test
- Require you to study a specified reading list

DEVELOPING AN INDIVIDUALIZED STUDY PROGRAM

The Sat II: Literature Subject Test is primarily a test to measure your *skills* in understanding literature. Developing such skills—or as in this case, groups of interdependent skills—requires an understanding of yourself (how *you* learn), an understanding of the test (what is expected of you), and a strategy (a plan to use this understanding of yourself and of the test to your advantage). Also, this plan should incorporate both a long-term perspective and a short-term perspective that takes into account the practical mechanics of taking a test.

A fundamental first step, then, in preparing to take the SAT II: Literature Subject Test is for you to design a study program that is individualized to capitalize on your strengths and to overcome your weaknesses. What follows is a four-step guide to developing such a plan that will be appropriate for you.

STEP 1. LEARN ABOUT YOURSELF.

How do you normally prepare for a skills test? What would you consider to be your most effective study methods? Make a list of the ways that you have used successfully in the past to prepare to take tests. Evaluate each method to see if it would be practical for you in preparing to take the SAT II: Literature test.

In addition, consider some of the following ideas to help you prepare:

Include a sound diet, adequate rest, and proper exercise in your study plan. These healthy habits can improve test performance.

Include some "time off" periods for relaxation when you are studying. Giving your mind a chance to relax periodically can help you think clearly and learn faster.

Develop an organized plan of action for preparing to take the test. An organized plan can include

a. identifying what skills you need to learn,

b. finding ways to practice those skills and to evaluate periodically how you are doing, and

c. establishing goals and a time schedule (what you want to accomplish by what dates).

NOTE: Turn to the Introduction on pages viii–ix for a plan of action using Barron's *How to Prepare for SAT II: Literature.*

Reward yourself when you do well and enjoy your study time. A good attitude toward what you are studying enhances learning. Reading literature can be a very enjoyable activity. Also, try adding some entertaining projects that you can look forward to in your study plan, such as watching the movie version of a book you have read. Is the movie version different from the story in the book? Why do you think the changes were made? Identifying such changes are part of understanding how the literary elements can be used. Look for literature-based games on the market, or perhaps you would enjoy developing your own games aimed at improving reading skills and understanding literary works. There are many ways you can get excited about what you are studying.

Concentrate on learning new information and skills. Taking the diagnostic and practice tests such as those in *How to Prepare for SAT II: Literature* can help you determine what concepts you have already mastered. Another way for you to know whether you really understand a concept is to explain it to someone else. How would you explain what a *simile* is, for example, to another student or to a younger brother or sister? Are you able to explain clearly to someone else what the meaning of a given line of poetry is? Your literature classes may give you opportunities for this type of practice.

STEP 2. LEARN ABOUT THE TEST.

The SAT II: Literature Subject Test consists of about 60 multiple-choice questions, with five answer choices (A through E) for each question. The question stem might be worded in two ways:

1. As a question, such as "What is the MEANING of 'establishment' as it is used in line 2?"

2. As an incomplete sentence, such as "The vehicle of the metaphor in line 3 is"

There are three different kinds of multiple-choice questions that may appear on the test:

1. Regular multiple-choice questions

What is the speaker's attitude? (Question stem)

(A) Angry   (A through E answer choices)
(B) Raucous
(C) Profane
(D) Morbid
(E) Defensive

Someone once compared the regular multiple-choice question to a series of five true-false questions because essentially you are examining each answer choice to see if it is true or false. Usually, the true answer choice is the correct one. In these questions, however, you may encounter more than one answer choice that is to some degree true or correct, in which case you would select the answer choice that is best.

2. NOT or EXCEPT questions

All the following appear in lines 1–4 EXCEPT
(A) personification
(B) simile
(C) metaphor
(D) paradox
(E) apostrophe
Which of the following uses of language does NOT appear in lines 1–4?
(A) Personification
(B) Simile
(C) Metaphor
(D) Paradox
(E) Apostrophe

Some test questions might contain the words EXCEPT, LEAST, or NOT. In these questions, you are looking for the response that does not apply to the situation or that is inappropriate to the question stem—just the opposite of a regular multiple-choice question.

3. Roman numeral questions

In this passage, the rose is
 I. an emblem
 II. a vehicle for metaphor
 III. an allegorical representation
(A) I only   (B) II only   (C) I and III only
(D) II and III only   (E) I, II, and III

Sometimes, because the literary elements involve many different perspectives (especially figurative language), a question will test your skills in recognizing multiple MEANINGS and different perspectives. In these questions, you will be given several possible statements that are labeled with Roman numerals and the answer choices will present either individual statements or combinations of statements as possible correct answer choices. In this case, you are to evaluate each statement, decide which statement or statements are correct, then select the answer choice that contains the Roman numeral(s) of these correct or most appropriate statement(s).

The practice tests in this book will provide you some opportunity to work with each of these three different types of multiple-choice questions. Here are a few tips to keep in mind:

- Read through all the answer choices—do not stop when you reach the "correct" answer. Reason: Answer Choice B, for example, may indeed be "correct"; however, in multiple-choice questions you may be looking for the answer that is most accurate among more than one "correct" answer. You may later find that Answer Choice E is a better answer than B!
- After you read through all the answer choices, eliminate all those that are clearly not the correct answer choice.
- Compare those answer choices that are left, taking close note of key words in the question stem, including requirements such as "What is the effect…"
- Some testing authorities recommend that if you cannot decide on a final answer, continue with the next question, then return if time allows.
- Keep in mind that:
  1. You get one point for each correct answer.
  2. You lose one-fourth of one point for each wrong answer.
  3. Omitted questions and questions for which you mark more than one answer choice are not counted.

About Test Questions...

In order to prepare for the SAT II: Literature Subject Test, you need to develop reading comprehension skills. The test is designed to measure how well you understand literary selections, recognize the ways in which the seven literary elements are used within those selections, and understand the effects of those uses.

Naturally, a general knowledge of the ways in which test questions can be asked is helpful because familiarity with format can increase your sense of confidence and enable you to focus on understanding the contents of the test selections without the distraction of an unfamiliar question structure. The premise upon which this book is written, however, is that, once acquainted with a variety of possible test question formats, the student preparing to take the SAT II: Literature Subject Test should focus test preparation time and effort on increasing comprehension skills.

By this time, students preparing to take the SAT II: Literature Subject Test are probably already familiar with many of the perspectives from which questions might be asked. Here are a few such perspectives:

1. A question might directly ask the student to identify a literary device, a word MEANING, or some other directly stated identification. In such questions, the answer choices would be lists of terms or definitions. For example, you might have to recognize that "the car coughed, groaned, and winked its lights" is personification or that a "parley" is a discussion.
2. A question might indirectly test your knowledge of literary devices or word MEANINGS by asking you to select the effects their use has in the work. The personification of the car in the above example might make the car seem cute or comic, whereas the connotations surrounding use of the word "parley" might suggest conflict between the people speaking. How it is used in CONTEXT is the key.
3. Another way in which direct understanding of material can be indirectly tested is by asking questions concerning how use of one literary element affects another. Again, in the personified car illustration, a USE OF LANGUAGE has the effect of making the car seem cute or comic. You might be asked to recognize that this contributes to making the TONE of the entire work seem frivolous.
4. Part of reading comprehension is understanding relationships and, as such, is a very significant test perspective. Questions might ask you to recognize contrasts of parts or ideas, sequences or progressions of thought, parallelisms in constructions or ideas, and the roles of connotation in these relationships, to name a few.

How might these questions be worded? The possibilities vary with the literary works upon which they are based. As can be seen, then, an effective way to prepare for the SAT II: Literature Subject Test is to focus on learning the basics of literary analysis and developing reading comprehension skills so that you understand the selec-

tion's MEANING, the literary devices used, and their effects, regardless of how the test questions are asked.

This book is designed with the goal of helping you develop these skills so that you will increase your test-taking skills and build your confidence based on understanding reading selections. As a result, although the question formats of the diagnostic and practice tests that follow are aligned to the question structures (EXCEPT/LEAST/NOT, regular multiple-choice, and Roman numeral) that are already familiar to most test takers and that are identified by the College Board as being used in the SAT II: Literature Subject Test, the wording of the questions does not model after any particular tests. The questions and their answer choices in the diagnostic and practice tests in this book are governed by the selections and the evidence of the literary elements as they are used in those selections and serve to illustrate and provide practice in working with questions worded from different perspectives. Obviously, however, to achieve the goal of increasing your test-taking and reading comprehension skills, it is necessary to use some traditional words and phrases (such as "the CONTEXT of," "the effects of," references to contrasts and relationships, and others) that are so essential to the MEANING of the selections.

About Vocabulary

The importance of enlarging your vocabulary cannot be overstated. *Students have made incorrect answer choices on questions they might have otherwise answered correctly because they did not understand the MEANING of a word used in the question stem or answer choices.*

In understanding and discussing works of literature, vocabulary can be divided into the following four areas:

1. Basic literary terms and related vocabulary
2. Advanced literary terms and related vocabulary
3. Extensive, general vocabulary
4. Period vocabulary and poetic diction

What you need to know in each of the four areas
1. Basic Literary Terms and Related Vocabulary

You should be able to recognize and understand basic literary terms and their uses for taking the SAT II: Literature test. Part III ("Interpretive Skills and Critical Reading") in this book contains definitions and illustrations of basic literary terms.

Not everyone agrees on which literary terms are "basic." You should, however, be able to define and identify at least the following literary terms and their related vocabulary (grouped by literary element). Refer to the Index for additional pages.

Literary Element: MEANING
(Terms found on pages 61–67)

Types of purpose
  descriptive/expressive
  expository/informative
  narrative
  argumentative
  persuasive
Levels of meaning
  literal
  allegorical
  symbolic
  figurative
Theme
Motif   (page 23)
Thesis
Paraphrase

Literary element: FORM
Prose (Terms found on pages 69–75)

Sequence
  chronological sequence
  climactic order
  deductive order
  inductive order
  problem-solving sequence
  spatial sequence
  topical order
  mixed order
Organizing principles
  analogy
  cause and effect
  comparison/contrast
  definition
  description
  analysis and classification
  example
  induction
  deduction
  narration
  process (analysis)
Structure
Genre
Essay
Biography

Autobiography
  diaries
  journals
  letters
  memoirs
  confessions
Novel
Novelette
Short story
Anecdote
Narrative plot (prose)
  exposition
  complication
  conflict
  climax
  resolution
Tragedy
Comedy
Satire
Romance
Realism
Tale
Tall tale
Fable
Folktale
Parable

Poetry (Terms found on pages 76–96)

Rhythm
Rhyme scheme
Prose (in contrast)
Prose poetry
Free verse
Qualitative verse
Stanza
Epic poetry
Dramatic poetry
Lyric poetry
Dramatic monologue
Elegy
Ode
Sonnet
Haiku
Hymns
Songs
Ballads
Light verse
Parody
Limerick
Epigram
Epigraph
Concrete poetry

Acrostic poetry
Riddles
Satire

Drama (Terms found on pages 96–109)

Narrative plot (drama)
   exposition/introduction
   conflict/exciting force
   rising action/complication
   climax/crisis/turning point
   falling action
   resolution/dénouement
Foreshadowing
Flashbacks
Intrigue
Suspense
Surprise
Discovery
Monologue
Soliloquy
Scenes
Tragedy
Comedy
Romantic comedy
Realistic comedy
Realism
Farce
Fantasy

Literary element: NARRATIVE VOICE
(Terms found on pages 110–124)

Point of view
Omniscient/limited omniscient
Speaker/narrator
Dramatic monologue
Prologue
Epilogue

Literary element: TONE
(Terms found on pages 130–143)

Mood
Atmosphere
Onomatopoeia
Alliteration
Assonance
Cacophony
Euphony

Literary element: CHARACTER
(Terms found on pages 145–163)

Characterization
Hero(ine)

Villain(ess)
Protagonist
Antagonist
Stereotype
Caricature

Literary element: USE OF LANGUAGE
(Terms found on pages 165–192)

Imagery
Image
Figurative language
Literal language
Analogy
Simile
Metaphor
Mixed metaphor
Allegory
Allusion
Parody
Symbol
Rhetoric
Rhetorical questions
Anachronism
Hyperbole (overstatement)
Meiosis (understatement)
Paradox
Oxymoron
Irony (dramatic and verbal)
Diction
Anthropomorphism
Personification
Euphemism
Euphony

Literary element: MEANING(S) IN CONTEXT
(Terms found on pages 193–203)

Denotation
Syntax
Connotation
Implication
Inference
Jargon   (page 24)

Note: Beyond basic definitions (such as that a simile is a comparison using "like" or "as"), you need to be able to recognize when the concepts behind the literary terms are being used and the effects their uses create.

For example, you should be able to recognize that "The woman felt like a small child whose pet dog was missing" contains a simile that in context might make the woman seem in a state of panic, hurt, and fear with perhaps implied elements of emotional immaturity. A resulting test question might ask the following question:

In the line, "The woman felt like a small child whose pet dog was missing," comparing the woman to a child who lost her pet has the effect of
(A) condemning her anger
(B) making the woman seem unstable
(C) limiting her options for response
(D) emphasizing a sense of worry
(E) reinforcing a sense of disillusionment

If the woman has just lost something of great value to her, the answer might be (D) (losing a pet can cause worry); however, you cannot be sure without the context. What if the paragraph from which this sentence is taken is describing in detail the woman having hallucinations of friends who had left her life thirty years earlier? A woman feeling "like a small child whose pet dog was missing" in these circumstances would perhaps make her seem more "unstable" [answer choice (B)].

2. Advanced Literary Terms and Related Vocabulary

You do *not* need to memorize advanced literary terms for taking the SAT II: Literature test. Part III ("Interpretive Skills and Critical Reading") in this book, however, does include definitions and illustrations of some advanced literary terms for three reasons:

a. You can use them for analyzing selections and improving your work in your literature classes.
b. Understanding how they are used and the effects they create, even if you do not remember the terms themselves, can help increase your reading perception in preparation for the SAT II: Literature test.
   For example, you probably do not need to memorize the term *prosody* (the study of rhythms and sounds of poetry) or learn the names of the stressed/unstressed patterns and meters used by poets (illustrated on pages 77–78). However, on page 79 you will find two practice test questions that illustrate the importance of understanding the *effects* of a writer's use of these "advanced" literary concepts.
c. As mentioned in the previous discussion under "Basic Literary Terms and Related Vocabulary," not everyone agrees on which literary terms are "basic." For example, you might not find the literary term *apostrophe* included on

some "basic" lists; but the College Board does include *apostrophe* as an incorrect answer choice in a sample test question in the booklet "Taking the SAT II: Subject Tests" (1998–1999). *Apostrophe* is defined and illustrated on page 184 of this book.

3. Extensive, General Vocabulary

A well-developed general vocabulary can enhance reading comprehension. Understanding the meanings of words can enable you to do better in your classes and to do better on the SAT II: Literature test.

Perhaps the most direct and effective way to increase your vocabulary is to adopt a sense of language awareness when you read. Just memorizing words and meanings may have little lasting value. On the other hand, as you are reading works of literature, class assignments, magazine articles, or even the daily newspaper, make note of new words as they are used in context. By associating the words with how they are used, you can increase your vocabulary in a meaningful way. Begin looking for opportunities to use these words in your own class work and personal writings.

4. Period Vocabulary and Poetic Diction

The SAT II: Literature test may contain selections written during the Renaissance through the twentieth century. As discussed in detail on pages 20–28, the meanings of many words and how they are used have changed dramatically over the centuries and also on a regional basis.

How can you, as a modern reader, learn to understand the meanings of words and how they are used in a poem written, for example, in 1650? An effective method is to develop context skills:

First, practice reading period literature. Although modern words are easier to understand in many cases, you need to practice to develop the skills necessary to understand period literature.

Second, identify all the words and phrases used that you do not understand, then guess at their meanings, using the context of the passage.

Finally, use an unabridged dictionary to see if you guessed correctly.

For example, here is a stanza from Shakespeare's "The Phoenix and the Turtle"

Let the priest in surplice white
That defunctive music can,
Be the death-divining swan,
Lest the requiem lack his right.

Using the context of the stanza, what do you think the following words mean?

surplice: _____
defunctive: _____
death-divining: _____
swan: _____
requiem: _____

Now look each of these words up in the unabridged dictionary. How do your definitions compare? Did you find that "defunctive" is an obsolete adjective pertaining to funerals? Are you sure you know what a "swan" is? A look in the unabridged dictionary reveals that a swan is not just a water bird, but also is a talented poet or singer. Notice the word "music" in line two. In the context, which meaning of swan do you think Shakespeare intended?

The unabridged dictionary is one of the most valuable tools available to the student learning to understand and analyze British and American literature. The unabridged dictionary can reveal the MEANINGS of selections using words that are infrequently used in today's language, words that have changed in MEANING, words that are obsolete, and words that have multiple MEANINGS, one (or more) of which is (are) not commonly used.

After you experience the pleasure of unlocking the MEANING of a poem or essay, by investigating unfamiliar vocabulary in the unabridged dictionary, you may find that your skills in using CONTEXT clues to MEANING will increase. The ability to use CONTEXT clues can add to your comprehension skills beyond learning isolated word MEANINGS, so that unfamiliar words on the SAT II: Literature Subject Test will be manageable and will not interfere with understanding the selections and the accompanying questions. Of course, the added benefit of developing these skills is their transfer to other subjects and areas of life in which reading comprehension is important.

STEP 3. DEVELOP A LONG-RANGE STUDY PLAN.

You may want to include some of the following techniques and suggestions in your long-range study plan:

- Include an "overview" period to become acquainted with the content.

- Identify personal goals and specific objectives.
- Establish a timetable to ensure that no areas are overlooked and that no areas receive too much attention at the expense of others.
- Develop a schedule that includes:
  1. Adequate rest and relaxation
  2. Proper eating habits
  3. Exercise
  4. A balance of social activity (perhaps including group study) and solitude (for intensive concentration)
- Organize literary study groups.
- Work on vocabulary enrichment. (Make flash cards, game cards, and other study aids.)
- Enroll in one or more literature classes.
- Make periodic self-evaluations. (This book provides two diagnostic tests and several practice tests that can be used for this purpose.)
- Periodically revise the study plan to suit changing needs.
- Prepare study places that are clean, pleasant, well lit, and conducive to concentrated study without distractions.
- Develop a system of personal note taking, including, for example, outlines of main points, names of outstanding literary selections, and problem areas.
- Include library research: You may want to become familiar with the library resources available to you, including literary anthologies, literary indexes (such as the *Index to Literary Biography,* Granger's *Index to Poetry,* Chicorel's *Index to Poetry*), and literary bibliographies, as well as actual selections by individual authors.
- Plan extrinsic and intrinsic motivators.
- Seek help from teachers.
- Review literature textbooks.
- Plan for review of the literary elements.

STEP 4. DEVELOP A SHORT-RANGE STUDY PLAN.

Your short-range plan should include two major areas:

1. Prepare a checklist of things you need to do the day *before* and the day *of* the test. You may want to consider including such things as:
   - Plan and lay out comfortable clothes and shoes the night before the test.

- Confirm the day, time, and location of the test.
- Assemble the materials required, such as pencils.
- Avoid cram sessions.
- Get a good night's sleep.
- Adhere to the dietary pattern that will ensure *your* best performance. (For example, many people work best with a moderately sized, well-balanced breakfast.)

2. Prepare a mental checklist of things you need to remember *during the test*. You may want to consider including such things as:
   - Listen to all verbal instructions very carefully.
   - Read all instructions before beginning.
   - Pace yourself, not lingering too long over "problem" questions.
   - Maintain your concentration and keep focused.
   - Remain calm and maintain perspective.
   - Read all question stems and answer choices completely.
   - Watch for questions containing NOT or LEAST.
   - Do not worry about a "problem" question while working on another; give each question its "fair chance."
   - Periodically check the number of the question you are answering to the number on the answer sheet to be sure that you are answering in the correct space.

The previous pages suggest how you might develop a study plan and some of the study helps the plan might include. The main point, however, is that *you* should develop a plan and that the plan should be individualized to suit your personal needs.

Reading comprehension and interpretive skills—the core of the SAT II: Literature Subject Test—can significantly increase your understanding in history, science, government, and other important fields of study. Also, the skills you learn in preparing for the SAT II: Literature Subject Test can be used to develop a well-rounded professional career beyond the postsecondary campus, where effective communication (defined as transmitting and receiving information) translates into successful employment experiences and enhanced personal enrichment. In such areas of study as law, medicine, education, business, and technology, you need to understand what you read; and what you will be reading will come in many FORMS. By developing your own organized approach to studying for the SAT II: Literature Subject Test, you can better prepare for the test and better prepare for your future academic and professional pursuits.

PREPARING FOR THE LITERATURE TEST

Areas Addressed by
the Literature Test

Diagnostic Test I:
Literature

AREAS ADDRESSED BY THE LITERATURE TEST

Part II: Preparing for the Literature Test defines basic terms, discusses structural concepts, and provides systematic self-evaluation and practice in literary analysis.

FOCUS

A literary work can unfold to reveal layers of MEANING, stimulating the reader to go beyond the work itself; or it can stand alone, beautiful and stark in rich simplicity.

You need critical reading skills to understand literary selections. Of course, these skills include fundamental reading comprehension and advanced verbal abilities that are important to the basic understanding of any written work; however, the focus of the SAT II: Literature Subject Test is *interpretive skills.*

Why do you need to develop interpretive skills? Literature contains hidden treasures, filled with mysteries to be revealed and intrigues to be discovered. As a reader, you are an adventurer on a quest—to find what treasures are buried within each literary selection. Interpretive skills are the tools that are essential to finding these treasures, and the reader who develops and practices interpretive skills will uncover the many secrets of MEANING and experience literature has to offer.

SCOPE

Interpretive skills involve learning to examine and analyze the literary elements that work together in a selection. What are these literary elements? The College Board, in its *Official Guide to SAT II: Subject Tests,* points out seven major literary elements that will be the basis for questions asked in the SAT II: Literature Subject Test. These literary elements are MEANING; FORM; NARRATIVE VOICE; TONE; CHARACTER; USE OF LANGUAGE; and MEANINGS OF SENTENCES, LINES, PHRASES, AND WORDS IN CONTEXT (hereinafter called MEANING(S) IN CONTEXT).

One of the purposes of this book is to help you identify and explicate (explain in detail) each of these seven literary elements when they are at work in literary selections. The selections included are weighted toward period literature written prior to 1900 and were selected from a variety of sources for the purpose of illustrating the seven literary elements in many different contexts.

You may begin by taking an overview approach to the seven literary elements. The following questions are grouped by literary element. They will give you an idea of the information you will be seeking when you analyze a literary selection.

MEANING:

- What is the work about—its theme?
- What effect or impression does the work have on the reader?
- What is the argument or summary of the work?
- What is the writer's intent?

FORM:

- How has the writer organized the literary work to achieve the effect or to express the MEANING?
- How is the work structured or planned—as prose or as verse? As topics or as scenes? As a long narrative or as several short stories or episodes?
- Into what genre—type or category—could the work be placed?
- What method of organization or pattern of development was used within the structure of the work?

NARRATIVE VOICE:

- Who is telling the story?
- How is the speaker or narrator characterized (his or her CHARACTER revealed)? By

action or by description? Expressed or implied?
- From what perspective is the story told? By a person outside the story or by someone actually involved in the narrative?
- Is the speaker, the one telling the story, and the writer of the work the same person?
- If the writer and the speaker are two different individuals, are their attitudes toward the subject, the events, and the readers the same or different?

TONE:

- What is the writer's attitude toward the material, subject, or theme?
- What is the speaker's attitude (if different from the writer) toward the material, subject, or theme? Toward the reader?
- Is the TONE playful? Serious? Angry? Formal? Pleading? Joyful?
- What is the atmosphere of the work (the way in which the mood, setting, and feeling blend together to convey the prevailing TONE)?

CHARACTER:

- Who are the people in the work?
- How do dialogue (what he or she says) and action (what he or she does) reveal a CHARACTER'S personality traits?
- Is there a principal CHARACTER?
- What is the CHARACTER'S motivation?
- Is the CHARACTER'S personality revealed directly by the speaker telling the reader or indirectly by the CHARACTER'S own words and deeds (requiring the reader to come to conclusions about the CHARACTER based on dialogue and action)?

USE OF LANGUAGE:

- Does the selection include any imagery (the use of sensory images to represent someone or something)?
- What figures of speech does the writer use, and what effect do they have on the MEANING of the selection?
- How does the writer use diction—word choice—to convey MEANING?

MEANING(S) IN CONTEXT:

- What is the impact of the SENTENCES, LINES, PHRASES, AND WORDS as they are used in the selection?
- Did the writer intend the words used to convey the MEANINGS normally assigned to those words (the denotations)?
- Did the writer intend that some words would imply additional, associated MEANINGS for the reader (connotations)?
- What is the significance of those implications to the MEANING of the selection and the intent of the writer?
- How does the use of denotation, connotation, and syntax (how the words are structured and grouped to create meaningful thought units) relate to the style of the selection?
- Does the language of the selection include any elements of propaganda?

The Literary Elements—Working Together for Unity

Have you ever tasted a well-made sweet-and-sour sauce? You can identify the sweet taste. You can identify the sour taste. Yet these two identifiable tastes join together and unify the sauce to produce a unique blend that is a flavor of its own. Much in the same way, each of the literary elements can be identified individually; however, they also join together to unify the writing and to produce a blend that is unique to that particular work.

After the first diagnostic test, this guide defines and discusses in a somewhat isolated manner each of the seven literary elements necessary to interpretive skills development. Literature, however, is not static. It is a dynamic marriage of concepts and ideas. As a result, interpretation and critical analysis demand that the reader recognize the interrelatedness of these literary elements.

How are the seven literary elements interrelated, and how do they provide unity to a literary work?

1. SHARED CONCEPTS

Literary elements contain concepts that are shared, working together to add shades of MEANING, new or different perspectives, and increased insight into the focus and intent of the writer. For example, an allegory can be a FORM or genre of writing that has dual MEANING, a story in which the CHARACTERS, as well as the setting and narrative line, all represent someone or something else (an extended metaphor). Allegory can also be a USE OF LANGUAGE when it is used as a literary technique or strategy within some other FORM or genre.

Another example of this interdependency of use and thought is the revealment of CHARACTER. A writer can reveal the personality of a CHARACTER by the effective use of FORM, perhaps by the structure of the plot (how the CHARACTER acts when this or that happens), by the selection of a genre (for example, fulfilling the reader's expectations of what the personality of the main male CHARACTER in a typical romance should be), or even the method of organization (such as the writer revealing the CHARACTER'S personality through narration or examples of the CHARACTER'S own words in dialogue, thus allowing the reader to determine the CHARACTER'S attitudes).

2. SHARED FUNCTIONS

Irony (when reality is different from appearance—things are not what they seem) can be included as a technique working within several of the literary elements. The TONE of a selection might be ironic, using perhaps sarcasm (words that are the exact opposite of what the speaker means, such as telling someone who just made a dreadful mistake, "You really used your brains this time!") to produce an ironic effect. Such use of an ironic TONE could directly affect the MEANING of the selection. Also, NARRATIVE VOICE can work together with TONE to project irony, particularly when the attitude of the speaker in the work is different from the attitude of the writer of the work. Then again, irony must be considered a USE OF LANGUAGE, oftentimes developed through gross overstatement (like saying that a water well is "so deep it goes to China") or understatement (such as calling Beethoven's *Fifth Symphony* a "catchy little tune").

You need to recognize that the literary elements affect one another. For example, FORM can affect MEANING and CHARACTER can affect TONE. These relationships are so important that the literary elements are capitalized throughout this book so that you will recognize their interdependency.

3. SHARED DEFINITIONS

Separating the literary elements into neat compartments is indeed difficult. Likewise, defining the elements is equally difficult, because the interrelatedness and blending of use and FORM have led literary critics to vary considerably in defining not only the focus, but also the scope each literary element can and should entail. The elements of TONE and NARRATIVE VOICE are excellent examples of the wide range of interwoven definitions that these concepts can include.

Definitions of TONE include:

- The speaker's attitude toward the reader/listener
- The writer's attitude toward the subject
- The writer's attitude toward the reader/listener
- The speaker's attitude toward the subject
- A device to develop mood and atmosphere (for example, the result of the use of figures of speech—USE OF LANGUAGE—in a selection)
- The musical elements (rhyme and rhythm) in literature
- How a literary selection is supposed to be read aloud, hence "TONE of VOICE"

Definitions of VOICE include:

- The speaker's attitude toward the reader/listener and toward the subject (therefore projecting a TONE)
- The sense the reader gets of a writer's presence when the speaker's attitude and the writer's attitude toward the subject differ (in which case, the VOICE may disagree with the TONE)
- The sense the reader gets of the writer's presence
- The point of view from which a selection is narrated
- The persona (mask-voice) of the writer (expressing the TONE)
- A characteristic of a writer's style
- The thoughts of a poet to himself, the thoughts of a poet to the reader/listener, or the thoughts of a CHARACTER in a poem
- A writer's style characterized by using active VOICE (as in, "I threw the ball") or passive VOICE ("The ball was thrown to me") to project his or her point of view

USE OF LANGUAGE and MEANINGS IN CONTEXT are also elements of literary analysis that are difficult to define apart from one another. For instance, in the sentence, "John's attitude was a malignant growth spreading throughout the organization," the writer is comparing John's attitude to cancer. This type of comparison is a USE OF LANGUAGE called a metaphor. But how can the concept of metaphor (an implied comparison) be defined without recognizing the impact of the connotations (MEANINGS IN CONTEXT) that such a comparison brings to mind for the reader?

In fact, the same two comparisons (USE OF LANGUAGE) can convey different connotations based on the CONTEXT in which the comparisons are presented. Examine the simile (a comparison using *like* or *as*), "thin as a rail." In the first situation, a twenty-five-year-old man has recently lost 150 pounds on the advice and under the guidance of his doctor. He meets his aunt for lunch and she laughingly exclaims upon seeing the healthy-looking young man, "Julio, you're as thin as a rail!" What are the connotations of this USE OF LANGUAGE, based on the CONTEXT? In the second situation, a fifteen-year-old girl, 5 feet, 2 inches tall, has used starvation diets to reduce from 120 to 82 pounds. Her concerned mother takes her to see the family doctor. Upon seeing the girl enter the office, the nurse, who has known the girl since birth, gasps, "Young lady, you're as thin as a rail!" How has CONTEXT changed the connotations of this USE OF LANGUAGE?

An additional bond between USE OF LANGUAGE and MEANINGS IN CONTEXT that makes independent definition difficult is the relationship between the intent of the writer and the comprehension of the reader. Does the writer's USE OF LANGUAGE convey the MEANING IN CONTEXT that he or she intends? What does the USE OF LANGUAGE mean to the reader? Are the reader's perceptions of what the writer intends to say colored by the connotations and implications born in the reader's own past experiences and environment?

Time and Culture

Beyond the seven literary elements, or perhaps as a foundation for them, is the impact of different periods of time and of different cultures on language and writing.

The SAT II: Literature Subject Test includes selections taken from English and American literature, as well as from other literature written in English.

These selections are to be poetry, prose, drama, and other literary forms written during the Renaissance through the twentieth century. *Students are not expected to have pre-read or studied literary selections, and the test does not include questions concerning literary periods or movements, authors' biographies, or literary criticism.*

Important clues to understanding literary selections are lost, however, when the reader does not:

1. Understand *historical references*
2. Recognize *period motifs* and *conventions*
3. Identify *regional, ethnic,* and *national accents* or *dialects*
4. Realize how *words change in* MEANING *over time and space*
5. Appreciate *cultural differences*

HISTORICAL REFERENCES

Understanding historical references in literature is the work of a lifetime. Yet, recognizing that both American and British literature have gone through definable periods, considering why the various works and authors are grouped within each period as they are, and seeking to find what events may have influenced the writers within the various periods can be very useful in developing interpretive skills.

Begin by looking at some of the highlights of world events and of the periods of American and English literature (since 1500) that are shown in the following chart.

For exact dates and historical details, consult the many handbooks, glossaries, encyclopedias, and even dictionaries available that provide charts, summaries, and descriptions of the literary periods. Upon such a study, you will discover that literature is divided into major historical ages or periods and that each of these ages or periods often contains "movements" as the artists and writers of the age respond to the changes in the social and political environments that surround them.

Sources vary; however, most agree upon the dates and information on page 21.

Although you do not need to memorize literary or historical periods for the test, think about the significance of history to literature. What major events were happening in America, in England, and in the world during various literary periods? How do you think these events might have influenced writers at the time? For example, what effect might the Vietnam War have had on the literature written during what some literary critics call the Counterculture

LITERATURE AND WORLD EVENTS

1500   ENGLISH RENAISSANCE
- England's Golden Age
  Elizabeth I (1558–1603)
  (Shakespeare and Raleigh)

- Cortés conquers Aztecs (1521)
- Magellan sails around the world (1522)
- Counter-Reformation (1545)

1600   ENGLISH RENAISSANCE CONTINUES TO 1660
- Jacobean Age of King James I (1603–1625)
- Caroline Age (1625–1649)
- English Commonwealth Period (1649–1660)

RESTORATION ENGLAND: 1660–1700
- Neoclassicism in art and literature

- Thirty Years' War (1618)
- English Civil War (1642)

- "Glorious Revolution" (1688)
  King William of Orange

AMERICAN COLONIALISM
- Captain John Smith and Cotton Mather

- Jamestown colony (1607)
- Pilgrims arrive in America (1620)

1700   ENGLISH NEOCLASSICISM CONTINUES TO 1798
- Augustan Age (1700–1745)—emphasis on
  Latin literature (Age of Pope)
- Age of Sensibility (1745–1798)
  Samuel Johnson

AMERICAN COLONIALISM ENDS (1775); NATIONALISM BEGINS
- Franklin and Jefferson

- Seven Years' War (1756–1763)
- French Revolution (1789)

- American Revolution (1775)

1800   ENGLISH ROMANTIC PERIOD TO 1832
- Revolt against Neoclassicism in art and
  literature
- Wordsworth and Byron

AMERICAN TRANCENDENTALISM AND ROMANTICISM (1823–1865)
- Ralph Waldo Emerson
- Holmes and Poe

VICTORIAN ENGLAND (1832–1901)
- Emphasis on respectability
- Dickens, Browning, Rossetti

AMERICAN REALISM (1865–1900)
- Art and literature mirror life
- Twain and Hawthorne

- Napoleon defeated (1815)

- Mexican War (1846–1848)
- American Civil War (1861–1865)

- German Empire established (1871)

- Spanish-American War (1898)

1900   EDWARDIAN ENGLAND (1901–1910)
- Emphasis on elegance
- Yeats and Kipling

AMERICAN NATURALISM TO 1930
- Literature includes environmental
  realism

ENGLAND'S GEORGIAN AGE TO 1940
MODERN LITERATURE (1914–1965)
POSTMODERN LITERATURE (1965–)

- World War I (1914–1918)
- Great Depression (1929)
- Hitler in power (1933)
- American New Deal (1933)
- World War II (1939–1945)
- Berlin Wall (1961–1990)
- Kennedy assassinated (1963)
- King march on Selma, Alabama (1965)
- Vietnam War (1964–1975)

Movement in America? What do you think the TONE of their writing might be? Why might the impact of Vietnam have been different on writers in England than on those in the United States?

Investigate some of the events, contributions, or literary developments that set each period, sub-period, or movement apart from the others. For instance, during the Renaissance, scholars were fascinated with the Greek classics, Henry VIII and Elizabeth I instituted Protestantism in England, and people were "caught up" in the excitement of the "discovery" by Columbus of a new continent in 1492. How might the Greek classics and Protestantism have influenced the writings of the day?

One event that significantly influenced the literature of the day was the shipwreck of the *Sea Adventure* off Bermuda in 1609. Scholars believe that William Shakespeare was inspired by the accounts of this disaster when he penned *The Tempest* (1623), possibly his last play written alone. Other writings include *A True Declaration of the Estate of the Colonie in Virginia* (the official report of the Virginia Company), *A Discovery of the Barmudas* (by Silvester Jourdain), and *News from Virginia* (by Richard Rich in 1610).

During the Elizabethan Age, writers were very influenced by the happenings of the times. The defeat of the Spanish Armada in 1588 caused a surge in English nationalism, but in Colonial America attention was given to documenting the theologies, philosophies, and history-in-progress that were shaping a "new" world.

Also, make appropriate use of the marginal notes and glosses available with many literary anthologies. These "explanations" often help the reader identify and put into perspective the historical significances and influences at play within a work. They enable the reader to build a backlog of information that can be used to develop new interpretive skills.

But how does this knowledge increase your interpretive skills? An awareness of the events, thoughts, or conditions that may have influenced a writer helps you to understand motivation and perhaps even purpose or MEANING in what he or she has written. As the writer reveals attitudes, historical CONTEXT and perspective put you in a better position to know where the writer is "coming from." For example, knowing that critics believe Spenser (a writer during the Renaissance) and Shelley (a Romantic writer) were influenced by the philosopher Plato might be very useful in understanding their attitudes, word choices, and references.

Another reason a historical perspective helps increase interpretive skills is that many times writers refer to events, places, and people (sometimes even to other writers) without explaining their significance—upon the assumption that the reader will understand the reference. Often writers make references for a contemporary audience and, as a result, have the attitude "Doesn't everybody know that?" When, in *The Vanity of Human Wishes,* Samuel Johnson writes:

In full-blown dignity, see Wolsey stand,
Law in his voice, and fortune in his hand: **(lines 99–100)**

he assumes that the reader knows that Thomas Cardinal Wolsey was a powerful Lord Chancellor under King Henry VIII. Knowing the story of Wolsey, his rise and eventual fall, enables the reader to better understand Johnson when he writes:

Speak thou, whose thoughts at humble peace repine,
Shall Wolsey's wealth, with Wolsey's end be thine?
Or liv'st thou now, with safer pride content,
The wisest justice on the banks of Trent?
For why did Wolsey, near the steeps of fate,
On weak foundations raise the enormous weight?
Why but to sink beneath misfortune's blow,
With louder ruin to the gulfs below?   **(lines 118–128)**

Likewise, what point is biographer James Boswell making in *The Life of Samuel Johnson, L. L. D.,* when he writes "When I [Boswell] had him [Johnson] fairly seated in a hackney coach with me, I exulted as much as a fortune hunter who has got an heiress into a post chaise with him to set out for Gretna Green"? What is so special about Gretna Green? His comment becomes clearer when the reader learns that Gretna Green was a place in Scotland where couples could go to be married in a hurry by the local blacksmith or innkeeper—a place a fortune hunter would definitely want to take an heiress.

Acquiring some historical literary background can sharpen the reader's senses and help the reader better understand the author's use of literary elements. In the previous example, Boswell uses going to Gretna Green, a reference with which he assumes his readers are familiar, as part of a simile to show how intensely glad he was to have Johnson in the post chaise with him. Earlier in the same account, Boswell wants a friend to invite Dr. Johnson to a dinner party to which his friend had planned to invite a notorious and controversial figure in Parliament named John Wilkes. Boswell writes:

Notwithstanding the high veneration which I entertained for Dr. Johnson, I was sensible that he was sometimes a little actuated by the spirit of contradiction, and by means of that I hoped I should gain my point. I was persuaded that if I had come upon him with a direct proposal, "Sir, will you dine in company with Jack Wilkes?" he would have flown into a passion, and would probably have answered, "Dine with Jack Wilkes. Sir! I'd as soon dine with Jack Ketch."

Who is Jack Ketch? He was a public hangman, whose name was well known to Boswell's learned contemporaries in 1791; but Boswell does not explain this reference to his twenty-first-century readers. Authors today are writing about such people, places, and ideas as the Big Apple, John Glenn's return to space, *60 Minutes,* the Big Easy, the boob tube, and Oprah Winfrey. Will people two hundred years from now understand the significance of these references? Should a writer assume that the reader will have some background knowledge? What would happen to an author's style of writing if he or she tried to explain every reference used?

PERIOD MOTIFS AND CONVENTIONS

Different periods of literary history have brought with them identifiable motifs and themes, as well as conventions and traditions. Even though you do not need to memorize period motifs and conventions for the SAT II: Literature test, being able to recognize when these motifs and conventions are being used can help you to form expectations and to determine whether those expectations are being met.

First, examine motifs and themes.   A *motif* is a figure or element that recurs in literary works; the *theme* of a work is its main idea or concept. (Theme will be discussed later in Part III.) Certain motifs and themes have enjoyed popularity among writers during certain periods, whereas the use of others spans generations.

Some common motifs include:

- Loathly lady motif—an ugly girl turns out to be a beautiful woman; the ugly duckling becomes a beautiful swan in the children's tale (closely related to the Cinderella motif).
- *Ubi sunt* motif—the motif of mourning a lost past (sometimes used in lyric poetry); these poems often include the question "Where are…?" (Latin: *Ubi sunt*) such as "Where are the carefree days of youth?"

- *Carpe diem* motif—MEANING "seize the day" because of the brevity of life. An example of the *carpe diem* motif is Edmund Waller's "Song: Go, lovely rose!" written in 1645.

SONG

Go, lovely rose!
Tell her that wastes her time and me
    That now she knows,
When I resemble her to thee
How sweet and fair she seems to be.

    Tell her that's young,
And shuns to have her graces spied,
    That hadst thou sprung
In deserts, where no men abide,
Thou must have uncommended died.

    Small is the worth
Of beauty from the light retired;
    Bid her come forth,
Suffer herself to be desired,
And not blush so to be admired.

    Then die! that she
The common fate of all things rare
    May read in thee;
How small a part of time they share
That are so wondrous sweet and fair!

- Magic spell motif—music makes the girl fall in love; an apple causes a princess to fall asleep.
- Wake-up motif—one lover urging the other to awake, a motif found in an *aubade*, a song at dawn. For example, Shakespeare's *"Hark, Hark! the Lark"*:

HARK, HARK! THE LARK

Hark, hark! the lark at heaven's gate sings,
    And Phoebus 'gins arise,
His steeds to water at those springs
    On chaliced flowers that lies;
And winking Mary-buds begin
    To ope their golden eyes:
With every thing that pretty is,
    My lady sweet, arise!
    Arise, arise!

- Star-crossed lovers—a boy and girl fall in love but are doomed to tragedy because their families are feuding (*Romeo and Juliet,* the Hatfields and McCoys, and *West Side Story*).

Motifs may include a sense of formula. You can expect the princess to awake when kissed by her prince, the frog to become a prince when kissed by the beautiful girl.

Second, look at the role of conventions   (plots and genres, CHARACTERS, verse forms, styles or literary devices that recur in literature) and of traditions (a way to group literary works because they share themes or concerns).

Conventional plots and genres include many different FORMS, such as the romance in which girl falls in love with boy, boy is momentarily distracted by a heartless, conniving female, but boy realizes in the end that the heroine is the true love of his life. Although variations on conventional plots are seemingly endless, what cop-and-robber story can be complete without a chase scene or what western without a barroom brawl? The reader knows what is going to happen—what to expect.

Conventional CHARACTERS are often not difficult to identify: *stock CHARACTERS in fiction* (types of CHARACTERS that are usually found in certain literary FORMS—the tall, handsome leading man in a romance or the heart-of-gold saloon girl in a western). Conventional FORMS also can give the reader a sense of anticipation, such as in the *epic poem*. Three standard features of an epic poem are that the poet (1) moves right into the middle of the action and conflict without explaining the situation, (2) consults a muse for help, and (3) includes a superman-type epic hero whose fate is to overcome tremendous odds for the sake of a grand purpose. Sometimes a *conventional style* or *literary device* is used within a conventional FORM. An example would be the epic epithet (a description of CHARACTER traits to identify a person) within an epic poem. Conventions within drama include the soliloquy in which a CHARACTER speaks, but is "heard" only by the audience.

To identify a literary *tradition* is to attempt to group works that share certain themes or ideas. There are many possible ways to identify traditions, sometimes even by the way they employ certain conventions, as in the Courtly Love Tradition in which religious vocabulary is a convention used to put the object of affection "on a pedestal." A few traditions you might look for are Neoclassical, Pastoral, and Satiric Traditions, as well as the English, European, Western, and Modern Traditions.

REGIONAL, ETHNIC, AND NATIONAL DIALECTS

In order to understand a literary selection, the reader must recognize the importance of regional, ethnic, and national dialects to MEANING. Word choices and dialects vary greatly not only between England and America, but also within England and America. A Texan, accustomed to ordering *soda water,* might get a moment's hesitation from a waiter in Ohio, where *pop* is the common usage. Not recognizing regional differences in dialect and vocabulary can lead to confusion and lack of communication, as demonstrated by the young couple who moved from the Midwest to Texas. They searched the classified ads in local newspapers for land for sale, but were disappointed that many places were described as having "tanks." Picturing large, aboveground water tanks, the couple did not even bother to look at these properties until they discovered that "tank" is the "Texas lingo" for pond or small lake. A building supply store chain is taking these regional differences in vocabulary so seriously that its advertising explains that "wallboard," "drywall," and "gypsum" refer to the same product. It might have included "Sheetrock" (trademark) and "plasterboard" as synonyms, also.

Many times writers will attempt to convey to the reader the *dialect* (the speech of a region) or *accent* (the ways words are actually pronounced) by use of vocabulary choices and spelling variations (to show pronunciation). What elements can determine a person's dialect or accent?

1. Ethnicity or nationality—a Frenchman speaking English with a "French accent"
2. Regional differences—an Oklahoma accent compared to a Brooklyn accent; use of *y'all* in the South, *you guys* in the Midwest, and *you 'uns* in the Ohio River Valley

In addition, authors also attempt to convey in writing ways of speaking and accents that are the result of:

3. Education—usually seen in word choice as well as in pronunciation—note the speech patterns of American journalist William F. Buckley, Jr.
4. Occupation—"buzzwords" or word choices peculiar to an occupation being a predominant feature of the dialect, including technical terminology called **jargon**

5. Time, such as
   a. Periods of English—the Queen's English of Victorian England, for example, compared to Modern English
   b. The "Generation Gap" illustrated by the speech of the Beat Generation, the hippies, the yuppies, and the preppies. Compare the "surf talk" of Annette Funicello in the beach party movies of the late 1950s and 1960s to the "surf talk" of "Valley Girls" in the 1980s.

Look at an excerpt from "The Cotter's Saturday Night," a poem by the eighteenth-century Scottish poet Robert Burns:

Belyve, the elder bairns come drapping in,
    At service out, amang the farmer's roun';
Some ca' the pleugh, some herd, some tentie rin
    A cannie errand to a neibor town:
    Their eldest hope, their Jenny, woman-grown,
In youthfu' bloom, love sparkling in her e'e,
    Comes hame, perhaps to shew a braw new gown,
Or deposite her sair-won penny-fee,
To help her parents dear, if they in hardship be.

What word choices and variations in spellings has Burns used to convey native dialect? In the Scottish dialect, "bairns" are children, "Belyve" means soon, "rin" is run, a "braw new gown" is one that is fine, with sore-won spelled "sair-won." Can you find the MEANINGS of the other words of Scottish dialect used in this stanza?

Studying regional dialects, as well as changes in dialects and variations in vocabulary that are the result of time, is a very complex task. A student of literature, however, should learn to recognize some of the more widely used dialects and accents as they are translated into print, because these attempts at conveying spoken words to the reader can be clues to region and time.

As you read various literary selections, begin taking note of the ways in which the writers, through dialect and accent, convey the time and place of their stories. Notice how they use word choices and spelling.

CHANGES IN MEANINGS OF WORDS OVER TIME AND SPACE

As mentioned previously, time is an element that helps shape a person's dialect. Recognizing that words change in MEANING both denotatively (literal MEANINGS) and connotatively (associated MEAN-INGS) is so important to understanding a literary selection that the subject warrants further discussion.

Linguistic scholars have identified English (a Germanic language) as part of the Indo-European family of languages. English language history is divided into periods: Old English, Middle English, Modern English from 1500 to 1800, and Modern English from 1800 to the present. Although *selections for the SAT II: Literature Subject Test are taken from Modern English only,* notice the progression and changes the English language has undergone since the Old English period:

1. The Old English Period (A.D. 449–1100)
British Celts, under attack by the Picts and Scots (Irishmen), called on fierce Germanic warriors when the Romans would not provide adequate help in A.D. 449. After driving out the Picts and Scots, these Germanic Angles, Saxons, and Jutes took over England and established the seven kingdoms of Kent, Essex, Sussex, Wessex, East Anglia, Mercia, and Northumbria (names that appear throughout English literature—even in those works written in Modern English).

The following poem, written in Old English, was penned sometime between A.D. 658 and 680 and illustrates how radically different the English of this period was compared to English today.

CÆDMON'S HYMN

Nu sculon herigean	heofonrices Weard
Meotodes meahte	and his modgeþanc
weorc Wuldor-Fæder	swa he wundra gehwæs
ece Drihten	or onstealde
He ærest sceop	ielda bearnum
heofon to hrofe	halig Scyppend
ða middangeard	moncynnes Weard
ece Drihten	æfter teode
firum foldan	Frea aelmihtig

2. The Middle English Period (A.D. 1100–1500)
Middle English began shortly after the Norman Conquest (William the Conqueror) in 1066. Naturally, the impact was felt in the language, especially in vocabulary. During this time, the dialect of London became a standard for English; however, writers continued to use their regional dialects (North, South, Kent, West Midland, and East Midland) almost until the end of the period.

Examine these lines of Chaucer's "General Prologue" to *The Canterbury Tales,* written in 1386. Do you recognize any of the words?

A good man was ther of religioun,
And was a povre PERSOUN of a toun;
But riche he was of holy thoght and werk.
He was also a lerned man, a clerk,
That Cristes gospel trewely wolde preche;
His parisshens devoutly wolde he teche.

3. Modern English (A.D. 1500–1800)

The SAT II: Literature Subject Test may include selections taken from works written during the Renaissance, which (as a period in British literature) lasted from about 1500 to 1660, corresponding in part to the first half of the Modern English language period.

The English language underwent important changes during this time, especially changes in pronunciation, perhaps the most radical change being what linguists call "the Great Vowel Shift." But while English was changing significantly in pronunciation, spelling in the 1500s was not keeping pace.

Notice the first sentence of a paragraph written by Bankkes in 1525 in a "botanical" book called *Herball*:

Rofemary.

This herbe is hote and dry/take the flowres and put them in a lynen clothe/ & fo boyle them in fayre clene water to ẙ halfe & coole it & drynke it/for it is moche worth agaynft all euylles in the body.

The earliest English dictionaries appeared in this period, with Robert Cawdrey's *A Tabel Alphabeticall* leading the way in 1604; however, English spelling and usage was not standardized until Samuel Johnson was commissioned in 1746 to write *A Dictionary of the English Language*. Note Johnson's definition of *enthusiasm*:

ENTHU'SIASM. n. I. A vain belief of private revelation; a vain confidence of divine favor or communication.

Enthusiasm is founded neither on reason nor divine revelation, but rises from the conceits of a warmed or overweening brain.—Locke.

Has this word changed in MEANING since the mid-1700s?

4. Modern English (1800 to present)

In terms of FORM and structure of English, the Modern English Period has seen little radical change, with FORMS of standardized English being sustained in both England (where British Standard is taught in schools) and in the United States (where American English is the offspring of the British-speaking colonists and explorers of the seventeenth century).

Surprising to some, words in American usage have found their way into the British vocabulary, partly as a result of advanced communications, commerce, and American technology. Even so, there are significant differences between British and American word choices even in Modern English (note the British *posh frock*, the American *fancy dress*) and, of course, pronunciation. Spelling is another area of difference, due in part to Noah Webster, who took the *u* out of *colour, armour,* and *neighbour,* changed *-re* to *-er* in *theatre, centre*, and *manoeuvre,* and changed the *c* to *s* in *defence,* to cite just a few of his influences.

British English and American English have undergone and continue to undergo tremendous changes in the denotative and the connotative values of English words. How and why do words change MEANINGS and how are new words added to the English vocabulary? Here are a few of the more common ways:

1. Words often have more than one MEANING, and usage can add even more MEANINGS. A case in point is the word *firebreak*, a forest fire fighting term referring to a barrier (often a gap in the combustible trees or vegetation) meant to stop a fire. The key players in the Nuclear Age, however, have extended this word, giving it an additional, new MEANING: a barrier or gap separating conventional warfare and nuclear war, meant to stop nuclear confrontation.

    Sometimes words gain so many MEANINGS that they become very generalized and no longer carry the preciseness of MEANING that they once conveyed. Some people would use the word *love* as an example.

2. Obviously, the MEANINGS of a word can also be reduced, becoming rare, archaic, or even obsolete. *Buckle* (verb) is an example, as it appears in Webster's *New Twentieth Century Dictionary* (Unabridged).

    In fact, an entire word form can become obsolete, such as *brut* in its verb form (MEANING to *browse*) or *bruckled* (an adjective MEANING *grimy*). Very rarely today is a little stream called a *brun*. And look at the word *corn*: corn once meant *grain*; then it came to mean *Indian corn* or *maize* in America, *wheat* in England, and *oats* in Scotland.

3. Entirely new words can be coined or added to the language, often due to new technologies, explorations, or any circumstances in which a never-before-communicated idea must be expressed, illustrated by the word *Kodak,* "invented" by George Eastman in 1888.

4. Words once thought to have negative connotations can be elevated in the public's perception and become respectable for use (*nice* once meant *ignorant*) or the opposite when words fall into disrepute (*hussy* once meant *housewife*).

5. Words can come into use to avoid the negative connotations of harsher words. For example, the Irish began referring to *the little people* rather than saying *fairies*. The kinder, gentler word is called a *euphemism*. This genteelism is a significant factor in the language and literature of Victorian England, where, for instance a piano *leg* was called the less suggestive word *limb*.

6. New uses of prefixes, suffixes, and compounding can add to a language's vocabulary. Note: *panorama, snacketeria,* and *splashdown.*

7. Words also can be added to a vocabulary by abbreviation or clipping (*exam* for *examination*), blending (*broasted = broiled + roasted*), and by using acronyms (NOAA = National Oceanic and Atmospheric Administration).

8. Borrowing from other languages has been a significant influence on English. These borrowings include such words as *fork* (*furca*) from Latin, *frankfurter* from German, *raffle* (*rafle*) from French, *spaghetti* from Italian, and *serape* from Mexican-Spanish.

Of how much importance is recognizing the changes English has undergone to understanding literature? Consider the use of the word *petty* in this statement written during the mid-1700s by Samuel Johnson in *A Dictionary of the English Language:*

Swift, in his *petty* treatise on the English language, allows that new words must sometimes be introduced, but proposes that none should be suffered to become obsolete. [emphasis added]

What attitudes come to mind when Johnson calls Swift's treatise "petty"? *Petty* can mean *unimportant;* however, it can also mean simply *small* in size or length. How would this definition change the MEANING of the statement?

CULTURAL DIFFERENCES

An American answering the telephone may utter any number of responses, ranging from a simple "hello" to stating his or her name and asking "May I help you?" In England, however, you may hear the person answering the phone recite (rapidly) the telephone number that has been rung. Recognizing such cultural differences enables the reader to better understand plot and CHARACTER and allows the reader to form cultural expectations.

The word *culture* has many MEANINGS and shades of MEANING—so many, in fact, that the term has become rather imprecise. Yet for the purpose of literary analysis, the reader can look at culture as a body of concepts, skills, and institutions that make a particular people in a particular place and/or period of time an identifiable group or civilization.

How significant is culture to literary analysis? Sometimes an understanding of the culture of the writer is extremely important to recognizing the very attitudes of an entire work, for example, recognizing the English devotion to the British monarchy.

Cultural contrasts can help sharpen perceptions, and sometimes identifying these contrasts is important to literary MEANING. A case in point is Boswell's reference to a *turnspit* in *The Life of Samuel Johnson, L. L. D.:*

A man whom he had never seen before was employed one night to sit up with him. Being asked next morning how he liked his attendant, his answer was, "Not at all, Sir: the fellow's an idiot; he is as awkward as a turnspit when first put into the wheel, and as sleepy as a dormouse."

In the Western American culture of the past century or so, readers are familiar with the image of a person carefully turning buffalo or beef over an open campfire. To Boswell's contemporaries, however, the image of a dog (usually a relative of a terrier), called a turnspit, running on a treadmill to turn a roasting spit, was equally familiar. By using this reference, the writer makes a colorful point, for what could be more awkward than a dog just learning to run a treadmill?

Parenthetically, the value of identifying cultural points that are shared by peoples and time should also be noted. A relevant instance is found in lines 79–80 of Samuel Johnson's *The Vanity of Human Wishes* in which Johnson refers to the mid-1700 practice of morning receptions used by statesmen to grant inteviews and to meet friends and political allies.

Love ends with hope, the sinking statesman's door
Pours in the morning worshiper no more;

A comparison can be made to the current American practice of politicians who routinely participate in breakfasts for the press and civic groups, where they can present their points of view under congenial and (hopefully) nonthreatening circumstances. Johnson here refers to the "sinking statesman's door"—a place where "the morning worshiper" no longer comes—a statesman who no longer draws the crowds of reporters and no longer receives invitations to address local civic groups, political party receptions, or crowds of admirers.

Focus and Scope in Summary

The focus of the SAT II: Literature Subject Test is interpretive skills. One way to develop interpretive skills is to learn to identify and understand the various forms of the seven basic literary elements that are the basis for questions in the SAT II: Literature Subject Test—MEANING; FORM; NARRATIVE VOICE; TONE; CHARACTER; USE OF LANGUAGE; and MEANINGS OF SENTENCES, LINES, PHRASES, AND WORDS IN CONTEXT. These literary elements can be individually studied, but they cannot be totally isolated from one another in either function or definition.

Selections for the SAT II: Literature Subject Test are to be taken from poetry, prose, drama, and other literary FORMS in English literature, American literature, and other literature written in English, during the Renaissance through the twentieth century. Although you do not have to study specific literary selections and will not be tested on the literary periods, authors' lives, or literary criticism, a reader can gain helpful insight and clues to MEANING in literary selections, clues that can help develop interpretive skills, by being alert to the importance of historical references, period motifs and conventions, accents and dialects, changes in word MEANINGS, and cultural differences.

What method can you use to gain these insights? First, *read extensively*. The more you read literary selections from the various periods and cultures, the better your ability to understand the people, events, and places of the times. Then, *reread* the selections, identifying, analyzing, and applying the principles of critical analysis that lead to mastery of interpretive skills. You can use the definition and discussion section that follows Diagnostic Test I to examine individually each of the seven literary elements at the core of critical analysis.

Next is a 60-question Diagnostic Test. Use this test to become acquainted with the literature test's format and focus and to assess your prior knowledge of the basic literary elements.

DIAGNOSTIC TEST I: LITERATURE

The purpose of the following Diagnostic Test is to:

1. Introduce you to the format and structure of the test
2. Acquaint you with the types of questions that may be asked
3. Illustrate and explain the content of questions that are based on interpretive thinking skills
4. Help you identify your strengths—and your weaknesses—in critical reading and the seven major literary elements

Diagnostic Test I is not intended to be an easy test, but one that will present you with an opportunity to use evaluative skills over a wide range of literary devices, including symbolism and connotative word MEANINGS. Some of the test is written to provide you with examples and experience in dealing with questions in which shades of MEANING, minute details, and subtle distinctions make selecting the correct answer difficult without careful discernment in reading both the literary excerpt and the question with its answer choices.

You need to know that you need to know. Do not be concerned over any questions that you miss; the answers are explained following the test and can be used to further your learning and experience in literary analysis. Also, the concepts behind the questions are elaborated upon, developed, reviewed, and/or reinforced throughout the book.

In order to take this test, remove the answer sheet (see page 31) to record your answers. Allow yourself one hour (using a timer or clock to time yourself).

Be sure to use your most effective test-taking strategies, those that you find are right for you (for help in test taking, see Developing an Individualized Study Program, page 7), and be sure to read all directions carefully.

Remember: You may *not* use other papers, books, or reference materials of any kind.

After you complete the test, use the Answer Key (see page 43) to check your answers and to determine your raw score. Then use the Analysis: Diagnostic Test I (see page 47) to help you evaluate your answer choices.

ANSWER SHEET FOR DIAGNOSTIC TEST I

1. Ⓐ Ⓑ Ⓒ Ⓓ Ⓔ
2. Ⓐ Ⓑ Ⓒ Ⓓ Ⓔ
3. Ⓐ Ⓑ Ⓒ Ⓓ Ⓔ
4. Ⓐ Ⓑ Ⓒ Ⓓ Ⓔ
5. Ⓐ Ⓑ Ⓒ Ⓓ Ⓔ
6. Ⓐ Ⓑ Ⓒ Ⓓ Ⓔ
7. Ⓐ Ⓑ Ⓒ Ⓓ Ⓔ
8. Ⓐ Ⓑ Ⓒ Ⓓ Ⓔ
9. Ⓐ Ⓑ Ⓒ Ⓓ Ⓔ
10. Ⓐ Ⓑ Ⓒ Ⓓ Ⓔ
11. Ⓐ Ⓑ Ⓒ Ⓓ Ⓔ
12. Ⓐ Ⓑ Ⓒ Ⓓ Ⓔ
13. Ⓐ Ⓑ Ⓒ Ⓓ Ⓔ
14. Ⓐ Ⓑ Ⓒ Ⓓ Ⓔ
15. Ⓐ Ⓑ Ⓒ Ⓓ Ⓔ
16. Ⓐ Ⓑ Ⓒ Ⓓ Ⓔ
17. Ⓐ Ⓑ Ⓒ Ⓓ Ⓔ
18. Ⓐ Ⓑ Ⓒ Ⓓ Ⓔ
19. Ⓐ Ⓑ Ⓒ Ⓓ Ⓔ
20. Ⓐ Ⓑ Ⓒ Ⓓ Ⓔ

21. Ⓐ Ⓑ Ⓒ Ⓓ Ⓔ
22. Ⓐ Ⓑ Ⓒ Ⓓ Ⓔ
23. Ⓐ Ⓑ Ⓒ Ⓓ Ⓔ
24. Ⓐ Ⓑ Ⓒ Ⓓ Ⓔ
25. Ⓐ Ⓑ Ⓒ Ⓓ Ⓔ
26. Ⓐ Ⓑ Ⓒ Ⓓ Ⓔ
27. Ⓐ Ⓑ Ⓒ Ⓓ Ⓔ
28. Ⓐ Ⓑ Ⓒ Ⓓ Ⓔ
29. Ⓐ Ⓑ Ⓒ Ⓓ Ⓔ
30. Ⓐ Ⓑ Ⓒ Ⓓ Ⓔ
31. Ⓐ Ⓑ Ⓒ Ⓓ Ⓔ
32. Ⓐ Ⓑ Ⓒ Ⓓ Ⓔ
33. Ⓐ Ⓑ Ⓒ Ⓓ Ⓔ
34. Ⓐ Ⓑ Ⓒ Ⓓ Ⓔ
35. Ⓐ Ⓑ Ⓒ Ⓓ Ⓔ
36. Ⓐ Ⓑ Ⓒ Ⓓ Ⓔ
37. Ⓐ Ⓑ Ⓒ Ⓓ Ⓔ
38. Ⓐ Ⓑ Ⓒ Ⓓ Ⓔ
39. Ⓐ Ⓑ Ⓒ Ⓓ Ⓔ
40. Ⓐ Ⓑ Ⓒ Ⓓ Ⓔ

41. Ⓐ Ⓑ Ⓒ Ⓓ Ⓔ
42. Ⓐ Ⓑ Ⓒ Ⓓ Ⓔ
43. Ⓐ Ⓑ Ⓒ Ⓓ Ⓔ
44. Ⓐ Ⓑ Ⓒ Ⓓ Ⓔ
45. Ⓐ Ⓑ Ⓒ Ⓓ Ⓔ
46. Ⓐ Ⓑ Ⓒ Ⓓ Ⓔ
47. Ⓐ Ⓑ Ⓒ Ⓓ Ⓔ
48. Ⓐ Ⓑ Ⓒ Ⓓ Ⓔ
49. Ⓐ Ⓑ Ⓒ Ⓓ Ⓔ
50. Ⓐ Ⓑ Ⓒ Ⓓ Ⓔ
51. Ⓐ Ⓑ Ⓒ Ⓓ Ⓔ
52. Ⓐ Ⓑ Ⓒ Ⓓ Ⓔ
53. Ⓐ Ⓑ Ⓒ Ⓓ Ⓔ
54. Ⓐ Ⓑ Ⓒ Ⓓ Ⓔ
55. Ⓐ Ⓑ Ⓒ Ⓓ Ⓔ
56. Ⓐ Ⓑ Ⓒ Ⓓ Ⓔ
57. Ⓐ Ⓑ Ⓒ Ⓓ Ⓔ
58. Ⓐ Ⓑ Ⓒ Ⓓ Ⓔ
59. Ⓐ Ⓑ Ⓒ Ⓓ Ⓔ
60. Ⓐ Ⓑ Ⓒ Ⓓ Ⓔ

DIAGNOSTIC TEST I

Directions: The following questions test your understanding of several literary selections. Read each passage or poem and the questions that follow it. Select the best answer choice for each question by blackening the matching oval on your answer sheet. **Special attention should be given to questions containing the following words: EXCEPT, LEAST, NOT.**

Questions 1–10 are based on the following passage.

He was pitching the chill abominations into the bath-tub, pleased by the vindictiveness of that desolate flapping sound; and in the midst
line his wife serenely trotted in, observed serenely,
(5) "Why Georgie, dear, what are you doing? Are you going to wash out the towels? Why, you needn't wash out the towels. Oh, Georgie, you didn't go and use the guest-towel, did you?"
It is not recorded that he was able to answer.
(10) For the first time in weeks he was sufficiently roused by his wife to look at her.
Myra Babbitt—Mrs. George F. Babbitt—was definitely mature. She had creases from the corners of her mouth to the bottom of her chin,
(15) and her plump neck bagged. But the thing that marked her as having passed the line was that she no longer had reticences before her husband, and no longer worried about not having reticences. She was in a petticoat now,
(20) and corsets which bulged, and unaware of being seen in bulgy corsets. She had become so dully habituated to married life that in her full matronliness she was as sexless as an anemic nun. She was a good woman, a kind woman, a
(25) diligent woman, but no one, save perhaps Tinka her ten-year-old, was at all interested in her or entirely aware that she was alive.
After a rather thorough discussion of all the domestic and social aspects of towels she
(30) apologized to Babbitt for his having an alcoholic headache; and he recovered enough to endure the search for a B.V.D. undershirt which had, he pointed out, malevolently been concealed among his clean pajamas.
(35) He was fairly amiable in the conference on the brown suit.
"What do you think, Myra?" He pawed at the clothes hunched on a chair in their bedroom, while she moved about mysteriously
(40) adjusting and patting her petticoat and, to his jaundiced eye, never seeming to get on with her dressing. "How about it? Shall I wear the brown suit another day?"
"Well, it looks awfully nice on you."

Babbitt
by Sinclair Lewis

1. The "line" Mrs. Babbitt has passed in line 16 probably refers to her

(A) battle against growing older
(B) no longer loving her husband
(C) acceptance of the familiarity in her life
(D) weight problem
(E) attitude toward men

2. Of the literary devices listed below, which is used in lines 23–24 to describe Mrs. Babbitt?

(A) Metaphor
(B) Personification
(C) Paradox
(D) Simile
(E) Apostrophe

3. Babbitt pointed out that his undershirt had "malevolently been concealed among his clean pajamas" (lines 33–34) probably because he

(A) wanted to stop his wife from helping him
(B) felt irritable over the inconveniences he was experiencing
(C) really believed Mrs. Babbitt had hidden his undershirt
(D) was reacting positively to his wife's matronly presence
(E) thought the closet needed to be cleaned and reorganized

4. Lines 39–42 indicate that Babbitt's attitude toward his wife is sometimes

(A) hostile
(B) impertinent
(C) passive
(D) aggressive
(E) impatient

5. The TONE of "Well, it looks awfully nice on you" (line 44) in the CONTEXT in which it is said sounds

(A) resentful
(B) conciliatory
(C) argumentative
(D) retaliatory
(E) enthusiastic

6. The use of the word "pawed" (line 37) results in which of the following effects?

(A) Exposes his bearlike qualities
(B) Provides comic relief within the episode
(C) Implies that there are animalistic elements in Babbitt's civilized personality
(D) Represents the struggle between civilized and uncivilized behavior
(E) Proves that Babbitt is no better than an animal

7. The purpose of the statement made in line 9 can be seen as which of the following?

(A) As an insight into the mute impotence of Babbitt's personality
(B) As an impertinence on the part of Babbitt
(C) As an understatement used to project an ironic TONE
(D) As a cynical observation intended to reinforce the superficial nature of Babbitt
(E) As a suggestion of how awe-struck Babbitt is of his wife

8. The word "hunched," as it is used in line 38, is

(A) an allusion to Mrs. Babbitt
(B) a simile
(C) a metaphor
(D) a paradoxical term
(E) personification

9. The effect of alliteration in lines 39–40 is to

(A) change the TONE of the episode
(B) provide a contrast between Babbitt's movements and those of his wife
(C) symbolize the poetic elements of Babbitt's life
(D) emphasize the lack of parallel sentence structure
(E) stress the importance of Myra's movements

10. The word "jaundiced" in line 41 produces which of the effects listed below?

(A) To establish Babbitt as an ill man
(B) To reinforce the image of Babbitt's ill mood
(C) To symbolize Babbitt as a victim of circumstances
(D) To indicate that Babbitt viewed his wife through the eyes of reality
(E) To suggest that Babbitt was aggressively hostile toward Myra

Questions 11–19 are based on the following poem.

Proof to No Purpose

You see this gentle stream, that glides,
Shoved on, by quick-succeeding tides:
Try if this sober stream you can
line Follow to th' wilder ocean,
(5) And see, if there it keeps unspent
In that congesting element.
Next, from that world of waters, then
By pores and caverns back again
Induct that inadultrate same
(10) Stream to the spring from whence it came.
This with a wonder when ye do,
An easy, and else easier too:
Then may ye recollect the grains
Of my particular remains,
(15) After a thousand lusters hurled,
By ruffling winds, about the world.

by Robert Herrick

11. The central denotative theme of the poem addresses the subject of

    (A) water cycles
    (B) how oceans are formed
    (C) seasons and weather of the world
    (D) life cycles
    (E) the instabilities of life

12. As seen in lines 3 and 5, the speaker's attitude toward the silent auditor seems to be somewhat

    (A) mocking
    (B) challenging
    (C) loving
    (D) deferential
    (E) churlish

13. Within the CONTEXT of this poem, the speaker's "remains" in line 14 can be seen as his

    I.   work left to be done
    II. remnant of material possessions
    III. dead body
    IV. surviving writings

    (A) I only
    (B) II only
    (C) II, III, and IV only
    (D) II and III only
    (E) III and IV only

14. As the word is used in line 14, "particular" describes the speaker's "remains" as all the following EXCEPT

    (A) apart from others
    (B) personal
    (C) special rather than general
    (D) precise
    (E) considered separately

15. What is the outcome of the speaker's use of the phrase "unspent/In that congesting element" (lines 5–6)?

    (A) The use influences the reader to regard the stream as lost forever in the ocean.
    (B) The use creates a sense of nature's economy.
    (C) The use establishes an alliterative pattern with line 7.
    (D) The use contradicts the return of the stream to its source in line 10.
    (E) The use makes the stream seem like an exhausted person in an overcrowded situation.

16. Figuratively, the stream represents

    (A) part of the water cycle
    (B) the source for the ocean
    (C) people in a state of innocence
    (D) literary works
    (E) the natural elements of life

17. Of the literary devices listed below, which is used in line 3?

    (A) Parody
    (B) Allusion
    (C) Personification
    (D) Apostrophe
    (E) Assonance

18. The octosyllabic construction of the poem (eight syllables per line) contributes to its

    (A) sense of conformity
    (B) hypnotic effect
    (C) cyclical TONE
    (D) TONE of urgency
    (E) regulated imagery

19. In the poem's title, "to No Purpose" means

    (A) irrelevant
    (B) unresolved
    (C) without design
    (D) untalented
    (E) misdirected

Questions 20–26 are based on the following passage.

SETTING: *Morning-room in* Algernon's *flat in Half-Moon Street.*
The room is luxuriously and artistically furnished.

LADY BRACKNELL   It really makes no matter, Algernon. I had some crumpets with Lady Harbury, who seems to me to be living entirely for pleasure now.

(5) ALGERNON   I hear her hair turned quite gold from grief.

LADY BRACKNELL   It certainly has changed its color. From what cause I, of course, cannot say.

(10)   ALGERNON *crosses and hands tea.*

Thank you. I've quite a treat for you tonight, Algernon. I am going to send you down with Mary Farquhar. She is such a nice woman, and so attentive to her
(15) husband. It's delightful to watch them.

ALGERNON   I am afraid, Aunt Augusta, I shall have to give up the pleasure of dining with you tonight after all.

LADY BRACKNELL [*frowning*]   I hope not,
(20) Algernon. It would put my table completely out. Your uncle would have to dine upstairs. Fortunately he is accustomed to that.

ALGERNON   It is a great bore, and, I need hardly say, a terrible disappointment to me,
(25) but the fact is I have just had a telegram to say that my poor friend Bunbury is very ill again. [*Exchanges glances with* Jack] They seem to think I should be with him.

LADY BRACKNELL   It is very strange.
(30) This Mr. Bunbury seems to suffer from curiously bad health.

ALGERNON   Yes; poor Bunbury is a dreadful invalid.

LADY BRACKNELL   Well, I must say,
(35) Algernon, that I think it is high time that Mr. Bunbury made up his mind whether he was going to live or to die. This shilly-shallying with the question is absurd. Nor do I in any way approve of the modern

(40) sympathy with invalids. I consider it morbid. Illness of any kind is hardly a thing to be encouraged in others. Health is the primary duty of life. I am always telling that to your poor uncle, but he never seems to take much
(45) notice...as far as any improvement in his ailments goes. I should be much obliged if you would ask Mr. Bunbury, from me, to be kind enough not to have a relapse on Saturday, for I rely on you to arrange my
(50) music for me. It is my last reception, and one wants something that will encourage conversation, particularly at the end of the season when everyone has practically said whatever they had to say, which, in most
(55) cases, was probably not much.

The Importance of Being Earnest
by Oscar Wilde

20. Lady Bracknell's attitude can be seen as

(A) anxious
(B) opinionated
(C) sympathetic
(D) encouraging
(E) resentful

21. Lady Bracknell's air of authoritative condescension is ironic because

I.   she knows it is "at the end of the season" and everyone has had his or her say, which is not much (lines 52–55)
II. Algernon as well as Algernon's uncle do not seem to respect or obey her orders
III. she is unable to determine the cause of Lady Harbury's change in hair color

(A) I only
(B) II only
(C) III only
(D) I and II only
(E) I, II, and III

22. What does the stage direction [*Exchanges glances with* Jack] in line 27 tell you about Algernon's CHARACTER?

    (A) He is far more worried about Bunbury than he wants his aunt to know.
    (B) He is not really worried about Bunbury, but still feels it is his duty to go.
    (C) He is sincere about not wanting to miss dining with his aunt.
    (D) He may not be telling the truth about Bunbury.
    (E) He does not want to appear ungrateful to his aunt.

23. Based on the speaker's TONE, how should Algernon's use of verbal irony in lines 5–6 be regarded?

    (A) A mean-spirited hatred
    (B) A childish rambling
    (C) A witty repartee
    (D) A titillating discourse
    (E) A ludicrous burlesque

24. Lady Bracknell's comments throughout the passage reveal her to be

    (A) pious
    (B) obsequious
    (C) indecisive
    (D) sympathetic
    (E) pompous

25. The stage direction [*Exchanges glances with* Jack] in line 27 indicates that Jack might be Algernon's

    (A) confidant
    (B) villain
    (C) protagonist
    (D) antagonist
    (E) *vers libre*

26. The expressions "shilly-shallying" (lines 37–38), "modern sympathy" (lines 39–40), and "primary duty" (lines 42–43) produce which of these effects?

    (A) They strengthen Lady Bracknell's argument, making it obvious that in a contest of wills she would win.
    (B) They underscore Lady Bracknell's opinion that good health is the decided result of attitude.
    (C) They suggest that to be ill is to lack sympathy for others.
    (D) They provide a contrast to Algernon's obvious deep concern for his ill friend.
    (E) They imply motivation on Lady Bracknell's part to help people overcome their illnesses.

Questions 27–35 are based on the following poem.

My Friend, the Things That Do Attain

My friend, the things that do attain
The happy life be these, I find:
The riches left, not got with pain;
The fruitful ground; the quiet mind;
(5) The equal friend; no grudge, no strife;
No charge of rule, nor governance;
Without disease, the healthy life;
The household of continuance;

The mean diet, no dainty fare;
(10) Wisdom joined with simpleness;
The night dischargéd of all care,
Where wine the wit may not oppress:

The faithful wife, without debate;
Such sleeps as may beguile the night;
(15) Content thyself with thine estate,
Neither wish death, nor fear his might.

       by Henry Howard, Earl of Surrey

27. The central theme of the poem is the

    (A) resplendent nature of a happy life
    (B) finding a happy life in "the mean estate"
    (C) self-denial necessary to pursue a happy life
    (D) contrast of a sumptuous life against a meager existence
    (E) beguiling nature of "the rich estate"

28. How does the personification of death affect the MEANING in line 16?

   (A) The inevitability of death is emphasized.
   (B) The ultimate end of both friend and speaker are revealed.
   (C) Death becomes the friend of the poet.
   (D) Pain (line 3), disease (line 7), and wine (line 12) all play into death's hands.
   (E) Death, as someone not to be feared, is less threatening than an abstract concept.

29. Which of the following statements summarizes the relationship of lines 1–2 to the rest of the poem?

   (A) They establish the rhyme pattern.
   (B) They set a pattern of contrasts.
   (C) They introduce the topic.
   (D) They reveal an attitude of covetousness.
   (E) They reinforce a sense of tension.

30. Another way of saying "The household of continuance" (line 8) is

   (A) an unbroken home
   (B) family wealth
   (C) genetically based good health
   (D) a large inheritance
   (E) a family estate

31. In the poem's CONTEXT, "pain" (line 3) can be thought of as all the following EXCEPT

   (A) physical hurt
   (B) punishment
   (C) mental anguish
   (D) expiation
   (E) penalty

32. "Wisdom joined with simpleness" (line 10) is a(n)

   (A) metaphor for a simple life
   (B) metrical accent within the stanza
   (C) paradox to emphasize that a simple life is wise
   (D) hyperbole to emphasize the great value of simplicity
   (E) ironic point of departure within the theme

33. The attitude of "I" (line 2) to "My friend" (line 1) can be seen as

   (A) conciliatory
   (B) impatient
   (C) didactic
   (D) critical
   (E) impersonal

34. The word "beguile," as it is used in line 14, conveys which of the following ideas?

   I.   Pass the time pleasingly
   II. Relieve weariness in
   III. Deceive or cheat

   (A) I only
   (B) II only
   (C) III only
   (D) I and II only
   (E) I, II, and III

35. Line 6 refers to

   (A) the peace that comes from not charging items, thus reducing debt
   (B) not engaging in attacks and warlike behavior
   (C) avoiding political activities
   (D) not taking on the responsibilities of being in control or in a position of authority
   (E) resistance to rules and forms of government

Questions 36–44 are based on the following passage.

As it happens we had been having a number of cases of diphtheria in the school to which this child went during that month and we were
line all, quite apparently, thinking of that, though
(5) no one had as yet spoken of the thing.
    Well, I said, suppose we take a look at the throat first. I smiled in my best professional manner and asking for the child's first name I said, come on, Mathilda, open your mouth and
(10) let's take a look at your throat.
    Nothing doing.
    Aw, come on, I coaxed, just open your mouth wide and let me take a look. Look, I said opening both hands wide, I haven't anything
(15) in my hands. Just open up and let me see.

Such a nice man, put in the mother. Look how kind he is to you. Come on, do what he tells you to. He won't hurt you.

At that I ground my teeth in disgust. If only
(20) they wouldn't use the word "hurt" I might be able to get somewhere. But I did not allow myself to be hurried or disturbed but speaking quietly and slowly I approached the child again.
(25) As I moved my chair a little nearer suddenly with one catlike movement both her hands clawed instinctively for my eyes and she almost reached them too. In fact she knocked my glasses flying and they fell, though
(30) unbroken, several feet away from me on the kitchen floor.

Both the mother and father almost turned themselves inside out in embarrassment and apology. You bad girl, said the mother, taking
(35) her and shaking her by one arm. Look what you've done. The nice man...

For heaven's sake, I broke in. Don't call me a nice man to her. I'm here to look at her throat on the chance that she might have
(40) diphtheria and possibly die of it. But that's nothing to her. Look here, I said to the child, we're going to look at your throat. You're old enough to understand what I'm saying. Will you open it now by yourself or shall we have
(45) to open it for you?

Not a move. Even her expression hadn't changed. Her breaths however were coming faster and faster. Then the battle began.

"The Use of Force"
by William Carlos Williams

36. The primary effect of the absence of quotation marks around the dialogue is

(A) confusion over who said what
(B) stream-of-consciousness narration
(C) an omniscient point of view
(D) a stylistic device to build tension and anticipation
(E) a melodramatic style

37. "I" in this selection can best be identified as

(A) a school psychologist
(B) a doctor or nurse
(C) a school administrator
(D) the child's teacher
(E) a friend of the family

38. "As I moved my chair a little nearer suddenly with one catlike movement both her hands clawed instinctively for my eyes and she almost reached them too" (lines 25–28). This sentence includes all the following EXCEPT

(A) personification
(B) metaphor
(C) simile
(D) first person narrative
(E) active voice

39. In lines 18 and 20, use of the word "hurt" seems to elicit in the speaker a sense of

(A) unmanageable rancor
(B) resigned acceptance
(C) tenacious unyielding
(D) restrained repugnance
(E) nonchalance

40. The TONE of "He won't hurt you" (line 18) can be considered

(A) patronizing
(B) accusatory
(C) impertinent
(D) passive
(E) responsive

41. All the following conflicts are revealed in this passage EXCEPT

(A) resistance to aggression
(B) fear of the unknown
(C) distrust in adult authority
(D) embarrassed pride
(E) impertinent cruelty

42. During the course of this episode, the speaker's attitude changes from

(A) professional naïveté to detached repugnance
(B) professional competence to apologetic resignation
(C) controlled anger to uncontrolled wrath
(D) restrained professionalism to unrestrained self-will
(E) detached professionalism to emotionally involved

43. The setting of this episode is probably

(A) the child's home
(B) a clinic
(C) the hospital
(D) the doctor's office
(E) an emergency room

44. Which of the following best explains the difference in the speaker's and the writer's purpose in use of diction in line 10 ("let's") and line 12 ("Aw, come on")?

(A) The speaker is patronizing and the writer is establishing his arrogance.
(B) The speaker wants to gain the child's trust, but the writer is setting the TONE for the episode.
(C) The speaker's attitude is being established by the writer's contemptuously ironic TONE.
(D) The speaker and writer are one; therefore, the purpose is the same.
(E) The speaker and the writer are in conflict over the purpose.

Questions 45–54 are based on the following poem.

That Time of Year

That time of year thou mayst in me behold
When yellow leaves, or none, or few, do hang
Upon those boughs which shake against the cold,
line Bare ruined choirs, where late the sweet birds sang.
(5) In me thou see'st the twilight of such day
As after sunset fadeth in the west;
Which by and by black night doth take away,
Death's second self, that seals up all in rest.
In me thou see'st the glowing of such fire,
(10) That on the ashes of his youth doth lie,
As the deathbed whereon it must expire,
Consumed with that which it was nourished by.
This thou perceiv'st, which makes thy love more strong,
To love that well which thou must leave ere long.

by William Shakespeare

45. Lines 5, 9, and 13 contain changes in

(A) internal rhyme
(B) voice
(C) end rhyme scheme
(D) rhythm
(E) scansion

46. The progression of "ruined" (line 4) to "fadeth" (line 6) to "expire" (line 11) can be seen as

(A) a resistance to death
(B) a progression of life to death
(C) love transcending death
(D) the instability of life
(E) fear of death

47. The poem's subject is

(A) dead trees
(B) sunsets
(C) dying fires
(D) making love grow stronger
(E) approaching death

48. In lines 1–4, the speaker compares the coming of winter to

(A) a winter landscape
(B) a leafless tree
(C) a time when birds leave
(D) his own period of old age
(E) his inability to engage in youthful activity

49. In lines 5–8, the speaker uses twilight as a

   (A) symbol of depression
   (B) metaphor for approaching death
   (C) personification of death
   (D) representation of his state of mind
   (E) transitional device

50. Of the following literary identifications, which best describes the ashes as they are used in lines 9–12?

   I.   A metaphor for life that is spent
   II. The termination of the sunset
   III. A symbol of youth

   (A) I only
   (B) II only
   (C) III only
   (D) I and II only
   (E) I, II, and III

51. What is the speaker's TONE in lines 1–4?

   (A) Arrogant
   (B) Ironic
   (C) Shocked
   (D) Lonely
   (E) Encouraged

52. What is the effect of the progression from "yellow leaves" to "none" to "few" in line 2?

   (A) It emphasizes the lateness of the season.
   (B) It shows that the speaker's vision is not clear.
   (C) It represents unfulfilled dreams.
   (D) It implies human uncertainties about life and death.
   (E) It contrasts the "ruined choirs" in line 4.

53. Lines 13–14 relate to the rest of the poem in which of the following ways?

   (A) They summarize the point that when death is near, love should intensify.
   (B) They intensify the sadness of the autumn, sunset, and dying fires.
   (C) They reinforce the sense of struggle for life.
   (D) They introduce love as an answer for old age and death.
   (E) They serve to change both subject and attitude.

54. How does the personification of sleep in line 8 affect the MEANING?

   (A) Sleep becomes a friend offering rest and solace.
   (B) The comparison to a sunset is intensified.
   (C) The speaker reinforces his struggle for life.
   (D) Sleep is made more threatening as a reflection or shadow of death.
   (E) Sleep resists death and makes night less threatening.

Questions 55–60 are based on the following passage.

[Passage from George Washington's Farewell Address delivered to his cabinet on September 17, 1796]

The unity of government which constitutes you one people is also now dear to you. It is justly so, for it is a main pillar in the edifice of
line your real independence, the support of your
(5) tranquility at home, your peace abroad, of your safety, of your prosperity, of that very liberty which you so highly prize.

But as it is easy to foresee that from different causes and from different quarters much pains
(10) will be taken, many artifices employed, to weaken in your minds the conviction of this truth, as this is the point in your political fortress against which the batteries of internal and external enemies will be most constantly
(15) and actively (though often covertly and insidiously) directed, it is of infinite moment that you should properly estimate the immense value of your national union to your collective and individual happiness....
(20) The name of American, which belongs to you in your national capacity, must always exalt the just pride of patriotism more than any appellation derived from local discriminations. With slight shades of
(25) difference, you have the same religion, manners, habits, and political principles. You have in a common cause fought and triumphed together. The independence and liberty you possess are the work of joint
(30) councils and joint efforts, of common dangers, sufferings, and successes.

55. "The unity of government which constitutes you one people is also now dear to you. It is justly so, for it is a main pillar in the edifice of your real independence, the support of your tranquility at home" (lines 1–5). Of the following statements concerning Washington's comment, all are correct EXCEPT which statement?

(A) They are aphoristic.
(B) They state a conclusion.
(C) They serve to establish the TONE.
(D) They establish distance between speaker and subject.
(E) They contain metaphorical language.

56. In this selection, the speaker's TONE can be considered

(A) paternal and patriotic
(B) patronizing and discouraging
(C) intensely ironic
(D) enthusiastically optimistic
(E) disappointed

57. The "truth" described in lines 11–12 probably is that

(A) tranquility, peace, and safety are highly prized
(B) some people may try to undermine truth
(C) happiness is of immense value
(D) various interest groups try to weaken government unity
(E) independence depends upon unity of government

58. Of the statements that follow, which is the best description of the relationship between the first paragraph and the second?

(A) The second paragraph simply reiterates the main point of the first paragraph.
(B) The second paragraph creates a sense of emotional tension.
(C) Both paragraphs serve to support a change in public policy.
(D) The point of the first paragraph renders moot the main idea of the second paragraph.
(E) The second paragraph introduces an optimistic TONE.

59. What organizational pattern does the speaker use to persuade his audience?

(A) Classification
(B) Process analysis
(C) Conclusion-premise relationship
(D) Spondaic stress
(E) Metrical scan

60. What is the literary function of the phrase "political fortress" in lines 12–13?

(A) Metaphor for a system of beliefs under attack
(B) Reference to independence
(C) Hyperbole for truth
(D) Literary allusion to governmental systems
(E) Affective fallacy

ANSWER KEY: DIAGNOSTIC TEST I

Step 1. Score Your Test

- Use the following table to score your test.
- *Compare* your answers to the correct answers in the table:
- ✓ Place a check in the "Right" column for those questions you answered correctly.
- ✓ Place a check in the "Wrong" column for those questions you answered incorrectly. (For quick reference later, you may also want to circle the number of each question you missed.)
- If you omitted answering a question, leave both columns blank.

Step 2. Analyze Your Test Results

- *Read* the portions of the "Analysis: Diagnostic Test I" (analysis follows the scoring table) that apply first to those questions you missed.
- *Scan* the rest of the analysis for those questions you answered correctly. This analysis identifies the correct answer, the literary element tested by each question, and briefly discusses the answer choice(s).

Step 3. Learn from Your Test Results

- *Circle* the question number on the Answer Key Table (if you have not already done so) for each of the questions you answered incorrectly. Which literary elements were these questions testing?

Obviously, due to the interrelated scope and definitions of the seven literary elements, many of the questions are actually testing more than one literary element. Consequently, these identifications serve only as a guide to areas to *begin* your study—to pinpoint "problem" areas and to make your study plan more effective.

- *Review* the seven literary elements.

For Further Help in Literary Elements:	See Page:
1. MEANING	61
2. FORM	69
3. NARRATIVE VOICE	110
4. TONE	126
5. CHARACTER	145
6. USE OF LANGUAGE	165
7. MEANING(S) IN CONTEXT	193

You may want to plan your study program by first working through the study materials provided in this book for those literary elements that you missed on the test. You should, however, eventually *review all seven literary elements* as part of your complete study program.

ANSWER KEY: DIAGNOSTIC TEST I

Scoring			Literary Element Tested						
Right	Wrong	Answer	1	2	3	4	5	6	7
		1. C							*
		2. D						*	
		3. B							*
		4. E				*			
		5. B				*			
		6. C					*		

ANSWER KEY: DIAGNOSTIC TEST I

Right	Wrong	Answer	1	2	3	4	5	6	7
		Scoring				Literary Element Tested			
		7. C						*	
		8. E						*	
		9. B						*	
		10. B							*
		11. D	*						
		12. B			*				
		13. C						*	
		14. D							*
		15. E						*	
		16. D						*	
		17. C						*	
		18. C				*			
		19. A							*
		20. B			*				
		21. B						*	
		22. D					*		
		23. C				*			
		24. E					*		
		25. A					*		
		26. B							*
		27. B	*						
		28. E						*	
		29. C		*					
		30. A							*
		31. D							*

ANSWER KEY: DIAGNOSTIC TEST I

Scoring			Literary Element Tested						
Right	Wrong	Answer	1	2	3	4	5	6	7
		32. C						*	
		33. C			*				
		34. D							*
		35. D							*
		36. D				*			
		37. B			*				
		38. A						*	
		39. D			*				
		40. A				*			
		41. E	*						
		42. E			*				
		43. A				*			
		44. B			*				
		45. C		*					
		46. B		*					
		47. E	*						
		48. D						*	
		49. B						*	
		50. A						*	
		51. D				*			
		52. D							*
		53. A		*					
		54. D						*	
		55. D						*	
		56. A				*			

ANSWER KEY: DIAGNOSTIC TEST I

Scoring			Literary Element Tested						
Right	Wrong	Answer	1	2	3	4	5	6	7
		57. E							*
		58. B		*					
		59. C		*					
		60. A						*	

TO OBTAIN YOUR RAW SCORE:

_____ divided by 4 = _____
Total wrong   Score W

_____ minus _____ = _____
  Total right   Score W   Score R

Round Score R to the nearest whole number for
the raw score.

HOW DID YOU DO?

55–60 = Excellent
44–54 = Very Good
35–43 = Above Average
23–34 = Average
15–22 = Below Average

ANALYSIS: DIAGNOSTIC TEST I

NOTE: The scope and definition of each of the literary elements sometimes can differ among the literary critics (see discussion in Part II, Areas Addressed by the Literature Test section). As a result, the rationale behind what constitutes a correct or an incorrect answer also may differ. Many of the questions in Diagnostic Test I are testing your skills in more than one literary element. Also, each answer analysis might be viewed from more than one perspective. Consequently, this analysis should be used as only a part of your study program.

1. **C** Element 7 (MEANINGS IN CONTEXT) Mrs. Babbitt has accepted the familiarity of her life. Nothing in this passage indicates that she is waging a "battle" against growing older, that she no longer loves her husband, or that she has a defined attitude toward men. Although she obviously has a weight problem, some clues to identifying what line she has passed are found in lines 18–19 (she "*no longer worried* about not having reticences") and line 22 (and had become "*dully habituated* to married life")—emphasis added.

2. **D** Element 6 (USE OF LANGUAGE) "…as sexless as an anemic nun" is a comparison using *as*—a simile.

3. **B** Element 7 (MEANINGS IN CONTEXT) Clues to Babbitt's irritability are found in line 2 ("pleased by the vindictiveness"), line 11 ("roused"), line 31 ("alcoholic headache"), line 35 ("fairly amiable"), and lines 40–41 ("his jaundiced eye").

4. **E** Element 4 (TONE) Although Babbitt's attitude seems hostile in lines 1–11, his observation in lines 41–42 ("never seeming to get on with her [Myra's] dressing") indicates impatience.

5. **B** Element 4 (TONE) Myra's serene nature, described as good, kind, and dilligent (lines 24–25), and apologetic attitude in lines 30–31 are indicators that her comment was made in a conciliatory TONE.

6. **C** Element 5 (CHARACTER) The verb "paw" has many shades of MEANING involving such concepts as clumsiness, roughness, overintimacy, and waving in the air. To paw something has definite connotations associated with the behavior of animals, whether it be the crushing paws of a bear, the tearing paws of a cougar, or the pawing hooves of a horse. These connotations suggest that Babbitt does, indeed, have some primitive, animalistic elements in his behavior and personality. Remember to select the *most complete* answer.

7. **C** Element 6 (USE OF LANGUAGE) How is Babbitt feeling? Vindictive (line 2) over wet towels. What is Myra's reaction? She seems totally unaware of his mood, completely misinterprets his actions, and babbles on about the towels. "It is not recorded that he was able to answer" is an understatement of Babbitt's anger (such an understatement is called *meiosis*)—he was really too angry to speak, thus making an ironic TONE. Understatement or meiosis is a figure of speech in which the speaker gives the subject far less importance than it has in reality. Generally, the effect is irony. Remember Mark Twain's famous ironic understatement "The reports of my death are greatly exaggerated"?

8. **E** Element 6 (USE OF LANGUAGE) "Hunched" gives clothes (inanimate objects) a human characteristic—personification (E).

9. **B** Element 6 (USE OF LANGUAGE) Alliteration in these lines is the repetition of the initial consonant sounds in "moved…mysteriously" and "patting…petticoat." Alliteration is a poetic device that contributes to a sense of rhythm in a work. In this case, this subtle hint at poetic rhythm further contrasts Myra to her husband, who is characterized by such harsh movements as pitching wet bath towels with vindictiveness and pawing clothes.

10. **B** Element 7 (MEANINGS IN CONTEXT) Jaundice not only is an illness associated with liver damage and characterized by yellowing of the eyes, but also is a reference to an ill attitude or state of mind (B).

11. **D** Element 1 (MEANING) Although you might be tempted to select answer A because the first twelve lines do, indeed, contain an eloquent (but incomplete) description of the earth's water cycle, this answer is inadequate because the question stem asks about

the *central* theme—the one that is the structural support for the entire poem. Seasonal aspects and weather of the world are mentioned, but the central theme is reflected in the last four lines that reveal that lines 1–12 are being used with the cycles of life—answer D.

12. **B** Element 3 (NARRATIVE VOICE) The poem evidences the speaker as one who is trying to make a point. First, he uses the water cycle analogy to establish what would seem to be a rather straightforward metaphor. Notice, however, the TONE in which he addresses the silent auditor, particularly in lines 3 and 5: "Try if…you can…And see…." Couple this TONE with the forceful use of "Then" in line 13 when he says "Then may ye recollect the grains/Of my particular remains" [emphasis added] and you will discover a speaker whose attitude is challenging (B). What do you think has caused this attitude?

13. **C** Element 6 (USE OF LANGUAGE) Obviously, the "remains" of the speaker can be seen as his dead body (III), the "grains" of which he challenges the silent auditor to "recollect." Also, an argument might be made that upon the speaker's death, his remnant of material possessions (II) would be left to be recollected (brought together); however, on a highly figurative level, the "remains" can be seen as the speaker's surviving writings (IV) that are "particular" (personal) and that the silent auditor would "recollect" (recall or remember) after "a thousand lusters" (fame or renown) "hurled by ruffling winds" (disturbing or rippling air that bears trends or information).

14. **D** Element 7 (MEANINGS IN CONTEXT) Answers A through E are all definitions of "particular"; consequently, CONTEXT is essential to determining which MEANING is not applicable to this situation. A major clue is in the description of the stream that flows into and becomes part of the ocean, but then returns to the springs from which it originated. Likewise, the speaker suggests that the silent auditor "recollect" (implying a gathering again) his "particular remains"—those that are separated from those mixed in the "world of waters" (line 7) or "about the world" (line 16). This association of ideas

supports selection of definitions that reflect this sense of individualism: apart from others (A), personal (B), special rather than general (C), and considered separately (E). Precise (D) does not conform to the established association.

15. **E** Element 6 (USE OF LANGUAGE) The word spent means to be exhausted or without energy. To be "unspent," then, would mean to have energy. The speaker contends that the silent auditor should "see, if there it [the stream] keeps unspent"—remains full of energy—"in that congesting [overcrowded] element" of the ocean. This subtle personification renders the stream to seem like an exhausted person in an overcrowded situation (E).

16. **D** Element 6 (USE OF LANGUAGE) On a literal level, the stream flows as a source for the ocean. On a figurative level, the root of its MEANING can be found in the last four lines of the poem in which the speaker establishes two levels of MEANING: (1) based on the life cycle of the human body and (2) based on his personal literary works ("particular remains") and their recollection. Using this second level as a basis, the stream can be seen as literary works (perhaps the personal works of the speaker) that gently flow into the "wilder ocean" (line 4) of the world's body of literary conventions and criticisms where it (line 5) becomes exhausted "In that congesting [overcrowded] element" (line 6). Eventually, it returns to the "spring from whence it came" (inspiration?—line 10).

17. **C** Element 6 (USE OF LANGUAGE) Personification is giving human attributes to nonhumans: "sober stream." Also, the repeated initial consonant(s) is an example of alliteration.

18. **C** Element 4 (TONE) The speaker uses several literary devices (including alliteration, assonance, regular rhythm and rhyme, diction, and octosyllabic construction) to project the smooth, cyclical TONES that extend to support the imagery of the poem's figurative MEANING—answer C.

19. **A** Element 7 (MEANINGS IN CONTEXT) The phrase "to the purpose" means something is relevant or pertinent (as: Is that remark to the purpose?). Consequently, "to

no purpose" would be something that is irrelevant. What do you think is the significance of the title to the poem's literal and to its figurative MEANINGS?

20. **B** Element 3 (NARRATIVE VOICE) Lady Bracknell has very distinct opinions (B). Notice her opinions about Lady Harbury, about Algernon's reason not to dine with her, about Mr. Bunbury's illness, and about her reception guests.

21. **B** Element 6 (USE OF LANGUAGE) Irony, in this case, involves the difference between the way Lady Bracknell views herself and the way she is viewed by those around her. She obviously has an air of authority (note that she does not hesitate even to order people to be healthy) and a sense of condescension (note her air of superiority over her reception guests). But do those around her respect her opinions or orders? Algernon refuses her invitation to dine and his uncle does not heed her advice.

22. **D** Element 5 (CHARACTER) In determining motivation and CHARACTER, CONTEXT is extremely important. How sincere is Algernon about his "sick" friend? Clues can be found in Lady Bracknell's comments that Bunbury's illness is "very strange" (line 29), that he suffers from "*curiously* bad health" (lines 30–31—emphasis added), and that he brushes with death frequently (lines 36–38)... perhaps Algernon is not telling the truth.

23. **C** Element 4 (TONE) In answering this question, the first step is to determine what is ironic in Algernon's statement. Verbal irony occurs when the speaker's MEANING is different from what he or she says, usually revealing the speaker's attitude or opinion on the subject. One can assume that Lady Harbury has been through a traumatic event (causing her grief or what would normally be expected to cause her grief). In such circumstances, a person's hair generally does not turn gold from grief. Also, note that Lady Bracknell points out that Lady Harbury "seems to me to be living entirely for pleasure now," so Algernon is aware that Lady Harbury is not really grieving at all. His comment that "her hair has turned quite gold from grief" really means that grief had nothing to do with her hair turning gold. Although his comment, when coupled with

that of Lady Bracknell, is suggestive that Lady Harbury is acting in a way unbecoming a person in grief, his observation is by no means titillating (exciting) or burlesque (an amusing imitation of a literary work). Does anything in his dialogue indicate that he hates her (A)? Does he ramble on about it? No, he simply makes this witty reply (C), then drops the subject.

24. **E** Element 5 (CHARACTER) A pompous CHARACTER is one who is self-important (an exaggerated sense of her own importance). This trait can be seen in Lady Bracknell's attempts to control others: She tells Algernon "I am going to send you down with Mary Farquhar" (lines 12–13). She is willing to make her husband dine upstairs to balance her table. She even commands sick people to control their illnesses for her convenience and to facilitate her dinner party plans.

25. **A** Element 5 (CHARACTER) A confidant (A) is someone in a play who acts to establish the CHARACTER of someone else by being a sounding board, by reacting with the other CHARACTER, or by some other means revealing the personality of the more dominant or main CHARACTER. In this case, Jack simply being there to exchange glances gives the reader/viewer clues into Algernon's personality and motives.

26. **B** Element 7 (MEANINGS IN CONTEXT) Nothing in the selection supports the idea that Lady Bracknell's strong will prevails over that of others—except perhaps over Algernon's uncle at dinner. Neither is "deep concern" on the part of Algernon established. Although Lady Bracknell may be motivated to help Algernon's uncle be healthy, these strongly connotative words do reveal that Lady Bracknell believes people should not encourage illness in others by expressing sympathy, but rather invalids should make health a duty and simply decide to be well (B). Lack of sympathy on the part of ill people is not discussed.

27. **B** Element 1 (MEANING) The structure of this poem helps to define its central idea: first, the writer sets forth his topic—these are the "things" that make a happy life. He then lists those things, all of which are found in a simple, humble lifestyle, or in other words, "the mean estate" (B).

28. **E** Element 6 (USE OF LANGUAGE) Personification is the attributing of human qualities to inanimate objects or abstract ideas. The unknown and abstract can be very frightening; however, by encouraging the reader to think of death in human terms is to make it less fearful, less threatening. Be aware, though, that CONTEXT is *very* important in recognizing the effects of personification or of any literary USE OF LANGUAGE. The CONTEXT of this poem allows the personification of death to render death less threatening, but the CONTEXT of another work might mean that such personification would turn death into a monster.

29. **C** Element 2 (FORM) In this particular poem, the complete rhyme scheme or pattern cannot be determined from just the first two lines—the rhyme pattern of the entire poem needs to be examined. Neither covetousness (D) nor contrast (B) are revealed here, and tension also is not an element (E). The first two lines do, however, introduce the topic (C).

30. **A** Element 7 (MEANINGS IN CONTEXT) The central idea of the poem is that a simple, humble life can be very happy; therefore, wealth (B), an inheritance (D), and an estate (E) are in antithesis to the speaker's main point. Although no inherited diseases or illnesses would make for a happy situation, a household (home, family, and the affairs of the home) of continuance (an unbroken succession) would be a home not broken (by anger or separation).

31. **D** Element 7 (MEANINGS IN CONTEXT) (A), (B), (C), and (E) can all be associated with pain; but expiation (D) is a condition of having made reparation or amends for wrongdoing and, as such, could be considered a *release from pain* of guilt.

32. **C** Element 6 (USE OF LANGUAGE) Being "simple" is often viewed as the opposite of being "wise." Here the concepts of simpleness and wisdom are used in a paradox to point out that simpleness (from the perspective of simplicity in living) can, in fact, be quite wise.

33. **C** Element 3 (NARRATIVE VOICE) A conciliatory attitude (A) has connotations of winning over or placating, implying that some division has taken place. Yet there is no indication in this poem of any separation between the two people in thought, emotion, or action having taken place, except the difference of opinion concerning lifestyles *implied* by the poet's sense of need to write this poem expounding the benefits of a simple lifestyle. Neither does the speaker seem impatient (B) or impersonal (E). Although he may be somewhat critical (again, by implication) of the high stress life of wealth, his attitude mostly is didactic (C) as he wants to instruct his friend—to teach him about the pursuit of happiness.

34. **D** Element 7 (MEANINGS IN CONTEXT) In a "night discharged of all care" (line 11) the time would be passed pleasingly (I) and would relieve weariness (II), but would not deceive or cheat (III).

35. **D** Element 7 (MEANINGS IN CONTEXT) A "charge" is a responsibility or duty when in a position of "rule" or in a position of governance (control and the exercise of authority). A simple life, then, would mean avoiding the "headaches at the top"—positions of responsibility.

36. **D** Element 4 (TONE) Stream of consciousness (B) is a narrative method describing the thoughts going through a CHARACTER'S mind. In this story, no quotation marks are used around the give-and-take dialogue of the CHARACTERS, not just the doctor's thoughts. This is not confusing (A), melodramatic (E), or an omniscient point of view (C). It is, however, a stylistic device that allows the reader to be visually unencumbered, causing a more rapid, conversational flow that builds both dramatic tension and nervous anticipation for the reader during this life-and-death confrontation.

37. **B** Element 3 (NARRATIVE VOICE) "I" in the narrative is a health-care worker, probably a doctor or a nurse. Clues to the identity of "I" are found throughout: "my best professional manner," (lines 7–8), someone trained to be able to recognize the symptoms of diphtheria, and "we" in line 1, indicating inclusion in a group involved in the health care of school children.

38. **A** Element 6 (USE OF LANGUAGE) This first-person account (written "I") in the active VOICE (E) does contain a metaphor

(comparing her hands to a cat's claws) and a simile (comparing her movement to those of a cat, "catlike," a comparison using "like"); however, it does not contain any personification—giving human qualities to inanimate objects or ideas.

39. **D** Element 3 (NARRATIVE VOICE) The word "hurt" elicits restrained ("But I did not allow myself to be hurried or disturbed") repugnance ("I ground my teeth in disgust") from the speaker.

40. **A** Element 4 (TONE) The parents' unspoken fears (first paragraph) and care for the child (evidenced by their seeking medical treatment for her) contribute to making their TONE a patronizing (A) blend of pleading and urging when the mother says "Come on, do what he tells you to. He won't hurt you" in front of the speaker.

41. **E** Element 1 (MEANING) (A), (B), (C), and (D) are all causes of conflict: The more physical the speaker becomes, the greater the child's resistance (A); fear of the unknown (Does she have deadly diphtheria?) permeates the room (B); the care-based arguments put forth do not elicit a response so the child must not trust the care of either her parents or the speaker (C); and the parents are greatly embarrassed over the child's behavior, thus causing them to actually work counter to the speaker's efforts (D). None of the CHARACTERS, however, exhibit impertinent cruelty.

42. **E** Element 3 (NARRATIVE VOICE) Although he did progressively change from controlled to less controlled stages of anger, a more striking change is from his somewhat detached (but friendly) professionalism ("I smiled in my best professional manner") to becoming very emotionally involved (note last two paragraphs).

43. **A** Element 4 (TONE) Notice that the speaker's glasses flew across the kitchen floor, making the probable setting the child's home.

44. **B** Element 3 (NARRATIVE VOICE) Diction is word choice and, as such, can be used for a variety of purposes. The speaker uses the first person plural objective case personal pronoun "us" (let's = let us) to create a sense that he and the child are "in this together." Also, the slang phrase "Aw, come on" establishes a friendly, pleading TONE of VOICE,

all aimed at gaining her trust. The author, on the other hand, is trying to elicit a response from the reader by setting a TONE for the episode. This use of diction works together with other elements in the selection (such as setting and characterization) to establish the TONE (B). An important note: The speaker and the author can be two separate and distinctly different VOICES—even in a first person NARRATIVE. Although sometimes the speaker and the writer are "one," keep in mind that the speaker in a selection quite often determines his or her words and actions within the confines of the setting and CHARACTERS of the narrative. The writer, however, also has the reader in mind as he or she uses different literary devices (such as diction) to create the desired effect.

45. **C** Element 2 (FORM) This 14-line, iambic pentameter poem's end rhyme scheme is in the tradition of the English (sometimes called Shakespearean) sonnet. Consequently, the end rhyme pattern changes in lines 5, 9, and 13:

line	1	behold	a
line	2	hang	b
line	3	cold	a
line	4	sang	b
line	5	day	c
line	6	west	d
line	7	away	c
line	8	rest	d
line	9	fire	e
line	10	lie	f
line	11	expire	e
line	12	by	f
line	13	strong	g
line	14	long	g

HINT: Once you have identified a poem as a sonnet, the end rhyme scheme *sometimes* can be a clue to MEANING and structure. English sonnets can be identified by an abab cdcd efef gg rhyme scheme, dividing the 14 lines into three quatrains (four-line sections) and a concluding couplet (two lines). The structure is a vehicle for a step-by-step progression of ideas that is either summarized or reversed by the final couplet. If, on the other hand, the sonnet's rhyme scheme divides it into two parts (an octave of eight lines or two four-line quatrains with a sestet of six lines), often with an abbaabba cdecde rhyme scheme, then the sonnet is Italian (sometimes called Petrarchan). In an Italian sonnet, you can anticipate that the first 8 lines will contain either a statement or a question that will be answered, explored, or somehow addressed in the last six lines. Also, you might look for the two sections to provide a contrast of ideas.

English Sonnet		Italian Sonnet	
a		a	
b		b	
a		b	
b		a	makes a
		a	statement or
c		b	asks a question
d	progression	b	
c	of ideas	a	
d			
		(sometimes contrasts ideas)	
e			
f		c	
e		d	
f		e	explores
		c	concept or
g	summary or	d	answers
g	reversal	e	question

Not all sonnets are in this FORM; however, identification of the rhyme scheme can provide clues to help you answer questions about the poem's MEANING and structure. Question 46 and its analysis exemplify finding the progression of ideas leading to the summary or reversal in an English sonnet.

46. **B** Element 2 (FORM) This poem is a sequence of three metaphors comparing old age and approaching death to a season of the year (when things are still there but "ruined"), to the end of a day (a briefer period, when light "fadeth"), and to the dying down of a fire (that can be extinguished in a brief moment, when the life of the fire "expire[s]").

47. **E** Element 1 (MEANING) This poem is primarily about old age and death. Trees, sunsets, and fires are used as vehicles within the poem.

48. **D** Element 6 (USE OF LANGUAGE) We are to "behold" "in me" (the speaker) "That time of year." How can a time of year be seen in a person? This poem is built upon a conven-

tional metaphor that has been used many times in literature and in the popular culture:

> spring = birth and youth
> summer = prime of life
> fall = retirement and "golden years"
> winter = old age and death

FORMS of this metaphor can be found in poetry, in music (note Frank Sinatra singing "It Was a Very Good Year"), and even in expressions such as "a May-December romance."

49. **B** Element 6 (USE OF LANGUAGE) The metaphor here is an implied comparison: the speaker's approaching death is like the twilight after sunset—a time just before death comes in line 8. Sunrise and sunset representing life and death is another conventional metaphor commonly found in literature (note the song "Sunrise, Sunset").

50. **A** Element 6 (USE OF LANGUAGE) The reader sees in the speaker the "fire" (line 9) that lies on the "ashes of his youth" (line 10); consequently, if the fire is his life, the ashes are what remains of the life that is spent or gone.

51. **D** Element 4 (TONE) The leaves of summer have yellowed, fallen, and no doubt blown away (line 2) and the birds with their sweet songs are gone (line 4), leaving the tree (representing the speaker) alone—shaking against the cold (line 3).

52. **D** Element 7 (MEANINGS IN CONTEXT) The speaker wants the reader to "behold" (line 1) in him the "time of year" (line 1)— obviously the late fall of life. But in this request, he must also look at himself. At first he sees how late in the season it is (the trees have "yellow leaves"). Then he observes "or none," suggesting an emotional sense of loss. Yet he adds "or few" leaves "do hang." Why? Is he not yet ready to face completely "bare" limbs (line 4)? This suggests human uncertainties about life and death on the part of the speaker.

53. **A** Element 2 (FORM) This final couplet makes the point of the poem—the summary concept that when someone is old and dying, like a tree in winter (lines 1–4), the sun about to set (lines 5–8), and a fire going out (lines 9–12), this condition should "make thy love more strong" (line 13).

54. **D** Element 6 (USE OF LANGUAGE) The personification (the giving of human qualities) to sleep "that seals up all in rest" (line 8) makes sleep more threatening as "Death's second self" (line 8).

55. **D** Element 6 (USE OF LANGUAGE) Washington makes an implied comparison (a metaphor) in these lines, likening unity of government to a support pillar and likening real independence to an edifice or large building. In so doing, he states a conclusion: real independence requires unity of government (B). He states a principle (unity of government is a main support of real independence) in a concise, somewhat aphoristic manner (A). The rather impassioned, definitely persuasive TONE (C) is established in part by the use of "dear" and "It is justly so." These lines do not, however, establish distance between speaker and subject (D). On the contrary, use of the word "also" implies that unity of government was "dear" to the speaker some time ago.

56. **A** Element 4 (TONE) The speaker's fatherly (paternal) concern for the well-being of his fellow-Americans can be seen in the second paragraph where he expresses concern that you "should properly estimate the immense value of your national union to your collective and individual happiness…." The patriotic TONE is throughout, particularly in the third paragraph in which he directly addresses "the just pride of patriotism."

57. **E** Element 7 (MEANINGS IN CONTEXT) The "truth" that "different causes" will try "to weaken in your minds" is that "unity of government… is a main pillar in the edifice of your real independence"—independence depends upon unity of government (E).

58. **B** Element 2 (FORM) The first paragraph makes the reader emotionally care about government unity by associating it with such connotatively charged words as "peace… safety…prosperity." Then the second paragraph poses a threat to "that very liberty which you so highly prize," a threat of artifices (tricks), a threat of minds weakened to "truth," a threat of "batteries of internal and external enemies…." Making the reader care, then posing a threat creates a sense of emotional tension.

59. **C** Element 2 (FORM) Of the four FORMS or types of composition (narration, description, exposition, and argumentation), this portion of Washington's speech is mostly argumentative; his purpose is to convince his listeners of the truth of his proposition. Writers can include the elements of several methods of organization in argumentation; however, argumentation generally has at its core the examination of a possible relationship between a conclusion and a premise (evidence from which the conclusion can be drawn.) One conclusion-premise relationship in this passage is:

Conclusion: "The unity of government…is dear to you."

Premise: [because it makes possible] "your real independence…your tranquility at home, your peace abroad…."

Do you see any other conclusions and premises?

60. **A** Element 6 (USE OF LANGUAGE) The speaker uses a military metaphor (an implied comparison) to describe the threats against the "truth" of government unity. He describes their systems of beliefs as a "political fortress" and the tricks and attempts on the part of the "internal and external enemies" to destroy those beliefs as "batteries" (tactical military weapons).

PART III

INTERPRETIVE SKILLS AND CRITICAL READING

Overview

Understanding Prose, Poetry, and Drama

Literary Elements
    Number One: MEANING
    Number Two: FORM
    Number Three: NARRATIVE VOICE
    Number Four: TONE
    Number Five: CHARACTER
    Number Six: USE OF LANGUAGE
    Number Seven: MEANING(S) IN
               CONTEXT

Putting the Seven Literary
   Elements to Work
Writing to Learn
Interpretive Skills and Critical
   Reading in Conclusion

OVERVIEW

The purpose of the Interpretive Skills and Critical Reading section is to examine individually each of the seven literary elements. The following pages:

1. Introduce and define each literary element
2. Discuss and illustrate the basics involved in understanding what each literary element is and how it can be used (*including defining the basic terms listed on page 11*)
3. Discuss and illustrate those features of the literary elements used in prose
4. Discuss and illustrate those features of the literary elements used in poetry
5. Discuss and illustrate those features of the literary elements used in drama
6. Guide you in asking the right questions as you read literary selections so that you can practice identifying the elements
7. Provide hints concerning ways to address the literary elements being discussed, possible test questions, and exceptions and special situations you may encounter when studying works that illustrate the literary elements

The College Board expects you to recognize basic literary terminology (such as simile and personification). Do not, however, be alarmed if some of the terms in this section are unfamiliar to you. You do not have to memorize all the terms and their definitions, but the concepts behind the terms can be useful for insightful reading and expressive writing. Consequently, in addition to explanations of basic literary terms, some more advanced terms are included for your use.

1. Use these terms for reference when analyzing literary selections for literature classes, papers, study groups, and self-study.
2. Use them also for developing a sensitivity to the wide variety of literary devices. For example, you probably will not be expected to identify by name or to define on the actual test such terms as aposiopesis and paraposiopesis, two related terms based on when a speaker stops in mid-sentence (terms defined in "Literary Element Number Six: USE OF LANGUAGE," see pages 178 and 179). An awareness of the shades of difference between these two literary devices, however, can lead the reader to examine *why* a speaker stops in mid-sentence or to recognize the possible *effect* of that device. Is the speaker too scared to continue? Does the speaker stop to express emotion? Perhaps the speaker stops intentionally to comment directly on his or her own emotional state? These are clues to determining the CHARACTER of the speaker—an element that may be the subject of possible test questions. Developing a sensitivity to the many literary devices that writers use is a skill that can be helpful in understanding what you read and in preparing to take the SAT II: Literature Subject Test.

UNDERSTANDING PROSE, POETRY, AND DRAMA

The SAT II: Literature Subject Test is to consist of about 45 to 50 percent poetry, 45 to 50 percent prose, and 0 to 10 percent drama selections on the average.

Prose is expression (whether written or spoken) that does not have a *regular* rhythmic pattern. Prose does have rhythm but its rhythm lacks any sustained regularity and is not meant to be scanned.

Poetry is expression that is written in verse, often with some FORM of regular rhythm. The basis of poetic expression is a heightened sense of perception or consciousness.

Do all poems have regular rhythm? No. Do all poems take verse form? No. How, then, can you distinguish between prose and poetry? Both prose and poetry are forms of communication. Consequently, they share many elements as the prose writer or poet uses whatever means will most effectively convey his or her thoughts. As a result, prose and poetry can be seen as two levels or planes, each going in opposite directions, but partially overlapping at their common ends. Eventually prose pulls elements from poetry and poetry pulls elements from prose until each reaches a finite point at which prose becomes poetry and poetry becomes prose.

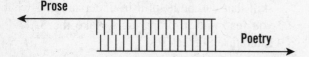

For example, look at this prose poem (a poem without traditional line divisons or lengths). Notice the prose elements at work, such as both left and right margin justification (each line starts and finishes at the same point) and paragraph indentation.

BELL-TONES

Bells have been ringing and marking time in my life. Bells to come for and bells to go by. Bells to ring and bells to hear. Easy bell-tones turn to clattering bells ringing, finally becoming muted into many soft death knells.

I started with Tinker Bell, then listened to school bells between playing in fields of bluebells. Happy bells ringing;

proms, parties, and dancing, playing happily and listening to the ringing of sleigh bells. Church bells comforting and confirming and wedding bells promising our love Always; such joy, bluebonnets and baby bonnets, with happy baby bells on baby booties.

Dinner bells called me; laundry bells startled me; cake timers beckoned me; liberty bells stirred me; jingle bells amused me until all the bells jangled and wrangled metallic as door bells and telephone bells ringing in pairs demanded me.

Then bells rang for help…time to get up, time to sleep, time to eat, time to leave, time to escape danger, time to come and time to go. Bells marked the hours and the times of my life. Now the beautiful bluebells in fields are calling me once again, mute bells singing soft notes as Church bells sound in blissful bell-tones, while we are waiting for the joyful ringing rapture of the Resurrection.

by L. E. Myers

Where would you place this prose poem on the diagram?

Although visually made to look like prose, this prose poem contains such major poetic elements as personification ("bluebells...calling me"), onomatopoeia ("jangled and wrangled metallic"), and alliteration ("baby bells on baby booties") and the intensity of MEANING characteristic of poetry, such as symbolism (the bell itself as a symbol of life's major events) and other uses of language such as the oxymoron ("mute bells"). The MEANING is reflected and intensified by elements of rhythm throughout the work, such as the back-and-forth bell-like movement in "time to sleep, time to eat, time to leave...."

Now read this descriptive prose excerpt from Sharon Curtin.

There is nothing to prepare you for the experience of growing old. Living is a process, an irreversible progression toward old age and eventual death. You see men of eighty still vital and straight as oaks; you see men of fifty reduced to gray shadows in the human landscape. The cellular clock differs for each one of us, and is profoundly affected by our own life experiences, our heredity, and perhaps most important, by the concepts of aging encountered in society and in oneself.

The aged live with enforced leisure, on fixed incomes, subject to many chronic illnesses, and most of their money goes to keep a roof over their heads. They also live in a culture that worships youth.

A kind of cultural attitude makes me bigoted against old people; it makes me think young is best; it makes me treat old people like outcasts.

Hate that gray? Wash it away!

Wrinkle cream.

Monkey glands.

Face-lifting.

Look like a bride again.

Don't trust anyone over thirty.

I fear growing old.

Feel Young Again!

I am afraid to grow old—we're all afraid.

What poetic devices has Curtin used? What effect do these devices produce? Where would you place this work on the diagram?

Obviously, a clear-cut distinction between prose and poetry is difficult to establish; you need to be constantly alert to the poet's use of prose techniques and the prose writer's borrowing of poetic devices. Yet, whenever possible you should learn to distinguish the literary elements that are used particularly in prose from those that are more widely used in poetry. Each one has elements that are unique, concepts that are important first to recognize and then to use as ways to gain MEANING and insight.

The following lists summarize some of the key distinguishing features of prose and poetry. Use these lists to compare and contrast these two FORMS writers use to convey MEANING.

Poetry has (or can have)

- Imaginative elements
- Significance and levels of MEANING
- A regularity of rhythm
- Intensity
- Unity
- Poetic diction ("poetic" language [such as archaisms, epithets, and periphrases used by eighteenth-century poets] once used by English writers, but no longer used except perhaps to create irony)
- Poetic license (liberties poets take in varying from standardized diction, rhyme, spelling, syntax, and mechanics)
- Sense impressions and heightened consciousness
- Concrete language
- Versification (meter, rhyme, and stanza forms)
- Sentences divided into lines (verse-lines/lineation)
- Stanzas
- Bound speech
- Sound patterning
- Syntactic deployment
- Both MEANING and sound

Prose has (or can have)

- Rhythmic pattern (but not regular or sustained) called *prose rhythm*
- Consciously shaped writing
- Logical grammatical order
- Connected (not listed) ideas
- Levels of diction
- "Style"
- Rhetorical accent (When the accent is determined by the intent or MEANING, for example, "She gave the keys to <u>you</u>?" implies that the speaker is surprised at who is the recipient of the keys. Compare: "She <u>gave</u> the keys to you?" questions whether she really did give the keys or "<u>She</u> gave the keys to you?" questions who actually gave the keys.)
- Modes or types of formal organization (These "formal" organizations can range from loosely structured everyday discourse through carefully structured exposition.)
- A primary function: to communicate information
- Sentences
- Paragraphs

Drama is a story intended to be acted out on a stage. Some critics include pantomime (silent acting), whereas others specify that drama requires dialogue. Drama also requires a plot, a setting, and CHARACTERS.

Drama is divided into two very broad categories, each with its own characteristics:

1. Comedy. Generally, comedy refers to plays that amuse us and/or have happy endings.
2. Tragedy. In a tragic play, the protagonist is disastrously overcome by some catastrophe.

As with prose and poetry, drama is a dynamic FORM that provides a rich source of elements that can be used by the poet and prose writer, as well as by the dramatist. Obviously, elements of both comedy and tragedy can be found in prose fiction and in narrative poetry. The dramatist can also, however,

HOW LANGUAGE SAVED A NATION

English prose is the result of the courage and farsighted thinking of a young hero named Alfred the Great, the ninth century King of Wessex. In the 870s, the Danes were vigorously attacking the English-speaking kingdoms. Should they have war, there would not have been any English-speaking kingdoms left. The English language was in danger of extinction. King Alfred managed to push back the Danes from Wessex, but he knew that without the help of the Englishmen surrounding Wessex, the treaty the Danes had signed would not save them. What could he do?

In a brilliant move to unify the kingdoms against the Danes, King Alfred consolidated the people on the basis of their "Englishness," with the English language at the heart of their new awareness of national identity. In a sense, King Alfred used the English language to establish and at the same time save a nation. Once the people were united against the Danes, Alfred moved boldly ahead. He replaced Latin with English, had English chronicles written to give the people a sense of history, established a standardized English writing system and earned for himself the title of "founder of English prose" by writing (in A.D. 887) the first example of completed English prose (*Handbook*).

Whereas the Danes were a threat to the English-speaking people and their language as a nation, Latin was a threat to English prose within the nation. Obviously, Alfred's promotion of English over Latin as an impetus for national unity did much to help English prose in its struggling stages. Even after English prose became more prevalent, however, its forms and syntax were significantly influenced by Latin.

incorporate elements of prose and poetry within the development of the drama. Take the use of poetic FORMS in drama as an example. In Elizabethan drama, Marlowe's lower-class CHARACTERS speak in prose, but the "Good and Bad Angels" speak in blank verse. Of William Shakespeare's plays, a large number are written in blank verse. Shakespeare used poetic elements throughout his dramas to create moods, to project CHARACTER, to develop plot, and even to signal the mechanical elements of the play. This can be seen in his ingenious use of couplets to cue entrances and to close scenes. A striking example is in Shakespeare's *The Tragedy of Julius Caesar*. Notice the dramatic impact of Shakespeare's use of couplet at the moment when the struggle between Caesar and Marcus Brutus ends with Brutus committing suicide:

Act V Scene V

MARCUS BRUTUS. Hence! I will follow.
>   [*Exeunt* CLITUS, DARDANIUS, *and* VOLUMNIUS.]
> I prithee, Strato, stay thou by the lord:
> Thou art a fellow of a good respect;
> Thy life hath had some smatch of honour in it:
> Hold, then, my sword, and turn away thy face,
> While I do run upon it. Wilt thou, Strato?

STRATO. Give me your hand first: fare you well, my lord.

MARCUS BRUTUS.
>   Farewell, good Strato.—Caesar, now be still:
> I kill'd not thee with half so good a will.
>   [*He runs on his sword, and dies.*]

Prose, poetry, and drama are vehicles a writer can use to carry out his or her purpose. Many patterns and devices can be used within each of these vehicles to accomplish this purpose. In other words, writers use and manipulate literary techniques within each vehicle to establish or alter the MEANING, FORM, VOICE, TONE, CHARACTER, USE OF LANGUAGE, and the MEANINGS WITHIN CONTEXT to further their purpose.

As you read and incorporate into your personal study program the following discussion of the seven literary elements, keep in mind that the mixing and blending of purpose, overall FORM, patterns of development, and literary techniques is at the core of literary expression. Interpretive skills involve identifying those purposes, FORMS, patterns of development, and literary techniques as they are used in a literary selection. Critical reading also involves analyzing how effectively these elements have been used.

LITERARY ELEMENT NUMBER ONE: MEANING

SAMUEL FOOTE (1720–77)

Charles Howard of Greystock published a silly book he called 'Thoughts'. He meets Foote at a coffee-house. 'And have you read my *Thoughts*?' says he. 'No,' replies the other, 'I wait for the second volume.'—'And why so?'—'Because I have heard', says Foote, 'that Second Thoughts were best.'

The purpose of writing is communication. Whether the literary selection is in the FORM of prose, poetry, or drama, the writer is communicating. That communication, that purpose on the part of the writer, forms an important part of the MEANING of the work. One of the first steps, then, in determining MEANING is to identify the writer's purpose.

There are four types of writing based on its purpose or function:

1. The descriptive or expressive purpose

In description, the prose writer, poet, or dramatist attempts to "paint a picture with words." Description, however, is also an important way to convey abstract concepts. Description can be factual (describing, for example, the color and dimension of an object) or it can be impressionistic (such as expressing what love feels like). Although descriptive or expressive writing may make extended use of descriptive adjectives and be characterized by powerful action verbs, it is not necessarily "wordy." A tightly written work that makes use of carefully chosen figurative language can be *very* expressive. Notice the rich textures of MEANING in these four lines from a poem by Percy Bysshe Shelley:

From thy nest every rafter
Will rot, and thine eagle home
Leave thee naked to laughter,
When leaves fall and cold winds come.

2. The expository or informative purpose

Exposition explains something. This book is expository: the purpose of this work is to explain about the major literary elements and to inform about the SAT II: Literature Subject Test as it relates to those literary elements. Most instructional textbooks are written with an expository purpose. The expository writer includes ideas and facts about the focus subject. Encyclopedias, newspapers, and business reports are all written to inform the reader.

3. The NARRATIVE purpose

A narrator tells a story. The story may focus on an incident or brief episode (as in an anecdote), the story might chronicle a hero's adventurous relationship to the history of a nation (as in an epic poem), or it might follow the history of a family's generations (as in a saga). An important element of narration is time—events unfolding through time.

4. The argumentative and/or persuasive purpose

Notice that argumentation can be joined to persuasion, but it also can be distinguished from persuasion. A writer or speaker uses argumentation to convince readers or hearers of the truth (or falsehood) of a proposition. The purpose of persuasive writing, however, is to convince the reader or hearer that some action must be taken. The writer's purpose might simply be to convince you that what he or she is saying is true, such as that the spotted owl is an endangered species. But the writer's purpose may also include persuading you to take some action, such as pressuring your local representative to support legislation that would set aside protected habitats for the spotted owl. Expository or informative writing focuses on the subject, whereas persuasion focuses on the reader or listener. Oration, a passionately presented formal speech, illustrates how an argumentation can be developed. Although oration has lost favor in today's culture, orations once rang out in courtrooms, churches, and other public forums. Its seven-part structure includes an attention-getting introduction, a narration aimed at giving the facts, an exposition or definition, a clarification of the issues, a confirmation to present the pros and cons, a refutation of the opponent's arguments, and a summary.

Although a literary selection may be identified as predominantly one of these four types of composition, seldom is a work exclusively one type. Generally, the writer uses elements of the other three types to aid in the development of the main purpose. For instance, description is frequently used in narration; describing details about oppressive heat, black water, and clinging leeches helps the narrator tell his or her story of convicts escaping a swamp-bound prison camp. An expository writer, aiming to "tell the facts," can narrate an anecdote (an episode or event) to help the reader better understand the information; and political writers often incorporate illustrative narration in their persuasive speeches.

A current trend among writers of informative articles in popular magazines is to begin their articles with anecdotes designed to capture the reader's interest before presenting the facts of the topic. The topics range from the humorous to the serious; the anecdotes range from abbreviated personal experiences of the writer to complex incidences in the lives of others.

Diana Townsend-Butterworth's article on "Are You a Good Role Model?" in *Family Circle* magazine begins:

Angela smiles down at her infant son, Joey. Joey smiles back. Fast forward by two years: Joey is in his stroller when a neighbor's golden retriever wanders over. Angela leans down and says, "Good dog," as she pats the dog and scratches him behind the ears. Joey reaches out and pats the dog's head. "Good dog," he mimics. Fast forward again: Joey, a first grader now, is helping his mother wrap Christmas presents to take to children in a homeless shelter.

She continues the article by moving into the focus and informative aspects of the topic:

Angela is not merely teaching her son to smile, to say "Good dog," and to wrap presents; she is also modeling language, affection, social responsibility and the importance of caring about the needs and feelings of others.

In *Woman's Day* magazine, Loraine Stern, M.D., writes:

Exactly a year ago, on January 17, I learned firsthand about how to cope with disaster.

After describing her own experience during one of California's famous earthquakes, Stern lists and describes specific steps people can take for "Surviving a Disaster—Together."

Shirley Redmond, in another *Woman's Day* magazine article, uses anecdote to persuade her readers in "It's *Not* Just the Thought":

When, for the third Christmas in a row, a relative sent my daughter a red velvet dress, I was furious. Bethany, with her tangerine-colored hair and pale skin, never dresses in shades of red or orange. She looks ill when she even stands near something that color.

When I made my feelings known to my husband, he shrugged and offered the requisite, "Oh well, I guess it's the thought that counts." But as far as I'm concerned, the maxim has holes in its logic. And it's high time we quit using it as an excuse for habitual thoughtlessness.

After you have identified in broad terms the type(s) of writing used in a literary selection, try to narrow your focus to determine what the work is about and what the writer is trying to achieve.

In the excerpt from Redmond's article, what is the writer hoping to achieve? What is the MEANING of the selection? By using a narrative anecdote as an attention-getting illustration, she supports the main point of her argument: "the maxim [I guess it's the thought that counts] has holes in its logic." What is she intending to persuade her readers to do?— "quit using it as an excuse for habitual thoughtlessness."

Test questions concerning the MEANING of this brief excerpt might read:

What is the subject of this passage?

(A) A maxim
(B) A Christmas gift
(C) Habitual thoughtlessness
(D) Bethany's hair color
(E) A thoughtless gift

Although all five answer choices are involved in the MEANING of the selection, the maxim, the Christmas gift, Bethany's hair color, and the thoughtless gift itself are only supportive or illustrative evidence behind the main subject: habitual thoughtlessness (C).

The main point of the passage is that

(A) Bethany has tangerine-colored hair
(B) Bethany's relative was thoughtless
(C) red and orange do not suit Bethany
(D) the speaker's husband responded with an expected answer
*(E) people use an old saying as an excuse for thoughtlessness

Determining the MEANING of a work also involves looking at its *effect*. The emotional impact, the impression the work leaves on the reader, is part of its effect. Skillful writers will plan a certain effect—perhaps drawing from the reader's feelings of anger, aversion, joyful laughter—by careful use of the literary elements and the techniques available to the writer within those elements. Yet, sometimes an effect happens unintentionally, without the writer's deliberate plan or even conscious knowledge. This is because MEANING is a two-sided concept. On one side you have the writer, someone with a topic to discuss, a point to make, an agenda to fulfill. When you look for the purpose in a work, you are looking at the writer's intent. But on the other side of MEANING is the reader, someone who often comes to the work without pre-knowledge of the writer's intent, but someone who does generally have some preconceived thoughts or opinions. For the reader, the focus is on the work itself and what effect the work has on him or her. Read this poem by William Oldys:

THE FLY
An Anacreontic

Busy, curious, thirsty fly,
Gently drink, and drink as I;
Freely welcome to my cup,
Could'st thou sip, and sip it up;
Make the most of life you may,
Life is short and wears away.
Just alike, both mine and thine,
Hasten quick to their decline;
Thine's a summer, mine's no more,
Though repeated to threescore;
Threescore summers when they're gone,
Will appear as short as one.

by William Oldys

What is the effect of this poem on you? How might "The Fly" affect another reader? How might the reader's age affect his or her views of this poem and the speaker's MEANING? (Anacreontic means in the easy style of the Greek poet Anacreon.)

How would you answer the following question concerning this poem's MEANING?

The focus of this poem is

(A) the speaker's fondness for a fly
(B) a fly drinking from the speaker's cup
(C) the fly's impending death
(D) the relative brevity of life
(E) the speaker's impending death

Each of the above five answer choices correctly addresses some level of MEANING in this poem. The best description of the poem's focus, however, is the answer choice that summarizes the speaker's intent or main point. Why does the speaker fondly welcome the fly to drink from his cup (A and B)? Because the fly's life is short (C). Why does the speaker care that the fly's life is short? Because the speaker's life also seems short (E). What is the effect (emotional impact) of this comparison on the poem's MEANING? It establishes, in relation to the life cycle, a similarity between the speaker and the fly: that whether life lasts a summer or threescore summers, life is relatively short; therefore, the correct answer choice is D.

Another way to determine the MEANING of a literary selection is to look for different levels of MEANING and to determine how each may or may not work within the author's purpose. Some levels of MEANING are:

1. The literal MEANING
This level of MEANING is based on taking the work at its "face value"—without examining any figurative levels.

2. The allegorical MEANING
At the allegorical level, particularly in narrative works, each object, person, place, and event represents something else, with the CHARACTERS of the narrative personifying abstract qualities. An entire work may be allegorical (as, for example, in *Pilgrim's Progress* in which the man named Christian meets Mr. Worldly Wiseman—a story in which people and places represent the qualities after which they are named) or a literary selection may have or incorporate a few allegorical elements.

3. The symbolic MEANING
Symbols have dual MEANINGS, the literal or face value MEANING and a representative MEANING—the symbol stands for something else. "Old Glory, Mother, and apple pie" are symbols of down-home American patriotism. A symbol represents something else, but in a less structured way than an allegory.

4. The figurative MEANING
At the figurative level the writer strives for a special MEANING other than the standard or literal

MEANING of the words. These special MEAN-INGS (tropic MEANINGS) are brought about by the use of tropes. Some tropes include simile (a comparison using "like" or "as"—lips as red as a rose) and metaphor (an implied comparison—rose-red lips). Tropes will be examined in more detail in a later section in this book.

These four levels of MEANING, and possibly other levels as well, can, depending on how they are used, affect in a very narrow sense the MEANING of specific elements of a work; or they can affect the MEANING of the entire selection.

Read the following poem by Tennyson.

DARK HOUSE

Dark house, by which once more I stand
    Here in the long unlovely street,
    Doors, where my heart was used to beat
So quickly, waiting for a hand,

line

(5) A hand that can be clasped no more—
    Behold me, for I cannot sleep,
    And like a guilty thing I creep
At earliest morning to the door.

He is not here; but far away
(10) The noise of life begins again,
    And ghastly thro' the drizzling rain
On the bald street breaks the blank day.

                by Alfred, Lord Tennyson

What is the literal MEANING of this poem? The speaker is standing by a dark house on a rainy morning.

Do you see any symbolic MEANINGS in the poem? What might the "dark house" represent? Could it symbolize death? Are there any other symbolic, figurative, or allegorical levels of MEAN-ING? Consider the possibility:

Why do you think that the speaker isolates "Doors" in line 3? What do the doors represent? How does this relate to "door" in line 8? What is ironically significant in the speaker's inability to sleep (line 6)? Why does the speaker emphasize "hand" in lines 4–5? What might the hand represent? What other words and PHRASES do you see that carry levels of MEANING additional to the literal MEANING?

As the examination of MEANING has so far shown, MEANING can be defined in several ways. **"What is the MEANING?"** can be answered by determining:

1. The author's purpose
2. The effect of the work on the reader or listener
3. The level(s) of MEANING working within the selection

A fourth way MEANING can be determined is by recognizing that a literary selection is made up of parts. These parts may be external structure (such as chapters in a novel, stanzas in a poem, or acts and scenes in a play) or they may be internal (such as plot in a narrative). Each of these parts can have MEANING independent of or contributing to the MEANING of the work as a whole. Sometimes the MEANING of a selection is the sum of its parts—sometimes the MEANING can be determined by a key portion of the work. In a testing situation, you may be asked to determine the MEANING of an entire selection—or of just a portion of that selection. You may be asked to identify how the MEAN-ING of each part contributes to the whole, or how it contrasts that MEANING.

To look at a practical example, reread the poem for questions 45–54 in Diagnostic Test I (see page 40) a Shakespearean sonnet called "That Time of Year."

First, examine lines 1–4. What is the MEANING of these four lines? At a figurative level, the speaker is in a stage of life that is like the fall of the year when trees shed their leaves and birds leave in migration.

What is the MEANING of lines 5–8? This stage of life is also like the twilight. (Notice that on a symbolic level sleep represents death.) Lines 9–12? The speaker's life can, as well, be described as a dying fire (again, on a figurative level). The final couplet? When death is so near, love should intensify. Now look at the poem as a whole. How do these parts work together to create the MEANING of the whole?

MEANING IN PROSE

Fiction

Prose fiction is often narrative, generally in the form of a novel or short story. In such works, the writer sometimes makes a statement (called the **theme**) that is intended to summarize or assert to the reader some main point, doctrine, or generalization about life, love, religion, the condition of the world, and so forth. Occasionally, the writer will directly state the theme, but more often it is implied in plot development and characterization. Unlike **topic** (the subject of the story, such as war, love, business, or children), the theme is what the story is about—its plot, setting, and CHARACTER blended with the writer's perceptions to make a statement about the subject.

In some prose fiction, the theme can be seen as the "moral of the story." To cite an instance, *Aesop's Fables* are noted for the concise nature of their theme statements. Also, theme is referred to as "the message" of the story. The narrative, then, exemplifies or makes concrete an otherwise abstract idea.

Some topics or subjects are so popular that you will see themes developed within them over and over again. Here are just a few examples.

Survival—In these stories an individual family or group of people must survive such disasters as shipwrecks on deserted islands, plane crashes into swamps, earthquakes, tidal waves, floods, volcanoes, getting lost in mountains, being stranded in unfamiliar territory, and attacks by wild animals. Emphasis is usually placed on the elements of human behavior that are often revealed in life-threatening situations, such as bravery, cowardice, loyalty, and ingenuity. Some famous works written on this topic include *Robinson Crusoe* and *The Swiss Family Robinson*.

Children raised by animals—This is a very old topic in literary history in which a child is somehow lost, abandoned, or in some other way separated from parents and civilization and is adopted and raised by animals, often wolves or apes. A well-known example is the *Tarzan of the Apes* series of novels based on the CHARACTER Tarzan. The stories often portray the children (who may become adults in the story) as having great integrity or innocence in contrast to civilization.

UFO invasions and abductions—stories in which Earth is contacted by other-world beings that generally take one of two directions: the aliens are characterized as evil invading forces who want to destroy humans or as kindly, misunderstood visitors that are targets for people who want to destroy them out of fear or ignorance. The UFO story is represented by *War of the Worlds*.

Lost pets—In stories based on this subject, a family pet (usually a dog or cat, but occasionally a larger animal such as a horse) is lost or stolen and must undergo grand adventures and display remarkable courage and seeming intelligence as it overcomes and escapes captors, natural elements, and other such obstacles to return home. Family values and loyalty are important elements in these stories. The *Lassie* series included many examples of this popular topic.

End of the world—Seen in a variety of CONTEXTS, these stories usually involve a man-made disaster (ecological, biological, or nuclear) in which only a few people survive and must face the horrors of a world in which civilization and its amenities are destroyed.

Good versus evil—This is another very old concept that has been addressed in an almost endless variety of ways. A common FORM is the law versus the lawless. In this variation, the law is often represented by law enforcement officers, for example, the Canadian Mounted Police, and the lawless by criminals ranging from train robbers in western genres to drug dealers in more modern stories. These plots usually involve chases that culminate in a final battle in which often (but not always) the law prevails.

Nonfiction

The theme, the central idea of the work, is also called the **thesis** in nonfiction prose. The thesis refers to the writer's position on the subject. The thesis may be directly stated or may be implied; it might lead off the first paragraph of the selection or the author might "build" his or her main points to a concluding thesis. How a thesis is developed relates directly to the writer's purpose (descriptive, informative, narrative, or argumentative/persuasive).

Although the thesis may be directly stated, discovering the thesis in a nonfiction narrative occasionally is similar to finding the implied theme in a fiction narrative. Finding the thesis in argumentation and persuasive writing, however, requires further discussion. In argumentation, the writer's main purpose is not just to explain something, but to convince the reader that his or her thesis—or *proposition*—is true. Although the writer might use elements of exposition, narration, or description to support the proposition, the main purpose is to "argue the point." Consequently, the thesis or proposition is a statement of the generalization that the writer is attempting to prove or is a statement of the specific conclusion the writer wants you to make.

How writers do this is discussed under FORM, but read the following Preface to Richard Shenkman's *"I Love Paul Revere, Whether He Rode or Not"* by Warren Harding.

> Imagine for a moment it is 1923. Al Capone is assembling an army of gun-toting henchmen in Chicago. (They will number 700 before he is through.) Cotton farmers in the South are sunk in depression. The Ku Klux Klan is on the rise. Newspaper headlines tell of corruption in the Veterans Bureau (the director has had to resign). Rumors in the capital hint of the coming Teapot Dome Scandal. (Eventually two secretaries in the cabinet will go to jail, convicted of corruption.)
>
> But these are not the things that concern the president of the United States. What worries Warren Harding—touring the country on a campaign swing that will prove to be his last—is a recent attack on the legend of Paul Revere. An iconoclast had noted that Revere never completed the ride made famous by Longfellow. Before giving warning to Concord, Revere was discovered by the British and captured. Harding, however, told the crowd he didn't care. "I love the story of Paul Revere," the president intoned in his most presidential-sounding voice, "whether he rode or not."
>
> Americans today are less scandalized by iconoclasm than Harding was. But we are less cynical than we think we are. Indeed, the evidence suggests we are just as susceptible to mythology as Americans in the past.
>
> The danger is not that we have myths. They tell us who we are and what we cherish and all people have them. The danger is hiding from the fact that they are myths.

What is the thesis or proposition of Shenkman's argument? What do you think, based on the preface, this book is mainly about?

Based on Shenkman's thesis, how would you answer this question regarding the selection's MEANING?

The speaker's main point in the selection is that

(A) Harding should have concentrated on real issues
(B) people should differentiate fact from myth
(C) Americans should avoid myth as dangerous
(D) iconoclasms are dangerous
(E) myths should be cherished

(The correct answer is B.)

MEANING IN POETRY

What does a poem "mean"? Answers to this question vary with the critics asked; however, here are some of the elements you can look for to identify MEANING in a poem:

1. Poets used to write a prose paraphrase that summarizes the plot or states the MEANING of the poem. Such a statement is called the *argument* of the poem. Modern poets may not provide an argument for a poem, but writing a prose summary and perhaps even a paraphrase in some cases will help you to determine MEANING.
2. Try to identify the poem's:
   - Subject or topic, such as love, death, or birth.
   - Theme (how the poet treats the subject). You might summarize (write a one- or two-sentence summary) a paraphrase of the poem (the line-by-line or stanza-by-stanza MEANING of the poem expressed or explained in your own words) to establish the theme, for example, a simple life is best or unrequited love can make you sick.
   - Motifs (if any)—elements that recur in poetry, such as *carpe diem* ("seize the day") themes.
   - Use of poetic devices, such as rhythm and rhyme, as they relate to and affect the MEANING.

As a practical application, read the following poem by Walt Whitman and (1) identify the subject, (2) write a paraphrase, and (3) identify the theme.

A NOISELESS PATIENT SPIDER

A noiseless patient spider,
I marked where on a little promontory it stood isolated,
Marked how to explore the vacant vast surrounding,
line It launched forth filament, filament, filament, out of itself,
(5) Ever unreeling them, ever tirelessly speeding them.

And you O my soul where you stand,
Surrounded, detached, in measureless oceans of space,
Ceaselessly musing, venturing, throwing, seeking the spheres to connect them,
Till the bridge you will need be formed, till the ductile anchor hold,
(10) Till the gossamer thread you fling catch somewhere, O my soul.

The Subject

At first glance, the subject is a spider—on a literal level. But is a spider *really* the poet's subject, or is a spider the means he uses to metaphorically approach another, more abstract subject? Examine the paraphrase for clues.

The Paraphrase

Lines 1–5—The speaker watched a spider spin a web. Lines 1–2—The speaker saw a spider standing alone on a promontory. Line 3—The spider checked out its surroundings. Lines 4–5—It spun a web.

Lines 6–10—The speaker's soul is detached and is seeking to be attached. Lines 6–7—The speaker's soul is standing detached in space. Line 8—His soul is checking out his surroundings. Lines 9–10—His soul is seeking to become attached to something.

Now, based on the paraphrase, what is the subject? It can be stated many ways: "anchoring of the soul," "isolation," or perhaps stated simply "the soul."

The Theme

Based on the paraphrase, the theme is a product of a structural metaphor. In the first stanza, the speaker describes how a spider is isolated in space, spinning a web. This forms the basis for the metaphor, the implied comparison. In the second stanza, he describes how the soul is isolated in space, attempting to fling "the gossamer thread"— to become attached (like a spider spinning its web). The spider spinning its web is a *vehicle*; the soul seeking attachment is the *tenor* of the metaphor. (These terms will be discussed in detail in the Literary Element Number Six: USE OF LANGUAGE.)

One way the theme, then, might be stated is that the soul, like a spider, is isolated and detached, trying to make connections with its surroundings.

MEANING IN DRAMA

In drama written for television and movies, the main idea (the literal MEANING) is a summary statement called a "hook." In *Close Encounters of the Third Kind* the hook is aliens telepathically contacting humans, with the narrative culminating in an actual encounter. Hooks may revolve around any number of topics, ranging from social issues to famous personalities. But to find the MEANING in literary drama, the hook serves only as a starting point. The action, setting, and CHARACTER work with the plot to establish MEANING in drama.

As with poetry, sometimes the writer provides an argument, a plot summary or statement of MEANING; but most often the reader or audience is left to draw MEANING from the performance itself—a point that should be underscored—drama is intended to be performed. As a result, all the elements present in the telling of the NARRATIVE are geared in drama to the performance.

At the center of literary drama and its MEANING is conflict. This conflict (the good guys vs. the bad guys, the obstacles to overcome, the love of winning, and so forth) will naturally affect the MEANING of the play.

The MEANING may result from how the CHARACTERS deal with the conflict. For instance, think about a play in which the hook is two ghetto-born brothers who each must face and deal with a legacy of abuse and poverty. One brother strives for immediate gratification by joining street gangs and drug dealers, eventually being killed by an overdose of drugs. The other brother exercises self-discipline and works his way through college to become a successful businessman and father. At this point the MEANING might be that the way to overcome a life of abuse and poverty is through perseverance and self-discipline. What if, however, the play continues and the successful brother returns to the ghetto to do community-service work and is killed by a senseless, drive-by shooting? Now MEANING is being affected not by how the CHARACTERS deal with the conflict but by how the setting and forces within the plot structure work together with the conflict to overcome the CHARACTERS. In this case the MEANING changes to be a very pessimistic view that regardless of the struggle, the forces of poverty and abuse cannot be overcome (an example of dramatic irony).

When trying to find MEANING in a dramatic selection, remember that a play is intended to be performed. Consequently, you should first find the hook, then look for MEANING.

QUESTIONS TO APPLY YOUR LEARNING

As you practice reading literary selections, ask these questions to help you identify and understand MEANING:

1. Which type of writing does the author use— descriptive/expressive purpose, expository/informative purpose, narrative purpose, or argumentative and/or persuasive purpose?
2. Does the writer use any of the other types of writing to more effectively convey MEANING?
3. What is the work about (stated in a PHRASE and in a statement)?
4. What does the writer hope to achieve?
5. What is the effect of the work?
6. What is the literal, "face value" MEANING of the selection?
7. Can you identify any other levels of MEANING in this selection?
8. How does the MEANING of the parts contribute to the MEANING of the whole selection?
9. If the work is prose fiction, what is the topic (subject)? the theme?
10. If the work is prose nonfiction, what is the topic (subject)? the thesis?
11. In an argumentation, what is the writer's proposition?
12. Has the poet included a statement of argument?
13. If the work is a drama, what is its "hook"?
14. How do the actions, settings, and CHARACTERS work with the plot of the drama to influence the MEANING?

ADDITIONAL HELPFUL POINTS TO REMEMBER

- Look for extensive use of symbolic levels of MEANING in the works written in mid-nineteenth century America. (For instance, Walt Whitman, Henry David Thoreau, and Ralph Waldo Emerson used romantic symbolism and their works provide excellent practice in identifying these symbols.)
- Be alert to questions about MEANING.

  The answer choices may require you to select a single word or PHRASE that sums up the topic of the selection, for example, marriage, death, persecution, loyalty. Some may be looking for a statement of the theme (the thesis or statement of the propositions). Still others may be describing the various levels of MEANING at work in the selection.
- When looking for the theme in narrative fiction, be alert for possible sub-themes (generalizations that can be drawn from or supported by the story but are not the main theme; sub-themes may support the main theme or may be independent of it.) Also, watch for motifs (such as conventional situations).
- If the question of MEANING deals with an epic poem, look for the speaker to begin his or her narration with a statement of argument (the epic theme) just before asking a muse for inspiration and asking an epic question.

LITERARY ELEMENT NUMBER TWO: FORM

LINES WRITTEN IN RIDICULE OF CERTAIN POEMS

Wheresoe'er I turn my view,
All is strange, yet nothing new;
Endless labor all along,
Endless labor to be wrong;
Phrase that time has flung away,
Uncouth words in disarray,
Tricked in antique ruff and bonnet,
Ode, and elegy, and sonnet.

by Samuel Johnson

Ode...elegy...sonnet—their misuse in poorly executed works led Samuel Johnson to write these critical lines about "Phrase that time has flung away" and about "Uncouth words." Yet, when well written, these FORMS of literary expression can stir emotions from deep within the reader or hearer.

While MEANING might be called the "what?" (as in "What is the writer trying to say?") in a literary selection, FORM can surely be called the "how?" ("How does he or she say it?"). FORM includes many different patterns of development or methods of organization—ways in which the writer attempts to achieve his or her purpose(s). These purposes generally include (1) self-expression, (2) providing information, (3) persuasion, and (4) entertainment (or creation of a literary work). As a result, the basic organizing principles of FORM are governed to a greater or lesser degree by purpose. The reason for this is easy to explain: Some FORMS of writing communicate certain MEAN-INGS better than others. There can be more than one level of MEANING; consequently, the FORM of a literary selection can be viewed from different perspectives.

PERSPECTIVE ONE
ORGANIZING PRINCIPLES

How does the writer develop his or her thoughts as they relate to the purpose? The summary on page 70 in a very simplified manner sets forth some of the organizing principles commonly used by writers to develop their thoughts within a literary work.

Also, as you identify and study the organizing principles being used in a literary selection, give attention to *sequence* or *order* of presentation. Here are some of the most common ways writers sequence their work:

1. Chronological sequence—tells what happened according to time
2. Climactic order—arranged from the least important to the most important
3. Deductive order—arrangement based on deductive reasoning (from the general to the specific)
4. Inductive order—arrangement based on inductive reasoning (from the specific to the general)
5. Problem-solving sequence—presents a problem, then suggests or explains the solution
6. Spatial sequence—describes a location
7. Topical order—presents ideas by topics
8. Mixed order—arrangement that is a blend of patterns

THINK ABOUT THIS—LITERARY FORM AND THE READER

You probably are aware of whether you are a visual learner who appreciates a hands-on approach or an auditory learner who benefits most from lectures and verbal communication. In addition, each reader has talents, skills, experiences, and personal interests that directly and indirectly affect his or her comprehension and learning (interests that may result from the joy experienced in exercising a particular ability or skill or that may result from the pleasure found in meeting a challenge to that ability or skill).

As you read different literary selections, can you see ways the writers use FORM to appeal more effectively to their readers? Perhaps a use of prose rhythm enhances the work's auditory appeal (a very effective device in rhetorical writing), or the use of an outline for a plan of action within a persuasive essay provides a visual structure. Does the writer appeal to any of your talents, skills, experiences, or personal interests within the body of the work?

ORGANIZING PRINCIPLES

Basic Organization Principle:	Definition:	Example:
Analogy	Comparisons using the known to explain or clarify the unknown	Fried frog legs (the unknown) taste a lot like fried chicken (the known).
Cause and Effect (Causal Analysis)	Establishing a relation between outcomes and the reasons behind them	She fired him (effect) because he drank on the job (cause).
Comparison/Contrast	Pointing out similarities and differences of subjects	His management style is bold, like Kennedy's (comparison), but less organized (contrast).
Definition	Clarifying by using synonyms or by pointing out uniqueness within a general class	Mucilage, liquid glue, (synonym) was used to hold the in-laid pieces of the mosaic—a picture (general class) that's made of inlaid pieces (unique feature).
Description	Using words to convey sensory impressions or abstract concepts	The temperature was −32°F (objective description), with a frigid wind blowing blankets of snow over the ice (subjective description).
Analysis and Classification (Division)	Dividing a subject into parts (analysis) or grouping information by class	The elements of Earth's crust are mostly oxygen and silicon (analysis). Gold, silver, and copper, which are all found in the ground, have been known to man for many years (classification).
Example	Using illustrations to clarify, explain, or prove a point	A case in point is this column of this summary.
Induction	Reasoning that arrives at a general principle or draws a conclusion from the facts or examples	He was late for supper, late for our wedding, and even a late delivery when he was born (examples)—that man is habitually late (conclusion)!
Deduction	Reasoning that uses a syllogism (two premises and a conclusion)	Premise I: When it rains over 5 inches, the river floods. Premise 2: It has rained 6 inches. Conclusion: The river is overflowing its banks.
Narration	Telling what happened or is happening in chronological order (recounting events or telling a story)	I walked to the refrigerator, opened the door, pulled out the turkey, and spilled an open carton of milk.
Process (Analysis)	Explaining how something happened or happens (works)—sometimes instructional in purpose	First, cream the sugar and butter. Next, add eggs and milk; then blend in the sugar, flour, and baking powder. Finally, pour into the cake pan and bake at 350° for 50 minutes.

These basic organizing principles and sequence patterns can be used by prose writers and poets, as well as dramatists. How they are used sometimes will determine the paragraph and chapter divisions of the prose work, the stanzas of a poem, or the scenes and acts of a play.

PERSPECTIVE TWO
STRUCTURE AND GENRE

The organizing principles discussed in perspective one weave in and out of the writer's craft in varying amounts and to differing degrees, but the elements of the second perspective of FORM (structure and genre) work to make the literary selection a whole. Structure provides unity; genre provides labels for identification and a basis for certain expectations.

Structure is sometimes used as a synonym for FORM. For some, structure is an integral part of style. Regardless, structure refers to the plan, the framework of the writing. Often the structure can be identified simply by an outline or by the verse FORM. The formal study of structure (whose basis has been identified as binary or binomial) can, however, become very complex, particularly when investigating the "Structuralism Movement" that incorporates elements of structural linguistics and structural anthropology into the study of structure. (If you find structuralism interesting, there are many books on the subject, including *Structuralism in Literature: An Introduction* by Robert Scholes, 1974.) *Structure* as used in this book, however, refers to the general plan of a work of literature.

Genre, on the other hand, refers to identifying literary selections by (1) structure, (2) technique and use of organizing principles, and (3) subject matter.

These groupings and their resulting labels are very useful as descriptive devices for identification, particularly the genre classifications that contain anticipated characteristics that give the reader clues to MEANING, CHARACTER, and the other literary elements.

Like so many other interdependent aspects of literary study, however, a work is often a blend of genres; you may not be able to wrap a literary selection in one tidy package and label it "Genre: Western," for example. Remember the "singing cowboy" movies starring Roy Rogers and Dale Evans? These westerns also incorporated elements of romance (boy gets girl at end of movie), musicals (both of the lead players sang), and comedy (generally a "sidekick" that acted as a "comic relief" to the drama). Many long-running television "sitcoms" (situation comedies) address social and family issues by blending elements of comedy and drama (note *Family Matters* and the *Bill Cosby Show*). You may have no difficulty identifying *The Perry Mason Movies* and *Murder, She Wrote* as belonging to the murder-mystery genre, but where would you place *Northern Exposure?*

The College Board has specified that the SAT II: Literature Subject Test will include selections from three major genre groups: **prose**, **poetry**, and **drama**. Under these three "umbrella" genres you will find many other genres. In preparing for the SAT II: Literature Subject Test, you may need to be able to identify the major characteristics of the main genres.

FORM IN PROSE

Nonfiction

Here is a listing of a few of the genres written in nonfiction with brief descriptions of their characteristic structures, techniques, and subject matters. As you read a literary selection, try to identify not only the genre or blend of genres employed by the writer, but also make note of what structures, techniques, and organizing principles have been utilized that are characteristic of that genre.

1. Genre: Essay
Characteristics:

- Defined as a brief prose composition
- Restricted topics
- Purpose: discussion or persuasion
- Often contains a thesis statement
- Addressed to general audience
- Two types:
  a. Formal essay—serious TONE, scholarly, organized
  b. Informal essay—intimate TONE, everyday topics, humor, less structure

EXAMPLES: The French writer Montaigne's *Essais (Essays)* appeared in 1580, and Francis Bacon began the English essay in 1597. *Essays,* especially the enlarged 1612 and 1625 editions, includes many **aphorisms** (concise statements intended to make a point). For examples of periodical essays, go to Joseph Addison and Sir Richard Steele (*The Tatler* and *The Spectator*—eighteenth century). Keep alert for their use of humor and satire. Other important British essayists include Jonathan Swift, Thomas Fuller, Abraham Cowley, John Locke, William Cowper, Robert Burton, Sir Thomas Browne, John Milton, Sir William Temple, John Dryden, Daniel Defoe, and Anthony Ashley Cooper (Earl of Shaftesbury). Be sure to include some American essayists in your study of the essay. Washington Irving's *The Sketch Book* (1820) and Thoreau's *Walden* (1854) provide excellent examples for comparison and contrast of styles. William F. Buckley, Jr. is a prolific modern essayist, and you can go to such magazines as *The New Yorker* and *Scientific American* as well as to other serious magazines and newsletters for essays on a wide range of topics.

2. Genre: Biography
Characteristics:

- Defined as the story of a person's life as told or recorded by another
- Word first used by Dryden (1683) and defined as "the history of particular men's lives"

EXAMPLES: To see how the biography genre changed over the years, compare the first English biography (William Roger's *Life of Sir Thomas More*) written in the sixteenth century with Boswell's use of **anecdote** (using brief narration of single episodes to tell about interesting events in Johnson's life) and **ana** (gossip and other sayings). The Pulitzer Prize has had a category for biographers and autobiographers since 1917.

Another genre that should be explored is the CHARACTER. These short CHARACTER sketches describe the ideal or sometimes less than ideal of humanity as demonstrated or embodied by the person being described. They often have such titles as "A Wise Man" or "A Glutton." These were very popular in the early part of the seventeenth century. Richard Aldington's *A Book of Characters* (1924) anthologizes the CHARACTER, and you can find examples among the writings of Bishop Joseph Hall.

3. Genre: Autobiography
Characteristics:

- Defined as the story of one's own life
- Subtypes of autobiography:
  a. **Diaries**—an intimate account of day-to-day life, including thoughts

b. **Journals**—chronological logs of day-to-day events (also, some scholarly periodicals such as *The Journal of Medicine*)
c. **Letters**—notes and epistles; correspondence from one person to another
d. **Memoirs**—recollections that center around certain other persons or events in the life of the writer
e. **Confessions**—autobiographical recollections of matters that are normally held private

EXAMPLES: Autobiographies and memoirs are written to be published, whereas dramas, journals, and letters are more personal, with (in the case of letters especially) perhaps only a few people at most reading them. You may, in addition to looking at the most obvious autobiographies, such as those of Franklin and Adams, be interested in some letters written during various periods of literary history or written by noted writers (such as those of Charles Dickens or Lord Byron and perhaps the diary of Samuel Pepys).

4. Genre: Criticism
Characteristics:

- Defined as studies that analyze and comment upon works of art and literature
- Rhetoric and diction—the subject of critics in Renaissance England

EXAMPLES: In the sixteenth century, a battle raged between English scholars (called "purists"), who would not allow any borrowing from other languages to contaminate English diction, and the Inkhornists, who extensively favored incorporating Latin and Greek words into the English vocabulary. Criticism often reflects the moods and trends of the period in which it is written, and literary critics (those who write criticisms) sometimes polarize into "schools" or groups that subscribe to various theories or who prefer certain methods of critical analysis. Historically, Dr. Benjamin Johnson in the eighteenth century and Matthew Arnold in the nineteenth century wrote critical essays. A noted twentieth-century critic is Northrop Frye.

5. Genre: Informational Text
Characteristics:

- Factual
- Structured by topical outline (if subject allows)

- Can include extensive use of example, analogy, and description, but most organizing principles can be effectively used

EXAMPLES: An instructional text is a type of informational text aimed at teaching. Sometimes these types rely heavily on process analysis for the purpose of the reader following instructions.

Also, note the importance of the **chronicle** to the body of English literature. These forerunners of the modern history genre were significant since the time of King Alfred and provided rich resource materials for Shakespeare and other writers. (Note: *Mirror for Magistrates.*) Chronicles that record events year by year are called **annals**. Some "histories" have been awarded the Pulitzer Prize (such as Carl Sandburg's *Abraham Lincoln: the War Years* and Stanley Karnow's *In Our Image: America's Empire in the Philippines*). There also has been a Pulitzer Prize category for "General Nonfiction" since 1962.

Fiction

Fiction is an imaginative literary narrative that can be in the FORM of prose, poetry, or drama. Most prose fiction falls into one of several types based primarily on length:

1. Novel
An extended prose narrative that is fiction. The first English novel was *Pamela* (*Virtue Rewarded*) by Samuel Richardson. (Generally, novel-length works are divided into chapters.)

2. Novelette
Shorter than the novel, more tightly structured. Sometimes called a short novel, it generally consists of about 15,000 to 50,000 words.

3. Short story
Ranges from 500 (in the short-short story) to 15,000 words. The short story is very tightly structured with a formal development.

4. Anecdote
A narrative of a single episode (an incident). Once referring simply to gossip, today anecdote refers to any episodic narrative and is very popular among magazine article writers as an attention-getting device to introduce their subjects. Also, political speech writers use the anecdote to enliven what

might be otherwise "dull," issue-based speeches; and, if the narrative is about someone with whom the audience can identify, they use the anecdote as a means of persuasion.

Perhaps the single most important structural element in narrative fiction is *plot*—a summary of the action of the story, including the words and deeds of the CHARACTERS.

But what precipitates this action? Why does the reader care about the words and deeds of the CHARACTERS? Conflict. The motivating, driving force that involves both CHARACTERS and (if written well) involves the readers in the narrative is **conflict**. Conflict makes readers care. Conflict means opposition: person vs. person, person vs. group, person vs. environment, person vs. nature, or person vs. self. Generally, when reading a narrative, the reader begins to anticipate the conflicts in the plot, selects a "side" that he or she thinks is "right," evaluates the CHARACTERS to see which "side" each is on, identifies which CHARACTER(S) he or she wants to "win," and eventually may even begin to identify with that CHARACTER. The plot, then, with conflict as its driving force, provides unity for the work as a whole.

In its simplest, most predictable FORM, a narrative plot might look like this:

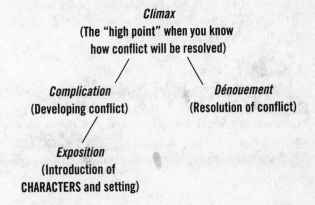

How can the plot line for a narrative be summarized? In a stereotypical "paperback" romance it might be: Jasmine is a beautiful, single professional woman on vacation in Hawaii (*Exposition*). She meets Roberto, the dark, handsome, rich sugar baron who sweeps her off her feet until Susan, Jasmine's rival for Roberto's affections, causes a misunderstanding that makes Roberto doubt Jasmine's love (*Complication*—developing conflict that obviously is the longest part of the narrative). Roberto discovers Susan's treachery while Jasmine is headed in a taxi to the airport to leave his life forever (*Climax*—the reader knows how this is going to end). Roberto races to the airport and reconciles with Jasmine just in time to live happily ever after (*Dénouement*). Some genres have very predictable plot lines. For example, how would you summarize the plot line for a Charles Bronson-type cop-and-robber movie? Or a typical western? (Such a plot summary is sometimes called an **epitome** and each section of the narrative is an **episode**.)

Predictable narrative story lines are sometimes called formula plots. They consist of variations on the same plot line story after story. As you read narrative fiction, however, watch for departures from the expected plot line. Sometimes writers will depart from the usual plot structure in order to achieve a specific effect. In fact, most plots (whether traditonal or those that are departures from the usual) will aim to create some effect. Five significant examples (but by no means an exhaustive list) of effects that are the result of plot are:

1. Tragedy
In a tragic narrative, humans do not and cannot overcome inevitable failure, although they may demonstrate grace and courage along the way.

2. Comedy
A comic effect is produced when the plot leads the CHARACTERS into amusing situations, ridiculous complications, and a happy ending.

3. Satire
A narrative is satiric when it makes a subject look ridiculous. The subjects being derided can range from an individual to all mankind and those societies that have been formed. (Swift's *Gulliver's Travels,* written in 1726, is an example of indirect satire.)

4. Romance
A romantic narrative (called a *prose romance*) has clear distinctions between the "good guys and the bad guys," an adventurous plot, and events that occasionally demand that the reader believe the otherwise unbelievable. (For instance, *Wuthering Heights,* written by Emily Brontë in 1847 is a famous romance.)

5. Realism
A realistic narrative is in contrast to the romance. It tries to mirror real life, not present life as the reader thinks or wishes it could be. In realism, the leading

CHARACTERS are not necessarily beautiful or handsome, rich or talented. The plot revolves around events that face people everyday in a real world.

In narrative fiction, the writer uses **genre** (a narrative identified by structure, technique, and subject matter) to achieve a tragic, comedic, satiric, romantic, realistic, or some other effect. The genres available to writers are numerous. The following listing highlights the characteristics of some of the more common fictional narrative genres you may encounter and provides some examples.

1. Genre: Picaresque
Characteristics:

- Autobiographical—first person NARRATIVE
- A rascal as the main CHARACTER who does not change
- Adventurous episodes
- The main CHARACTER lives by wits
- Generally lacks formal structure
- The main CHARACTER is called a picaroon (picaro)

EXAMPLES: *The Adventures of Tom Sawyer,* Fielding's *Jonathan Wild,* and Daniel Defoe's *Moll Flanders* fit this genre.

2. Genre: Stream of consciousness
Characteristics:

- Major technique: interior monologue
- Reports the nonverbalized flow of thoughts of the CHARACTER(S)
- Thoughts are erratic, illogical
- Introspection
- Focus: inner consciousness

EXAMPLES: As you investigate the stream-of-consciousness novel, try to identify the influences of Freudian psychology at work in the more modern examples. Examples of stream of consciousness are in the writings of James Joyce, Virginia Woolf, and Laurence Sterne.

3. Genre: Bildungsroman
Characteristics:

- German for "novel of formation"
- Once called "apprenticeship novel"
- An account of growing up
- Called *Künstlerroman* when the protagonist is an artist or writer

EXAMPLES: James Joyce's *Portrait of the Artist as a Young Man* and Dickens's *Great Expectations*

4. Genre: Regional

Characteristics:

- Setting (including regional dialogues) has significant impact on CHARACTER and on plot structure

EXAMPLES: Some of the works of William Faulkner fit this genre. Also, notice the way such writers as Mark Twain combine the regional novel with other FORMS.

5. Genre: Social

Characteristics:

- Plot centers on social environment
- Plot incorporates persuasive language—calls for social reform

EXAMPLES: The Lost Generation during the decade after World War I ended produced many social novelists.

Some other genres include:

- Detective—Also called crime stories, murder mysteries, and "whodunits," the plot focuses on solving a crime, often murder (Sir Arthur Conan Doyle, Agatha Christie).
- Psychological—Plot tells not only what happens, but also why it happens, concentrating on motivation.
- Problem—Plot centers on solving a problem.
- Novels of
  a. Sensibility—Plot focuses on emotion.
  b. CHARACTER—Plot focuses on CHARACTER.
  c. Manners—Plot focuses on a social class.
  d. Incident—Plot focuses on episodes.
  e. The Soil—Plot focuses on rural regional struggle to survive.
- Sociological—A type of problem novel, it purports to have the solutions for specified problems in society.
- Propaganda—Plot is subordinated to the role of a vehicle to put forth a particular doctrine.
- Western—"Dime novels" are set in the American West.
- Gothic—Plot centers on ghostly castles, medieval settings, and romantic knights bound by chivalry.

- Epistolary—Plot is carried out through a series of letters between or among the CHARACTERS.
- Science Fiction—Plot centers on science fantasy, such as time machines, aliens, or mutants.
- Suspense—Also called "edge-of-your-seat" stories, the plot keeps the reader in a somewhat sustained sense of suspense or anticipation. In serials in which there is a break in the plot between episodes, the reader or viewer may be left at a "cliff-hanger"—a point at which the suspense level is high, thus encouraging the reader or viewer to continue the story to see what happens. (A famous television "cliff-hanger" is the "Who Shot J. R.?" episode in the American soap opera *Dallas*.)
- Utopia—Plot depends upon a fictional, perfect world. (Contrasted with *dystopia* in which the fictional world is far less than perfect, as in Orwell's *1984*.)

As previously mentioned, writers often blend elements (including the structure, technique, and subject matter) of more than one genre to create the desired effect(s) and to fulfill their purpose(s). Generally speaking, however, the shorter narratives require tighter, more economical structures. Some shorter genres include:

1. The *tale* that centers on an outcome—As a result of this focus, the tale may not be as tightly structured as some of the other short narrative genres. Look to O'Henry for some example tales.
2. The *tall tale* that centers on the exaggerated feats of (generally) American heroes—Examples include such CHARACTERS as Paul Bunyan and Davy Crockett (although some tall tales have been written in other countries).
3. The *fable* that centers on a moral—The moral is often stated in an *epigram* put forth by the writer or one of the CHARACTERS at the end (called a beast fable when the CHARACTERS in the fable are talking animals). Examples include the famous fables of Aesop.
4. The *folktale* that is a narrative that originally was transmitted orally—Elements of the folktale are commonly found in tall tales and fables.
5. The *parable* that teaches a lesson by using very tightly structured allegory—As pointed out by Professors William Harmon and the late C. Hugh Holman of the University of North Carolina at Chapel Hill in *A Handbook to Liter-*

ature (Macmillan Publishing Company, 1992), the most famous parables are those of Jesus Christ. (Examples include the "Prodigal Son," the "Parable of the Sowers," and the "Parable of the Workers.")

6. The *legend* that relates the life of the hero—people whose lives are of legendary "proportions."

7. The *myth* that once was believed to be true but is now accepted as fiction—These stories are generally of anonymous origin and include supernatural elements.

FORM IN POETRY

FORM in poetry can be seen on two levels. On the one level poetry, like prose, can be grouped into many different genres or types based to a great extent on structural techniques (organizing principles) and subject matter. But because of the intensity of poetry (intensity of MEANING, sound, and FORM), each poem should also be examined on a second level by identifying the elements of FORM that are unique to that individual poem.

Each poem's MEANING is to a greater or lesser degree affected by its FORM. Because economy of language and the other parameters within which the poet must work are of such impact on the poem's FORM, and conversely, the poem's FORM can so greatly impact its language and MEANING, this individualized approach is both necessary and greatly desirable in preparing for the SAT II: Literature Subject Test. You may need to be able to identify the FORM of a poem, and you may also need to be able to identify how the FORM affects the poem's MEANING.

Four common areas that you can examine to determine a poem's FORM as it relates to and affects MEANING are rhythm, rhyme scheme, physical FORM, and genre (defined by patterns of rhythm, rhyme, physical FORM, and subject).

Rhythm

Poetry has rhythm—a variation of stressed and unstressed sounds that has some type of regular pattern. Generally, the stressed sounds or syllables (accents) recur regularly and, almost as a natural consequence, cause grouping of the stressed sounds into units. In music, these units are often counted aloud by the piano student learning rhythm. These groupings of accented and unaccented syllables are fundamental to the driving beat of hard rock, the toe-tapping cadence of a Texas two-step, and the slow rhythm of the blues. Rhythm can directly affect people's moods (and perhaps their perceptions?) and different people prefer and enjoy or avoid and dislike different rhythms.

The musical unit became a "signature" of the late bandleader Lawrence Welk (whose program, *The Lawrence Welk Show,* has been syndicated on the Public Broadcasting System for many years). He would direct his orchestra to begin with a smile, a raised swirl of his baton, and "a one-and-a-two-and-a...."

The emphasis on musical units continued with the reggae music of 1970s Jamaica and the rap music begun in the 1980s in New York City. Notice the strong regularity of this rap-style work:

So you gotta take a test
And you wanna do your best
Work hard'n you'll be knowin'
That to college you'll be goin'

As you examine poetic rhythm patterns, however, you will also encounter variation. Sometimes the variation simply breaks the monotony of the "beat." Sometimes it changes the mood and consequently affects the MEANING. But at times, variation is used counter to the regular rhythm to the point that it becomes "unrhythmical."

Determining the rhythm in a poem is somewhat different from determining the accented syllables in everyday speech patterns. Natural rhythms of speech depend greatly upon such individual considerations as regional dialects. Prose rhythm is determined largely by the accents of the words as they would normally be spoken and by rhetorical accent, the emphasis placed on words and syllables because of their meaning. (An example of rhetorical accent might be: "Roger is _so_ popular..._Everybody_ knows Roger!") But *metrical accent*, the rhythm patterns found in poetry, is influenced by the varying levels of both syntax (word choice) and concepts that work within the tightly woven elements of poetic FORM.

Several factors will influence which syllables are stressed or accented in a line of poetry. These include the normal accents associated with the word, particularly in polysyllabic words, such as *es-tab-lish* or *stee-ple* (when the poet uses CONTEXT to change the normal accent of a word, it is called *wrenched accent*), the grammatical function of the words (prepositions and articles are generally not stressed as strongly as nouns and verbs), rhetorical accents (stresses based on MEANING), and metrical accents (stresses established in the CONTEXT of the poem). The study of the rhythms and sounds of poetry is called **prosody**; the system used to describe rhythm is called **scansion**. When you **scan** a line of poetry, you first identify which kind of **foot** is being used. A foot is the unit formed by a strong stress or accent and the weak stress(es) or unaccented syllable(s) that accompany it. You identify the type or kind of foot that is being used as you "walk" along the individual line of poetry.

To illustrate, *scan* the first stanza of "The Wife of Usher's Well."

There lived a wife at Usher's Well,
   And a wealthy wife was she;
She had three stout and stalwart sons,
   And sent them o'er the sea.

The first step in scanning is to determine the accented or stressed sounds. This is done by placing an accent mark over each stressed syllable. (Remember: you are finding the "beat" of the poem.)

```
      /       /        /        /
There lived a wife at Usher's Well,
         /        /        /
   And a wealthy wife was she;
      /         /          /
She had three stout and stalwart sons,
         /         /       /
   And sent them o'er the sea.
```

Next, identify the unstressed syllables by placing an X over each.

```
  X   /  X  /  X  /  X   /
There lived a wife at Usher's Well,
   X X   / X  /  X  /
   And a wealthy wife was she;
 X   /  X   /   X   /  X  /
She had three stout and stalwart sons,
   X  /   X   /   X  /
   And sent them o'er the sea.
```

Now look for a pattern. In this poem, there seems to be a pattern of an unstressed syllable followed by a stressed syllable. Divide the groups of unstressed and stressed syllables into *feet* by using a slash mark (called a *virgule*.)

```
  X    /  X   / X  / X   /
There lived / a wife / at Ush / er's Well,
    X X  /  X   /   X  /
   And a weal / thy wife / was she;
 X  /   X    /    X   /  X   /
She had / three stout / and stal / wart sons,
    X  /   X   /   X  /
   And sent / them o'er / the sea.
```

At this point, you can identify what kind of foot is used in the poem. There are many different kinds of feet, but the most common to English poetry are illustrated by L. E. Myers in the following five stanzas called "Stressed and Unstressed":

"Stressed and Unstressed"

Iambic foot (X /) unstressed, stressed

```
X  / X / X / X   /
Iambic is a line of verse,
     X  / X  /  X    /
   That first is weak, then strong.
X  /  X   /   X  / X  /
If this light rhyme you do rehearse,
    X   / X / X   /
   You're sure to do no wrong.
```

Anapestic foot (X X /) unstressed, unstressed, stressed

```
  X  X  /  X X /  X  X  / XX /
With two weak and a strong we will learn anapest,
    X X /  X  X   /  X X /
   As we take this small verse right along.
 X  X  /  X  X  /  XX / XX  /
Feel the beat, mark the stress, anapest is the best,
    X X /  X  X  /  X X /
   With a rhythm that can be a song.
```

Trochaic foot (/ X) stressed, unstressed

```
   /   X  /  X   /  X / X
Strong then weak should bring no terror—
     /    X / X / X
   Verse that is trochaic.
 /  X   /   X  / X / X
Up then down—you will not error—
     / X / X  / X
   Never be prosaic!
```

Dactylic foot (/ X X) stressed, unstressed, unstressed

```
 /  X   X   / X X  / X  X   / X X
He could write verses like Alfred, Lord Tennyson,
```

/ X X / X X / X X / X X
Dactylic foot that could march clear to Dennison.
/ X X / X X / X X / X X
Rhythms he kept and to rhyme he was dutiful—
/ X X / X X / X X / X X
That's why his work was so strong and so beautiful.

Spondaic foot (/ /) stressed, stressed

X / X / X / X /
When two successive syllables
X / X X / X X / X /
with equal strong stresses occur in verse,
/ / / X /
Strong, strong, spondee foot
/ X / X /
comes to mind at first.

Pyrrhic foot (X X) unstressed, unstressed: Although not basic meters, spondaic and pyrrhic feet can occur as variants from the standard feet. Some experts in scanning argue that true pyrrhic foot does not exist because every foot must have an accented syllable.

Because the preceding stanza from "The Wife of Usher's Well" is predominantly groups of unstressed then stressed syllables, *it is written in iambic foot.*

After determining the type of foot, you need to identify how many feet are *in each line.*

Traditionally: one foot   = monometer
two feet   = dimeter
three feet = trimeter
four feet   = tetrameter
five feet   = pentameter
six feet   = hexameter
seven feet = heptameter
eight feet = octameter

Look at the first line of "The Wife of Usher's Well":

There lived / a wife / at Ush / er's Well,

There are four feet in this line: tetrameter. Consequently, the *meter* or *metrical pattern* of line one is iambic tetrameter. Notice the metrical patterns of the entire stanza:

Iambic tetrameter—There lived/ a wife/ at Ush/er's Well,
Iambic trimeter—and a weal/thy wife/ was she;
Iambic tetrameter—She had/ three stout/ and stal/wart sons,
Iambic trimeter—and sent/ them o'er/ the sea.

Because iambic and anapestic meters end on a high stress, they are often referred to as the *rising meters* or rhythms, whereas dactylic and trochaic are *falling meters* or rhythms. The meter used, the metrical pattern, can directly affect the mood, the TONE, and/or the MEANING.

What are some specific instances in which the metrical pattern is used to affect MEANING and/or TONE of a *verse* (a literary work written in meter)? Some examples include:

1. Poems in which the poets use the metrical pattern to contribute to a *comic effect*:
   • anapestic foot and iambic tetrameter

I DO NOT LOVE THEE, DR. FELL

I do not love thee, Dr. Fell,
The reason why I cannot tell;
But this I know, and know full well,
I do not love thee, Dr. Fell.

by Tom Brown

   • a trochaic line that ends with the unstressed syllable
2. Pauses that affect the "pace" of a poem: When a poem has a very long pause within a line, it is called **caesura** (shown as / / in scansion).
3. Use of substitute feet: This happens when a line scans predominantly, for example, iambic; but the poet has substituted some other foot somewhere within the line. The poet then returns to iambic (or whatever the predominant foot is) until he or she again substitutes another foot. The effects can vary. For instance, when the predominant beat carries you along like a waltz, the substitute might be jarring—or at the very least might get your attention.
4. The direct use of meter to contribute to MEANING: Notice how the bold use of spondee adds intensity to these lines of Tennyson's "Break, Break, Break."

Break, break, break,
    On thy cold gray stones, O Sea!
And I would that my tongue could utter
    The thoughts that arise in me.

O well for the fisherman's boy,
    That he shouts with his sister at play!
O well for the sailor lad,
    That he sings in his boat on the bay!
And the stately ships go on

To their haven under the hill;
But O for the touch of a vanished hand,
   And the sound of a voice that is still!

Break, break, break,
   At the foot of thy crags, O Sea!
But the tender grace of a day that is dead
   Will never come back to me.

The use of spondee in relation to the poem's MEANING can be tested by the following question:

The contrast in rhythm of the first line of the last stanza to the rhythm of the second stanza serves to

(A) accentuate the harshness of the speaker's mood about his position in life
(B) change the poem's emphasis from the speaker to the sea
(C) weaken the speaker's argument
(D) heighten the impact of the sea's danger
(E) reinforce that the sea represents normal life

(The correct answer is A.)

Now, examine Richard Lovelace's "Going to the Wars" to see how he used rhythm to affect MEANING. What follows is one way this poem could be scanned. Note that some poems are scanned differently by different critics. For example, the very first line might also be scanned:

   / X /   / X / X /
Tell me not (Sweet) I am unkind.

Going to the Wars

  X / X   / X / X /
1. Tell me not (Sweet) I am unkind,
    X   / X / X/
2.   That from the nunnery
  X /   X   / X / X /
3. Of thy chaste breast, and quiet mind,
    X / X / X/
4.   To war and arms I fly.

    / X X / X / X /
5. True; a new mistress now I chase,
    X / X / X /
6.   The first foe in the field;
  X / X / X / X /
7. And with a stronger faith embrace
    X / X / X /
8.   A sword, a horse, a shield.

    X / X/ X / X /
9. Yet this inconstancy is such,
     X / X   / X /
10.   As you too shall adore;
  X / X / X   / X /
11. I could not love thee (Dear) so much,
    X / X / X /
12.   Loved I not honour more.

Lines 1, 3, 5, 7, 9, and 11 are iambic tetrameter; lines 2, 4, 6, 8, 10, and 12 are iambic trimeter. Each line ends with a strong stress, called a **masculine ending**. (A line that ends with a weak stress is a **feminine ending**.)

Notice the natural pauses in both thought and reading at the ends of lines 1, 3, and 4 in the first stanza, lines 5, 6, and 8 in the second, and lines 9, 10, 11, and 12 in the third stanza. Lines such as these are called **end-stopped**. On the other hand, examine how the lack of natural pause at the end of line 2 pulls the reader to line 3. This movement of thought and rhythm is called a **run-on line**. Line 7 also is a run-on line (called *enjambement* in French). Can you spot any significant departures or breaks in the rhythm of this poem? Look at line 5. The poet uses two devices that break the rhythm; the semicolon is a clue to a very strong, lengthy pause—a *caesura*. Also, the usual iambic foot has been inverted to create a trochee (trochaic foot). Such a dramatic change in an otherwise predictable rhythm is a definite clue to a shift in thought—a change in MEANING.

A test question might read: The speaker uses a break in tempo in line 5 to suggest that he

(A) is conceding the point to his mistress
(B) is angry because he must go to war
(C) is shifting from a defensive to an offensive position
(D) resents the position in which war places him
(E) realizes his mistake

Have you ever argued a position using a negative drone of words until you break the tension with "Yes! I feel this way because . . ."? Were you able to "feel" the startled response such a shift makes?

In the first stanza the speaker is being defensive—he is "not...unkind" (line 1). But the second stanza's change in rhythm, his abrupt "True; a new mistress now I chase," (line 5) marks a dramatic and somewhat startling shift in the TONE of his position: Yes! I must leave...I have an honorable reason to go. (Also startling: "a new mistress")

Before leaving this poem, look at line 8. Can you see any subtle differences between this line and the last lines of the first and last stanzas (lines 4 and 12)—differences that might contribute to MEANING?

One final word about rhythm. Scanning a poem for its metrical patterns is very useful; however, do not forget that a poem is a literary work and as such also should be read and enjoyed as a whole. Maintain a balance: Yes, you need to be able to disassemble a poem into its component parts to see how it "works," but do not deny yourself the pleasure of getting "caught up" in the rhythm of a poem. You may be surprised by the depth of MEANING and reflections of TONE a whole work approach can reveal. You also may find that practicing using poetic elements (such as rhythm and rhyme) in writing your own poetry is very beneficial to your skill development. As stated by William Cowper in "The Task":

THE TASK

There is a pleasure in poetic pains
Which only poets know. The shifts and turns,
Th' expedients and inventions, multiform,
line To which the mind resorts, in chase of terms
(5) Though apt, yet coy, and difficult to win—
T'arrest the fleeting images that fill
The mirror of the mind, and hold them fast,
And force them sit till he has pencil'd off
A faithful likeness of the forms he views;
(10) Then to dispose his copies with such art,
That each may find its most propitious light,
And shine by situation, hardly less
Than by the labour and the skill it cost;
Are occupations of the poet's mind
(15) So pleasing, and that steal away the thought
With such address from themes of sad import,
That, lost in his own musings, happy man!
He feels th' anxieties of life, denied
Their wonted entertainment, all retire.
(20) Such joys has he that sings, But ah! not such,
Or seldom such, the hearers of his song.
Fastidious, or else listless, or perhaps
Aware of nothing arduous in a task
They never undertook, they little note
(25) His dangers or escapes, and haply find
There least amusement where he found the most.

                                    by William Cowper

"What should I write about?" you ask. You may find many subjects in your daily life—some serious or some light, as is John Fletcher's "Do Not Fear to Put Thy Feet":

Do not fear to put thy feet
Naked in the river sweet;
Think not leech, or newt or toad
Will bite thy foot, when thou hast troad;
Nor let the water rising high,
As thou wad'st in, make thee cry
And sob, but ever live with me,
And not a wave shall trouble thee.

Rhyme Scheme

Although many definitions of rhyme are functional in the study of poetry, rhyme as it relates to and influences FORM can be foundationally defined as when two or more words have a sound in common or echo one another. The degree to which words "rhyme" is affected, of course, by pronunciation. As a result, the student of English and American literature must have an awareness of how pronunciations have changed in time, how pronunciations differ nationally between American English and British English, and how pronunciations differ regionally. Essentially, the argument is summarized by the questions, "Did you pick a 'tomato' (long *a*) or 'tomawto' from your garden?" and "Is your mother's sister your 'aunt' (pronounced as *ant*) or your 'awnt'"? Rigidity in opinion concerning what constitutes "correct" pronunciation of words can greatly affect the enjoyment of a poem, whether the differences are subtle as in *quinine* (American *kwi-nin* with long *i* in both syllables, British *kwin-en* with short *i* in the first syllable and long *e* in the last) or whether the differences are striking, as in *clerk* (American pronunciation usually rhyming with *work*, British pronunciation usually rhyming with *lark*), used by John Donne in "And though fowl now be scarce, yet there are clerks, / The sky not falling, think we may have larks."

In addition to recognizing basic rhyme, you need to be able to identify some of the major rhyme FORMS and how they are used.

End rhymes are when the rhyming words fall at the ends of two or more lines of verse:

But were some child of yours alive that *time*,
You should live twice—in it, and in *my rhyme*.

Echo verse employs a FORM of end rhyme used commonly in the 1500s and 1600s in which the closing syllables of a line are repeated to form the next line:

THE ECHO

About the tow'r an' churchyard wall,
   Out nearly overright our door,
A tongue ov wind did always call
   Whatever we did call avore.
The vaice did mock our neames, our cheers,
   Our merry laughs, our hands' loud claps,
An' mother's call "Come, come my dears"
         —*my dears*;
   Or "Do as I do bid, bad chaps"
         —bad chaps.

                  by William Barnes

In some echo poems, the echo's repeated syllables serve to answer a question posed in the previous line:

   For the Candidate
      Echo! How can I show my support
              to devote it?
               Vote it.

Internal rhymes are two or more rhyming words within a line of verse:

Off to the right, we see the dawn's light;
An upturned face, tears not a trace.

Another example is: My *wealth* is *health* and perfect ease....

Masculine rhyme is rhyme of a single stressed syllable that generally is forceful: look, cook; sing, bring; sob, rob; sweet, treat.

Feminine (or *double*) **rhyme** is rhyme of a stressed then unstressed syllable and, as a result, is softer than masculine rhyme: looking, cooking; feature, creature.

Compound rhyme is rhyme of both pairs of compound components: fish broth, dishcloth; corkscrew, pork stew.

Triple rhyme is rhyme of a stressed followed by
            /   /
two unstressed syllables: bacteria, diptheria. (Take note of the way rhyme blends with rhythm for a
                 / X X X
pleasing effect in such words as mandatory and
   / X X X
obligatory.)

Perfect rhyme (also called true or pure rhyme) is an exact alignment of sounds, whereas **imperfect rhyme** (also called partial, slant, or half rhyme) is only a close alignment:

And when he'd ride in the *afternoon*
I'd follow with a hickory *broom*,

Eye rhymes (also called **visual rhyme**) look like they should rhyme (and at one time perhaps did) but do not, such as *horse, worse* or as in the first two lines of:

Shall a woman's virtues *move*
Me to perish for her *love*?
Or, her well-deserving known,
Make me quite forget mine own?

Rime riche (also called *identical rhyme*) consists of words that sound the same but have different spellings and meanings: seas, sees; hare, hair; their, there; heart, hart. Rime riche is sometimes identified as one of the many ways writers can make a "play on words," and *rime riche* lies at the heart of a pun.

Notice Shakespeare's use of *rime riche* as an internal rhyme in these lines from *The Rape of Lucrece:*

That for his prey to pray he doth begin,
As if the heavens should countenance his sin.

Historical rhymes are words that once rhymed, but due to pronunciation shifts no longer rhyme: *tea* once rhymed with *day*.

Forced rhymes are those that are "invented" by the poet. Along with eye rhyme and imperfect rhyme, forced rhymes are examples of *poetic license*—when a poet departs from the usual use of rhyme, diction, syntax, and other such conventions.

PITY THE POOR RACCOON

Pity the poor raccoon.
He could run fast 'cause he stayed slim and trim;
But one day right at noon he heard a loon's tune
That bedazzled and mystified him.
"What's that sound?" he bemused, for he felt quite amused
'Til a hound heard the sound when Raccoon left the ground.
He was trapped! He was cornered! But he wasn't forlornered.
The hound saw a flash and his teeth he did gnash
For the prey he had treed just turned tail and fleed.

by L. E. Myers

Notice the pairing of "cornered" with "forlornered" and of "treed" with "fleed" in "Pity the Poor Raccoon."

After you have identified the poet's use of rhyme, you can then work out the *rhyme scheme* or pattern of the end rhyme of each line. To illustrate determining the rhyme scheme of a poem examine, line by line, Robert Browning's "Meeting at Night":

Line 1: *The gray sea and the long black land;*
The line ends with the word *"land"* and is assigned the letter **a**.

Line 2: *And the yellow half-moon large and low;*
Because *"low"* does not rhyme with *"land,"* it is given the letter **b**.

Line 3: *And the startled little waves that leap*
"Leap" does not rhyme with *"low"* or *"land,"* so it is given the letter **c**.

Line 4: *In fiery ringlets from their sleep,*
"Sleep" and *"leap"* do rhyme; therefore, "leap" is given the letter **c**, also.

Line 5: *As I gain the cove with pushing prow,*
Line 5 picks up the rhyme of line 2 (*"prow"* and *"low"*—eye-rhyme) and is consequently labeled **b**.

Line 6: *And quench its speed i' the slushy sand.*
This last line of the first stanza ends with *sand,* rhyming with line 1. This line is given the letter **a**.

The rhyme scheme, then, of the first stanza is **a b c c b a**.

Now look at the second stanza.

Line 7: *Then a mile of warm sea-scented beach;*
Because *"beach"* does not rhyme with *"land"* (the **a** rhyme), with *"low"* (the **b** rhyme), or with *"leap"* (the **c** rhyme), line 7 is given the letter **d**.

Line 8: *Three fields to cross till a farm appears;*

"Appears" does not rhyme with any of the previous lines, so it is also given a new letter, **e**.

Line 9: *A tap at the pane, the quick sharp scratch*
Again, *"scratch"* does not rhyme with any other line, so it is given the letter **f**.

Line 10: *And blue spurt of a lighted match,*
Return to a rhyme with *"scratch"* and give the line the letter *f*.

Line 11: *And a voice less loud, through its joys and fears,*
"Fears" and "appears" (line 8) rhyme so line 11 is given an **e**.

Line 12: *Than the two hearts beating each to each!*
The final line of the second stanza picks up the rhyme of line 7 (*"beach"* and *"each"*) and is assigned the letter **d**.

The rhyme scheme of the last stanza is **d e f f e d**.
The rhyme scheme, then, of "Meeting at Night" is:

First stanza		Second stanza	
…land	**a**	…beach	**d**
…low	**b**	…appears	**e**
…leap	**c**	…scratch	**f**
…sleep	**c**	…match	**f**
…prow	**b**	…fears	**e**
…sand	**a**	…each	**d**

What effect does an **abccba deffed** rhyme scheme have on the reader (or listener)? One effect might be that because the third and fourth lines of each stanza introduce rhyme to the poem's structure (FORM), the reader pauses (perhaps even imperceptibly) or may have a sense of anticipation of a new direction that will either complement or contrast the first two lines. In the pattern of "Meeting at Night," however, a new direction is *not* taken as you return in the fifth line to rhyme with the second line and in the last line of the stanza to rhyme with the first line.

What are some of the possible effects? Emphasis…unity of thought…perhaps using the rhyme scheme to contribute to the TONE. Subliminally, the cyclical nature of the rhyme scheme may give the reader a sense of movement and expectation— an expectation that is fulfilled—that is emotionally satisfying in the first stanza when the speaker comes ashore and the last stanza when he is reunited with the one waiting for him. This sense of movement, expectation, and fulfillment that results from the rhythm and rhyme and their effects on and interaction with the MEANING of the poem can form the basis for a test question.

A test question about "Meeting at Night" might read:

In this poem, the relationship of lines 1–4 to lines 5–6 and of lines 7–10 to lines 11–12 reflect the speaker's progression from

(A) danger to safety
(B) understanding to fear
(C) resistance to acceptance
*(D) challenge to attainment
(E) communication to noncommunication

Notice in lines 1–4 that the speaker is in a challenging situation: at sea surrounded by "startled little waves that leap in fiery ringlets"; however, he "gain[s] the cove" and makes it ashore in lines 5–6. This progression from challenge to attainment is mirrored in the second stanza as he is challenged to cross the beach and fields and to gain the attention of the one lighting the match in lines 7–10, then attains reunion in lines 11–12.

How do you determine the rhyme scheme in a poem when the pronunciations of one or more of the end-line words are unfamiliar to you due to regionalisms or changes in pronunciation over time or when the rhyme is imperfect? How do such situations affect the rhyme scheme? Here is a stanza from Shakespeare's "The Phoenix and the Turtle":

Let the priest in surplice white
   That defunctive music can,
   Be the death-divining swan,
Lest the requiem lack his right.

"White," "can," "swan," and "right"—what seems to be an *abca* rhyme scheme: When you look at the next two stanzas, however, the rhyme scheme appears to be somewhat different. (Because the rhyme schemes of individual stanzas are being compared, each stanza will begin with "a" for the first line.)

And thou treble-dated crow,	a
That thy sable gender makest	b
With the breath thou givest and takest,	b
'Mongst our mourners shalt thou go.	a
Here the anthem doth commence:	a
Love and constancy is dead;	b
Phoenix and the turtle fled	b
In a mutual flame from hence.	a

You might surmise, based on the CONTEXT of the rhyme scheme of the other stanzas, that the poet intends "can" and "swan" to rhyme for an **abba** pattern. When dealing with possible historical rhyme, eye rhyme, or imperfect rhyme, you need to look first at the CONTEXT (the established rhyme scheme of the poem—a process called **correspondence**) and then at the MEANINGS of the line in which the rhyme appears. A word search in the *Oxford English Dictionary* or in some other etymological dictionary might reveal a change in pronunciation due to time or a difference in pronunciation due to nationality/regionalism. If you eliminate the possibility of rhyme affected by pronunciation changes and must decide the poet's intent, MEANING can be a valuable clue. Examine the MEANING of the line in the CONTEXT of the stanza: the poet may be using the break from the established rhyme pattern for a specific *effect*, such as a shift in MEANING, as a contrast, or simply as an attention-getting device.

IF BY DULL RHYMES OUR ENGLISH MUST BE CHAINED

If by dull rhymes our English must be chained,
And, like Andromeda, the sonnet sweet
Fettered, in spite of painéd loveliness,
Let us find out, if we must be constrained,
Sandals more interwoven and complete
To fit the naked foot of poesy:
Let us inspect the lyre, and weigh the stress
Of every chord, and see what may be gained
By ear industrious, and attention meet;
Misers of sound and syllable, no less
Than Midas of his coinage, let us be
Jealous of dead leaves in the bay wreath crown;
So, if we may not let the Muse be free,
She will be bound with garlands of her own.

by John Keats 1795–1821

Physical FORM

The physical FORM of a poem—what it looks like on a page—can greatly affect its MEANING and can even affect its "label" of "a poem."

Although the distinction between prose and poetry has already been addressed, the physical FORM of poetry cannot be discussed without examining the range of FORMS that exists between these two extremes:

Prose: Prose is written from margin to margin. Thoughts are written in complete sentences. Sentences are grouped into paragraphs. Paragraphs are arranged into subsections (under subheadings—particularly in nonfiction works). Subsections are joined to make chapters. Chapters are grouped under larger sections or parts. The sections or parts go together to form a book.

> **Book**
> > **Sections or parts**
> > > **Chapters**
> > > > **Subsections**
> > > > > **Paragraphs**
> > > > > > **Sentences**

Poetry: Poetry has a regular rhythm that can be measured and a rhyme scheme. A poem is written in lines that may—or may not—contain sentences or sentence fragments. Based on metrical patterns, rhyme schemes, and/or thought units, a poem is divided into stanzas. (Some poets refer to poem divisions that are regular and rhymed as stanzas, but when the subdivision is irregular and unrhymed, they may call it a **strophe**.) Generally, the rhyme scheme and metrical pattern of the initial stanza are repeated in subsequent stanzas. As previously mentioned, this is called **correspondence**, and greatly facilitates identifying, for example, the rhyme scheme in a poem in which one of the end-line words has changed in pronunciation. By looking at another stanza, you can easily determine where the word in question fits in the established rhyme scheme and metrical pattern.

> **Poem (Section—for example, book, canto)**
> > **Stanza (Strophe)**
> > > **Lines**
> > > > **Metrical feet**

A discussion of some of the various FORMS that you will find within and between these two extremes (prose and poetry) follows.

Prose poetry

Is it prose or is it a poem? Viewed by some critics as "impossible—no such thing," the prose poem would seem to be an **oxymoron**, a contradiction in terms. Poetry written in paragraphs (with left and right margin justification), without the line breaks of regular verse, the prose poem relies on its compact intensity and repetition of rhyme and figurative elements. ("Bell-Tones" is a previously cited example.)

Free verse

Free verse is just that—free of a regular meter. Also called "open form" or *vers libre*, free verse is characterized by short, irregular lines, no rhyme pattern, and a dependence on the effective and more intense use of pauses, words selected not only for MEANING but for how that MEANING is intensified by their position in the poem. Notice the use of free verse in "Know Yourself" by L. E. Myers:

KNOW YOURSELF

There is a
truth
with us
and in us.
Is this the truth?

There is a
lie
with us,
but not in us.
Is this the truth?

Blank verse

Blank verse is written in iambic pentameter, but with no rhyme pattern. It is the major verse FORM used by Shakespeare in his plays. In blank verse, divisions are referred to as **verse paragraphs** (although the verse paragraph can also be in free verse). Blank verse made its appearance in English literature first in drama, then epics, and since has been used frequently in a wide variety of long poems. For example, here is an excerpt from William Wordsworth's rather lengthy "Lines Composed a Few Miles above Tintern Abbey on Revisiting the Banks of the Wye During A Tour, July 13, 1798."

Five years have passed; five summers, with the length
Of five long winters! and again I hear
These waters, rolling from their mountain-springs
With a soft inland murmur, Once again
Do I behold these steep and lofty cliffs,
That on a wild secluded scene impress
Thoughts of more deep seclusion; and connect
The landscape with the quiet of the sky.

Qualitative Verse

This verse has a measurable rhythm with an identifiable rhyme scheme. The poem is presented in a known stanza. The verse is accentual-syllabic: it depends on (1) how many syllables are in each line and (2) the accented and unaccented syllables forming patterns. (Do not confuse this with *quantitative verse* that imitates Greek and Latin versification, depending on the duration of sound.)

A significant aspect of FORM in poetry is FORM of the stanza. Among the most common stanza FORMS are:

- **Couplets**—Two grouped lines that rhyme (called *distich* if they do not rhyme)

- **Heroic couplets**—Couplets written in iambic pentameter (very popular in English poetry during the 1800s and 1900s):

  X / X / X / X / X /
  Which gives the watchword to his hands full soon,
  X / X / X / X / X /
  To draw the cloud that hides the silver moon.

Stanza:	No. of Lines:	Meter:	Rhyme Scheme:
Ballad	4	lines 1 and 3 iambic tetrameter	abcb
		lines 2 and 4 iambic trimeter	
Elegiac	4	iambic pentameter	abab
Terza Rima	3	iambic pentameter	aba, bcb, cdc, ded,…
Rhyme Royal	7	iambic pentameter	ababbcc
Ottava Rima	8	iambic pentameter	abababcc
Spenserian	9	lines 1–8 iambic pentameter	ababbcbcc
		line 9 iambic hexameter (an Alexandrine)	

Other terms referring to the number of lines in a stanza include:

tristich (triplet) — three lines
quatrain — four lines
quintain (quintet) — five lines
sextain (sestet) — six lines

Genre

The major genres of poetry are defined by patterns of rhythm, rhyme, physical FORM, and subject.

There are three major groups or divisions of poems, classifications that can be further subdivided into many different genres:

- Epic poetry (written in the narrative mode)
- Dramatic poetry (written in the dramatic mode)
- Lyric poetry (written in the lyric mode)

Epic poetry

An epic poem is a long poem written in the narrative mode. The characteristics of an epic poem include:

- Elevated style
- Adventurous plot
- Heroic figures
- A legendary main CHARACTER
- An expansive setting
- Supernatural "machinery"
- The narrative as an "objective" account

Epic poetry usually follows a "formula" and utilizes a variety of epic conventions:

- A statement of the theme (called the *argument*) begins the epic.
- An *epic question* is posed to "invoke" a Muse.
- The story begins in the middle of the action, with explanations given later.
- The main CHARACTERS give very long, very formal speeches.
- The names of warriors, ships, and so forth are listed.
- Throughout the narrative, the poet uses very complex, multi-level *epic similes* (extended comparisons).

Folk epics (traditional or primary epics) were handed down orally and often are of uncertain authorship. Literary epics are imitations of these. The importance of the epic to English poetry should not be underestimated. In the Renaissance, the epic was highly esteemed by critics and has influenced English writers over the years. To cite an example, Milton was influenced by Virgil's *The Aeneid* when he wrote *Paradise Lost* in 1667.

The length and complexity of an epic, however, is quite imposing, hence the birth of the **mock epic** or **mock heroic** poem. FORMS of high burlesque, these poems apply the conventional FORMS and styles of an epic to comparatively mundane, unimportant subjects. The grandiose treatment of insignificant subjects creates a comic disparity.

The influence of the epic poem on other narrative poem modes is arguable. Some narrative poems are rooted deeply in the epic traditions; others are not. Poems in the narrative mode range from folkloric poems to beast-fables in verse to "court epics" to verse novels (such as Elizabeth Barrett Browning's *Aurora Leigh*).

Dramatic poetry

Some critics argue that the label "dramatic poetry" is somewhat ambiguous. Of course, the term refers to poems that are dominated in content, style, and structure by the dramatic FORM and/or by the many possible dramatic techniques, such as dialogue and blank verse. Other critics would go so far as to include poetic drama (plays written in verse) under this large category that is held together by the special elements of the dramatic mode. What constitutes the dramatic mode?

- The work presents an abrupt change.
- The TONE is influenced by the emotional involvement that arises from the interaction of the CHARACTERS and the conflict of the situation.
- The plot line follows the rise and fall of the main CHARACTER.

The dramatic mode of poetry (whether poems that are dramatic or poetic drama) can include:

- Dialogue written in verse (usually blank verse in the poetic drama)
- Monologues—long speeches uttered by one person

Unlike poems that contain dramatic elements, poetic drama is meant to be acted out. Works such as Shelley's *Prometheus Unbound* (written in 1820) and Milton's *Samson Agonistes* (written in 1671), however, are dramas that are *not* meant to be acted out. This genre is called the **closet drama**.

Lyric poetry

In the lyric mode, the TONE is reflective, at times even introspective, with the speaker discussing an experience or expounding upon an idea. Originally referring to songs sung to lyre music, now the term *lyric* refers to expressive, short nonnarrative poems; however, lyric also includes longer works such as some elegies. Lyric poetry includes a blend of elements:

- Melodious TONE
- Spontaneously expressed emotion
- Unified structure (harmonious)
- Individualized
- Subjective

The broad range of poetic FORMS that fall under the label of lyric poetry is impressive; but although not all lyric poetry is intended to be sung, the intrinsic musical elements of lyric poetry that are rooted in its musical origins should be recognized (although not overstated). Some of the subclasses of lyric poetry include:

Dramatic monologue: A persona (someone who is not the poet) unintentionally reveals his or her CHARACTER by expressing a poem at a critical moment. There may or may not be a silent auditor—the person to whom the monologue is being addressed. In Robert Browning's "My Last Duchess" the silent auditor is an agent for negotiating the Duke's next marriage arrangement.

Notice some of the literary elements at work in this small excerpt from Tennyson's "Ulysses." Written in the first person, the speaker is Odysseus (Ulysses), a Greek hero of the Trojan War and the King of Ithaca.

ULYSSES

It little profits that an idle king,
By this still hearth, among these barren crags,
Matched with an agéd wife, I mete and dole
Unequal laws unto a savage race,
That hoard, and sleep, and feed, and know not me.
I cannot rest from travel; I will drink
Life to the lees. All times I have enjoyed
Greatly, have suffered greatly, both with those
That loved me, and alone; on shore, and when
Through scudding drifts the rainy Hyades
Vexed the dim sea. I am become a name;
For always roaming with a hungry heart
Much have I seen and known—cities of men
And manners, climates, councils, governments
Myself not least, but honored of them all—
And drunk delight of battle with my peers,
Far on the ringing plains of windy Troy.
I am a part of all that I have met;
Yet all experience is an arch wherethrough
Gleams that untravelled world, whose margin fades
For ever and for ever when I move.

Dramatic monologues, by definition, can be sources for test questions over CHARACTER—a case in which knowledge of FORM helps the reader to gain insight into another literary element:

In the poem "Ulysses," the speaker reveals that he

(A) does not frequently leave his responsibilities as king
(B) considers himself an adventurer
(C) is not well liked among his people
(D) shuns battle and confrontation
(E) deeply respects his subjects

(The correct answer is B.)

Elegy: A lament over the death of someone (although elegy once referred to poems written in elegiac meter—lines that alternate hexameter and pentameter).

Read the first stanza of Thomas Gray's "Elegy Written in a Country Churchyard." Notice his use of the elegiac stanza (four lines of iambic pentameter with an abab rhyme scheme).

The curfew tolls the knell of parting day,
    The lowing herd wind slowly o'er the lea,
The plowman homeward plods his weary way,
    And leaves the world to darkness and to me.

Elegies include some love poems about death. Subtypes of elegy include:

* ***Dirges:*** Short songs expressing grief over someone

* ***Pastoral elegy:*** Poems in which both the deceased and the mourners are presented as shepherds. These elegies often include mythology as part of the poetic structure.

Ode: A complex, serious, long lyric poem modeled after Pindar (the Greek poet) whose complex songs (originally used in dramatic poetry) were divided into numerous three-part units consisting of the strophe, antistrophe, and epode. The English ode has three FORMS:

* ***Regular or Pindaric ode:*** Includes one stanza pattern for strophe and antistrophe, whereas epode is in another stanza pattern.

* ***Irregular ode:*** Each stanza has its own pattern —the most common ode FORM in English since it was first done in 1656 by Abraham Cowley.

* ***Horatian (homostrophic) ode:*** One repeated stanza type that may vary within the established pattern. These odes are calmer— less passionate—than Pindar's odes.

Odes are very unified with just one theme handled in an extremely dignified manner. The purpose of many odes is to eulogize someone or something, such as Alexander Pope's "Ode on Solitude."

Happy the man, whose wish and care
    A few paternal acres bound,
Content to breathe his native air,
            In his own ground.

Whose herds with milk, whose fields with bread,
    Whose flocks supply him with attire,
Whose trees in summer yield him shade,
            In winter fire.

Blest, who can unconcern'dly find
    Hours, days, and years slide soft away,
In health of body, peace of mind,
            Quiet by day,

Sound sleep by night; study and ease,
    Together mixed; sweet recreation;
And innocence, which most does please
            With meditation.

Thus let me live, unseen, unknown,
    Thus unlamented let me die,
Steal from the world, and not a stone
            Tell where I lie.

Sonnet: A 14-line iambic pentameter poem. There are three main types of sonnet:

1. The **Italian (Petrarchan) sonnet** consists of an octave (eight lines) or a set of two quatrains (four lines each) in an abbaabba rhyme scheme that asks a question or presents a statement that is answered or somehow addressed by the concluding sestet (six lines) or set of two tercets (three lines each). Notice Wordsworth's use of the sonnet FORM in "Nuns Fret Not."

        X   / X   / X   /   X   / X   /
    Nuns fret not at their convent's narrow room;   a
    And hermits are contented with their cells;   b

And students with their pensive citadels;   b
line Maids at the wheel, the weaver at his loom,   a
(5) Sit blithe and happy; bees that soar for bloom,   a
High as the highest Peak of Furness-fells,   b
Will murmur by the hour in foxglove bells: b
In truth the prison, into which we doom   a
Ourselves, no prison is: and hence for me,   c
(10) In sundry moods, 'twas pastime to be bound   d
Within the Sonnet's scanty plot of ground;   d
Pleased if some Souls (for such there needs must be)   c
Who have felt the weight of too much liberty,   c
Should find brief solace there, as I have found.   d

First, in lines 1–9, Wordsworth tells the reader that some "imprison" themselves by choice (nuns, hermits, students)—hence if by choice, then they are not really in prison (lines 8–9). He concludes in lines 10–14 that the "prison" of the sonnet (the confines of structure required to write in this FORM) is actually a "solace" from "the weight of too much liberty,"—poems lacking the tight structure of a sonnet.

2. The **English (Shakespearean) sonnet** consists of three quatrains (four lines each) concluding with a couplet in an abab cdcd efef gg rhyme scheme. You can expect the final couplet either to summarize the theme variations in the first three quatrains or to be epigrammatic. An example from Shakespeare:

Why is my verse so barren of new pride,   a
So far from variation or quick change?   b
Why, with the time, do I not glance aside   a
line To newfound methods and to compounds strange?   b
(5) Why write I still all one, ever the same,   c
And keep invention in a noted weed,   d
That every word doth almost tell my name,   c
Showing their birth, and where they did proceed?   d
O, know, sweet love, I always write of you,   e
(10) And you and love are still my argument;   f
So all my best is dressing old words new,   e
Spending again what is already spent: f
For as the sun is daily new and old,   g
So is my love still telling what is told.   g

Lines 1–4 ask why the speaker does not try new methods of verse. (Notice the connotative implications of the first line: "Why is my verse so barren of *new pride,*"—Does he consider trying new FORMS of verse a means of pride?) Lines 5–8 ask why he still writes the same—to

the extent that his work is easily identified as his. (Consider: These questions may be *rhetorical*, in other words, he may not expect a reply, but may be using the interrogative to emphasize his point. The rhetorical question will be discussed in more detail in a later section.) Lines 9–12 bring the reader to the subject of his writings: "you"—with the implication that there are only so many ways to describe his love. The concluding couplet is slightly aphoristic as he likens the sun, which is old yet is seen new each day, to how he expresses his love.

3. The **Spenserian sonnet** consists of the three quatrains being linked by a continuing rhyme scheme, namely abab bcbc cdcd ee.

LIKE AS A HUNTSMAN AFTER WEARY CHASE

X / X / X / X / X /
Like as a huntsman after weary chase,   a
Seeing the game from him escaped away,   b
Sits down to rest him in some shady place,   a
line With panting hounds beguiléd of their prey: b
(5) So, after long pursuit and vain assay,   b
When I all weary had the chase forsook,   c
The gentle deer returned the self-same way,   b
Thinking to quench her thirst at the next brook: c
There she, beholding me with milder look,   c
(10) Sought not to fly, but fearless still did bide;   d
Till I in hand her yet half trembling took,   c
And with her own good-will her firmly tied.   d
Strange thing, meseemed, to see a beast so wild,   e
So goodly won with her own will beguiled.   e

by Edmund Spenser

Once again, the concluding couplet summarizes the speaker's point. In your study of the sonnet, be aware of the sonnet sequence (also called the sonnet cycle)—a device used by Shakespeare and Spenser. These cycles consist of a series of sonnets that are related by theme or some other means.

Here is a brief overview of the more common genres of poetry. Most are lyric; however, some include elements of the epic (narrative mode) and drama (dramatic mode).

Haiku: A single-stanza, three-line, (originally Japanese) lyric poem of 17 syllables. The subject is generally impressionistic of a scene in nature or a natural object:

Line 1 with five syllables
Line 2 with seven syllables
Line 3 with five syllables

HAIKU

Hear their sad refrain
  To capture sense with a sound.
    Doves before the rain.

by C. Myers-Shaffer

Poems set to music

1. **Hymns:** Religious songs. Hymns have appeared in both rhymed and unrhymed qualitative verse, as well as in prose.
2. **Songs:** Lyric poems meant to be sung. Songs are typically short and emotional on topics that range from love to hate, dancing to mourning, work to play.

DRINK TO ME ONLY WITH THINE EYES

Drink to me only with thine eyes,
  And I will pledge with mine;
Or leave a kiss but in the cup
  And I'll not look for wine.
The thirst that from the soul doth rise
  Doth ask a drink divine;
But might I of Jove's nectar sup,
  I would not change for thine.
I sent thee late a rosy wreath,
  Not so much honoring thee
As giving it a hope that there
  It could not withered be;
But thou thereon didst only breathe,
  And sent'st it back to me;
Since when it grows, and smells, I swear,
  Not of itself, but thee!

by Ben Jonson

Some works labeled as songs, however, cannot actually be sung, such as "The Love-Song of J. Alfred Prufrock" by T. S. Eliot. **Folk songs** are those of unknown authorship.

3. **Ballads:** Narrative songs that may be sung or simply recited. The ballad tradition can be found worldwide.
   Characteristics of the ballad:
   - Theme: courage or love
   - Little description or characterization
   - Incremental repetition (repetition of WORDS, LINES, or PHRASES for effect)

FORM of ballad:
- The ballad stanza: usually iambic foot in four lines (quatrain) with an abcb rhyme scheme (sometimes based on approximate rhyme or on assonance and consonance)—lines 1 and 3 have four accented syllables; lines 2 and 4 have three accented syllables
- Use of *refrain* (repetition of WORDS, PHRASES, or LINES at intervals)
- Sometimes has a concluding or summary stanza
- Stock descriptive PHRASES

Types of ballads:
a. **Popular ballad:** A narrative folk song
b. **Broadside ballad:** A song
   - Topic: A current event, well known person or debated issue
   - Tune: Well known
   - Printed on one side of a sheet of paper
c. **Literary ballad:** An imitation of the popular ballad, but written by a "poet"

Because anonymous folk ballads are part of our oral tradition, the same ballad can surface from different regions, times, or peoples in different FORMS. The seventeenth century "Barbara Allen" is such a folk song. One version is in ten stanzas:

BARBARA ALLEN

Stanza one: In Scarlet town, where I was born,
  There was a fair maid dwellin',
Made every youth cry *Well-a-way*!
  Her name was Barbara Allen.

Stanza two: All in the merry month of May,
  When green buds they were swellin',
Young Jemmy Grove on his death-bed lay,
  For love of Barbara Allen.

Stanza three: He sent his man in to her then,
  To the town where she was dwellin';
"O haste and come to my master dear,
  If your name be Barbara Allen."

Stanza four: So slowly, slowly rase she up,
  And slowly she came nigh him,
And when she drew the curtain by—
  "Young man, I think your're dyin'."

Stanza five: "O it's I am sick and very very sick,
  And it's all for Barbara Allen."—
"O the better for me ye'se never be,
  Tho' your heart's blood were a-spillin'!

Stanza six: "O dinna ye mind, young man," says she,
                "When the red wine ye were fillin',
                That ye made the healths go round and round,
                And slighted Barbara Allen?"

Stanza seven: He turned his face unto the wall,
                And death was with him dealin':
                "Adieu, adieu, my dear friends all,
                And be kind to Barbara Allen!"

Stanza eight: As she was walking o'er the fields,
                She heard the dead-bell knellin';
                And every jow the dead-bell gave
                Cried "Woe to Barbara Allen."

Stanza nine: "O mother, mother, make my bed,
                O make it saft and narrow:
                My love has died for me to-day,
                I'll die for him to-morrow.

Stanza ten: "Farewell," she said, "ye virgins all,
                And shun the fault I fell in:
                Henceforth take warning by the fall
                Of cruel Barbara Allen."

Now compare this nine-stanza version:

BONNY BARBARA ALLAN

Stanza one: It was in and about the Martinmas time,
                When the green leaves were a falling,
                That Sir John Graeme, in the West Country,
                Fell in love with Barbara Allan.

Stanza two: He sent his man down through the town,
                To the place where she was dwelling;
                "O haste and come to my master dear,
                Gin ye be Barbara Allan."

Stanza three: O hooly, hooly rose she up,
                To the place where he was lying,
                And when she drew the curtain by,
                "Young man, I think you're dying."

Stanza four: "O it's I'm sick, and very, very sick,
                And 'tis a' for Barbara Allan."
                "O the better for me ye's never be,
                Tho your heart's blood were a spilling.

Stanza five: "O dinna ye mind, young man," said she,
                "When ye was in the tavern a drinking,
                That ye made the healths gae round and
                    round,
                And slighted Barbara Allan?"

Stanza six: He turned his face unto the wall,
                And death was with him dealing:

"Adieu, adieu, my dear friends all,
    And be kind to Barbara Allan."

Stanza seven: And slowly, slowly raise she up,
                And slowly, slowly left him,
                And sighing said she could not stay,
                Since death of life had reft him.

Stanza eight: She had not gane a mile but twa,
                When she heard the dead-bell ringing;
                And every jow that the dead-bell geid,
                It cry'd "Woe to Barbara Allan!"

Stanza nine: "O mother, mother, make my bed!
                O make it soft and narrow!
                Since my love died for me today,
                I'll die for him tomorrow."

Notice the similarities:

Version one		Version two
Stanza three	and	Stanza two
Stanza four	and	Stanza three
Stanza five	and	Stanza four
Stanza six	and	Stanza five
Stanza seven	and	Stanza six
Stanza eight	and	Stanza eight
Stanza nine	and	Stanza nine

These changes due to the oral tradition can be seen in "The Cowboy's Lament" when compared to "The Dying Cowboy" (nineteenth century). Compare the first stanzas of each:

THE COWBOY'S LAMENT

As I walked out in the streets of Laredo,
As I walked out in Laredo one day,
I spied a poor cowboy wrapped up in white linen,
Wrapped up in white linen as cold as the clay.

~ ~ ~ ~ ~

THE DYING COWBOY

As I rode out by Tom Sherman's bar-room,
As I rode out so early one day,
'Twas there I espied a handsome young cowboy,
All dressed in white linen, all clothed for the grave.

For an example of the literary ballad, read these first four stanzas of Coleridge's *The Rime of the Ancient Mariner*, Part I.

It is an ancient Mariner
And he stoppeth one of three.

"By thy long gray beard and glittering eye,
Now wherefore stopp'st thou me?

The Bridegroom's doors are opened wide,
And I am next of kin;
The guests are met, the feast is set:
May'st hear the merry din."

He holds him with his skinny hand,
"There was a ship," quoth he.
"Hold off! unhand me, gray-beard loon!"
Eftsoons his hand dropt he.

He holds him with his glittering eye—
The Wedding-Guest stood still,
And listens like a three years' child:
The Mariner hath his will.

4. **Chansons:** Simple poems meant to be sung.
5. **Epithalamium poems:** Songs written to celebrate a marriage
6. **Madrigals:** Love poems meant to be sung *a cappella* (without instrumental accompaniment) by five to six singers, their voices blending and weaving in and out of the melody:

TAKE, O! TAKE THOSE LIPS AWAY

Take, O! take those lips away,
    That so sweetly were forsworn,
And those eyes, the break of day,
    Lights that do mislead the morn;
But my kisses bring again,
        Bring again,
Seals of love, but sealed in vain,
        Sealed in vain.

by William Shakespeare

7. **Rhapsody:** Once referring to epic poetry that is sung, now rhapsody refers to very emotional poems or any sequence of literary expressions that have been arbitrarily joined together.
8. **Serenades:** Evening songs
9. **Aubades:** Early morning songs, such as Shakespeare's "Hark, Hark, the Lark"
10. **Jingles:** The short, easy-to-sing songs used to sell products. Notable jingles on television include songs to sell toothpaste and hamburgers. (Jingles can have negative connotations—have you ever had a jingle in your mind that you could not seem to stop repeating?)

Light verse: Poems intended to be humorous or witty. Types of light verse include:

1. *Vers de societe*: these are characterized by:
   • brief length
   • playful mood
   • social relationships as the subject
   • sophisticated style
   • terse TONE
   • brisk and generally rhymed rhythm
2. **Parody:** A comic or satiric imitation of a more serious work that ridicules a work, an author, or a style.

   A parody can be fun to write, especially when the original poem has a very pronounced rhythm or mood. Edgar Allan Poe's "The Raven" has such a distinctive rhythm pattern that it works well in parody. Here is the first stanza of the original poem:

Once upon a midnight dreary, while I pondered, weak
    and weary,
Over many a quaint and curious volume of forgotten lore,
While I nodded, nearly napping, suddenly there came a
    tapping,
As of some one gently rapping, rapping at my chamber
    door.
"'Tis some visitor," I muttered, "tapping at my chamber
    door—
        Only this and nothing more."

Here is a parody of the preceding stanza:

Once upon a schoolday dreary, while I studied, weak and
    weary,
Over many a quaint and curious volume of literature,
Feeling grisly, grim and grumbling, suddenly there came
    a rumbling,
A gruesome gripping kind of rumbling, rumbling that was
    premature.
"'Tis my stomach," then I muttered, "rumbling here so
    premature—
        Candy bars will be the cure."

3. **Limerick:** A poem of five anapestic lines with an aabba rhyme scheme. Lines 1, 2, and 5 are trimeter; lines 3 and 4 are dimeter. (Note: If the limerick is only four lines, the third line generally will have some internal rhyme.) The limerick is a FORM of nonsense verse.

```
X X  /  X X  /  X X  /
I sat next/ to the Duch/ess at tea.          a
X X  /  X X  /  X X  /
It was just/ as I thought/ it would be:      a
    X  / X  X  / X X
    Her rumblings ab/dominal                 b
    X  / X X  / X X
    Were simply phe/nomenal                  b
  X  /  X X  /  X X  /
And ev/eryone thought/ it was me.            a
```

This limerick illustrates the use of **substitution**, when the poet substitutes a different foot in place of the one established by the pattern already used. The pattern established in lines 1 and 2 of anapestic trimeter would allow the reader to assume that line 5 would also be anapestic trimeter. The first foot of line 5, however, is an iamb "substituted" for an anapest.

4. **Occasional verse:** Generally written for specific occasions, such as coronations, birthdays, and deaths. For official occasions, the English poet laureate is expected to write the occasional poem. An often-cited occasional poem was written in 1681 by Andrew Marvell. The poem, "An Horatian Ode upon Cromwell's Return from Ireland," is based upon Cromwell's return to England in 1650, at which time he prepared to go to battle against the Scots.

5. **Epigrams:** Short poems that are characteristically witty with a twist in the thought at the end. An epigram, however, can also be defined as simply a clever saying used for a variety of purposes, including to eulogize, to compliment, or to satirize.

This anonymous Latin epigram sums up the point:

Three things must epigrams, like bees, have all,
A sting, and honey, and a body small.

6. **Epitaph:** Generally a short poem (an epigram) intended for a tombstone (or as if for carving on a tombstone). The epitaph may be comic:

MY OWN EPITAPH

Life is a jest; and all things show it.
I thought so once; but now I know it.

by John Gay

Some epitaphs are both lengthy and serious:

AN EPITAPH UPON A YOUNG MARRIED COUPLE, DEAD AND BURIED TOGETHER

To these, whom death again did wed,
This grave's their second marriage-bed.
For though the hand of fate could force
'Twixt soul and body a divorce,
It could not sunder man and wife
'Cause they both livéd but one life.
Peace, good reader, Do not weep.
Peace, the lovers are asleep.
They, sweet turtles, folded lie
In the last knot love could tie.
And though they lie as they were dead,
Their pillow stone, their sheets of lead,
(Pillow hard, and sheets not warm)
Love made the bed; they'll take no harm;
Let them sleep, let them sleep on.
Till this stormy night be gone,
Till th'eternal morrow dawn;
Then the curtains will be drawn
And they wake into a light,
Whose day shall never die in night.

by Richard Crashaw

William Blake wrote an epitaph in which he compares his subject to an epigram:

HER WHOLE LIFE IS AN EPIGRAM

Her whole life is an epigram: smack, smooth & neatly
   penned,
Platted quite neat to catch applause, with a sliding
   noose at the end.

7. **Epigraph** (motto): The quotation or inscription on a statue, on a coin, before chapter headings, and on title pages of books.

8. **Clerihew:** Named after the writer of detective fiction (Edmund Clerihew Bentley). The subject of the Clerihew is the name of a person. The name appears on the first line of the quatrain. The rhyme scheme is aabb with no regular meter.

Sir Humphrey Davy
Detested gravy
He lived in the odium
Of having discovered sodium.

9. **Nonsense verse:** Poems characterized by:
- Strong rhythm
- No logic
- Words that are coined, invented, or borrowed (without regard to appropriateness) from other languages

Visual poems: The physical shape affects MEANING.

1. **Shaped verse** (Renaissance emblem poetry): The words are shaped to fit MEANING.

THE ALTAR

A broken ALTAR, Lord, Thy servant rears,
Made of a HEART, and cemented with tears;
Whose parts are as Thy hand did frame;
No workman's tool hath touched the same.
A HEART alone
Is such a stone
As nothing but
Thy power doth cut.
Wherefore each part
Of my hard HEART
Meets in this frame,
To praise Thy name:
That, if I chance to hold my peace,
These stones to praise Thee may not cease.
O, let Thy blessed SACRIFICE be mine,
And sanctify this ALTAR to be Thine.

by George Herbert

2. **Concrete poetry** (pattern poems): Highly graphic, modern poems that are also graphic art.

A
l
p h a
b
et
Soup

A Bowl Can Do Each Friend Good
Hot In January—Knowing Life's
Mean, Nasty—Only Please
Quick—Run Straight To
Universal Values With
Xtra Yummy Zoups
(-oops-)

by L. E. Myers

3. **Acrostic poems:** Poems in which the first letter of each line when read down joins to spell a word.

ACROSTIC

L   Little maidens, when you look
O   On this little storybook,
R   Reading with attentive eye
I   Its enticing history,
N   Never think that hours of play
A   Are your only HOLIDAY,

A   And that in a HOUSE of joy
L   Lessons serve but to annoy:
I   If in any HOUSE you find
C   Children of a gentle mind,
E   Each the others pleasing ever—

E   Each the others vexing never—
D   Daily work and pastime daily
I   In their order taking gaily—
T   Then be very sure that they
H   Have a life of HOLIDAY.

by Lewis Carroll
Christmas 1861

Riddles: Poems presented as mental puzzles meant to be solved. What is L. E. Myers describing in "That Sound"?

THAT SOUND

What fun camping out—
Wild animals all about.
Then it gets dark
In the National Park.

And after all are fed,
You're tired and ready for bed.
The tents are all in a row
And into bed you all go.

You hear that sound
And out of bed you bound.
It's still quite early—
Only about four-thirty.

That sound came from who-o-o
Just in time to scare you.
A quivering sound that's eerie:
The dark makes you leery.

The others hear it, too—
That same sound that scared you.
Please try to identify
That strange and scary cry.

by L. E. Myers

Satire: Poems that embody a satiric outlook. Formal verse satire, sometimes didactic in TONE, satirize some vice. Look for *Horatian* satire (gentle ridicule) in the poetry of W. H. Auden. *Juvenalian* satire is very formal, very cutting, whereas *Menippean* satire uses plot, dialogue, and a mixture of prose and verse.

Jonathan Swift, well known for his ability to satirize, penned "A Satirical Elegy" in 1722. This was written "On the Death of a Late Famous General"—John Churchill. Churchill was a member of royalty (Duke of Marlborough) and an English military hero whose CHARACTER was eventually called into question.

A SATIRICAL ELEGY
On the Death of a Late Famous General

His Grace? impossible? what dead?
Of old age too, and in his bed?
And could that Mighty Warrior fall?
And so inglorious, after all!
Well, since he's gone, no matter how,
The last loud trump must wake him now;
And, trust me, as the noise grows stronger,
He'd wish to sleep a little longer.

And could he be indeed so old
As by the newspapers we're told?
Threescore, I think, is pretty high;
'Twas time in conscience he should die.
This world he cumbered long enough;
He burnt his candle to the snuff;
And that's the reason, some folks think,
He left behind *so great a stink*.

Behold his funeral appears,
Nor widow's sighs, nor orphan's tears,
Wont at such times each heart to pierce,
Attend the progress of his hearse.
But what of that, his friends may say,
He had those honors in his day;
True to his profit and his pride,
He made them weep before he died.

Come hither, all ye empty things,
Ye bubbles raised by breath of Kings,
Who float upon the tide of state,
Come hither, and behold your fate.
Let pride be taught by this rebuke,
How very mean a thing's a Duke;
From all his ill-got honors flung,
Turned to that dirt from whence he sprung.

Invective poems: Personal attacks or lampoons (satires against individuals).

Panegyric poems: Poems that praise someone or something, especially public figures and institutions.

Epideictic poetry: Special occasion poems:

- **Encomiums** are poems (often in the FORM of odes) that eulogize.
- **Epithalamiums** are poems (that can be songs) that celebrate a wedding.

Complaint: A lyric poem (usually a monologue) in which the poet complains about the state of the world, his individual situation, or his mistress.

A COMPLAINT BY NIGHT

Alas! so all things now do hold their peace,
Heaven and earth disturbèd in no thing.
The beasts, the air, the birds their song do cease;
The nightès chare the stars about doth bring;
Calm is the sea; the waves work less and less.
So am not I, whom love, alas! doth wring,
Bringing before my face the great increase
Of my desires, whereat I weep and sing,
In joy and woe, as in a doubtful ease:
For my sweet thoughts sometime do pleasure bring;
But by and by, the cause of my disease
Gives me a pang, that inwardly doth sting,
When that I think what grief it is again,
To live and lack the thing should rid my pain.

by Henry Howard, Earl of Surrey

Confessional poems: A contemporary FORM that deals with very private matters.

Palinode: A poem or song that retracts a previous work, oftentimes retracting an ode.

Metaphysical poetry: Philosophical poetry written in the seventeenth century as a revolt against Elizabethan love poetry. Characterized by:

- The *metaphysical conceit*
- Psychological analysis
- Subjects: love and religion
- Use of the shocking
- Simple diction
- FORM: an argument
- Style: rough

DEATH, BE NOT PROUD

Death, be not proud, though some have callèd thee
Mighty and dreadful, for thou art not so,
For those whom thou think'st thou dost overthrow
Die not, poor Death, nor yet canst thou kill me.
From rest and sleep, which but thy picture be,
Much pleasure, then from thee much more must flow;
And soonest our best men with thee do go—
Rest of their bones and souls' delivery!
Thou'rt slave to fate, chance, kings and desperate men,
And dost with poison, war, and sickness dwell,
And poppy or charms can make us sleep as well,
And better than thy stroke; why swell'st thou then?
One short sleep past, we wake eternally,
And death shall be no more: Death, thou shalt die!

by John Donne

A type of metaphysical poetry is the *meditative poem,* written with Renaissance poetic techniques about religious topics for religious ceremonies.

Verse epistles: Poems written as letters from the poet to (usually) a friend.

Didactic poetry: Poems meant to instruct.

Georgic poems (didactic-descriptive): Poems that teach about rural life, science, art, or some skill for the purpose of praising rural life. This is in contrast to the **pastoral poem** that tries to fictionalize country life. Georgics that detail a specific place are *topographical.*

Stanza   FORMS from France

1. **Rondeau**—a poem of 15 lines in three stanzas.

   - Lines 9 and 15 begin a refrain.
   - Rhyme scheme: aabba aabc aabbcc.
   - Eight-syllable lines.

   Alternate FORMS of rondeau have 12 lines (abba abc abbac) and the *rondeau redouble (*six quatrains of abab rhyme scheme, lines 1–4 form the last lines of quatrains 2, 3, 4, and 5).

2. **Villanelle**—a poem of 19 lines.

   - Lines 6, 12, and 18 repeat line 1.
   - Lines 9, 15, and 19 repeat line 3.
   - Rhyme scheme: aba' aba aba' aba aba' abaa'

YOUR BEST FOR THE TEST

As you prepare for the literature test,	a
You will need to develop a plan	b
That will help you to realize your best.	a
line To pursue learning make knowledge a quest,	a
(5) A goal your whole lifetime to span	b
As you prepare for the literature test.	a
You may want to play and to rest;	a
But keep focused on works that you scan	b
That will help you to realize your best.	a
(10) Some works you may find you detest	a
Poems so hard to understand, no one can—	b
As you prepare for the literature test.	a
Now, we have one thing to suggest:	a
Just go back to your individual plan	b
(15) That will help you to realize your best.	a
Keep your zeal and keep your zest.	a
Remember—you can, yes, you can!	b
As you prepare for the literature test	a
That will help you to realize your best.	a

3. **Triolet**—a poem of eight lines.

   - Lines 7 and 8 repeat lines 1 and 2.
   - Line 4 repeats line 1.
   - Rhyme scheme: ab aa abab.

TRIOLET

Easy is the triolet,	a
If you really learn to make it!	b
Once a neat refrain you get,	a
line Easy is the triolet.	a
(5) As you see!—I pay my debt	a
With another rhyme. Deuce take it,	b
Easy is the triolet,	a
If you really learn to make it!	b

by W. E. Henley

This book has defined and/or illustrated a wide variety (although not all) of the genres of poetry.

For the test, you may need to know literary genres—perhaps to identify a sample or to define the terms. You also need to recognize:

1. When the poet makes a change in rhythm or the rhyme scheme, this change may indicate an important shift, break, or significant reinforcement in MEANING, TONE, or other literary element.

2. Certain genres carry with them expectations concerning structure (FORM) and, as a result, identifying the genre is a clue to the MEANING, TONE, or other literary element that is characteristic of and inherent to that particular genre. In other words, clues to answering test questions over MEANING, TONE, or the other literary elements sometimes can be found when there is a change in rhythm or rhyme scheme or can be found from the expectations you can have concerning subject and structure that are peculiar to a specific genre. Always bear in mind, however, that there are exceptions to the rules.

FORM IN DRAMA

Drama—a play—is a literary composition or story that is intended to be acted out by actors or players (usually) on a stage.

Drama was present in ancient Greek Dionysian religious ceremony, but modern drama is more closely a product of Western European medieval drama, a new FORM that was developed from Christian Church ritual in the ninth century.

Dramatic Structure

"Dramatic structure," of course, refers to *plot*. To confine a discussion of dramatic structure to just the narrative line of the play, however, is perhaps an oversimplification of the subject. Several other elements work together to form and at the same time counter one another to influence the structure of a play. For example, most plays are intended to be performed in a theater, in a movie, or on television, and each of these milieus has an inherent impact upon dramatic structure.

Even the physical format is significant:

Play
    Acts (the major divisions of a play)
        Scenes and/or episodes

Just as in prose narrative, the plot of a drama centers around conflict: person vs. person, person vs. group, person vs. environment, person vs. nature, or person vs. self. Each event is arranged within the dramatic structure to move along the story line of the plot—the action—and to have some impact upon the audience.

The structure of a typical stage play might look like this:

1. Exposition, introduction, or status quo

During the opening of the play the setting is established and the audience meets the main CHARACTERS. Sometimes the story begins in the conflict; sometimes you only get clues of the conflict to come. The opening scene does, however, develop a sense of credibility by "filling you in" on the circumstances that motivate the actors. Also, the introduction sets the TONE. In the movie, *E. T.*, the exposition introduces the audience to a mother and her children in an average American home setting and endears the viewer to a gentle, supernatural, slightly comical alien who just wants to "phone home."

2. Conflict or exciting force

The **conflict** is the point at which you recognize a threat to something and/or to someone you have come to care about in the introduction or to something or someone that you are, in the course of the story, coming to care about. Obstacles are placed in the way of the protagonist (the main CHARACTER). These obstacles may arise from another person, a group, nature, the environment, or from psychological conflicts that are generated within the protagonist. Called the **exciting force**, it sets into motion the rising action in the play. Being able to identify the exciting force in the structure of a drama is very important because it gives the CHARACTERS motivation for their words and deeds and it gives the audience motivation to care.

What are some common exciting forces used in plays? (This list is not exhaustive of the possibilities—only illustrative of some of what has been done.)

- In plots in which the conflict is person vs. person or group, the exciting forces might be competition (rivalry), pursuit (a chase or stalking), rebellion, revenge, love, hate, betrayal, war, or persecution.
- In plots in which the conflict is person vs. environment or nature, the exciting forces might be a catastrophe, grief over death or loss, survival, or rescue.
- In plots in which the conflict is person vs. self, the exciting forces might be self-sacrifice, greed, ambition, love, hate, or rebellion.

HINT: In preparing to answer test questions concerning the conflict (exciting force) in a story, you need to identify it from two perspectives: (1) in general terms, such as "The exciting force is rebellion," and (2) in specific terms, such as "Joe is rebelling against conforming to the values of his friends." For example, in the film *E. T.* the exciting force is a chase. More specifically, government agents discover the possible existence of an alien and the chase begins as they try to capture E. T.

3. Rising action or complication

Once the exciting force has set the action in motion, the struggle builds dramatic tension toward a confrontation. This stage in the dramatic structure consists of a series of emotional highs and lows, with each high gaining intensity. This conflict becomes more complicated. How? In escaping a sinking ship, for example, the hero goes through a series of progressively more dangerous "near-misses" and "close calls," being rescued each time. Or the hero is in a love triangle and gets caught in a series of events involving suspicion, conspiracy, and deception. In the movie *E. T.,* the alien is hunted by government authorities and "barely" escapes as the pursuers close in on the children and the alien that they are hiding.

4. Climax, crisis, or turning point

Then it happens—the inevitable moment of confrontation. This is the point of *climax*—the turning point in the plot—the point at which there is a reversal from rising action to falling action.

HINT: Be aware that the word *climax* actually has more than one usage in literary analysis. Climax is a synonym for crisis when you are determining the structure of a story or a drama, but climax can also refer to the point of highest intensity for the reader or audience—a point that might come before or after the crisis. In the case of *E. T.*, the emotional climax or point of highest intensity might be when the alien "dies." The structural climax (crisis or turning point), however, might be when the alien revives because it is at this point his "fortunes" have reversed. Although more "near misses" ensue, you know that somehow he will make it.

5. Falling action

Briefer than rising action, the falling action may still have some suspenseful moments, but for the most part gives the reader or audience a sense of completion, with the various unsettled issues at work within the plot reaching some state of resolution. In *E. T.,* there is one last race to the spaceship and a moment for farewells to be said.

6. Resolution or Dénouement

The hero has won or lost; issues are resolved; order is restored. The alien goes home.

How the structure is handled depends on many factors, including the length of the play and the intended audience, the use of dramatic elements, the settings, and the genre of the play.

Length and Audience

In a typical three-act play, both the exposition and the introduction of the conflict may occur in Act I. The conflict may continue into Act II, with rising action leading to the point of crisis (the turning point) happening just before the curtain closes on the second act. Act III, then, is left to the falling action and the resolution.

The structure of a five-act tragedy cannot be better explained than by Gustav Freytag's (1863) *Technik des Dramas:*

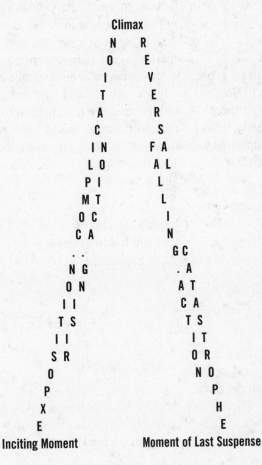

The intended audience—or rather the medium used to convey the enactment of the drama to the audience—is very important to structure. Stop and think about the structural challenges facing the writer of drama for television. At a stage performance, the audience arrives with the expectation of sitting and watching a performance through—with perhaps a few brief intermissions at most. Most big-screen movie theaters have no intermission (or maybe one popcorn break). During a two-hour television movie, however, there is a two- to three-minute intermission every 15 minutes and a longer break for commercials on the hour and sometimes on the half hour. Viewers see these breaks as opportunities to talk, to get a snack, or to "channel surf," but for the writer these intermissions are better described as *interruptions* in the dramatic structure. These breaks interrupt the continuity of the play and as a result pose a risk of losing the viewers. The result? A simplification of plot and an intensification of structure. The writer must "hook" the viewer into coming back to the story despite distractions like commercials and the refrigerator—particularly on the hour (and to a lesser degree the half hour) when the viewer anticipates slightly longer commercial breaks.

With these elements in mind, the structure of a television movie or program might look like the following. The numbers of segments, lengths and frequencies of commercials, and plot structure given here are generalizations intended to demonstrate how such elements influence one another and must be coordinated. Actual programming structures vary greatly from network to network, based upon such widely ranging factors as subject, target audience, and time slot in which the program is to be broadcast.

Sample program structure:

Segment one
13 minutes: Exposition, Introduction of Conflict and Exciting force

(3-minute commercial)

Segment two
11 minutes: Rising action
End with a crisis that hints at a larger crisis ahead

(3-minute commercial)

Segment three
11 minutes: Resolution of previous crisis; hint at upcoming larger crisis; end with rising action crisis

(2-minute commercial)

Segment four
10 minutes: Intensify previous crisis; more hints at larger crisis; end with major cliff-hanger before on-hour break

(5-minute commercial on the hour)

Segment five
13 minutes: Immediate gratification of cliff-hanger; revelation of magnitude of larger crisis; end with emotional rising action crisis as plan to solve problem is revealed

(2-minute commercial)

Segment six
12 minutes: Rising action crisis continues; intensity of larger crisis continues to increase; CHARACTERS start implementing plan; abrupt jolt when plan fails

(3-minute commercial)

Segment seven
12 minutes: Begin with new surge of crisis after plan fails; rising action crisis continues; end with turning point (crisis solved)

(3-minute commercial)

Segment eight
13 minutes: CHARACTERS discuss implications of crisis and solution on future; minor crisis resolved; end of story

Dramatic Elements

A playwright's understanding of structure is not complete without a sense of awareness of the many techniques and devices—dramatic elements—available to create various effects. Here are just a few:

Foreshadowing: Hints at the future that can build anticipation and tension in the audience. In the movie *Back to the Future,* foreshadowing is very cleverly used in a psychologically reversed way as events in the present "foreshadow" events in the past.

Flashbacks: Descriptions or enactments of past events for the purpose of clarifying the situation, usually as it relates to the conflict.

Intrigue: A scheme designed by one of the CHARACTERS, the success of which depends on another CHARACTER'S innocence or ignorance of the situation. The usual result is a complication in the plot.

In medias res: The first scene opening in the middle of the action.

Suspense: Establishing caring on the part of the viewers for one or more of the CHARACTERS, then presenting events that create a sense of uncertainty concerning what will happen to them.

Double plots: Especially evident in Elizabethan drama—use of a *subplot* or second plotline weaving in and out of the main plot.

Surprise: Once the audience has a sense of expectation, events happen that are not expected.

Reversal: Also called *peripety*—when the main CHARACTER either fails or succeeds.

Discovery: When the main CHARACTER finally realizes the reality of the situation.

Deus ex machina: Once referring to the Greek practice of physically lowering a "god" to the stage at the end of the play to solve all the problems, today it refers to a contrived element in the plot used to resolve a problem.

Monologue: When an actor delivers a speech in the presence of other CHARACTERS who listen, but do not speak.

Three unities: Although not adhered to by many playwrights, French and Italian critics of the sixteenth and seventeenth centuries believed that a play needs three unities to achieve verisimilitude (believability):

1. Unity of action (first suggested by Aristotle)
2. Unity of place (a single location)
3. Unity of time (the play portraying no longer than a 24-hour period)

Dramatic conventions: The elements of a play that the audience knows merely represent reality, but is willing to accept them as real for the sake of the story: actors representing the CHARACTERS of the story, the stage set representing a real location in time and space, suspended time or jumps forward or backward in time, Italians in Italy speaking English, and other such conventions.

The aside: When an actor speaks directly to the audience, however, the rest of the actors on stage supposedly cannot hear him or her. Assumed to be truthful, the aside was used in Renaissance drama to let the audience know the actor's inner feelings and was used in the nineteenth century to interject elements of comedy or melodrama.

Soliloquy: When an actor delivers a speech when he or she is alone, expressing thoughts.

Complications: Causing conflict by introducing new CHARACTERS, information, or events.

Scenes: Portions of an act, sometimes triggered by the clearing of the stage for the next "scene." Some types of scenes include *relief scenes* that allow the audience to relax briefly in the tension of the drama and *balcony scenes*. (Remember *Romeo and Juliet*?)

HINT: Comic relief scenes are widely used in English drama. Be aware that sometimes their purpose is to ease tension, but also they can add a sense of poignant sadness. Such a scene could lead to test questions concerning CHARACTER, MEANING, or TONE.

Music: A mainstay of the musical drama, however, early tragedies had both dancing and choral singing. Also, background music is used extensively in television, movies, and on the stage to set the mood and TONE. Music can help psychologically establish the setting: the theme from *Bonanza* for a western, a minuet for a period play, native drums for Africa, an Italian opera for Italy, an Irish reel for Ireland, and Cajun music for New Orleans.

Setting

The setting of a story refers to the time and place of the story and of the socioeconomic background of the CHARACTERS. In drama, *setting* also refers to the means necessary to translate the story to the audience.

In the theater, this translation depends greatly upon illusion—using lights, costumes, props, and so forth to allow the viewers to suspend reality for a brief time and to accept the story as real.

For the religious plays and classical drama enacted in Elizabethan and Jacobean theaters of the sixteenth and seventeenth centuries, there were very few props and painted backdrops. Playwrights depended upon trapdoors, some sound effects, music, mechanical contrivances (to raise and lower

CHARACTERS), and dialogue to establish the setting of the story. Due to lack of sufficient lighting, there were no evening performances and only "special" CHARACTERS (representing, for example, animals and royalty) in the almost all-male acting troupes wore costumes. The stage was in an open-air public theater that included an area for some of the audience to stand and galleries with seats also available.

The Puritans closed the English theaters in 1642; however, when they reemerged in 1660 (the Restoration), they had a new look, a new subject, and a new audience. The religious plays and classical dramas of Elizabethan theater gave way to the bright and colorful Comedies of Manners (influenced by French and Italian Neoclassicism), with actresses playing female roles, prose dialogue, and audiences that were predominantly upper classes and royalty. So lacking in "propriety" were some of these plays that by the eighteenth century, people were protesting. The Restoration saw a change in the theater itself, with an indoor construction that included balconies. A skylight allowed daylight to illuminate the stage for the afternoon performances, but this meant actors tended to gravitate toward the forestage area where the light was best. Costumes were elaborate, and by the eighteenth century, the theaters grew in size to seat more people.

The approach of the 1800s (and well into the nineteenth century) brought a reaction against the rules of Neoclassicism and the Age of Reason. This less restrictive style and attitude ushered in Romanticism. The plays of the period are loosely structured and characterized by tragic love affairs, the use of dramatic effects such as intrigue, and dialogue written in poetry rather than prose (although the melodrama—also a product of the nineteenth century literary world and considered to be of less literary value—was usually written in prose with the hero overcoming the obstacles by the end of the play). With Romanticism came a new sense of adventure in the production of plays as well. No longer were performances limited to daylight as the theaters were lit with lime, gas, and carbon arc lights. New attention was paid to costuming with attempts at historical accuracy and the audiences (now composed of people from all classes) were thrilled with elaborately painted stage scenes.

People soon tired of the idealism of Romanticism and as the century progressed, they began to turn to Realism, especially as seen in the plot "formulas" of Eugene Scribe (French). The plays of Realism lost the freedoms of their predecessors in favor of highly structured FORMS and prose dialogue with the plot trying to mirror real life. Naturalism emerged, whose playwrights presented a more victimized portrait of the lower classes in plays that focused on that victimization rather than on the structure of the plot. As the literary world approached the twentieth century, electricity gave new freedoms to stage production and contributed to the new attention to reality in plots, scenery, and acting. Experimental theaters emerged in which attempts were made to make the play seem so real as to make the audiences temporarily forget that they were watching a play.

The cycles of innovation and reaction against those innovations continued as the Symbolists reacted against the harshness of Naturalism by using Symbolism to convey MEANING and as the Expressionists reacted against Realism by writing plays aimed at psychologically calling for social change. Some of their drama became quite didactic (as in Epic Theater). Also, around this time the Theater of the Absurd emerged—a strange blend of satire, symbolism, and dream imagery. Despite these reactions, however, FORMS of Realism have been carried into the modern theater as have a variety of other FORMS and styles. The settings for modern plays incorporate a wide range of costumes, props, sets, and other materials to convey the story to the audience.

There are three different types of stages that vary with location, but the following sketches will give you an idea of the basic principles of each:

ARENA STAGE

Just the actors and audience—the arena stage places the play on an "island" in a sea of viewers. With the physical possibilities of setting greatly reduced, plays produced on an arena stage depend on a few props, costumes, the words of the play, and the delivery by the actors.

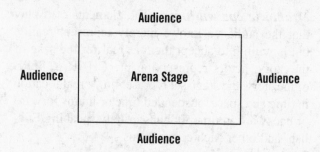

Also called the "theater in the round," the arena stage is the popular choice for the circus and boxing matches. Historically, the arena was used for some of the earliest harvest festival dramas and medieval rounds.

THE THRUST STAGE

The thrust stage (also called the open stage or platform stage) projects into the audience, reducing the use of the wings and fly galleries, although they may or may not be there. These stages enable very economical productions. The "runway" upon which winners of beauty pageants, such as Miss America, Miss U.S.A., and Miss Universe, traditionally take their "victory walks" are types of thrust stages. Versions of the open stage appeared historically in China, Italy, Japan, and the playhouses of Elizabethan England.

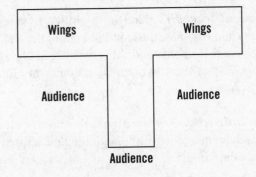

PROSCENIUM STAGE

In the proscenium-arch stage (also called the picture-frame stage), the auditorium is separated from the stage. View from audience (notice picture-frame effect):

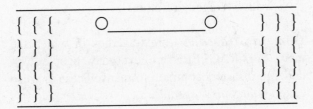

Aerial view of the Proscenium Stage:

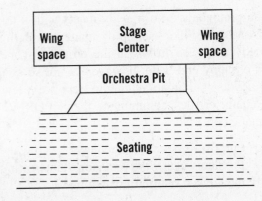

This type of stage can be found in many of the older American public school auditoriums and in the "legitimate" theater. Its obvious advantages include providing the means for elaborate settings and greater "illusion."

With the twentieth century, however, came a new opportunity—and challenge—for dramatists: *motion pictures*. Whether intended for movie theaters or television, motion pictures and advancing technology are inseparably linked. Even in the first silent films, the tremendous potential of this medium was clearly evident.

Unlike in a stage production, the filmmaker has the advantages of being able to use exterior scenes, *real* props (such as elephant herds), and computer graphics (such as those used in such movies as *E.T., Jurassic Park,* and *Star Wars*). Movies can be filmed on location, and if an actor forgets a line the scene can be retaken.

But perhaps one of the major disadvantages to filmmaking is the lack of intimacy with the audience that is a natural part of a live theater performance. Not possible is the give-and-take rapport among the actor, the audience, and indirectly the writer. Not possible are the changes to what did not "work" in last night's performance before tonight's production. The greater distance between writer and audience translates into structural changes: the writer must "hook" the audience in some other way—perhaps by intensity of dialogue, by the use of "kept me on the edge of my seat" action, by captivating graphics, or by restructuring the plot.

Genre

One cannot look at the genre of drama played out on English and American stages without first looking at the history of drama in England—more specifically the Elizabethan popular theater.

The Early Church in England, in celebrating Christmas and Easter, developed special music in which choir groups would musically "respond" to one another. Sometimes a soloist would "answer" the choral group, or vice versa. This back-and-forth musical conversation eventually suggested to the Early Church the concept of dialogue. Soon costumes and settings were added and people began to "act out" their roles in dramas.

In the world without television, radio, or computer video games, such performances provided grand entertainment—crowds grew in number, spilling out into the church yards. Eventually, the secular communities became involved, starting festivals at which dramatic episodes were enacted in cycles of plays. The subjects for these "mystery" or "miracle" plays were still based on events in the Bible, and production fell into the hands of various trade guilds.

Secular involvement began to be reflected in these productions—at first with minor changes, like adding comic or tragic scenes that are not in the Bible; but eventually they became completely secular works. The first formal tragedy written and enacted in England was in 1561, *Gorboduc,* by Thomas Sackville and Thomas Norton, in the "tragedy of blood" tradition of Seneca, a first-century stoic philosopher.

Upon this basis, then, evolved the drama of England and eventually that of the United States.

Some literary critics have pointed out that the MEANING of the term, *dramatic literature* is contradictory because *literature* refers to written works whereas *drama* refers to performed works. Yet, the interwoven nature and mutual dependence of literature and drama defined as such still provides a basis for study—and for testing. The makers of the SAT II: Literature Subject Test list drama as a genre that may constitute 0 to 10 percent of the selections tested.

Drama can take two different fundamental FORMS under which many other genres fall: *tragedy* and *comedy.*

TRAGEDY

In a tragedy, the protagonist (the hero or heroine) is overcome in the conflict and meets a tragic end. The TONE is serious and builds in the audience a fatalistic sense of the inevitability of the outcome and, as a result, is sometimes frightening. Yet the inescapable aspects of the catastrophe serve as a *catharsis* that somehow inexplicably purges the viewer of pity and fear. The significance, then, is not that the protagonist meets with an inevitable catastrophe, but rather the degree to which he or she deals with the conflict and the tragedy with dignity, courage, and honor.

What are the basic ingredients of a tragedy?

- Mode: narrative
- Protagonist: a *tragic hero,* honorable, high CHARACTER, a person of conscience
- Catastrophe: the tragic conclusion of the conflict—usually death of the hero or heroine
- Catharsis: the purging of feelings of pity and fear through the vehicle of the play

- Spectacles: grand displays used to grab the attention of the audience
- Reversal: the point when the protagonist's situation changes from good to bad
- Hamartia: the protagonist's fatal error or the mistake made (for whatever reason) that leads to his or her downfall; e.g., *hubris*—too much self-confidence that results in mistakenly not taking heed to a warning
- Recognition: simultaneous with the reversal, the protagonist's recognition of the truth of the situation

Also, tragedy elicits pity and fear from the audience, and the protagonist begins in a state of happiness and falls into a state of unhappiness or death.

Classical tragedies   are those written *by* ancient Greeks and Romans, those written *about* the ancient Greeks and Romans, and those written *in the style and FORM of* those written by the ancient Greeks and Romans.

Romantic tragedies   are those that are not classical and include many of the tragedies written in Elizabethan England.

Revenge tragedies   are characterized by:

- Senecan technique
- Plot line: father revenges son at direction of son's ghost or son revenges father at direction of father's ghost
- Sensationalized murders (the most extreme called "tragedy of blood")

Domestic tragedies   are tragedies in which the main CHARACTERS are everyday people who undergo disasters common to many. These are also called *bourgeois tragedies.*

COMEDY

If the protagonist of a tragedy meets with a tragic end, one would like to simplify matters by defining comedy as a play in which the protagonist meets with a happy end. Life, however, is not so simple and neither is dramatic comedy. Here are a few of the characteristics common to many FORMS of dramatic comedy:

- Purpose—to amuse the viewer
- Problems facing the protagonist interesting to the viewer, but not threatening

- Subject—generally a somewhat realistic view of peoples' lives, including the disparities between what they should be and what they are
- Emotional involvement of audience—a balance between two elements:
  1. A superficial involvement based on relevance to their own lives and on familiarity
  2. Detachment arising from less involvement with the fate of the protagonist (as contrasted to the high levels of emotional involvement of the audience with the fate of the tragic protagonist)
- Intellectual laughter
- Style—friendlier as contrasted to the exalted style of tragic drama
- Includes a sustained plot
- Uses *humor*—laughter invoked by a good-natured look at the inconsistencies in human nature and of life
- Uses *wit* (in non-comedic FORMS referring to wisdom, but in comedy referring to the bright, intelligent use of words to invoke laughter)

The degree to which humor is used, the FORM it takes, and the manner of presentation are fundamental to *high comedy,* a "serious" FORM that intends the laughter to be *at* the CHARACTERS—at their ridiculous conduct or attitudes—laughter that is intellectual, but not mocking. In contrast, *low comedy* is just plain fun with jesting and clownish behavior. Plays can be predominantly high or low comedy, or elements of either (or both) can be incorporated into more serious FORMS. Compare the elements of low comedy used in the slapstick television plays of *I Love Lucy* to the high comedic elements used in *Cheers* in which the viewer laughs not just at the silly but also at the incongruous actions and attitudes of a group of people who interact with one another in lives that revolve around a bar. When Lucille Ball's plan backfires and the scene leaves her with a cream pie in the face, the audience laughs with abandon at the silliness of her situation. When the viewer laughs at jokes that reveal Norm is a "fixture" at the Cheers bar, however, one laughs with a different sense of humor—a somewhat serious, thoughtful laughter about a man whose beer and social interaction at a bar has taken precedence over his wife, job, and home.

An example of how both high and low comedy can be used is the television sitcom *Family Matters.* Steven Urkel's CHARACTER depends upon exten-sive use of low comedy, for instance, when he causes the entire Winslow family to fall into a heap in the middle of the living room floor and asks, "Did I do that?" Elements of high comedy are also used throughout as the comedy and laughter revolves around family issues (Should Eddie go to college?) and moral issues (Should Carl tell his wife the truth about his job promotion test results?). The use of high comedy makes the viewer think.

Comedy can take many FORMS and, of course, examples of each can be found in any age. Yet, some FORMS were more prevalent in certain literary periods:

Literary Age:	Comic FORM:
Sixteenth Century (particularly Elizabethan England)	Romantic Comedy
Seventeenth Century	Realistic Comedy
Eighteenth Century	Comedy of Manners Sentimental
Nineteenth Century	Burlesque Operetta

The following takes a look at each of these comic FORMS:

Romantic comedy: The plot revolves around a love story with a happy ending. Shakespeare's *As You Like It* is a notable example. Notice: A peculiar characteristic of the romantic comedy is that the heroine often will pretend (for whatever reason) that she is a man. An interesting reversal on the convention is the trend in the modern romantic comedy to have the hero mask as a woman, as in *Tootsie* and *Mrs. Doubtfire.*

Realistic comedy: A reaction that began late in the sixteenth century against romantic comedy, this FORM is based on real life, usually in London, and is characterized by a cynical TONE and extensive use of satire. An example is Ben Jonson's *The Alchemist.* Jonson also joined George Chapman to introduce a new FORM of realistic comedy called the *Comedy of Humours.* These plays focus on the *humour* or predominant CHARACTER trait of the protagonist: melancholic, sanguine, choleric, and phlegmatic. For further information concerning the four humours, see Literary Element Number Five: CHARACTER page 154.

Comedy of manners: A realistic FORM practiced during the Restoration (late seventeenth century) and then later for two revivals (late in the eighteenth century and again late in the nineteenth century.) Its name is indicative of its subject: the contrived, self-conscious manners of society. The CHARACTERS tend to be stereotypes, with heavy use of satire, clever dialogue, and forbidden, illicit love. The comedy of manners is also called *Restoration comedy*.

Sentimental comedy: Reacting to the immorality extant in the comedies of manners, this FORM came to be called "reformed comedy" that aimed to restore virtue to the comic stage. The result was a FORM steeped in sentimentality, with "perfect" heroes and contrived plots that destroyed the dramatic reality of the plays. *The Conscious Lovers* by Richard Steele is an example.

Burlesque: At the center of burlesque is difference—the difference between the style of the work and its subject, in other words, an elevated style for a base subject or a base style for an elevated subject. In drama, this FORM of comedy has many devices available, including song and dance routines and bawdy humor. An often cited example of burlesque in drama is *The Beggar's Opera* by John Gay.

Operetta: Also called the Comic Opera, this colorful musical production, such as those of Gilbert and Sullivan, blends dialogue with singing in plots that are often romantic.

Other FORMS of dramatic comedy include:

- *Comedy of intrigue* (also called the *comedy of situation)* in which the twists and turns of the plot line supersede the CHARACTERS involved in the situations.
- *Farce-comedies* in which farce (low comedy when the humor is based on the silliness of the situation) is central to the play. The CHARACTERS generally are exaggerated stereotypes who get into unbelievable situations that often result in "slapstick" comedy. *Charlie's Aunt* by Brandon Thomas (1892) is a farce, and such sitcoms as *Three's Company* employ elements of farce-comedy.
- *Court comedies*, written for royal command performances, in which a clever style and light TONE work together with a plot somewhat devoid of action and with elements of mythology and contrasting characterization.

- *Commedia dell'arte* in which stock CHARACTERS (played by Italian actors) were given a scenario or main idea of the plot and improvise the dialogue. Although Italian in origin, these improvisations greatly influenced Elizabethan dramatic comedy.
- *Satiric comedy* in which satire is used to make ridiculous the root causes of social problems, particularly dysfunctional political policies, social customs, and contemporary thinking.

Neither writers nor critics have found all plays to fit neatly into either the comic or the tragic mold. Both FORMS can properly include elements of the other, sometimes to the point that they are called **tragicomedy**. This FORM was used in Elizabethan and Jacobean England and is characterized by inclusion of both CHARACTERS from the higher classes usually found in tragedy and CHARACTERS from the lower classes found in comedy.

Also, there is the threat of inevitable tragedy, but a plot line that ends with a victorious protagonist (often after some melodramatic turn of events). The tragicomedy as a dramatic FORM is attributed to Beaumont and Fletcher in the first decade of the seventeenth century. Killigrew's *The Prisoner* and Shakespeare's *The Winter's Tale* are both tragicomedies.

Other FORMS of drama can be classified as either tragedy or comedy. One example is the **chronicle play**. Based on sixteenth-century chronicles (historical records), these Elizabethan dramas were characterized by enactments of battles, funerals, and other historical events. Some incorporate the elements of the romantic comedy; others are clearly tragedies. Yet a third group of chronicle plays, called the **history play**, is not comic nor tragic. Perhaps the most famous examples of chronicle plays are based on *Chronicles of England, Scotland, and Ireland,* first published in 1578 by Raphael Holinshed, then revised in 1587. These revised chronicles became a major historical source for thirteen of Shakespeare's plays.

Also, based in part on Holinshed's *Chronicles* are Shakespeare's *King Lear, Cymbeline,* and *Macbeth.* According to Holinshed, Lear "was admitted ruler over the Britons in the year of the world 3105, at what time Joas reigned in Judah" and Cymbeline "was of the Britons made king after the decease of his father in the year of the world 3944, after the building of Rome 728, and before the birth of our Saviour 33."

ENGLISH HISTORY AS SEEN IN SHAKESPEARE'S DRAMAS

Play	Covers	Play written in
King John	1199–1216	ca. 1591
King Richard II	1398–1400	1595
King Henry IV, Part I	1402–1403	1597
King Henry IV, Part II	1403–1413	1598
King Henry V	1413–1422	1599
King Henry VI, Part I	1422–1453	ca. 1590
King Henry VI, Part II	1445–1455	ca. 1591
King Henry VI, Part III	1455–1471	ca. 1592
King Richard III	1471–1485	ca. 1593
King Henry VIII	1520–1544	1613

Another FORM that can be tragedy or tragicomedy is the Restoration *heroic drama*. These attention-getting productions with settings in exotic places, such as Morocco, feature a hero torn between love and duty. Heroic dramas can include a sinister, evil male antagonist (a villain) who may be the father of the heroine and an equally evil female antagonist (a villainess) who tries to win the protagonist's affections. In further terms of FORM, the dialogue is often in heroic couplets and overflowing with hyperbole.

The *interlude* (a type of play written in the fifteenth and sixteenth centuries) is part of the transition that drama underwent in FORM as it moved from the Church to the secular world and is significant to the development of realism in drama. These short, witty plays sometimes were simply a dialogue between two players. In Tudor England they were performed at special banquets. (Later *masques*—expensive spectacles or dramatic exhibitions in which the CHARACTERS wore masks—were the court entertainment for Elizabeth I, James I, and Charles I. Ben Jonson eventually developed the *antimasque,* a comparatively uncivilized version in which low comedy and the grotesque were employed to contrast the elegance of the masque.)

A FORM that is most often a comedy, the *melodrama* can also be an element in a tragedy. The melodrama means "a play with music" and was used in a period of English history when, during the nineteenth century, plays were allowed to be performed only in Patent Theaters (a monopoly) due to the Licensing Act, but musicals could be performed anywhere. By adding music and song, these dramas could be legally performed. Romantic and extreme in emotion, an argument could be made that the very early silent movies, characterized by the beautiful girl being tied to a railroad track by the evil villain who wants her land (greed) and her hand (in marriage) as a pianist performs live music to heighten the mood, are a FORM of melodrama.

Pantomime is drama acted out without words. These mixtures of drama and dance were popular in England in the 1700s, but were especially enjoyed in Elizabethan drama as single episodes used for dramatic effect in spoken drama. This use is called the *dumb show.* The pantomime as a FORM has survived into this century through silent films and such comedic actors as Charlie Chaplin and Red Skelton. Also, aspiring actors can be seen *miming* for money on street corners in major international cities.

As you study FORM in literature, you will doubtless encounter many trends, movements, themes, and conventions (they are known by many different labels) that group certain works from prose, poetry, and drama together. You can benefit by recognizing the effect these "elements in common" can have. Following is a sample of such groupings.

Pastoral literature: A life apart from the urban mainstream; rural setting; country people.

1. Pastoral poems—poems about shepherds and rural life (many written between 1550 and 1750)
2. Pastoral elegies—poems using pastoral imagery to mourn a death
3. Pastoral drama—(also called pastoral plays) plays that use shepherds and the conventions of pastoral poems
4. Pastoral romance—shepherds and pastoral conventions in a long prose narrative (for example, *Rosalynde* by Thomas Lodge)

Literature of the absurd: Poems, prose, and plays that emphasize an existential sense of isolation, using such devices as black humor (morbid and grotesque humor) to show the writer's view of the absurdity of life.

Escape literature: Poems, prose, and plays with the main purpose to allow the reader to escape real life.

Genteel tradition: American poems, prose, and plays that stress conventional correctness.

History literature: Poems, prose, and plays based on history (prose FORMS can include historical fiction and historical novels).

Local color writing: Predominantly American poems, prose, and drama based on regionalisms, such as dialect, dress, and geographical setting.

QUESTIONS TO APPLY YOUR LEARNING

As you practice reading literary selections, ask these questions to help you identify and understand FORM:

1. What organizing principles did the writer use?
2. How is the selection sequenced or ordered?
3. Is there any faulty reasoning present?
   - If so, is it by the writer, the speaker, or a CHARACTER?
   - Is the faulty reasoning intentional or unintentional?
   - Is it intended to mislead the reader or to reveal CHARACTER?
   - How does it affect the MEANING?
4. If the selection is a narrative, how would you summarize the plot?
5. Into what genre(s) does the selection fit? Why?
6. If the selection is a poem, is there a significant rhyme scheme? Any variations in the rhyme scheme? Does this affect the MEANING, TONE, and so forth?
7. In a poem, what is the metrical scan? Are there any variations in the rhythm? Does the rhythm affect the MEANING, TONE, and so forth?
8. What is the structure of the poem?
9. If the selection is a play, what is the plot development? What is the exciting force? The turning point?

ADDITIONAL HELPFUL POINTS TO REMEMBER

Be alert to the validity of the reasoning of a writer—some things that are written are not valid—some things that are written are not true. You need to be able to distinguish:

1. Valid arguments (logical conclusions based on true premises) from logical fallacies (errors in reasoning due to false premises or illogical consequences)
2. Whether the invalidity of the faulty thinking is intentional or unintentional

3. Whether the valid or invalid argument is the VOICE of the speaker or the VOICE of the writer and whether they agree

VOICE will be discussed in a later section, but at this point you need to be able to identify some of the more common logical fallacies you may encounter in literary selections. Whether they be persuasive speeches, powerful short stories, or expressive poems, logical fallacies are sometimes hidden (intentionally or unintentionally) within literary works. These fallacies might serve the purpose of the writer or they may simply reveal faulty thinking on his or her part. The presence of logical reasoning is FORM contributing to, shaping, and developing MEANING. Logical fallacies are flaws (or misuses of organizing principles) in form that affect MEANING.

When you are asked a question about the MEANING in a selection, you need to be alert to any logical fallacies—any flaws in FORM (misuses of organizing principles) that might affect the MEANING.

HERBERT SPENCER
(1820–1903)

In a discussion which took place at a reception at G. H. Lewes's, somebody asserted that everyone had written a tragedy. Lewes agreed with the statement, saying, 'Yes, everyone—even Herbert Spencer.'—'Ah,' interposed Huxley, 'I know what the catastrophe would be—an induction killed by a fact.'

- MEANING can be affected by FORM, so watch for questions that are based on this relationship.
- Some writers use elements of one genre as literary devices within another. For example: autobiography is a nonfiction account of a person's own life, but in the novel *Moll Flanders*, Defoe uses autobiography as a literary device. Some fiction novels are actually autobiographical. Also, the diary has been used as a literary device in fiction.
- Watch for literary works that lie in a gray area between fiction and nonfiction. For example, historical fiction or a historical novel *is fiction* that has historical people, places, and events interwoven. Also, watch for fictional biography, autobiographical fiction, *Roman à clef* (a novel about real people but written as though it were fiction—such as Hemingway's *The*

A Validity Checklist

When reading a selection, look for:

- Consistency of thought
- Fairness
- Ambiguous thinking, such as
  1. Statements that have more than one MEANING, for example, "Several beautiful paintings are being hung in the lobby. Yours will be hung in the back office." (Regional dialects can sometimes be the source of these miscommunications.)
  2. Misuse of personification, such as, "The company will have to take better care of its employees for me to work there." (People within companies make policies to take care of people.)
  3. Statements that are inappropriate in their CONTEXT (as a lady is shopping and the clerk says, "That dress does *wonders* for your shape"). Note that when such statements are made intentionally, they can create a FORM of verbal irony or can be sarcasm.
  4. Changing MEANINGS OF WORDS (Alice: He certainly is calm and collected about raising money for his rent. Jayne: He's collected, all right, from Moris, and Jules, and from me!)
  5. Assumptions that if something is true of the whole, then it is also true of the parts or that something true of the parts can be generalized to the whole, for example, "The Pizza Dilly is a great pizza place, so we will get the pizza we ordered delivered on time." (Even "great" places can have an occasional late delivery.) The pizza has extra of my favorite cheese, so it will be delicious. (What if the crust is burned?)

- Misrepresentations of the facts (distortions), such as
  1. Assuming a premise is true without proof
  2. Taking words out of CONTEXT
  3. Exaggerating a statement out of CONTEXT
  4. Diverting attention from the real issue by introducing a false issue
  5. Calling names or attacking the credibility of a person
  6. Making generalizations based on assumptions or on too little evidence
  7. Asking a "loaded question" that by simply answering implies guilt ("Have you stopped stealing from your neighbor?")
  8. Establishing double standards through connotatively charged words (Why is one person called "thrifty" or "frugal" while another is called "cheap" or "tight" with money, when both exhibit the same spending habits?)
  9. Comparing dissimilar things as though they are similar
  10. Omitting facts or ignoring alternatives
  11. Presenting coincidence as a cause-and-effect relationship
  12. Attempting to influence the reader through a sense of pity, ignorance, fear, expertise, or some other emotion, all based on false or misleading information
  13. Stereotyping
  14. Oversimplifying
- Remember:
  a. Sometimes faulty reasoning is for the purpose of misleading the reader.
  b. Sometimes these errors in reasoning, however, are made by people within a story or by a speaker other than the writer—thus revealing CHARACTER.

Sun Also Rises), and the nonfiction novel (Truman Capote's *In Cold Blood* or Karen Blixen's, a.k.a., Isak Dinesen's *Out of Africa*).

- When reading a selection, be sure to establish clearly the main plot of a narrative. In a framework story, there is a story within another story, for example: A group of girls camp out and tell ghost stories around the campfire. Each ghost story is a narrative "framed" by the narrative of the girls telling the stories.

  The significance of the frame to the intent and effect of the work can vary. It might be used simply as a reason to tell the ghost stories—or perhaps one main ghost story told by the eldest girl. Or it may become the main plot of the selection if the girls go on to have experiences beyond just telling stories—for example, an attack by a bear, an encounter with Africanized ("killer") bees, or a visit by an uninvited guest, such as a skunk.

  Some famous frame tales can be found in the writings of Joseph Conrad. (Also, see Mark Twain's "Jim Baker's Blue Jay Yarn.")

  Another structural device used by fiction writers is the subplot. A subplot is a less important plot working within the structure of the main plot. Some work with the main plot; and others are to some degree independent of it. Also, be aware that some writers may have multiple subplots working throughout the main plot.

- Watch for use of the term *argument* in a multiple sense. Argumentation is commonly known as one of the four modes of writing (exposition, narration, description, and argumentation). Argumentation aims to convince the reader, and when the argument is flawed (either by inaccuracy in fact or FORM) the error is called a **fallacy**. Argument also refers to using either authority or syllogisms and analogies to prove whether a proposition is true or false. But Shakespeare and Milton used the word *argument* to refer to the theme of a literary work.

- Because of the physical confines of the test structure, the prose selections for the SAT II: Literature Subject Test are limited in length. Short passages (particularly if the selections are excerpts from larger works) could limit the types of questions concerning structure and method of organization that can be asked. Be sure to include in your study an examination of paragraph structure and development. Practice identifying organizational methods not only of, for example, short essays, but also those structural elements that are used within sets or groups of paragraphs within larger works.

- Use these questions to differentiate *realism, farce,* and *fantasy:*

FORM:	Can it happen?	Does it ever happen?
Realism	yes	yes
Farce	yes	no
Fantasy	no	no

- When you see **triple rhyme** in a poem, often the TONE will be satirical and/or humorous rather than serious.

- Poems with **sprung rhythm** are a special challenge to scanning. Sprung rhythm allows only single stressed syllables (monosyllabic), the trochee, the dactyl, and the first *paeon* (one stressed syllable followed by three unstressed syllables) because the rhythm is based only on the number of stressed syllables per line and not on the number of unstressed syllables. The advantages? It produces a rhythm very close to natural speech rhythms. The disadvantages? Sprung rhythm is *very* difficult to scan. For example, you might want to research the poems of Gerard Manley Hopkins, the poet who coined the term sprung rhythm. Be sure to look at the rhythm of "Pied Beauty" by Hopkins:

PIED BEAUTY

Glory be to God for dappled things—
   For skies of couple-color as a brinded cow;
     For rose-moles all in stipple upon trout that swim;
Fresh-firecoal chestnut-falls; finches' wings;
   Landscape plotted and pieced—fold, fallow, and plow;
     And all trades, their gear and tackle and trim.

All things counter, original, spare, strange;
   Whatever is fickle, freckled (who knows how?)
     With swift, slow; sweet, sour; adazzle, dim;
He fathers-forth whose beauty is past change:
     Praise him.

       by Gerard Manley Hopkins

- As you try to identify the speaker (particularly for test questions concerning NARRATIVE VOICE), be especially alert in identifying the "I" in a lyric poem. The speaker—even in a poem written in the first person—may not be the poet, but rather an invented CHARACTER.

- Remember: The focus in a *dramatic monologue* is on the speaker's unintentional revealment of his or her CHARACTER. If the poem is a *dramatic lyric,* however, the focus is on the speaker's argument rather than his or her temperament. This subtle difference between otherwise similar FORMS might be important for questions about MEANING and CHARACTER. An example of the dramatic monologue is Browning's "My Last Duchess." A dramatic lyric is John Donne's "The Flea."

- When you see the word "folk," this is a clue that the literary work, usually a (folk-) ballad, drama, epic, lore, song, or tale, is: (1) of unknown authorship and (2) the product of the oral tradition.

- Do not be confused by the term "folklore." **Folklore** was not used as a literary term until the nineteenth century, and it refers to many different genres that include a people's traditions. These traditions, of course, are filled with customs, beliefs, and rituals. As a result, they have given rise to innumerable formula plots, conventions, motifs, and literary traditions.

  Folklore includes (to name a few):

popular ballads	riddles
cowboy songs	nursery rhymes
stories	legends

- Do not confuse the **ballad** (a narrative song) with the **ballade**—a French verse FORM that was used to a limited extent by Chaucer; however, the FORM was never used extensively in English poetry.

- There is some controversy among critics concerning the roles of **parody** and **burlesque**.

Some see parody as a variety of high burlesque, but other critics see parody as the literary opposite to burlesque in that a parody mocks style by keeping the writing in the target style but selecting a "silly" subject. Burlesque, on the other hand, lowers the style. Parody is, then, a FORM of travesty (ridicule of a subject by a mismatch of style with topic). Once travesty is so defined, burlesque is cited as the travesty of a literary FORM; parody is the travesty of a specific work.

- Although many use **plot** and **story** interchangeably, you may need to know the subtle difference between the two. A story is the narration of events according to their *sequence in time.* A plot, on the other hand, is a narration of events with emphasis on causal relationships.

- Use your knowledge of FORM to help you study drama. As you read drama selections, you know that pivotal plot elements occur at certain points. The exposition most often is in the beginning—the first scene of the first act. Also, during the first act you may be able to pinpoint the conflict and the exciting force. If the crisis or turning point happens at the end of the next to the last act (as is sometimes but not always the case), then the falling action and resolution will play out in the final act and the acts previous to the turning point will consist of rising action with a series of complications. These complications or points of dramatic impact will often be placed just at the end of each act because structurally this heightens their effectiveness in keeping the plot moving and in holding the audience's attention. Consequently, read the last one or two pages of script at the closing of each act carefully—these portions of dialogue may contain important revelations of CHARACTER, theme, and uses of the other literary elements.

LITERARY ELEMENT NUMBER THREE: NARRATIVE VOICE

GEORGE MEREDITH
(1828–1909)

Robert Louis Stevenson numbers *The Egoist* among the books which have most powerfully influenced him, and owns to having read it seven or eight times. 'Meredith read me some chapters', he says, 'before it was published, and at last I could stand it no longer. I interrupted him, and said, "Now, Meredith, own up—you have drawn Sir Willoughby Patterne from me!" Meredith laughed, and said, "No, no, my dear fellow, I've taken him from all of us, but principally from myself."'

NARRATIVE VOICE, in its most narrow sense, is who is telling the story. But NARRATIVE VOICE in action is far more than just the "narrator," and if you take away the restrictions implicit in the word "NARRATIVE," you will find the fascinating world of VOICE, a place of illusion where the speaker may not be quite who or what he or she seems.

NARRATIVE VOICE IN PROSE

Before discussing the *impact of determining the speaker from the writer*, and the *significance of the speaker's attitude*, it is important to look at the foundation of NARRATIVE VOICE: *point of view* and how point of view can relate to the *characterization of the narrator*.

Point of View

Also called the *focus* of a narrative, point of view refers not only to who is telling the story (in other words, the narrator), but also to how the narrator relates to the story in terms of the action of the plot and in terms of how much he or she knows about what is going on both in the story and in the minds of the CHARACTERS in the story.

Pretend that the "world" of a story is represented by this illustration:

The world of the NARRATIVE	The world outside the NARRATIVE

The place, time, CHARACTERS, and events of the story all exist within "the world of the NARRATIVE." The "world outside the NARRATIVE" is where the readers exist. The narrator, then, stands between the reader and the story; and his or her aim is to tell the reader a story, to describe the CHARACTERS and events as they move around within the confines of the world of the narrative while the reader watches and listens.

How does the narrator do this? There are several ways. The narrator might tell the story from a **third person limited** (also called **limited omniscient**, **centered**, or **central consciousness**) point of view. This type of story is written using third person pronouns (he, she, they, him, her, them) and is evidenced by such narrative constructions as "He said this or that" or "She walked to the fireplace." The third person narrator is telling the story from outside the world of the CHARACTERS. The narrator describes to the reader what goes on in that narrative world. Also, the narrator is able to tell the reader the thoughts, opinions, motives, and inner feelings of *one* of the CHARACTERS in the story, someone who often is the main CHARACTER or protagonist of the story. Suppose the major CHARACTERS are Pam, Bob, and Sue, with Sue being the main CHARACTER. The following illustration places Sue at the focus point in the narrative world:

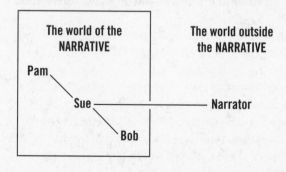

The narrator, who is not a CHARACTER in the story, tells the reader what Bob and Pam do and say (generally as these elements relate to Sue), but more importantly he or she tells *about* Sue—her consciousness—to the point that the reader can "understand" Sue or perhaps even relate to her. The reader learns (through the narrator sharing Sue's thoughts, opinions, and feelings with the reader) how Sue is dealing with the relationships and events that affect her and how she perceives the world around her. The reader sees the other CHARACTERS through Sue's eyes.

Now examine this excerpt from Scott Carpenter's *The Steel Albatross.* As you read, try to identify the main CHARACTER and how the narrator treats him differently from the other CHARACTERS.

But the real trouble began when they finally arrived at the swimming pool, where Kraus was waiting with a three-gallon bucket at his feet and one of his death's-head grins spread across the lower half of his face.

"This," he said conversationally, "is an easy one. And to prove it, I'll show you how it goes."

He jumped into the water, grabbed the bucket from the side, filled it with water, positioned it between his legs. Then, with both hands on the handle, he turned on his back to swim, effortlessly, from one end of the pool to the other, using only a lazy frog-kick.

"Now you," Kiwi [Kraus] said, climbing out of the pool and handing the bucket to the smallest man in Rick's crew, a fireman second from St. Louis whose name was Durant.

Durant froze. And Rick couldn't blame him. He was one of the "sinkers" in the group, a hard-muscled rooster who had barely managed to pass the basic swimming tests. Full of water, the bucket would act as a true sea-anchor; no way was the little man going to be able to carry it anywhere without using his arms to swim. He knew Kraus must be aware of that—and must know, too, that a man like Durant would never give up, short of actually drowning.

Rick looked at Durant, then at Kiwi, and back at Durant, realizing suddenly that both men were looking at him. Durant was blank faced, but clearly hoping his platoon commander would find some way of taking him off the hook. And Kiwi, not so blank, was also waiting.

And then Rick understood. Deliberately striking an instructor except in disarmed-combat drill was an automatic bilge; no trial, no questions. Just a quick out. Kiwi had casually positioned himself in range of any punch Rick might care to throw, waiting for him to take the one action that would assure his elimination from the course. And Rick very much wanted to oblige. The fingers of his right hand curled in anticipation, and he could feel his left heel screwing itself into the earth. But the blow never landed; instead, Rick sneezed.

It was a loud one, and it had just the effect Rick had hoped: Kiwi turned toward him, lungs sucking in air to fire a blast in Rick's direction, and took a single step that brought him a full foot closer than he had been—which was when Rick sneezed for the second time. Kraus went down for the count.

The force of the second sneeze had bent Rick double at just the right moment to allow the hardest point of his forehead to collide with the vulnerable spot just above Kraus's nose.

The chief instructor went down suddenly, but got up slowly. He was in the sick bay for two hours…and when he returned, although he said the actual damage appeared to be minimal, the nose still showed signs of bleeding at the smallest excuse.

Which saddened Rick. He'd really intended to flatten it permanently.

The narrator tells the reader:

1. What Rick, Kiwi, and Durant say
2. What Rick, Kiwi, and Durant do
3. What Rick thinks (Notice the fifth, seventh, and last paragraphs.)
4. What Kraus thinks *as perceived by Rick* ("He knew Kraus must be aware of that—and must know, too, that a man like Durant would never give up, short of actually drowning.")
5. What Durant thinks as *perceived by Rick* ("Rick looked at Durant…Durant was…clearly hoping his platoon commander would find some way of taking him off the hook.")

The technique of the narrator in literary narrative revealing the main CHARACTER'S thoughts was affected in the late nineteenth century by psychologist William James. Based on the earlier thinking of Alexander Bain, he put forth the concept of **stream of consciousness,** the flow of thoughts that people experience, thoughts that range from the unintelligible to the very rational and well articulated. By the turn of the century, works began to include long passages in which the main CHARACTERS engage in lengthy passages of introspection. Stream-of-consciousness techniques have been used well into the twentieth century. One such technique is the *interior monologue* in which the main CHARACTER'S thoughts are reported as they occur—often in vague terms with sometimes (but not always) illogical order and a lack of grammatical clarity.

Both James Joyce and William Faulkner used stream-of-consciousness techniques in their writings. Here is a sample from Faulkner's short story, "Barn Burning."

They were running a middle buster now, his brother holding the plow straight while he handled the reins, and walking beside the straining mule, the rich black soil shearing cool and damp against his bare ankles, he thought *Maybe this is the end of it. Maybe even that twenty bushels that seems hard to have to pay for just a rug will be a cheap price for him to stop forever and always from being what he used to be;* thinking, dreaming now, so that his brother had to speak sharply to him to mind the mule:

Maybe he even won't collect the twenty bushels. Maybe it will all add up and balance and vanish—corn, rug, fire; the terror and grief, the being pulled two ways like between two teams of horses—gone, done with for ever and ever.

Another third person point of view is the **third person unlimited** (also called **omniscient**) point of view, in which the narrator knows everything about everyone in every situation and feels free to reveal this information at will to the reader.

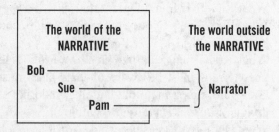

The reader no longer needs to rely upon Sue's observations; the narrator can directly reveal the thoughts, motives, and actions of Pam and Bob.

Another popular stance of the narrator is called **first person** point of view.

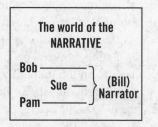

The first person narrator might be the main CHARACTER, one of the minor CHARACTERS, or simply an observer. Written in the first person "I," the readers can easily "identify" with the person telling the story and eventually become "a part" of the narrative. But when the narrator is also one of the CHARACTERS, the reader is *limited* in his or her view of the "NARRATIVE world" (in others words, the "world" of the CHARACTERS in the story) to one as seen by an active participant in that world. This view, however, is one that generally has

a heightened sense of both realism and sometimes (but not always) credibility.

Characterization of the Narrator

Regardless of the point of view used, the narrator can be characterized in several other ways. Sometimes the narrator is **self-conscious**, one who deliberately allows the reader to know that the work is a fictional account or goes so far as to point out the elements of narration at work. Read as an example this first paragraph of *The Posthumous Papers of the Pickwick Club* by Charles Dickens:

The first ray of light which illumines the gloom, and converts into a dazzling brilliancy that obscurity in which the earlier history of the public career of the immortal Pickwick would appear to be involved, is derived from the perusal of the following entry in the Transactions of the Pickwick Club, which the editor of these papers feels the highest pleasure in laying before his readers, as a proof of the careful attention, indefatigable assiduity, and nice discrimination, with which his search among the multifarious documents confided to him has been conducted.

The narrator points to himself as "the editor of these papers"—in the third person addressing "his readers."

Also, note the first paragraph of *Oliver Twist,* how the narrator refers to the writing process:

Among other public buildings in a certain town, which for many reasons it will be prudent to refrain from mentioning, and to which I will assign no fictitious name, there is one anciently common to most towns, great or small: to wit, a workhouse; and in this workhouse was born: on a day and date which I need not trouble myself to repeat, inasmuch as it can be of no possible consequence to the reader, in this stage of the business at all events: the item of mortality whose name is prefixed to the head of this chapter.

These paragraphs are found near the end of *Oliver Twist,* in which the narrator talks of "this tale" and describes his writing of the conclusion:

The fortunes of those who have figured in this tale are nearly closed. The little that remains to their historian to relate, is told in few and simple words.

…   …

And now, the hand that traces these words, falters, as it approaches the conclusion of its task: and would weave, for a little longer space, the thread of these adventures.

I would fain linger yet with a few of those among whom I have so long moved, and share their happiness by endeavouring to depict it. I would show Rose Maylie in all the bloom and grace of early womanhood, shedding on her secluded path in life such soft and gentle light, as fell on all who trod it with her, and shone into their hearts. I would paint her the life and joy of the fireside circle and the lively summer group; I would follow her through the sultry fields at noon, and hear the low tones of her sweet voice in the moonlit evening walk; I would watch her in all her goodness and charity abroad, and the smiling untiring discharge of domestic duties at home; I would paint her and her dead sister's child happy in their mutual love, and passing whole hours together in picturing the friends whom they had so sadly lost; I would summon before me, once again, those joyous little faces that clustered round her knee, and listen to their merry prattle; I would recall the tones of that clear laugh, and conjure up the sympathising tear that glistened in the soft blue eye. These, and a thousand looks and smiles, and turns of thought and speech—I would fain recall them every one.

Test questions concerning the attitudes or points of view of the self-conscious narrator might be very directly stated:

What is the narrator's attitude toward Rose Maylie?

(A) Passionate
(B) Affectionate
(C) Amorous
(D) Zealous
(E) Dispassionate

(The correct answer is B.)

What is the effect of a self-conscious narrator on the reader? Because the narrator sometimes "lets you in" on the structural and more intimate aspects of telling the story (such as confessing that "the hand that traces these words, falters"), the reader is very likely to develop a bond with the narrator, an association that oftentimes increases the reader's sense of confidence in the narrator's credibility as a witness of the events of the story. The reader may tend to take for granted that the accounts and opinions, the observations and conclusions of the narrator are both accurate and true.

Although the reader may have a tendency to believe that the narrator is *always* credible and correct in his or her opinions, this may not always be the case. Sometimes the narrator has an erroneous understanding of the situation. Take, as an example, works in which the narrator is the main CHARACTER and the reader must rely upon his or her perspective. In such cases, the main CHARACTER, through whose eyes the reader sees the "world" of the story, may have a distorted view of things—is perhaps naive, too self-confident, mentally unstable, or even immature. Such a narrator is characterized as **unreliable** or **fallible**. An example is Huck Finn in *The Adventures of Huckleberry Finn*. Henry James makes extended use of the unreliable narrator, especially in some of his short stories and in *The Turn of the Screw*.

In addition, a narrator can be characterized as either **intrusive** or as **unintrusive** (objective, impersonal). As the name implies, the intrusive narrator gives opinions concerning the words and deeds, the personalities and motives, and the events and circumstances at work in the story. Sometimes these comments will even take the FORM of an essay that engages in "editorializing," and his or her comments are generally regarded as truthful or reliable.

Notice how the narrator interjects his opinions in this excerpt from *Oliver Twist*:

Although I am not disposed to maintain that the being born in a workhouse, is in itself the most fortunate and enviable circumstance that can possibly befall a human being, I do mean to say that in this particular instance, it was the best thing for Oliver Twist that could by possibility have occurred. The fact is, that there was considerable difficulty in inducing Oliver to take upon himself the office of respiration,—a troublesome practice, but one which custom has rendered necessary to our easy existence; and for some time he lay gasping on a little flock mattress, rather unequally poised between this world and the next: the balance being decidedly in favour of the latter. Now, if, during this brief period, Oliver had been surrounded by careful grandmothers, anxious aunts, experienced nurses, and doctors of profound wisdom, he would most inevitably and indubitably have been killed in no time. There being nobody by, however, but a pauper old woman, who was rendered rather misty by an unwonted allowance of beer; and a parish surgeon who did such matters by contract; Oliver and Nature fought out the point between them. The result was, that, after a few struggles, Oliver breathed, sneezed, and proceeded to advertise to the inmates of the workhouse the fact of a new burden having been imposed upon the parish, by setting up as loud a cry as could reasonably have been expected from a male infant who had not been possessed of that very useful appendage, a voice, for a much longer space of time than three minutes and a quarter.

The unintrusive narrator is quite the opposite of the intrusive; he or she reports without personal comment the words and deeds of the CHARACTERS in the CONTEXT of the events of the story. Is there such a thing as a totally unintrusive narrator? Possibly not. The connotative values of word choices alone reflect a certain degree of personal opinion; however, when the narrator refrains from direct statements of opinion and at least attempts the straight-forward telling of the story, the reader can (perhaps with reservation) *characterize* the narrator as unintrusive. Look to some of Ernest Hemingway's short stories for examples of the unintrusive narrator.

Until this point, you have examined briefly the *characterization* of the narrator or speaker including;

1. From what point of view (first person or third person) the story is being told
2. To what degree the narrator knows the minds of the CHARACTERS (third person limited or third person unlimited narrator)
3. To what extent the narrator is self-conscious, pointing out his or her role in telling the story
4. To what degree the narrator is seen as a credible witness (ranging from the usually very credible self-conscious narrator to the not credible unreliable narrator)
5. To what degree the narrator gives his or her opinions (intrusive or unintrusive narrator)

The role of the writer of the story, however, also needs to be addressed.

The Speaker or the Author—Whose VOICE?

Narrative writers must, in addition to determining from what point of view the story is to be told, decide what method(s) they will use to present the various parts of the narrative (presentation of the setting, the action, and the dialogue). Two of the more common means writers employ are the *panoramic method* and the *scenic method*.

Panoramic method In this method, the writer summarizes conversations and events for the reader by using exposition. Here is an isolated excerpt from George Eliot's *Middlemarch:*

These peculiarities of Dorothea's character caused Mr. Brooke to be all the more blamed in neighbouring families for not securing some middleaged lady as guide and companion to his nieces. But he himself dreaded so much the sort of

superior woman likely to be available for such a position, that he allowed himself to be dissuaded by Dorothea's objections, and was in this case brave enough to defy the world—that is to say, Mrs Cadwallader the Rector's wife, and the small group of gentry with whom he visited in the north-east corner of Loamshire. So Miss Brooke presided in her uncle's household, and did not at all dislike her new authority, with the homage that belonged to it.

Some elements of the panoramic method used in the preceding paragraph include:

1. The writer tells the reader that Mr. Brooke is criticized by his neighbor, rather than allowing the reader to "listen in on" the neighbors actually discussing the issue.
2. The reader is told that Dorothea objected to a guide and influenced Mr. Brooke, but their conversation is not included.
3. The reader learns that Mr. Brooke defied the Rector's wife; however, the reader does not see the encounter or hear their words.
4. The writer tells the reader that Miss Brooke likes her position ("Miss Brooke…did not at all dislike her new authority…"—a USE OF LANGUAGE called **litotes**, when understatement results from negative affirmation—"did not dislike" means that she "did like"), but does not convey to the reader any scenes (actions and direct dialogue) to demonstrate the point.

Rather than reporting the actual words and actions of Dorothea, Mr. Brooke, the neighbors, and the Rector's wife, the writer summarizes the conversations and events for the reader.

Scenic method In contrast to this is the **scenic method**. In its pure form, the **self-effacing author** is one whose existence is totally unrealized by the reader because the story is told objectively, using the *scenic method*. The effect of the scenic method is very dramatic as the author (writer) typically describes the setting and perhaps presents an insightful look into the inner mind of the main CHARACTER, then launches directly into action and dialogue (like scenes in a play) to tell the story. The scenic method is employed in *The Portrait of a Lady* by Henry James (an often-cited example) and is used in various FORMS by writers yet today, such as Payne Harrison's *Thunder of Erebus*.

This conversation between two sisters has scenic elements at work in the following excerpt taken from *Middlemarch* by George Eliot:

'Pray open the large drawer of the cabinet and get out the jewel-box.'

The casket was soon open before them, and the various jewels spread out, making a bright parterre on the table. It was no great collection, but a few of the ornaments were really of remarkable beauty, the finest that was obvious at first being a necklace of purple amethysts set in exquisite gold-work, and a pearl cross with five brilliants in it. Dorothea immediately took up the necklace and fastened it round her sister's neck, where it fitted almost as closely as a bracelet; but the circle suited the Henrietta-Maria style of Celia's head and neck, and she could see that it did, in the pier-glass opposite.

'There, Celia! you can wear that with your Indian muslin. But this cross you must wear with your dark dresses.'

Celia was trying not to smile with pleasure. 'O Dodo, you must keep the cross yourself.'

'No, no, dear, no,' said Dorothea, putting up her hand with careless deprecation.

'Yes, indeed you must; it would suit you—in your black dress, now,' said Celia, insistingly. 'You *might* wear that.'

'Not for the world, not for the world. A cross is the last thing I would wear as a trinket.' Dorothea shuddered slightly.

'Then you will think it wicked in me to wear it,' said Celia, uneasily.

'No, dear, no,' said Dorothea, stroking her sister's cheek 'Souls have complexions too: what will suit one will not suit another.'

'But you might like to keep it for mamma's sake.'

'No. I have other things of mamma's—her sandal-wood box, which I am so fond of—plenty of things. In fact, they are all yours, dear. We need discuss them no longer. There—take away your property.'

Celia felt a little hurt. There was a strong assumption of superiority in this Puritanic toleration, hardly less trying to the blond flesh of an unenthusiastic sister than a Puritanic persecution.

'But how can I wear ornaments if you, who are the elder sister, will never wear them?'

'Nay, Celia, that is too much to ask, that I should wear trinkets to keep you in countenance. If I were to put on such a necklace as that, I should feel as if I had been pirouetting. The world would go round with me, and I should not know how to walk.'

Celia had unclasped the necklace and drawn it off. 'It would be a little tight for your neck; something to lie down and hang would suit you better,' she said, with some satisfaction. The complete unfitness of the necklace from all points of view for Dorothea, made Celia happier in taking it. She was opening some ring-boxes, which disclosed a fine emerald with diamonds, and just then the sun passing beyond a cloud sent a bright gleam over the table.

The dialogue and action are self-explanatory. In the scenic method the writer "fades" into the background as the dynamic dialogue and action move the story from scene to scene, allowing the reader to be swept along by the story and to forget the author's existence.

Had the author wanted to write the previous dialogue in the panoramic method, he might have written: "After a minor quarrel with Celia, Dorothea refused to keep her mother's cross necklace."

Many times literary narrative, especially lengthy novels, will use both methods (scenic and panoramic), depending upon the effect desired by the writer and by the confines dictated by the plot. For instance, when action is a significant element, when a rapid exchange of conversation will intensify the story, elements of the scenic method are vital. What if, however, the story is spanning three generations of a family as they migrate from Europe to America, living through significant historical events, personal triumphs, and tragedies? Can every important event and meaningful conversation be reported like scenes in a play? Obviously, works of such magnitude sometimes *require* the author to summarize events and conversations, to use the panoramic method.

Establishing that the writer can elect to use scenic and/or panoramic methods to present a narrative is an important first step to understanding some of the essential structural decisions that face a writer. Another very important decision that a writer must make is to decide on a narrator or speaker. (Some literary critics use the terms *narrator* and *speaker* interchangeably, whereas others prefer to reserve *speaker* to refer to the one speaking in a nonnarrative work.)

Some readers mistakenly assume that the writer and the narrator (speaker) are the same. This is not always the case. Sometimes the author and narrator are the same, but at other times they are two distinctly different VOICES. When the NARRATIVE is in the first person, with a CHARACTER being the one telling the story as the narrator or speaker, identifying the VOICE of the writer as different from that of the narrator can be very difficult.

The story world can be used to illustrate on a very basic level and to build, step-by-step, a basis for this distinction. Suppose the story is a first-person NARRATIVE actually being told by the person who is living the events. This autobiographical story is told live as the events happen—as a news reporter does at the scene of an ongoing news story. The present tense adds a TONE of excitement. The story might include elements of stream-of-consciousness writing, also. Here is an excerpt of Elaine's account of being trapped in a burning building:

I hope this microphone is still working and I'm still on the air...

I am looking at the locked door. I can almost see how hot it must be! If I try to touch it, I'll get burned. The fire is raging on the other side. Jayne is screaming for someone to unlock the door. Smoke is choking me—my eyes are smarting with thick black fumes that blanket my head. I hear Roel calling my name....

"I" (Elaine) is the narrator, the main CHARAC-TER, and (because this is an autobiographical story), the author.

The world of the NARRATIVE	The world outside the story
Jayne	
Elaine the narrator, CHARACTER, and author	
Roel	

Now look at the difference a simple change in verb tense can make. Once again suppose this is a real-life event that happens to Elaine; however, rather than telling the story as it happens, she waits until the fire trucks leave and writes her story for broadcast much later—perhaps the next day:

I tried the microphone, but it wouldn't work. I looked at the locked door. I could almost see how hot it must have been. If I had tried to touch it, I would have gotten burned. The fire was raging on the other side. Jayne was screaming for someone to unlock the door. Smoke was choking me—my eyes smarted with the thick fumes that blanketed my head. I heard Roel calling my name.

The main CHARACTER is still Elaine, but what about the narrator and author? In the first account, the narrator and author are Elaine *as she lived the experience*. In the second account, the author is Elaine *after the experience*, taking the role of a narrator telling about herself as a CHARAC-TER at a previous time.

A story can be told by a participant from his or her perspective while it is happening; however, as soon as time elapses, the story can be retold only as an account in which the participant has a dual role:

first as the person who was in the story and second as the narrator who is now outside of the world (the time and place) in which the events occurred.

Where should Elaine appear on the illustration in her role as narrator? Who is telling the story?

The world of the NARRATIVE	The world outside the story
Jayne	
Elaine the CHARACTER	Elaine the author and narrator (remembering the events)
Roel	

Now that a distinction has been established between the CHARACTER and the author/narrator in a first person account, the illustration can be taken one step further. Suppose that Sally Smith, as an author, wrote the account of the events of the fire, placing Elaine Brown as a major CHARAC-TER in the story. Elaine Brown is the main CHAR-ACTER narrating the story (written in the first person); however, Sally Smith is the author:

The world of the NARRATIVE	The world outside the story
Jayne	
Elaine Brown the CHARACTER and narrator	Sally Smith the author
Roel	

Because the story is in first person, you might easily assume that when the CHARACTER/narrator tells us that "I thought this or I did ..." that these words are the thoughts and actions of the writer of the story, but this is clearly not the case. Because Sally Smith (author) is writing the words and actions of Elaine Brown (CHARACTER), those words and actions (whether in past or present tense) are those of a CHARACTER in the story and may or may not reflect Sally Smith's opinions, even though they are written in the first person. The narrator and the author are two different VOICES. This forms the basis for distinguishing *between the narrator (speaker) and the writer.* Unlike television talk shows, however, in which the program ends with an announcement that "The views expressed by the guests on this program are not necessarily those of this station or its management," distinguishing in a first person NARRATIVE the VOICE of the author from that of the CHARACTER who narrates the story can only be accomplished through examining CONTEXT and the particulars of the account.

Sometimes the speaker and the author can arguably be viewed as the same VOICE. For example, in Charles Dickens's *David Copperfield* (a story that Dickens based on some of his own life experiences and in which he expresses many of his own personal views), Dickens has written in the first person:

DAVID COPPERFIELD
by
Charles Dickens
I Am Born.

Whether I shall turn out to be the hero of my own life, or whether that station will be held by anybody else, these pages must show. To begin my life with the beginning of my life, I record that I was born (as I have been informed and believe) on a Friday, at twelve o'clock at night. It was remarked that the clock began to strike, and I began to cry, simultaneously.

In consideration of the day and hour of my birth, it was declared by the nurse, and by some sage women in the neighbourhood who had taken a lively interest in me several months before there was any possibility of our becoming personally acquainted, first, that I was destined to be unlucky in life; and secondly, that I was privileged to see ghosts and spirits; both these gifts inevitably attaching, as they believed, to all unlucky infants of either gender, born towards the small hours on a Friday night.

I need say nothing here, on the first head, because nothing can show better than my history whether that prediction was verified or falsified by the result. On the second branch of the question, I will only remark, that unless I ran through that part of my inheritance while I was still a baby, I have not come into it yet. But I do not at all complain of having been kept out of this property; and if anybody else should be in the present enjoyment of it, he is heartily welcome to keep it.

So in this story Dickens is the author, David is the main CHARACTER, and David is the speaker who tells the story using the first person pronoun "I" as if he is the author. David is Dickens's **persona**: in other words, he is a CHARACTER who narrates the story for the author. As Dickens's persona, David the narrator and Dickens the author have the same VOICE.

In other situations the speaker and author do not share the same VOICE. Read carefully the following excerpt from "A Modest Proposal," written in 1729 by Jonathan Swift at a time when landowners were turning deaf ears to the suffering of homeless Irish who were victims of a three-year drought.

It is a melancholy object to those who walk through this great town or travel in the country, when they see the streets, the roads, and cabin doors, crowded with beggars of the female sex, followed by three, four, or six children, all in rags and importuning every passenger for an alms. These mothers, instead of being able to work for their honest livelihood, are forced to employ all their time in strolling to beg sustenance for their helpless infants, who, as they grow up, either turn thieves for want of work, or leave their dear native country to fight for the Pretender in Spain, or sell themselves to the Barbados.

I think it is agreed by all parties that this prodigious number of children in the arms, or on the backs, or at the heels of their mothers, and frequently of their fathers, is in the present deplorable state of the kingdom a very great additional grievance; and therefore whoever could find out a fair, cheap, and easy method of making these children sound, useful members of the commonwealth would deserve so well of the public as to have his statue set up for a preserver of the nation.

But my intention is very far from being confined to provide only for the children of professed beggars; it is of much greater extent, and shall take in the whole number of infants at a certain age who are born of parents in effect as little able to support them as those who demand our charity in the streets.

As to my own part, having turned my thoughts for many years upon this important subject, and maturely weighed the several schemes of other projectors, I have always found them grossly mistaken in their computation. It is true, a child just dropped from its dam may be supported by her milk for a solar year, with little other nourishment; at most not above the value of two shillings, which the mother may certainly get, or the value in scraps, by her lawful occupation of begging; and it is exactly at one year that I propose to provide for them in such a manner as instead of being a charge upon their parents or the parish,...they shall on the contrary contribute to the feeding, and partly to the clothing, of many thousands.

* * *

I am assured by our merchants that a boy or a girl before twelve years old is no salable commodity; and even when they come to this age they will not yield above three pounds, or three pound and half a crown at most on the Exchange; which cannot turn to account either to the parents or the kingdom, the charge of nutriment and rags having been at least four times that value.

I shall now therefore humbly propose my own thoughts, which I hope will not be liable to the least objection.

I have been assured by a very knowing American of my acquaintance in London, that a young healthy child well nursed is at a year old a most delicious, nourishing, and wholesome food, whether stewed, roasted, baked, or boiled; and I make no doubt that it will equally serve in a fricassee or a ragout....

How would you answer this practice test question?

Of the attitudes listed, which is the attitude of the speaker toward his readers?

(A) Overbearing self-confidence
(B) Aggressive hostility
(C) Confident conviction
(D) Feigned sincerity
(E) Ribald frivolity

(The correct answer is D.)

Swift is the author; "I" is the speaker. Does this speaker, however, represent Swift's true opinions? Obviously not. Note the shocking nature of the speaker's proposal, particularly when he exposes his "plan" for turning children into a food source in the last paragraph of the excerpt, a totally alien concept to any civilized people. The writer might have directly said, "You are allowing these children to starve and to be treated like animals," but would such direct words have had the attention-getting effect and the same shame-producing impact that his proposal elicits? In the case of "A Modest Proposal," the author and the speaker do not share the same VOICE.

This is an example of the **naive narrator**, a CHARACTER who narrates in the first person as if he or she is the author, but whose opinions, actions, or thoughts are so naive or so obtuse (as in this case) that they ironically make the point of the author. If the naive narrator is a child whose simplicity of thought could conceivably end in tragedy, however, the result might be pathos rather than irony.

As you can see, then, even in a first person NARRATIVE, there is the VOICE of the speaker and the VOICE of the author. In other words, the first person speaker/narrator can be a *persona* of the writer/author, a persona who *may or may not* project the experiences or views of the author. Sometimes the difference is easy to recognize, as when the story is the first person account of a ten-year-old girl's experiences training a horse on a New Mexico ranch, and the story is written by a middle-aged male writer living in central New York. But sometimes the difference is not so easily distinguished.

The difference between the VOICE of the speaker and the VOICE of the author is no less important to address in the third person NARRATIVE than in the first person account. Because the story is told in the third person ("he said," "she said"), the "sense" of the author and the speaker might easily become blurred into one VOICE, especially when the narrator is omniscient. Wayne C. Booth's concept of the **implied author**—that author who is an imaginary, idealized person whose existence is sensed by the reader from the work as a whole—as opposed to the real author who is not as "ideal" as the implied author—is important to keep in mind at this point. In a third person NARRATIVE, the potential exists for there to be three "different" VOICES: (1) the main CHARACTER'S thoughts and actions, (2) the opinions and perspectives of the narrator who is telling the story, and (3) the personal opinion and structural concerns of the author.

To summarize, there are three different VOICES at work in a narrative: the writer, the speaker/narrator, and the CHARACTER. For example, in the NARRATIVE VOICE structure in the *Sherlock Holmes* mysteries of Sir Arthur Conan Doyle, you will find:

1. Doyle—the writer
2. Dr. Watson—the speaker/narrator, a CHARACTER in the story and *persona* for Doyle
3. Holmes—the main CHARACTER

The world of the NARRATIVE	The world outside the story
Watson **CHARACTER** narrator	
	Sir Arthur Conan Doyle Author
Holmes main **CHARACTER**	

When reading a passage from one of these mysteries, a relevant question might be (if, for example, the passage is Watson speaking), is this the VOICE of Dr. Watson, the persona for Doyle (the writer) speaking? (When the author creates a fictional CHARACTER who writes the story or book, the device is called the **putative author**. Diedrich Knickerbocker is Washington Irving's putative author in *A History of New York*.)

The Attitude of the Speaker

In examining such questions about NARRATIVE VOICE, one step further must be taken—a step beyond just identifying whose VOICE is speaking—to determine what that VOICE is trying to say: *the attitude of the speaker*. VOICE in this respect is an element in both the narrative FORM and in nonnarrative works, as well. The difference in *the attitude of the speaker* (the VOICE of the speaker) and the attitude of the writer (the writer's VOICE) results in irony in Swift's essay, "A Modest Proposal" (an example of VOICE affecting a work to create an ironic TONE). Clearly, the main CHARACTER or the speaker does not always VOICE the opinions of the author.

If the speaker is also the main CHARACTER, then determining his or her VOICE (*the attitude of the speaker*) is important to CHARACTER revelation.

VOICE IN POETRY

Another area in which determining the VOICE and the attitude of the speaker is important is in poetry, particularly in the lyric poem. VOICE in narrative poetry has many of the same considerations as in its narrative prose FORM; however, VOICE in lyric poetry has some significant differences. As proposed by T. S. Eliot, VOICE in poetry encompasses three different perspectives: (1) the silent contemplations of the poet, (2) the MEANING conveyed from the poet to the reader/hearer, and (3) the role of the persona that the poet uses in the poem.

W. B. YEATS
(1865–1939)

Sometimes I told myself very adventurous love-stories with myself for hero, and at other times I planned out a life of lonely austerity, and at other times mixed the ideals and planned a life of lonely austerity mitigated by periodical lapses. I had still the ambition, formed in Sligo in my teens, of living in imitation of Thoreau on Innisfree, a little island in Lough Gill, and when walking through Fleet Street very homesick I heard a little tinkle of water and saw a fountain in a shop-window which balanced a little ball upon its jet, and began to remember lake water. From the sudden remembrance came my poem *Innisfree*, my first lyric with anything in its rhythm of my own music.

As mentioned in the discussion of FORM, lyric poems are nonnarrative works that express the speaker's feelings, state of mind, thoughts, and other expressions, and are written generally in the first person. The usage of the first person "I" in the lyric poem does not necessarily mean that the poet is the speaker (just as the first person narrator of a story is not always the author). In the lyric poem, although some argument can be made that the author's life cannot help but be reflected in the words of the lyric speaker, the temptation to overstate the case should be resisted in favor of recognizing the lyric speaker as part of the poem as a whole as the speaker addresses the situation to produce an effect.

The Dramatic Monologue
Perhaps recognition of the lyric speaker can best be illustrated by looking closely at a type of lyric poem called the *dramatic monologue*. The characteristics of the dramatic monologue are

1. Persona (called the lyric speaker and *not* referring to the poet) who expresses the lyric at some dramatic moment or in a situation
2. A one-sided conversation in which the clues in the lyric reveal that this poem is part of a conversation addressed *to* someone, but only the lyric of the (persona) speaker can be heard—the other people in the one-sided conversation are *silent* auditors
3. Revelation of the lyric speaker's CHARACTER (usually unintentional) through what he or she says

This revelation of the lyric speaker's CHARACTER demonstrates the significance of looking at VOICE from the perspective of the *speaker's attitude* to the MEANING of a dramatic monologue. Bear in mind that very often the lyric speaker is a famous person—someone with whose life or circumstances the contemporary readers or hearers of the poem would have been expected to be familiar.

Read this often referenced dramatic monologue by Robert Browning called "My Last Duchess." The lyric speaker is *not* Browning, but rather a sixth-century Italian duke named Alfonso II. He was married to a fourteen-year-old girl who died when she was just seventeen. Her death has been described as "suspicious"; however, Duke Alfonso went on to negotiate an arrangement to marry a member of Austrian royalty. He used an agent for these negotiations; that agent is the silent auditor to whom this lyric poem is addressed:

MY LAST DUCHESS

That's my last Duchess painted on the wall,
Looking as if she were alive. I call
That piece a wonder, now: Fra` Pandolf's hands
line   Worked busily a day, and there she stands.
(5)   Will't please you sit and look at her? I said
"Fra` Pandolf" by design, for never read
Strangers like you that pictured countenance,
The depth and passion of its earnest glance,
But to myself they turned (since none puts by
(10)   The curtain I have drawn for you, but I)
And seemed as they would ask me, if they durst,
How such a glance came there; so, not the first
Are you to turn and ask thus. Sir, 'twas not
Her husband's presence only, called that spot
(15)   Of joy into the Duchess' cheek: perhaps
Fra` Pandolf chanced to say "Her mantle laps
Over my lady's wrist too much," or "Paint
Must never hope to reproduce the faint
Half-flush that dies along her throat": such stuff
(20)   Was courtesy, she thought, and cause enough
For calling up that spot of joy. She had
A heart—how shall I say?—too soon made glad,
Too easily impressed; she liked whate'er
She looked on, and her looks went everywhere.
(25)   Sir, 'twas all one! My favor at her breast,
The dropping of the daylight in the West,
The bough of cherries some officious fool
Broke in the orchard for her, the white mule
She rode with round the terrace—all and each
(30)   Would draw from her alike the approving speech,
Or blush, at least. She thanked men,—good! but thanked
Somehow—I know not how—as if she ranked
My gift of a nine-hundred-years-old name
With anybody's gift. Who'd stoop to blame
(35)   This sort of trifling? Even had you skill
In speech—which I have not—to make your will
Quite clear to such an one, and say, "Just this
Or that in you disgust me; here you miss,
Or there exceed the mark"—and if she let
(40)   Herself be lessoned so, nor plainly set
Her wits to yours, forsooth, and made excuse,
—E'en then would be some stooping; and I choose
Never to stoop. Oh sir, she smiled, no doubt,
Whene'er I passed her; but who passed without
(45)   Much the same smile? This grew; I gave commands
Then all smiles stopped together. There she stands
As if alive. Will't please you rise? We'll meet
The company below, then I repeat,
The Count your master's known munificence
(50)   Is ample warrant that no just pretense

Of mine for dowry will be disallowed;
Though his fair daughter's self, as I avowed
At starting, is my object. Nay, we'll go
Together down, sir. Notice Neptune, though,
(55)   Taming a sea-horse, thought a rarity,
Which Claus of Innsbruck cast in bronze for me!

by Robert Browning

Now, examine the poem to answer the following questions:

1. Can you *distinguish between the speaker and the writer?*

    The FORM (a dramatic monologue) dictates this distinction: the poet (Browning) has used a persona, a lyric speaker in the person of the Duke.

2. What in the poem reveals the speaker's attitude?

    Some lines are obvious; however, look for the more subtle hints at his CHARACTER, for example, notice how easily he glides from the painting of his late wife to discussing another work of art—the bronze statue (lines 54–56).

3. Are there any clues to what Browning's attitude toward the Duke might be?

    Be sure to look for clues arising from the choice of words he had the Duke speak or from the elements of CHARACTER Browning (the poet) chose to have this lyric speaker reveal.

4. Finally, what role does the silent auditor serve here?

    Notice lines 1, 5–7, 12–13, 35–41 (Is "you" referring specifically to the silent auditor—the marriage agent to whom he is speaking?), 51–52.

The Direct Address

As you examine poems for elements of VOICE, do not overlook some of the more obvious mechanical devices that can indicate the role of the speaker, such as use of quotation marks and of dialogue between two or more people. "Lord Randal," an anonymous work written sometime in the fifteenth century, illustrates a dialogue of two individual VOICES, neither of which is the poet speaking directly to the reader:

LORD RANDAL

"O where hae ye been, Lord Randal, my son?
O where hae ye been, my handsome young man?"
"I hae been to the wild wood; mother, make my bed soon,
For I'm weary wi hunting, and fain wald lie down."

"Where gat ye your dinner, Lord Randal, my son?
Where gat ye your dinner, my handsome young man?"
"I din'd wi my true-love; mother, make my bed soon,
For I'm weary wi hunting, and fain wald lie down."

"What gat ye to your dinner, Lord Randal, my son?
What gat ye to your dinner, my handsome young man?"
"I gat eels boiled in broo; mother, make my bed soon,
For I'm weary wi hunting, and fain wald lie down."

"What became of your bloodhounds, Lord Randal, my son?
What became of your bloodhounds, my handsome young man?"
"O they swelld and they died; mother, make my bed soon,
For I'm weary wi hunting, and fain wald lie down."

"O I fear ye are poisond, Lord Randal, my son!
O I fear ye are poisond, my handsome young man!"
"O yes! I am poisond; mother, make my bed soon,
For I'm sick at the heart, and I fain wald lie down."

In "Lord Randal" the *direct address* used in CONTEXT identifies the two speakers as a mother and her son.

Now read this anonymous ballad, "The Three Ravens." The unabridged dictionary reveals that "derrie" has no specific meaning, but is just a word sometimes used in the refrains of ballads and that a "leman" is a lover. After reading the poem, identify the speakers and establish their attitudes as well as the possible attitudes of the poet.

THE THREE RAVENS

There were three ravens sat on a tree,
   Downe a downe, hay downe, hay downe.
There were three ravens sat on a tree,
line   With a downe.
(5) There were three ravens sat on a tree,
They were as blacke as they might be.
   With a downe derrie, derrie, derrie, downe, downe.

The one of them said to his mate,
"Where shall we our breakfast take?"

(10) "Downe in yonder greene field,
There lies a knight slain under his shield.

"His hounds they lie downe at his feete,
So well they can their master keepe.

"His haukes they flie so eagerly,
(15) There's no fowle dare him come nie."

Downe there comes a fallow doe,
As great with yong as she might goe.

She lift up his bloudy hed,
And kist his wounds that were so red.

(20) She got him up upon her backe,
And carried him to earthen lake.

She buried him before the prime,
She was dead herselfe ere even-song time.

God send every gentleman,
(25) Such haukes, such hounds, and such a leman.

Here are some of the possible questions and answers concerning the preceding poem.
1. Who are the speakers?

- A narrator in lines 1–8 and 16–25
- Two ravens in dialogue (lines 9–15)

2. What are the attitudes of the speakers?
The ravens: How do they view the slain knight? As a potential meal (lines 9–11). What is their attitude toward the hounds and hawks? As preventing them from approaching the dead knight (line 15). Also however, note line 13—does the speaking raven possibly admire the hounds?

Discussion question: Why is the poem called "The Three Ravens" and three ravens sit in the tree in line 1, but only two ravens speak? What is the role of the third raven?

The narrator: How does the narrator view the ravens? He or she relates their situation and dialogue in a straightforward manner. What is his or her attitude toward the knight? The slain knight is almost ignored. The speaker does not reveal how the knight died nor describe the knight's CHARACTER (as in "brave" or other such descriptive words). What attitude toward the "fallow doe" is revealed? Her noble actions are carefully detailed (lines 16–23) and admired (lines 24–25). Toward the hawks and hounds? They, too, are admired.

3. What is the attitude of the poet?
Clues for discussion:

- A "fallow doe" represents the knight's lover. Why does the poet select this imagery?
- Ravens are prevented from feeding on a slain knight by his hounds and hawks. What does this say about the CHARACTER of the knight and the poet's seeming lack of direct portrayal of him?

A practice test question:

In the poem, the attitude of the "fallow doe" toward the slain knight is emphasized for its

(A) suicidal tendencies
(B) compassion

(C) self-sacrifice
(D) loyalty
(E) fearlessness

Her attitiude of loyalty (D) toward her dead knight is emphasized by the last line in which she is grouped with his hawks and hounds who were so loyal in protecting his body even after death.

Discussion question: In the CONTEXT of the poem as a whole, what is ironic about the fact that the "fallow doe" is "great with yong" (note spelling—line 17) and dies (line 23)?

One final element of VOICE as it applies to poetry needs to be mentioned: VOICE as it relates to *style*. Some refer to this element of VOICE as the poet's "trademark"—those elements that combine to make the work of a particular poet identifiable. An example would be the "everyday man-next-door" perspective used by Robert Frost.

VOICE IN DRAMA

There are divergent views concerning the role of NARRATIVE VOICE in drama. On the one hand, there are those who see VOICE strictly as a determination of the relationship of the person who is telling the story to what is going on in the story. As such, narrative prose and poetry have speakers or narrators—mediators of the action who convey the story to the readers. Drama, however, lacks a narrator in the same sense as prose and poetry because in a drama, the audience sees events and conversations being acted out without intervention. In this view, NARRATIVE VOICE is not an element of drama. How can you determine the *characterization of the speaker* and the attitude of the speaker if there is no speaker?

The opposing view would contend that there is a speaker even in drama—more difficult to perceive perhaps, but nonetheless a factor in the dramatic structure. How can you determine the speaker in a drama? Trying to establish the point of view is fruitless: the point of view refers to who is telling the story (first or third person). Because in a drama the CHARACTERS act out their own stories, the NARRATIVE is not "narrated" and as a result is not first person or third person. There generally is a main CHARACTER; however, you do not see the world of the play through his or her eyes except for the few clues you may gather from the main CHARACTER'S words.

In order to determine the *attitude of the speaker*, the NARRATIVE VOICE, in a play, some look to the dramatist's use of dramatic conventions, especially the use of the chorus, the choral-character, the prologue, and the epilogue.

The Chorus

The **chorus** originally was composed of singers (and dancers) but eventually underwent a progression of FORMS until it came to be editorial-type comments, foreshadowing, and points for plot development recited between acts by a single actor in Elizabethan drama. The chorus sometimes contains clues to the attitude of the "speaker." (Remember, however, that the "speaker" in a drama must be viewed in a totally different perspective from the point-of-view perspective that can be used in narrative prose, narrative poetry, and even to a certain extent lyric poetry, in which there is clearly a "speaker" who is telling the story or expressing the lyric.) Just as other dramatic conventions are used to substitute for reality (methods used by the dramatist to make the play seem "real" or devices used that the audience is expected to accept as substitutions for reality), the chorus is used to provide those elements that are lost in the absence of a true "NARRATIVE speaker." As such, the chorus can provide a sense of the speaker's perspective, the NARRATIVE VOICE, the *attitude of the speaker*.

Here is the chorus from the Prologue before Act I Scene I of *Romeo and Juliet* and the chorus from before Act II Scene I of the same.

ACT I PROLOGUE
[*Enter*] CHORUS
CHORUS.

Two households, both alike in dignity,
In fair Verona, where we lay our scene,
From ancient grudge break to new mutiny,
line Where civil blood makes civil hands unclean.
(5) From forth the fatal loins of these two foes
A pair of star-crost lovers take their life;
Whose misadventured piteous overthrows
Doth with their death bury their parents' strife.
The fearful passage of their death-mark'd love,
(10) And the continuance of their parents' rage,
Which, but their children's end, naught could remove,
Is now the two hours' traffic of our stage;

The which if you with patient ears attend,
What here shall miss, our toil shall strive to mend. [*Exit*]

ACT II PROLOGUE
[*Enter*] CHORUS
CHORUS.

Now old desire doth in his death-bed lie,
And young affection gapes to be his heir;
That fair, for which love groan'd for, and would die,
line With tender Juliet matcht, is now not fair.
(5) Now Romeo is beloved, and loves again,
Alike bewitched by the charm of looks;
But to his foe supposed he must complain,
And she steal love's sweet bait from fearful hooks:
Being held a foe, he may not have access
(10) To breathe such vows as lovers use to swear;
And she as much in love, her means much less
To meet her new-beloved any where:
But passion lends them power, time means, to meet,
Tempering extremities with extreme sweet. [*Exit*]

Notice the role of the first chorus:

1. It sets the scene (line 2).
2. It foreshadows the ending (line 7).
3. It tells the length of the play (line 12).
4. It gives the cause of the tragedy (lines 1, 3).
5. It promises more detail (lines 13–14).
6. It editorializes through use of connotatively charged words ("grudge," "mutiny," "unclean," and "piteous").
7. It directly addresses the tragedy of the story (lines 10–11).

Now examine the role of the chorus for Act II. Based on these two uses of the chorus, what might the *attitude of the speaker,* his NARRATIVE VOICE, be in this play? Also, note that both choruses are written in traditional sonnet FORM.

The Choral-Character
A more recent development of the chorus convention is the use of the **choral-character**. The choral-character is actually a CHARACTER in the play who takes over the role of the chorus, providing the audience with insight into the action, motivations, consequences, and indirectly into the speaker's VOICE.

The Prologue
The **prologue** was used commonly in Restoration and eighteenth-century drama. A CHARACTER would directly address the audience before the first scene, giving the listeners information significant to their understanding of the plot. Sometimes the prologue would be written not by the authors but by noted literary friends.

The Epilogue
The **epilogue** was given by a CHARACTER at the end of the play. Often the epilogue will in a sense "court" the audience by expressing wishes for goodwill. Although epilogues did not survive to any extent in the twentieth century, they were used extensively in the seventeenth and eighteenth centuries. Here is the epilogue spoken by the King in Shakespeare's *All's Well That Ends Well:*

EPILOGUE
Spoken by the King.

The king's a beggar, now the play is done:
All is well ended, if this suit be won,
That you express content; which we will pay,
With strife to please you, day exceeding day:
Ours be your patience then, and yours our parts;
Your gentle hands lend us, and take our hearts.

How would you summarize the *attitude of the speaker* toward his audience? Toward the plot of the play?

In summary, finding the NARRATIVE VOICE at work in a literary selection involves

1. Identifying the speaker or speakers
2. Identifying the point of view of the speakers
3. Determining the role of the author
4. Determining the speaker's attitude

A discussion of NARRATIVE VOICE, especially as it is used in the *characterization of the speaker,* would not be complete, however, without also addressing grammatical VOICE.

Most students of literature are familiar with active VOICE and passive VOICE: When the subject does the action in a sentence or in the condition named by the verb, the VOICE of the verb is active. (I threw a ball.) When the subject receives the action, the VOICE of the verb is passive. (The ball was thrown by me.) Passive VOICE constructions are made with the past participle and a form of the verb *to be:* was thrown. Much of the writing done in English is in the active VOICE and the occasional shift to passive VOICE can be very effective, particularly when emphasis is to be placed on the object, as in *"The difficult test was passed by the student"* (emphasis is on the test) or when the actors (of the action) are not known, as in "Many books have been written this year" (Who wrote the books?).

Largely an element of a writer's style, overuse of the passive VOICE can affect the TONE of a narrative and, as a result, might influence the reader's perception of the NARRATIVE VOICE and particularly the speaker's attitude. Compare these two versions of the same paragraph:

Version One:

The ball was hit by Jim, but it was immediately caught by the outfielder. Roars were heard from the crowd. Tears streaming down his face were awkwardly wiped away by Jim's gloved hand. The truth was finally realized by him: the championship game was lost.

Version Two:

Jim hit the ball, but the outfielder caught it immediately. The crowd roared. Jim's gloved hand awkwardly wiped away the tears streaming down his face. He finally realized the truth: the championship game was lost.

In a narrative, the use of active VOICE helps to intensify the action (a function of TONE) and hold the reader's attention, whereas overuse of the passive VOICE misdirects attention away from Jim—the main subject of the sample narrative. But controlled use of passive VOICE can be useful: the shift from active to passive in the last sentence effectively serves to catch the reader's attention that something is different (in this case a significant point is being made). In narrative writing, as this example illustrates, use of active and passive VOICE has significant implications on the reader's perceptions of TONE and MEANING.

QUESTIONS TO APPLY YOUR LEARNING

As you practice reading literary selections, ask these questions to help you identify and understand NARRATIVE VOICE:

1. From what point of view is this story being told?
2. Who is the main CHARACTER?
3. Who is the speaker?
4. Are the speaker and the author the same person?
5. What is the attitude of the author?
6. If the attitudes of the author and speaker differ, what is the effect?
7. Are there any stream-of-consciousness techniques present? If so, what is the effect?
8. Is the narrator intrusive or unintrusive?
9. Is the narrative written in the scenic method with a self-effacing author or in the panoramic method?
10. Is the point of view (if applicable) limited or unlimited third person?
11. Is the narrator credible? Naive?
12. Does the persona project the views of the author?
13. Does the NARRATIVE VOICE affect the TONE?
14. If the selection is a lyric poem, who is the speaker? What is the speaker's attitude?
15. Is the poem a dramatic monologue? Why or why not?
16. If a play, are there any dramatic conventions present that might project a NARRATIVE VOICE?

ADDITIONAL HELPFUL POINTS TO REMEMBER

- *Never* assume that the speaker and the author are the same person—even when the work is written in the first person.
- When the test question asks you to select the best description of the speaker's attitude:
  1. Be sure that you have clearly understood the *identity of the speaker* of the passage.
  2. Examine the passage to be sure that you are identifying the speaker's attitude toward the concept in the test question and *not* some other concept, for example, if the question asks you to describe the speaker's attitude toward his cat, be careful that you extract from the passages those clues concerning his attitude *toward his cat* and not toward something else mentioned in the passage, such as his dog.
- In preparing for test questions in which you must describe the speaker's attitude, be sure to enrich your vocabulary with descriptive adjectives relating to attitudes. Learn the definitions (you may already be familiar with their dictionary definitions), but also learn

what CHARACTER traits are the foundations for such labels. For example, what words and actions would a person with a *deferential* attitude exhibit? You could use the following list to start your vocabulary study on attitudes. Also, see the list of other words in the study plan section of this book.

A speaker's attitude might be:

assertive	dictatorial
boisterous	dilatory
bravado	insolent
callous	irascible
censorious	irrational
churlish	optimistic
complaisant	pacifiable
condescending	petulant
derisive	sanctimonious
derogatory	sanguinary

- Watch for shifts in points of view in a selection, particularly in lyric poetry. A change from the third person to first person pronouns (from "he" or "they" to "I" or "we"), for example, is important to MEANING and can affect the identification of the speaker and the speaker's attitude.
- As with identifying the speaker's attitude, when the test question asks you to select a description of the narrator's attitude, be sure you understand the identity of *the narrator.* For example, here is an excerpt from *The Pickwick Papers* (Dickens):

THE PICKWICK PAPERS
by
Charles Dickens

"My secret was out; and my only struggle now, was for liberty and freedom. I gained my feet before a hand was on me, threw myself among my assailants, and cleared my way with my strong arm as if I bore a hatchet in my hand, and hewed them down before me. I gained the door, dropped over the banisters, and in an instant was in the street.

"Straight and swift I ran, and no one dared to stop me. I heard the noise of feet behind, and redoubled my speed.... When I woke I found myself here—here in this gay cell where the sun-light seldom comes, and the moon steals in, in rays which only serve to show the dark shadows about me, and that silent figure in its old corner. When I lie awake, I can sometimes hear strange shrieks and cries from distant parts of this large place. What they are, I know not; but they neither come from that pale form, nor does it regard them. For from the first shades of dusk 'till the earliest light of morning, it still stands motionless in the same place, listening to the music of my iron chain, and watching my gambols on my straw bed."

At the end of the manuscript, was written, in another hand, this note:—

[The unhappy man whose ravings are recorded above, was a melancholy instance of the baneful results of energies misdirected in early life, and excesses prolonged until their consequences could never be repaired....It is only matter of wonder to those who were acquainted with the vices of his early career, that his passions, when no longer controlled by reason, did not lead him to the commission of still more frightful deeds.]

In this selection, part of a manuscript is written in the first person, followed by a commentary (the "note") written in the third person by someone else in reference to the writer of the manuscript. A question concerning the narrator's attitude would probably be referring to the writer of the commentary. Be aware, however, that there is yet a third VOICE that, although this limited excerpt reveals very little about his or her attitude, the existence of this person needs to be recognized: Who is the VOICE that says, "At the end of the manuscript, was written, in another hand, this note:"?

Practice questions concerning this selection might include:

The attitude of the speaker "I" in the first two paragraphs is

(A) optimistically exuberant
(B) angerly resistant
(C) intensely forlorn
(D) respectfully submissive
(E) earnestly imploring

What is the attitude of the commentator toward the "unhappy man" in the last paragraph?

(A) Judgmental
(B) Sympathetic
(C) Hostile
(D) Defensive
(E) Compassionate

(The correct answers are respectively C and A.)

LITERARY ELEMENT NUMBER FOUR: TONE

ROBERT BURTON
(1577–1640)

The author of *The Anatomy of Melancholy* is said to have laboured long in the writing of this book to suppress his own melancholy, and yet did but improve it; and that some readers have found the same effect. In an interval of vapours he would be extremely pleasant, and raise laughter in any company. Yet I have heard that nothing at last could make him laugh but going down to the Bridge-foot in Oxford, and hearing the barge-men scold and storm and swear at one another, at which he would set his hands to his sides, and laugh most profusely. Yet in his college and chamber so mute and mopish that he was suspected to be *felo de se*.

TONE refers, in its most narrow sense, to the attitude of the literary speaker toward his or her listener. When identifying the TONE or trying to describe the TONE (of VOICE) used, generally such descriptors as happy, sad, ironic, abstruse, sincere, playful, straightforward, *formal, informal,* serious, condescending, and many more descriptive words are used. Usually the TONE is described as, for example, "He has a somber TONE of VOICE." In other words, TONE answers the question: How does the literary speaker "sound" to the listener? As the phrase "TONE of VOICE" implies, *sound* in this CONTEXT does include an auditory impression; however, because most literary expressions (other than those in the oral traditions, speeches, drama, and poems meant to be read aloud) are intended to be read silently, sound also refers to the impression that is conveyed. Hence the question can be restructured to read: What impression is the literary speaker conveying to the reader? How does the literary speaker *seem* to the reader? A subtle implication here is that the TONE (of VOICE) somehow will reveal information about the speaker's opinion of the intelligence and sensitivity of the reader or listener. For example, an adult might use a condescending TONE of VOICE with a child. Even an apology can be turned into further hostility through the TONE (of VOICE) used. "I beg your pardon" can be sincere words of regret or they can be sarcastically spoken. In listening to a speaker, you can distinguish his or her TONE (of VOICE) through the verbal inflections and facial expressions used. How can you tell what TONE a speaker is using in a written selection? Sometimes the writer will use graphic means to convey TONE, such as italicizing words to show the speaker's verbal inflections. Also, the writer may use description to portray the attitude of the CHARACTER in the written work. As in other aspects of analysis, CONTEXT is very important to determining a CHARACTER'S/speaker's TONE (of VOICE). Just as a person in an argument might say, "Did you hear the TONE she used with me?"— the TONE of VOICE in a literary selection is an element of communication with the reader (or with another CHARACTER in the story). TONE (of VOICE) also implies that there is an auditor.

When considering the NARRATIVE VOICE, the reader needs to establish who is speaking and how that speaker might be *characterized (recognizing the difference between the speaker and the writer* and identifying the attitude of the *speaker*). The concept of TONE is an almost inseparable element of VOICE, one that includes the speaker's attitude and extends to encompass the entire work.

TONE, atmosphere, mood, feeling: there is a great disagreement among literary scholars about how interchangeably these terms can be used. At one extreme are writers who consider these elements as synonyms; at the other extreme are those who would differentiate their shades of meaning. If the VOICE refers to who is speaking and the speaker's or writer's attitude in terms of what is being said, then perhaps TONE might be defined as the speaker's or writer's attitude in terms of *how* he or she "sounds" saying it, contributing to atmosphere, mood, and feeling.

Defined as such, TONE works on several different levels. There is a TONE found in:

- Dialogue between CHARACTERS as they interact (their TONE of VOICE)
- Specific words, PHRASES, and sentences used at specific points as an expression of the writer's, narrator's, or speaker's TONE of VOICE

- Each individual CHARACTER'S attitude
- The TONE of the work as a whole

What elements contribute to make the TONE of a work?

1. *The speaker*

The speaker has an attitude toward the subject. *How* he or she expresses that attitude projects a TONE. If the speaker's attitude is, for example, condemning of those who hunt for sport, his or her TONE when describing a hunting scene might influence the readers to regard the act as grisly or morbid. The NARRATIVE VOICE is condemning; the TONE is morbid. In contrast, if the speaker's attitude is admiring of hunters, his or her TONE when describing a hunting scene might make the act appear adventurous or necessary (for food or protection). The NARRATIVE VOICE is admiring; the TONE is exciting.

2. *The author*

The author also has an attitude toward the subject. How the author expresses that attitude, however, depends upon the relationship of the speaker to the writer. If the speaker is the author's persona expressing his or her own views, the TONE is more likely that expressed by the speaker. When the speaker speaks and acts *in contrast to* the views of the author, this discrepancy or difference in VOICE creates an ironic TONE. Swift's "A Modest Proposal" is an example.

3. *The theme or subject*

Some themes or subjects carry with them intrinsic elements of TONE, for instance, death usually has an unhappy TONE and birth generally a happy TONE. You should not assume, however, that a work about death is always in a negative TONE: the TONE is a product of many elements that work together, including the author's intent. The speaker's approach and the author's use of literary elements can turn a work about death into a celebration of life or, as in Henry Vaughan's poem, "Peace," written in the mid-1600s, an anticipation of peace.

PEACE

My soul, there is a country
   Far beyond the stars,
Where stands a wingèd sentry
   All skilful in the wars;
There above noise, and danger
   Sweet peace sits crowned with smiles,
And one born in a manger
   Commands the beauteous files;
He is thy gracious friend,
   And (O, my Soul, awake!)
Did in pure love descend
   To die here for thy sake.
If thou canst get but thither,
   There grows the flower of peace,
The rose that cannot wither,
   Thy fortress, and thy ease;
Leave then thy foolish ranges,
   For none can thee secure,
But one, who never changes,
   Thy God, thy life, thy cure.

by Henry Vaughan

4. *The CHARACTERS*

The CHARACTERS in a work (what they say and do) and how they are characterized (what is said about them) can significantly influence the TONE of a work. The individual temperaments of the CHARACTERS, how they act and react, what they say and how they say it are all important elements of TONE. Here is an excerpt of dialogue from *The Old Curiosity Shop* by Charles Dickens.

"I can't see anything but the curtain of the bed," said Brass, applying his eye to the keyhole of the door. "Is he a strong man, Mr. Richard [Dick Swiveller]?"

"Very," answered Dick.

"It would be an extremely unpleasant circumstance if he was to bounce out suddenly," said Brass. "Hallo there! Hallo, hallo!"

While Mr. Brass, with his eye curiously twisted into the keyhole, uttered these sounds as a means of attracting the lodger's attention, and while Miss Brass plied the hand-bell, Mr. Swiveller put his stool close against the wall by the side of the door, and mounting on the top and standing bolt upright, began a violent battery with the ruler upon the upper panels of the door.

Suddenly the door was unlocked on the inside and flung violently open. Miss Sally dived into her own bedroom; Mr. Brass, who was not remarkable for personal courage, ran into the next street, and finding that nobody followed him, armed with a poker or other offensive weapon, put his hands in his pockets, walked very slowly all at once, and whistled.

Meanwhile Mr. Swiveller, on the top of the stool, drew himself into as flat a shape as possible against the wall and looked, not unconcernedly, down upon the single gentleman, who appeared at the door growling and cursing in a very awful manner, and, with the boots in his hand, seemed to have an intention of hurling them downstairs. This idea, however, he abandoned, and he was turning into his room again, still growling vengefully, when his eyes met those of the watchful Richard.

"Have *you* been making that horrible noise?" said the single gentleman.

"I have been helping, sir," returned Dick, keeping his eye upon him.

"How dare you then," said the lodger. "Eh?"

To this, Dick made no other reply than by inquiring whether the lodger held it to be consistent with the conduct and character of a gentleman to go to sleep for six-and-twenty hours at a stretch, and whether the peace of an amiable and virtuous family was to weigh as nothing in the balance.

"Is my peace nothing?" said the single gentleman.

"Yes, sir, indeed," returned Dick, yielding, "but an equal quantity of slumber was never got out of one bed and bedstead, and if you're going to sleep in that way, you must pay for a double-bedded room."

"Come here, you impudent rascal," was the lodger's answer as he reentered his room.

"Can you drink anything?" was his next inquiry.

Mr. Swiveller replied that he had very recently been assuaging the pangs of thirst, but that he was still open to "a modest quencher," if the materials were at hand. Without another word spoken on either side, the lodger took from his great trunk a kind of temple, shining as of polished silver, and placed it carefully on the table.

Greatly interested in his proceedings, Mr. Swiveller observed him closely. Into one little chamber of this temple he dropped an egg, into another some coffee, into a third a compact piece of raw steak from a neat tin case, into a fourth he poured some water. Then, with the aid of a phosphorus box and some matches, he procured a light and applied it to a spirit lamp which had a place of its own below the temple; then he shut down the lids of all the little chambers, then he opened them; and then, by some wonderful and unseen agency, the steak was done, the egg was boiled, the coffee was accurately prepared, and his breakfast was ready.

"Hot water—" said the lodger, handing it to Mr. Swiveller with as much coolness as if he had a kitchen fire before him, "—extraordinary rum—sugar—and a travelling glass. Mix for yourself. And make haste."

Dick complied, his eyes wandering all the time from the temple on the table which seemed to do everything, to the great trunk which seemed to hold everything. The lodger took his breakfast like a man who was used to work these miracles, and thought nothing of them.

"The man of the house is a lawyer, is he not?" said the lodger.

Dick nodded. The rum was amazing.

"The woman of the house—what's she?"

"A dragon," said Dick.

"I want to do as I like, young man," he added after a short silence; "to go to bed when I like, get up when I like, come in when I like, go out when I like—to be asked no questions and be surrounded by no spies. In this last respect, servants are the devil. There's only one here?"

"And a very little one," said Dick.

"Let them know my humour," said the single gentleman, rising. "If they disturb me, they lose a good tenant. Good day."

"I beg your pardon," said Dick, halting in his passage to the door, which the lodger prepared to open. "—But the name," said Dick, "in case of letters or parcels—"

"I never have any," returned the lodger.

"Or in case anybody should call."

"Nobody ever calls on me."

"If any mistake should arise from not having the name, don't say it was my fault, sir," added Dick, still lingering.

"I'll blame nobody," said the lodger, with such irascibility that in a moment Dick found himself upon the staircase, and the locked door between them.

Mr. Brass and Miss Sally were lurking hard by, having been, indeed, only routed from the keyhole by Mr. Swiveller's abrupt exit. As their utmost exertions had not enabled them to overhear a word of the interview, they hurried him down to the office to hear his account of the conversation.

Notice how the conversation between Dick Swiveller and the nameless lodger contributes to TONE: The lodger refers to Dick as a "impudent rascal," seems antisocial ("Is my peace nothing?" "I never have any [letters or parcels]" "Nobody ever calls on me.") and wants his own way ("I want to do as I like, young man"), yet he invites Dick to have a rum with him. Dick, on the other hand, blends a lack of intimidation and a wide-eyed amazement at the lodger's "temple." Combined with the comical scene of Dick, Brass, and Miss Sally trying to awaken the lodger, the interaction of the CHARACTERS serves to make the TONE both amusing and entertaining. Also, the actions and instructions of the nameless lodger add a slightly mysterious TONE to the episode.

5. The USE OF LANGUAGE and MEANING of the language in CONTEXT

How words are used in a selection, the connotations, the figurative language, all contribute directly to setting the TONE. For example, look at how the MEANINGS of the language in CONTEXT sets the TONE in this excerpt from a communication sent by Benjamin Franklin to Lord Kames of England in April of 1767.

But America, an immense territory, favored by nature with all advantages of climate, soil, great navigable rivers and lakes, etc., must become a great country, populous and mighty; and will, in a less time than is generally conceived, be able to shake off any shackles that may be imposed on her, and perhaps place them on the imposers. In the meantime, every act of oppression will sour their tempers, lessen greatly, if not annihilate, the profits of your commerce with them, and hasten their final revolt; for the seeds of liberty are universally sown there, and nothing can eradicate them.

The CONTEXT of the communication is the growing resistance of the American colonists to British rule. First, Franklin describes America as "immense…favored by nature…a great country, populous and mighty"—in other words, a formidable nation. Then he introduces the element of time and uses figurative language to state that "any shackles…imposed" on America may eventually be placed "on the imposers"—a very connotatively harsh metaphor that compares Britain's relationship to America as enslavement, and that the slaves may turn and enslave their masters. He then points out that "oppression" might even "annihilate, the profits of your commerce"—a threat to Britain's financial base in America. Again, he links the element of time ("hasten") to the impending "final revolt." He concludes the excerpt with another powerful metaphor comparing liberty to sown seeds that cannot be eradicated (another strongly connotative word).

In the CONTEXT of the excerpt, what is Franklin's (the speaker's) attitude (the NARRATIVE VOICE) toward England? Disapproving, unintimidated, one of warning. What is his TONE (in what manner does he convey this attitude)? In a threatening TONE…a bold TONE…an uncompromising TONE…a confident TONE.

6. The sound of the language

The rhythm and rhyme also affect the TONE of a work, just as they affect the TONE of music. This element of language has been referred to as its TONE *color* and has been compared to the timbre in music. Just as certain musical selections can make people want to dance and others can give listeners the "blues," the rhythm and rhyme in literary selections (even in prose) can bring to the reader or listener certain TONES. Notice the TONE of the poem (page 66) about "A Noiseless Patient Spider." Contrast how Whitman uses rhythm, rhyme, alliteration, and other sound devices to contribute to the TONE with this excerpt from "Upon a Spider Catching a Fly":

Thou sorrow, venom elf:
  Is this thy play,
To spin a web out of thyself
    To catch a fly?
      For why?

I saw a pettish wasp
  Fall foul therein,
Whom yet thy whorl-pins did not clasp
  Lest he should fling
    His sting.

      …   **by Edward Taylor**

7. The setting

Setting in a literary selection refers to:

- Geographical location: This includes area or region, the general locale, descriptions of architecture, flora and fauna, floor plans, furniture arrangements, weather conditions, and so forth.
- Time: This may refer to a historical period, time of day, season of the year, projection into the future, period of life (such as the time of "mid-life crisis"), or even a nonexistent time (used extensively in the science fiction genre).
- Socioeconomic conditions: These are revealed, generally, on two different levels: First, there are those conditions and circumstances that relate directly to the CHARACTERS. These include their occupations, family lives, lifestyles, and social interactions. Second, there is the larger society that surrounds and affects the microcosm of the CHARACTERS. This larger societal structure includes its predominant mores and the general social and work environments.

Although setting is generally associated with narrative writing, some aspects of setting, particularly those of socioeconomic conditions, can affect the TONE even in nonnarrative works. As an example, some works that describe local social customs, employing elements of local color writing and regionalism (nineteenth-century American narrative movements), definitely have a TONE based on setting, despite their lack of a traditional narrative story line.

Some literary scholars refer to the elements of setting (particularly those elements of setting that can be pictured or seen "in the mind's eye" in lyric poetry) that are present in any literary work as the opsis of the work. But whether in a narrative or non-narrative FORM, one of the significant influences of setting on TONE is the emotional impact of the setting—emotions elicited from either the CHARACTERS or the reader in response to the setting. The effects on TONE of some settings are dramatic and easy to identify: the romantic TONE of a deserted island, the frightening TONE of a lonely graveyard on a stormy night, the harsh TONE of an inner city ghetto, the warm TONE of a family gathering on Christmas Eve. Some, however, are more subtle, changing, or perhaps even unexpected, as when the romantic island becomes a place of fear and hardship when food and water supplies dwindle or when the harsh TONE of the inner city ghetto changes to a warm, caring TONE as residents join together to overcome their adversities.

The complexity of what constitutes TONE should, at this point, be obvious. As previously mentioned, TONE, *atmosphere, mood,* and *feeling,* although used synonymously by some, reflect shades of MEANING for others.

Mood can refer to an emotional state, especially as projected by the CHARACTERS in the work: "Joyce is in a foul mood" or "Eric is in a happy mood." Moods, of course, can change (as can many of the other elements of TONE) within the work. As the attitude of the author toward the subject is revealed, his or her mood might be seen as self-righteous, defiant, proud, noble, or even reactionary, to name a few. When the author's VOICE is different from that of the main CHARACTER or the speaker, the mood might differ from the TONE (of VOICE) used by the author. For example, the mood of the speaker in "A Modest Proposal" (on pages 117–118) could be described as helpful, conciliatory, and serious, but the TONE of the author (Swift) is satiric, whose mood (quite possibly) was angry and indignant when he put pen to paper.

On the other hand, **feeling** has been defined as an intellectual state: the attitude of the author toward his subject on an intellectual rather than on an emotional basis. Conversationally, this might be approached with the question, "What is your *feeling* on the subject?" to which the respondent would express his or her views.

The setting, the TONE (of VOICE) of the author and speaker, the emotional moods of the author, the speaker, and/or the CHARACTERS, and the feelings of the author blend together to give the work its **atmosphere**—that prevailing and pervasive ambience that gives the reader the basis for expectation.

Atmosphere is often described using such terms as "mysterious," "romantic," "gloomy," "horrifying," "intellectual," and other expressions depicting these types of effects. When movie critics label a motion picture as a "feel-good movie," they are referring to its atmosphere.

What follows is Edgar Allan Poe's "The Raven" in its entirety. Teachers, critics, and anthology editors for generations have pointed to "The Raven" as an American "classic" because of its distinctive use of rhythm, rhyme, and alliterative elements that contribute to its TONE.

First, read the poem for enjoyment. Notice the use of internal rhyme: "dreary" and "weary"; "napping," "tapping," and "rapping"; "remember," "December," and "ember"; "morrow," "sorrow," and "borrow." In the third stanza, listen to the effects of "silken, sad, uncertain rustling." But how do these elements work together to give the poem its atmosphere? How would you describe the atmosphere of "The Raven"?

THE RAVEN

Stanza:

1   Once upon a midnight dreary, while I pondered, weak
      and weary,
      Over many a quaint and curious volume of forgotten lore,
   While I nodded, nearly napping, suddenly there came a
      tapping,
      As of some one gently rapping, rapping at my
      chamber door.
   "'Tis some visitor," I muttered, "tapping at my chamber
      door—
      Only this and nothing more."

2   Ah, distinctly I remember it was in the bleak December,
      And each separate dying ember wrought its ghost
      upon the floor.
   Eagerly I wished the morrow; vainly I had sought to borrow
      From my books surcease of sorrow—sorrow for the
      lost Lenore,
   For the rare and radiant maiden whom the angels name
      Lenore—
      Nameless *here* for evermore.

3   And the silken, sad, uncertain rustling of each purple
      curtain
      Thrilled me—filled me with fantastic terrors never
      felt before;
   So that now, to still the beating of my heart, I stood
      repeating,
      "'Tis some visitor entreating entrance at my chamber
      door—

Some late visitor entreating entrance at my chamber
door—
　This it is and nothing more."

4　Presently my soul grew stronger: hesitating then no longer,
　　"Sir," said I, "or Madam, truly your forgiveness I
　　implore;
　But the fact is I was napping, and so gently you came
　　rapping,
　　And so faintly you came tapping, tapping at my
　　chamber door,
　That I scarce was sure I heard you"—here I opened
　　wide the door—
　　Darkness there and nothing more.

5　Deep into that darkness peering, long I stood there,
　　wondering, fearing,
　　Doubting, dreaming dreams no mortal ever dared to
　　dream before;
　But the silence was unbroken, and the stillness gave no
　　token,
　　And the only word there spoken was the whispered
　　word "Lenore!"
　This I whispered, and an echo murmured back the word
　　"Lenore!"
　　Merely this and nothing more.

6　Back into the chamber turning, all my soul within me
　　burning,
　　Soon again I heard a tapping, somewhat louder than
　　before.
　"Surely," said I, "surely that is something at my window
　　lattice;
　　Let me see, then, what thereat is, and this mystery
　　explore—
　Let my heart be still a moment and this mystery explore—
　　'Tis the wind and nothing more."

7　Open here I flung the shutter, when, with many a flirt and
　　flutter,
　　In there stepped a stately Raven of the saintly days of
　　yore.
　Not the least obeisance made he, not a minute stopped
　　or stayed he,
　　But with mien of lord or lady perched above my
　　chamber door—
　Perched upon a bust of Pallas just above my chamber
　　door—
　　Perched and sat, and nothing more.

8　Then, this ebony bird beguiling my sad fancy into smiling
　　By the grave and stern decorum of the countenance
　　it wore,
　"Though thy crest be shorn and shaven, thou," I said,
　　"art sure no craven,

Ghastly, grim, and ancient Raven, wandering from the
　nightly shore:
Tell me what thy lordly name is on the night's Plutonian
　shore!"
　Quoth the Raven, "Nevermore."

9　Much I marveled this ungainly fowl to hear discourse so
　　plainly,
　　Though its answer little meaning, little relevancy bore;
　For we cannot help agreeing that no living human being
　　Ever yet was blessed with seeing bird above his
　　chamber door—
　Bird or beast upon the sculptured bust above his
　　chamber door—
　　With such name as "Nevermore."

10　But the Raven, sitting lonely on the placid bust, spoke only
　　That one word, as if his soul in that one word he did
　　outpour.
　Nothing further then he uttered, not a feather then he
　　fluttered;
　　Till I scarcely more than muttered, "Other friends
　　have flown before:
　On the morrow he will leave me, as my hopes have flown
　　before."
　　Then the bird said, "Nevermore."

11　Startled at the stillness broken by reply so aptly spoken,
　　"Doubtless," said I, "what it utters is its only stock
　　and store,
　Caught from some unhappy master whom unmerciful
　　Disaster
　　Followed fast and followed faster till his songs one
　　burden bore,
　Till the dirges of his hope that melancholy burden bore
　Of 'Never—nevermore.'"

12　But the Raven still beguiling my sad fancy into smiling,
　　Straight I wheeled a cushioned seat in front of bird
　　and bust and door;
　Then, upon the velvet sinking, I betook myself to linking
　　Fancy unto fancy, thinking what this ominous bird of
　　yore,
　What this grim, ungainly, ghastly, gaunt, and ominous
　　bird of yore
　　Meant in croaking "Nevermore."

13　This I sat engaged in guessing, but no syllable
　　expressing
　　To the fowl, whose fiery eyes now burned into my
　　bosom's core;
　This and more I sat divining, with my head at ease
　　reclining

On the cushion's velvet lining that the lamplight
gloated o'er,
But whose velvet-violet lining with the lamplight gloating
o'er,
She shall press, ah, nevermore!

14   Then, methought, the air grew denser, perfumed from an
unseen censer
Swung by seraphim whose foot-falls tinkled on the
tufted floor.
"Wretch," I cried, "thy God hath lent thee—by these
angels he hath sent thee
Respite—respite and nepenthe from thy memories of
Lenore!
Quaff, oh quaff this kind nepenthe, and forget this lost
Lenore!"
Quoth the Raven, "Nevermore."

15   "Prophet!" said I, "thing of evil! prophet still, if bird or
devil!
Whether Tempter sent, or whether tempest tossed
thee here ashore,
Desolate yet all undaunted, on this desert land
enchanted—
On this home by Horror haunted—tell me truly, I
implore:
Is there—is there balm in Gilead?—tell me—tell me, I
implore!"
Quoth the Raven, "Nevermore."

16   "Prophet!" said I, "thing of evil—prophet still, if bird or
devil!
By that Heaven that bends above us, by that God we
both adore,
Tell this soul with sorrow laden if, within the distant
Aidenn,
It shall clasp a sainted maiden whom the angels
name Lenore:
Clasp a rare and radiant maiden whom the angels name
Lenore!"
Quoth the Raven, "Nevermore."

17   "Be that word our sign of parting, bird or fiend!" I
shrieked, upstarting:
"Get thee back into the tempest and the Night's
Plutonian shore!
Leave no black plume as a token of that lie thy soul hath
spoken!
Leave my loneliness unbroken! quit the bust above
my door!
Take thy beak from out my heart, and take thy form from
off my door!"
Quoth the Raven, "Nevermore."

18   And the Raven, never flitting, still is sitting, *still* is sitting
On the pallid bust of Pallas just above my chamber
door;
And his eyes have all the seeming of a demon's that is
dreaming,
And the lamp-light o'er him streaming throws his
shadow on the floor;
And my soul from out that shadow that lies floating on
the floor
Shall be lifted—nevermore!

by Edgar Allan Poe

Now examine the poem for some of the elements of TONE (of VOICE) and NARRATIVE VOICE that have been discussed. These questions can help you prepare for the types of questions concerning VOICE, TONE, atmosphere that might appear on the SAT II: Literature Subject Test. (Note: On the SAT II: Literature Subject Test, questions are in multiple-choice format rather than short answer and fill-in-the-blank format.) How would you fill in the following blanks and answer the accompanying questions?

1. "I" can best be described as _____
   _____.

2. The attitude of "I" toward Lenore is best described as _____
   _____.

3. The attitude of "I" toward the raven changes
   from _____ to
   _____ in the poem.

4. The attitude of the author toward the speaker is
   best described as _____
   _____.

5. The attitude of "I" toward the unknown visitor
   is best described as _____
   _____ in stanza 4.

6. What changes in TONE are introduced in the
   twelfth stanza? _____
   _____

7. How does the theme influence the TONE? ___

_____

8. How does the setting influence the TONE? ___

_____

9. The speaker's TONE suggests that the raven is

_____.

10. The TONE of the speaker in the second stanza is best described as_____.

11. The TONE of the speaker in the eighth stanza is best described as _____.

12. The TONE of the speaker in the fifteenth stanza is best described as_____.

13. The TONE of the speaker in the last stanza is best described as _____.

14. What is the TONE of the entire poem? _____

_____

Finally, look at the structural elements as they relate to TONE and atmosphere.

1. Examine the rhyme scheme. What is its effect on the atmosphere? _____

_____

2. Examine the rhythm. How does it affect the atmosphere? _____

_____

3. Alliteration and assonance refer to the repetition of consonant and vowel sounds respectively. How does the use of alliteration and assonance affect the atmosphere of this work?

_____

_____

4. Notice the use of italics in the second, thirteenth, and (especially) the last stanzas. What are the effects of each? _____

_____

_____

5. Write a stanza-by-stanza paraphrase, writing one sentence for each stanza, putting the point of each in your own words.

Stanza 1. _____

_____

Stanza 2. _____

Stanza 3. _____

_____

Stanza 4. _____

_____

Stanza 5. _____

_____

Stanza 6. _____

_____

Stanza 7. _____

_____

Stanza 8. _____

_____

Stanza 9. _____

_____

Stanza 10. _____

_____

Stanza 11. _____

_____

Stanza 12. _____

_____

Stanza 13. _____

_____

Stanza 14. _____

_____

Stanza 15. _____

_____

Stanza 16. _____

_____

Stanza 17. _____

_____

Stanza 18. _____

_____

6. Write a plot summary in one or two paragraphs and consider how the plot affects the atmosphere.

_____

_____

_____

7. Notice the poignant impact of stanza 16. Also, look at the use of the words "quaff" and "nepenthe" in stanza 14. The significance of word MEANING in this stanza is very important to understanding what is being conveyed to the reader. What is the author telling the reader? Does this information change the atmosphere and mood?_____

_____

_____

_____

_____

_____

Because TONE is partly the result of attitude, an investigation of its role in a literary work is not complete without a look at its role in the author's *style*. Style is a significant element in both NARRATIVE VOICE and TONE (of VOICE):

- NARRATIVE VOICE—the writer's or speaker's attitude
- TONE (of VOICE)—how the writer or speaker "sounds" (intellectually and emotionally) expressing that attitude to the auditor (listener)
- *Style*—how the writer uses the literary elements to express his or her attitude

Although a writer may try to emulate another author's style, like snowflakes, no two writers' styles are *exactly* alike. The labels readers place on a particular writer's style can be based on a wide range of factors. For example, you might associate the style of a writer with his or her purpose (a scientific style, a journalistic style, a didactic style). Sometimes a writer consistently works in the same genre and one comes to describe his or her style based on that genre (a romantic style or a swashbuckler style). If a writer tries to emulate the work of a particular literary period, school, or favorite writer, you might label the style accordingly (a

Shakespearean style, a New Formalism style). Also, readers tend to label the style of a writer based on their overall impression of the "sense" they get of elements that are generally consistent throughout that particular author's work. You might label his or her writing style as imaginative (or unimaginative), exciting (or dull), sensitive (or insensitive). Once a writer has established a recognizable style, readers tend to measure each of his or her new works to see how it measures against their perception of his or her style. Readers then talk about whether the new work is consistent with or is a departure from the writer's "style."

Literary scholars, however, take a more analytical approach to style, which will be discussed as TONE is examined in prose, poetry, and drama.

TONE IN PROSE

As previously discussed, TONE is *how* the writer or speaker "sounds" to the auditor in expressing his or her attitude (NARRATIVE VOICE). The TONE can reveal the speaker's opinion of the listener or reader. This is a significant factor in the writer's style (the way in which the writer uses literary elements to express his or her attitude).

Traditionally, literary scholars labeled style in terms of levels:

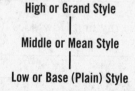

High or Grand Style
|
Middle or Mean Style
|
Low or Base (Plain) Style

The level of style used was dictated by the genre, the context or circumstances, and the social rank of the speaker.

Northrop Frye has pioneered an important variation on this view of style by categorizing the style before the level is determined:

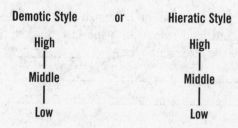

Demotic Style   or   **Hieratic Style**

High   **High**
| |
Middle   **Middle**
| |
Low   **Low**

In this view of style, the work is first determined to be either *demotic*, meaning that it uses the syntax and mechanics of ordinary speech, or *hieratic*, meaning that it uses more formal literary constructions. Once assigned a category, the level of the writing style is then determined within the category. In such a view, the significance of the speaker's or writer's TONE in prose is self-evident.

What follows are several prose selections. The first is an excerpt from a speech delivered by President John F. Kennedy on July 25, 1961 in a broadcast to the American people. The second selection is the introduction to Sir Walter Scott's *Ivanhoe*. The final passage is a paragraph of *The Scarlet Letter* by Nathaniel Hawthorne.

After each selection is presented, its TONE and how the TONE and style are interrelated will be discussed. As you read each selection and think about the accompanying discussions concerning TONE and style, an interesting aspect of the subject to think about is the extent of the writer's intent. Did the writer consciously and deliberately use the elements of style discussed to affect the TONE or were these effects the result of subconscious elements, such as passion for the subject, or the result of basic understanding of the writing process as it relates to producing certain effects in the minds and emotions of the hearers or readers? Perhaps this question cannot be answered, but the degree to which the writer consciously or unconsciously uses style to produce certain effects certainly merits discussion.

THE BERLIN CRISIS
by
John F. Kennedy

Seven weeks ago tonight I returned from Europe to report on my meeting with Premier Khrushchev and the others. His grim warnings about the future of the world, his aide-mémoire on Berlin, his subsequent speeches and threats which he and his agents have launched, and the increase in the Soviet military budget that he has announced have all prompted a series of decisions by the administration and a series of consultations with the members of the NATO organization. In Berlin, as you recall, he intends to bring to an end, through a stroke of the pen, first our legal rights to be in West Berlin and secondly our ability to make good on our commitment to the two million free people of that city. That we cannot permit...

West Berlin is 110 miles within the area which the Soviets now dominate—which is immediately controlled by the so-called East German regime.... We are there as a result of our victory over Nazi Germany—and our basic rights to be there deriving from that victory include both our presence in West Berlin and the enjoyment of access across East Germany. These rights have been repeatedly confirmed and recognized in special agreements with the Soviet Union. Berlin is not a part of East Germany but a separate territory under the control of the allied powers. Thus our rights there are clear and deep-rooted. But in addition to those rights is our commitment to sustain—and defend, if need be—the opportunity for more than two million people to determine their own future and choose their own way of life.

Thus, our presence in West Berlin, and our access thereto, cannot be ended by any act of the Soviet government. The NATO shield was long ago extended to cover West Berlin—and we have given our word that an attack in that city will be regarded as an attack upon us all.

For West Berlin—lying exposed 110 miles inside East Germany, surrounded by Soviet troops and close to Soviet supply lines—has many roles. It is more than a showcase of liberty, a symbol, an island of freedom in a Communist sea. It is even more than a link with the Free World, a beacon of hope behind the Iron Curtain, an escape hatch for refugees.

West Berlin is all of that. But above all it has now become— as never before—the great testing place of Western courage and will, a focal point where our solemn commitments stretching back over the years since 1945 and Soviet ambitions now meet in basic confrontation.

It would be a mistake for others to look upon Berlin, because of its location, as a tempting target. The United States is there; the United Kingdom and France are there; the pledge of NATO is there—and the people of Berlin are there. It is as secure, in that sense, as the rest of us—for we cannot separate its safety from our own....

We do not want to fight, but we have fought before. And others in earlier times have made the same dangerous mistake of assuming that the West was too selfish and too soft and too divided to resist invasions of freedom in other lands. Those who threaten to unleash the forces of war on a dispute over West Berlin should recall the words of the ancient philosopher: "A man who causes fear cannot be free from fear."...

So long as the Communists insist that they are preparing to end by themselves unilaterally our rights in West Berlin and our commitments to its people, we must be prepared to defend those rights and those commitments. We will at all times be ready to talk, if talk will help. But we must also be ready to resist with force, if force is used upon us. Either alone would fail. Together, they can serve the cause of freedom and peace...

Thus, in the days and months ahead, I shall not hesitate to ask the Congress for additional measures or exercise any of the executive powers that I possess to meet this threat to peace. Everything essential to the security of freedom must be done; and if that should require more men, or more taxes, or more controls, or other new powers, I shall not hesitate to ask them. The measures proposed today will be constantly studied and altered as necessary. But while we will not let panic shape our policy, neither will we permit timidity to direct our program.

First, the reader should look at how the subject affects the TONE of this speech. Soviet Premier Nikita Khrushchev was making threats concerning free world rights in West Berlin. The threats were of the nature that the situation might have led to a major military confrontation. The subject? The threat of war. The resulting TONE? Serious, urgent, grave.

Next, look at the speaker's attitude toward the subject and his attitude toward his listeners to see how the TONE is affected. He describes Khrushchev's rhetoric at their meeting as "grim warnings," indicating that he views the Premier's position as threatening. He says that Khrushchev would end legal rights in West Berlin "through the stroke of the pen"— connotative of an overbearing (perhaps even capricious?) attitude on the part of the Premier. He points out America's right and need to be a presence in West Berlin. His attitude toward the subject? America is justified in resisting the threats made against West Berlin. The resulting TONE? Confident, resolved.

The President has essentially three groups of listeners to this speech: the world community (who are poised, listening to see what America and the American President will do), Communist powers (particularly Premier Khrushchev), and the American people. To the world community he points out that he recognizes West Berlin as "the great testing place of Western courage and will"—a matter of "commitment"; however, he also forms psychological alliance with much of the free world. To the Communists and Khrushchev he sends the message: "We have fought before." To the American people he gives assurances ("We will at all times be ready to talk, if talk will help"); he prepares Americans for the possibility of war ("But we must also be ready to resist with force, if force is used upon us") and for the sacrifices that might be ahead ("more men...more taxes...more controls..."). His attitude toward his listeners? He seems to view the world community as both spectators and (particularly NATO, the United Kingdom, and France) as

allies, the Communist regime as a threat, and the American people as needing to know where they stand. The resulting TONE? Responsible (to the world community), brave, unflinching (to the Communist aggressors), forthright (to the American people).

Because he is speaking to three different audiences—three groups of listeners—he uses elements of style to facilitate his message, to communicate three distinct messages to three different groups without ever addressing his remarks directly to any one of them. President Kennedy uses several stylistic devices to accomplish this: two will be examined here.

Notice in the first paragraph the sentence "His grim warnings...have all prompted a series of decisions...." The syntax of this sentence cannot be closed until almost the end of the sentence. Use of this style in the first paragraph establishes a formal TONE in which he introduces the gravity of his topic to all three audiences simultaneously. In the second paragraph, however, he changes (particularly in the first and second sentences) to a more loosely joined construction that could have a period before the end of the sentence and still be complete in terms of syntax. The more relaxed style helps to shift the focus as he explains to the world community in a more conversational TONE why America is justified in its position in West Berlin. Although he does not use extreme forms of syntax, such as the periodic sentences of Boswell in the late eighteenth century and the nonperiodic sentences in the style of Addison, his subtle use of syntax helps to change the TONE.

Also, most of the speech is written in a *hypotactic* style, a use of subordinate PHRASES, clauses, and conjunctions that establish relationships (often cause and effect). At precise times, however, he quite effectively changes to a more *paratactic* style (no subordination or conjunctions—other than perhaps *and*—are used between sentences) that very subtly changes the TONE. For example, notice the effect of his use of the hypotactic style and paratactic style in this paragraph:

It would be a mistake for others to look upon Berlin, because of its location, as a tempting target. The United States is there; the United Kingdom and France are there; the pledge of NATO is there—and the people of Berlin are there. (parataxis) It is as secure, in that sense, as the rest of us— for we cannot separate its safety from our own.... (hypotaxis)

As you can see, the speaker in this speech uses *subtle* changes in his use of stylistic elements to alter his TONE to convey the message to the intended audiences more effectively.

How might questions about TONE in this selection be written? Here are a few possibilities:

- Based upon the speaker's TONE, the listener should consider Soviet intentions to be

  (A) amusing and trivial
  (B) aggressive and threatening
  (C) committed and respectable
  (D) uncontrollable and unstoppable
  (E) inevitable and ambitious

- Of the following statements, all are true of the CONTEXT of this speech EXCEPT that the

  (A) message is intended to inform the American people
  (B) speaker is unintimidated
  (C) purpose is to state America's position in the conflict
  (D) last two paragraphs suggest that peaceful resolutions are possible
  (E) TONE is mocking

- When the speaker says "We do not want to fight, but we have fought before," his TONE can be described as

  (A) disinterested
  (B) disrespectful
  (C) intrepid
  (D) offensive
  (E) pusillanimous

(The correct answers are, respectively, B, E, and C.)

IVANHOE
by
Sir Walter Scott

In that pleasant district of merry England which is watered by the river Don, there extended in ancient times a large forest, covering the greater part of the beautiful hills and valleys which lie between Sheffield and the pleasant town of Doncaster. The remains of this extensive wood are still to be seen at the noble seats of Wentworth, of Wharncliffe Park, and around Rotherham. Here haunted of yore the fabulous Dragon of Wantley; here were fought many of the most desperate battles during the Civil Wars of the Roses; and here also flourished in ancient times those bands of gallant outlaws whose deeds have been rendered so popular in English song.

Such being our chief scene, the date of our story refers to a period towards the end of the reign of Richard I., when his return from his long captivity had become an event rather wished than hoped for by his despairing subjects, who were in the meantime subjected to every species of subordinate oppression. The nobles, whose power had become exorbitant during the reign of Stephen, and whom the prudence of Henry the Second had scarce reduced into some degree of subjection to the crown, had now resumed their ancient license in its utmost extent; despising the feeble interference of the English Council of State, fortifying their castles, increasing the number of their dependants, reducing all around them to a state of vassalage, and striving by every means in their power to place themselves each at the head of such forces as might enable him to make a figure in the national convulsions which appeared to be impending.

The situation of the inferior gentry, or franklins, as they were called, who, by the law and spirit of the English constitution, were entitled to hold themselves independent of feudal tyranny, became now unusually precarious. If, as was most generally the case, they placed themselves under the protection of any of the petty kings in their vicinity, accepted of feudal offices in his household, or bound themselves, by mutual treaties of alliance and protection, to support him in his enterprises, they might indeed purchase temporary repose; but it must be with the sacrifice of that independence which was so dear to every English bosom, and at the certain hazard of being involved as a party in whatever rash expedition the ambition of their protector might lead him to undertake. On the other hand, such and so multiplied were the means of vexation and oppression possessed by the great barons, that they never wanted the pretext, and seldom the will, to harass and pursue, even to the very edge of destruction, any of their less powerful neighbours who attempted to separate themselves from their authority, and to trust for their protection, during the dangers of the times, to their own inoffensive conduct and to the laws of the land.

A circumstance which greatly tended to enhance the tyranny of the nobility and the sufferings of the inferior classes arose from the consequences of the Conquest by Duke William of Normandy. Four generations had not sufficed to blend the hostile blood of the Normans and Anglo-Saxons, or to unite, by common language and mutual interests, two hostile races, one of which still felt the elation of triumph, while the other groaned under all the consequences of defeat. The power had been completely placed in the hands of the Norman nobility by the event of the battle of Hastings, and it had been used, as our histories assure us, with no moderate hand. The whole race of Saxon princes and nobles had been extirpated or disinherited, with few or no exceptions; nor were the numbers great who possessed land in the country of their fathers, even as proprietors of the second or of yet inferior classes. The royal policy had long been to weaken, by every means, legal or illegal, the strength of a part of the population which was justly considered as nourishing the most inveterate antipathy to their victor. All the monarchs of the Norman race had shown the most marked predilection for their Norman subjects; the laws of the chase, and many others, equally unknown to the milder and more free spirit of the Saxon constitution, had been fixed upon the necks of the subjugated inhabitants, to add weight, as it were, to the feudal chains with which they were loaded. At court, and in the castles of the great nobles, where the pomp and state of a court was emulated, Norman-French was the only language employed; in courts of law, the pleadings and judgments were delivered in the same tongue. In short, French was the language of honour, of chivalry, and even of justice, while the far more manly and expressive Anglo-Saxon was abandoned to the use of rustics and hinds, who knew no other. Still, however, the necessary intercourse between the lords of the soil, and those oppressed inferior beings by whom that soil was cultivated, occasioned the gradual formation of a dialect, compounded betwixt the French and the Anglo-Saxon, in which they could render themselves mutually intelligible to each other; and from this necessity arose by degrees the structure of our present English language, in which the speech of the victors and the vanquished have been so happily blended together; and which has since been so richly improved by importations from the classical languages, and from those spoken by the southern nations of Europe.

This state of things I have thought it necessary to premise for the information of the general reader, who might be apt to forget that, although no great historical events, such as war or insurrection, mark the existence of the Anglo-Saxon as a separate people subsequent to the reign of William the Second, yet the great national distinctions betwixt them and their conquerors, the recollection of what they had formerly been, and to what they were now reduced, continued, down to the reign of Edward the Third, to keep open the wounds which the Conquest had inflicted, and to maintain a line of separation betwixt the descendants of the victor Normans and the vanquished Saxons.

In this first person narrative excerpt, what is the speaker's subject? He is setting the scene for the story. The scene is England "toward the end of the reign of Richard I" when nobles had "exorbitant" power over the people. Such social conditions create a TONE that is serious. What is the speaker's TONE of VOICE regarding the subject? He does not refrain from connotative word choices that *editorialize*—revealing his opinion of the conditions in England at the time: outlaws described as "gallant," "depairing subjects," "oppression," "despis-

ing the feeble interference of the English Council of State," "reducing all around them to a state of vassalage" (the position of a vassal being subservient to the feudal lord). The resulting TONE? a condemnatory TONE toward the nobles. (Also, the speaker refers to the position of the independence of franklins, the inferior gentry, as "now unusually precarious"—giving the reader a sense of anticipation of trouble ahead.) This condemnatory TONE is extended to include the speaker's opinion of the Norman-French in racial terms. In this regard, the speaker describes, in a rather patriotic TONE, the Saxon constitution as "milder and more free spent" and the Anglo-Saxon tongue as "more manly and expressive," as compared to Norman-French.

How do CHARACTERS influence the TONE in this selection? At this point—the introduction of the narrative—no CHARACTERS (other than the first person narrator) have been introduced. This in itself is significant to setting the TONE of the story because the narrator has invested significant effort in establishing the TONE of the setting in its historical CONTEXT. This gives the reader reason to *anticipate* that the focus of the narrative is on, not exclusively the CHARACTERS, but also on how the events of the time and place (as they are historically significant) affect the lives of the CHARACTERS and how, in turn, the lives of the CHARACTERS may (or may fail to) affect historical events and outcomes. The narrator even directly states that he "thought it necessary" to inform readers of the historical CONTEXT of the "line of separation" between the Normans and Saxons.

In examining the style of the narrative, you will find that the writer uses very little figurative language, but relies heavily upon connotative word choices, particularly in the contrast of the TONE established in the first paragraph (the TONE projected by the description of a beautiful place of fabulous events) with the following paragraphs (the TONE projected by introduction of a blight imposed upon that beautiful place by hated conquerors).

Now read the following excerpt from *The Scarlet Letter* by Nathaniel Hawthorne:

The Grass Plot before the jail, in Prison Lane, on a certain summer morning, not less than two centuries ago, was occupied by a pretty large number of the inhabitants of Boston; all with their eyes intently fastened on the iron-clamped oaken door. Amongst any other population, or at a later period in the history of New England, the grim rigidity that petrified the bearded physiognomies of these good people would have augured some awful business in hand. It could have betokened nothing short of the anticipated execution of some noted culprit, on whom the sentence of a legal tribunal had but confirmed the verdict of public sentiment. But, in that early severity of the Puritan character, an inference of this kind could not so indubitably be drawn. It might be that a sluggish bond-servant, or an undutiful child, whom his parents had given over to the civil authority, was to be corrected at the whipping-post. It might be, that an Antinomian, a Quaker, or other heterodox religionist, was to be scourged out of the town, or an idle and vagrant Indian, whom the white man's fire-water had made riotous about the streets, was to be driven with stripes into the shadow of the forest. It might be, too, that a witch, like old Mistress Hibbins, the bitter-tempered widow of the magistrate, was to die upon the gallows. In either case, there was very much the same solemnity of demeanour on the part of the spectators; as befitted a people amongst whom religion and law were almost identical, and in whose character both were so thoroughly interfused, that the mildest and the severest acts of public discipline were alike made venerable and awful. Meagre, indeed, and cold, was the sympathy that a transgressor might look for, from such bystanders at the scaffold. On the other hand, a penalty which, in our days, would infer a degree of mocking infamy and ridicule, might then be invested with almost as stern a dignity as the punishment of death itself.

How does Hawthorne project the TONE in this dramatic scene? The use of structure is important to the TONE of this work. He reveals the CHARACTER of the people first by comparison and contrast: their morbid preoccupation with the jail in times past or by another people would have been precipitated by "the anticipated execution of some noted culprit," but these people—*these* people would be drawn to the jail for a glimpse of the punishment of someone for any of a number of much lesser crimes. The list of things they deem worthy of such punishment defines the values and CHARACTER of this group of people.

"Their eyes intently fastened on the iron-clamped oaken door" causes us to picture a silent, grim mob staring to see the criminal's fate. The list of crimes and the consequences that might have been the cause of the people's interest in the jail makes the reader picture horrific scenes of whippings, scourgings, and hangings. Use of such descriptive words as "Meagre, indeed, and cold, was the sympathy" and "the grim rigidity that petrified the bearded physiognomies" makes the reader picture stony faces inflicting pain in an unyielding

manner. What is Hawthorne's style in this excerpt? He *makes the reader picture the scene* using a blend of structural and connotative devices including CHARACTER revelation. The result is a distinctive TONE or atmosphere.

Which of the pairs of adjectives below identifies the TONE of the passage?

(A) Lively and sporting
(B) Solemn and entreating
(C) Resentful and challenging
(D) Ominous and foreboding
(E) Respectful and encouraging

(The correct answer is D.)

TONE IN POETRY

[W. B.] Yeats never had the remotest idea of taking care of himself. He would go all day without food unless someone remembered it for him, and in the same way would go on eating unless someone checked him. That first winter, a hard one, he would come to see me, [Katherine Tynan] five miles from Dublin, striding along over the snow-bound roads, a gaunt young figure, mouthing poetry, swinging his arms and gesticulating as he went. George Russell complained to me the other day that Willie Yeats had said somewhere of him, and printed it, that he used to walk about the streets of Dublin swinging his arms like a flail, unconscious of the alarm and bewilderment of the passers-by. It was Willie's own case. I remember how the big Dublin policemen used to eye him in those days, as though uncertain whether to 'run him in' or not. But, by and by, they used to say, 'Shure, 'tisn't mad he is, nor yet drink taken. 'Tis the poethry that's disturbin' his head,' and leave him alone.

Many of the same elements at work to establish the TONE in prose are also significant in its development in poetry: subject, the speaker's perspective, CHARACTERS, the USE OF LANGUAGE, and the setting. Although it can be effectively used to influence the TONE in prose, however, the one element that has significant impact on the TONE of a poem is the sound of the language (rhythm and rhyme).

One needs to look no further than the limerick to probe the effect of rhythm and rhyme on TONE. Whereas the MEANING is at the root of a limerick's humorous impact (its funny TONE), the impact of the rhythm and rhyme scheme on its TONE cannot be denied:

A YOUNG LADY OF SPAIN

There was a young lady of Spain
Who was dreadfully sick on a train,
   Not once, but again
   And again and again,
And again and again and again.

                              Anon.

THERE WAS A YOUNG FELLOW NAMED HALL

There was a young fellow named Hall,
Who fell in the spring in the fall;
   'Twould have been a sad thing
   If he'd died in the spring,
But he didn't—he died in the fall.

                              Anon.

Also look to nursery rhymes for TONES set by rhythm and rhyme. These musical rhythms and easy-to-complete rhymes create a wide range of TONES (ranging from comforting to scary) that captivate children's attention:

I HAD A LITTLE NUT TREE

I had a little nut tree,
   Nothing would it bear
But a silver nutmeg
   And a golden pear;

The King of Spain's daughter
   Came to visit me,
And all for the sake
   Of my little nut tree.

Notice the musical rhyme of "Sing a Song of Sixpence."

SING A SONG OF SIXPENCE

Sing a song of sixpence,
   A pocket full of rye;
Four and twenty blackbirds,
   Baked in a pie.

When the pie was opened,
   The birds began to sing;
Was not that a dainty dish
   To set before the king?

The king was in his counting-house,
   Counting out his money;

The queen was in the parlor,
   Eating bread and honey.

The maid was in the garden,
   Hanging out the clothes,
There came a little blackbird
   And snapped off her nose.

Now compare the amusing and lighthearted TONES projected in the nursery rhymes "I Had a Little Nut Tree" and "Sing a Song of Sixpence" with that of the following nursery rhyme:

THERE WAS A MAN

There was a man of double deed
Sowed his garden full of seed.
When the seed began to grow,
'Twas like a garden full of snow;
When the snow began to melt,
'Twas like a ship without a belt;
When the ship began to sail,
'Twas like a bird without a tail;
When the bird began to fly,
'Twas like an eagle in the sky;
When the sky began to roar,
'Twas like a lion at the door;
When the door began to crack,
'Twas like a stick across my back;
When my back began to smart,
'Twas like a penknife in my heart;
When my heart began to bleed,
'Twas death and death and death indeed.

The speaker in "There Was a Man" projects the TONE of a victim, but in "As I Went over the Water" the speaker has in today's slang what might be called "an attitude."

As I went over the water,
   The water went over me.
I saw two little blackbirds
   Sitting on a tree;
One called me a rascal,
   And one called me a thief,
I took up my little black stick
   And knocked out all their teeth.

TONE in poetry cannot be examined without addressing the verbal and musical aspects of poetry, whether the poem is sung or read aloud—its TONE color (called timbre in music).

In songs, ballads, and other styles of poetry set to music, the TONE is influenced greatly by the arrangement of the music itself. Examples include the emotional impact of rhythm and blues, the playful TONE of an English children's ballad like "The Fox Went Out on a Chilly Night," the agitated TONE in some rap music, the humorous TONE in country and western's "Tennessee Bird Walk," the hauntingly sad TONE of Patsy Cline singing "I Fall to Pieces," the serious TONE of a tragic opera, the inspiring TONE of a gospel song, and the reverent TONE of a hymn like "Amazing Grace."

Poems not intended to be sung, however, can also rely on verbal and musical elements to project a TONE. Rhythm and rhyme have been discussed at length in a previous section; the significance of rhythm, "the beat" of a poem to establishing the TONE of a poem can easily be seen. Rhyme, too, has obvious tonal qualities. You do need to recognize, though, that there is more to the "sound" of a poem as it relates to the TONE it projects than just rhythm and rhyme. TONE in a poem is also a product of *sound effects* (their uses and tonal qualities). Here are a few of the more commonly found sound effects:

1. Onomatopoeia

Although onomatopoeia does refer to words that imitate sounds: "buzz," "roar," "sweep," "hiss," "rattle," its significance to TONE is far more than this simple definition conveys. It also includes what some scholars refer to as *sound-symbolism* (although recent trends in literary analysis prefer the expression *icon* over *symbol* when referring to this aspect of written representation of sound). Regardless, onomatopoeia refers to words, lines, and passages whose sound, size, movement, and overall effect denote the sense or MEANING. The sounds work together to carry the MEANING. Tennyson's *The Princess* ("Come Down, O Maid"—1847):

**"...The moan of doves in immemorial elms,
And murmuring of innumerable bees."**

Notice how, in this first stanza of a poem written by Robert Burns in the late eighteenth century, the sounds work together to carry its MEANING and to establish the TONE:

AFTON WATER

**Flow gently, sweet Afton, among thy green braes,
Flow gently, I'll sing thee a song in thy praise;
My Mary's asleep by thy murmuring stream,
Flow gently, sweet Afton, disturb not her dream.**

by Robert Burns

The sounds here seem to have a "feel" about them that relates to the MEANING and results in a TONE.

2. Phonic echo devices

There are three major devices in which sound is repeated or "echoes":

- *Alliteration*—the initial consonant or consonant cluster sounds in stressed syllables are repeated (generally in successive or closely associated stressed syllables).

**Lo, how I hold mine arms abroad,
Thee to receive ready yspread!**

In its more extreme FORM, alliteration becomes the "tongue twister"—those consonant-packed lines that you may attempt to repeat "real fast" without "tripping" on your tongue: "Peter Piper picked a peck of pickled peppers" and "She sells sea-shells by the sea-shore." For a variety of reasons many people are attracted to alliteration, and examples can be found in many FORMS in addition to poetry. Alliteration is used by the broadcast media as an attention-getting device, by advertisers to help a slogan stay in the consumer's mind, and by writers in general to lighten material that might otherwise be dry or boring. For example, a newspaper might use "The Top Ten Terrific Tomatoes to Try This Time for Your Texas Territory" to head a variety and region chart for growing tomatoes in Texas. A jingle for a new car wash named "Curly Carl's" that is in competition with "Sudsy Sam" might be

**Curly Curl can keep your car,
Scrubbed, sparkling like a star.
No scuffs, no scum, no scrapes, no stratches,
So Sudsy Sam still tries to match us.**

Once again, the sounds have a "feel" that relates to the MEANING and results in a TONE.

Here is a stanza from John Skelton's "Lullay, Lullay, Like a Child" (written sometime in the late 1400s or early 1500s), a poem rich in alliteration:

My darling dear, my daisy floure,
   Let me, quod he, lie in your lap.
Lie still, quod she, my paramoure,
   Lie still hardlie, and take a nap.
   His head was heavy, such was his hap.
All drowsy dreaming, drowned in sleep.
That of his love he took no keep,
   With hey lullay, lullay, like a child,
   Thou sleep'st too long, thou art beguiled.

- *Assonance*—the same (or similar) vowel sounds are repeated in nearby words (usually in stressed syllables). Unlike rhyme, which has similarity of both vowel and final consonant sounds (for example, "book" and "took"), assonance repeats only the vowel sounds and ends with different consonant sounds. Notice the use of elements of rhyme, alliteration ("w"), and assonance in this anonymous ballad:

HELEN OF KIRCONNELL

I wish I were where Helen lies,
Night and day on me she cries;
O that I were where Helen lies
   On fair Kirconnell lea!

"I" and "night" both contain the long *i* sound. This assonance is emphasized in the rhyme of "lies" with "cries." You also may find assonance a popular substitution for end rhyme, especially in the ballad FORM:

His hounds they lie downe at his *feete*,
So well they can their master *keepe*.

- *Consonance*—final consonant sounds of stressed syllables are repeated while the preceding vowels are different. Consonance is often used in conjunction with alliteration (as in *reader* and *rider*); however, initial alliteration is not always a factor (as in *learn, torn*). The aural appeal can be heard in George

Wither's use of consonance in the last stanza of "Shall I Wasting in Despair" in which *d, r, v, l,* and *t* are repeated:

Great, or good, or kind, or fair,
I will ne'er the more despair,
If she love me, this believe,
I will die, ere she shall grieve.
If she slight me when I woo,
I can scorn, and let her go.
      For, if she be not for me,
      What care I for whom she be?

(Note also that the basis for "eye rhyme" often is consonance: *gone, stone.*)

3. Cacophony and dissonance

These two sound effects can be examined in terms of comparison and contrast. Both terms refer to harshness of sounds that produce an unpleasant or unsettling TONE. A sound has dissonance when it is harsh, inharmonious, or discordant with the sounds and rhythm that surround it. A sound has cacophony when it is simply harsh in and of itself, regardless of the sounds and rhythms that surround it. Cacophony is often an accident; dissonance, on the other hand (discordance with surrounding sounds and rhythms), can be very deliberate.

Note the conscious use of dissonance in "Broken-Down Car":

A budget bruised, bent blistered broken relic needin' fixin'.
Dented dimpled dinges from fender benders galore—grief
      over grime and time.

Courage: There goes cash on four tires.
Frame and bumpers lookin' good—not me still under hood.

Clank…grind…bang…grime grating against metal and skin.
Squirting oil and squirming torso—pain.

Start and stop motor again—not a gain, sorry mess
Headin' for the Junk-heap next, I guess!

                                    by C. Myers-Shaffer

Cacophony, harsh sounds (words) that are unpleasant in and of themselves, can result from many things, such as too many unvoiced plosives in a poem. Some poets feel that overuse of *s* or *sh* sounds have a cacophonic effect and consequently try to avoid them.

4. Euphony

Euphony refers to sounds that are pleasing and easy to pronounce, producing a pleasant TONE. Sounds exhibiting euphony (the opposite of cacophony) generally contain more vowel sounds (thought to have more "sonority" or resonance than consonants and to cause more vibration or "voicing" sounds) and lean toward the liquids, nasals, and semivowels (*l, m, n, r, v, w*), with the voiced consonants being heard as "softer" (*b, d, g, v, z*) and the unvoiced consonants as "harsher" (*p, t, k, f, s*). Poetry exhibiting euphony tends also to avoid difficult-to-pronounce sound combinations and to stress sound patterns that include repetitions.

In determining the euphony of a selection, its sense of a pleasing TONE, do not overlook the part MEANING sometimes contributes to that sense of pleasantness. One poem that many consider "pleasant" to the tongue and ear is "The Raven," although the TONE is very disquieting.

TONE IN DRAMA

As with poetry, drama shares with prose (particularly with the narrative FORMS) many elements that help to set the TONE, such as setting, USE OF LANGUAGE, and CHARACTER revelation. But drama has one unique feature that can definitely affect the TONE—both of the individual elements of the play and of the play as a whole: drama is meant to be acted on a stage by players. As a result, the playwright can include stage directions instructing the actors concerning facial expressions, gesture, and TONE of VOICE to use for delivery of the lines of dialogue. Even if the viewer misses the MEANING of the words, he or she can still gain a sense of their TONE by hearing the way they are *actually spoken*. Add to this that the viewer does not need to imagine the setting; the stage can be set up to replicate (to varying degrees) the setting so that he or she can actually *see* the place (or at the very least suggestions of the place). The result? A sense of TONE based on the audience's physical, intellectual, and emotional senses.

QUESTIONS TO APPLY YOUR LEARNING

As you practice reading literary selections, ask these questions to help you identify and understand TONE:

1. Who is the speaker?
2. What is the TONE (of VOICE) of the speaker in the entire work?
3. Can the TONE (of VOICE) of the author be identified? If so, does it differ from the TONE (of VOICE) of the speaker?
4. With what TONE (of VOICE) does each of the CHARACTERS address one another?
5. How does the USE OF LANGUAGE and/or MEANING of the language in CONTEXT contribute to the TONE?
6. Do the rhythm, rhyme, and other sound effects contribute to the TONE in this work?
7. How does the setting contribute to the TONE in this work? What, if applicable, is the work's atmosphere?
8. How does the writer's style contribute to the TONE of this work?

ADDITIONAL HELPFUL POINTS TO REMEMBER

- Become familiar with descriptive adjectives that relate to TONE of VOICE (both of a speaker's TONE and of the TONE of a work). A list of such words might include:

adulatory	egotistical	morose
amatory	embittered	ominous
amorous	enamored	polemic
antagonistic	flirtatious	querulous
appreciative	forbearant	remorseful
belligerent	indulgent	saponaceous
cajoling	infatuated	sardonic
choleric	inhospitable	scandalous
compassionate	insidious	scurrilous
contentious	irritable	surly
coquettish	magnanimous	tranquil
defamatory	malicious	unctuous
depreciatory	menacing	
dyspeptic	minatory	

- Notice that many of the words that describe the TONE of a work or the TONE of VOICE a speaker uses also describe the style and/or the level of diction used. For example, *concise* can refer to the TONE, the style, the syntax, and the diction, with each usage looking at the words of the selection from a slightly different perspective.
- Be sure to understand clearly the perspective from which the question concerning TONE is being asked. For example, it might ask:

  1. The TONE of the speaker and/or author
  2. The TONE of the selection (as a whole)
  3. The TONE of one of the CHARACTERS
  4. The TONE of a specific word, phrase, sentence, or portion of the passage
  5. What conclusion or judgment should be made regarding something in the passage *based on the speaker's* TONE
  6. What role TONE plays in the MEANING of the selection
  7. How a change in TONE might change the MEANING of the selection

LITERARY ELEMENT NUMBER FIVE: CHARACTER

A legendary Burmese potter became jealous of the prosperity of a washerman. Determined to ruin him, the potter induced the king to issue an order requiring the man to wash one of his black elephants white. The washerman replied that according to the rules of his vocation he would need a vessel large enough to hold the elephant, whereupon the king commanded the jealous potter to provide one. Though carefully fashioned, it crumbled to pieces beneath the weight of the giant beast. He made many more vessels, but each was crushed in the same way. Eventually the potter was ruined by the very scheme he had devised to defame the man he envied.

(from *Our Daily Times with God*, 1988)

A CHARACTER is a person (or a being given the characteristics of a person) who appears in, acts and/or speaks in, narrates, or is referred to in a literary work. **Characterization** is the methods or combinations of methods used to portray that person or being.

Distinctive Traits

The basis for characterization is the revelation of the CHARACTER'S *identifying traits,* the mental and ethical (including moral) traits (qualities or characteristics) of the individual. CHARACTER traits, their definitions, the involvement of implied moral judgment, and identification of what is their source (and what elements work together to shape a person's "CHARACTER") is the subject of debate among cultural psychologists and others who research the subject.

Some view CHARACTER as a product of heredity; others see it as a product of environment. Which is the predominant factor in CHARACTER development is arguable and interesting to keep in mind when reading literary works in which the author, through various literary means, reveals his or her bias on the subject in the course of presenting CHARACTERS in the work. How readers and writers view CHARACTER traits (as good or bad, as desirable or undesirable) is oftentimes a result of their home environments and of the cultures in which they live. The literary works that are the focus of the SAT II: Literature Subject Test are taken from English and American literature: In England and the United States, traditionally, CHARACTER and traits of CHARACTER are defined in terms that are inherent in the Judeo-Christian tradition.

How do you define CHARACTER traits? A person's temperament, disposition, and distinctive personal and social traits can be viewed as a function of his or her (1) attitudes, (2) emotional states, (3) response mechanisms, and (4) intrinsic values. All these elements combine to make an individual's personality. Within each of these areas is a continuum of traits that range (based on cultural and family traditions as well as on personal perceptions) between two extremes. Although this treatment of the subject is by no means exhaustive, here are a few considerations to be made regarding each area:

1. Attitudes

A CHARACTER'S attitudes in terms of CHARACTER are his or her mental positions or feelings with regard to self, other people, objects, or a subject. Conversation often includes talk about a person's attitude as being "good" or "bad" (as in "My son has such a bad attitude"), as being "productive" or "unproductive," as being "responsive" or "unresponsive," and the list goes on. Evidently, there are many degrees of productivity and responsiveness; however, people frequently tend to make generalizations that polarize their perceptions of a person's attitude to either the "positive" or the "negative."

When test questions ask you to identify a CHARACTER'S:

viewpoint	feeling	bearing
opinion	conclusion	position
posture	mien	assumption
presumption	impression	judgment
demeanor	notion	standpoint
stance	idea	appearance
sentiment	pose	

(to name a few), they may be asking you to identify his or her attitude.

How can an attitude be described? Some possibilities include:

positive (attitudes):	negative (attitudes):
productive	unproductive
responsive	unresponsive
good	bad
kind	unkind
soft	firm
helpful	helpless
lenient	strict
inspired	uninspired
godly	irreverent
constructive	destructive
forgiving	unforgiving
happy	sad

The discussion of attitudes as they relate to CHARACTER also includes those attitudes that are not individual in nature. A group of people (such as a family or community), a nation, or a literary work can have a prevailing attitude. Sometimes this is referred to as the "climate"—the political climate might be referred to as liberal or conservative; the intellectual climate might be referred to as decaying; the moral climate as strict; the climate of opinion as "going against" a particular stance; the climate of the stock market as "bullish." A prevailing attitude or "climate" can also sometimes be identified in a literary work. Of course, the groups of CHARACTERS within the work itself may also project a "climate" in and of itself—a prevailing attitude. When this prevailing attitude is seen consistently throughout the works of a particular writer, you might attribute this as part of his or her style. Sometimes the literary climate will produce groups of writers who share a prevailing attitude in their works, thus giving birth to a movement or tradition. An example might be the "tradition of black humor" that includes works by Kurt Vonnegut, Thomas Pynchon, and playwright Harold Pinter—works that in comically dealing with grotesque, horrid situations project attitudes (and as a result TONE) that are both angry and bitter.

2. Emotions

The emotions of a CHARACTER are his or her intense feelings. These emotions may include states of excitement, states of emotional attachment or dissociation, states of stability or instability, states of emotional insulation, states of emotionalism, and degrees of emotional appeal.

Here are some clues to a CHARACTER'S emotional state:

- References to his or her sentiments, impressions, experiences, or a "deep sense" concerning something might reflect the CHARACTER'S emotional feelings.
- References to degrees of stimulation and exhilaration might reflect his or her state of excitement.
- References to a CHARACTER'S (negative or positive) transference of feelings, identification with others (individuals or groups), introjection or projection might reflect his or her state of attachment; and references to schizophrenia, multiple personalities, split personalities, double or dual personalities, personality disorganization, disconnection, and personality disintegration might relate to the CHARACTER'S state of dissociation.
- References to his or her feelings of inferiority, inadequacy, moral deficiency, emotional immaturity, lability, or pathological mendacity might reflect the CHARACTER'S lack of stability—a state of instability.
- References to signs of escapism (flight and withdrawal), isolation, defense mechanisms, fantasy (dreamlike thinking), sublimation, rationalization, and negativism might reflect a CHARACTER'S state of emotional insulation.
- References to anxiety, hysteria, melancholia, depression, preoccupation, apathy, lethargy, stupor, euphoria, indifference, detachment, or elation might reflect his or her state of emotionalism.
- References to the CHARACTER'S nature in terms of his or her demonstrativeness, sensationalism, or sense of the dramatic (melodrama) might influence the perception for the reader (or self-perception) of that CHARACTER'S degree of emotional appeal.

Of course, certain attention must be paid to psychologically based inferences and direct characterizations that reflect a CHARACTER'S defects in the areas of personality (including pathological personality types, such as maladjusted, inferior, perverse, antisocial, sociopathic, psychotic, alcoholic, masochistic, and so forth) and social adjustment (assaultive reactions and antisocialism, among others). In order to fully appreciate and to adequately identify the emotional state(s) of a literary CHARACTER, then, sometimes requires some familiarity with symptoms of neuroses (such as traumatic, anxiety, obsessive-compulsive, occupational, fright, phobic), psychosomatic disorders (such as bulimia), disturbances in emotions (such as anxiety or hysteria), thoughts (such as delusions or mental blocks), and psychomotor disorders (such as convulsions or twitching), and mental states such as amnesia, somnambulism, and trances.

Fundamental, however, to the examination of a CHARACTER'S emotions is first the degree to which the individual exhibits feelings or lack of feelings. Also, of great importance to distinguishing CHARACTER traits is to identify the role of hope—and of hopelessness—in that CHARACTER'S perspective of life.

Sometimes a CHARACTER has emotions that are reflected in almost all he or she says, does, or thinks. But these emotions, as with attitudes, can polarize to the "positive" or to the "negative." Generally, the following emotions are regarded as "positive" because they are rooted in feelings:

affection	warmheartedness	vehemence
passion	sentiment	gusto
sensitivity	fervor	zeal
sympathy	ardor	responsiveness
tenderness	cordiality	demonstrativeness

But even "positives" can be "too much":

mawkishness	insipidity
sentimentality	melodrama
"mush"	emotionalism
"wearing one's heart on one's sleeve"	

At the other extreme are those emotions connotatively regarded as "negative" because of their lack of feeling:

soullessness	callousness
emotionlessness	hardness
heartlessness	hardheartedness
frigidity	obduracy
cold-heartedness	imperviousness
cold-bloodedness	apathy
untouchability	listlessness
unresponsiveness	lethargy
unimpressionability	indifference

The degree to which these emotions (the emotions that stem from feelings or from the lack of feelings) can be viewed as "positive" or "negative," however, depends greatly on CONTEXT.

The role of hope and of its opposite, hopelessness, on CHARACTER development and revelation should not be underestimated. Hope is a powerful motivating force as seen in last-minute plays that win the championship game or in acts of heroism that save lives or win wars; and being in a state of hope-lessness can be equally powerful, as seen in lives that have lost meaning, suicides, and unfulfilled dreams.

What words are connotative of a CHARACTER'S sense of hope?

expectation	reliance	assurance
trust	assumption	dreams
confidence	optimism	faith

Are all hopes justified? Is the CHARACTER deluding himself or herself? Consider such words as:

bubble	fool's paradise	pipe dream

Words connotative of hopelessness:

impossibility	disappointment	cynical
despair	defeated	gloominess
desperation	pessimistic	irrevocability
despondent	irretrievable	incorrigible
forlorn	incurable	disconsolate

Sometimes understanding the role of hope in a CHARACTER'S life is very important to understanding his or her role in the work.

Another term you may encounter when examining a CHARACTER'S emotional state is *disposition.* "Emotional state" is connotative of that person's feelings *at a particular time*—his or her emotional state may be happy today, unhappy tomorrow. In contrast, a CHARACTER'S disposition is connotative of his or her feelings as well as *natural attitudes toward life* that are somewhat consistent throughout his or her life. Although we may say that George, for example, might be unhappy today, he generally has a "happy disposition," outlook on life, or temperament.

3. Response mechanisms

How does the CHARACTER respond physically and emotionally to life? CHARACTER traits that are revealed by the CHARACTER'S response to the world about him or her can, as with attitudes and emotions, be discussed by examining the extremes.

- To what degree does the CHARACTER exhibit signs of stress when put under pressure? These CHARACTER traits include, for example, agitation, perturbation, trepidation fury, frenzy, excitation, exhilaration, or explosion. In contrast, the CHARACTER might react with dispassion, even-temperedness, impassiveness, nonchalance, composure, serenity, self-confidence, offhandedness, placidity, or staidness.

- How nervous does the CHARACTER become? A nervous CHARACTER has agitation or, trepidation, is unnerved, unstrung, demoralized, or shaken. In the opposite case the CHARACTER is steady, calm, unflinching, steel-nerved, or relaxed.
- Is the CHARACTER patient or impatient? Tolerant or intolerant? Resigned or anxious?

Other CHARACTER traits that are revealed by a CHARACTER'S response mechanisms include:

honest (dishonest)	rejoicing (lamenting)
fight (flight)	happy (sad)
brave (cowardly)	cheerful (solemn)
courageous (fearful)	contented (discontented)
wise (foolish)	social (unsocial)
faithful (unfaithful)	hospitable (inhospitable)
rash (cautious)	companionable (secluded)
pleasant (unpleasant)	courteous (discourteous)
witty (dull)	forgiving (unforgiving,
humorous (boring)	revengeful, retaliatory)
pitying (pitiless)	giving (taking, envious,
regretful (glad)	jealous, resentful)

4. Intrinsic values

CHARACTER traits can also arise from examining the CHARACTER'S intrinsic values: those traits that result from the value judgments made in the heart of the person—what is really important (or not important) to him or her. At their core are fundamental concepts: home, family, country, religion, fellowman, self, and other value-type concepts.

How the reader perceives the CHARACTER traits that are part of the CHARACTER'S intrinsic values is largely a product of the attitudes, emotions, and response mechanisms the character has exhibited in word and deed within the selection. These perceptions can lead to generalizations about the person, based on his or her attitudes, emotions, and response mechanisms exhibited; and these generalizations then become judgments of "what kind of person he or she is." Are these generalizations, based on those CHARACTER traits, always accurate statements of that person's intrinsic values? The appropriateness of these conclusions is debatable, but nonetheless, these conclusions are often reached.

Based on the CHARACTER traits revealed by a CHARACTER'S attitudes, emotions, and response mechanisms in a literary selection, the reader may conclude that the CHARACTER is trustworthy, a criminal, a proud man, a humble boy, a fastidious girl, an honorable woman, a shallow person, a devil—or a saint. Once the reader has generalized the exhibited traits of CHARACTER to mean that the person is "honorable" or "moral" or "shallow," the reader then tends to assume that this person will most likely exhibit the characteristics of "honor" or of "morality" or of "shallowness" in most situations because, the reader assumes, these characteristics arise from the person's intrinsic value system.

METHODS OF CHARACTERIZATION

SAMUEL JOHNSON

Mrs. Digby told me that when she lived in London with her sister Mrs. Brooke, they were, every now and then, honoured by the visits of Dr. Samuel Johnson. He called on them one day, soon after the publication of his immortal dictionary. The two ladies paid him due compliments on the occasion. Among other topics of praise, they very much commended the omission of all naughty words. 'What! my dears! then you have been looking for them?' said the moralist. The ladies, confused at being caught, dropped the subject of the dictionary.

As previously discussed, a CHARACTER is a person (or a being given the characteristics of a person) who appears in, acts and/or speaks in, narrates, or is referred to in a literary work. Oftentimes the CHARACTERS in a work can be identified by the role they play in relation to the story:

Hero—the leading male CHARACTER who exhibits superior qualities

Heroine—the leading female CHARACTER who exhibits superior qualities

Superhero(ine)—a larger-than-life hero(ine), usually supernatural

Villain(ess)—a CHARACTER who is often characterized as evil and is in opposition to the hero(ine)

Antihero(ine)—a hero(ine) who is more ordinary than the traditional hero(ine)

Protagonist—the hero(ine)

Antagonist—the villain(ess)

These seven terms are commonly used when talking about the chief CHARACTERS in a literary work. The following are other terms, however, with which you should be familiar:

Flat CHARACTER: A flat CHARACTER is only two-dimensional, described without the kind of details you would need to see him or her as an individual. These roles are often played by "extras" in movie and television productions, although sometimes named stars will assume these roles as "cameo" spots.

Round CHARACTER: In extreme contrast to the flat CHARACTER, the round CHARACTER is three-dimensional, complex, as lifelike as the literary medium allows. Unlike the flat CHARACTER, the round CHARACTER is complex and changes or grows in the course of the story. (Naturally, shades of "flatness" or "roundness" abound along the continuum between these two extremes, with the plot and the intent of the writer largely dictating the degree to which a CHARACTER is developed. Generally, the main CHARACTERS are "round.")

Stock CHARACTER: A conventional stereotype CHARACTER, the stock CHARACTER, is expected to appear in certain literary FORMS, such as the "prince charming" in fairy tales. A stock CHARACTER is one that is frequently used in literary traditions, but who does not necessarily represent a particular class or group.

Type CHARACTER: A type CHARACTER embodies or exhibits the characteristics of a particular class or group of people. A type CHARACTER may be very individualized and unpredictable in personality and action, and still be representative of the class or group to which he or she belongs. Television situation comedies, as well as more serious shows, abound with type CHARACTERS: Dr. Quinn in *Dr. Quinn, Medicine Woman* is a type who represents the professional women who were forerunners of the twentieth-century women's movements; Corky on *Murphy Brown* represents women raised after stereotypical models of women's roles (such as being a beauty contest queen) but who are attempting success in less traditional, more professional roles; the six children in *Step by Step* are types of children who are attempting to adjust to their parents' remarriage and to their own assimilation into a "blended" family.

Stereotype CHARACTER: Unlike the type CHARACTER, the stereotype is predictable, one who is repeated without variation and who lacks originality: the "tough" woman who (behind her crusty exterior) is softhearted; the leading man who is "tall, dark, and handsome"; the "absent-minded" professor. The stock CHARACTER is a stereotype that arises from certain literary conventions, but stereotypes may also be the product of political and social trends and national mores, as well.

Look for a moment at the nation's perception of a "hero." A hero is traditionally portrayed as someone who is honorable and brave. Writers of certain literary FORMS have for many years characterized high-ranking military and political leaders (princes, kings, knights, generals, soldiers, and presidents) as men of honor and respect, willing to sacrifice self for country. They became heroes who were given stereotypical characteristics: tall, handsome, brave, strong, and brilliant military strategists and ingenious survivalists whether in jungles or deserts. Even those who were not-so-handsome or not-so-tall would still, under fire, exhibit the stereotypical characteristics of a hero. Such stereotypes depend upon a perception of military and political leaders as true heroes worthy of the honor and respect they receive.

Now that you have an overview of CHARACTER traits, and a few of the basic labels by which CHARACTERS are identified, you can examine the *techniques* that a writer can use to present a CHARACTER and to reveal his or her CHARACTER traits and/or the *ethos* or CHARACTER (emotions), of either the writer or speaker.

Characterization—CHARACTER development in a story—can be accomplished through many different methods or techniques:

1. Disclosure of CHARACTER through stereotyping

This method of characterization involves identifying a CHARACTER with a group about which you have certain cultural assumptions (stereotypes). If a CHARACTER is, as an illustration, a West Texas cowboy who is visiting Boston for the first time, the reader might make certain assumptions concerning his dress, speech, and CHARACTER traits that are based on stereotypical conceptions of what the reader "thinks" a West Texas cowboy is like and of how he or she "thinks" he would manage in Boston. Obviously, this method of characterization can work for—or counter to—the purpose of the writer.

2. *Disclosure of CHARACTER through exposition*

Sometimes the author or speaker will simply tell the reader about the CHARACTER. These explanatory messages from the author or speaker might include descriptions of the person's background, motivating forces, personality traits, relationships, and physical characteristics. Generally, a person tends to accept these characterizations as truthful and accurate until proven to be otherwise by the CHARACTER'S own words, revealed thoughts, and actions.

An example of characterization through exposition can be seen in these few paragraphs taken from the early nineteenth-century American short story "Rip Van Winkle" by Washington Irving:

In that same village, and in one of these very houses (which, to tell the precise truth, was sadly time-worn and weather-beaten), there lived, many years since, while the country was yet a province of Great Britain, a simple, good-natured fellow, of the name of Rip Van Winkle. He was a descendant of the Van Winkles who figured so gallantly in the chivalrous days of Peter Stuyvesant, and accompanied him to the siege of Fort Christina. He inherited, however, but little of the martial character of his ancestors. I have observed that he was a simple, good-natured man; he was, moreover, a kind neighbor, and an obedient, hen-pecked husband. Indeed, to the latter circumstance might be owing that meekness of spirit which gained him such universal popularity; for those men are most apt to be obsequious and conciliating abroad, who are under the discipline of shrews at home. Their tempers, doubtless, are rendered pliant and malleable in the fiery furnace of domestic tribulation; and a curtain-lecture is worth all the sermons in the world for teaching the virtues of patience and long-suffering. A termagant wife may, therefore, in some respects, be considered a tolerable blessing; and if so, Rip Van Winkle was thrice blessed.

Certain it is, that he was a great favorite among all the good wives of the village, who, as usual with the amiable sex, took his part in all family squabbles; and never failed, whenever they talked those matters over in their evening gossipings, to lay all the blame on Dame Van Winkle. The children of the village, too, would shout with joy whenever he approached. He assisted at their sports, made their playthings, taught them to fly kites and shoot marbles, and told them long stories of ghosts, witches, and Indians. Whenever he went dodging about the village, he was surrounded by a troop of them, hanging on his skirts, clambering on his back, and playing a thousand tricks on him with impunity; and not a dog would bark at him throughout the neighborhood.

The great error in Rip's composition was an insuperable aversion to all kinds of profitable labor. It could not be from the want of assiduity or perseverance; for he would sit on a wet rock, with a rod as long and heavy as a Tartar's lance, and fish all day without a murmur, even though he should not be encouraged by a single nibble. He would carry a fowling-piece on his shoulder for hours together, trudging through woods and swamps, and up hill and down dale, to shoot a few squirrels or wild pigeons. He would never refuse to assist a neighbor even in the roughest toil, and was a foremost man at all country frolics for husking Indian corn, or building stone fences; the women of the village, too, used to employ him to run their errands, and to do such little odd jobs as their less obliging husbands would not do for them. In a word, Rip was ready to attend to anybody's business but his own; but as to doing family duty, and keeping his farm in order, he found it impossible.

A question concerning Rip's CHARACTER might read:

What irony does the speaker use to characterize Rip Van Winkle?

(A) That Rip's wife was especially nagging
(B) That children liked Rip
(C) That Rip would work for others but not for his own family
(D) That Rip played games
(E) That Rip had a kind nature and conciliatory disposition

(The correct answer is C.)

Vocabulary check: What do the CHARACTER-revealing words "obsequious" and "termagant" mean in the first paragraph? Once again, a knowledge of word MEANINGS is important to understanding characterization within a story.

At about the same time Irving was writing in America, Jane Austen (a writer of the Romantic Period) was in England writing this characterization in her novel of manners, *Persuasion:*

Vanity was the beginning and the end of Sir Walter Elliot's character; vanity of person and of situation. He had been remarkably handsome in his youth; and, at fifty-four, was still a very fine man. Few women could think more of their personal appearance than he did; nor could the valet of any new made lord be more delighted with the place he held in society. He considered the blessing of beauty as inferior only to the blessing of a baronetcy; and the Sir Walter Elliot, who united these gifts, was the constant object of his warmest respect and devotion.

His good looks and his rank had one fair claim on his attachment; since to them he must have owed a wife of very superior character to any thing deserved by his own. Lady Elliot had been an excellent woman, sensible and amiable; whose judgement and conduct, if they might be pardoned the youthful infatuation which made her Lady Elliot, had never required indulgence afterwards.—She had humoured, or softened, or concealed his failings, and promoted his real respectability for seventeen years; and though not the very happiest being in the world herself, had found enough in her duties, her friends, and her children, to attach her to life, and make it no matter of indifference to her when she was called on to quit them.—Three girls, the two eldest sixteen and fourteen, was an awful legacy for a mother to bequeath; an awful charge rather, to confide to the authority and guidance of a conceited, silly father. She had, however, one very intimate friend, a sensible, deserving woman, who had been brought, by strong attachment to herself, to settle close by her, in the village of Kellynch; and on her kindness and advice, Lady Elliot mainly relied for the best help and maintenance of the good principles and instruction which she had been anxiously giving her daughters.

Lady Elliot's CHARACTER is largely

(A) silly
(B) infatuated
(C) disrespectful
(D) vain
(E) pragmatic

(The correct answer is E.)

3. Disclosure of CHARACTER through the CHARACTER'S actions

What does the CHARACTER do at times of crisis? How does he or she react to conflict? To everyday situations? To extraordinary situations? A significant element to consider when examining characterization by actions of a CHARACTER is the tendency toward being judgmental of the CHARACTER based on what the reader thinks he or she would do in like circumstances. The value of such moral and ethical judgments in better understanding the CHARACTER is yet another area of debate. Such excursions into the area of "If I were in this situation I would…" can, however, provide interesting grounds for plot analysis and self-examination.

Before making a value judgment based on a generalization concerning his or her CHARACTER (such as "He is destructive" or "She is too lenient"), examine the person's actions to try to identify what

individual CHARACTER traits are revealed by those actions (such as "He exhibited anger and frustration when he destroyed the statue" or "She exhibited kindness, but also seemed intimidated when she did not punish her daughter for taking the car without permission"). Hasty generalizations that do not take into account CONTEXT, cause-and-effect relationships, and the individual personality traits that blend together within an action can lead to faulty conclusions concerning the CHARACTER.

You can, however, learn a great deal about a CHARACTER from the way in which he or she reacts in different circumstances and situations. In this excerpt from Jane Austen's *Persuasion,* what elements of Mary's CHARACTER are revealed by the way that she treats Anne? What do Mary's actions reveal about her personality?

Something occurred, however, to give her a different duty. Mary, often a little unwell, and always thinking a great deal of her own complaints, and always in the habit of claiming Anne when any thing was the matter, was indisposed; and foreseeing that she should not have a day's health all the autumn, entreated, or rather required her, for it was hardly entreaty, to come to Uppercross Cottage, and bear her company as long as she should want her, instead of going to Bath.

4. Disclosure of CHARACTER through the CHARACTER'S words

You also can deduce a great deal about a CHARACTER'S personality from his or her own words. But as with the other elements of characterization, do not overlook the significance of CONTEXT and motivation when examining a CHARACTER'S words. You need to address such questions as:

• To whom is he or she speaking?
• Are his or her words true reflections of how the CHARACTER feels or thinks?
• Is there any indication that he or she is putting forth a false CHARACTER?
• What motivation might the CHARACTER have for deception?

In addition, look for unintentional revelation of CHARACTER. Sometimes a CHARACTER will reveal significant hidden aspects of his or her personality from words spoken in an unguarded moment or during a heated argument.

Here is a conversation that takes place in *Persuasion.* What do Anne, Mary, and Lady Russell unintentionally reveal about themselves in this exchange? Remember that this revelation may not be unintentional on the part of the writer.

'Oh! he talks of you,' cried Charles, 'in such terms,'—Mary interrupted him. 'I declare, Charles, I never heard him mention Anne twice all the time I was there. I declare, Anne, he never talks of you at all.'

'No,' admitted Charles, 'I do not know that he ever does, in a general way—but however, it is a very clear thing that he admires you exceedingly.—His head is full of some books that he is reading upon your recommendation, and he wants to talk to you about them; he has found out something or other in one of them which he thinks—Oh! I cannot pretend to remember it, but it was something very fine—I overheard him telling Henrietta all about it—and then "Miss Elliot" was spoken of in the highest terms!—No Mary, I declare it was so, I heard it myself, and you were in the other room.— "Elegance, sweetness, beauty," Oh! there was no end of Miss Elliot's charms.'

'And I am sure,' cried Mary warmly, 'it was very little to his credit, if he did. Miss Harville only died last June. Such a heart is very little worth having; is it, Lady Russell? I am sure you will agree with me.'

'I must see Captain Benwick before I decide,' said Lady Russell, smiling.

'And that you are very likely to do very soon, I can tell you, ma'am,' said Charles. 'Though he had not nerves for coming away with us and setting off again afterwards to pay a formal visit here, he will make his way over to Kellynch one day by himself, you may depend on it. I told him the distance and the road, and I told him of the church's being so very well worth seeing, for as he has a taste for those sort of things, I thought that would be a good excuse, and he listened with all his understanding and soul; and I am sure from his manner that you will have him calling here soon. So, I give you notice, Lady Russell.'

'Any acquaintance of Anne's will always be welcome to me,' was Lady Russell's kind answer.

'Oh! as to being Anne's acquaintance,' said Mary, 'I think he is rather my acquaintance, for I have been seeing him every day this last fortnight.'

'Well, as your joint acquaintance, then, I shall be very happy to see Captain Benwick.'

'You will not find any thing very agreeable in him, I assure you, ma'am. He is one of the dullest young men that ever lived. He has walked with me, sometimes, from one end of the sands to the other, without saying a word. He is not at all a well-bred young man. I am sure you will not like him.'

'There we differ, Mary,' said Anne. 'I think Lady Russell would like him. I think she would be so much pleased with his mind, that she would very soon see no deficiency in his manner.'

'So do I, Anne,' said Charles. "I am sure Lady Russell would like him. He is just Lady Russell's sort. Give him a book, and he will read all day long.'

'Yes, that he will!' exclaimed Mary, tauntingly. 'He will sit poring over his book, and not know when a person speaks to him, or when one drops one's scissors, or any thing that happens. Do you think Lady Russell would like that?'

Lady Russell could not help laughing. 'Upon my word,' said she, 'I should not have supposed that my opinion of any one could have admitted of such difference of conjecture, steady and matter of fact as I may call myself. I have really a curiosity to see the person who can give occasion to such directly opposite notions. I wish he may be induced to call here. And when he does, Mary, you may depend upon hearing my opinion; but I am determined not to judge him before-hand.'

'You will not like him, I will answer for it.'

What role does Charles play in this passage? How would you describe his CHARACTER?

5. *Disclosure of CHARACTER through the CHARACTER'S thoughts*

A CHARACTER'S own thoughts (through such devices as interior monologue and stream of consciousness) can be a rich source for insight into motivation and CHARACTER; however, be alert for elements of self-delusion on the part of the CHARACTER. Also, be aware of the role that *perception* plays in thought. A CHARACTER'S perception includes:

- Awareness of the environment through his or her physical senses
- Realizations of events, activities, and conversations
- Insight into the deeper meanings of the words and events that occur
- Comprehension of the significance of these words and events

A CHARACTER'S thoughts can be penetrating, discerning, and discriminating or they can be shallow, undiscerning, and indiscriminating.

In the CONTEXT of the situation, is the person sagacious and shrewd? Sensible? Sensitive? Knowing? Discriminative? Or is his or her thinking shallow? Insincere? Insensitive? Indiscriminative?

Again, examine an excerpt from *Persuasion*. What does Anne reveal about herself with her thoughts?

Captain Benwick had some time ago been first lieutenant of the Laconia, and the account which Captain Wentworth had given of him, on his return from Lyme before; his warm praise of him as an excellent young man and an officer, whom he had always valued highly, which must have stamped him well in the esteem of every listener, had been followed by a little history of his private life, which rendered him perfectly interesting in the eyes of all the ladies. He had been engaged to Captain Harville's sister, and was now mourning her loss. They had been a year or two waiting for fortune and promotion. Fortune came, his prize-money as lieutenant being great,—promotion, too, came at *last*; but Fanny Harville did not live to know it. She had died the preceding summer, while he was at sea. Captain Wentworth believed it impossible for man to be more attached to woman than poor Benwick had been to Fanny Harville, or to be more deeply afflicted under the dreadful change. He considered his disposition as of the sort which must suffer heavily, uniting very strong feelings with quiet, serious, and retiring manners, and a decided taste for reading, and sedentary pursuits. To finish the interest of the story, the friendship between him and the Harvilles seemed, if possible, augmented by the event which closed all their views of alliance, and Captain Benwick was now living with them entirely. Captain Harville had taken his present house for half a year, his taste, and his health, and his fortune all directing him to a residence unexpensive, and by the sea; and the grandeur of the country, and the retirement of Lyme in the winter, appeared exactly adapted to Captain Benwick's state of mind. The sympathy and good-will excited towards Captain Benwick was very great.

'And yet,' said Anne to herself, as they now moved forward to meet the party, 'he has not, perhaps, a more sorrowing heart than I have. I cannot believe his prospects so blighted for ever. He is younger than I am; younger in feeling, if not in fact; younger as a man. He will rally again, and be happy with another.'

6. Disclosure of CHARACTER through the words of others

A lot can be learned about a CHARACTER by "listening in" on what other CHARACTERS have to say about him or her.

In this excerpt, the reader learns something of the CHARACTER of Captain Wentworth (in *Persuasion*):

Anne found Captain Benwick getting near her, as soon as they were all fairly in the street. Their conversation, the preceding evening, did not disincline him to seek her again; and they walked together some time, talking as before of Mr Scott and Lord Byron, and still as unable, as before, and as unable as any other two readers, to think exactly alike of the merits of either, till something occasioned an almost general change amongst their party, and instead of Captain Benwick, she had Captain Harville by her side.

'Miss Elliot,' said he, speaking rather low, 'you have done a good deed in making that poor fellow talk so much. I wish he could have such company oftener. It is bad for him, I know, to be shut up as he is; but what can we do? we cannot part.'

'No,' said Anne, 'that I can easily believe to be impossible; but in time perhaps—we know what time does in every case of affliction, and you must remember, Captain Harville, that your friend may yet be called a young mourner—Only last summer, I understand.'

'Ay, true enough,' (with a deep sigh) 'only June.'

'And not known to him, perhaps, so soon.'

'Not till the first week in August, when he came home from the Cape,—just made into the Grappler. I was at Plymouth, dreading to hear of him; he sent in letters, but the Grappler was under orders for Portsmouth. There the news must follow him, but who was to tell it? not I. I would as soon have been run up to the yard-arm. Nobody could do it, but that good fellow, (pointing to Captain Wentworth.) The Laconia had come into Plymouth the week before; no danger of her being sent to sea again. He stood his chance for the rest—wrote up for leave of absence, but without waiting the return, travelled night and day till he got to Portsmouth, rowed off to the Grappler that instant, and never left the poor fellow for a week; that's what he did, and nobody else could have saved poor James. You may think, Miss Elliot, whether he is dear to us!'

Use caution, however, in accepting the words of other CHARACTERS—be sure to examine their motives (and the possibility of differences in their perceptions) for how their personal interest might affect their words concerning the CHARACTER in question, especially when the CHARACTER who is speaking holds a different opinion or a different value system than that of the person about whom he or she is speaking. The hidden agenda of the speaker, the possibility of misrepresentation of the person who is the subject of the conversation, can only be discerned by CONTEXT.

Here Anne (of *Persuasion*) overhears Wentworth and Louisa talking about Louisa's sister, Henrietta:

Anne, really tired herself, was glad to sit down; and she very soon heard Captain Wentworth and Louisa in the hedge-row, behind her, as if making their way back, along the rough, wild sort of channel, down the centre. They were speaking as they drew near. Louisa's voice was the first distinguished. She seemed to be in the middle of some eager speech. What Anne first heard was, 'And so, I made her go. I could not bear that she should be frightened from the visit by such nonsense. What!—would I be turned back from doing a thing that I had determined to do, and that I knew to be right, by the airs and interference of such a person?—or, of any person I may say. No,—I have no idea of being so easily persuaded. When I have made up my mind, I have made it. And Henrietta seemed entirely to have made up hers to call at Winthrop to-day—and yet, she was as near giving it up, out of nonsensical complaisance!'

'She would have turned back then, but for you?'

'She would indeed, I am almost ashamed to say it.'

'Happy for her, to have such a mind as yours at hand!—After the hints you gave just now, which did but confirm my own observations, the last time I was in company with him, I need not affect to have no comprehension of what is going on. I see that more than a mere dutiful morning-visit to your aunt was in question;—and woe betide him, and her too, when it comes to things of consequence, when they are placed in circumstances, requiring fortitude and strength of mind, if she have not resolution enough to resist idle interference in such a trifle as this. Your sister is an amiable creature; but *yours* is the character of decision and firmness, I see. If you value her conduct or happiness, infuse as much of your own spirit into her, as you can.

This revealing passage gives the reader insight into not necessarily Henrietta's personality, but rather into Captain Wentworth's and Louisa's *perception* of Henrietta's personality. As a result, the reader also learns a great deal about these two CHARACTERS as well—concerning their beliefs and value systems. Another interesting note: Wentworth, in his conversation with Louisa, speaks directly to her concerning *her* personality ("but yours is the CHARACTER of decision and firmness"). Not uncommon are conversations in which a CHARACTER will compliment (or else criticize) the CHARACTER of the other speaker. Again, be sensitive to the role of perception and motive.

7. Disclosure of CHARACTER through the use of setting

The effects of the stereotypes associated with CHARACTERS from certain regional settings (environments) have already been briefly touched upon in the discussion of *disclosure of CHARACTER through stereotypes*. The setting can to varying degrees be a factor in predicting CHARACTER. Setting can also contribute to the elements that stimulate change in CHARACTERS and be, as a result, significant to the story line. Even in those stories in which the CHARACTERS do not change, as such, the setting can act as an agent of revelation of CHARACTER.

An example might be a story set in a remote area of the Rocky Mountains. A group of people are on a back-to-nature excursion. Encounters with hardships that are a natural possibility in such a setting (a flash flood, a member falling and becoming injured, an attack by wild animals, running out of food, or becoming lost) can bring out in the CHARACTERS' personalities tendencies toward bravery or cowardice, stamina or weakness, selflessness or selfishness, and other traits.

In real life, people are constantly affected by their environment—the settings around them. Likewise, the setting can affect CHARACTERS in literature.

As you see, characterization can be accomplished by telling or by showing, through dialogue, action, examinations of motivating forces, and through many other means. CHARACTER can be revealed through direct mention of the CHARACTER trait or it can be inferred indirectly through behavior.

THE FOUR HUMOURS

The concept of humours is based on early theories of physiology: there are (according to old theories of cosmology) four elements in the universe. The humours need to be in balance because if any one humour predominates, it can lead to sickness and disease and can affect personality. The following chart summarizes these theories.

Element	Characteristic	Humour	Personality*
earth	cold, dry	black bile	melancholic—depressed, gloomy, gluttonous, sentimental
air	hot, moist	blood	sanguine—cheerful, hopeful, amorous
fire	hot, dry	yellow bile	choleric—angry vengeful, impatient
water	cold, moist	phlegm	phlegmatic—stoic, apathetic, impassive, dull, cowardly

* A person was said to be of a sanguine personality, for example, if that humour was predominant. A well-balanced person has all four humours in balance.

The four elements and the four humours are significant to the Comedy of Humours and to many other FORMS of prose, poetry, and drama throughout English and (to a certain extent) American literature as a device used by writers to identify the personalities of CHARACTERS.

Jane Austen, for example, refers to his "sanguine temper" in this description of Captain Wentworth in *Persuasion:*

Captain Wentworth had no fortune. He had been lucky in his profession, but spending freely, what had come freely, had realized nothing. But, he was confident that he should soon be rich;—full of life and ardour, he knew that he should soon have a ship, and soon be on a station that would lead to every thing he wanted. He had always been lucky; he knew he should be so still.—Such confidence, powerful in its own warmth, and bewitching in the wit which often expressed it, must have been enough for Anne; but Lady Russell saw it differently.— His *sanguine temper, and fearlessness of mind, operated very differently on her. She saw in it but an aggravation of the evil. It only added a dangerous character to himself. He was brilliant, he was headstrong.—Lady Russell had little taste for wit; and of any thing approaching to imprudence a horror. She deprecated the connection in every light.

Based on this passage, a practice test question might read:

Captain Wentworth is characterized as having what personality type?

(A) Sentimental
(B) Hopeful
(C) Vengeful
(D) Apathetic
(E) Cowardly

(The correct answer is B.)

Up to this point, the focus has been on the *techniques* of characterization over substance, viewing CHARACTERS as a "part" of a story and viewing characterization as a means to an end without really addressing CHARACTERS and characterization as they blend into the literary work to create a unified whole.

As pointed out by novelist Kit Reed in *Mastering Fiction Writing,* writers sometimes "become" the CHARACTERS in their stories, just as actors may "become" the CHARACTERS that they are portraying. This is a very interesting and useful perspective for the reader of literature as well as for the writer. The reader also brings his or her own experi-ence to the work and, to greatly varying degrees, "becomes" the CHARACTERS.

Generally, the reader does form some type of relationship with the CHARACTERS. In many respects, the degree of involvement you may have with the CHARACTERS and the extent of whatever aesthetic distance may be between CHARACTER and reader quite often rests in the hands of the writer. For example, the writer may use the literary elements and characterizations in such a way as to make the reader actually experience a sense of participation in the story—to "become," through **empathy,** that CHARACTER. Sometimes this is accomplished through vivid descriptions of experiences that are common to both the reader and the CHARACTER. For instance, the reader can empathize with the Beadsman in the first stanza of John Keats's "The Eve of St. Agnes" because the reader can vicariously "feel" the cold as it is described:

St. Agnes' Eve—Ah, bitter chill it was!
The owl, for all his feathers, was a-cold;
The hare limped trembling through the frozen grass,
And silent was the flock in woolly fold:
Numb were the Beadsman's fingers, while he told
His rosary, and while his frosted breath,
Like pious incense from a censer old,
Seemed taking flight for heaven, without a death,
Past the sweet Virgin's picture, while his prayer he saith.

The reader's *sympathy* in this CONTEXT includes a sense of emotional agreement (empathy). In "Lord Randal," the anonymous fifteenth-century ballad, the reader can certainly feel pity and grief both for the poisoned child and for his mother; however, the reader generally does not identify with them or "feel" what they are feeling, although the emotion of the last stanza is very moving:

"O I fear ye are poisond, Lord Randal, my son!
O I fear ye are poisond, my handsome young man!"
"O yes! I am poisond; mother, make my bed soon,
For I'm sick at the heart, and I fain wald lie down."

(Note: "Make my bed soon" is an expression said to refer to making a coffin—a bed for the sleep of death, with *bed* also referring to the grave.)

Of course, the CHARACTER can also elicit feelings of antipathy from the reader—aversion, dislike, distrust, disassociation, and as a result, distance from the reader.

Another element in this question of involvement of the reader with the CHARACTER is **pathos**. Modern slang would probably call many scenes of pathos real "tearjerkers," but pathos does occur when a passage (or scene) "captures the heart" of the reader or audience with intense feelings of sorrow and pity, as when Little Nell dies in *The Old Curiosity Shop* by Charles Dickens:

The old man looked from face to face, and his lips moved; but no sound came from them in reply.

"If we were knit together then," pursued the younger brother, "what will be the bond between us now! And even," he added in an altered voice, "even if what I dread to name has come to pass—even if that be so, or is to be—still, dear brother, we are not apart, and have that comfort in our great affliction."

By little and little, the old man had drawn back towards the inner chamber, while these words were spoken. He pointed there, as he replied, with trembling lips.

"You plot among you to wean my heart from her. You never will do that—never while I have life. I have no relative or friend but her—I never had—I never will have. She is all in all to me. It is too late to part us now."

Waving them off with his hand, and calling softly to her as he went, he stole into the room. They who were left behind drew close together, and after a few whispered words followed him. They moved so gently, that their footsteps made no noise; but there were sobs from among the group, and sounds of grief and mourning.

For she was dead. There, upon her little bed, she lay at rest. The solemn stillness was no marvel now.

Her couch was dressed with here and there some winter berries and green leaves, gathered in a spot she had been used to favour. "When I die, put near me something that has loved the light, and had the sky above it always." Those were her words.

The old man held one languid arm in his, and had the small hand tight folded to his breast, for warmth. It was the hand she had stretched out to him with her last smile—the hand that had led him on through all their wanderings. Ever and anon he pressed it to his lips; then hugged it to his breast again, murmuring that it was warmer now; and as he said it he looked, in agony, to those who stood around, as if imploring them to help her.

But she was dead, and past all help, or need of it.

Pathos, fundamentally, is a response from the heart of the individual, yet pathos or the lack of pathos is also often a reflection of society and the norms and cultures of the age. Dickens and the readers of his day lived in a world without television, ac-

tion news reports, and big-screen movie theaters. As a result, stage productions, concerts, and reading were major outlets for the feelings and interests of the people. The readers of *The Old Curiosity Shop* during the period when it was first written reacted strongly to Little Nell's death. According to one historian, one reader wrote in his diary that he had never read such painful words, whereas another reader threw his copy of the book out of a train window in his grief. Writers of the time record that American readers were also deeply affected—a crowd of concerned people gathered at a New York pier to shout questions at an arriving ship concerning Little Nell's fate. These reactions show that they had become personally involved with the CHARACTER Little Nell as if she were a real person. Compare their reactions to the death of Little Nell to world reactions to the tragedy of Nicole and O. J. Simpson. Have people been conditioned as a society to perceive events differently? Like the original readers of Little Nell's death, society sometimes fuses fiction and reality, but has that erasing of the line that divides fiction from reality produced different effects in people's perceptions today as compared to the past?

Finally, involvement of the reader with a CHARACTER is also greatly influenced by the degree of probability that exists surrounding the words, thoughts, deeds, and circumstances of the CHARACTER. For the reader to become involved, to care about the story and the CHARACTER, these elements must all have a degree of probability—they must be convincing. The importance of probability is nowhere greater seen than in the area of CHARACTER development.

As you read various literary selections in preparation for the test and for your own enjoyment and enrichment, you will find that CHARACTER as seen in full works is quite often not static, but a changing dual element that involves both you (as the reader) and the CHARACTER in the work. The element of change is at the root of CHARACTER *development*:

1. CHARACTER development involves the writer's exposition of various CHARACTER traits and the revelation of these traits to the reader as the work progresses.
2. CHARACTER development also involves the concept of the person in the literary work *being* a developing CHARACTER. In other words, certain aspects of what the reader

would consider his or her CHARACTER change as a result of events in the narrative. Whether a person can change personality, disposition, or other like elements of CHARACTER is questionable (hence directly affects the credibility of the characterization of the CHARACTER unless masterfully done), but changes of attitude, emotional states, and some response mechanisms are common and necessary to making a CHARACTER seem real to the reader. Such changes can be the critical turning point of the story.

CHARACTER development, as already mentioned, must be *credible*—rooted in probability. Although credibility can be established—or destroyed—in many ways, there are a few areas that are considered pivotal to establishing the probability of a CHARACTER'S development (hence the credibility of the entire work):

1. Did the CHARACTER have sufficient motivation to change?

For the reader to be convinced that a CHARACTER really has changed, he or she must also be convinced that there is some reason to change: directly stated, CHARACTER change often is seen as a cause-and-effect relationship. To see the effect (the change) without seeing the cause or without being convinced that what is being presented as the cause is sufficient motivation (reason) for the change, weakens the credibility of the work.

An example can be seen in a western movie that was played on cable television channels in the United States. In this movie, a group of cattle rustlers injure the hero, who then hides until nightfall. After dark, he "gets the draw" on the three rustlers (two experienced outlaws and one novice), who are sleeping around the campfire. Bleeding profusely, the hero shoots one rustler, injuring him slightly, then demands a horse for his escape. The horse is brought, but the hero collapses from the loss of blood and falls to the ground with the three cattle rustlers looking down on him. The novice asks if they should kill the hero, to which the leader of the outlaws replies that no—you do not shoot a man who is a real "hombre," a real man. Instead, the leader of the cattle rustlers (who was making large sums of money stealing cattle) makes plans to move on to Mexico (leaving the country) and to leave the

wounded hero at the campsite. The novice asks if he might go with them but the outlaw leader tells him to stay to take care of the wounded hero and to learn to become a "real man" like the hero, then once he becomes "half the man" the hero is, he can once again ride with the outlaws. The writer of this story wants the viewer to believe that these criminals would be willing not only to spare the life of a man who is trying to stop them but also would voluntarily give up a lucrative cattle stealing operation, actions motivated by their respect for the hero's manliness (courage, determination). The home audience responded with comments like "Yeah, sure," but does the motivation for change in the CHARACTERS lack credibility?

2. Was there sufficient time (in terms of "story time") for the CHARACTER change to be realistic and probable?

People can suddenly change, but unless the reader or audience is thoroughly convinced of the motivation, such abrupt changes as that in the cowboy movie previously discussed under *"sufficient motivation,"* leave the audience with an uneasy sense of incredulity. Of course, a writer is faced with the problem of translating "real time" (two hours for a movie, three to four hours to read an average novel, for example) into "story time" that may involve days, weeks, years, or generations. There are some techniques available to the writer to give the reader a sense of protracted time, such as weaving subplots in and out of the main story or changing points of view; however, regardless of the methods used, the reader needs to be convinced that the CHARACTER who has changed or who is changing has a realistic amount of time in which to make these changes.

Sometimes this is expressed as a "gradual awakening or dawning of the truth" of a situation, especially when a change in attitude is the result of learning a before-hidden truth (a truth that was either accidentally or deliberately concealed from the CHARACTER or was consciously or subconsciously avoided by a CHARACTER who "refuses to see the truth").

3. Has the reader been given adequate information about the CHARACTER to make the change seem believable?

A story, because of the physical confines of the medium, is a "slice of life." Even in stories that follow a CHARACTER from birth to death, only certain amounts of the details of that life can be presented. Consequently, "filling in" the reader on the parts not chronicled in detail is important to establishing the credibility of a CHARACTER change.

One method to do this is the use of **flashback**, such as dream sequences, recollections by a CHARACTER, and other means in which past events are detailed. (Sometimes the flashback can be almost the entire story, for example, the story might begin with the main CHARACTER awaiting sentencing after a jury trial. He sits "remembering" the events that lead to that point, then concludes with the judge's pronouncement of sentence.) Another means a writer can use to achieve credibility for change is the effective use of **foreshadowing**, a means of preparing the reader or audience for upcoming events. Foreshadowing devices include the clues in a mystery or a prevailing atmosphere, among others.

JAMES BRUCE (1730–94)

Bruce's book [*Travels to Discover the Source of the Nile, 5 volumes, 1790*] is both dull and dear. We join in clubs of five, each pays a guinea, draw lots who shall have it first, and the last to keep it for his patience.

Bruce's overbearing manner has raised enmity and prejudices; and he did wrong in retailing the most wonderful parts of his book in companies. A story may be credible when attended with circumstances, which seems false if detached.

I was present in a large company at dinner, when Bruce was talking away. Someone asked him what musical instruments were used in Abyssinia. Bruce hesitated, not being prepared for the question; and at last said, 'I think I saw one lyre there.' George Selwyn whispered... 'Yes; and there is one less since he left the country.'

CHARACTER IN PROSE

A discussion of the role of CHARACTER in prose must begin with at least a brief mention of the seventeenth- and eighteenth-century literary FORM called the "CHARACTER." The CHARACTER is brief, very descriptive, and focuses on a person who embodies a particular virtue, vice, or CHARACTER trait.

Also, the reader needs to be aware that the term CHARACTER refers to places as well as to people, such as "That wonderful Italian restaurant on the corner has a lot of CHARACTER." By extension, an entire literary work might be said to have CHARACTER—and, as such, identifying "CHARACTER" is appropriate even in nonnarrative prose that does not include people as CHARACTERS. Arguably, such references to CHARACTER in a nonnarrative essay actually incorporate elements of TONE, VOICE, and author's style, particularly when the analysis of CHARACTER is, for example, "His essay is characterized by a somber tone that conflicts with the trivial nature of the subject and by a propensity toward the macabre."

Having said this, now look more closely at one method you can use to analyze CHARACTER in a narrative prose selection. Following are the introductory paragraphs of Agatha Christie's *Dead Man's Folly*. Make a list of all the information about Poirot, Miss Lemon, and finally Mrs. Oliver that you can gain from this selection.

DEAD MAN'S FOLLY
by
Agatha Christie

It was Miss Lemon, Poirot's efficient secretary, who took the telephone call.

Laying aside her shorthand notebook, she raised the receiver and said without emphasis, "Trafalgar 8137."
(5) Hercule Poirot leaned back in his upright chair and closed his eyes. His fingers beat a meditative soft tattoo on the edge of the table. In his head he continued to compose the polished periods of the letter he had been dictating.

Placing her hand over the receiver, Miss Lemon
(10) asked in a low voice,

"Will you accept a personal call from Nassecombe, Devon?"

Poirot frowned. The place meant nothing to him.

"The name of the caller?" he demanded cautiously.
(15) Miss Lemon spoke into the mouthpiece.

"Air raid?" she asked doubtingly. "Oh, yes—what was the last name again?"

Once more she turned to Hercule Poirot.

"Mrs. Ariadne Oliver."
(20) Hercule Poirot's eyebrows shot up. A memory rose in his mind: windswept grey hair…and eagle profile…

He rose and replaced Miss Lemon at the telephone.

"Hercule Poirot speaks," he announced grandiloquently.
(25) "Is that Mr. Hercules Porrot speaking personally?" the suspicious voice of the telephone operator demanded.

Poirot assured her that that was the case.

"You're through to Mr. Porrot," said the voice.

Its thin reedy accents were replaced by a magnificent
(30) booming contralto which caused Poirot hastily to shift the receiver a couple of inches further from his ear.

"M. Poirot, is that really you?" demanded Mrs. Oliver.

"Myself in person, Madame."

"This is Mrs. Oliver. I don't know if you'll remember
(35) me—"

"But of course I remember you, Madame. Who could forget you?"

"Well, people do sometimes," said Mrs. Oliver. "Quite often, in fact. I don't think that I've got a very distinctive
(40) personality. Or perhaps it's because I'm always doing different things to my hair. But all that's neither here nor there. I hope I'm not interrupting you when you're frightfully busy?"

"No, no, you do not derange me in the least."
(45) "Good gracious—I'm sure I don't want to drive you out of your mind. The fact is, I need you."

"Need me?"

"Yes, at once. Can you take an airplane?"

"I do not take airplanes. They make me sick."
(50) "They do me, too. Anyway I don't suppose it would be any quicker than the train really, because I think the only airport near here is Exeter which is miles away. So come by train. Twelve o'clock from Paddington to Nassecombe. You can do it nicely. You've got three
(55) quarters of an hour if my watch is right—though it isn't usually."

"But where are you, Madame? What is all this about?"

"Nasse House, Nassecombe. A car or taxi will meet you at the station at Nassecombe."
(60) "But why do you need me? What is all this about?" Poirot repeated frantically.

"Telephones are in such awkward places," said Mrs. Oliver. "This one's in the hall ….People passing through and talking ….I can't really hear. But I'm expecting you.
(65) Everybody will be so thrilled. Goodbye."

There was a sharp click as the receiver was replaced. The line hummed gently.

With a baffled air of bewilderment, Poirot put back the receiver and murmured something under his breath.
(70) Miss Lemon sat with her pencil poised, incurious. She repeated in muted tones the final phrase of dictation before the interruption.

"—allow me to assure you, my dear sir, that the hypothesis you have advanced—"
(75) Poirot waved aside the advancement of the hypothesis.

"That was Mrs. Oliver," he said "Ariadne Oliver, the detective novelist. You may have read—" but he stopped, remembering that Miss Lemon only read improving books and regarded such frivolities as
(80) fictional crime with contempt. "She wants me to go down to Devonshire today, at once, in"—he glanced at the clock—"thirty-five minutes."

Miss Lemon raised disapproving eyebrows.

"That will be running it rather fine," she said. "For
(85) what reason?"

"You may well ask! She did not tell me."

"How very peculiar. Why not?"

"Because," said Hercule Poirot thoughtfully, "she was afraid of being overheard. Yes, she made that quite
(90) clear."

"Well, really," said Miss Lemon, bristling in her employer's defence. "The things people expect! Fancy thinking that you'd go rushing off on some wild goose chase like that! An important man like you! I have
(95) always noticed that these artists and writers are very unbalanced—no sense of proportion. Shall I telephone through a telegram, 'Regret unable leave London?'"

Her hand went out to the telephone. Poirot's voice arrested the gesture.

(100)   **"*Du tout!*" he said. "On the contrary. Be so kind as to summon a taxi immediately." He raised his voice. "Georges! A few necessities of toilet in my small valise. And quickly, very quickly. I have a train to catch."**

The main CHARACTER, of course, is Hercule Poirot. Those acquainted with the works of Agatha Christie will recognize Poirot as a (or, as Poirot would probably say, "*the*") famous Belgian detective, living in England. But even without this background information, the reader can gather several clues to his identity as a CHARACTER and to his personality from the CONTEXT of the selection:

- He has an office and a secretary (paragraph 1).
- He attends to detail. ("…he continued to compose the polished periods of the letter he had been dictating"—lines 7–8.)
- He screens his calls. ("[He] demanded cautiously" to know the name of the caller—line 14.)
- He is somewhat pompous. (He gave his name on the phone "grandiloquently."—line 24.)
- He has a good memory. (He remembers Mrs. Oliver.)
- He gets airsick (line 49).
- He is intuitive concerning Mrs. Oliver's not explaining why she did not want to be overheard.
- He is in London (line 97).
- He is multilingual (line 100).
- He has a personal attendant named Georges (line 102).
- He has revealed that he has a mind of his own.
- He is going by train.

The next CHARACTER is Miss Lemon:

- She is efficient (line 1).
- She is professional. (Notice her telephone style.)
- She does not have a sense of curiosity about the mysterious phone call (line 70).
- She reads only "improving books."
- She considers fictional crime as frivolous and views it with "contempt" (lines 79–80).
- She feels confident enough in her position to show disapproval with her body language (line 83) and to question her employer concerning a phone call ("For what reason?"—lines 84–85).
- She is loyal ("bristling in her employer's defence"—lines 91–92).

- She is impressed with Poirot's importance (line 94).
- She does not respect artists and writers (lines 95–96).
- She does not hesitate to say no to others (lines 96–97).

Finally, the CHARACTER of Mrs. Oliver:

- She is in Nassecombe, Devon (lines 11–12).
- She has "grey hair…an eagle profile…" (line 21).
- She has a "booming contralto" voice (line 30).
- She is uncertain whether Poirot will remember her (lines 34–35).
- She has a low self-image (lines 38–41).
- She changes hairstyles (and perhaps color?) frequently (lines 40–41).
- She seems to be unaware that *derange* also means "to upset or to disarrange" as well as "to make insane" (lines 45–46). Consider this: Is she really unaware or is she making a jest?
- She, too, gets airsick (line 50).
- She assumes Poirot will come immediately on short notice (lines 50–56). This self-assurance seems to be contradictory to the low self-image she shows in lines 38–41.
- She knows the train schedule (line 53).
- Her watch usually is not right (lines 55–56).
- She will have Poirot picked up (lines 58–59).
- She is calling from a "hall" with people about (line 63).
- She is a detective novelist (lines 76–77).
- She does not tell him why she wants him to come (line 86).

CHARACTER IN POETRY

In addition to the CHARACTER revelation that is a part of narrative poetry, there is the concept of **ethos** that involves the reader's (or hearer's) impression of the moral CHARACTER of the speaker. As such, this is related to the perception of persona or the speaker's VOICE, particularly in lyric poetry. CHARACTER, even in the case of an implied author, is significant to poetry as well as to prose.

What insight can you gain about the CHARACTER of the speaker of these lines? (Take particular note of the last stanza.) How would you summarize his system of values?

STILL TO BE NEAT

Still to be neat, still to be dressed,
As you were going to a feast;
Still to be powdered, still perfumed;
Lady, it is to be presumed,
Though art's hid causes are not found,
All is not sweet, all is not sound.

Give me a look, give me a face
That makes simplicity a grace;
Robes loosely flowing, hair as free;
Such sweet neglect more taketh me
Than all th' adulteries of art.
They strike mine eyes, but not my heart.

by Ben Jonson

Here is a sample practice question:

Referring to cosmetics and elaborate grooming as "adulteries of art" emphasizes the speaker's

(A) easygoing nature
(B) moralistic attitudes
(C) rigid CHARACTER
(D) lack of refinement
(E) disdain for the unnatural

(The correct answer is E.)

Now examine this poem for a more subtle revelation of the speaker's personality:

INVITING A FRIEND TO SUPPER

Tonight, grave sir, both my poor house and I
Do equally desire your company;
Not that we think us worthy such a guest,
line But that your worth will dignify our feast,
(5) With those that come, whose grace may make that seem
Something, which else could hope for no esteem.
It is the fair acceptance, sir, creates
The entertainment perfect, not the cates.
Yet shall you have, to rectify your palate,
(10) An olive, capers, or some better salad
Ushering the mutton; with a short-legged hen,
If we can get her, full of eggs; and then,
Lemons, and wine for sauce: to these, a cony
Is not to be despaired of for our money;
(15) And though fowl now be scarce, yet there are clerks,
The sky not falling, think we may have larks.
I'll tell you of more, and lie, so you will come:
Of partridge, pheasant, woodcock, of which some
May yet be there; and godwit if we can:
(20) Gnat, rail, and ruff, too. Howsoe'er, my man

Shall read a piece of Vergil, Tacitus,
Livy, or of some better book to us,
Of which we'll speak our minds, amidst our meat;
And I'll profess no verses to repeat:
(25) To this, if aught appear, which I not know of,
That will the pastry, not my paper, show of.
Digestive cheese, and fruit there sure will be;
But that which most doth take my muse and me,
Is a pure cup of rich Canary wine,
(30) Which is the Mermaid's now, but shall be mine:
Of which had Horace, or Anacreon tasted,
Their lives, as do their lines, till now had lasted.
Tobacco, nectar, or the Thespian spring,
Are all but Luther's beer, to this I sing.
(35) Of this we will sup free, but moderately,
And we will have no Pooly or Parrot by;
Nor shall our cups make any guilty men,
But at our parting, we will be as when
We innocently met. No simple word
(40) That shall be uttered at our mirthful board
Shall make us sad next morning, or affright
The liberty that we'll enjoy tonight.

by Ben Jonson

Notice, for example, his humility ("my poor house" in line 1), respect for his guest (lines 3–4), willingness to spare no expense to please his guest. Also, he is the type of person who enjoys the classics and intellectual discussion (lines 21–23). ("Mermaid" in line 30 is a reference to a tavern.) What other clues to the speaker's CHARACTER or personality can you find?

_____

_____

_____

_____

_____

_____

_____

_____

_____

CHARACTER IN DRAMA

Although drama generally lacks the more direct communication between writer and reader that typifies works not intended to be acted out, there are ways in which the "CHARACTER" of the CHARACTERS in a play can be revealed.

Certain styles of drama carry with them CHARACTERS whose personalities are expected to be exhibited in set ways. Such classic stock CHARACTERS include the **alazon** who is a braggart, the **eiron** who is a self-deprecatory CHARACTER, the **pharmakos** who is a victim of circumstances, the **bomolochos** who is a buffoon, and the **agroikos** who is either rustic or easily deceived.

Also CHARACTERS can reveal their thoughts (and hence elements of their personality traits) through such devices as:

1. A *confidant*—generally a friend, who "draws out" the person into talking about private matters

2. A *foil*—a contrasting CHARACTER, who through that very contrast causes the viewer to see more clearly the personality of another CHARACTER

3. An *aside*—in which a CHARACTER directly addresses the audience

4. A *soliloquy*—in which a CHARACTER, alone on stage, delivers a speech that reveals his or her thoughts

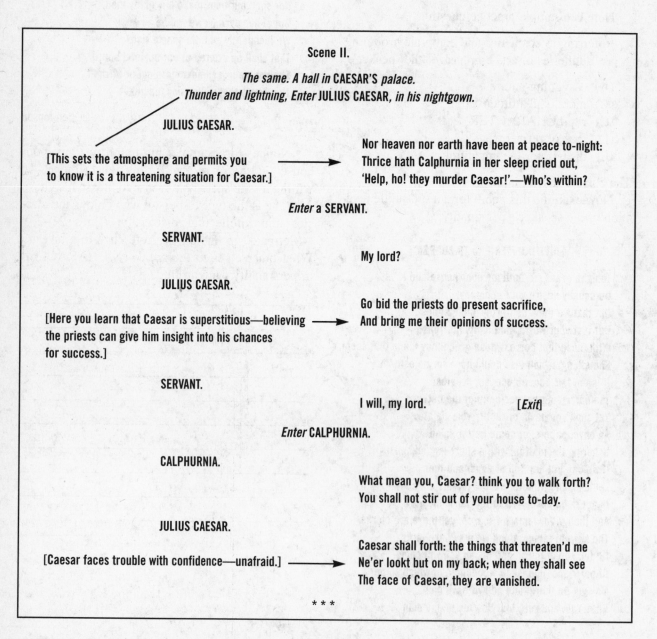

Scene II.

The same. A hall in CAESAR'S *palace.*
Thunder and lightning, Enter JULIUS CAESAR, *in his nightgown.*

JULIUS CAESAR.

[This sets the atmosphere and permits you to know it is a threatening situation for Caesar.]

Nor heaven nor earth have been at peace to-night:
Thrice hath Calphurnia in her sleep cried out,
'Help, ho! they murder Caesar!'—Who's within?

Enter a SERVANT.

SERVANT.

My lord?

JULIUS CAESAR.

[Here you learn that Caesar is superstitious—believing the priests can give him insight into his chances for success.]

Go bid the priests do present sacrifice,
And bring me their opinions of success.

SERVANT.

I will, my lord.   [*Exit*]

Enter CALPHURNIA.

CALPHURNIA.

What mean you, Caesar? think you to walk forth?
You shall not stir out of your house to-day.

JULIUS CAESAR.

[Caesar faces trouble with confidence—unafraid.]

Caesar shall forth: the things that threaten'd me
Ne'er lookt but on my back; when they shall see
The face of Caesar, they are vanished.

* * *

Of course action and dialogue are also of immeasurable importance in determining the personality of a CHARACTER and in establishing whether he or she is **static** (unchanging) or **developing** (changing). Because you can actually "see" the CHARACTER onstage, you have the advantage of being able to determine those personality traits that are evidenced by facial expression, TONE of VOICE, body language, dress, and bearing or demeanor.

A very small excerpt from Act II Scene II of Shakespeare's *Julius Caesar* appears on page 162. Although the selection is brief, notice the insight into Caesar's personality that is revealed.

QUESTIONS TO APPLY YOUR LEARNING

As you practice reading literary selections, ask these questions to help you identify and understand CHARACTER:

1. Who are the CHARACTERS? (names, ages, occupations, and so forth)
2. What role does each play? (hero, villain, or other)
3. What attitudes do you see at work in each of the CHARACTERS? Emotions? Response mechanisms? Intrinsic values?
4. Is the CHARACTER stock? Type? Stereotype?
5. Is the CHARACTER flat or round?
6. How is each CHARACTER characterized?
7. What "humour" would you assign each CHARACTER?
8. Is the CHARACTER static or changing?

ADDITIONAL HELPFUL POINTS TO REMEMBER

- Watch for **fictive** CHARACTERS. A fictive CHARACTER is a romanticized, idealized version of a real person. Fictive CHARACTERS also may be "types," because they represent a group, a historical period, or some other element. The "noble savage" of American writers like James Fenimore Cooper is an example of a fictive CHARACTER who is an idealized representation of American Indians in the wilderness.

- As with the other literary elements, do not forget the significance of vocabulary to understanding questions about CHARACTER.
- Two terms to remember: A **dynamic** CHARACTER is one who changes; a **static** CHARACTER is one who does not change.
- As you read literary selections to practice for the test, be aware that in some circumstances drawing conclusions concerning a CHARACTER'S motivation based on an excerpt of a work may be misleading. Sometimes the true "CHARACTER" of a CHARACTER can only be determined from the work as a whole, because the clues to CHARACTER taken from an excerpt out of CONTEXT are the result of the circumstances. Here are three examples:
  1. An excerpt may show a CHARACTER to be sweet, kind, and caring. CONTEXT might reveal that the CHARACTER is being "two-faced" because he or she has a selfish hidden agenda and ulterior motives.
  2. An excerpt may show a CHARACTER to have a distinctive VOICE with a forceful personality. CONTEXT might reveal that the CHARACTER, perhaps even unconsciously, has elements of a dual personality. (This is not necessarily indicative of a personality disorder. Many people will answer the telephone or attend a business meeting using a more formal style of language, TONE of VOICE, and overall demeanor than the characteristics that they exhibit in the more casual atmosphere that surrounds close friends and family.)
  3. An excerpt may show a CHARACTER who has courage and resolve (in other words, strong motivation) for a change or an action. CONTEXT might reveal that the CHARACTER had good intentions, but ultimately lacked sufficient resolve and motivation or that subsequent factors interfered with or lessened that drive for executing the change.
- Watch for **caricature** in characterization. In caricature, a CHARACTER is not believable because one CHARACTER trait dominates his or her personality to the extreme.
- When looking for clues to CHARACTER, become sensitive to the role of tension or conflict (in addition to action) as it relates to the more complex CHARACTERS in the

story. The more subtle sides of personality—of CHARACTER—are often revealed in response to tension.

- A way to get to know CHARACTERS in a literary selection and to practice identifying the elements of personality and CHARACTER development at work in a story or drama is to read a selection, then work out a CHARACTER analysis. A CHARACTER analysis consists of a list of prepared questions that, once completed, will give you a highly detailed description of the CHARACTER. The questions might range from physical appearance to how the CHARACTER feels about his or her profession to the CHARACTER'S romantic life.

  Television and movie scriptwriters Jurgen Wolff and Kerry Cox in *Successful Script Writing* (Writer's Digest Books, 1988) have developed a CHARACTER analysis that, although intended for use by scriptwriters in planning their CHARACTERS when writing scripts, is *very* useful for the reader in search of a better understanding of CHARACTER.

- When determining CHARACTER in a selection, be sure to establish the following information as a background:
  1. The point of view used in the selection
  2. The VOICE
  3. The speaker's attitude

- "CHARACTER" can also refer to places and things, such as people may refer to a restaurant as having "a lot of CHARACTER." Here is an occasion when the writer actually refers to the CHARACTER of the ocean.

A DESCENT INTO THE MAELSTRÖM
by
Edgar Allan Poe

…As the old man spoke, I became aware of a loud and gradually increasing sound, like the moaning of a vast herd of buffaloes upon an American prairie; and at the same moment I perceived that what seamen term the *chopping* character of the ocean beneath us, was rapidly changing into a current which set to the eastward. Even while I gazed, this current acquired a monstrous velocity. Each moment added to its speed—to its headlong impetuosity. In five minutes the whole sea, as far as Vurrgh, was lashed into ungovernable fury; but it was between Moskoe and the coast that the main uproar held its sway. Here the vast bed of the waters, seamed and scarred into a thousand conflicting channels, burst suddenly into phrensied convulsion—heaving, boiling, hissing—gyrating in gigantic and innumerable vortices, and all whirling and plunging on to the eastward with a rapidity which water never elsewhere assumes except in precipitous descents.

LITERARY ELEMENT NUMBER SIX: USE OF LANGUAGE

A DESCENT INTO THE MAELSTRÖM
by
Edgar Allan Poe

The ordinary accounts of this vortex had by no means prepared me for what I saw. That of Jonas Ramus, which perhaps the most circumstantial of any, cannot impart the faintest conception either of the magnificence, or of the horror of the scene—or of the wild bewildering sense of *the novel* which confounds the beholder. I am not sure from what point of view the writer in question surveyed it, nor at what time; but it could neither have been from the summit of Helseggen, nor during a storm. There are some passages of his description, nevertheless, which may be quoted for their details, although their effect is exceedingly feeble in conveying an impression of the spectacle.

You are traveling in the American Midwest and open the newspaper to learn about the area. There are the grocery store ads: This week's featured item in the bakery—apple pie.

A crust, cooked apples, cinnamon.

You have not had fresh apple pie in a long time. You can see it in your mind's eye now: hot apple pie, rich pastry crust that flakes apart when your fork hits it. Steam rises from the slice and softly brushes your cheek as the slice is lifted from the rest of the pie— and it smells *so-o-o* good. You begin to breathe deeper: aromas of hot cinnamon and vanilla and baked apples swirl around your head. Maybe add a thick slice of American cheese that melts down into the apples and sauce. No, better yet—a big scoop of rich vanilla ice cream that melts and makes a creamy, thick sauce all around the chunks of steamy apples, mixing with the cinnamon in great big swirls of flavor. Your mouth waters in anticipation of that first bite. After all, it's your duty to eat a slice of fresh-baked apple pie, because what represents America better than the flag, Mom, and apple pie?

Welcome to the world of **imagery**.

Roughly defined, imagery—the use of images—refers to the mental pictures you get as a result of words. An image can be **literal**, a standard MEANING like the mental picture of apples and cinnamon baked in a pastry crust for an apple pie, or it can be **figurative**, like the American love of country associated with apple pie. Imagery can refer to visual pictures that come to mind, or it can also include all the sensual qualities (kinesthetic/motion, auditory/hearing, thermal/heat, tactile/touch, gustatory/taste, and olfactory/smell). Imagery can also refer to the abstract, the nonsensual qualities that can come to mind, such as love, hate, peace, fear, and other emotions.

An **image**, then, is the mental representations that certain words and certain USES OF LANGUAGE produce. Imagery is a collection of images. Look at the collection of images used in the preceding apple pie illustration. You see the pie (visual), smell the pie (olfactory), feel the steam (tactile), and taste the pie (gustatory). Taking the concept of appealing to more than one of the physical senses one step further, when one sense is described by terms usually associated with another sense, such a mixture of sensory images is called **synaesthesia**: "a red-hot candy." Imagery can also take on patterns as the images are used throughout a work or can be seen as **image-clusters** (recurring groupings of images) that can actually affect the TONE of a work.

To summarize: Words create images in people's minds, some of which are literal and some of which are figurative.

Figurative Language

Figurative language is using the choice of words to bring to mind figurative imagery. What constitutes figurative language? As has been clearly established, definitions and the assignment of various literary concepts to specific categories is an area of controversy among literary scholars—and figurative language is no exception. Some generalizations can be made, however, for the purpose of facilitating the study of figurative language.

Figurative language can be divided into three main categories:

1. Figures of thought (also called tropes)

A trope is the MEANING a word has *other than* its literal meaning. Trope refers to change or turn, in other words, using a word in other than its literal sense, such as in comparison. For example, when the romantic young lover compares his girlfriend's blue eyes to "cornflowers on a sunny day," the word *cornflower* is no longer restricted to a blue flower (the literal meaning). It now is a trope (a figure of thought) with another, figurative meaning.

2. Figures of speech (also called rhetorical figures or schemes)

Rhetorical figures depart, not from the literal MEANING of the words, but from the standard usage or order of the words (or some other departure other than in MEANING), thus making a special effect. An example of such figures of speech is the rhetorical question—a question normally begs reply, but in the rhetorical question, no reply is expected; the question is being asked to emphasize the obvious, albeit unspoken answer.

3. Figures of sound

These devices include the sound effects discussed in the section on FORM, Literary Element Number Two, including alliteration, assonance, and consonance.

Graphically, one view of figurative language might look like this:

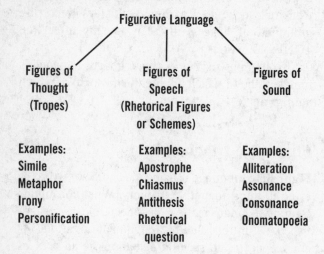

There is a trend away from this view, however, largely due to the confusion generated by the tendency of many to refer to figures of speech as a more inclusive term under which tropes and rhetorical figures fall as major categories:

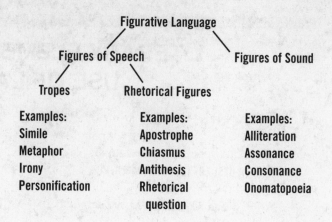

Although you need to be aware of the former triadic view of figurative language, the latter assignment of terms will be used in this discussion. Also, you should realize that placement of the various figures of speech under the category of trope or rhetorical figure does not meet with universal consensus among scholars. For example, one literary dictionary might place the **zeugma** (see figures of speech based on syntax, chart, page 184) under trope, whereas another would identify it as a rhetorical figure. Regardless, figures of speech are of major significance both to understanding and to appreciating a literary work; and you need to recognize their use and their effect.

Figures of Speech

Here are some of the major figures of speech you may encounter:

1. Figures of speech based on analogy

Analogy, which has its origin in mathematics, involves explaining the unknown and unfamiliar by drawing comparisons to the known and familiar. When in mathematics you figure $\frac{a}{b} = \frac{c}{d}$ a (an analogue) is to b in the same relationship as c (another analogue) is to d; therefore, although a and c are not necessarily identical, they are similar because a has the same relationship to b that c has to d.

Analogies are drawn to explain, to describe, to argue, and to justify; however, whatever the purpose in making the comparison, at the root of analogy are two distinct units of thought: the **vehicle** and the **tenor**.

The tenor is the subject or idea you are trying to explain, and the vehicle is the means by which you explain it. If you try to describe a zebra by comparing it to a horse with stripes, the zebra is the tenor and the horse is the vehicle. Likewise, if you wanted to explain some abstract concept, such as rage, you might compare it to a consuming fire: Tenor? Rage. Vehicle? Fire.

- **Simile** is a comparison using "like" or "as." This trope can be found in most FORMS of literature as people attempt to communicate by making direct, unveiled analogies. This is perhaps the result of a psychological need to try to understand the unknown by associating it with elements of the known. A person who has never tasted buffalo meat might ask someone who just ate a buffalo burger, "What does it taste *like?*" The answer, "It tastes *like* a very strong beef burger," is a simile.

Similes are characterized by their directness, as in the opening couplet of Henry Constable's sixteenth-century poem:

HOPE, LIKE THE HYENA

Hope, like the hyena, coming to be old,
Alters his shape, is turned into despair.

The speaker compares hope that is delayed ("old") to a hyena that changes shape *like* hope changes into despair. What is the tenor? Hope. Its vehicle? The hyena.

Sometimes the simile is sustained for an entire stanza or even an entire poem. Here is the first stanza of Thomas Lodge's "Love in My Bosom." The vehicle is a bee. What is the tenor?

LOVE IN MY BOSOM

Love in my bosom like a bee
   Doth suck his sweet;
Now with his wings he plays with me,
   Now with his feet.
Within mine eyes he makes his nest,
His bed amidst my tender breast;
My kisses are his daily feast,
And yet he robs me of my rest.
   Ah, wanton, will ye?

Here is Shakespeare's "Sonnet 118." Can you identify his vehicle and tenor?

Like as, to make our appetites more keen,
With eager compounds we our palate urge;
As, to prevent our maladies unseen,

line We sicken to shun sickness when we purge;
5   Even so, being full of your ne'er-cloying sweetness,
To bitter sauces did I frame my feeding;
And, sick of welfare, found a kind of meetness
To be diseased, ere that there was true needing.
Thus policy in love, to anticipate
(10) The ills that were not, grew to faults assured,
And brought to medicine a healthful state,
Which, rank of goodness, would by ill be cured;
But thence I learn, and find the lesson true,
Drugs poison him that so fell sick of you.

Be sure to use the clues to MEANING that are found through FORM—especially the Shakespearean sonnet rhyme scheme. Also, note the use of "Like as" and "As" (lines l and 3)—setting up the comparison, the use of "Even so" and "Thus" (lines 5 and 9)—setting up relationships of ideas, and the use of "But" (line 13)—setting up a contrast in thought.

- **Metaphor**, unlike the direct nature of the simile, is an *implied* comparison: rosy-red lips (tenor—lips; vehicle—a red rose). Recognition of the tenor-vehicle relationship is more subtle, yet sometimes is clearly stated as in this third stanza from Thomas Nashe's sixteenth-century "Adieu, Farewell Earth's Bliss":

Beauty is but a flower
Which wrinkles will devour;
Brightness falls from the air,
Queens have died young and fair,
Dust hath closed Helen's eye.
I am sick, I must die.
   Lord, have mercy on us!

A practice test question might directly ask you to identify the comparison being made:

"A flower" in line 1 is used as a vehicle to describe

(A) brightness
(B) Queens
(C) beauty
(D) Helen
(E) wrinkles

(The correct answer is C.)

The answer choices may ask you to identify the vehicle in more abstract terms:

"A flower" in line 1 is compared to

(A) time
(B) love
(C) personality
(D) appearance
(E) royalty

(The correct answer is D.)

An important approach to understanding any USE OF LANGUAGE is to determine the *effects* of its use. Consequently, a practice test question might read:

Comparing beauty to a flower in line 1 has the effect of

(A) emphasizing the natural elements of beauty
(B) making beauty seem fragile
(C) elevating beauty to a higher symbolic level
(D) limiting beauty to natural elements
(E) exaggerating beauty's impact

CONTEXT will help you select answer B (the correct answer) over A (an answer that may seem to be correct): use of "but" in the sense of "nothing more than" or "merely" and the clear reference to a flower's fragility in line 2—"wrinkles will devour."

At other times the metaphor (like simile) can be a **controlling image**. A controlling image is a metaphor—or image—that runs throughout a work. The controlling image in Shakespeare's "Sonnet 97" is a simile comparing the speaker's absence from his love to the winter season:

How like a winter hath my absence been
From thee, the pleasure of the fleeting year!
What freezings have I felt, what dark days seen!
What old December's bareness everywhere!
And yet this time removed was summer's time,
The teeming autumn, big with rich increase,
Bearing the wanton burden of the prime,
Like widowed wombs after their lords' decease:
Yet this abundant issue seemed to me
But hope of orphans and unfathered fruit;
For summer and his pleasures wait on thee,
And, thou away, the very birds are mute.
Or, if they sing, 'tis with so dull a cheer,
That leaves look pale, dreading the winter's near.

In Michael Drayton's "To Nothing Fitter," the controlling image is more complex, with metaphoric comparisons being made on several levels: The subject of the poem ("thee") is compared to a rich son (lines 1–2) who inherits and squanders wealth (lines 3–7). The subject's wealth, however, is his "love, that is on the unworthy placed"—another metaphor. Now align lines 7–8 with the final two lines (13–14): What metaphor is at work here?

TO NOTHING FITTER

To nothing fitter can I thee compare
Than to the son of some rich pennyfather,
Who having now brought on his end with care,
line Leaves to his son all he had heaped together;
(5) This new-rich novice, lavish of his chest,
To one man gives, doth on another spend,
Then here he riots, yet amongst the rest
Haps to lend some to one true honest friend.
Thy gifts thou in obscurity dost waste,
(10) False friends thy kindness, born but to deceive thee,
Thy love, that is on the unworthy placed,
Time hath thy beauty, which with age will leave thee;
Only that little which to me was lent
I give thee back, when all the rest is spent.

Sometimes a tenor will have more than one vehicle: "His attitude was ice-cold, rock-hard, and knife-sharp." Anthony Munday uses over twenty vehicles in "I Serve a Mistress":

I serve a mistress whiter than the snow,
 Straighter than cedar, brighter than the glass,
Finer in trip and swifter than the roe,
 More pleasant than the field of flowering grass;
More gladsome to my withering joys that fade,
Than winter's sun or summer's cooling shade.

Sweeter than swelling grape of ripest wine,
 Softer than feathers of the fairest swan,
Smoother than jet, more stately than the pine,
 Fresher than poplar, smaller than my span,
Clearer than beauty's fiery pointed beam,
Or icy crust of crystal's frozen stream.

Yet is she curster than the bear by kind,
 And harder-hearted than the agèd oak,
More glib than oil, more fickle than the wind,
 Stiffer than steel, no sooner bent but broke.
Lo! thus my service is a lasting sore;
Yet will I serve, although I die therefore.

Mixed metaphors are the result of a blend of incongruous vehicles for the same tenor. Mixed metaphors can be effectively used, but when poorly done, a mixed metaphor can produce undesirable effects: "She watched the eagle sail the sea of air currents with eggbeater movements and calypso rhythms." Comparing the air currents (the tenor) to the sea (the vehicle) is a common metaphor: however, this poor bird's flight (the tenor) is being compared to three very incongruous vehicles: a ship ("sail"), an eggbeater ("egg-beater movements"), and dance music ("calypso rhythms"). You may find mixed metaphors in prose narratives, such as "She sailed into the room and clawed through the books on the tables."

As is evident, the extent that metaphoric language is developed—its complexity and its subtlety of use—varies greatly. The **epic simile** is a very formal simile in which the vehicle is developed so extensively that the reader loses sight of the original relationship between it and its tenor. The TONE of the epic simile is ceremonial; the style copies that of Homer (hence you may find sources that refer to the epic simile as the Homeric simile). John Milton includes the epic simile in *Paradise Lost*.

You also may encounter the term **conceit**. Originally referring simply to a concept, the idea of a conceit has undergone a change in status. A conceit is a very intricate parallel drawn between two otherwise *dissimilar* concepts or things. These poetic metaphors were found, during the 1700s and 1800s, to be too artificial and strained. Conceit is viewed with more neutrality today, with some contemporary poets making very effective use of it, particularly in American poetry. There are two types of conceit. The Petrarchan conceit (named after the Italian poet Petrarch) was a favorite of Renaissance English poets—especially in their love sonnets, either for imitation or for contempt. The comparisons in Petrarchan conceits are highly exaggerated, as in:

ELEGY

My prime of youth is but a frost of cares,
    My feast of joy is but a dish of pain,
My crop of corn is but a field of tares,
    And all my good is but vain hope of gain;
        The day is past, and yet I saw no sun,
        And now I live, and now my life is done.

by Chidiock Tichborne

In great contrast to the Elizabethan Petrarchan conceits are the metaphysical conceits that often were the controlling images used by the metaphysical poets of the seventeenth century. The vehicles for these conceits were taken from the complexities of life with witty, sometimes shocking, comparisons. John Donne used the metaphysical conceit extensively, as in "The Flea" (1633):

THE FLEA

Mark but this flea, and mark in this
How little that which thou deny'st me is;
It sucked me first, and now sucks thee,
And in this flea our two bloods mingled be;
Thou know'st that this cannot be said
A sin, nor shame, nor loss of maidenhead,
    Yet this enjoys before it woo,
    And pampered swells with one blood made of two,
    And this, alas, is more than we would do.

Oh stay, three lives in one flea spare,
Where we almost, yea more than, married are.
(note)→ This flea is you and I, and this
Our marriage bed, and marriage temple is;
Though parents grudge, and you, we're met
And cloistered in these living walls of jet.
    Though use make you apt to kill me,
    Let not to that, self-murder added be,
    And sacrilege, three sins in killing three.

Cruel and sudden, hast thou since
Purpled thy nail in blood of innocence?
Wherein could this flea guilty be,
Except in that drop which it sucked from thee?
Yet thou triumph'st, and say'st that thou
Find'st not thyself, nor me, the weaker now;
    'Tis true; then learn how false, fears be;
    Just so much honor, when thou yield'st to me,
    Will waste, as this flea's death took life from thee.

by John Donne

In your reading, you also may find some use of metaphor in which the tenor is not directly named but only implied. These sophisticated comparisons are called **implicit metaphors** and you must rely upon CONTEXT for MEANING. In a work about a young woman's growing affection for a young man, a descriptive line might read "The bud drowned in the seas of distrust and envy." The *bud* is a vehicle for an implied tenor that can only be determined by the situation: undeveloped love. In contrast, the second metaphor at work here has directly stated tenors (distrust and envy) for its vehicle (seas).

Also, a metaphor can "die." **Dead metaphors** are those that are so commonplace that the reader no longer perceives the fact that the vehicle and tenor do not match: "pig-headed attitude," "the skin of one's teeth," "the core of the subject," "to set your heart on…," "the long arm of the law."

When metaphors are extended into narrative FORM in which the actual story and its elements (actions, places, people, and things) represent elements outside the story, often with the CHARACTERS and events representing ideas, the work is called an **allegory**. John Bunyan's *Pilgrim's Progress* is a famous allegory in which the journey of "Christian" (a CHARACTER in the story) from the City of Destruction to the Celestial City allegorizes the Christian doctrine of salvation.

- **Personification:** In personification (also called **prosopopoeia**, if the figure being personified speaks) inanimate objects or abstract ideas are given human characteristics. In the third stanza of "The Aged Lover Renounceth Love" (Lord Thomas Vaux's sixteenth-century work), age and "lusty life" are both personified:

For age with stealing steps
  Hath clawed me with his crutch,
And lusty life away she leaps
  As there had been none such.

Age is given the human characteristics of walking and hitting someone with a crutch. Lusty life—youth—is given the human characteristic of leaping.

In a testing situation, you may be asked to identify that the object or idea is being personified. Tests also may include questions concerning the effects of the personification:

"Lusty life," as a CHARACTER in lines 3–4, of the above stanza seems

(A) uncaring
(B) happy
(C) athletic
(D) an illusion
(E) deceptive

The personification of "age" in lines 1–2 emphasizes

(A) that no one escapes age
(B) the speaker's acceptance of age
(C) universal carnality
(D) age's feeble condition
(E) age's furtive nature

(The correct answers are respectively A and E.)

In Robert Browning's "In the Doorway," a fig-tree is personified:

Our fig-tree, that leaned for the saltness, has furled
  Her five fingers,
Each leaf like a hand opened wide to the world
  Where there lingers
No glint of the gold, summer sent for her sake:
How the vines writhe in rows, each impaled on its stake!
My heart shrivels up, and my spirit shrinks curled.

When you are working with personification in a work (whether in poetry or in prose), do not stop with just identifying what is being personified and what human characteristics that object or concept is being given. A test question concerning personification might tell *you* what personification is being used in the work and ask you to determine the effect of its use. After some thought, a reason for this is easy to see: Personification is figurative language that personalizes the work to the reader. By giving that object or abstract concept human qualities, it has something in common with *people* —an association that is bound to create in the reader some sort of reaction. That effect might be positive (as when death is personified as a comforting friend), negative (as when death is personified as a sinister CHARACTER), ironic, or any number of other possible effects. The sea can be personified as a friend or an enemy, as brave or cowardly, as calm or angry.

How can you tell the effect of personification in a work? Generally, writers use personification for a purpose, and that purpose, in turn, is related to the effect. First, look for the MEANING: very often the effect of the personification will be used to further the MEANING. If the MEANING of a work is that for a loved one to part is a tragedy, the writer might personify the sea upon which the person sails away as a sinister enemy. Also, look at TONE: the personification might be used to amplify the TONE. For example, a frightening TONE might be served by a sea personified as brooding and angry. Similarly, the speaker's VOICE is an element. CONTEXT, then, is pivotal to finding the effect of personification.

In Sir Phillip Sidney's sixteenth-century poem "Loving in Truth," he personifies Invention, Nature, and Study:

Loving in truth, and fain in verse my love to show,
  That she, dear she, might take some pleasure of my pain,

Pleasure might cause her read, reading might make her
know,

line   Knowledge might pity win, and pity grace obtain,

(5)   I sought fit words to paint the blackest face of woe,
Studying inventions fine, her wits to entertain,
Oft turning others' leaves, to see if thence would flow
Some fresh and fruitful showers upon my sunburnt brain.
But words came halting forth, wanting Invention's stay;

(10)   Invention, Nature's child, fled step-dame Study's blows;
And others' feet still seemed but strangers in my way.
Thus great with child to speak, and helpless in my throes,
Biting my truant pen, beating myself for spite:
"Fool," said my Muse to me, "look in thy heart and write."

What is the *effect* of this personification? The first four lines set up the situation: The speaker wants to write a poem that will show the woman he loves how much he loves her. Lines 5–8 outline that he studied "inventions" and "others' leaves" (other poets' writings) for ideas, but his brain is "sunburnt"—what today might be called "writer's block" or "burnout." Lines 9–10 (the lines that contain the personification) reveal that although he wanted "Invention" (originality) which is "Nature's child" (unlearned, natural) to stay, it "fled" from "step-dame Study's blows." Line 11 confirms that copying the style of others' works did not help him. He compares himself to a pregnant woman in line 12, his message wants so to be delivered; he is desperate by line 13. But line 14 makes his point: originality must come from within.

Within this CONTEXT, what is the *effect* of personifying Invention and Nature? One possible effect is to make originality, as "Nature's child" seem innocent (as a child), nonthreatening and desirable. The personification of Study, on the other hand, heightens the perception that the speaker has lost his fresh approach (perhaps) to imitation of others' works (a "step-dame" relationship to Invention in contrast to Invention as "Nature's child"—a natural relationship). The effect of the personification of Invention, Nature, and Study is to emphasize that writing a poem is a natural process from within rather than an artificial process.

- **Reification** is a means of describing abstract ideas as if they were concrete things. Reification cuts through the FORMS of analogous relationships, sometimes using metaphor (for example, "Life is a flowing stream"), sometimes personifying the abstraction (as in, "Love wonders the lonely paths in my heart"). The effect, regardless of the type of analogy used, is to give the reader a sense of tangible reality for otherwise difficult to explain ideas.

- **Allusion** is a reference in a literary work to some person, place, thing, or event outside the work, or to some other literary work. These references illustrate or emphasize through comparison or contrast, but when there is discrepancy between the subject and the allusion, the effect can be ironic.

Some literary scholars contend that allusions can be directly stated references or that they can be inferences; however, the current trend seems to be to emphasize the role of indirect references that cause the reader to call upon memory (and its associated emotions, connotations, feelings, and TONES) as allusion (as figures of speech) over what might be more accurately described as direct quotation or direct reference.

There are several different kinds of allusion. **Topical allusions** are based on current events and serve a significant role in the stand-up comedy routines of such performers as David Letterman, Jay Leno, and other late-night television talk show hosts. **Personal allusions** are references to events, facts, and other information in the writer's own life. Obviously, the significance of many topical and personal allusions are lost to readers of later generations. **Allusions to historical events and personages, other works** (the writers, the works themselves, or the styles of the works), and **documented information**, however, have a sense of timelessness, although realizing the full significance may require a broad base of knowledge on the part of the reader.

Allusions can be culturally based or they can be more universal in nature. Sometimes the title of a work holds an allusion that sets the TONE, subject, or VOICE of its content: The title of John Ashbery's 1965 poem "Civilization and Its Discontents" is an allusion to Sigmund Freud's book of the same title that addresses instinct and civilization.

Some allusions are popular among writers and are used over the centuries. The Trojan War, its CHARACTERS and circumstances, has remained a rich source of allusion for both prose and poetry for many generations. These two stanzas from Thomas Nashe's "Adieu, Farewell Earth's Bliss" (1592) are characteristic:

Beauty is but a flower
Which wrinkles will devour,
Brightness falls from the air,
Queens have died young and fair,
(allusion) → Dust hath closed Helen's eye.
I am sick, I must die.
Lord, have mercy on us!

Strength stoops unto the grave,
(allusion) → Worms feed on Hector brave,
Swords may not fight with fate,
Earth still holds ope her gate.
Come! come! the bells do cry.
I am sick, I must die.
Lord, have mercy on us!

One way an allusion can be tested:

In line 5, "Helen" is presented as

(A) a woman who became ill and died
(B) famous for growing flowers
(C) a woman symbolic of beauty
(D) the speaker's lover
(E) the victim of a dust storm

(The correct answer is C.)

The allusion to Helen as beautiful and Hector as brave has been used so extensively as to become traditional "types" of beauty and bravery.

Another source for allusion is the systems of Greek and Roman mythology. For example, Matthew Arnold's "Memorial Verses," for the day that William Wordsworth died (April 27, 1850) alludes to the Titans of Greek myth to emphasize the "Titanic" size (Colossal—very large) of the strife described in this excerpt from the second stanza:

When Byron's eyes were shut in death,
We bowed our head and held our breath.
He taught us little; but our soul
Had *felt* him like the thunder's roll.
With shivering heart the strife we saw
Of passion with eternal law;
And yet with reverential awe
We watched the fount of fiery life
(allusion) → Which served for that Titanic strife.

Allusion can also be accomplished through writing in the same style, rhythm, and other elements of another work. Not to be confused with **parody** (as discussed in the section on FORM, Literary Element Number Two, see page 91), in which the composition imitates another work for the pur-

pose of ridicule, allusion of this type calls to mind the other work, with (hopefully) the associated connotations, feelings, and effects desired by the writer. This is done occasionally in gospel music. For example, a modern gospel song might begin or include within its stanza a few strains in the style of "Rock of Ages" or "Amazing Grace." Or the effect might be gained by quoting another work with a slight change in, for example, words or rhythm.

The works of ancient writers, the paintings of famous artists (such as Degas, El Greco, and Brueghel), the stoic philosophies of Seneca, wars, politics—these are just a sampling of the sources from which writers pull their allusions. Yet one source of literary allusion stands out, both because of its prevalence in terms of numbers of references in English and American literature and because of its influence as a prevailing belief system: the Bible.

Old English translations were available during the seventh century. Although there were many English versions in between, the first *printed* English Bibles were not available until the sixteenth century with William Tyndale's English translation of the New Testament in 1525–1526.

In 1611, England's King James the First sponsored an English translation from the Greek "New Testament" and Hebrew "Old Testament." The King James Version, also called the Authorized Version, is the most popular English Bible and a "best-seller" yet today.

The significance of the King James Version as a work of great literature has been acknowledged by writers and critics throughout the generations. The Bible's themes and language (part prose, part verse) are exceptional, and as stated in *Words with Power* (published in 1990, Harcourt Brace Jovanovich, Publishers) by famed literary critic and professor Northrop Frye of the University of Toronto, "few would deny that some of the greatest poetry the world has ever seen is included in it [the Bible]."

Literary study went through a period in which, although recognition of the literary merits of the Bible as "a" work of literature was readily acknowledged, the study and recognition of biblical influences on the literary heritage of England and America were neglected—and perhaps to a certain extent even rejected. Viewed as "a" great work of literature, the King James Bible can be read or ignored; viewed as a major influence on English literature of the last four centuries, it must be addressed. From this perspective, then, the recent trend among some literary scholars is to at last include this formerly neglected area of literary study.

Professor Frye makes this very strong statement in *The Great Code* (published in 1982, 1981, Harcourt Brace Jovanovich, Publishers): "I soon realized that a student of English literature who does not know the Bible does not understand a good deal of what is going on in what he reads: the most conscientious student will be continually misconstruing the implications, even the meaning." Although not all writers did use or are using the Bible as a source for allusions, a significant number of important works of English and American literature indisputably include biblical references and allusions that range from occasional biblical references to literature in which the very structures of the works themselves rely upon the readers' knowledge of the Bible for understanding the writers' MEANINGS.

Based on Judeo-Christian traditions, the English-speaking culture assimilated many of the principles, values, and teachings of the Bible. As a result, both religious and secular writings oftentime reflect these influences. Some biblical PHRASES and concepts often used include:

- The apple of my eye
- A Judas
- A prophet has no honor in his own country
- The salt of the earth
- Hiding your light under a bushel
- Man does not live by bread alone
- Turning water into wine
- Walking on water
- Casting the first stone
- My brother's keeper
- A house divided cannot stand
- Standing against a Goliath
- Forty years in the wilderness
- Being thrown to the lions
- Being thrown into the fiery furnace
- Trying to pass a camel through the eye of a needle
- The patience of Job
- Wisdom of Solomon
- A coat of many colors

This list could go on and on. After years of usage in secular writing, readers today and even some of the speakers and writers incorporating these ideas into their writing may not recognize that these PHRASES and concepts are found in the Bible.

One significant factor that separates the Bible from other works that have become the basis for or influential factors on other literary works (such as the influence of Holinshed's *Chronicles* on Shakespeare, as discussed in a previous section, see page 104) is the pervasiveness of the Bible's influence. This is a book that affected to varying degrees a people's belief system and, as a result, influenced history with a major impact on that people's literature. That these beliefs would be incorporated into their literature on many different levels was inevitable.

Professor William Harmon and the late C. Hugh Holman of the University of North Carolina at Chapel Hill give us further insight into the subject on pages 49–52 of *A Handbook to Literature*, Sixth Edition (1990, Macmillan Publishing Company) in which they address the Bible both as a work of literature and as an influence on writers spanning many generations, citing several noted twentieth-century American novelists.

Some of the biblical analogies are direct references, as in Edwin Morgan's "Message Clear" (1968) based on "The Gospel according to John" 11:25 (chapter 11, verse 25) and in Lord Byron's "The Destruction of Sennacherib," a poem based on the account in II Kings chapters 18 and 19 of the destruction of King Sennacherib of Assyria by God when the king attacked Jerusalem. Others, though, include not only allusionary references, but also reflect a Bible-based belief system. What allusions to scripture do you see in this poem?

LEAVE ME, O LOVE

Leave me, O Love, which reachest but to dust,
And thou, my mind, aspire to higher things;
Grow rich in that which never taketh rust:
line Whatever fades but fading pleasure brings.
(5)   Draw in thy beams, and humble all thy might
To that sweet yoke where lasting freedoms be;
Which breaks the clouds and opens forth the light
That doth both shine and give us sight to see.
    O take fast hold; let that light be thy guide
(10) In this small course which birth draws out to death,
And think how evil becometh him to slide,
Who seeketh heav'n, and comes of heav'nly breath.
    Then farewell, world, thy uttermost I see;
    Eternal Love, maintain thy life in me.

by Sir Philip Sidney

Examining one-by-one the allusions at work in this poem the reader finds:

(Line 1)   Love (personified, hence carnal) "reachest but to dust" alludes to Genesis 3:19.

(Line 2)   The mind aspiring to higher things alludes to Colossians 3:2.

(Lines 3 and 4)   Treasures in Heaven do not rust—an allusion to Matthew 6:19–20.

(Line 5)   A call to the humbling of might alludes to Luke 14:11 and I Peter 5:5.

(Line 6)   The yoke is an allusion to Matthew 11:28–30.

(Lines 7 and 8)   These allusions are to the return of Jesus (Luke 21:27–28), the light of God (Ephesians 5:14, II Timothy 1:10, I John 1:5), and John 1:4.

(Line 9)   Taking "fast hold" alludes to Hebrews 4:14 and the light as guide alludes to Psalm 48:14 and Luke 1:79.

(Line 10)   This line alludes to the brevity of carnal life (Psalm 103:15–16).

(Line 11)   This line alludes to John 3:20.

(Line 12)   "Heavenly breath" is an allusion to Genesis 2:7 and John 20:22.

(Lines 13 and 14)   These lines allude to Matthew 28:20 and I John 5:4, with Eternal Love being an allusion to I John 4:16 and Romans 8:38-39 and with "thy life in me" alluding to John 14:23 and 15:10, I John 2:24–25, 5:11–12, and John 3:16.

The MEANING in this poem appears to be the speaker's expounding upon Romans 6:23, and as you can see, the MEANING of the poem is lost without an understanding of the speaker's scriptural allusions. Many times the scriptural allusions will be interspersed in a work. Even then, however, a familiarity with the Bible can be pivotal to understanding the references used.

Prose writers, too, within the Judeo-Christian tradition of England and America rely heavily on the King James Bible as a source for literary allusion. Most Americans are familiar with Patrick Henry's most famous speech in which he challenged "Give me liberty, or give me death!" Notice his extensive use of biblical allusion in these excerpts from the speech:

LIBERTY OR DEATH
by
Patrick Henry

Mr. President, it is natural to man to indulge in the illusions of hope. We are apt to shut our

An allusion to: eyes against a painful truth and listen to the song of that siren, till she transforms us into beasts. Is this the part of wise men, engaged in a great and arduous struggle for liberty? Are we disposed to be of the number of those, who,

Mark 8:18 → having eyes, see not, and having ears, hear not, the things which so nearly concern their temporal salvation? For my part, whatever anguish of spirit it may cost, I am willing to know the whole truth, to know the worst and to provide for it.

I have but one lamp by which my feet are guided, and that is the lamp of experience. I know of no way of judging of the future but by the past. And judging by the past, I wish to know what there has been in the conduct of the British ministry for the last ten years to justify those hopes with which gentlemen have been pleased to solace themselves and the House? Is it that insidious smile with which our petition has been lately received? Trust it not, sir; it will

Luke 22:47→ prove a snare to your feet. Suffer not yourselves
48 to be betrayed with a kiss. Ask yourselves how this gracious reception of our petition comports with these warlike preparations which cover our waters and darken our land. Are fleets and armies necessary to a work of love and reconciliation? Have we shown ourselves so unwilling to be reconciled that force must be called in to win back our love? Let us not deceive ourselves, sir. These are the implements of war and subjugation, the last arguments to which kings resort....If we wish to be free—if we mean to preserve inviolate those inestimable privileges for which we have been so long contending—if we mean not basely to abandon the noble struggle in which we have been so long engaged, and which we have pledged ourselves never to abandon until the glorious object of our contest shall be obtained, we must fight! I repeat it, sir, we must fight! An

Psalm 46:7→ appeal to arms and to the God of Hosts is all
11 that is left us!

* * *

It is in vain, sir, to extenuate the matter.
Jeremiah 6→ Gentlemen may cry, peace, peace!—but there
14 and 8:11 is no peace. The war is actually begun! The next gale that sweeps from the north will bring to our ears the clash of resounding arms! Our brethern are already in the field! Why stand we here idle? What is it that gentlemen wish? What would they have? Is life so dear, or peace so sweet, as to

be purchased at the price of chains and slavery? Forbid it, Almighty God! I know not what course others may take, but as for me: *Give me liberty, or give me death!*

Regardless of the reader's personal beliefs, the value of a familiarity with this great and lasting work—the Authorized, King James Version of the Bible—to the serious student of English and American literature needs to be considered.

- Nomenclature—by what names people, places, things, and ideas are called. Among the Anglo-Saxon peasants of early England, people were addressed by their first names; however, English family names (surnames) came into use during the fourteenth century.

At first these surnames indicated heritage, with "son of" used as an affix to the father's name: son of Jacob became Jacob<u>son</u>, son of Erik became Erik<u>son</u>, and the trend continued with such names as John<u>son</u>, and Richard<u>son</u>. Then people became known by the name of where they lived (Hill, Rivers, Austin, London), by occupation (Weaver, Harper, Thatcher)—or, as in Scotland, identified by the occupation of their fathers: McPherson, meaning "son of (Mc) the parson (Pherson)."

Evidently, in their search for means of identification, the English named themselves based on practical associations. This sense of the practical is carried into the literary figures of speech that deal with what to call—how to identify—things, places, and most especially people. Some of these figures of speech reflect popular usage; others are more literary based.

The **kenning** originated as an Old Germanic descriptive or figurative phrase used in Old English in such works as *Beowulf*. The phrase serves as a synonym in place of the simple or ordinary name, such as "the foamy-necked" or "the sea-farer" for *ship*. Generally, a kenning is an example of **periphrasis**, meaning that it is an indirect, sometimes wordy, way of stating something. (An example of periphrasis would be to refer to a pen as "a procurer of gains and debts, and love requited." Also, such statements as "I would if I could but I can't so I won't" or "I am most desirous to make your acquaintance" are periphrasic.)

A kenning will often include **metonymy**—when a closely associated name of an object is used in place of a word, such as referring to a king as "the ring giver" or "the crown," or to his position of au-

thority as "the throne." In the United States, people often refer to the executive branch of the federal government or to the president as "the White House." James Shirley uses metonymy in this seventeenth-century poem "The Glories of Our Blood and State":

> The glories of our blood and state
> Are shadows, not substantial things;
> There is no armour against fate;
> Death lays his icy hand on kings:
> metonymy → Sceptre and crown
> Must tumble down,
> And in the dust be equal made
> metonymy → With the poor crooked scythe and spade.

A practice test question might read:

"Scythe and spade" in the last line contextually refers to

(A) damaged equipment
(B) death
(C) farm implements
(D) the working man
(E) fate

(The correct answer is D.)

"Sceptre and crown" is a metonymy for the king, whereas "scythe and spade" is a metonymy for the working man.

You also may encounter **synecdoche**, a trope in which the name of a part represents the whole or the name of the whole represents the part. Workers may be referred to as "hands." A country's "ears and eyes" are its spies. A "roof over your head" is a home, and a musical producer might refer to the lead singer as "the voice."

Antonomasia is a figure of speech used extensively in politics. In antonomasia, a proper name is used to represent an idea, such as "Watergate" refers to an entire network of events during the 1970s. Sometimes the antonomasia is a person's name, as when western movie enthusiasts say "There aren't any John Waynes in movies anymore"—John Wayne representing (a type of) the rugged, "all-male" western hero who exhibits certain expected characteristics. Occasionally, the antonomasia will come in the form of an **epithet** (a periphrasic descriptive adjective, noun, or noun phrase describing a particular characteristic of a person or thing). An epithet might be to describe a puzzle as a "brain-twister," a home as a "sanctuary from the storm," or an admired leader as a "shining beacon of light." An epithet is often used as a substitution for a proper name, for example when, in referring to Elvis Presley, tabloid headlines read "The King of Rock'n'Roll Spotted in White House Tour Group." Note that the epithet is not restricted to just the negative name-calling normally associated with the term.

A **symbol** (in contrast to metaphor that serves to illustrate) is a type of image that begins with some objective thing that calls to mind a second level of MEANING, a level of MEANING that oftentimes embodies abstract concepts, that in turn elicit from the reader a range of emotions.

Some symbols are universal. Here is a limited sampling:

In this third stanza of "The Canonization," John Donne uses two traditional symbols: the eagle to represent strength and the dove to represent purity.

> Call us what you will, we are made such by love.
>   Call her one, me another fly,
> We're tapers too, and at our own cost die;
> → And we in us find th'eagle and the dove.
>   The phoenix riddle hath more wit
>   By us; we two, being one, are it.
> So to one neutral thing both sexes fit,
>   We die and rise the same, and prove
>   Mysterious by this love.

Generally, symbols depend for their associated MEANINGS upon the CONTEXT of the literary work in which they are used.

UNIVERSAL SYMBOLS

Symbol	MEANING Level one	MEANING Level two	*Possible Emotions
1. National flag	Cloth with pattern	Represents country	Pride, patriotism
2. Sea	Large body of water	Represents countless people	Fear of invasion, pity on the masses
3. Red rose	Flower	Represents love	Sentimentalism, special person
4. Purple	Color	Represents royalty	Respect, honor
5. Wedding ring	Gold band worn on left hand	Represents a state of being married	Fidelity, loyalty
6. Longhorned steer	Steer with long, curved horns	Represents football team at a Texas school	School loyalty and rivalry
7. *Yellow	Color	Represents cowardice and fear	Shame, dishonor
		also	
		Slow down	Caution
		and	
		Homecoming, reunion (ribbons)	Support, honor, and happiness

* Notice that the same symbol can have both negative or positive connotations depending on usage or CONTEXT.

2. Figures of speech based on rhetoric

In its broadest sense, rhetoric relates directly to persuasion; in other words, the USE OF LANGUAGE for the purpose of persuading the readers or hearers. Rhetoric, as a "school of thought" in which there are certain principles and certain persuasive devices aimed at effective discourse, probably began to be studied sometime during the fifth century. Aristotle dealt extensively with the subject, defining it as "discovering all the available means of persuasion in any given case." Implied in the definition is the idea that there are, indeed, specific, identifiable techniques or devices that a writer or speaker can use to persuade people to agree with his or her point of view.

Also implicit in this view is the notion that in order to effectively agree with a point, rhetoric must deal in some way with:

- Effective proof and information
- Effective arrangement of the information
- Effective presentation of the information in terms of syntax, diction, and mechanics

Finally, rhetoric traditionally has three main categories or types:

Deliberative rhetoric is aimed at moving the hearers or readers to some action either for or against a specific public policy.

Forensic rhetoric is aimed at proving someone's guilt or innocence. (From television crime shows, you may recognize forensic medicine as medical evidence at crime scenes that can be used to prove or disprove in a court of law a suspect's involvement in a crime—his or her guilt or innocence.)

Epideictic rhetoric is aimed at displaying rhetorical skills at some special occasion by praising (or perhaps condemning) a person or group.

Of course, all the literary elements can contribute to the effectiveness of a rhetorical work. Likewise, most figures of speech can be used to further the purpose—to persuade the readers or listeners. There are some figures of speech, however, that are generally considered rhetorical in nature.

- **Rhetorical questions** are those asked, not for the purpose of eliciting an expressed answer, but rather for their rhetorical effect: an emphasis of the speaker's point. When, as a case in point, a man stops another on the street, asking for the correct time and the second man holds up his wrist to show that he does not have a watch and says "How should I know?" no answer is expected, but the point could be: "You are being unreasonable in expecting me to know what time it is." (Determination of intent, of course, in a case such as this, would depend a great deal on the facial expressions and TONE of VOICE used by the man when he says "How should I know?"—did he smile and shrug, indicating he, too, was at a loss about the time; or did he growl the words with a snarl on his face, indicating a hostile "don't bother me" attitude?)

The "Give me liberty, or give me death!" speech of Patrick Henry uses the rhetorical question extensively. Sir Thomas Wyatt, in "And Wilt Thou Leave Me Thus?" bases both title and poem on a rhetorical question:

And wilt thou leave me thus?
   Say nay, say nay, for shame!
   To save thee from the blame
   Of all my grief and grame.
And wilt thou leave me thus?
   Say nay! say nay!

And wilt thou leave me thus,
   That hath loved thee so long
   In wealth and woe among?
   And is thy heart so strong
As for to leave me thus?
   Say nay! say nay!

And wilt thou leave me thus,
   That hath given thee my heart,
   Never for to depart
   Neither for pain nor smart;
And wilt thou leave me thus?
   Say nay! say nay!

And wilt thou leave me thus,
   And have no more pity
   Of him that loveth thee?
   Helas! thy cruelty!
And wilt thou leave me thus?
   Say nay! say nay!

- **Amplification** is a device used by teachers extensively—and is used throughout this study guide. In amplification, a word, concept, point, or idea is defined or explained, then the initial definition or explanation is followed by another, more detailed explanation. Amplification is rhetorically effective for several reasons:

- The restatement emphasizes the importance of the idea.
- The restatement clarifies the idea, thus enabling the reader or listener to better understand it.
- The restatement facilitates the reader's or listener's retention of the idea.

The additional details in the restatement can include more facts, an illustration, another figure of speech, a change in diction or level of language, and other devices.

In this excerpt from James Madison's June 6, 1788 speech, Madison (who favored a Federal constitution) is arguing against a speech made the previous day by Patrick Henry in which Henry spoke against ratification:

I must confess I have not been able to find his usual consistency in the gentleman's argument on this occasion. He informs us that the people of the country
line are at perfect repose; that is, every man enjoys the
(5) fruits of his labor peaceably and securely, and that everything is in perfect tranquility and safety. I wish sincerely that this were true. If this be their happy situation, why has every state acknowledged the contrary? Why were deputies from all the states sent to
(10) the general convention? Why have complaints of national and individual distresses been echoed and reechoed throughout the continent? Why has our general government been so shamefully disgraced and our Constitution violated? Wherefore have laws been
(15) made to authorize a change, and wherefore are we now assembled here? A federal government is formed for the protection of its individual members. Ours has attacked itself with impunity. Its authority has been disobeyed and despised.

Madison points out that Henry "informs us that the people of the country are at perfect repose." He **amplifies** "perfect repose" in lines 4–7. He gives an example using figurative language ("fruits of his labor") and amplifies with a generalization. Interestingly, Madison then uses a series of rhetorical questions that attack the amplification Madison supplied to Henry's assertion that the country is "at perfect repose."

(Another rhetorical device Madison employs is a FORM of repetition called **palilogy**: notice the effect when he keeps repeating "Why…? Why…? in lines 8–12.)

- **Aposiopesis.** You are in a supermarket. A child is screaming, and you can hear the parent's exasperated, high-pitched, slightly threatening TONE, "If you don't stop it, I'll...." Or you hear children playing and one squirts water on the other. The victim starts chasing the attacker and cries, "Wait'll I catch you... I'm gonna...." This is aposiopesis. It is a very deliberate trailing off of the speaker's voice—an incomplete sentence—stopping midway in a sentence.

In rhetorical writing, what purpose does this serve? One obvious purpose is to allow the hearer to supply his or her own words—a technique that can emphasize the point. Also, it allows a speaker to convey MEANING, to express a message without actually putting it into words that can be later quoted—or misquoted—a very advantageous situation in some circumstances. James Fenimore Cooper uses aposiopesis in *The Pilot:*

"There are men, who have never worn the servile livery of Britain, sir, whose names are as fondly cherished in America as any that she boasts of," said Katherine, proudly; "ay, sir, and those who would gladly oppose the bravest officers in the British fleet."

"I contend not against your misguided reason," said Colonel Howard, rising with cool respect. "A young lady who ventures to compare rebels with gallant gentlemen engaged in their duty to their prince, cannot escape the imputation of possessing a misguided reason. No man—I speak not of women, who cannot be supposed so well versed in human nature—but no man who has reached the time of life that entitles him to be called by that name, can consort with these disorganizers, who would destroy everything that is sacred—these levellers who would pull down the great to exalt the little—these Jacobins, who—who—"

"Nay, sir, if you are at a loss for opprobrious epithets," said Katherine, with provoking coolness, "call on Mr. Christopher Dillon for assistance; he waits your pleasure at the door."

Colonel Howard turned in amazement, forgetting his angry declamations at this unexpected intelligence, and beheld, in reality, the sombre visage of his kinsman, who stood holding the door in his hand, apparently as much surprised at finding himself in the presence of the ladies as they themselves could be at his unusual visit.

Vocabulary check: What does "opprobrious epithets" mean as used by Katherine in the third paragraph?

Another aspect significant to rhetorical writing is delivery, particularly of speeches. An important aspect of a speech is establishing the rapport with the hearers. There are ways in which a speaker can use delivery (the way in which the speech is given) to claim the attention of the audience. One way is to plan moments of silence or deliberate pauses, causing the hearers to continue the unspoken thought. Of course speeches given prior to modern recording means were delivered with only written copies (for example, of the Gettysburg Address); however, you can become sensitive to the point at which a speaker may have paused during his or her verbal discourse. Developing such awareness can help the reader to identify key points in the speaker's argument.

Clarence Darrow, in 1924, was opposed to capital punishment. The situation of the following excerpt was an appeal to the court on behalf of two teenagers who had been convicted of killing another teenager:

I do not know how much salvage there is in these two boys. I hate to say it in their presence, but what is there to look forward to? I do not know but what Your Honor would be merciful if you tied a rope around their necks and let them die; merciful to them, but not merciful to civilization, and not merciful to those who would be left behind. To spend the balance of their days in prison is mighty little to look forward to, if anything. Is it anything? They may have the hope that as the years roll around they might be released. I do not know. I do not know.

What would be the effect if he paused each time he said "I do not know"? (Why do you think he kept repeating "I do not know"?)

Paraposiopesis is when the interruption is an actual expression of emotion. In addition, sometimes the speaker mentions his or her inability to express his or her emotion at the point at which the sentence is broken off (for example, "I don't know what to say..."). This usage is called **aporia**, a rhetorical device described in the *Webster's New Twentieth Century Dictionary* (Unabridged). It is also cited by *The New Princeton Encyclopedia of Poetry and Poetics* (1993) as a figure that becomes **adynaton**, an expression of impossibility (for example, "When elephants fly, I'll...").

Notice how the speaker in "My Last Duchess" searches for words when he says: "A heart—how shall I say?—too soon made glad."

Another example: Sinclair Lewis's main CHARACTERS react emotionally in "Virga Vay & Allan Cedar":

"Oh, sweet, be careful! It might explode!"
"Yes, it—" Then he shouted. "Listen at us! As if we cared if we got blown up now!"

Graphically, (sometimes but not always) aposiopesis is shown with ellipsis (...), or with an em dash (—) or even a double dash (— —). Not all use of ellipsis and dashes, however, are indicative of aposiopesis, but are depending on MEANING and CONTEXT.

- **Apophasis** occurs when the speaker makes a point by pretending to deny it. For instance, "If I did not know you are an honest person, I would think you took that money," or "I would have to conclude your participation in this plan was with knowledge and premeditation, were it not for our long years of friendship and trust."
- **Anachronism** refers to violations of time and space in which an event or person is placed in the wrong time. When these violations appear in movies and television, viewers include them in a broad category of cinematic error called "bloopers." Examples of anachronistic-type bloopers are when the soldiers defend the fort against an Indian attack in 1855 by setting up a Gatling gun (not invented until 1861) or when Geronimo (not born until 1829) attacks a fort in 1820. Such anachronisms can be found in prose, poetry, and drama. For instance, what is the anachronism in this excerpt from Shakespeare's *Julius Caesar?*

MARCUS BRUTUS.	Alas, good Cassius, do not think of him: If he love Caesar, all that he can do Is to himself,—take thought, and die for Caesar: And that were much he should; for he is given To sports, to wildness, and much company.
TREBONIUS.	There is no fear in him; let him not die; For he will live, and laugh at this hereafter.
	[Clock strikes.]
MARCUS BRUTUS.	Peace! count the clock.
CASSIUS.	The clock hath stricken three.
TREBONIUS.	'Tis time to part.

A clock that can strike the hour? In Caesar's Rome?

Here is John Keats's "On First Looking into Chapman's Homer." Can you find the anachronism?

Much have I travelled in the realms of gold,
And many goodly states and kingdoms seen;
Round many western islands have I been
Which bards in fealty to Apollo hold.
Oft of one wide expanse had I been told
That deep-browed Homer ruled as his demesne;
Yet did I never breathe its pure serene
Till I heard Chapman speak out loud and bold:
Then felt I like some watcher of the skies
When a new planet swims into his ken;
Or like stout Cortez when with eagle eyes
He stared at the Pacific—and all his men
Looked at each other with a wild surmise—
Silent, upon a peak in Darien.

HINT: Who discovered the Pacific Ocean?

But do not mistakenly assume that all anachronisms are accidental errors—some are quite purposeful with "poetic license"—a rhetorical means that can have desired effects, such as Mark Twain's extended use of anachronism in *A Connecticut Yankee in King Arthur's Court* for an ironic effect.

- **Litotes** is a favorite of Anglo-Saxon writing. In litotes, a sense of understatement is achieved through negative affirmation (the negative of the opposite), which actually confirms or increases the importance of what is being discussed:

Litotes	*Meaning*
not bad	good
not fat	thin
not least	great
not unbecoming	appropriate
not the smartest	stupid

Of course, much of the rhetorical effect of litotes depends upon its use in CONTEXT. For example, the effect of litotes might be ironic:

Two people are running for political office. The person representing Party X makes extensive use of unfair (or unethical) campaign practices, whereas the person representing Party Y runs a "clean" campaign. The Party X candidate appears to be ahead in the polls and declares himself to be "Number One." Despite Party X candidate's lead, he decides to make public a story he heard from unconfirmed sources that would be damaging to the Party Y candidate, almost eliminating him from the race. Upon publishing this information, the Party Y candidate not only clearly establishes to the public the wrongful nature of the allegations, but does so with such grace and dignity that he leaps ahead in the polls. At Party Y headquarters, the candidate inquires about the Party X candidate's current standing, to which a party worker replies, "Well, let's just say he's not Number One!"

- **Hyperbole** (overstatement or exaggeration) and **meiosis** (understatement) are tropes that can be used for a wide variety of both serious and comic effects.

Hyperbole can be especially comic: Texans, as a case in point, are noted for their use of hyperbole, exaggeration, in a state where "the men are braver, the sky is bluer, the steaks are bigger, and the women are prettier than anywhere else in the world." Some stand-up comedians who perform before live audiences make extensive use of hyperbole. An example is the comedian who begins his routine by bragging about how hot he makes his chili, to which the audience shouts "How hot is it?" Comedian: "It's *so* hot it'll melt your spoon!"

Sometimes hyperbole is sincere, as when a lover wants to emphasize the extent of his or her love, or ironic. Read this first stanza of Andrew Marvell's "To His Coy Mistress":

TO HIS COY MISTRESS

→ Had we but world enough, and time,
   This coyness, Lady, were no crime.
   We would sit down, and think which way
   To walk, and pass our long love's day.
   Thou by the Indian Ganges' side
   Should'st rubies find: I by the tide
   Of Humber would complain. I would
→ Love you ten years before the Flood:
   And you should if you please refuse
→ Till the conversion of the Jews.
   My vegetable love should grow
→ Vaster than empires, and more slow.
→ And hundred years should go to praise
   Thine eyes, and on thy forehead gaze.
→ Two hundred to adore each breast:
→ But thirty thousand to the rest.
   An age at least to every part,
   And the last age should show your heart.
   For, Lady, you deserve this state;
   Nor would I love at lower rate.

by Andrew Marvell

Its opposite, **meiosis** or understatement, treats a serious subject as though it is much less important than it is. Often meiosis projects a derogatory manner (unlike litotes, which, through negation, frequently elevate the importance of their subjects); however, CONTEXT may dictate any number of effects, such as irony. The effect of the understatement in the last stanza of Thackeray's "Sorrows of Werther" is based on the incongruity of Charlotte's reaction to a man's death over her.

SORROWS OF WERTHER

Werther had a love for Charlotte
   Such as words could never utter;
Would you know how first he met her?
   She was cutting bread and butter.

Charlotte was a married lady,
   And a moral man was Werther,
And, for all the wealth of Indies,
   Would do nothing for to hurt her.

So he sighed and pined and ogled,
   And his passion boiled and bubbled,
Till he blew his silly brains out,
   And no more was by it troubled.

Charlotte, having seen his body
   Borne before her on a shutter,
Like a well-conducted person,
   Went on cutting bread and butter.

           by William Makepeace Thackeray

- **Paradox,** an important element in metaphysical poetry and in epigrammatic writing, is a statement that seems to contradict itself, yet is actually true. Statements of paradox occur in conversations in everyday life: a couple may look at a pug-faced dog in a store window and exclaim "He's so ugly he's cute!"

The second stanza of Chidiock Tichborne's sixteenth-century "Elegy" is built upon paradoxial relationships:

My tale was heard and yet it was not told,
   My fruit is fallen and yet my leaves are green,
My youth is spent and yet I am not old,
   I saw the world and yet I was not seen;
      My thread is cut and yet it is not spun,
      And now I live, and now my life is done.

An **oxymoron** occurs when words, terms, or expressions appear to be self-contradicting: bittersweet, a dry martini, sweet-and-sour, love-hate relationships, passive resistance, jumbo shrimp, or a kind ogre.

Sometimes you will find passages in which the speaker makes extensive use of oxymorons, as Romeo's speech in *Romeo and Juliet* (Act I Scene I) in which he speaks in such terms as "loving-hate" and "cold fires." More often, though, the oxymoron will be used with more restraint, primarily for the contradictory effect that produces such feelings as an emphasized sense of confusion, frustration, or determination (to name a few). CONTEXT, once again, is a prime determinant of the effect. Also, be alert for the "play on words" that so many times is within the oxymoron. The fourth stanza of Sir Thomas Wyatt's "Marvel No More" ends with an oxymoronic play on words, as does Shakespeare's "Sonnet 40" in line 13.

MARVEL NO MORE

Marvel no more although
   The songs I sing do moan,
For other life than woe
   I never provèd none.

And in my heart also
   Is graven with letters deep
A thousand sighs and mo,
   A flood of tears to weep.

Now may a man in smart
   Find matter to rejoice?
How may a mourning heart
   Set forth a pleasant voice?

Play who that can that part:
   Needs must in me appear
How fortune, overthwart,
   Doth cause my mourning cheer. ←

           by Sir Thomas Wyatt

SONNET 40

    Take all my loves, my love, yea, take them all;
    What hast thou then more than thou hadst before?
    No love, my love, that thou mayst true love call;
line All mine was thine before thou hadst this more.
(5) Then, if for my love thou my love receivest,
    I cannot blame thee for my love thou usest;
    But yet be blamed, if thou thyself deceivest
    By wilful taste of what thyself refusest.
    I do forgive thy robbery, gentle thief,
(10) Although thou steal thee all my poverty;

And yet love knows it is a greater grief
To bear love's wrong than hate's known injury.
→ Lascivious grace, in whom all ill well shows, ←
Kill me with spites; yet we must not be foes.

by William Shakespeare

- **Irony** is a concept that involves opposites. The many types of irony form two distinct categories: **situational** or **dramatic irony**, in which the result following a sequence of events is the opposite of what is expected, and **verbal irony**, in which the speaker uses words that express the opposite of what is actually meant.

First, examine a few of the many FORMS situational irony can take. Ironic situations are a mainstay of popular comedy. The acting comedy of Lucille Ball, for example, relied heavily on situational irony as a source of humor. Often Lucy, who wanted to be part of her husband's nightclub act, would devise a plan to be part of the show. Rather than achieving her expected results, however, her plans usually ended with Lucy locked in a closet, hanging from a balcony, or in some other embarrassing situation.

Occasionally, a situation is ironic when someone who intends harm against another becomes the victim of his or her own plan, for instance, when the angry teenager is splashing paint on his neighbor's car, but an unexpected wind causes the paint to blow back on his own parked car, ruining the finish. Sometimes, if the person's attitudes or motives are unjustified and he becomes the victim of an ironic situation, he is said to have "gotten what he deserves."

Situational irony can be sad or even poignant, as when parents secure weapons to protect their children from danger, only to have a child injured or killed by one of those same weapons. On very subtle levels, situations can be intrinsically ironic, such as when the undeserving, cowardly, or lazy are rewarded while the deserving, brave, or industrious are punished.

Sometimes irony results from making false assumptions, and the very presence of an ironic outcome might lead you to examine the validity of the assumptions you have made.

Examine the following short excerpt from Rachel Carson's *Silent Spring* (1962).

Now at last, as it has become apparent that the heedless and unrestrained use of chemicals [insecticides] is a greater menace to ourselves than to the targets, the river which is

the science of biotic control flows again, fed by new streams of thought.

What situation is ironic in this passage? What makes this situation ironic?

The irony of this situation revolves around using chemicals to destroy insect populations. Note the connotative clues given: using the words *heedless* and *unrestrained* to describe the use of chemicals. Insecticides were developed and used to create a healthier, insect-free environment; but those same chemicals were "a greater menace to ourselves than to the targets"—an ironic situation.

Verbal irony occurs when the speaker says the opposite of what he or she means. How can you tell that verbal irony is at work in a statement? One clue is through the speaker's "ironic" TONE of VOICE and through facial expression. The effect of the irony is a product of the speaker's intent.

For instance, a married couple plans to meet another couple at a restaurant for dinner. The wife arrives first, as usual for this couple. The other couple arrives and asks about her overdue husband. "He'll be here in a moment, I'm sure," she says with a laugh and wink, "Steve is *never* late!" Obviously from her TONE, body language, and emphasis on never, Steve generally is late (a knowledge that, by implication, is shared by the other couple); however, his wife is not distressed but rather views this as a comical part of Steve's personality. But what if her attitude is different—perhaps critical because Steve's habitual tardiness had caused the couple serious social, business, and family problems? "He'll be here in a moment, I'm *sure*" she says through clenched teeth, her gaze rolling toward the ceiling in disdain. "*Steve* is *never* late!" The TONE is hostile; the intent is critical. When the intent of the irony is to criticize by use of praise, the FORM is called **sarcasm**. (The sarcastic TONE of Robert Browning's "Soliloquy of the Spanish Cloister" is an oft-cited example, as is Swift's "A Modest Proposal.")

Verbal irony, although sometimes described as "tongue in cheek," is not always sarcastic in TONE or intent. The irony may be the result of **understatement**, also called **meiosis**, ("I think we have a little water in the basement"—when the basement contains a 3-foot deep flood), in which the irony intensifies the MEANING of what is said, the result of **overstatement**, also known as **hyperbole**, ("This pimple outshines a neon sign!"), in which the irony lessens the importance of the MEANING of what is said, or the result of **contradiction in CONTEXT** (such as describing a cruel, uncaring person in terms that are endearing).

Whether verbal or situational, sometimes the irony is readily apparent, as in Chief Seattle's words (1854):

There was a time when our people covered the land as the waves of a wind-ruffled sea cover its shell-paved floor, but that time long since passed away with the greatness of tribes that are now but a mournful memory. I will not dwell on, nor mourn over, our untimely decay, nor reproach my pale-faced brothers with hastening it as we too may have been somewhat to blame....

Our good father at Washington—for I presume he is now our father as well as yours, since King George has moved his boundaries further north—our great and good father, I say, sends us word that if we do as he desires he will protect us....

But very often verbal irony is subtle and difficult to recognize. In Andrew Marvell's "To His Coy Mistress," the speaker begins with:

Had we but world enough, and time,
This coyness, Lady, were no crime.
We would sit down, and think which way
To walk, and pass our long love's day.

He concludes the poem, however, by saying:

Thus, though we cannot make our sun
Stand still, yet we will make him run.

What is ironic about the speaker's words? Upon what is this irony based? These words are ironic because they are based upon contradiction in CONTEXT: at first the speaker bemoans how short the time—there is not enough time for her to be coy (an implication from the statement that "Had we but world enough, and time,..."). But he concludes that because they cannot stop the sun (a symbol for time), their love will make time go faster (the sun run)—an irony in the speaker's argument.

The relationship of verbal irony to MEANING is, at this point, self-evident, as demonstrated by a master of verbal irony, Alexander Pope. Here is his "Epigram from the French." What verbal irony is at work here?

EPIGRAM FROM THE FRENCH

Sir, I admit your gen'ral rule
That every poet is a fool.

But you yourself may serve to show it,
That every fool is not a poet.

by Alexander Pope

Perhaps the speaker's auditor has stated that all poets are fools—a generalization that would include the speaker. Does the speaker really agree ("admit your gen'ral rule")? The final couplet confirms that he is speaking ironically, as he indulges in a generalization that the auditor (probably not a poet) is proof that not all fools are poets.

3. Figures of speech based on syntax

Although diction refers to word choice (vocabulary), syntax refers to how the words are arranged into patterns. A few of the more common figures of speech that depend on syntax are summarized in the chart on page 184.

What effects can you expect from the use of figures of speech based on syntax? Figures such as antithesis and apostrophe can, depending on CONTEXT, project a formal TONE or render the work more or less emotional. Hyperbatons and hypallages can add a sense of confusion, particularly when the speaker is portraying a state of mental anxiety, as an example. Sleights of "and" can be witty, provocative, or disruptive, again based on CONTEXT. Of course, the chart on page 184 is only a partial list of the many effects syntax-based figures can have in a work.

Diction

Diction refers to the enunciation or exact articulation of words and also refers to word choice. Diction, in terms of its significance to studying and understanding literature, can be discussed from several perspectives, including diction as a USE OF LANGUAGE, poetic diction, and diction as it relates to MEANINGS OF SENTENCES, LINES, PHRASES, AND WORDS IN CONTEXT (particularly as diction and syntax interact to produce a writer's style).

Diction—the writer's word choice—can be based on many different sources, levels, and purposes: sources for words can range from Germanic to Latinate, archaic to modern, eclectic "borrowed expressions" (such as a Gallicism, which is a borrowing from French) to those of Anglo-Saxon origin, and so forth. The levels can range from formal to informal, technical to nontechnical, standard to nonstandard.

FIGURES OF SPEECH BASED ON SYNTAX

Figure of Speech	Characteristic Syntactical Structure	Examples
1. Antithesis	Balance of contrasting terms; parallelism	O, change thy thought, that I may change my mind!
2. Apostrophe	Direct address to an auditor (called invocation if to a muse)	My pen, take pain a little space. To follow that which doth me chase.
3. Hyperbaton	Transposition or rearrangement of normal sentence order	Which when she entered, although the younger except, none could attain, fixed the smile for the rest….
4. Hypallage	An epithet or qualifier placed next to less proximate of a group of nouns	"the Gypsy's wondering curse" for "the wondering Gypsy's curse"
5. Sleight of "and"	Tropes that use co-ordinating conjunctions For example, the zeugma: • Same grammatical relation, but different idiomatic use • Two different verbs • Subject-verb agreement problem	 • He will pay Jane her due and her rent. • He bussed the table in the restaurant and the children to school. • You or she is going to have to leave.

The purpose could be for literal communication or for figurative MEANING, for expression of opinion or for teaching, for contemplation or for spurring to action.

As a USE OF LANGUAGE, diction (word choice) plays an obvious role, particularly in imagery and figures of speech. Sometimes the change of a single word can make—or destroy—the TONE or the MEANING of a selection, hence a writer's diction is generally aimed at producing a desired effect, an effect that may go beyond the literal MEANING of the word choice.

To some degree, diction can be viewed as isolated word choices. For example, a **malapropism** is the use of a word that is inappropriate for the CONTEXT, but that resembles a word that is appropriate. The effect, of course, of using the incorrect word can be amusing (as when Norm Crosby fills his routine with malapropisms—for the purpose of making the audience laugh) or it can be embarrassing when the error in word choice is unintentional. When the malapropism is used in the dialogue of a CHARACTER, the effect depends upon the situation of the story: the malapropism might serve to enlighten the reader and/or the other people engaged in the dialogue concerning the CHARACTER'S educational level, as an example. Richard Brinsley Sheridan's Mrs. Malaprop in *The Rivals* (1775) is the CHARACTER whose constant misuse of words,

such as "a progeny of learning," gave rise to the expression "malapropism." In the case of Mrs. Malaprop, she was trying to display mastery of a large vocabulary.

Can you spot any malapropisms in this excerpt from *Romeo and Juliet,* Act II Scene III? What is the effect?

NURSE. By my troth, it is well said;—'for himself to mar,' quoth a'?—Gentlemen, can any of you tell me where I may find the young Romeo?

ROMEO. I can tell you; but young Romeo will be older when you have found him than he was when you sought him: I am the youngest of that name, for fault of a worse.

NURSE. You say well.

MERCUTIO. Yea, is the worst well? very well took, i'faith; wisely, wisely.

NURSE. If you be he, sir, I desire some confidence with you.

BENVOLIO. She will indite him to some supper.

MERCUTIO. A bawd, a bawd, a bawd! So-ho!

The first malapropism is the nurse's use of *confidence* where she most likely means *conference.* The effect this malapropism has on Benvolio is to cause him to mock her by deliberately using a malapropism: "indite" for "invite."

Diction also deals with the sounds of the words, their pronunciation/enunciation. Some words have changed in pronunciation. **Metathesis** is a change in which sounds within a word change position. This change might affect the spelling, such as in Old English, *bird* was spelled and pronounced *bridd*. At other times, however, the metathesis is not accorded the validity of a spelling change, but rather is simply a product of a regional or ethnic dialect. When this is the case, the writer might indicate the dialect by writing the word as it is phonetically pronounced by the CHARACTER in dialogue. For instance, a CHARACTER might pronounce *predict* as *perdict* or *pretty* as *perty*. The effect of phonetically "spelling out" a CHARACTER'S use of metathesis is to give the reader more insight into that CHARACTER as an individual.

Related to metathesis is the **spoonerism**, named after Dr. W. A. Spooner (New College, Oxford). In a spoonerism, the speaker accidentally exchanges the initial consonants of two or more words: "a dork way" for a "work day," a "sunken drop" for a "drunken sop," or "libeled rafter" for "ribald laughter." Unlike metathesis, however, the spoonerism has a more limited effect in dialogue, except in the case of very specialized characterization.

Four terms relate to omitting letters in words:

Apocope is omitting final letter(s) or syllable(s) of a word, as in *thro'*. **Aphaeresis** is omitting unstressed syllable(s) at the beginning of a word, as in *'til*.

Syncope is omitting a letter or syllable from the middle of a word, as in "e'en" for "even," for the purpose of meter, to avoid the reduplication of a letter when a suffix is added, or as a natural result of a word passing from Latin to English or of shortening a word; and **elision** is omitting part of a word, frequently when two or more words are run together, as in "th'world" for "the world":

"The general balm th'hydroptic earth has drunk."

"When by thy scorn, O murd'ress, I am dead,
 And that thou think'st thee free."

"Thou call'st for more."

"Like th'other foot, obliquely run."

"For 'tis my outward soul."

"And now, like am'rous birds of prey."

Puns are word choices that are referred to as a "play on words"—two words have the same sound but very different MEANING. The use of these words often elicits a smirky smile and gutteral groan on the part of the hearers, and for a very long time puns were held in low esteem; but in current discussion they enjoy a higher status. Although frequently used for comic effect, puns can be used quite seriously, particularly as used in literature written prior to the eighteenth century. Famous writers of puns include John Donne, Shakespeare, Bennett Cerf, Ezra Pound, and T. S. Eliot.

Puns rely, of course, on the CONTEXT for their witty overtones because the CONTEXT gives significance to *both* MEANINGS: A married couple is driving down a country road on a beautiful spring day. They are engaged in a lively discussion in which the husband, who is driving, is describing at length with some "picky" details what he feels is wrong with the plan his wife just proposed for their upcoming vacation. Just as he makes what he feels is a most convincing argument ("You get off from work thirty minutes earlier than I do, so I should get to select where we go on vacation"), they approach two small rabbits playing in the middle of the road. One rabbit streaks to the right while the other bunny races to the left. "Darling," she smiles sweetly, "You are *splitting hares!*"

An often quoted pun appears in *Romeo and Juliet*, Act III Scene I when Mercutio is wounded:

ROMEO.   Courage, man; the hurt cannot be much.

MERCUTIO.   No, 'tis not so deep as a well, nor so wide as a church-door; but 'tis enough, 'twill serve: ask for me to-morrow, and you shall find me a grave man.

What is the pun at work here? "Grave" can refer to either a "serious" man (as, indeed, his wound is a serious situation) and to a man in his grave. Do you see any other figures of speech here?

Here is John Donne's "A Hymn to God the Father." What puns can you find?

Wilt Thou forgive that sin where I begun,
    Which was my sin, though it were done before?
Wilt Thou forgive that sin, through which I run,
    And do run still, though still I do deplore?
        When Thou hast done, Thou hast not done,
            For I have more.

Wilt Thou forgive that sin which I have won
    Others to sin, and made my sin their door?
Wilt Thou forgive that sin which I did shun
    A year, or two: but wallowed in, a score?

When Thou hast done, Thou hast not done,
  For I have more.

I have a sin of fear, that when I have spun
  My last thread, I shall perish on the shore;
But swear by Thy self, that at my death Thy Son
  Shall shine as he shines now, and heretofore;
    And, having done that, Thou hast done;
      I fear no more.

A very obvious pun appears in the final stanza: "Son" and *sun*. (Keep in mind that the pun as a literary device can be *very* serious.) There is another pun at work throughout this poem—hint: look again at the poet's name.

Diction also refers to the level of words used: vocabulary that is high, plain, or low. As you study diction and its effect on literature, you will find that many different descriptive systems have been developed to try to identify the different levels of diction that writers and speakers use:

1. Diction can be described by dialect.
Dialects are the speech patterns (including diction, grammatical constructions, and accents) of a defined geographical region or group.

Generally, this descriptive system identifies *Standard English* as the speech used by the mainstream professionals of the age in question. The "standard" often cited to exemplify twentieth-century Standard English is that of speech-trained television and radio journalists—hence the informal expression "Walter Cronkite English." *Nonstandard English,* then, could be said to be all language that does not conform to this standard.

Standard English can be formal, general, or informal in level with diction playing a significant role in the determination. For example, general English often includes the use of the **vernacular**, the jargon of the person's profession or the diction that is specific to the region. Informal English is marked by colloquial expressions, slang, and clipped words that are sometimes drawn from nonstandard usage. Nonstandard English consists of colloquial expressions, slang, and clipped words plus diction that is characteristically considered "nonstandard," such as *ain't.* The grammatical constructions of Nonstandard English do not conform to the rules of Standard, particularly in the use of pronouns and subject-verb agreement, or to the rules of standardized spelling. Keep in mind, however, that words and constructions considered Non-

standard today may well have been considered Standard (or vice versa) in a previous period. Because the pronoun "they" was once considered to be a singular pronoun, "If a person laughs, they must be happy" would be considered a Standard usage. Even double negatives and "ain't" were once a part of Standard English.

2. Diction can be described by purpose.
The purpose of language is communication. Consider the use of technical terms, so useful and appropriate for instructing or enlightening professionals in a given field, (terms that become an "-ese" as in "educationese" or "doctorese" to the untrained layperson). Oftentimes the reader or hearer will respond to technical language with the plea "Can you put that in plain English?" As a result of advanced technology (home computers with ROM-drive and VCRs), technical writers (a very lucrative field in which professional writers write reports, instruction manuals, instructional charts, and articles) are being called upon to "translate" the technical world of science and technology into a language that can be understood by the nontechnical world.

The diction used in this book is technical to the extent that its purpose is to help prepare people to take a standardized test over the technical elements of a defined body of literature. Naturally, most technical diction will be found in nonnarrative prose writing; however, it can also be found in some surprising packages. Take, as an example, this poem in which Samuel Taylor Coleridge gives "Metrical Feet: Lesson for a Boy" (1806). "Derwent" is his son.

METRICAL FEET
LESSON FOR A BOY

Trōchēe trĭps frŏm lōng tŏ shōrt;
From long to long in solemn sort
Slōw Spōndēe stālks; strōng fŏot! yet ill able
Ēvĕr tŏ cōme ŭp wĭth Dāctўl trĭsўllăblē.
Ĭāmbĭcs mārch frŏm shōrt tŏ lōng—
Wĭth ă lēap ănd ă bōund thē swĭft Ānăpēsts thrōng;
One syllable long, with one short at each side,
Ămphĭbrăchўs hāstes wĭth ă stātelў stride—
Fīrst ănd lāst bēĭng lōng, mĭddle shōrt, Āmphĭmācer
Strīkes hĭs thūndĕrĭng hōofs lĭke ă prōud hĭgh-brĕd Rācer.
If Derwent be innocent, steady, and wise,
And delight in the things of earth, water, and skies;
Tender warmth at his heart, with these meters to show it,
With sound sense in his brains, may make Derwent a poet—

May crown him with fame, and must win him the love
Of his father on earth and his Father above.
   My dear, dear child!
Could you stand upon Skiddaw, you would not from its whole
   ridge
See a man who so loves you as your fond S. T. COLERIDGE.

by Samuel Taylor Coleridge

3. Diction can be described by TONE.

The diction of communication can give the work a formal or an informal TONE. Formal writing depends upon diction that is higher level vocabulary, whereas informal writing engages casual diction, such as the **colloquial expressions**, **idiomatic diction** (based on tradition rather than on logic, for instance, "call off," "get on," or "set about"), and **slang** (vernacular language) of everyday speech.

Before leaving diction as a USE OF LANGUAGE, some words need to be said about a relatively recent trend in literary "awareness": sexist vs. nonsexist writing, especially in the area of social titles and descriptive labels.

Today, "Ms.," "chairperson," "business people," and other such nonsexist terms are in broad general use. As you read period literature, however, you will find social titles and descriptive labels that are gender based. You also will discover that some titles and labels underwent changes in both MEANING and status over the years. As a result, you will miss important clues to understanding a selection if you do not recognize the MEANING of the title or label *as used in the period in which the work was written*. For example, when did *man* change from referring predominantly to *mankind* (both sexes included) to referring to an *adult male*? When Thomas Jefferson wrote "All men are created equal," what did *he mean?*

Space precludes an exhaustive look at how the perceptions of gender in terms of roles, status, and customs have changed over time and how these perceptions are reflected in literature (such as the personification of machines and nature as female, with hurricanes being named with male as well as female names being a relatively recent practice). Yet, there are a few terms that need to be addressed:

- Man, woman

As this chart shows, man originally meant human being (male or female), but came to mean male. A female might be referred to (in early English writings) as a man.

	Old English writing:	Eighteenth-century writing:
Adult male:	wer	man*
Adult male person:	waepman	man
Humankind (male and female being inclusive):	man	man
Adult female person:	wifman	woman
Adult female:	wif	wife

* By the nineteenth century, *man* was used mostly as a synonym for *male,* especially in legal matters.

Man, then, continued to some degree to refer to humankind, but in popular practice gradually came to mean an adult male. The problem comes in reading period literature: when the writer refers to man, is he or she referring to just adult males or also referring to females?

In the literature of the last half of the twentieth century, some writers very slowly gained an awareness of "sexist language." As a result, readers taught during this period of greater sensitivity may tend to mirror this view when reading the writings of other periods: to assume that a seventeenth-century writer means humankind when referring to man could be a mistake. This may or may not be the case, particularly in issues of interpretation of the law.

- He, she

Originally, they was used as a singular pronoun: "If a person comes, they should be shown in" or "Each person should speak their minds." Grammarians, however, objected to the lack of pronoun-antecedent agreement, hence the assignment of he to fill this syntactical role.

He (as used in the sixteenth century) did not refer to both sexes (as today "he" can mean both men and women, for example, "When a person drives a car, he should obey the traffic laws"). This may reflect the fact that the first English grammar books (written in the sixteenth and seventeenth centuries) were written by males for male readers (few females could read or write).

He as used in the previous example sentence to refer to both male and female in a general, more inclusive sense was not introduced until the eighteenth century and not extensively used until the nineteenth century, when an Act of Parliament decreed that females would be included in masculine-gender words. Abuses of this order, however, have occurred.

• Mrs., Miss, Ms., Madam

Today, a mistress (a noun) refers to the head of a household or to a woman having an affair with a man other than her own husband. Although mistress (used as a noun) did refer to a prostitute in the 1600s and 1700s, it also was a social title commonly used before the woman's name:

Mistress (abbreviations Mrs. and Miss)

Mrs. — used to address a married or unmarried adult female
Miss — used to address female children

By the end of the 1700s, the social customs began to take the FORM that is seen today:

Mrs. — used to address a married female
Miss — used to address an unmarried female

In the 1800s, Mrs. came to be used before the husband's full name (as in Mrs. John Smith) to refer to the wife. Not until the mid-twentieth century was Ms. used to refer to a woman whether married or unmarried. Madam (Ma'am) is a FORM of polite address to a woman and has also ironically been used as the title of a woman who has a house of prostitution.

• Master, Fellow, Esquire

Historically, master was the masculine equivalent of mistress; however, recent attention is being paid to acknowledging that women, too, can show "mastery" in certain areas and hence can be addressed as master. Male children may be referred to as master; and in period literature, an owner of slaves is often referred to as master.

Fellow, an Old English word, originally was sex neutral, referring to a partner or co-worker. Although modern connotations associate the term as more masculine (possibly due to the FORM fellowman), fellow was used to refer to a male or female (including a wife).

An esquire (esq.) was a male attendant to an English knight or one of the English landed gentry (with esquiress—the female FORM—referring in rather limited use to a variety of positions, such as a mourner or a slave girl). Today, esquire might appear after the name of an attorney (in practice in the United States), whether male or female.

What conclusion can be reached concerning sexism and diction? Obviously, awareness of the issue has been the impetus to change; however, as a student of period literature, do not impose today's consciousness on yesterday's norms. If you are seeking to gain insight into the MEANING of a work, try to view the diction used in the CONTEXT of the period in which it was written.

USE OF LANGUAGE IN PROSE, POETRY, AND DRAMA

Effects

Being able to name and define the different types of figurative language is important. Being able to recognize and label the different types of figurative language when they are used in a literary selection is also important. But being able to identify what *effect* the use of figurative language has within the literary work is crucial.

You may encounter on the SAT II: Literature Subject Test questions that are based on:

• Cause and effect relationships
• The *effects* of the USE OF LANGUAGE
• The effects of one literary element on another
• How the language affects our perception of the speaker
• The effects of CONTEXT on MEANING

You need to become comfortable with reading selections and looking for the *effects* the writer's USE OF LANGUAGE has on the other literary elements, particularly MEANING and TONE, as well as CHARACTERS and events within the selections.

Epiphany

A discussion of the *effects* of USE OF LANGUAGE should include at least brief mention of *epiphany*. Historically, epiphany first referred to the January sixth Church festival called by that name. Literally MEANING "a manifestation," epiphany came to mean a revelation of God's presence in the world.

What has this to do with the *effects* of the USE OF LANGUAGE in a literary work? James Joyce borrowed the term in the mid-twentieth century to describe a sudden revelation of some commonplace object. Since that time, the term has been used to describe the point at which the commonplace is revealed to be radiant. The term *epiphany* came to be used in the same way that the expression "*the moment*" was used in previous literary study. The role that the writer's USE OF LANGUAGE (the symbols, images, and other USES OF LANGUAGE) plays in facilitating this revelation—the moment or the epiphany—is self-evident. Joyce's *The Dubliners* is considered a collection of epiphanies, and William Wordsworth's "The Solitary Reaper" describes such a moment of revelation:

THE SOLITARY REAPER

Behold her, single in the field,
Yon solitary Highland Lass!
Reaping and singing by herself;
Stop here, or gently pass!
Alone she cuts and binds the grain,
And sings a melancholy strain;
O listen! for the vale profound
Is overflowing with the sound.

No nightingale did ever chaunt
More welcome notes to weary bands
Of travellers in some shady haunt,
Among Arabian sands:
A voice so thrilling ne'er was heard
In spring-time from the cuckoo-bird,
Breaking the silence of the seas
Among the farthest Hebrides.

Will no one tell me what she sings?—
Perhaps the plaintive numbers flow
For old, unhappy, far-off things,
And battles long ago:
Or is it some more humble lay,
Familiar matter of to-day?
Some natural sorrow, loss, or pain,
That has been, and may be again?

Whate'er the theme, the maiden sang
As if her song could have no ending;
I saw her singing at her work,
And o'er the sickle bending;—
I listened, motionless and still;
And, as I mounted up the hill,
The music in my heart I bore,
Long after it was heard no more.

by William Wordsworth

Poetic Diction

Poetic diction refers to language that is normally associated with poetry—that has a "poetic effect." The trend in modern writing is to use the diction of everyday speech; however, English poets of various periods (such as the Romantics) sought a "language of poetry" with an effect that would transcend that of everyday speech.

The poetic diction in vogue varied with the period and the group involved. Eighteenth-century writers, as an example, favored periphrasis (substituting ornate descriptions for ordinary expressions), personifications, and archaisms. The effect? An artificial, stilted FORM.

Poetic diction can be the basis of some very interesting word studies. Take the word "fain" as an example. A word study reveals that *fain* as a verb is obsolete; as an adverb it is used with <u>would</u> (She <u>would fain</u> have come with him tonight), but as an adjective it has two uses, both of which are identified as "archaic" and "poetic." "Fain" as an adjective can mean pleased or it can mean "making do," as expressed today. Usually "fain," when it means accepting less than desired circumstances, is accompanied by the infinitive form of the verb.

Christina Rossetti uses "fain" in this latter sense in "A Bed of Forget-Me-Nots":

Is LOVE so prone to change and rot
We are fain to rear Forget-me-not
By measure in a garden-plot?—

Dramatic Irony

Irony has already been discussed in some detail; however, the *effect* of dramatic irony merits some mention. In drama, irony takes a different FORM that, naturally, significantly influences the effect. Dramatic irony involves the audience having an awareness or knowledge of some information that is not known by the CHARACTERS in the play. The effect is *tragic* (tragic irony) when the very words spoken by a CHARACTER unwittingly foretell the coming disaster (unknown by the CHARACTER but known by the hearers).

Epiphany, poetic diction, dramatic irony—these are just a sampling of the many effects USE OF LANGUAGE can have in a work. In preparing for the SAT II: Literature Subject Test, recognizing effects should play an important role in your study plan.

QUESTIONS TO APPLY YOUR LEARNING

As you practice reading literary selections, ask these questions to help you identify and understand USE OF LANGUAGE:

1. Do you recognize any figures of speech based on analogy (similes, metaphors, personification, allusions, and so forth)?
2. Do you recognize any figures of speech based on rhetoric (rhetorical questions, amplifications, and so forth)?
3. Do you recognize any figures of speech based on syntax?
4. How would you describe the diction used in the selection?
5. What is the effect of each USE OF LANGUAGE that you found in the selection?

ADDITIONAL HELPFUL POINTS TO REMEMBER

- Love, time, and death are without doubt among the most widely personified concepts in literature. Yet, the range of effects the personification of these three topics can produce is almost as numerous as the poems in which they appear.

    Here are just a few examples—notice the different effects each has:

Love

(Love is sometimes portrayed as Cupid in literature, particularly poetry.)

1. The long love that in my thought doth harbour,
   And in mine heart doth keep his residence,
   Into my face presseth with bold pretence,
   And therein campeth, spreading his banner.

2. Farewell, Love, and all thy laws forever;
   Thy baited hooks shall tangle me no more:

3. Ring out your bells, let mourning shows be
        spread;
   For Love is dead.
       All Love is dead, infected
   With plague of deep disdain;

Worth, as nought worth, rejected,
And Faith fair scorn doth gain.

4. Then give me leave to love, and love me too
       Not with design
   To raise, as Love's cursed rebels do,
       When puling poets whine,
   Fame to their beauty, from their blubbered eyne.
   (Notice in the first line love is not personified;
       in the third line it is.)

5. Now at the last gasp of Love's latest breath,

6. Love, that doth reign and live within my thought,
   And built his seat within my captive breast,
   Clad in the arms wherein with me he fought,
   Oft in my face he doth his banner rest.
   But she that taught me love and suffer pain,
   My doubtful hope and eke my hot desire
   With shamefast look to shadow and refrain,
   Her smiling grace converteth straight to ire.
   And coward Love, then, to the heart apace
   Taketh his flight, where he doth lurk and plain,
   His purpose lost, and dare not show his face.
   For my lord's guilt thus faultless bide I pain,
   Yet from my lord shall not my foot remove:
   Sweet is the death that taketh end by love.

7. If I the death of Love had deeply planned,
   I never could have made it half so sure,

Death

(Death is commonly portrayed as a skeleton.)

1. For look, as Life, that pleasant dame, hath
       brought
   The pleasant years and days of lustiness,
   So Death, our foe, consumeth all to nought,
   Envying these, with dart doth us oppress,
   And that which is the greatest grief of all,
   The greedy gripe doth no estate respect,
   But where he comes he makes them down to
       fall,
   Nor stays he at the high, sharp-witted sect.

2. O death, rock me asleep,
       Bring me to quiet rest,
   Let pass my weary guiltless ghost
       Out of my careful breast.

3. Care-charmer Sleep, son of sable Night,
   Brother to Death, in silent darkness born,
   Believe my languish, and restore the light,
   With dark forgetting of my cares return.

4. But thy eternal summer shall not fade,
   Nor lose possession of that fair thou owest,
   Nor shall Death brag thou wander'st in his
      shade,

5. In me thou see'st the twilight of such day
   As after sunset fadeth in the west,
   Which by and by black night doth take away,
   Death's second self that seals up all in rest.

6. Now with the drops of this most balmy time
   My love looks fresh, and Death to me subscribes,
   Since, spite of him, I'll live in this poor rhyme,
   While he insults o'er dull and speechless tribes.

7. Death, Be Not Proud
   Death, be not proud, though some have callèd
      thee
   Mighty and dreadful, for thou art not so,
   For those whom thou think'st thou dost
      overthrow
   Die not, poor Death, nor yet canst thou kill me.
   From rest and sleep, which but thy picture be,
   Much pleasure, then from thee much more
      must flow;
   And soonest our best men with thee do go—
   Rest of their bones and souls' delivery!
   Thou'rt slave to fate, chance, kings and
      desperate men,
   And dost with poison, war, and sickness dwell,
   And poppy or charms can make us sleep as well,
   And better than thy stroke; why swell'st thou
      then?
   One short sleep past, we wake eternally,
   And death shall be no more: Death, thou shalt
      die!

Time

(Time is many times personified as an old man with
a scythe.)

1. When wasteful Time debateth with Decay,
   To change your day of youth to sullied night;

2. Devouring Time, blunt thou the lion's paws,
   And make the earth devour her own sweet
      brood;

3. Nativity, once in the main of light,
   Crawls to maturity, wherewith being crowned,
   Crookèd eclipses 'gainst his glory fight,
   And Time that gave doth now his gift confound.

4. When I have seen by Time's fell hand defaced

The rich proud cost of outworn buried age;

5. O! how shall summer's honey breath hold out
   Against the wrackful siege of battering days,
   When rocks impregnable are not so stout,
   Nor gates of steel so strong, but Time decays?
   O fearful meditation! where, alack,
   Shall Time's best jewel from Time's chest lie
      hid?
   Or what strong hand can hold his swift foot
      back?
   Or who his spoil of beauty can forbid?

6. Love's not Time's fool, though rosy lips and
      cheeks
   Within his bending sickle's compass come;

7. Fly envious Time, till thou run out thy race,

As you practice identifying figurative language
in literary selections, keep alert for the different *effects* produced by the personification of love, time,
and death.

- Spend some time with a variety of literary
  dictionaries, such as Holman and Harmon's *A
  Handbook to Literature,* Abram's *A Glossary
  of Literary Terms,* and *The New Princeton
  Encyclopedia of Poetry and Poetics.* No one
  book can exhaust the different perspectives of
  literary study. By cross-referencing several
  different sources, you will find examples illustrating the different figures of speech, literary movements, and many other areas
  important to your preparation for the SAT II:
  Literature Subject Test. You may need to consult several sources for examples and explanations of those areas that are new to you.
  Also, you may find in your library's computer
  the location of British and American anthologies (the Norton anthologies are extremely
  popular). You may enjoy spending some time
  browsing through the appendixes, glossaries,
  and explanatory matter that are part of many
  of these literary collections. You should find
  a wealth of information, often with full-con-
  text illustrations.

- Do not confuse **personification**, which is figurative language in which human characteristics are given to inanimate objects or abstract
  ideas, with **anthropomorphism**, which is
  presenting a nonhuman (such as an animal or
  a mythical god) as a human. The rabbit who
  declares that he is "late" in *Alice in Wonder-*

land is an anthropomorphism; the rabbit described by the hunter as "a worthy opponent who planned his strategy well—laughing at my clumsiness and disdaining the sophistication of my weapons" is being personified.

- For some fun with figures of speech, look for books and magazine articles that are collections of amusing ways to use language. For example, in the December 1994 issue of *Texas Monthly* magazine you will find "More Colorful Texas Sayings Than you Can Shake a Stick at: 622 wise and witty ways to talk Texan." These types of collections are great for releasing "study tension" and are enjoyable ways to view figurative vocabularies.

- Keep an *unabridged dictionary* within close reach when reading period literature for USE OF LANGUAGE. The slang of yesterday, for instance, may no longer carry the same MEANING today; however, an unabridged dictionary can help you better understand the diction used in other periods of time.

- Do not assume that every word or phrase that has "multiple MEANINGS" is an intentional attempt at figurative language. Sometimes such use is an **ambiguity**, the effect of which is confusion. Ambiguity can result from syntax problems, an unclear relationship between a pronoun and its antecedent, or a CONTEXT that does not clarify the intended MEANINGS of multiple-MEANING words. When the *intended effect* is to project a TONE or atmosphere that is confused, unclear, ambiguous, such ambiguities are useful; but if the intended effect is otherwise, such ambiguities can destroy the integrity of the work. The term *ambiguity* commonly refers to misuse of words with multiple MEANINGS and the term **plurisignation** refers to their effective use.

- You may encounter writers who use the word *type* (defined in this book in terms of a CHARACTER who represents a group) as a USE OF LANGUAGE: a synonym for *symbol*.

- Consider this topic for study group discussion: Cliches, figures of speech, and expressions that have been overused and have been labeled "trite" are often found in literature. There was a point in time, however, when a given figure of speech or expression would have been considered "fresh" and "new."

At what point does a clever or useful figure of speech or expression cross the line to become trite or a cliche? In discussion, keep in mind the various groups that use words, such as literary writers (essayists, poets, and others), journalists, and radio personalities. Also, address the historical perspectives: a poet used a figure of speech two hundred years ago that was fresh, new, and clever—so clever that his contemporaries and the generations that followed took the expression from CONTEXT and used it to the point that it is now considered trite. How does this affect your perception of the poet's original use of the expression? Is his poem of lesser importance today because of this? Do cliches have any place in the works of writers today? What do you anticipate will be the trite expressions of the future?

- Just as a mixed metaphor combines unlikely vehicles for the same tenor, a similar concept applies to the mixed figure in which unlikely figures of speech are blended together in use. It also might be called mixed imagery.

  "My new car is a lemon; she quits on me every chance she gets." (Mixed imagery: simile and personification)

- Do not confuse the **euphemism**, which is the replacing of an offensive expression with an inoffensive one, with **euphony**, which is the pleasant sound found in some works. This little poem may help you differentiate the two literary terms:

IS IT EUPHEMISM OR EUPHONY?

Is it euphemism or euphony?
  The answer has evaded me.
Euphemism, they say, is to render
  A harsh word into one kind and tender.
We don't say "leg"; we say a "limb."
  Don't call him "skinny," instead say "trim."
But when a poem has euphony,
  It simply "sounds" pleasant to you and me.
Now all your doubts should flee when you see:
  Is it euphemism or euphony?

                              by L. E. Myers

LITERARY ELEMENT NUMBER SEVEN: MEANING(S) IN CONTEXT

Read not to contradict and confute, nor to believe and take for granted, nor to find talk and discourse, but to weigh and consider. Some books are to be tasted, others to be swallowed, and some few to be chewed and digested:…

Of Studies
by Francis Bacon (1561–1626)

As with the other areas of linguistics (the study of language), such as **phonology** (the study of speech sounds) and **morphology** (the study of word formation), the final literary element's focus—**semantics** (the study of MEANINGS in language) and **syntax** (the arrangement of words into patterns) are both complex areas of study. Yet, there are some basics upon which you can build as you prepare to take the SAT II: Literature Subject Test.

Denotation

Simply stated, **denotation** is the basic or literal MEANINGS of a word. Note that this definition employs the plural MEANINGS—hence serves to emphasize what can be a major obstacle in the way of an exact interpretation of what a WORD, PHRASE, or LINE means in a literary selection.

Words often have multiple literal MEANINGS and only through careful exploration of the CONTEXT in which they are used can the reader learn the intended denotation (literal MEANING). An excellent example of the problems that can arise when the reader or listener is unaware of the multiple MEANINGS of a word appears in the brief exchange on the phone between Hercule Poirot and Mrs. Oliver in Agatha Christie's *Dead Man's Folly*:

[Mrs. Oliver] "…I hope I'm not interrupting you when you're frightfully busy?"

[Poirot] "No, no, you do not derange me in the least."

[Mrs. Oliver] "Good gracious—I'm sure I don't want to drive you out of your mind."

Mrs. Oliver does not seem to know that "derange" means to drive someone insane *and* to cause a disturbance. CONTEXT, however, makes it clear that Poirot intended the latter, not the former, denotation. Is she serious or is she trying to be humorous?

As Mrs. Oliver's conversation illustrates, a clear understanding of the multiple MEANINGS OF WORDS can be essential. As a result, the student preparing to take the SAT II: Literature Subject Test should include a study of denotation in his or her individualized study plan.

A word in isolation can have MEANING, but the MEANING depends on CONTEXT. Look at the multiple MEANINGS of *air* that appear in the *Merriam-Webster Dictionary*:

air n 1: the gaseous mixture surrounding the earth 2: a light breeze 3: MELODY, TUNE 4: the outward appearance of a person or thing: MANNER 5: an artificial manner 6: COMPRESSED AIR (—sprayer) 7: AIRCRAFT (—patrol) 8: AVIATION (—safety) 9: the medium of transmission of radio waves; also: RADIO, TELEVISION

1. We must measure the <u>air</u> pressure.
   ["the gaseous mixture surrounding the earth"]
2. The warm <u>air</u> of the ocean brushed her face.
   ["a light breeze"]
3. That song has a lovely <u>air</u> to it.
   ["MELODY, TUNE"]
4. He has a friendly <u>air</u>.
   ["the outward appearance of a person or thing: MANNER"]
5. He had a phony <u>air</u> about him.
   ["an artificial manner"]
6. He used an <u>air</u> sprayer to paint the car.
   ["COMPRESSED AIR (—sprayer)"]
7. She was a member of the <u>air</u> patrol.
   ["AIRCRAFT (—patrol)"]
8. The commission voted on <u>air</u> safety.
   ["AVIATION (—safety)"]
9. She was on the <u>air</u> last night.

["the medium of transmission of radio waves; also RADIO, TELEVISION"]

Obviously, one element of semantics is the *interplay* of dictionary MEANING and CONTEXT. Another element that is very significant to the denotation of words in CONTEXT is "sloppy" or careless use of words (diction) that is so often witnessed in everyday speech.

Eighteenth-century essayist William Cowper addresses use of everyday speech in "On Conversation":

Your talk to decency and reason suit,
Nor prate like fools or gabble like a brute.

In the comedy of the "Frenchman in London," which we were told was acted at Paris with universal applause for several nights together, there is a character of a rough Englishman, who is represented as quite unskilled in the graces of conversation; and his dialogue consists almost entirely of a repetition of the common salutation of "How do you do?"

* * *

I shall not attempt to lay down any particular rules for conversation, but rather point out such faults in discourse and behavior as render the company of half mankind rather tedious than amusing.

* * *

Everyone endeavors to make himself as agreeable to society as he can; but it often happens that those who most aim at shining in conversation overshoot their mark. Though a man succeeds, he should not (as is frequently the case) engross the whole talk to himself; for that destroys the very essence of conversation, which is talking together. We should try to keep up conversation like a ball bandied to and fro from one to the other, rather than seize it all to ourselves, and drive it before us like a football. We should likewise be cautious to adapt the matter of our discourse to our company, and not talk Greek before ladies, or of the last new furbelow to a meeting of country justices.

Lack of precision in day-to-day conversations has resulted in confusion over words that are similar both in their individual MEANINGS and in their shades of MEANING. The words assure, ensure, and insure are examples. These three words tend to be used interchangeably, yet each has its own MEANING:

Assure means to give a promise to a person— "Let me assure you that I'll be there on time."

Ensure means to make sure— "Your participation will ensure the success of the program."

Insure means to protect with insurance— "I must insure the house against flood damage."

Being able to differentiate such often confused words is important to understanding denotative MEANING. Even words that quite rightly might be grouped as synonyms can have shades of MEANING that should not be disregarded. The noun remnant illustrates the point. Remnant usually means a small amount left or a piece of fabric left on a bolt. Synonyms for "remnant" include residue, portion left, rest. Consequently, in "The remnant of the solution was in the bottle"—the words residue, portion left, or rest could quite appropriately be used in place of remnant. In "The store clerk put the remnant of the fabric on sale," "remnant," of course, refers to the rest of the fabric. But would the shades of MEANING—the denotations of remnant—allow a person, assuming that remnant has "rest" as a synonym, to say "I think I'll have a short remnant before dinner tonight"?

Denotation is a word's literal MEANINGS, including its shades of MEANING that depend upon CONTEXT for identity.

Another element of denotation (the literal MEANINGS OF WORDS) involves diction (the writer's or speaker's choice of words): the degree to which the words used are **specific** or **general**, and **concrete** or **abstract**.

- General words denote a group or class: cat
- Specific words denote members of a group or class: Siamese, tabby
- Concrete words denote people and things that are perceived by the five senses: a warm coat
- Abstract words denote concepts and ideas: pride, responsibility

Concrete words are easily defined; abstract words, however, often defy universally accepted definitions because they cannot be measured or described by physical senses. The more specific and concrete the diction used, the easier it is to establish the MEANINGS. Look at this series of five statements. Which statement contains the most easily defined underlined word?

1. "I like having protection around."
2. "I like having an animal around."
3. "I like having a dog around."
4. "I like having a Great Dane around."
5. "I like having my dog Killer around."

In the first statement, protection is very abstract as an idea and very general. It might refer to a barbed wire fence, to bodyguards, to bolted, steel doors, to a weapon or any number of other means of protection. The second sentence is far more concrete (animals can be seen, felt), but still is rather ambiguous, rather general. The third sentence begins to give a more specific, concrete picture—obviously this person likes having some type of dog around. What breed? Sentence four gives an even more concrete picture; however, the fifth sentence, in which there is a particular dog—named "Killer"—is both concrete and specific.

Based on the evidence, a first step to understanding MEANING(S) IN CONTEXT might be to read the selection for denotative MEANING: (1) making sure that you are aware of the multiple MEANINGS some words convey, (2) selecting the denotative MEANINGS as used in CONTEXT, (3) scanning for any words whose MEANINGS or shades of MEANINGS might be confused, and (4) identifying those words that are very general or abstract (as opposed to those specific or concrete).

As you look more closely at denotation, you will find that MEANING becomes a product of the writer's use of denotative MEANINGS and the levels of specificity and abstractness that are inherent in them. How, as an example, would you characterize the denotation of the diction used in Shakespeare's 27th Sonnet—as specific or general? As abstract or concrete?

27TH SONNET

Weary with toil, I haste me to my bed,
The dear repose for limbs with travel tired;
But then begins a journey in my head,
To work my mind, when body's work's expired:
For then my thoughts (from far where I abide)
Intend a zealous pilgrimage to thee,
And keep my drooping eyelids open wide,
Looking on darkness which the blind do see:
Save that my soul's imaginary sight
Presents thy shadow to my sightless view,
Which, like a jewel hung in ghastly night,
Makes black night beauteous, and her old face new.
   Lo, thus, by day my limbs, by night my mind,
   For thee and for myself no quiet find.

by William Shakespeare

The speaker gives the reader very little specific language here. He talks of his "bed...limbs...journey...pilgrimage...a jewel...," mostly terms that

relate more to the general than to the specific (such as, *What type of jewel? A diamond* that is clear yet catches light and color? Or a *ruby* that passionately blazes with flames of red?). At the same time, the level of abstractness is very high, with many of the words having denotative definitions that are ideas, conditions, relationships, qualities, and so forth: "Weary...toil...haste...dear repose...tired...work... expired...thoughts...abide...Intend...soul's imaginary sight...sightless view [oxymoron]...ghastly... beauteous...old...new...mind...quiet."

Levels of abstraction will vary in CONTEXT, depending upon the writer's use of specific examples that tend to make the writing more concrete. Writers, in other words, can clarify abstract concepts through use of specific examples, but also can increase the levels of abstraction by making generalizations.

Syntax

Diction is the choice of words used; **syntax** is their arrangement into patterns. Just as diction (vocabulary) has been grouped into different levels for ease in identification, certain grammatical patterns of words (syntax) have been identified and labeled.

As you read about syntax and its effects on literary MEANING, you will find some sources using the word **grammar** as a synonym for syntax. Although such usage is common, grammar actually involves not just syntax (study and description of the grammatical arrangement of words into patterns), but also includes **morphology** (study and description of word formation) and **phonology** (study and description of the sounds of words). In its fullest sense, then, syntax is the arrangement of words and the grammatical relationships of the words and the groups of words in a sentence.

You will encounter many different grammar systems, but each should in some way address the role of syntax to MEANING. Consider, as an example, what is commonly called "traditional grammar." This grammar system is based on Latinate and literary models and was developed by eighteenth- and nineteenth-century grammarians. In traditional grammar, there are eight parts of speech with rules governing how they should and should not be used. This is a contrast to "structural grammar" of the mid-twentieth century that concentrates on the patterns of syntax and sound as they actually are used (and not necessarily dictating how they "should" be used). Transformational-generative grammar emphasizes syntax by trying to examine and explain how the organization of sentences into such parts as PHRASES and words interact with those ideas that come to mind both to convey and to understand MEANING. (If you are interested in transformational-generative grammar, look to some of the work done by Noam Chomsky.)

Regardless of what system of grammar you prefer, there are a few general comments that can be noted concerning syntax and the role it plays in determining MEANINGS OF SENTENCES, LINES, PHRASES, AND WORDS IN CONTEXT.

Syntax (the arrangement of words into patterns in a sentence) also involves the **function** these words and groups of words serve within the sentence. Words and groups of words can serve in many different functions: **subject**, **verb**, **object**, **modifier**, **connective**, **complement**, and **absolute**.

In English, the most common sequence pattern is subject-verb-object. Other common sequence patterns include subject-verb-modifier/complement

Very often, but not always, the subject will appear before the verb. Exceptions include such constructions as "There are three mice in the room" in which the subject, "mice," comes after the verb "are." Verbs can be transitive and be followed by an object, intransitive and not be followed by an object, or linking and used to connect a complement (an adjective or noun) to the subject. Objects can be direct receivers of action (He threw the ball) or indirect receivers of action (He threw me the ball). *Complements* follow linking verbs.

Modifiers describe or limit, with adjectives and adverbs usually appearing before the word(s) they modify, with PHRASE and clause modifiers usually coming after—although exceptions to the generalization abound. Connectives include coordinating conjunctions that connect words that are in similar functions (such as two subjects: "Jane and John went home"), subordinating connectives that connect a subordinate clause to a main clause ("I can't continue unless you stop eating"), and transitional connectives ("There will be a test on Monday. As a result, she will not assign any further homework.")

Prepositions both connect and show a relationship of the word that follows to another word, quite often one that precedes ("The ball rolled under the table."—under tells where the ball rolled). Absolutes are not grammatically related to anything; they just "feel right" and somehow help the sentence ("No, I can't!" or "For crying out loud, do you expect him to believe her?").

As this review of functions implies, the functions of words and where they are placed in relation to the rest of the sentence significantly contribute to their relationship to one another and, as a result, to their MEANING. The function and the syntax, then, provide the CONTEXT for MEANING.

This can be illustrated by looking at the different types of sentences. First, some definitions:

1. The loose or common sentence

The loose or common sentence is the most used sentence structure in the English language. It generally is written in one of three basic FORMS, each of which can be expanded by coordinating similar structures into the sentence or by modifying parts of or the entire sentence with more information:

Subject	Transitive Verb	Object
The car	hit	a tree.

Subject	Intransitive Verb	
Susan	cried.	

Subject	Linking Verb	Complement
Roger	was	a student.
The dog	is	happy.
The book	is	there.

Effect: As the most common sentence structure used, there is a sense of met expectation (comfortable style due to familiarity). The writing tends to be "choppy" if most of the sentences contain little coordination or modification. Too much elaboration, however, results in a difficult, wordy style.

2. The periodic sentence

In contrast to the loose sentence in which the subject often appears early in the sentence, in the periodic sentence the subject and its verb come much later, and serve as a climactic statement to a series of subordinate clauses or PHRASES. The rhetorical benefits of "building" to the main point can clearly be seen:

Reaching deep within herself for some type of consolation, some small reflection of the pride and dignity that had once been the fighting edge of her courage, some reassurance that all was not lost, the *destitute woman opened the courtroom door*.

Effect: The rhetorical "build up" to the main point is dramatic.

3. The parallel sentence

Parallel sentences consist of a series of PHRASES, main clauses, or subordinate clauses:

The mother was *always laughing at his jokes, crying over his heartbreaks, and justifying his faults.*

The children laughed; the dog yelped; the young girl cried.

You should always remember *which key unlocks the chain, which chain binds the heart, and which heart breaks for you.*

Effect: The parallel sentence appeals to the reader's sense of logic in sequencing similar ideas or items and provides a sense of rhythm to the writing.

4. The balanced sentence

The balanced sentence is a type of parallel construction in which two major sentence elements that contrast with one another are balanced between a coordinating conjunction:

The river's ravishes stunned the older onlookers, *but* the water's pull mesmerized the younger ones.

Working on the project satisfied his sense of justice, *but* destroyed his sense of independence.

Effect: The balanced sentence, as a type of parallel sentence, provides a sense of rhythm to the sentence, but also provides emphasis or contrast—an element of logic.

The introductory paragraph of *A Tale of Two Cities* can be used to put this information into practical application. After reading the paragraph, identify what sentence structures are used and their effects on the MEANING.

A TALE OF TWO CITIES
by
Charles Dickens

It was the best of times, it was the worst of times, it was the age of wisdom, it was the age of foolishness, it was the epoch of belief, it was the epoch of incredulity, it was the season of Light, it was the season of Darkness, it was the spring of hope, it was the winter of despair, we had everything before us, we had nothing before us, we were all going direct to Heaven, we were all going direct the other way —in short, the period was so far like the present period, that some of its noisiest authorities insisted on its being received, for good or for evil, in the superlative degree of comparison only.

The bulk of the paragraph consists of a series of main clauses that are structured as loose or common sentences using a very simple, plain, easy-to-understand level of diction. This gives the reader a comfortable, nonthreatening beginning. Although so many short sentences would normally be "choppy," they have been joined together **mechanically** with commas (representing "and") and have been joined together **structurally** with parallel sentence construction.

We had:	It was: the best of times
everything before us	the worst of times
nothing before us	the age of wisdom
	the age of foolishness
	the epoch of belief
	the epoch of incredulity
We were:	the season of Light
all going direct to Heaven	the season of Darkness
all going direct the other way	the spring of hope
	the winter of depair

This results in a rhythm that literally pulls the reader along, far outweighing any staccato effect the short, loose sentences might have otherwise produced.

Next, examine the contents of the syntactical structure used in the excerpt. "It was" is the subject-verb for the first ten independent clauses. The subject-verb changes to "We had" and "We were" respectively in the final four independent clauses. What is the effect of this change? One possible effect is that the momentum builds with a series of paradoxical statements with "it"—a neutral, *third person* pronoun—as the subject. The change to "we"—a *first person* pronoun—is startling; it jars the reader from any "lull" the otherwise comfortable rhythm might have given him or her. Notice also how the paradoxes change from "time," "ages," "epochs," "seasons," "spring...winter," to "everything...nothing <u>before us</u>" and to the promise, "We were all going direct to Heaven" countered by the threat "We were all going direct the other way." The syntactical structure makes the reader comfortable, appeals to our sense of logic through parallel sentence structure, then gains the reader's attention first with a change in pronoun usage, followed by the abrupt break in syntax with the use of an absolute: "in short." What is the significance of the use of this absolute to the MEANING of the paragraph? It divides the paragraph structurally into two parts: the first part is a series of paradoxical relationships of a period that at first seems impersonal, but eventually comes to be on a more personal level as it relates to the "we" of the story. The second part summarizes that these paradoxes of that period are "like the present period"—a MEANING that personally involves the reader.

What sentence structures does Shakespeare use in his "Sonnet 64" and how do they affect MEANING?

SONNET 64

When I have seen by Time's fell hand defaced
The rich proud cost of outworn buried age;
When sometime lofty towers I see down razed,
line And brass eternal slave to mortal rage;
(5) When I have seen the hungry ocean gain
Advantage on the kingdom of the shore,
And the firm soil win of the watery main,
Increasing store with loss, and loss with store;
When I have seen such interchange of state,
(10) Or state itself confounded to decay,
Ruin hath taught me thus to ruminate,
That Time will come and take my love away.
This thought is as a death, which cannot choose
But weep to have that which it fears to lose.

by William Shakespeare

The first sentence is lines 1 through 12. Notice the parallel constructions:

Line 1 "When I have seen…"
Line 3 "When sometime lofty towers I see…"
Line 5 "When I have seen…"
Line 9 "When I have seen…"

These are subordinate clauses—so where are the subject and the verb of the sentence? They do not appear until line 11: "Ruin hath taught." Lines 1 through 12 consist of a periodic sentence in which the speaker "builds" to his point. This heightens the impact, then, of the MEANING of the concluding couplet that is a loose sentence, in structural contrast to the preceding periodic sentence.

Another element of syntax that is helpful to determining MEANING is the **transitional marker**. Transitional markers are relationship words—words that somehow establish some type of MEANING between the words that appear before the marker to those that follow. Naturally, these include that large group called the **conjunction**. Most readers are aware that <u>and</u> signals combining relationships or addition, whereas <u>but</u> signals an exception. Yet the careful student of literature should be aware that

whereas some transitional markers carry obvious MEANING, others have more subtle shades of MEANING that although they may be similar, are not exactly the same:

> <u>Thus</u> involves how, why, or to what extent something is done and suggests results.
> <u>Thence</u> implies a forward progression from a specified point in space or time.
> <u>Also</u> is a marker for additional information.
> <u>Moreover</u> indicates an excess beyond that designated previously.
> <u>Nevertheless</u> means despite the circumstances.
> <u>However</u> marks relationships of manner, degree, or exception.

As these few illustrations show, the transitional marker can affect MEANING. To demonstrate, read this first stanza of "Oft, in the Stilly Night" by Thomas Moore. How would the MEANING of the last four lines change if the speaker had used "Thence" rather than "Thus" in line 11?

OFT, IN THE STILLY NIGHT

Oft, in the stilly night,
Ere Slumber's chain has bound me,
Fond Memory brings the light
line Of other days around me;
(5) The smiles, the tears,
Of boyhood's years,
The words of love then spoken;
The eyes that shone,
Now dimmed and gone,
(10) The cheerful hearts now broken!
Thus, in the stilly night,
Ere Slumber's chain hath bound me,
Sad Memory brings the light
Of other days around me.

by Thomas Moore

A practice question might read:

In line 11, "Thus" points the reader to

(A) the element of time at work
(B) a degree of intensity of the speaker's emotion
(C) in what manner the speaker's night is spent
(D) new information concerning the speaker
(E) emotion beyond that previously expressed

(The correct answer is C.)

What if the speaker had used the transitional device "Also"? "Moreover"?

Some other clues to MEANING that can be found within the structure of sentences include:

What ideas are "important" as opposed to what ideas are not

Those ideas that the speaker considers important might be emphasized graphically with italics, underlining, capital letters, and graphic devices. Structurally, they might be placed in the main noun-verb structure of the sentence, with those ideas that are simply supportive to that main idea subordinated in subordinate clauses or modifying PHRASES.

Who or what is doing the action

When the speaker uses active VOICE, the reader knows who or what is doing the action; when the speaker uses passive VOICE, the identity of who or what is doing the action is de-emphasized—and the reader may not hear the "actor's" identity at all. In the sentence "It was agreed upon that the party would be canceled," the speaker does not tell the reader who canceled the party. In "The party was canceled by Bob and Ted," you learn who canceled the party, but the passive VOICE de-emphasizes Bob and Ted's role, placing greater emphasis on the subject: the party was canceled. In "Bob and Ted canceled the party," the emphasis is placed on Bob and Ted's role in the action of the sentence.

When the action takes place

Recognizing that the tense of a verb used (present, past, or future) affects MEANING may seem like an obvious observation; however, the shades of MEANING implicit in the different tenses, particularly the perfect tenses and the progressive *forms*, need to be addressed. *To review:*

Simple tenses convey what is happening <u>now</u>, what happened <u>before now</u>, and what will happen <u>after now</u>.

Simple present tense:	I work.	I ride.
Simple past tense:	I worked.	I rode.
Simple future tense:	I will work.	I will ride.

The simple present tense also is used when a future event has a set time ("The sale <u>starts</u> next Tuesday"), when the information is a general truth ("A yard <u>measures</u> 36 inches"), when the action happens regularly ("She <u>meets</u> her mother every afternoon after school"), or when the information is not dependent upon time ("The poet <u>speaks</u> of lace and satin in his latest work").

Perfect tenses are used when the action or state of being has already been completed or will be completed at a particular time.

Present perfect tense:	I have worked.
Past perfect tense:	I had worked.
Future perfect tense:	I will have worked.

The present perfect indicates that the action or state of being began in the past and its effects continue into the present. In past perfect, the action was completed prior to another action taking place. In future perfect, the action will be completed prior to a specific time. Perfect tense can also be expressed in the infinitive: to have worked.

Simple and perfect tenses can take the **progressive verb form** in which the action or state of being is ongoing:

Simple present progressive verb form:	I am walking.
Simple past progressive verb form:	I was walking.
Simple future progressive verb form:	I will be walking.
Present perfect progressive verb form:	I have been walking.
Past perfect progressive verb form:	I had been walking.
Future perfect progressive verb form:	I will have been walking.

Remember: The passive VOICE consists of past participle plus a form of *to be*.

Present passive VOICE: Mail is sent by John (present tense of *to be* with past participle).

Past passive VOICE: Mail was sent by John (past tense of *to be* with past participle).

Past progressive passive VOICE: Mail was being sent by John (past progressive of *to be* with past participle).

Knowing <u>when</u> the action or state of being occurs or occurred is very significant to MEANING(S) IN CONTEXT.

How does the tense used affect the MEANING in this selection?

Jayne was unaware that the keys were still in the lock, and she was equally unaware that the throbbing in her ears was

being made by the intensity of her own heartbeat. Where were those keys? A chilling wind brushed her face as she glanced toward the entrance to the garage.

"I will stay calm," she whispered, momentarily closing her eyes against painful, stinging tears. Her right index finger began to hurt, and she realized that she had been cutting it on the zipper-edge of the opening of her purse as she searched through it for her keys.

The story's primary tense is simple past: "Jayne was…the keys were…she was…." The throbbing in her ears; however, is past progressive passive (the throbbing…was being made by…). What are the effects of this tense? The sense of ongoing action of the progressive tense adds tension when presented in a CONTEXT connotative of danger— "a chilling wind," the need to "stay calm," emotion intense enough that she does not realize that she is hurting herself. What do the passive aspects of this construction do to the MEANING? They place the emphasis on the throbbing in her ears, rather than on its cause (her heartbeat). Notice the shift in emphasis if the construction is changed to simple past:…she was equally unaware that the intensity of her own heartbeat caused the throbbing in her ears. What tense does she use when she whispers "I will stay calm"? Its effect? Why is the tense of "she had been cutting it…" important to the MEANING of the selection?

Connotation

Denotations are the literal MEANINGS of words; *connotations* are their emotional MEANINGS. Sometimes *associations* result from a person's own nonverbal experiences. Such associations can be very powerful. A particular song might be associated with a first love. Certain foods can remind you of a person, an enjoyable vacation, or a particular place. Events in your life may be brought to mind when you hear a name, smell a fragrance, or experience a familiar feeling. Such associations can be positive or negative, but seldom without some type of emotional response.

Similarly, words can gain connotative MEANING for a person through his or her personal experiences. These connotations might be negative or positive, sad or happy, discouraging or encouraging—reflecting any number of emotional responses. Connotative MEANINGS also can be universal (shared by most people) or shared by some group (such as a nation, an organization, a race, a religion, or a profession or trade).

An example of connotative MEANINGS: Suppose you develop a new type of vacuum cleaner that you believe surpasses any other on the market. You would possibly refer to it as your "invention." Invention is a rather neutral word (because inventions can be either useful or nonuseful)—with perhaps slightly positive connotations that anyone who "invents an invention must be an inventive inventor"— a "feel-good" association of ideas. Someone (who is perhaps jealous of your success?) might come to see your new vacuum cleaner and later refer to it in conversation as your new "contrivance." Although technically accurate (a "contrivance" is a mechanical device or appliance), "contrivance" also carries with it some negative connotations related to its other definition: a scheme. Such a word is suggestive to the hearer of such questions as "Does this vacuum cleaner really work, or has this person just developed a scheme to make money?" Even the word invention, itself, which is neutral or somewhat positive in connotative value, can become negative in certain CONTEXTS, because another definition of "invention" involves something "made up."

Words, then, can stir emotions and can cause a person to make certain associations. A writer can elicit emotions from his or her readers simply by selecting connotatively charged words. This translates into tremendous power—power to influence beyond the effects of denotation.

1. For the public speaker, connotation can help persuade the hearers to adopt certain views and to take desired action. Connotation can be a very effective rhetorical device.

In 1837, Ralph Waldo Emerson gave a profoundly interesting address to the Harvard community in Cambridge, Massachusetts. His aim was to stir the "American Scholar" to become "Man Thinking."

The world—this shadow of the soul, or *other me*—lies wide around. Its attractions are the keys which unlock my thoughts and make me acquainted with myself. I run eagerly into this resounding tumult. I grasp the hands of those next me and take my place in the ring to suffer and to work, taught by an instinct that so shall the dumb abyss be vocal with speech. I pierce its order; I dissipate its fear; I dispose of it within the circuit of my expanding life. So much only of life as I know by experience, so much of the wilderness have I vanquished and planted, or so far have I extended my being, my dominion. I do not see how any man can afford, for the sake of his nerves and his nap, to spare any action in which he can partake. It is pearls and rubies to his discourse. Drudgery, calamity, exasperation, want are instructors in eloquence and wisdom. The true scholar grudges every opportunity of action passed by as a loss of power. It is the raw material out of which the intellect moulds her splendid products. A strange process, too, this by which experience is converted into thought, as a mulberry leaf is converted into satin. The manufacture goes forward at all hours…

I have now spoken of the education of the scholar by nature, by books, and by action. It remains to say somewhat of his duties. They are such as become Man Thinking. They may all be comprised in self-trust. The office of the scholar is to cheer, to raise, and to guide men by showing them facts amidst appearances….For all this loss and scorn, what offset? He is to find consolation in exercising the highest functions of human nature. He is one who raises himself from private considerations and breathes and lives on public and illustrious thoughts. He is the world's eye. He is the world's heart. He is to resist the vulgar prosperity that retrogrades ever to barbarism, by preserving and communicating heroic sentiments, noble biographies, melodious verse, and the conclusions of history….

What connotations, associated emotional responses, does his use of words, such as those that follow, bring to mind? "resounding tumult," "dumb abyss," "pearls and rubies," "the wilderness have I vanquished," "loss and scorn" "breathes and lives… illustrious thoughts," and "heroic…noble…melodious…"

Notice how the speaker uses connotation to establish a paradoxical relationship of "Drudgery, calamity, exasperation, want" as "instructors in eloquence and wisdom."

2. For the story writer, connotation can help the readers identify with the CHARACTERS in the narrative. For example, when the "young man" in a story "doesn't want to go to his house," the language is rather neutral, or perhaps a bit negative for some people who associate "young man" as a phrase used to address a boy who has been disobedient to adults, with the fact that he "doesn't want to go to his house" implying an attitude problem. What if you say "the little boy is afraid to go home"? Now the connotative MEANING is much more sympathetic, with "home" being connotative of safety and comfort, but this poor little fellow is "afraid" to go there!

What connotations about CHARACTER do you gain from this brief narrative selection?

Alice reached for the new dress and hummed softly under her breath as she slipped it on. She was amused by the contrast of her pallid skin against the shocking red silk.

To illustrate connotation, examine two words: "hummed" and "amused." "Alice…hummed softly…." What connotations are associated with humming? For many people humming implies happiness and indicates a personality that is perhaps playful. Now look at the description of Alice in her new dress—hardly a description of classical beauty—"pallid" being connotative of the paleness that comes from either having been ill or indoors too much. Yet, this CHARACTER is "amused" by the "contrast." What are the connotations concerning someone who is "amused" by her own less-than-perfect appearance?

One type of humming is a "drone" and a type of amusement is a "diversion." What if the sentence read "Alice…droned softly…, she was diverted by the contrast…"? How does this change of two words change the connotations about her CHARACTER?

Another example can be seen in *Silas Marner* (written by George Eliot), in which the narrator points out that the speaker's words "are coarser than his intentions," that connotations are an issue in the emotional nature of the communications involved. Also, what are the connotations of "susceptible feelings" as used in the second paragraph?

SILAS MARNER
by
George Eliot

'Well, my meaning is this, Marner,' said Godfrey, determined to come to the point. 'Mrs Cass and I, you know, have no children—nobody to be the better for our good home and everything else we have—more than enough for ourselves. And we should like to have somebody in the place of a daughter to us—we should like to have Eppie, and treat her in every way as our own child. It'ud be a great comfort to you in your old age, I hope, to see her fortune made in that way, after you've been at the trouble of bringing her up so well. And it's right you should have every reward for that. And Eppie, I'm sure, will always love you and be grateful to you: she'd come and see you very often, and we should all be on the look-out to do everything we could towards making you comfortable.'

A plain man like Godfrey Cass, speaking under some embarrassment, necessarily blunders on words that are coarser than his intentions, and that are likely to fall gratingly on susceptible feelings. While he had been speaking, Eppie had quietly passed her arm behind Silas's head, and let her hand rest against it caressingly: she felt him trembling violently. He was silent for some moments when Mr Cass had ended—powerless under the conflict of emotions, all alike painful. Eppie's heart was swelling at the sense that her father was in distress; and she was just going to lean down and speak to him, when one struggling dread at last gained the mastery over every other in Silas, and he said, faintly—'Eppie, my child, speak. I won't stand in your way. Thank Mr and Mrs Cass.'

A practice question:

"Susceptible feelings," as used in the second paragraph, connotes

(A) that Cass is feeling very emotional
(B) that Marner would agree to anything
(C) Eppie's insignificant role in Marner's life
(D) a sensitivity in Marner
(E) that Marner felt anger at Cass's manner

(The correct answer is D.)

3. For the nonnarrative prose writer, connotation can be a problem to avoid when neutrality is essential. Writers <u>use</u> words to communicate and sometimes connotation can actually hinder that communication. When the intended use is poetic, connotation is a useful element; but when the intended use is scientific, connotation can convey MEANINGS that are contrary to the point or perhaps even false. When the prose writer's aim is to instruct or to inform concerning processes and facts, avoiding additional connotative MEANING is essential.

4. For the poet, connotation can add another layer of MEANING to the work as a whole. Examine "Of the Birth and Bringing up of Desire" by Edmund De Vere, Earl of Oxford. What connotative MEANINGS <u>beyond</u> denotation are conveyed by such expressions as "pride and pomp," "sugared joy," "sad sighs," "Sweet thoughts, which liked me best," "gentle hearts," "muse alone," and "disdain"?

OF THE BIRTH AND BRINGING UP OF DESIRE

When wert thou born, Desire?
  In pride and pomp of May.
By whom, sweet boy, wert thou begot?
  By Self Conceit, men say.
Tell me, who was thy nurse?
  Fresh Youth, in sugared joy.

What was thy meat and daily food?
  Sad sighs and great annoy.
What haddest thou to drink?
  Unfeigned lovers' tears.
What cradle wert thou rocked in?
  In hope devoid of fears.
What brought thee to thy sleep?
  Sweet thoughts, which liked me best.
And where is now thy dwelling-place?
  In gentle hearts I rest.
Doth company displease?
  It doth, in many one.
Where would Desire then choose to be?
  He loves to muse alone.
What feedeth most thy sight?
  To gaze on favour still.
Whom finds thou most thy foe?
  Disdain of my good will.
Will ever age or death
  Bring thee unto decay?
No, no! Desire both lives and dies
  A thousand times a day.

by Edmund De Vere, Earl of Oxford

5. For some advertisers, connotation is a means to influence the public to buy. Local supermarket shelves are evidence of the affective overtones of connotative language used in product merchandising. Use of connotative language to manipulate people is widespread. Such use is one FORM of what William Lutz calls "doublespeak" in his book of the same name.

Public officials must exercise caution in using connotative word choices. This caution is reflected in such examples as police reports in which "suspects" of criminal activities are referred to as "actors." Special interests movements often use connotative language to put forth their agendas. In the last half of the twentieth century, during the women's movement, as an example, housewives (women who work at home raising children and running a family) were being referred to as "domestic engineers."

This brief overview of connotative language might be summarized with the following illustration:

<u>Positive connotation</u>	<u>Neutral</u>
an antique	an old chair

<u>Negative connotation</u>
junk

Implications

Implications and **inference** are two easily confused words that have related MEANINGS. An *implication* is an involvement or indication that is made indirectly by association; an *inference* is a conclusion drawn from facts or premises. The speaker implies (hints at, suggests) some idea from which the hearer or reader infers (receives, draws) a conclusion.

Implications can come in many different FORMS. Some writers, as a case in point, make a distinction between **implicit statements** in which such information as who, what, where, when, why, and how is implied through CONTEXT and **explicit statements** in which the writer, to put it in modern slang, "spells it all out." To tell someone that "sometimes water systems can become contaminated" is implicit; to tell someone that "the Health Department found unsafe levels of bacteria in the water system of the XYZ Restaurant and shut them down this morning" is more explicit.

Implications can be subtle or they can be easily seen. What implication does the speaker make in this sentence from a short story ("Liberty Hall") by Ring Lardner?

On the fourth awful day Ben gave out the news—news to him and to me as well as to our host and hostess—that he had lost a filling which he would not trust any but his own New York dentist to replace.

What is the speaker implying when she says "news to him"? Could it be that he really had not lost a filling but simply wanted an excuse to leave? In this case, finding the CONTEXT of the short story in which this sentence appears is the only way to realize the true MEANING and significance of this implication.

The implication made in this sentence from a short story ("An Outpost of Progress") by Joseph Conrad is far less subtle:

He had charge of a small clay storehouse with a dried-grass roof, and pretended to keep a correct account of beads, cotton cloth, red kerchiefs, brass wire, and other trade goods it contained.

What are the implications in the statement that he "pretended to keep a correct account"? The obvious answer is that although he led others to believe the accounts were accurate, they were not; and he knew that they were not. This much can be learned from the implications of "pretended." From these implications, can an inference be made concerning why he did this? Can an inference be made that he did not have the ability to keep accurate books and as a result tried to cover careless and perhaps unintended errors? Or can an inference be made that he deliberately misled others to cover embezzlement or to harm them financially? These questions cannot be answered and such inferences outside the CONTEXT in which the sentence was taken cannot be made.

MEANING(S) IN CONTEXT
IN PROSE, POETRY, AND DRAMA

Isolated words and PHRASES depend upon CONTEXT for both their level of MEANING and for their implied MEANINGS, as well as for any inferences that can be drawn from those implications. Prose sentences, too, can carry many different MEANINGS, depending on their CONTEXT. Here are some examples:

1. *The facts and nothing but the facts*

Some prose writing is purported to be fact. There are two very important elements you should keep in mind when looking at the MEANING IN CONTEXT of statements that are intended to be based on facts: First, *not all things asserted to be "facts" are true.* Second, *facts, in most cases, are verifiable—they can be proven as either true or false.* Of course, the first logical place to look for verification is the CONTEXT in which the statement is given; however, very often you must look elsewhere at observations, the records of others, the accounts of witnesses, and so forth (outside the CONTEXT) to determine the accuracy of the "facts."

2. *"In my opinion..."*

Not all speakers and writers state clearly that they are expressing an opinion rather than a fact. Yet, you can differentiate between facts and opinions and as a result, gain significant insight into their MEANING(S) IN CONTEXT. A statement based on the writer's opinion—on his or her judgment—cannot be verified as true or as false. How can the reader know, then, what such a statement means and whether to trust or to believe the statement? Very often, this determination is based on the credibility of the speaker or writer and on the CONTEXT or the circumstances in which the statement is made. Because the statement cannot be *verified* by CONTEXT or by means outside the CONTEXT, the reader must look at the speaker very closely: Is the speaker known to be reliable? What circumstances (events or concerns) surround the making of the statement? Might the speaker have a hidden agenda? Many more such questions can be asked about statements of opinion, the answers of which directly relate to and influence the MEANING, because this evaluation of the position of the speaker, in a sense, provides the CONTEXT.

Here is an illustration taken from a speech by Theodore Roosevelt in 1903 to the Leland Stanford Junior University in California. The topic is the preservation of forests:

California has for years, I am happy to say, taken a more sensible, a more intelligent interest in forest preservation than any other state. It early appointed a forest commission; later on some of the functions of that commission were replaced by the Sierra Club, a club which has done much on the Pacific coast to perpetuate the spirit of the explorer and the pioneer. Then I am happy to say a great business interest showed an intelligent and farsighted spirit which is of happy augury, for the Redwood Manufacturers of San Francisco were first among lumbermen's associations to give assistance to the cause of practical forestry. The study of the redwood which the action of this association made possible was the pioneer study in the cooperative work which is now being carried out between lumbermen all over the United States and the Federal Bureau of Forestry.

Based on CONTEXT, what does President Roosevelt mean when he says "California has for years...taken a more sensible, a more intelligent interest in forest preservation than any other state"?

The statement is obviously an opinion—for how can one verify "more sensible" or "more intelligent" in this CONTEXT? But look at his use of verifiable facts to support his opinion. The reader or listener can go to other sources to ascertain the forest commission's appointment, its functions compared to those of the Sierra Club, the assistance of the Redwood Manufacturers of San Francisco, and the pioneer study that they made possible. So what does he mean, based on CONTEXT, when he says that "California has…taken a more sensible, a more intelligent interest…"? He means that the government, service clubs, and lumbermen's associations

of California led the way with concrete, verifiable actions toward forest preservation.

3. "Well, what you really ought to do…"
Normative, directives—these both refer to statements that aim to influence the reader or listener either directly or indirectly to conform to some standard or a designated norm. Occasionally, these directives are straightforward in which the writer literally says that you should do this or that you ought to do that.

But very often directives and normatives are not so easily spotted, because, after all, their purpose is to influence—a purpose at the root of propaganda. Society, of course, must have norms or standards by which its members can live; however, it is important to be able to recognize when people are being directed and to what norms they are being directed to conform. Only then can the reader or listener make a conscious and informed choice as to conduct as it relates to these norms.

In this concluding paragraph of the speech by Roosevelt on forest preservation, what norms are being set for these young university men? What directives does the speech give them?

Citizenship is the prime test in the welfare of the nation; but we need good laws; and above all we need good land laws throughout the West. We want to see the free farmer own his home. The best of the public lands are already in private hands, and yet the rate of their disposal is steadily increasing. More than six million acres were patented during the first three months of the present year. It is time for us to see that our remaining public lands are saved for the home maker to the utmost limit of his possible use. I say this to you of this university because we have a right to expect that the best-trained, the best-educated men on the Pacific Slope, the Rocky Mountains and Great Plains states will take the lead in the preservation and right use of the forests, in securing the right use of the water, and in seeing to it that our land policy is not twisted from its original purpose, but is perpetuated by amendment, by change when such change is necessary in the line of that purpose, the purpose being to turn the public domain into farms each to be the property of the man who actually tills it and makes his home on it.

Notice the directives being set before them: (1) "taking the lead in the preservation and right use of the forests," (2) "securing the right use of the water," and (3) "seeing to it that our land policy is not twisted." Why? Because a norm has been set by the speaker in this speech: "We want to see the free farmer own his home" and "we have a right to expect that the best-trained, the best-educated men on the Pacific Slope, the Rocky Mountains and Great Plains states will take the lead…."

Poetic Syntax

Elements of poetic language are commonly found in prose. The use of metaphor, as an example, is found in this excerpt from a speech made by Booker T. Washington concerning slavery:

A ship lost at sea for many days suddenly sighted a friendly vessel. From the mast of the unfortunate vessel was seen a signal, "Water, water; we die of thirst!" The answer from the friendly vessel at once came back, "Cast down your bucket where you are." And a third and fourth signal for water was answered, "Cast down your bucket where you are." The captain of the distressed vessel, at last heeding the injunction, cast down his bucket, and it came up full of fresh, sparkling water from the mouth of the Amazon River. To those of my race who depend on bettering their condition in a foreign land or who underestimate the importance of cultivating friendly relations with the Southern white man, who is their next-door neighbor, I would say: "Cast down your bucket where you are"—cast it down in making friends in every manly way of the people of all races by whom we are surrounded.

Yet, there is a **poetic syntax** that by definition includes both the emotive language that speaks to the reader's emotions over and above the descriptive and expository neutrality of **referential** (also called **cognitive**) language and a use of syntax that focuses on its effect over its conformity to rules. Some literary scholars cite this freedom in the use of syntax as a major line drawn between prose and poetry. Regardless, the syntax of poetry is a product of FORM and a major contributor to MEANING. How do poets use syntax? A few notable ways include:

- Words that are normally assigned one function are used in an unusual function in a syntactical structure. For example, <u>was</u> normally functions as a verb and <u>lifetime</u> as a noun. The poet might assign <u>was</u> to the role of subject and use <u>lifetime</u> as a verb.

  <u>Was</u> is a lifetime ago…
  And she has <u>lifetimed</u> her existence away.

- Inversion of normal syntactical patterns, such as placing the modifier after rather than before the word it modifies:

This <u>Hermit good</u> lives in that wood
Which slopes down to the sea. [emphasis added]

Or placing the predicate modifier first in the sentence:

<u>Silent</u> is the house: all are laid asleep.
[emphasis added]

What would be the normal syntactical pattern for this structure?

With olives ripe the sauces
    Were flavored, without exception.

- Repetition of syntactical patterns:

MY MIND TO ME A KINGDOM IS

Some have too much, yet still do crave;
    I little have, and seek no more.
They are but poor, though much they have,
    And I am rich with little store.
<u>They poor, I rich; they beg, I give;</u>
<u>Thy lack, I leave; they pine, I live.</u>

[emphasis added]

by Sir Edward Dyer   (fifth stanza)

There are many more ways poets can use syntactical patterns to achieve their purposes; however, CONTEXT remains one of the most useful elements to determining MEANING, particularly when the poetic syntax makes MEANING more obscure.

QUESTIONS TO APPLY YOUR LEARNING

As you practice reading literary selections, ask these questions to help you identify and understand MEANINGS OF SENTENCES, LINES, PHRASES, AND WORDS IN CONTEXT.

1. Do you understand the denotations of all the words employed in the work?
2. What "shades of MEANING" are intended?
3. Do any of the words or PHRASES have multiple MEANINGS? Does CONTEXT support any of these alternate usages?
4. What is the level of abstraction (or concreteness) in the work? Specificity?

5. Are there any unusual syntactical patterns used? What is the effect?

6. What is the main clause (as opposed to those clauses that are subordinated)?

7. Who or what is doing the action (as applicable)?

8. When does the action take place (based on verb tense)?

9. Do any of the WORDS, PHRASES, or LINES carry with them connotative MEANINGS in this CONTEXT?

10. What implications are made in the CONTEXT of the work?

ADDITIONAL HELPFUL POINTS TO REMEMBER

- Do keep in mind that just as connotations can be based on individual experiences, on cultural groups, on national identity, and so forth, they also can be directly affected by *time.* Connotation is a function of diction—of word choice. As such, not only can denotations of words change over the years, but also the connotations can change.

  The color red is an example. Today red denotatively refers to a color. Connotatively you might think of red as a symbol for blood, fire, communism, or a warning to stop. But in the last century red also was a symbol for immorality (as in the story *The Scarlet Letter*). If today's reader were to read an account of a woman wearing a red dress, the reader would probably not take notice; however, such a dress would have very negative connotations for readers of the past, connotations that would reflect badly on the CHARACTER wearing the offending color.

  Conversely, being called a "hussy" today has negative connotations that did not exist back when a "hussy" simply referred to a "housewife."

- The poetic syntax of poetry selections for testing purposes most generally can be understood in CONTEXT; however, you may encounter in your personal study instances in which the poetic syntax unites with other USES OF LANGUAGE (such as complex imagery or dissonance) to make the MEANING obscure beyond identification. This is especially true of some twentieth-century poems that are deliberate interplays of syntax, symbolism, strange wordplays, and other such devices to produce a sense of obscurity. Although some historical use of obscurity was for the purpose of circumventing political censorship (such as the political commentaries "hidden" in the obscure language of some Renaissance English poets), very often such obscurity does not serve such a pragmatic function.

  Some poems, like some abstract art, do not necessarily have "a MEANING," but rather the MEANING is a product of what the individual reader or hearer brings to the work. In such cases, the CONTEXT is outside the poem. Other poems are so intimately a reflection of the poet's personal experiences that the full extent of the MEANING cannot be determined without knowledge of the event, people, or circumstances that inspired the work: the CONTEXT is the poet's life. For example, nineteenth-century poet Leigh Hunt wrote a poem called "Jenny Kissed Me":

  Jenny kissed me when we met,
     Jumping from the chair she sat in;
  Time, you thief, who love to get
     Sweets into your list, put that in:

  Say I'm weary, say I'm sad,
     Say that health and wealth have missed me,
  Say I'm growing old, but add,
     Jenny kissed me.

  Here is the story behind this little poem: "Jenny" was Mrs. Jane Welsh Carlyle. Leigh Hunt, her friend, fell ill with influenza, a disease that in the early 1800s claimed many lives. Mrs. Carlyle, who was quite concerned about her friend, was so excited upon seeing him recovered that she impulsively kissed Hunt, inspiring him to write "Jenny Kissed Me."

- Some test questions may test your understanding of **connotation** by giving you words used in the passage and asking you to select from among lists of ways the words (or PHRASES) have influenced MEANING.

PUTTING THE SEVEN LITERARY ELEMENTS TO WORK

LITERARY ANALYSIS IN PREPARATION FOR THE SAT II: LITERATURE TEST

Up to this point the seven literary elements have been discussed separately and briefly, illustrating some of the major considerations in each element to help prepare you for what you might encounter on the SAT II: Literature Subject Test. Yet, as you read and analyze English and American literature in preparation for the test, you need to develop a systematic approach that will deal with two challenges:

1. When working with literature outside the actual testing situation, you will encounter entire selections that can range in length from two lines to hundreds of pages.
2. Analyzing a work of literature to identify, understand, and discuss its use of the seven literary elements can be complex.

The purpose of this section is to model approaches to literary analysis that will deal with both these challenges. You might elect to study individually, to study as part of a group, or to use a combination of both. Regardless of your preferences in study plans, you need to establish a means to manage the task so that you use your literary analysis time efficiently.

In this section is a step-by-step approach to examining the seven literary elements in works of literature. Also, you will find several full-length selections: an essay, a short story, a lyric poem, and a narrative poem. These selections are much longer than many of the excerpts that you have encountered to this point and should give some idea how you can handle works of varying lengths. The suggestions that follow, of course, are just that—suggestions. Remember, you probably will want to develop your own study plan: just be sure to keep it manageable.

Step one. Make a preliminary list of genres.

You need a list of what kinds of literary works you want to analyze. This list needs to be short and prac-

tical so that you establish a sense of encouragement at the onset. For this section, four genres (already listed) have been chosen that represent narrative and nonnarrative prose and poetry. For this exercise, you may want to make just two selections—perhaps one poem and one short story—or maybe even begin with just one selection. Remember: You can increase your numbers of selections and range of genres as you gain proficiency in analysis and as you increase your adeptness in recognizing the seven literary elements and the effects of their use.

Step two. Make your selection(s).

A trip to the library is most likely necessary. If you desire or need help, the librarian can provide assistance in locating suitable selections. Suppose that you decide to begin with a narrative poem: Make a computer search to find names of poets who have written narrative poems since 1600. Also, you might ask your English/language arts teacher to suggest narrative poems for analysis. Look, as well, into anthologies of poems, stories, plays, and other literary genres. Anthologies contain literary works that are grouped according to such topics as a particular author (the collected works of Charles Dickens), nationality (American poems from the last century), theme (love poems), time ("modern" poetry), genre (collections of sonnets or groupings of political essays), and literary periods (works of the Romantics). The benefit of beginning with an anthology is that you can, in a time of calm reflection, see many comparable works together in one book.

You may want to begin collecting suggested reading lists; however, you may find that reading lists have fallen into disfavor among some literary educators because such lists are often not representative of the important body of ethnic and minority literature that is a part of both American and British literary traditions. Yet, these lists do include many of the works that have been considered "great" from one generation to the next. Although you perhaps should not overemphasize study of the works on recommended reading lists, they do provide convenient starting places for literary analysis. Also, you will find that many of the "classics" and award-winning works of literature have been analyzed by various literary critics over the years. After analyzing a work for the seven literary elements, you can use these analyses by the critics for comparison and contrast, helping you to identify even deeper levels of MEANING and extended USES OF LANGUAGE. You may even encounter a variety of opinions among the critics themselves. Allow yourself, however, to bring a fresh view to the work. Taking an alternative viewpoint concerning a literary work can be constructive to your study as long as you have paid attention to detail and considered all the facts. Be *sure* that you understand the words as they are used in the period in which the work was written.

Finally, if you have not already done so, become acquainted with the literary reference section of your library. You can use this section to help you make selection choices. For example, the *Reader's Encyclopedia of American Literature* contains titles of works with synopses, plus other helpful information. You might want to look into the *Oxford Companion to English Literature* and the *American Authors and Books 1640 to the Present Day,* among others. Cultivate these types of resources! They are useful not just for your preparation for the immediate testing situation; they are also important tools for your future academic career.

Step three. Read.

After you make your first selection, find a comfortable spot and read the work for pleasure. Do not at this point try to find the significance of every comma and adjective: just read it. Allow yourself to enjoy the effects of the words, the impact of the MEANING. After finishing, take a few minutes to reflect on the selection. What did you like about it? Dislike about it? Did it affect you personally in any way? Jot down your overall impressions. You can refer to these first impressions after you have examined the work in CONTEXT with the literary elements involved. An interesting exercise is to compare your first impressions with your opinions concerning the work after the selection has undergone the scrutiny of analysis.

Step four. Select an excerpt.

As you progress in literary analysis, you will want to analyze entire selections; however, in preparation for the SAT II: Literature Subject Test, learning to

select your own excerpts will make preparation far more manageable and will intensify the focus of your study.

There are no hard-and-fast rules for sectioning off an excerpt at this point, but here are a few general guidelines:

1. You can either select the excerpt at random or you can focus on a section that strikes you as especially interesting. As you practice your skills, you may notice, for example, that a particular paragraph includes effective use of personification and, because you understand this concept, you could elect to include that paragraph as part of the excerpt that you analyze. This is quite justifiable because identifying personification is only half the job. Just as significant (or, in the opinion of some literary analysts, more significant) to your analysis is identifying the *effects* of the personification on the other elements (such as MEANING) of the work (or of the excerpt). Do not, however, neglect the more challenging portions of the work—those that will make you stretch to find the significance. Remember: If you encounter a selection that you do not understand or if you find that you do not recognize, for example, the attitude of the speaker, you can go to a literature teacher for help and you can ask a librarian to assist you in locating (if available) the comments of literary critics concerning the work in question. You may find that the answers to your questions are in the basics: in word meanings as used in the period in which the selection was written, in identification of the speaker, or in the structural development of the work.

2. You can take more than one excerpt from a literary work, particularly if you find the work challenging. Also, you can work with the entire selection if the length is manageable, as in the case of some short stories, even though the selection might be much longer than a test excerpt would be.

3. If the work is prose, you may want to limit your excerpts to between 50 and 400 words. These numbers are not unchangeable, and if you find that adding or deleting another sentence or paragraph will help you in your analysis, by all means do so. One effective method to select an excerpt is to ask yourself this question: If I were to write the test questions, where would I start and stop this excerpt?

4. If the work is poetry, you may want to limit excerpts to between ten and fifteen lines, although a selection might be over forty lines. Again, which portion of the poem would you select to write questions concerning the literary elements that you have been studying? Of course, you will often find that poems in their entirety will fall within this range.

Step five. Analyze the excerpt.

Examine your excerpt for the use of the seven literary elements, one by one. Each of the seven previous chapters in this section details many of the common uses of the seven literary elements, and each chapter includes a "Questions To Apply Your Learning" set of questions to ask when reading a selection. At the end of this chapter you will find "A Quick Reference Guide to the Seven Literary Elements" (see page 225) that you can use for this purpose. Also, you can take a more generalized approach such as that modeled later in this section.

Step six. Think about test questions.

If you were writing test questions concerning a writer's use of the literary elements and their effects, which points would you consider important? You may want to compose (using the test questions in this volume as models) a few questions based on your analysis of the selection that would serve to increase your understanding of the literary elements involved.

Step seven. Discuss your analysis.

Verbalize your analysis with a teacher or in a study group. Study groups are especially effective in literary analysis. You can assign a genre or even a specific work to individuals who could first go through the steps outlined in this chapter, then present the results to the group. Another profitable exercise would be to have the "analyst" ask the group some SAT II-type questions to stimulate discussion.

If you encounter a selection in which you or those in your study group have difficulty understanding one or more literary elements being used, be sure to review the appropriate section or subject in this book. Check with your librarian to see if any critical essays or literary analysis books have been written about the writer or the selection in question that might better help you to understand the work.

Keep in mind that although your short-term focus is on the SAT II: Literature Subject Test, the work you do (the literary analysis approaches that you develop, the library resources that you cultivate) to prepare for the test can enable you to achieve in many other areas of academics and professional pursuits that depend upon reading comprehension. In addition, these skills can embark you into a lifetime of literary enjoyment.

You have just looked at seven steps aimed at making practice of skills in literary analysis more manageable. Now, a few aspects of the seven literary elements at work in an essay, a short story, a lyric poem, and a narrative poem will be briefly identified and discussed.

HINT: You will often find that a literary work is accompanied by a preface or introduction that discusses the life of the author, the literary times, the historical period, or the work itself. You may be tempted to skip right over this—after all, this information is not to be a focus of the SAT II: Literature Subject Test. If you omit this information, however, you will miss an opportunity to enlarge your understanding of literature and the English-speaking world that fostered it. Knowledge of the peoples and times in literature and the peoples and times that bore literature can empower you with a basis for the higher-level thinking skills (skills such as perceiving cause-and-effect relationships in history, society, government, economics) required for success in your future academic career and in your career beyond the postsecondary school campus.

Examining an Essay

Read the following essay.

THE CHARACTER OF NED SOFTLY
by
Joseph Addison (1672–1719)

(Paragraph)

(1) *Idem inficeto est inficetior rure,*
Simul poemata attigit; neque idem unquam
Æque est beatus, ac poema cum scribit:
Tam gaudet in se, tamque se ipse miratur.
Nimirum idem omnes fallimur; neque est quisquam
Quem non in aliqua re videre Suffenum
Possis.   —*Catullus, "de Suffeno," xx.14.*

(2)   Suffenus has no more wit than a mere clown when he attempts to write verses; and yet he is never happier than when he is scribbling: so much does he admire himself and his compositions. And, indeed, this is the foible of every one of us; for there is no man living who is not a Suffenus in one thing or other.

(3)   I yesterday came hither about two hours before the company generally make their appearance, with a design to read over all the newspapers; but, upon my sitting down, I was accosted by Ned Softly, who saw me from a corner in the other end of the room, where I found he had been writing something. "Mr. Bickerstaff," says he, "I observe by a late paper of yours, that you and I are just of a humor; for you must know, of all impertinences, there is nothing which I so much hate as news. I never read a gazette in my life; and never trouble my head about our armies, whether they win or lose, or in what part of the world they lie encamped." Without giving me time to reply, he drew a paper of verses out of his pocket, telling me, "that he had something which would entertain me more agreeably; and that he would desire my judgment upon every line, for that we had time enough before us until the company came in."

(4)   Ned Softly is a very pretty poet, and a great admirer of easy lines. Waller is his favorite: and as that admirable writer has the best and worst verses of any among our great English poets, Ned Softly has got all the bad ones without book: which he repeats upon occasion, to show his reading, and garnish his conversation. Ned is indeed a true English reader, incapable of relishing the great and masterly strokes of this art; but wonderfully pleased with the little Gothic ornaments of epigrammatical conceits, turns, points, and quibbles, which are so frequent in the most admired of our English poets, and practised by those who want genius and strength to represent, after the manner of the ancients, simplicity in its natural beauty and perfection.

(5)   Finding myself unavoidably engaged in such a conversation, I was resolved to turn my pain into a pleasure, and to divert myself as well as I could with so very odd a fellow. "You must understand," says Ned, "that the sonnet I am going to read to you was written upon a lady, who showed me some verses of her own making, and is, perhaps, the best poet of our age. But you shall hear it." Upon which he began to read as follows:

    "TO MIRA, ON HER INCOMPARABLE POEMS.

                    I

(6)   "When dress'd in laurel wreaths you shine,
        And tune your soft melodious notes,

        You seem a sister of the Nine,
        Or Phoebus' self in petticoats.

                    II

(7)   "I fancy, when your song you sing,
        (Your song you sing with so much art)
        Your pen was pluck'd from Cupid's wing;
        For, ah! it wounds me like his dart."

(8)   "Why," says I, "this is a little nosegay of conceits, a very lump of salt: every verse has something in it that piques; and then the *dart* in the last line is certainly as pretty a sting in the tail of an epigram, for so I think you critics call it, as ever entered into the thought of a poet." "Dear Mr. Bickerstaff," says he, shaking me by the hand, "everybody knows you to be a judge of these things; and to tell you truly, I read over Roscommon's translation of Horace's 'Art of Poetry' three several times before I sat down to write the sonnet which I have shown you. But you shall hear it again, and pray observe every line of it; for not one of them shall pass without your approbation—

        "When dress'd in laurel wreaths you shine.

(9)   "That is," says he, "when you have your garland on; when you are writing verses." To which I replied, "I know your meaning; a metaphor!" "The same," said he and went on—

        "And tune your soft melodious notes.

(10)   "Pray observe the gliding of that verse; there is scarce a consonant in it; I took care to make it run upon liquids. Give me your opinion of it." "Truly," said I, "I think it as good as the former." "I am very glad to hear you say so," says he, "but mind the next—

        "You seem a sister of the Nine.

(11)   "That is," says he, "you seem a sister of the muses; for, if you look into ancient authors, you will find it was their opinion that there were nine of them." "I remember it very well," said I; "but pray proceed."

        "Or Phoebus' self in petticoats.

(12)   "Phoebus," says he, "was the god of poetry. These little instances, Mr. Bickerstaff, show a gentleman's reading. Then, to take off from the air of learning, which Phoebus and the muses had given to this first stanza, you may observe, how it falls all of a sudden into the familiar, 'in petticoats'!

(13)   "Let us now," says I, "enter upon the second stanza; I find the first line is still a continuation of the metaphor—

        "I fancy, when your song you sing."

(14)   "It is very right," says he; "but pray observe the turn of words in those two lines. I was a whole hour in adjusting of them, and have still a doubt upon me whether in the second line it should be, 'Your song you sing;' or, 'You sing your song.' You shall hear them both—

> "I fancy, when your song you sing,
> (Your song you sing with so much art);

Or, "I fancy, when your song you sing,
> (You sing your song with so much art)."

(15)   "Truly," said I, "the turn is so natural either way, that you have made me almost giddy with it." "Dear sir," said he, grasping me by the hand, "you have a great deal of patience; but pray what do you think of the next verse—

> "Your pen was pluck'd from Cupid's wing."

(16)   "Think!" says I, "I think you have made Cupid look like a little goose." "That was my meaning," says he, "I think the ridicule is well enough hit off. But we come now to the last, which sums up the whole matter—

> "For, ah! it wounds me like his dart.

(17)   "Pray how do you like that 'Ah!' doth it not make a pretty figure in that place? 'Ah!'—it looks as if I felt the dart, and cried out as being pricked with it—

> "For, ah! it wounds me like his dart.

(18)   "My friend, Dick Easy," continued he, "assured me he would rather have written that 'Ah!' than to have been the author of the 'Æneid.' He indeed objected, that I made Mira's pen like a quill in one of the lines, and like a dart in the other. But as to that—" "Oh! as to that," says I, "it is but supposing Cupid to be like a porcupine, and his quills and darts will be the same thing." He was going to embrace me for the hint; but half a dozen critics coming into the room, whose faces he did not like, he conveyed the sonnet into his pocket and whispered me in the ear, "he would show it me again as soon as his man had written it over fair."

Although much longer than a test selection, such an essay as this is of manageable size to address in its entirety. Now, make an analysis of the seven literary elements as used in this essay. After you have completed your analysis, compare the points that you uncovered with those that follow.

Here are just a few points that you might consider in reading this essay:

1. MEANING

This is an entertaining essay that seems to aim at sharing with the reader an intellectually stimulating encounter between two men. Although the subject is poetry, the essay focuses on a poem written by Ned Softly and is concerned with an informal literary analysis of that poem. In addition to asking about the MEANING of the selection as a whole, test questions might be asked concerning the MEANING of the poem, particularly as it is viewed by each of the speakers.

2. FORM

As the title of the selection suggests, the FORM of this essay is the CHARACTER, traditionally defined as a short description of a "type" CHARACTER who exemplifies some vice or virtue. In this case, Addison individualizes the CHARACTER and combines it with a periodical essay FORM. The reader learns from introductory material (not reprinted here) that this essay appeared in *The Spectator*.

The essay is a narrative episode to the extent that the speaker is almost anecdotally relating his encounter and conversation with Ned Softly:

> I. Introduction (paragraph 3)
>   (A) Speaker is reading newspapers.
>   (B) Speaker is approached by Ned Softly.
> II. Body (paragraphs 4–17)
>   (A) Speaker and Ned read poem as a whole.
>   (B) Speaker and Ned make a line-by-line analysis of poem.
> III. Conclusion (paragraph 18)
>   (A) Speaker gives Ned a hint.
>   (B) Ned promises another encounter.

The structure of the lyric love poem is in two parts of four lines written in iambic pentameter with an abab cdcd rhyme scheme. Although identified by Ned as a "sonnet" (paragraph 5), this work contains only eight lines. The role of the quotation and introduction (paragraphs 1–2) will be addressed later.

3. NARRATIVE VOICE

Written in first person NARRATIVE, the speaker is a man of letters. Use of first person, the complementary words of Ned Softly, and the speaker's own words make him seem quite credible. The speaker's attitude toward Ned might be described as condescending: "a very pretty poet" (paragraph 4), "incapable" (paragraph 4), "pain" (paragraph 5), "so very odd a fellow" (paragraph 5). Although impossible to determine from an essay isolated from the historical context in which it was written, the reader might assume that when Ned Softly calls the speaker "Mr. Bickerstaff," the speaker is a mask or persona of the author.

4. TONE and 5. CHARACTER

The speaker's TONE (of voice) seems formal to modern perceptions, as becomes a late seventeenth-century man of letters. Yet, his patient indulgence with Ned, someone he obviously considers his inferior as "a true English reader, incapable of relishing the great and masterly strokes of this art," seems very conversational in TONE. The speaker's opinion of Ned is revealed and the TONE of his responses to Ned's conversation is set when he says, "Finding myself unavoidably engaged in such a conversation, I was resolved to turn my pain into a pleasure, and to divert myself as well as I could with so very odd a fellow." Because he cannot avoid the situation, he intends to use it for entertainment. This is also a revelation of CHARACTER on the part of Bickerstaff. On one hand he esteems himself knowledgeable enough to judge the learning of others, whereas on the other hand he has the capacity for what people today call "making lemons into lemonade"—turning unpleasant situations into pleasant ones through adopting a positive attitude. Realization of these elements of Bickerstaff's conversation with Ned might help in selecting answer choices concerning his TONE when he refers to Ned as one among "you critics" in paragraph 8, when he says that Ned has "made me almost giddy" with his use of words in paragraph 15, or when he says that Ned "made Cupid look like a little goose" in paragraph 16.

The revelation of Ned's CHARACTER and the TONE of his remarks are far less subtle than those of Bickerstaff. The reader learns some insight into Ned's CHARACTER through Bickerstaff's comments, notably:

- He likes "easy" lines.
- He likes Waller's poetry, but rather than the best verses, he has the "bad ones without book."
- He repeats poems "to show his reading."

The reader also learns about Ned's CHARACTER through his own words:

- He identifies with Bickerstaff's personality ("you and I are just of a humor").
- He is not interested in current events or the national interests.

- He elicits Bickerstaff's attention concerning his verses "without giving me time to reply." (This can be viewed in several ways: some people might label this aspect of his CHARACTER as overbearing or *pushy*. The reader also could cite such conduct as indicative of a self-centered personality, yet a case could be made that Ned is simply excited and overzealous concerning gaining Bickerstaff's approval.)
- He views the lady who is the object of his verse as an excellent poet ("perhaps, the best poet of our age"), indicating an appreciation for a work regardless of the sex of the poet.
- He looked to Horace's "Art of Poetry" to write his sonnet, indicating a "by the book" approach to an artistic endeavor.
- He is not satisfied with Bickerstaff's approval and complimentary words about the poem as a whole, but "shows off" the poem line by line.
- He reveals that he deliberately wants to "show a gentleman's reading" in the verses; he wants people to know that he is well read.
- He has "anguished" over each word of the poem (including diction and syntax): "I was a whole hour in adjusting of them [two lines]"— perhaps tendencies toward being a *perfectionist*.
- He is impressed by the opinions of others (such as Dick Easy).
- For some reason (one about which the reader can only speculate), he does not want to share his poem with other critics "whose faces he did not like."
- He has secretarial help ("his man" in paragraph 18).
- He appreciates help from Bickerstaff ("He was going to embrace me for the hint").
- He assumes that Bickerstaff will want to see the "sonnet" again.
- He is secretive about the "sonnet."

Many of these insights into Ned's CHARACTER help the reader to identify what TONE he uses in talking to Bickerstaff.

Taking the previously discussed elements into account, Bickerstaff's CHARACTER might be generalized as a man who is self-assured, respected, opinionated, and congenial. His CHARACTER sets a TONE of good-natured indulgence. Ned's CHARACTER could be generalized as a man who is impressionable, enthusiastic, eager to impress others, and fastidious about details. His CHARACTER adds a TONE of intense exuberance to the sketch.

Having established a background discussion of the use of CHARACTER and TONE in this essay, you should look once again at the FORM and VOICE. Look closely at the quote from *Catullus* and the commentary paragraph that follows it (paragraphs 1–2). Obviously Ned is characterized as a Suffenus type, one who admires himself (as a man of learning) and admires his own compositions, despite his lack of original talent. The commentary contains another insightful point: "there is no man living who is not a Suffenus in one thing or other." Does this mean that even Bickerstaff has elements of Suffenus in his CHARACTER?

In terms of FORM, the quotation and comment serve to introduce the CHARACTER trait(s) that are the focus of the sketch, to foreshadow "The Character of Ned Softly," and to summarize the main point by means of a generalization about the CHARACTER of man ("there is no man living who is not a Suffenus in one thing or other"). What is the effect of this use of FORM? One major effect is irony: Bickerstaff indirectly characterizes Ned as a Suffenus type, yet he, himself, must fall into the same "foible of every one of us…in one thing or other" that characterizes Suffenus and Ned.

In terms of VOICE, this introduction presents the reader with a challenge: who is speaking? If the speaker is Bickerstaff, the effect of the FORM is to reveal to readers an ironic tongue-in-cheek *awareness* on his part. If, on the other hand, the reader is listening to the VOICE of the writer of this CHARACTER sketch, the effect is even more profound because the writer is revealing his own view concerning Ned and Bickerstaff, as well as revealing the irony of Bickerstaff's *lack of awareness* of his own "foible."

6. USE OF LANGUAGE
This selection is rich in figurative language. A *few* uses include:

- "trouble my head" (paragraph 3)—slang
  Effect: a conversational TONE
- "nosegay of conceits" (paragraph 8)—metaphor
  Tenor: the poem, consisting of conceits (elaborate metaphors that were considered strained and artificial in the eighteenth and nineteenth centuries)

Vehicle: nosegay (small collection of flowers)
- "lump of salt" (paragraph 8)—metaphor
  Tenor: the poem
  Vehicle: lump of salt

Can you identify the comparison(s), including the tenor(s) and vehicle(s) in this line?

"…then the *dart* in the last line is certainly as pretty a string in the tail of an epigram,…" (paragraph 8)

- "a sister of the Nine" (paragraph 10)—literary allusion
  Effect: "an air of learning"
- "made Cupid look like a little goose" (paragraph 16)—simile
  Tenor: Cupid
  Vehicle: goose

7. MEANINGS OF SENTENCES, LINES, PHRASES, AND WORDS IN CONTEXT
One of the more obvious examples of the use of syntax in this selection is Ned's own discussion of word order when he debates between "Your song you sing with so much art" and "You sing your song with so much art." Can you identify the significance in syntactical terms of the one against the other?

In "You sing your song…," the function order is subject-verb-object, the most commonly used syntactical order that places emphasis on the subject (You). In contrast, "Your song you sing…" is in the object-subject-verb order. The result? Emphasis is placed on the song.

This selection contains many words, phrases, and lines that could be the subject of test questions aimed at MEANINGS IN CONTEXT. Read the following list and define the MEANING of each as used IN CONTEXT:

- "you and I are just of a humor" (paragraph 3)

Possible answers: A "humor" (often spelled *humour*) refers to the four humours or predominant features of a person's CHARACTER and personality. Ned believes that he and Bickerstaff share the same opinions on the subject.

- "a very pretty poet" (paragraph 4)

Possible answers: The CONTEXT is especially important in determining the use of the word *pretty* in this selection. Ned's CHARACTER has been established as someone who is a Suffenus type, enthusiastic about writing poetry and greatly admiring his own work. In this CONTEXT, "pretty" is an ironic word choice. "Pretty" means clever or artful—an opinion Ned holds of himself. The connotative definitions of "pretty," however, reinforce Bickerstaff's opinions concerning Ned: as a "pretty poet" his work sounds pleasant but does not have strength, or intensity. Also, do the names of the CHARACTERS in this work (Softly and Bickerstaff) have any significance to revelation of CHARACTER?

- "easy lines" (paragraph 4)

Possible answers: What are "easy" lines from a "pretty poet"? Such a poet would like lines that are not difficult to understand or difficult to write.

- "Ned Softly has got all the bad ones without book" (paragraph 4)

Possible answers: The clue to "without book" is found in the comment "which he repeats upon occasion, to show his reading and garnish his conversation." In other words, Ned has memorized (can repeat without looking at a book) Waller's worst verses so that he appears learned. This line would also make an excellent question concerning CHARACTER.

Examining a Short Story

The next selection is Edgar Allan Poe's famous short story "The Imp of the Perverse" published in 1845. You may have already read this story; however, now that you have studied the seven literary elements that form the basis for the SAT II: Literature Subject Test, you can examine this story from a different perspective, with a focus on developing skills to prepare you to take the Literature Test.

Read the story, then analyze the selection using the guidelines that follow.

THE IMP OF THE PERVERSE
by
Edgar Allan Poe

(1)   In the consideration of the faculties and impulses—of the *prima mobilia* of the human soul, the phrenologists have failed to make room for a propensity which, although obviously existing as a radical, primitive, irreducible sentiment, has been equally overlooked by all the moralists who have preceded them. In the pure arrogance of the reason, we have all overlooked it. We have suffered its existence to escape our senses, solely through want of belief—of faith;—whether it be faith in

Revelation, or faith in the Kabbala. The idea of it has never occurred to us, simply because of its supererogation. We saw no *need* of the impulse—for the propensity. We could not perceive its necessity. We could not understand, that is to say, we could not have understood, had the notion of this *primum mobile* ever obtruded itself;—we could not have understood in what manner it might be made to further the objects of humanity, either temporal or external. It cannot be denied that phrenology, and in great measure, all metaphysicianism, have been concocted *a priori*. The intellectual or logical man, rather than the understanding or observant man, set himself to imagine designs—to dictate purposes to God. Having thus fathomed to his satisfaction the intentions of Jehovah, out of these intentions he built his innumerable systems of mind. In the matter of phrenology, for example, we first determined, naturally enough, that it was the design of the Deity that man should eat. We then assigned to man an organ of alimentiveness, and this organ is the scourge with which the Deity compels man, will-I nill-I, into eating. Secondly, having settled it to be God's will that man should continue his species, we discovered an organ of amativeness, forthwith. And so with combativeness, with ideality, with causality, with constructiveness,—so, in short, with every organ, whether representing a propensity, a moral sentiment, or a faculty of the pure intellect. And in these arrangements of the *principia* of human action, the Spurzheimites, whether right or wrong, in part, or upon the whole, have but followed, in principle, the footsteps of their predecessors; deducing and establishing every thing from the preconceived destiny of man, and upon the ground of the objects of his Creator.

(2)   It would have been wiser, it would have been safer to classify, (if classify we must,) upon the basis of what man usually or occasionally did, and was always occasionally doing, rather than upon the basis of what we took it for granted the Deity intended him to do. If we cannot comprehend God in his visible works, how then in his inconceivable thoughts, that call the works into being! If we cannot understand him in his objective creatures, how then in his substantive moods and phrases of creation?

(3)   Induction, *a posteriori*, would have brought phrenology to admit, as an innate and primitive principle of human action, a paradoxical something, which we may call *perverseness*, for want of a more characteristic term. In the sense I intend, it is, in fact a *mobile* without motive, a motive not *motivirt*. Through its promptings we act without comprehensible object; or, if this shall be understood as a contradiction in terms, we may so far

modify the proposition as to say, that through its promptings we act, for the reason that we should *not*. In theory, no reason can be more unreasonable; but, in fact, there is none more strong. With certain minds, under certain conditions, it becomes absolutely irresistible. I am not more certain that I breathe, than that the assurance of the wrong or error of any action is often the one unconquerable *force* which impels us, and alone impels us to its prosecution. Nor will this overwhelming tendency to do wrong for the wrong's sake, admit of analysis, or resolution into ulterior elements. It is a radical, a primitive impulse— elementary. It will be said, I am aware, that when we persist in acts because we feel we should *not* persist in them, our conduct is but a modification of that which ordinarily springs from the *combativeness* of phrenology. But a glance will show the fallacy of this idea. The phrenological combativeness has for its essence, the necessity of self-defence. It is our safeguard against injury. Its principle regards our well-being; and thus the desire to be well, is excited simultaneously with its development. It follows, that the desire to be well must be excited simultaneously with any principle which shall be merely a modification of combativeness, but in the case of that something which I term *perverseness*, the desire to be well is not only not aroused, but a strongly antagonistical sentiment exists.

(4)   An appeal to one's own heart is, after all, the best reply to the sophistry just noticed. No one who trustingly consults and thoroughly questions his own soul will be disposed to deny the entire radicalness of the propensity in question. It is not more incomprehensible than distinctive. There lives no man who at some period, has not been tormented, for example, by an earnest desire to tantalize a listener by circumlocution. The speaker is aware that he displeases; he has every intention to please; he is usually curt, precise, and clear; the most laconic and luminous language is struggling for utterance upon his tongue; it is only with difficulty that he restrains himself from giving it flow; he dreads and deprecates the anger of him whom he addresses; yet, the thought strikes him that by certain involutions and parentheses, this anger may be engendered. That single thought is enough. The impulse increases to a wish, the wish to a desire, the desire to an uncontrollable longing, and the longing, (to the deep regret and mortification of the speaker, and in defiance of all consequences,) is indulged.

(5)   We have a task before us which must be speedily performed. We know that it will be ruinous to make delay. The most important crisis of our life calls trumpet-tongued, for immediate energy and action. We glow, we are consumed with eagerness to commence the work, with the anticipation of whose glorious result our whole souls are on fire. It must, it shall be undertaken to-day, and yet we put if off until to-morrow; and why? There is no answer, except that we feel *perverse*, using the word with no comprehension of the principle. To-morrow arrives, and with it a more impatient anxiety to do our duty, but with this very increase of anxiety arrives, also, a nameless, a positively fearful, because unfathomable craving for delay. This craving gathers strength as the moments fly. The last hour for action is at hand. We tremble with the violence of the conflict within us,—of the definite with the indefinite—of the substance with the shadow. But, if the contest have proceeded thus far, it is the shadow which prevails,—we struggle in vain. The clock strikes, and is the knell of our welfare. At the same time, it is the chanticleer-note to the ghost that has so long overawed us. It flies—it disappears—we are free. The old energy returns. We will labor *now*. Alas, it is *too late!*

(6)   We stand upon the brink of a precipice. We peer into the abyss—we grow sick and dizzy. Our first impulse is to shrink from the danger. Unaccountably we remain. By slow degrees our sickness, and dizziness, and horror, become merged in a cloud of unnameable feeling. By gradations, still more imperceptible, this cloud assumes shape, as did the vapor from the bottle out of which arose the genius in the Arabian Nights. But out of this *our* cloud upon the precipice's edge, there grows into palpability, a shape, far more terrible than any genius, or any demon of a tale, and yet it is but a thought, although a fearful one, and one which chills the very marrow of our bones with the fierceness of the delight of its horror. It is merely the idea of what would be our sensations during the sweeping precipitancy of a fall from such a height. And this fall—this rushing annihilation—for the very reason that it involves that one most ghastly and loathsome of all the most ghastly and loathsome images of death and suffering which have ever presented themselves to our imagination—for this very cause do we now the most vividly desire it. And because our reason violently deters us from the brink, *therefore*, do we the more impetuously approach it. There is no passion in nature so demoniacally impatient, as that of him, who shuddering upon the edge of a precipice, thus meditates a plunge. To indulge for a moment, in any attempt at *thought*, is to be inevitably lost; for reflection but urges us to forbear, and *therefore* it is, I say, that we *cannot*. If there be no friendly arm to check us, or if we fail in a sudden effort to prostrate ourselves backward from the abyss, we plunge, and are destroyed.

(7)   Examine these and similar actions as we will, we shall find them resulting solely from the spirit of the *Perverse*. We perpetrate them merely because we feel that we should *not*. Beyond or behind this, there is no intelligible principle: and we might, indeed, deem this perverseness a direct instigation of the arch-fiend, were it not occasionally known to operate in furtherance of good.

(8)   I have said thus much, that in some measure I may answer your question—that I may explain to you why I am here—that I may assign to you something that shall have at least the faint aspect of a cause for my wearing these fetters, and for my tenanting this cell of the condemned. Had I not been thus prolix, you might either have misunderstood me altogether, or, with the rabble, have fancied me mad. As it is, you will easily perceive that I am one of the many uncounted victims of the Imp of the Perverse.

(9)   It is impossible that any deed could have been wrought with a more thorough deliberation. For weeks, for months, I pondered upon the means of the murder. I rejected a thousand schemes, because their accomplishment involved a *chance* of detection. At length, in reading some French memoirs, I found an account of a nearly fatal illness that occurred to Madame Pilau, through the agency of a candle accidentally poisoned. The idea struck my fancy at once. I knew my victim's habit of reading in bed. I knew, too, that his apartment was narrow and ill-ventilated. But I need not vex you with impertinent details. I need not describe the easy artifices by which I substituted, in his bed-room candle-stand, a wax-light of my own making, for the one which I there found. The next morning he was discovered dead in his bed, and the coroner's verdict was,—"Death by the visitation of God."

(10)   Having inherited his estate, all went well with me for years. The idea of detection never once entered my brain. Of the remains of the fatal taper, I had myself carefully disposed. I had left no shadow of a clue by which it would be possible to convict, or even to suspect me of the crime. It is inconceivable how rich a sentiment of satisfaction arose in my bosom as I reflected upon my absolute security. For a very long period of time, I was accustomed to revel in this sentiment. It afforded me more real delight than all the mere worldly advantages accruing from my sin. But there arrived at length an epoch, from which the pleasurable feeling grew, by scarcely perceptible gradations, into a haunting and harassing thought. It harassed because it haunted. I could scarcely get rid of it for an instant. It is quite a common thing to be thus annoyed with the ringing in our ears, or rather in our memories, of the burthen of some ordinary song, or some unimpressive snatches from an opera. Nor will we be the less tormented if the song in itself be good, or the opera air meritorious. In this manner, at last, I would perpetually catch myself pondering upon my security, and repeating, in a low undertone, the phrase, "I am safe."

(11)   One day, while sauntering along the streets, I arrested myself in the act of murmuring, half aloud, these customary syllables. In a fit of petulance, I remodelled them thus:—"I am safe—I am safe—yes—if I be not fool enough to make open confession!"

(12)   No sooner had I spoken these words, than I felt an icy chill creep to my heart. I had some experience in these fits of perversity, (whose nature I have been at some trouble to explain,) and I remembered well, that in no instance, I had successfully resisted their attacks. And now my own casual self-suggestion, that I might possibly be fool enough to confess the murder of which I had been guilty, confronted me, as if the very ghost of him whom I had murdered—and beckoned me on to death.

(13)   At first, I made an effort to shake off this nightmare of the soul. I walked vigorously—faster—still faster—at length I ran. I felt a maddening desire to shriek aloud. Every succeeding wave of thought overwhelmed me with new terror, for alas! I well, too well understood that, to *think*, in my situation, was to be lost. I still quickened my pace. I bounded like a madman through the crowded thoroughfares. At length, the populace took the alarm, and pursued me. I felt *then* the consummation of my fate. Could I have torn out my tongue, I would have done it—but a rough voice resounded in my ears—a rougher grasp seized me by the shoulder. I turned—I gasped for breath. For a moment, I experienced all the pangs of suffocation; I became blind, and deaf, and giddy; and then, some invisible fiend, I thought, struck me with his broad palm upon the back. The long-imprisoned secret burst forth from my soul.

(14)   They say that I spoke with a distinct enunciation, but with marked emphasis and passionate hurry, as if in dread of interruption before concluding the brief but pregnant sentences that consigned me to the hangman and to hell.

(15)   Having related all that was necessary for the fullest judicial conviction, I fell prostrate in a swoon.

(16)   But why shall I say more? To-day I wear these chains, and am *here!* To-morrow I shall be fetterless!—*but where?*

Guidelines to Analysis

First, look at the selection as a whole and make some broad generalizations concerning use of the literary elements.

MEANING

1. Poe's purpose is to _____

_____

2. The effect on the reader is_____

_____

FORM

3. The genre is_____

_____

4. The elements of plot structure are

Exposition _____

Complication _____

Climax_____

Denouement _____

NARRATIVE VOICE

5. The point of view is _____

_____

6. The narrator's attitude is _____

_____

TONE

7. The TONE of the story is _____

_____

CHARACTER

8. The narrator's CHARACTER is best described

as _____

_____

USE OF LANGUAGE

9. What is the overall irony at work in this story?

_____

_____

_____

10. What is ironic about the narrator's account of his crime when compared to his account of his confession? (Be sure to address how this story fulfills the concept of *poetic justice* in that evil is punished.) _____

_____

_____

Obviously, when taking the actual SAT II: Literature Subject Test you will not have dictionaries or other such resources available to aid your understanding of a selection. When reading and analyzing period literature to develop your comprehension and test-taking skills, however, a comprehensive dictionary (preferably unabridged) and a set of upper-level encyclopedias (such as the *Encyclopaedia Britannica*) are valuable to help you understand the selection that you are analyzing and to help you develop a backlog of useful information, vocabulary, and interpretive insight.

This story provides an example. In the very first paragraph, the speaker refers extensively to *phrenology*. A check into reference sources will reveal that phrenology is the study of the lumps and bumps and dips and curves of the human skull in an effort to determine CHARACTER and the faculties of an individual. This so-called science was popular in the mid-nineteenth century and was practiced well into the twentieth. Consequently, a general knowledge of this popular belief system could prove helpful to understanding the import of references made to phrenology by writers of the period and is definitely significant to understanding its significance to MEANING in "The Imp of the Perverse."

To the phrenologist, the shape of the skull and its protuberances can be studied and used to analyze a person's CHARACTER and faculties. The faculties are divided into predispositions called propensities, emotions are the result of sentiments, and man's higher reason is the realm of the perceptive and reflective faculties. The phrenologist examines the cranial bumps on a person's head to determine where each of these faculties is located. There are thirty-five faculties in phrenology, and each portion of the brain in which a faculty is seated is called an organ.

In "The Imp of the Perverse," the speaker makes mention of these six organs:

1. *Alimentiveness* —faculty for seeking food
2. *Amativeness* —faculty for sexual desire
3. *Combativeness* —faculty for fighting
4. *Ideality* —faculty for conceiving ideals

5. *Causality* —faculty for determining the causes of effects

6. *Constructiveness* —faculty for constructing (Johann Spurzheim was a famous German phrenologist.)

Another concept that you may encounter in other writings is *a posteriori* as used in the third paragraph of "The Imp of the Perverse" and its opposite, *a priori*, used in the first paragraph:

a posteriori

- Meaning one is based on logic: inductive reasoning (beginning with effects and determining their causes).
- Meaning two is based on philosophy: determining something through empirical (observable) evidence or experience.

a priori

- Meaning one is based on logic: deductive reasoning (beginning with the cause and determining the effects) from a generalization to specific instances.
- Meaning two is based on philosophy: innate feelings and/or ideas determined before empirical evidence has been gathered or experience occurred.
- A third meaning is connotative: presuming something is true before knowing the facts.

Next, look at an excerpt in "The Imp of the Perverse" for possible questions concerning specific uses of the literary elements. You may select other excerpts as well, but consider a thorough look at the first paragraph.

What questions could be asked concerning use of the literary elements in this excerpt? Some possibilities include:

- What is this excerpt about?

- What is the attitude of "I" toward phrenologists?

- What is the speaker's TONE when he says that "We saw no *need* of the impulse"?

- How does the speaker characterize the "intellectual or logical" man?

- What does the speaker reveal about his own CHARACTER?

- What do the following words mean as used in CONTEXT?

  1. *prima mobilia* _____

  2. propensity _____

  3. Kabbala (also spelled cabala) _____

  4. supererogation _____

- What is the effect of the phrase "will-I nill-I"?

- According to the speaker, what is the reason that phrenologists and moralists have missed an important "propensity" of man? _____

- What is the difference, as presented in this paragraph, between the unidentified propensity and those that are identified? _____

- What is the speaker suggesting concerning the unidentified propensity when he says that "we could not have understood in what manner it might be made to further the objects of humanity, either temporal or external"? _____

- Based on the CONTEXT, what does the speaker mean when he says that phrenology and the systems of mind were "concocted *a priori*"? _____

_____

_____

An Extended Exercise

Select several other excerpts from this story and write lists of possible questions.

The following list contains a few points that might be important to developing questions. Keep in mind that you need to be able to identify literary elements and their effects, especially on MEANING and TONE.

A Few Points to Consider

Paragraph 2:

- What "(if classify we must)" suggests
- Comparison and contrast two views
- Effects of rhetorical devices
- Elements of logic

Paragraph 3:

- Identification of what elements are in paradox
- Determination of why an *a posteriori* approach would have revealed perverseness
- MEANINGS of "*mobile*" and "*motivirt*"
- Elements of irony
- Identification of the compelling force
- Use in CONTEXT of "admit"
- Identification of the fallacy
- Identification of the motive for combativeness

Paragraph 4:

- MEANINGS of "sophistry" and "radicalness" in CONTEXT
- MEANING of "circumlocution"
- Characterization of speaker
- Use of "one's own heart"
- Effect of "tantalize"
- MEANING of "laconic and luminous"

Paragraph 5:

- Effects of using everyday examples
- TONE of "It must, it shall be undertaken to-day, and yet"
- Implications of "craving"

- Identification of what is "definite" and "indefinite"
- Identification of "substance…shadow"
- MEANINGS of "knell of our welfare" and "chanticleer-note"
- Irony
- Effects of change in elements of style (especially syntax and sentence length)

Paragraph 6:

- Emotional impact of example
- Figurative use of "cloud"
- Literary allusion
- Use of "palpability"
- Figurative use of "chills the very marrow of our bones"—effect
- Effect of paradox in "delight of its horror"
- Cause and effect relationship
- Role of "*thought*"
- Structural use and effects of italics

Paragraphs 7 and 8:

- MEANING of "Beyond or behind"
- Identification of the "archfiend"
- Implication of a silent auditor
- Speaker's current situation
- MEANING of "prolix"
- Effect of "victims" and "Imp"
- Foreshadowing of "good" outcome—his confession

Paragraphs 9 and 10:

- Plot elements
- MEANING of "agency"
- Effect of "fancy" on characterization
- Effect of "impertinent"
- Characterization of speaker
- USE OF LANGUAGE: "shadow of a clue"
- Implications of "epoch"
- Relationship of "harassed" to "haunted"
- Use of analogy
- *Speaker's admission* that the murder was a sin

Paragraphs 11 and 12:

- TONE ("sauntering")
- Irony and foreshadowing ("arrested myself")
- Implication of "a fit of petulance"
- Effect of "icy chill creep to my heart" (personification)
- Significance of use of analogy

Paragraph 13:

- What occasioned his running
- Emphasis of "to *think*"
- The effect of simile
- What occasioned the chase
- Emphasis of "*then*"
- The effect of hyperbole
- CHARACTER revelation of secret bursting from soul

Paragraphs 14 through 16:

- Effect of "They"
- Connotations of "pregnant"
- Contrast of "chains…fetterless"
- MEANING of "distinct enunciation"
- Speaker's reference to "hangman and to hell"
- MEANING of "To-day" and "To-morrow"
- Implications of "*here*" and "*but where?*"

This list is only a partial treatment of the many uses of the literary elements that can contribute to the writer's style and that can affect the MEANING of the work. As you study through this list, see how many other uses of the literary elements are at work. Be sure to notice the changing moods of each individual paragraph. Also, be sure to address each sentence and each paragraph individually and to address them as they unify to become the work in its entirety, for example, the CHARACTER changes throughout the story as the speaker progresses to the point at which he begins to recognize the potential consequences beyond death for sins committed during life.

Examining a Lyric Poem

The third sample selection is "The Song of the Shirt" by Thomas Hood, a Victorian poet.

THE SONG OF THE SHIRT

(1) With fingers weary and worn,
    With eyelids heavy and red,
A Woman sat, in unwomanly rags,
    Plying her needle and thread—
        Stitch! stitch! stitch!
In poverty, hunger, and dirt,
And still with a voice of dolorous pitch
She sang the 'Song of the Shirt!'

(2) 'Work! work! work!
While the cock is crowing aloof!
    And work—work—work,
Till the stars shine through the roof!
It's O! to be a slave
    Along with the barbarous Turk,
Where woman has never a soul to save,
    If this is Christian work!

(3) 'Work—work—work
Till the brain begins to swim,
    Work—work—work
Till the eyes are heavy and dim!
Seam, and gusset, and band,
    Band, and gusset, and seam,
Till over the buttons I fall asleep,
    And sew them on in a dream!

(4) 'O, Men with Sisters dear!
    O, Men! with Mothers and Wives!
It is not linen you're wearing out,
    But human creatures' lives!
        Stitch—stitch—stitch,
In poverty, hunger, and dirt,
Sewing at once, with a double thread,
    A Shroud as well as a Shirt.

(5) 'But why do I talk of Death?
    That Phantom of grisly bone,
I hardly fear his terrible shape,
    It seems so like my own—
    It seems so like my own,
    Because of the fasts I keep;
O God! that bread should be so dear,
    And flesh and blood so cheap!

(6) 'Work—work—work!
    My labour never flags;
And what are its wages? A bed of straw,
    A crust of bread—and rags.
That shatter'd roof,—and this naked floor—
    A table—a broken chair—
And a wall so blank, my shadow I thank
    for sometimes falling there!

(7) 'Work—work—work!
From weary chime to chime,
    Work—work—work—
As prisoners work for crime!
    Band, and gusset, and seam,
    Seam, and gusset, and band,
Till the heart is sick, and the brain benumb'd,
    As well as the weary hand.

(8) 'Work—work—work,
In the dull December light,
    And work—work—work,
When the weather is warm and bright—

While underneath the eaves
   The brooding swallows cling,
As if to show me their sunny backs
   And twit me with the spring.

(9) 'O, but to breathe the breath
Of the cowslip and primrose sweet!—
   With the sky above my head,
And the grass beneath my feet;
For only one short hour
   To feel as I used to feel,
Before I knew the woes of want
   And the walk that costs a meal!

(10) 'O, but for one short hour!
A respite however brief!
No blessed leisure for Love or Hope,
   But only time for Grief!
A little weeping would ease my heart,
   But in their briny bed
My tears must stop, for every drop
   Hinders needle and thread!

(11) 'Seam, and gusset, and band,
Band, and gusset, and seam,
   Work, work, work,
Like the Engine that works by Steam!
A mere machine of iron and wood
   That toils for Mammon's sake—
Without a brain to ponder and craze
   Or a heart to feel—and break!'

(12) —With fingers weary and worn,
   With eyelids heavy and red,
A Woman sat, in unwomanly rags,
   Plying her needle and thread—
   Stitch! stitch! stitch!
   In poverty, hunger, and dirt,
And still with a voice of dolorous pitch,—
Would that its tone could reach the Rich!—
She sang this 'Song of the Shirt!'

by Thomas Hood

Questions concerning MEANING (What is the poem about?), NARRATIVE VOICE (What is the speaker's attitude? What is the woman's attitude?), TONE...these all need to be addressed. Of special note in this particular poem, however, is not just the USE OF LANGUAGE and the other literary elements, but the *effects* of those uses.

A rather useful method of approaching such a poem is to construct a cause-and-effect chart. In the "cause" column is listed the literary element and use, with the "effect" column describing its effect on such elements as the MEANING and TONE.

Cause	*Effect*
First stanza (lines 1–8)	
• Alliteration of <u>w</u> and <u>s</u>	• A "chain gang" rhythm that reinforces the sense of the monotony of the labor
• Repetition of <u>stitch</u>	
• Diction: "unwomanly" "dolorous pitch"	• In stark contrast to the imagery of a "woman" • In contrast to what one would expect of a "Song of the Shirt"

Notice that the speaker changes to the woman singing her song in the second stanza.

Cause	*Effect*
Second stanza (lines 9–16)	
• Diction: "aloof"	• Two levels of MEANING: 1. Distant in space 2. Distant in feeling • Contributing to a sense of physical and emotional isolation

Continuing with the second stanza, what are the *effects* of these *causes*?

Cause	*Effect*
• Break in rhythm: "It's O!"	_____ _____
• Contrast of "barbarous Turk" to "Christian work"	_____ _____

(HINT: In her isolated state of continued work, with whom does she identify? What is the significance of "If"?

Cause	Effect
Third stanza (lines 17–24)	_____
• Imagery: "the brain begins to swim"	_____
• Inverting "seam, and gusset, and band	_____
Sewing "in a dream"	_____

Now, you identify the cause-and-effect relationships in the remaining stanzas. Here are a few clues to important elements you might want to identify:

Cause	Effect
Fourth stanza: Addressing an auditor	
Linen as a symbol	
_____	_____
_____	_____
Fifth stanza: Personification of death	
_____	_____
_____	_____

Cause	Effect
Tenth stanza: Tears in a "briny bed"	
_____	_____
_____	_____
Eleventh stanza: Simile	
Literary allusion: Mammon	
A brain that ponders and crazes	
_____	_____
_____	_____
Twelfth stanza: "the Rich"	
_____	_____
_____	_____

Be sure to address this poem as a literary whole. What are the effects of the repetition of part of the first stanza in the last stanza? Do you see any over-all (central) contrasts, themes, or progressions of ideas in the poem?

(1) contrasts_____

_____

(2) themes _____

_____

(3) progressions_____

_____

The rich-poor contrast is obvious; however, look to stanza 9 for insight into the woman's change in circumstances. Also, you might want to discuss the role of hope/hopelessness in stanza 10.

Examining a Narrative Poem

"The Lady of Shalott" is a narrative poem by Alfred, Lord Tennyson:

THE LADY OF SHALOTT

PART I

On either side the river lie
Long fields of barley and of rye,
That clothe the wold and meet the sky;
And thro' the field the road runs by
    To many-tower'd Camelot;
And up and down the people go,
Gazing where the lilies blow
Round an island there below,
    The island of Shalott.

Willows whiten, aspens quiver,
Little breezes dusk and shiver
Thro' the wave that runs for ever
By the island in the river
    Flowing down to Camelot.
Four gray walls, and four gray towers,
Overlook a space of flowers,
And the silent isle imbowers
    The Lady of Shalott.

By the margin, willow-veil'd
Slide the heavy barges trail'd
By slow horses; and unhail'd
The shallop flitteth silken-sail'd
    Skimming down to Camelot:
But who hath seen her wave her hand?
Or at the casement seen her stand?
Or is she known in all the land,
    The Lady of Shalott?

Only reapers, reaping early
In among the bearded barley,
Hear a song that echoes cheerly
From the river winding clearly,
    Down to tower'd Camelot:
And by the moon the reaper weary,
Piling sheaves in uplands airy,
Listening, whispers, ' 'Tis the fairy
    Lady of Shalott.'

PART II

There she weaves by night and day
A magic web with colours gay.
She has heard a whisper say,
A curse is on her if she stay
    To look down to Camelot.
She knows not what the curse may be,
And so she weaveth steadily,
And little other care hath she,
    The Lady of Shalott.

And moving thro' a mirror clear
That hangs before her all the year,
Shadows of the world appear.
There she sees the highway near
    Winding down to Camelot:
There the river eddy whirls,
And there the surly village-churls,
And the red cloaks of market girls,
    Pass onward from Shalott.

Sometimes a troop of damsels glad,
An abbot on an ambling pad,
Sometimes a curly shepherd-lad,
Or long-hair'd page in crimson clad,
    Goes by to tower'd Camelot;
And sometimes thro' the mirror blue
The knights come riding two and two:
She hath no loyal knight and true,
    The Lady of Shalott.

But in her web she still delights
To weave the mirror's magic sights,
For often thro' the silent nights
A funeral, with plumes and lights
    And music, went to Camelot:
Or when the moon was overhead,
Came two young lovers lately wed;
'I am half sick of shadows,' said
    The Lady of Shalott.

PART III

A BOW-SHOT from her bower-eaves,
He rode between the barley-sheaves,
The sun came dazzling thro' the leaves,
And flamed upon the brazen greaves
    Of bold Sir Lancelot.
A red-cross knight for ever kneel'd
To a lady in his shield,
That sparkled on the yellow field,
    Beside remote Shalott.

The gemmy bridle glitter'd free,
Like to some branch of stars we see
Hung in the golden Galaxy.
The bridle bells rang merrily
    As he rode down to Camelot:
And from his blazon'd baldric slung
A mighty silver bugle hung,
And as he rode his armour rung,
    Beside remote Shalott.

All in the blue unclouded weather
Thick-jewell'd shone the saddle-leather,
The helmet and the helmet-feather
Burn'd like one burning flame together,
    As he rode down to Camelot.
As often thro' the purple night,
Below the starry clusters bright,
Some bearded meteor, trailing light,
    Moves over still Shalott.

His broad clear brow in sunlight glow'd;
On burnish'd hooves his war-horse trode;
From underneath his helmet flow'd
His coal-black curls as on he rode,
    As he rode down to Camelot.
From the bank and from the river
He flash'd into the crystal mirror,
'Tirra lirra,' by the river
    Sang Sir Lancelot.

She left the web, she left the loom,
She made three paces thro' the room,
She saw the water-lily bloom,
She saw the helmet and the plume,
    She look'd down to Camelot.
Out flew the web and floated wide;
The mirror crack'd from side to side;
'The curse is come upon me,' cried
    The Lady of Shalott.

PART IV

In the stormy east-wind straining,
The pale yellow woods were waning,
The broad stream in his banks complaining,
Heavily the low sky raining
   Over tower'd Camelot;
Down she came and found a boat
Beneath a willow left afloat,
And round about the prow she wrote
   The Lady of Shalott.

And down the river's dim expanse
Like some bold seër in a trance,
Seeing all his own mischance—
With a glassy countenance
   Did she look to Camelot.
And at the closing of the day
She loosed the chain, and down she lay;
The broad stream bore her far away,
   The Lady of Shalott.

Lying, robed in snowy white
That loosely flew to left and right—
The leaves upon her falling light—
Thro' the noises of the night
   She floated down to Camelot:
And as the boat-head wound along
The willowy hills and fields among,
They heard her singing her last song,
   The Lady of Shalott.

Heard a carol, mournful, holy,
Chanted loudly, chanted lowly,
Till her blood was frozen slowly,
And her eyes were darken'd wholly,
   Turn'd to tower'd Camelot.
For ere she reach'd upon the tide
The first house by the water-side,
Singing in her song she died,
   The Lady of Shalott.

Under tower and balcony,
By garden-wall and gallery,
A gleaming shape she floated by,
Dead-pale between the houses high,
   Silent into Camelot.
Out upon the wharfs they came,
Knight and burgher, lord and dame,
And round the prow they read her name,
   The Lady of Shalott.

Who is this? and what is here?
And in the lighted palace near
Died the sound of royal cheer;

And they cross'd themselves for fear,
   All the knights at Camelot:
But Lancelot mused a little space;
He said, 'She has a lovely face;
God in his mercy lend her grace,
   The Lady of Shalott.'

          by Alfred, Lord Tennyson

An identification of the plot line is appropriate to understanding the MEANING of a narrative poem. As an illustration, the following analysis *models* a very simple approach to identifying the plot in a narrative poem.

Exposition: Part I
Summary. Shalott is an island upriver of Camelot. The Lady of Shalott lives in a tower; people have not seen her, but know of her existence and have heard her sing.

Complication: Part II and Part III, stanzas 1–4
Summary. Part II introduces the curse on the Lady of Shalott. She does not know what will happen; however, she does know that she must not look directly out the window toward Camelot. Consequently, she views the world through a mirror and spends her time weaving a magic web in patterns that she sees in her mirror. Part III heightens the complication when she sees Sir Lancelot reflected in her mirror as he goes riding to Camelot.

Climax: Part III, final stanza
Summary. She looks to Camelot and the curse begins.

Denouement: Part IV
Summary. After preparing a boat, she casts herself adrift, sings her last song, and dies before reaching the first house in Camelot. Sir Lancelot, upon seeing her dead form, comments on her beauty.

In examining this poem on a line-by-line basis, make special note of Tennyson's use of *syntax*. Syntax is especially crucial to the climactic stanza (Part III, stanza 5), in which the subject-action verb repetition adds drama to the moment: "She left…she left…She made…she saw…She look'd…" Look at the second stanza of Part IV:

And down the river's dim expanse
Like some bold seër in a trance,
Seeing all his own mischance—

With a glassy countenance
Did she look to Camelot.

Do you recognize the sentence structure used here? Its effect? This is a periodic sentence in which the main subject and verb (*did she look*) come at the end of the sentence. Periodic sentences project a dramatic building of tension.

Also, "Shalott" appears in the last line of *every* stanza *except* stanza 4 of Part III, the last line before the climactic stanza. In this line, not "Shalott" but "Sir Lancelot" appears. What do you think is the significance of this to the poem's MEANING?

What other uses of *syntax* can you find in this poem? In USE OF LANGUAGE, what sad irony is at work in this poem?

A Summary to Help You Put It All Together

You can use many different methods to analyze selections. This book suggests several methods for you to use:

1. Use the "Questions to Apply Your Learning" sections that accompany each of the literary element discussions in Part III: Interpretive Skills and Critical Reading.
2. Follow the seven-step procedure discussed in this section.
3. Incorporate the procedures listed in the "Quick Reference Guide" that can be found at the end of this section.

In addition, this section *models* for you a few approaches to analyzing prose and poetry selections as you might find them in your literary studies.

Remember: The "best" way to analyze a work *varies* with each selection. Just be sure that you *do* address all seven of the literary elements on at least two levels:

1. *Identify their use.*
2. *Recognize the effects of their use.*

Finally, on the SAT II: Literature Subject Test you may encounter questions that address elements of opposition, pairs of words that illustrate contrasts in content, the opposition of words that suggests contrasts, and sequences of concepts. These questions might cut across the seven literary elements, sometimes testing your knowledge of FORM, other times examining *connotation* or some other element or combination of elements.

In developing skills to deal with these types of questions, you may be able to use your knowledge of FORM to an advantage. First, you might examine the passage or poem for divisions into parts, divisions made by paragraphing, rhyme scheme, a change in rhythm, transitional words, or some other structural break. Next, you can determine and paraphrase (put into your own words) the MEANING of each structural part of the passage or poem. By comparing and contrasting the MEANINGS of these parts and by determining their relationships to one another and to the work as a whole, you may gain insight into the elements of opposition and the progressions of ideas at work. This use of analysis can easily be seen when working with the sonnet FORM.

When FORM does not offer any clues to the elements of opposition or progression, you may find examining VOICE, TONE, and CHARACTER from several different perspectives can help. The elements of opposition might be found in the speaker's VOICE if it differs from that of the poet. It can also be found in the TONE if differing attitudes are reflected by the ways different things are said or if the atmosphere of one circumstance differs from that of another circumstance. In CHARACTER, sometimes elements of personality reveal opposition.

A QUICK REFERENCE GUIDE TO THE SEVEN LITERARY ELEMENTS

The literary elements briefly defined:

MEANING   involves the subject, theme, and purpose of a work on first a literal level, then on other levels, and the *effect* of the work on the reader.

FORM   is the genre, organization, sequence, and structure of a work.

NARRATIVE VOICE   includes the identities of the speaker, the author, and the main CHARACTER, and the attitudes or perspectives of each.

TONE   (of VOICE) is how the speaker and CHARACTERS "sound" ("playful," "serious," "angry"); the "atmosphere" projected by the subject, the setting, and the author's style; and how these elements combine to project a "feeling" from the entire work that produces an effect on the reader.

CHARACTER involves the people in a work and the means by which their attitudes, emotions, response mechanisms, and intrinsic values are revealed to the reader.

USE OF LANGUAGE is the use of figurative language, imagery, and diction to produce an effect.

MEANING(S) IN CONTEXT is the determination of how CONTEXT affects and is affected by denotation and connotation of words.

When reading a selection for **MEANING:**

1. Determine the purpose: descriptive/expressive, expository/informative, narrative, or argumentative/persuasive.
2. Determine the effect: the work is entertaining, disturbing, interesting.
3. Determine the literal MEANING:
   a. State the subject in a word or PHRASE.
   b. State the theme/thesis or hook in one sentence.
   c. Paraphrase each logical division (paragraph, subsection, stanza).
4. Determine any other possible levels of MEANING: allegorical, symbolic, figurative.

When reading a selection for **FORM:**

1. Determine if the work is prose, poetry, or drama.
2. Determine the method(s) of organization used: analogy, cause-and-effect, comparison/contrast, definition, description, analysis and classification, example, induction, deduction, narration, process analysis, (or other).
3. Determine the sequence used: chronological, climactic, deductive, inductive, problem-solving, spatial, topical, mixed, (or other).
4. Determine the nonfiction prose genre: essay (formal, informal), (auto)biography, criticism, informational, (or other).
5. Determine the prose narrative by length: novel, novelette, short story, anecdote, (or other).
6. Determine the prose structure:
   a. Outline nonfiction prose.
   b. Plotline prose narrative.
7. Determine the prose narrative effects: tragedy, comedy, satire, romance, realism, (or other).
8. Determine the prose narrative genre: picaresque, stream of consciousness, bildungsroman, regional, social, detective, novel of CHARACTER (incident, manners, sensibility, the soil),

psychological, problem, propaganda, western, gothic, epistolary, science fiction, suspense, utopia, tale, tall tale, fable, folktale, parable, legend, myth (or other).

9. Determine the structure of the poem:
   a. Scan for rhythm.
   b. Determine rhyme scheme.
   c. Look at physical FORM: prose poetry, free verse, blank verse, qualitative verse.
   d. Determine the stanza FORM: ballad, elegiac, terza rima, rhyme royal, ottava rima, Spenserian.
   e. Identify the genre: epic poem, dramatic poem, lyric poem, elegy, ode, sonnet (Italian/Petrarchan, English/Shakespearean, Spenserian), haiku, song, ballad, aubade, parody, limerick, epigram, epitaph, epigraph, shaped verse, satire, metaphysical poem.
10. Determine the dramatic structure of the play:
   a. Identify the plot: exposition/introduction, conflict/exciting force, rising action/complication, climax/turning point, falling action, resolution/denouement.
   b. Identify the length (acts, scenes, episodes) and audience format (stage production, television, movie).
   c. Identify the use of dramatic elements, such as foreshadowing, flashbacks, *in medias res,* double plots, reversals, dramatic conventions.
   d. Determine the dramatic genre: tragedy (classical, romantic, revenge, domestic), comedy (high or low, as well as romantic, realistic, comedy of manners, sentimental, burlesque, operetta), or tragicomedy.

When reading a selection for **NARRATIVE VOICE:**

1. Determine the point of view of the narrator: first person, third person limited, third person unlimited.
   a. Determine if the third person narrator is intrusive or unintrusive.
   b. Determine if the narrator is self-effacing, using the scenic method, or if the narrator uses the panoramic method.
   c. Determine if the first person narrator is credible.
2. Determine the relationship of the narrator/speaker, the writer, and the main CHARACTER.
3. Determine the narrator's/speaker's attitude.
4. Determine the writer's attitude.

5. Determine the main CHARACTER'S attitude.

When reading a selection for **TONE:**

1. Determine the speaker's TONE (of VOICE): formal, informal, playful, sincere.
2. Determine the TONE of the work:
   a. Describe the TONE of the subject.
   b. Describe the TONE of the subject's treatment.
   c. Describe the TONE of the setting.
   d. Determine the TONE(S) projected by the CHARACTERS.
   e. Determine the style: high, middle, low; demotic, hieratic.

When reading the selection for **CHARACTER:**

1. Determine each CHARACTER'S distinguishing traits:
   a. Describe attitudes (positive, negative, kind, unkind).
   b. Describe emotions (love, hate, stable, attached).
   c. Describe response mechanisms (fury, nonchalance, self-confidence).
   d. Describe intrinsic values, including a generalization of "what kind of person" he or she is.
2. Determine what techniques are used to reveal CHARACTER.
   a. Determine the CHARACTER'S identity, such as hero or stock.
   b. Determine any stereotypes.
   c. Identify CHARACTER revealed through exposition.
   d. Determine what actions reveal CHARACTER.
   e. Examine dialogue for CHARACTER revelation.
   f. Examine each CHARACTER'S thoughts (if revealed).
   g. Examine motives of each CHARACTER.
   h. Determine the impact (if any) of setting on CHARACTER.
3. Determine CHARACTER changes (development) in terms of:
   a. Motivation.
   b. Time.
   c. Insight.

When reading a selection for **USE OF LANGUAGE:**

1. Determine the literal MEANING of the work by section, paragraph, sentences, phrases, words (or other).
2. Examine the work for figures of speech based on analogy (simile, metaphor).
3. Examine the work for figures of speech based on rhetoric (rhetorical questions, amplification, aposiopesis).
4. Examine the work for figures of speech based on syntax (antithesis, apostrophe).
5. Describe the effects of each figure of speech used.
6. Describe the diction in terms of isolated word choices (Germanic source, puns, connotations).
7. Identify the level of diction in terms of dialect, purpose.

When reading a selection for **MEANING(S) IN CONTEXT:**

1. Identify denotative MEANINGS of all unknown words.
2. Determine the overall degree of specificity and concreteness.
3. Examine syntactical patterns for effects on MEANING.
4. Identify subordinated ideas.
5. Determine who does the action and when the action takes place.
6. Look for connotations.
7. Examine the selection for implications.

As previously stated, this section provides you with: 1. a reference source of definitions and examples of the seven literary elements at the focus of the SAT II: Literature Subject Test; 2. a seven-step procedure for analyzing literature in preparation to take the test; 3. four models of literary analysis; and 4. two detailed approaches based on analysis of each literary element used in a selection (the "Questions to Apply Your Learning" found in each section on the individual literary elements and "A Quick Reference Guide to the Seven Literary Elements" that you have just read).

WRITING TO LEARN THE LITERARY ELEMENTS

He who writes an epic poem must transport himself to the scene of action; he must imagine himself possessed of the same opinions, manners, prejudices, and belief; he must suppose himself to be the hero he delineates, or his picture can no longer be nature, and what is not natural cannot please.

**Preface to *The Battle of Marathon*, 1820
by Elizabeth Barrett Browning**

Writing to Learn is a self-study program developed specifically as a motivational tool to improve your reading comprehension skills to prepare you to take the SAT II: Literature test. At the same time, Writing to Learn is designed to make your study plan more interesting and satisfying.

There is a difference between Writing to Learn and a how-to-write program. You can receive writing instruction in your English classes and from books available on the subject of writing. Writing to Learn, in contrast, explains the reciprocal relationship between reading and writing and provides you with opportunities to use your own writing skills, drawing upon writing instruction from many different sources, to improve your reading comprehension and understanding of literature. In Writing to Learn you will explore how the literary elements work by placing yourself in the writer's role.

The following pages contain the Writing to Learn design:

SECTION ONE ("Writing to Learn: How Does It Work?") explains to you the educational concepts upon which Writing to Learn is based.

SECTION TWO is "Writing to Learn the Literary Elements: How to Use the Study Plan." It begins with establishing some goals; then the three major parts of a Writing to Learn Exercise (The Prewriting Review, Motivators, and the Active Learning Notes) are briefly described.

SECTION THREE consists of the Training Exercises for "Writing to Learn." First, detailed samples of Writing to Learn the Essay Training Exercises are given so that you can get an overall view. The Writing to Learn Autobiography Training Exercises begin with detailed samples, then guide and challenge you to begin incorporating your own ideas, giving you ownership of the plan. The remaining Training Exercises are lists of suggestions and tips for you to use in your own designs. The tips and suggestions given are in broad terms to stimulate your own ideas.

SECTION FOUR describes the "Seven Major Steps of a Writing to Learn Activity," including how your Active Learning Notes (developed as you write) can be used to help you develop skills for the SAT II: Literature test.

SECTION ONE. WRITING TO LEARN: HOW DOES IT WORK?

Some critics maintain that the best writers are those who know their subject and write from direct experience or who, at the very least, are able to incorporate themselves into their writing to such a degree that they psychologically become the character, are an integral part of the stated position, or are personally tied to the subject. A trend in thinking among educators is to extend this idea to improve learning in general. Some believe that the most successful students are those who directly experience what they are trying to learn or who are able to incorporate themselves into what they are trying to learn to such a degree that they mentally assume an active role in the subject.

Simply stated, **successful students are active rather than passive learners**. Passive learning has its place, of course. You could learn the rules of chess by reading a manual or by listening to a lecture on chess. You would learn even more if, after reading the manual or listening to the lecture, you watched a chess game. What if, however, you knew as you read the manual and watched the game that eventually you would be expected to play a few practice games of chess? Would this heighten your awareness and help you concentrate better?

Now take this illustration even further. As you actually played the practice games, do you think you would be learning the rules any better than by only reading the manual? What if, as you played the game, you knew that within a specified number of weeks, you would be expected to play in a tournament? Would this added stimulus help you concentrate on learning the rules?

This simplified example illustrates what current learning theory and research seems to be telling us about active learning. Add to this the already established idea that in order to learn new information, our brains need to organize the material by deciding what is important. This is often determined by some personal involvement, such as that present in active learning. Logically, then, one way to help your brain organize the material and to develop the skills you need to know to perform well on the SAT II: Literature test would be to add to your study plan active learning activities that will provide personal involvement.

This idea can be seen in the following Learning Involvement Chart.

As illustrated in the Learning Involvement Chart, if you know from the beginning of your study plan that you are going to write an editorial letter that may eventually be published in your local or school newspaper, your personal involvement should increase even more as you study this book, read and analyze the writings of others, and prepare to be able to answer questions on the SAT II: Literature test.

Focus on those areas that challenge and interest you the most and select one for an active learning activity that will provide the personal involvement you need to improve your comprehension skills for the test.

Also, you may discover that the active learning approach to study has a few unexpected benefits beyond doing well on the SAT II: Literature test. One benefit may be production of a written work that merits the attention of others because they find it informative, entertaining, or yes, even persuasive. Using active learning techniques is one method to make what might otherwise be an ordinary study plan more interesting. Perhaps the most compelling benefit is the resulting improvement in your overall reading and writing skills that should help you accomplish more in your other academic studies and career goals.

The pages that follow will provide you with a wide range of ideas for adding personal involvement to your study plan by Writing to Learn the seven literary elements. These ideas include new directions to take and resources for getting there. Space in this book will not allow detailed treatment of every possible genre. Writing to Learn, however, does focus on methods for you to utilize your own writing to learn to recognize, understand, and use the seven literary elements. The goal is for you to be able to use not only the ideas presented here, but also to recognize ideas and resources around you so that you can develop your own ways to add personal involvement to your study plan and translate that involvement into better preparation to take the test.

LEARNING INVOLVEMENT CHART

GOAL: To understand the seven literary elements to improve performance on the SAT II: Literature test.

Activity:	*Learning Involvement:*
BASIC ACTIVITY Read this manual and take the practice tests.	You will experience a certain degree of personal involvement due to impending test; however, comfort level is relatively high because practice tests are self-graded.
ADDED PERSONAL INVOLVEMENT #1 Using the seven literary elements described in this book, read written works and identify the literary elements and how they are used.	Personal involvement will depend largely upon group interaction. You may experience some degree of desire to do well before other members if you are in a study group. If a classroom paper is required (such as a literary analysis paper) or a classroom presentation, being graded will possibly be a motivating factor.
ADDED PERSONAL INVOLVEMENT #2 Using the applicable literary elements described in this book, write an essay aimed to persuade.	Personal involvement increases because expectations are being put on you to utilize what you have learned from a different perspective. You are no longer passively analyzing the work of others, but being expected to perform. Detail will become more important. Also, you will begin to see interrelationships between and among the literary elements, helping you to improve your comprehension skills.
ADDED PERSONAL INVOLVEMENT #3 Write a persuasive essay in response to a local community or school issue.	By focusing on a local community or school issue, your persuasive essay should reflect your opinion. This gives you ownership, plus a subject that probably involves your day-to-day life (increasing your personal involvement). Your motivation to use the applicable literary elements effectively should cause your understanding of them to increase and your writing to improve.
ADDED PERSONAL INVOLVEMENT #4 Write a persuasive essay in response to a local community or school issue and actually send it as an editorial letter to your local or school newspaper.	At this point, your personal involvement should cause you to construct your writing carefully, trying to use the applicable literary elements to their best advantage. What will the editor think of your article? Will your letter be published? If it is, what impression will it make on your family, friends, and the other readers of the paper? Have you used the literary elements effectively to persuade your readers? You should be learning the challenges, as well as the advantages, that the different literary elements present when they are used in persuasive writing and, consequently, be better able to recognize their uses in the writings of others as you prepare to take the SAT II: Literature test.

To help you utilize what you are learning by the Writing to Learn series of training exercises that follow, each exercise includes suggestions for you in making Active Learning Notes. The purpose of these notes is to direct your active learning to applying the seven literary elements as tested by the SAT II: Literature test to your own writing. The conclusion of this chapter includes a section in which you will use these Active Learning Notes to help you prepare directly for the SAT II: Literature test.

SECTION TWO. WRITING TO LEARN THE LITERARY ELEMENTS: HOW TO USE THE STUDY PLAN

The following Writing to Learn series of training exercises is aimed at helping you accomplish the following goals:

1. To incorporate more active learning activities into your study plan
2. To empower you to achieve greater reading comprehension skills because you have experienced the role of a writer
3. To enable you to produce writing as a worthwhile product and as a means of effective communication
4. To make your study plan more interesting
5. To enable you to perform better on the SAT II: Literature test
6. To use the reciprocal relationship of reading and writing to increase your performance in all your classes requiring these skills
7. To provide an activity that can be used for a special project in your literature (or other) classes as part of your preparation to take the SAT II: Literature test

You may want to use one or more portions of the following training exercises as presented; however, they should challenge you to examine what other writing opportunities are available to you and how they might help you gain the experience and motivation that will affect your study preparation for the SAT II: Literature test. You are ultimately responsible for your study program and how it affects your test performance. Students who actively engage in learning, those who are not satisfied with knowing that something works, but also want to know *why* and *how* it works, have discovered a great advantage: study for the sake of learning something new, performing better, and producing a worthwhile product can be both fun and motivating—and can mean better performance on standardized tests. The degree, then, to which these Writing to Learn training exercises benefit your study program is directly related to how you incorporate them on an individual basis.

I will therefore speak to you as supposing Lady Mary not only capable, but desirous of learning: in that case by all means let her be indulged in it. . . . Learning, if she has a real taste for it, will not only make her contented, but happy in it. No entertainment is so cheap as reading, nor any pleasure so lasting. She will not want new fashions, nor regret the loss of expensive diversions, or variety of company, if she can be amused with an author in her closet.

from a letter from the Lady Mary
Wortley Montagu to her daughter,
the Countess of Bute
January 28, 1753

The format of a Writing to Learn training exercise is both simple and straightforward:

1. Prewriting Review. A Writing to Learn exercise begins with a review of the major genre(s) and literary form(s) that will be the focus of the activities. This review includes (a) establishing definitions, seeking resources, and developing lists of major points concerning the literary form that might be helpful in skillful writing, (b) finding ways for you as a writer to identify with the work, thus making it your own, and (c) examining what possible options exist. This review provides background information for both your SAT II: Literature test preparation and for your own writing.
2. Motivators. Motivators take advantage of the personal involvement generated by knowing in advance that your writing has an ultimate purpose—a purpose that carries with it certain expectations of your knowledge and performance.

You will notice that writing contests, opportunities to submit work for publication, and other such high-profile ways to motivate your writing are included among the sample motivators in the following training exercises. Such activities can be very challenging and interesting. However, one of the benefits of Writing to Learn is that while you are preparing to take the SAT II: Literature test by learning different ways that the seven literary elements are used by writers, at the same time you will be learning how to incorporate and utilize the literary elements effectively in your own writing. As a result, the quality of your written communication should improve. Improved writing skills can mean improved work in whatever writing opportunities come your way. A motivator, then, might be entering a writing contest, or it might simply be preparing a well-constructed, effectively written paper for your history class.

Make your selection of subject based on your personal experience or knowledge. Of course, you may need to do some additional research.

3. Active Learning Notes. The last part of each training exercise consists of suggestions for Active Learning Notes. These notes have two major purposes:

   a. To help you utilize the seven literary elements in your writing
   b. To link your writing experience directly to preparing to take the SAT II: Literature test

As you review and prepare to write, are actually writing, and are editing what you have written, you should be taking Active Learning Notes; therefore, you will need a notebook specifically for this purpose. Your Active Learning Notes, and the notebook that contains them, probably will consist of many parts and should be a reflection of who you are as an individual. In this way you have established ownership of the work. Here are a few possibilities:

- As you review and collect information to prepare to write, include a section in your notebook to list resources and helpful activities. Be sure to include those ideas that come from your study group and teachers.
- Include a section to contain those graded class assignments and comments from your teachers concerning types of writing, subjects, or any information that might help you in your writing as it relates to learning the literary elements. Such a section would also be a logical place to collect test-taking tips and

strategies, such as the program described on pages 7–14 (Developing an Individualized Study Program) in this book.

- Much like the artist carries a sketchbook, a reader who is aiming to improve reading comprehension skills through motivated writing activities can keep a notebook of thoughts, ideas, and ways to use the literary elements, a catchy phrase that comes to mind, a description of something seen or heard, such as a beautiful flower or a heartbreaking scene. Writers sometimes keep paper and pens next to their beds in case a special idea occurs to them at night. All these types of notes would become part of your Active Learning Notebook to be used as resources for writing and for improving your reading comprehension skills.

Also, if you find that you enjoy the writing experience, you may want to record in your Active Learning Notes the reactions of others to your writing. For example, if your previously discussed letter to the editor is published and results in a series of letters from others responding to your ideas, you may want to clip them and add them (perhaps with comments) to your Active Learning Notes. This notebook can then become part of a writing portfolio.

Such a notebook containing successes and notes concerning areas needing improvement can be useful both in your short-term test preparation and class work goals, and in establishing experience and reputation as a writer—whether you view writing as a hobby, a career, or just as a useful skill in your future profession.

In addition to these suggestions, the Active Learning Notes will be used (as described in more detail in Section Four) as a means to translate your writing experience into preparing to take the SAT II: Literature test.

For further explanations concerning how to use Writing to Learn in your individual and group study plan, turn to page 259 and read the "Sample Writing to Learn Pattern." Also, the "Seven Major Steps of a Writing to Learn Activity" on page 267 will provide you with an overview perspective of the program.

SECTION THREE. TRAINING EXERCISES FOR WRITING TO LEARN

WRITING TO LEARN PROSE

Training Exercise Series A

WRITING TO LEARN NONFICTION: THE ESSAY

THE TURN OF A PHRASE

Historically, witty sayings and the essay go hand-in-hand. Sometimes the essayist quotes his or her memorable remarks from earlier writers, simply giving old sayings new importance; others ignite the fires of originality to express their points. Regardless, some of the sayings used by the essayist have remained in the popular culture for hundreds of years. An example? Read the following well-known saying. Can you guess what famous English writer used this saying in one of his essays?

> "If the hill will not come to Mahomet, Mahomet will go to the hill."

Did you recognize this version of "If the mountain will not come to Mohammed, Mohammed will go to the mountain"? This saying was used by Francis Bacon around 1600.

PREWRITING REVIEW

The Prewriting Review can help you

1. Prepare for the SAT II: Literature test, by giving you practice in identifying how essayists use the literary elements
2. Gain a writer's perspective by helping establish a foundation of information concerning the essay

Can you answer the following question: What is an essay?

Step 1. Reread pages 71–72 of this book.

Step 2. Ask your librarian to help you locate essays of various types so that you can read them to gain a sense of what forms essays can take. Also,

you should be able to locate collections of essays in textbooks on writing and reading.

Step 3. Consider the following points.

Point #1. A brief, selective overview of the modes or styles that the essay has taken:

Utilitarian mode/style in contrast to Grand mode/style

Brief, literal, aphoristic	Heavily structured, rhetorical, intense

Familiar mode/style in contrast to Euphuistic mode/style

Personal tone	Ornate, forced relationships

Historically, utilitarian and familiar styles were used to protest against the overdone styles of grand and euphuistic writing and gave rise to the modern mode/style that tends (in very general terms) to be brief in length and personal in tone.

Note: The first English essayist was Francis Bacon (*Essays*, 1597); therefore, the essay spans the entire time period covered by the SAT II: Literature test.

Point # 2. Today's essay often incorporates the following features:

- It is brief.
- It is an expression of a personal view rather than a simple presentation of facts.
- It relies heavily upon style (such as humorous style or logical style) to achieve purpose (such as to persuade or to explain).
- It can draw upon a wide variety of structural methods (examples include definition or analogy) and approaches (biographical, satirical), either in isolation or in combination.
- It can focus on broad conceptual subjects. An essay might, for example, express the writer's view on the arts, or narrow to bring into focus the writer's personal views concerning a particular topic, such as why readers should vote "yes" or "no" on a political issue.

Point #3. Practical applications of the essay.

Essays today can be found in many different forms, depending on their practical applications. The essay has, for example, definitely found a place in modern periodicals, such as the newspaper, newsletter, and magazine.

Types of essays found in periodicals

sports articles	personality profiles
medical reports	entertainment columns
humor columns	gardening features
book reviews	self-improvement features
editorials	guest opinion pages

Essays are also put to use in biographical sketches and political position papers of political candidates and in promotional fliers.

An increasingly popular practical application of the essay is in informational books in which each chapter consists of an essay written by a different author examining the main subject of the book from a particular point of view. These chapters, or more specifically, these collections of essays, are coordinated and arranged by an editor who then generally writes an introduction and perhaps a conclusion that intends to homogenize the diversity of views presented by the various writers into a summary of the subject for the reader.

If you look at your daily reading materials, you will probably find the essay in even more of its various forms: the profile of your favorite television star in *TV Guide,* the literary review of a book on the *New York Times* best seller list, and even the short autobiographical entries in your diary or journal.

Step 4. <u>Make the essay your own.</u>

By definition, an essay is a personal expression of the writer. You can, as a result, experiment with the essay's various forms, purposes, and practical applications to express your feelings and opinions on an unlimited list of subjects. By doing this, you may find that the essay will become a comfortable and useful means of expression that will help you define your own thinking while at the same time developing your reputation as a writer who can succinctly express a point of view toward a specified purpose or subject. Also, you may find that you will be more skillful at interpreting the points of view expressed by other essay writers—a useful skill for taking the SAT II: Literature test.

When you write (or read) an essay on any subject, consider these questions:

1. What are you (or the writer) trying to communicate?
2. Can you specifically state your personal opinion or view (or that of the writer) as a single sentence? (If not, should you refocus so that you can?)
3. Will the main point that you (or that the writer) want(s) to communicate contribute an original idea to what has already been written on the subject? Is your perspective (or that of the writer) fresh?
4. If facts are being presented, can you also analyze and/or interpret these facts to present a point of view?
5. Have you (or the writer) developed a structure, or mode of expression, that is appropriate to the practical application? For example, examine book reviews.

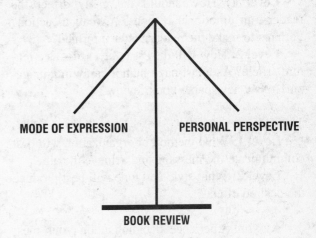

MODE OF EXPRESSION   PERSONAL PERSPECTIVE

BOOK REVIEW

Have you or the writer kept the personal perspective in balance with the mode of expression in a given book review? Can a writer express a personal opinion of a book that is being reviewed by structuring the essay using argument/persuasion? Or by beginning the essay with brief narration for a dramatic effect, then following with a combination of argument/persuasion and comparison/contrast?

Step 5. <u>Examine</u> your options.

The essay has so many faces that its popularity is easy to understand. Its many structural approaches aimed at almost any subject makes it a flexible means of communication that can be altered to the purposes of the writer with deceptive ease. Did you notice the use of the word "deceptive" in the last statement? How can writing an essay be deceptive? Because of its brevity and impact, a modern essay often appears to be the spontaneous expression of the writer. Much like the performance of a professional ice skater who glides across the ice with what appears to be such effortless ease, the well-written essay may be the product of hours of background preparation, as well as great skill in its actual writing.

Also, the very flexibility of the essay demands that the essayist make decisions on several different levels:

Message

Level 1: Will the essay deal with ideas or ideals, with the concrete or the abstract?

Level 2: Will the essay be on politics, education, technology, religion . . . ?

Aim

Level 1: How should the essay affect the reader—an emotional response? A call to action? Perhaps to make the reader better informed?

Level 2: How will the essay be used—as a feature article? As a last-page humor essay in a magazine? As a newspaper book review?

Method

Level 1: What method of organization will best communicate the message and achieve the aim?

Level 2: What style and tone will best produce the desired effect?

As you experience deciding upon your message, aim, and method *as a writer,* you also will be gaining greater insight *as a reader.* In developing the higher level thinking skills measured by the SAT II: Literature test, you may be able to identify more accurately a writer's possible intent and meaning as expressed in his or her choice of message(s), aim(s), and method(s) because you also have experienced making these choices.

When you approach writing an essay, you will probably want to have established a few parameters to the essay that will determine its structure, style, and tone. The following list, Essays in Review, may help you as it answers the questions "What does it (the essay) deal with?" and "What does it do?" for a rather wide-ranging sampling of essay types. Also included in the list are some tips for writing such essays, as well as suggestions for making each more interesting, and some sample topics.

You might rightfully ask the question, "Are these essay types really independent enough of each

other to be classified separately?" The obvious answer is no. Without doubt, the How-to Essay could also be a Teaching Essay, not only because we teach others how to do things, but also because an effective way to teach steps in a process is through giving concrete examples for the reader to follow. The name labels for the essay types in this list are convenient, but remember that often an essay will incorporate features of more than one essay type in order to make the point. However, clarity may demand that the essay adhere to one over-riding type that acts as a cohesive element throughout the writing.

ESSAYS IN REVIEW

How to use this list:

1. To prepare for the SAT II: Literature test, read a selection of essays; then using this list, identify for each:
   - The type of essay
   - What the essay deals with and what it does
   - The subject and the purpose
   - How the writer made the essay interesting or failed to do so
   - Thinking from a writer's perspective, which ideas seem to have been the most difficult for the writer to communicate
2. To prepare to write your own essay for your chosen Motivator (see pages 232–233, 238, 241, 243, 259, and 267 for ideas), select an essay type and a subject, then write an outline for a possible essay.
   - How can you make the essay interesting?
   - If you were to write this essay, which idea in your outline do you think would be the most difficult to communicate? Why?
   - What ways could you overcome this problem?

The How-To Essay

What does it deal with? . . . . . . A process
What does it do? . . . . Explains, clarifies
Tip: Be sure of the order, i.e., steps in logical sequence.
To make it interesting: Use illustrations, description, narration.

The following would be defined as How-To Essay topics:
   - How to successfully raise tulips in your region

- How to develop a better relationship with your brothers or sisters
- How to make the best pizza in town
- How to improve your grades in algebra
- How to clean your room in thirty minutes or less

The Example Essay

What does it deal with? . . Concrete examples of abstract ideas, definitions, and so forth

What does it do? . . . . . . Explains, clarifies

Tip: Be sure that your examples are relevant to what you are explaining.

To make it interesting: Make a connection with your readers by using specifics, if possible.

If concrete examples are used, the following would be defined as Example Essay topics:

- What is anger?
- What is the iron curtain?
- What are meteor showers?
- What is rain harvesting?
- What are "extenuating circumstances"?

Note the subtle difference between the Example Essay and the Definition Essay (described below).

The Definition Essay

What does it deal with? . . . Words, objects, abstract concepts

What does it do? . . . . Defines, explains

Tip: Be sure that you include not just synonyms, but also identify the word, object, or abstract concept as part of a *class* (love is an *emotion*) that has certain *distinguishing features* (love is an emotion that is a *warm, unselfish concern for another*).

To make it interesting: In addition to pointing out distinguishing features, define the words, objects, and abstract concepts through detail, such as examples that are easy to identify, comparison-contrast, pointing out examples that are *not* true illustrations.

If examples, synonyms, class identification, distinguishing features, and/or details are used, the following would be defined as Definition Essay topics:

- What is anger?
- What is the iron curtain?

- What are meteor showers?
- What is rain harvesting?
- What are "extenuating circumstances"?

The Comparison-Contrast Essay

What does it deal with? . . . Two or more subjects that have shared elements

What does it do? . . . . Compares, contrasts

Tip: Be sure that the subjects do have some substantial points in common.

To make it interesting: Pose questions to the reader that lead him or her to make the comparisons that make your point.

The following would be defined as Comparison-Contrast Essay topics:

- Is chocolate the best ice cream flavor?
- Will Candidate A be a better elected official than Candidate B?
- How does private day-care facilities compare to corporate employee day-care systems?
- Are women really better off than they were twenty years ago?
- The paintings of (new artist): are they a reflection of the works of Monet?

The "Why" Essay

What does it deal with? . . . Cause-and-effect relationships

What does it do? . . . . Explains, justifies

Tip: Be sure that your specified cause(s) are accurate, true, and can be proven.

To make it interesting: Use examples that are compelling because they withstand the scrutiny of "But what if . . ." questions.

The following would be defined as Why Essay topics:

- Global warming as a cause of more powerful hurricanes
- Why Americans need to be multilingual in the twenty-first century
- The effect of video games on preschool children
- What happens to our health when fluoride is added to the public water supply?
- Why are the world's frog populations disappearing?

The Relationship Essay

What does it deal with? . . Words, objects, abstract concepts
What does it do? . . . . Classifies, analyzes
Tip: Be sure that your classification categories do not overlap—that each category is distinctive and *every* example will fit into one of the categories.
To make it interesting: Use persuasive techniques to convince the reader that your categories are valid and that you do have a point to make.

The following would be defined as Relationship Essay topics:

- The three major types of modern American grocery stores—and the end of the corner market
- The types of people who become doctors
- The modern man as one of seven categories of adventurer
- Types of exercise and the role of walking in a home exercise program
- The types of women in America today and the role of America's stay-home mom

The Persuasion Essay

What does it deal with? . . The writer's opinion on a subject
What does it do? . . . . Argues, persuades
Tip: Be sure that you gather factual proof and establish provable cause-and-effect relationships as part of your background work.
To make it interesting: When establishing inferences (inductive and deductive reasoning), turn to respected experts in the field of your selected subject, people of reputation, to help you establish your point.

The following would be defined as Persuasion Essay topics:

- UFOs: an explainable phenomenon
- The need for more cancer research
- The need for a girls' basketball team
- Has the time come for stricter water conservation?
- Do you really want year-round school?

The Descriptive Essay

What does it deal with? . . Words, objects, abstract concepts
What does it do? . . . . Describes, explains

Tip: Be sure that you do not lose the point of your essay through aimless use of descriptive adjectives.
To make it interesting: Look to imagery techniques (simile, metaphor, personification), making vivid use of words and ideas that appeal to the senses.

The following would be defined as Descriptive Essay topics. Be sure to use the description *to make a point* about:

- Prom night
- A walk in the park
- Local flooding
- Trust
- People addicted to television

The Narrative Essay

What does it deal with? . . . Events, both real and imaginary
What does it do? . . . . Narrates[*], describes
Tip: Be sure that your narrative does relate an experience with some significance or that has a point.
To make it interesting: Sometimes (but not always) narratives written in the first person will draw in the reader and better create the desired effect(s).

The following would be defined as Narrative Essay topics:

- Your last shopping trip as it related to teenage economics
- A young boy who learns a lesson about sharing with his sister
- A girl's sense of adventure and how maturity can make a difference
- The camping trip that ended in disaster due to poor planning
- A botanist who finds a new plant species in her own backyard

As you can see from this list, you have many options concerning how to focus an essay. Once you begin utilizing these options, incorporating the seven literary elements as they are appropriate to your purpose, you will begin to recognize, understand, and perhaps even appreciate their use in the writings of other essayists.

Motivator #1. Write an essay to enter in an essay contest.

Comments: Essay contests are periodically sponsored by civic groups, newspapers, magazines, and schools

---

[*]What is the difference between a narrative essay and a short story? A narrative essay goes beyond the short story by using narrative techniques (dialogue, action sequence, descriptive elements, and so forth) and the story-line itself to make a point beyond mere entertainment.

throughout the United States. Your teachers or school librarian may know of upcoming events. Also, check with local civic clubs to see if their organizations are holding any essay contests.

Be sure to talk to the resource librarian of your public library and look into the latest edition of *Writer's Market* (Writer's Digest Books). You may be surprised at the variety of essay contests that are available to writers. Examples such as the Amelia Student Award (*Amelia Magazine*), open to students with previously unpublished essays (also poems and short stories), the Marine Corps Essay Contest, open to anyone with 3,000-word essays about the Marine Corps, and the Annie Dillard Award in Nonfiction (*The Bellingham Review*, Western Washington University) for essays on any subject of any length illustrate the great range of sponsors and subjects that are available.

Tip: If available, read essays that were winners of previous contests so that you can develop a sense of what has already been done successfully. Examine them for their use of the literary elements tested by the SAT II: Literature test.

ACTIVE LEARNING NOTES FOR MOTIVATOR #1

Begin writing your essay and consider the following:
Literary element #1. MEANING. (Review pages 65–66.)
Background decisions related to establishing meaning:
- What is the topic or subject?
- What is the purpose? Discussion? Persuasion? Entertainment?
- What effect on the readers do you want to achieve?
- Who is the audience?
- The thesis statement for this essay is as follows:

_____

_____

(When you write your essay, you may decide to imply your thesis, rather than to state it directly. Even so, you should be able to state your thesis in one concise sentence.)
- The major point(s) I want to make in this essay is (are) as follows:
  #1 _____
  #2 _____
- Supporting points:
  #1 _____
  #2 _____
  #3 _____

Literary Element #2. FORM. (Review pages 71–73.)
Obviously, the main form is the essay.
What type of essay? Formal or informal?
How many words?

What effect do you want to have on the reader? For example, an emotional response such as outrage or a light-hearted moment? Perhaps you want the reader to finish with a clearer understanding of the subject or with useful instructions for how to do something.

How can you organize your thesis, main points, and supporting points to achieve this effect?

Background decisions related to establishing meaning: What method or combination of methods of development will best achieve your purpose and desired effect?
- Points of argument
- Classification and analysis
- Points of persuasion
- Narration
- Description
- Cause-and-effect relationships
- Definition
- Comparisons/contrasts
- Explanations
- Example

DO YOU NEED AN OUTLINE?
An outline is an important tool that serves many different functions. It can mean the difference between an effectively written essay (defined as an essay that communicates the desired message and, if appropriate, elicits the desired responses in the reader) and an undirected meandering of words.

A very productive exercise that can help you develop comprehension skills for taking the SAT II: Literature test and at the same time help you to think from a writer's viewpoint is to outline an essay written by another writer. Use the outlining skills that you learned in your past English classes. See if you can identify the organizational pattern, the development of proofs, and the unifying elements. Does the structure break down at any point? How does this affect the meaning?

Some functions of the essay outline and its supporting data both in analyzing the writing of others and in your own writing include:
1. It can be used to prioritize research notes, highlighting those points that are germane and exposing those that are superfluous to the essay.
2. It can help identify points of faulty reasoning, such as incorrect classification, illogical inferences due to inductive/deductive reasoning based on false premises that lead to unsupportable conclusions, and so forth.

3. It can help you "play" with the essay's structure, trying different sequences and presentations to predict their potential effects.
4. It can point out areas of insufficient research, where facts are needed, illustrations would be helpful, or a new direction of thought needs to be taken.
5. It can help you define the less concrete elements of the essay, serving as a structural skeleton that you can flesh out to be an entertainer, a whimsical character, a stern-faced doctor, a persuasive authority, or whatever other persona will serve to elicit the effect you desire.
6. It can unify the essay by helping you to see its point of beginning that needs to captivate the reader's attention, its middle that needs to fulfill the reader's expectations, and its conclusion that needs to give the reader a sense of closure.
7. It can help you keep on the point, acting as a type of pattern that, once established, helps you stay within the desired lines of thought.

Literary element #3. NARRATIVE VOICE. (Review pages 110–119.)
Who is speaking in this essay?

The answer to this question depends largely upon the type of essay and your intended purpose.

First person point of view can be especially effective in narrative essays and, of course, are the mainstay of the editorial essay. You may find that your purposes are best served by allowing the points of the essay to carry themselves without the reader being distracted by an awareness of your presence as the writer. This is especially true in some instructional essays—and yet a common trend among essayists today is to expose him- or herself to the reader, forming an almost informal intimacy between writer and reader, like two old friends sitting down for a chat over a cup of coffee.

Literary element #4. TONE. (Review pages 134–139.)
What is your attitude toward your subject?

What is your attitude toward your audience?

How do you want your readers to feel after reading the essay?

How do you want your readers to view you? For example, are you sincere about your subject?

Literary element #5. CHARACTER. (Review page 158.)
Obviously, not all essays include characters in the narrative sense. Character as a literary element, however, still can be addressed from the following perspectives:

1. In the narrative essay, character should be dealt with just as in a short story.
2. Examine your outline. Does the subject and structure have any points at which adding an anecdotal incident involving a character would help to make your point?
3. Would using dialogue at any point in your essay add dramatic impact? Note: Essayists have even been known to carry on a type of conversation with the reader.

EXAMPLE:

I might ask you to carry my books, help me with my math homework, or give me a ride home on your bike. But would you consider, even for a moment, allowing me to invade your space with my music, my tastes in clothes, my likes and dislikes. I can see you shaking your head. What, you ask, is my point? My point is that....

4. Look at your intended essay from a larger perspective. How would you *characterize* it? Your answer might involve references to tone, voice, and style. How would an independent reader characterize your essay? Is it sentimental? Judgmental? Would your essay be characterized as apathetic? Optimistic? Perhaps cynical? How do you want readers to characterize your essay?

Literary element #6. USE OF LANGUAGE. (Review pages 165–188.)
Obviously, the use of figurative language, particularly words carrying multiple levels of meaning, can be especially effective in the essay because of its brevity and tightly-written structure.

How do you incorporate figurative language into an essay? Some writers are blessed with the ability "to turn a phrase." For most people, however, becoming adept at using figurative language effectively is a learned skill that takes practice. A few helpful SAT II: Literature test preparation exercises that will help you improve your own use of figurative language include:

1. Read and learn to recognize the use of figurative language in the writing of others.
2. However, at the same time evaluate their uses to determine their effectiveness. Even very clever language can be used ineffectively. You need to be able to identify what works and what does not work. This can be done in group discussion: using essays written in a variety of styles from several periods, identify the figurative uses of

language, then discuss their degrees of effectiveness.

3. Using your outline, identify potential areas in which development of an analogy or use of rhetorical devices, for example, might serve your purposes.

4. Examine your first draft of the essay. Are there any areas in which you can better convey your meaning and achieve the desired effect by using figurative language?

5. Ask your study group to discuss your use of language. Any problem areas? Any suggestions?

Literary Element #7. MEANING(S) IN CONTEXT. (Review pages 193–204.)

Once again, the short, compact nature of the essay by definition affects the significance of the words you use. The writer of a book-length manuscript has the luxury of numbers. When a book can be 15,000 words or more, the writer can put forth his or her point from multiple perspectives, using several different examples. The essayist, in contrast, is restricted by limited numbers of words, sometimes less than 500, and as a result must use precise language that conveys exact meanings. An example or illustration in an essay needs to be clear and must appeal to the understanding of the most people because length may dictate that only one example is possible.

Study every word, every phrase, every sentence of your essay. Ask yourself if any of the words used carry with them hidden connotations that might not suit your purposes. Or perhaps you do want the reader to make mental associations as he or she reads your essay. Of course, you want to take special care to use words that denotatively carry the meanings you want to convey. Yet, you do not want to overlook your use of syntax (see page 195). Does your essay have a natural rhythm to it that blends word choice and sentence structure to whisk the reader along to a satisfying or perhaps even challenging conclusion?

Significant point: You are, as this exercise progresses, attempting to use language (its connotations, figurative meanings, and context) in your own writing to influence the thinking of your readers. As you begin to think from the perspective of a writer, you can better recognize the uses of language and the meanings behind them in the literary works of the essayists. This comprehension skill is, of course, a direct focus of the SAT II: Literature test.

Motivator #2. Write an essay to send to the newspaper as a letter to the editor.

Comments: Why do people write letters to the editor of local or school newspapers? Some possible reasons include:

1. The writer feels strongly about a subject that he or she believes should be brought to the attention of the public.

2. The writer wants to sway public opinion.

3. The writer is responding to an article or letter previously published.

4. The writer wants to give credit to an individual, a business, a public figure, an institution or to voice a problem or protest.

5. The writer wants to "get it off his or her chest" concerning some issue.

6. The writer wants to clarify something that he or she believes is generally misunderstood.

7. The writer wants to see his or her name in print.

When you read a published letter or essay, apply the preceding list to help you determine what purpose the writer has in what and how he or she writes, the words used, or not used, to express his or her views. This examination of a writer's purpose from the viewpoint of a writer will help you develop skills in understanding meaning.

Naturally, there are more possible reasons for people to send letters to the editor than those just listed; however, you need to consider how directly related the motivation of the writer is to how he or she may have used the literary elements in writing the letter. Consequently, your initial steps (should you decide to write a letter to the editor) may need to be

1. to decide upon your subject and

2. to identify your true motivations in writing the letter.

Because letters to the editor are generally persuasive works that attempt to sway readers' opinions, the third logical prewriting step would be to establish for yourself your position on the subject. What is the opinion that you want your letter to convey?

If you are indecisive, do the research, speak to the people, read the materials that will enable you to establish an informed opinion. After you have enough information, put it in an order that will most likely appeal to the readers' sense of logic. Also, if the issue is new, how can you convince the readers to care about it and share your opinions?

Another consideration of the editorial letter is length. Perhaps one of the shortest essay forms, the letter to the editor must be long enough to be complete (introducing the subject, presenting your ideas, and concluding with a thought that has your readers thinking about your letter long after the newspaper goes to the recycling bin). Yet it must be short enough that the editor will consider printing it. A general rule of thumb when writing to editors: the shorter, the better. Also, consider making your main point early in your letter, especially if your letter is lengthy. An editor might "crop" or cut off the last few sentences or even the last paragraph of a lengthy letter. If the point that you want to make is at the end of your letter, you may find that your most important sentence will be missing in print.

ACTIVE LEARNING NOTES FOR MOTIVATOR #2

Begin writing your letter to the editor and consider the following:

Literary Element #1. MEANING. (Review pages 65–66.)
Background decisions related to establishing meaning:
  • Do you want to convince the readers of the truth of your position?
  • Do you want to persuade your readers to take action?

Identify your potential readers. Are they classmates, parents and teachers, the community at large? If you are submitting your letter to the local newspaper, what is the character (in the larger sense) of the paper's readership? Are they liberal, moderate, conservative? Are they actively engaged in technology (computers, the Internet, and so forth)? Once you have determined a profile of your potential readers, do any of these factors relate to potential preformed opinions that they might have concerning your topic? How might this affect your approach in your letter?

Literary Element #2. FORM. (Review pages 71–72.)
How many words? A call to the newspaper asking for the preferred length for letters to the editor and for the maximum number of words accepted might save you needless stress. Also, you might look at back issues to count words of those letters previously printed. Keep in mind, however, that a very lengthy (i.e., wordy) letter, unless extremely compelling in subject or written by a local celebrity, could be cropped (parts edited out or the end omitted) by the paper or simply not considered for publication at all.

What organizing principles (See page 70) can you use to establish your point? Because the letter is brief, you may want to take special care in writing the final sentence. What thought do you want to leave in the mind of the reader? You may want to restate your thesis—emphasizing your main point. Check your position for validity. (See page 107.)

Literary Element #3. NARRATIVE VOICE. (Review pages 110–119.)
The general rule is that the letter to the editor is written in the first-person, with yourself as speaker, with your name following the letter.

However, history has proven that there are exceptions. Sometimes editorial letters are signed by fictitious characters, with the writer assuming a persona to achieve, for example, a satiric effect. Although published as a pamphlet, Jonathan Swift's satirical essay "A Modest Proposal" is written by a tongue-in-cheek persona, and illustrates the type of devices that can be used. Such letters are put forth as from such fictitious characters as the Easter Bunny and Santa Claus or are signed by the famous Average Joe Citizen when the writer wants to establish a connection with the masses of readers, e.g., This writer "is one of us."

Although satiric essays and essays written by a persona may upon occasion be published, you may find that editors will view such special effects as contrivances rather than as clever writing and prefer a serious voice that is sincerely expressed. Humor will, in a letter to the editor, often best be developed as an extension of the humor intrinsically found in the subject. Humor then arises from your personal perspectives and observations concerning the subject, rather than through attention-getting gimmicks.

Read a variety of letters to the editor. Can you identify whether each of the writers is serious about the subject or is making light humor of the issue? Identifying the words that you would use as the writer of a similar essay/letter will help you to evaluate the use of such literary elements as Voice and Tone. From a writer's perspective, ask yourself such questions as "What is the author's attitude toward the subject?"

Literary Element #4. TONE. (Review pages 134–139.)
  • What is your attitude toward your subject?
  • What is your attitude toward your audience?
  • How do you want your readers to feel after reading your letter?
  • Does your writing style project the tone you desire?

The letter to the editor very often takes an informal style, one that projects an impression of authority and yet forms a connection between reader and writer. Your letter should flow smoothly and, at the same time, carry the weight of facts, logic, and credibility. According to William Hazlitt, an essayist in the early 1800s:

It is not easy to write a familiar style. Many people mistake a familiar for a vulgar style, and suppose that to write without affectation is to write at random. On the contrary, there is nothing that requires more precision, and, if I may so say, purity of expression, than the style I am speaking of. It utterly rejects not only all unmeaning pomp, but all low, cant phrases, and loose, unconnected, *slipshod* allusions. It is not to take the first word that offers, but the best word in common use; it is not to throw words together in any combinations we please, but to follow and avail ourselves of the true idiom of the language. To write a genuine familiar or truly English style, is to write as any one would speak in common conversation, who had a thorough command and choice of words, or who could discourse with ease, force, and perspicuity, setting aside all pedantic and oratorical flourishes. Or to give another illustration, to write naturally is the same thing in regard to common conversation, as to read naturally is in regard to common speech.

Literary Element #5. CHARACTER. (Review page 158.)
How would you characterize your letter? Is it angry? Do you sound amused? Does the letter project a sense of urgency?

Literary Element #6. USE OF LANGUAGE. (Review pages 165–188.)
In letters to the editor, a primary goal is to, as the title of William Brohaugh's book states, *Write Tight* (Writer's Digest Books, 1993).

You have no excess space for wordiness or redundant phrases. Consequently, figurative language can be especially useful in conveying more than one level of thinking with just a few words. However, figurative language can, at the same time, create complexities of thought that might alienate many of your readers. Examine each figurative device you use and ask the following questions:
1. Do I mean everything that this figurative device conveys?
2. Will my readers understand what I mean?

Literary Element #7. MEANING(S) IN CONTEXT. (Review pages 193–204.)

Perhaps William Hazlitt's words will give you a perspective on word choice as it relates to meaning:

The proper force of words lies not in the words themselves, but in their application. A word may be a fine-sounding word, of an unusual length, and very imposing from its learning and novelty, and yet in the connection in which it is introduced, may be quite pointless and irrelevant. It is not pomp or pretension, but the adaptation of the expression to the *idea* that clenches a writer's meaning:—as it is not the size or glossiness of the materials, but their being fitted each to its place, that gives strength to the arch; or as the pegs and nails are as necessary to the support of the building as the larger timbers, and more so than the mere showy, unsubstantial ornaments. I hate anything that occupies more space than it is worth.

The point? Suit your words to your topic and to your audience.

Motivator #3. Write an essay to send to a magazine.

Comments: Magazines are an excellent source of essays to examine in preparation for taking the SAT II: Literature test, and they also provide opportunities for you to view the subject as a writer would as you learn to recognize and use the literary elements.

Before looking at essays written specifically as articles in magazines, perhaps a discussion of magazines in general would be helpful. Magazines are grouped according to their purpose and intended audience.

SELECTED MAGAZINE TYPES

Category:	Purpose/Audience:	Example:
Consumer magazines	General information for the general public	*Seventeen*
Trade, technical, & professional journals	Profession- & trade-related information for professionals/ tradespeople	*Songwriter Magazine*
Company magazines	Produced by large companies for their employees, customers, and stockholders	*Caterpillar*

Often, company magazines are the product of company employees, and essays from people not directly connected to the organization are not encouraged, although exceptions do exist. However, the world of consumer and trade magazines is wide and varied, providing many opportunities for young, fresh voices. *Writer's Market,* for example, lists fifty different types of consumer magazines, ranging from aviation magazines to women's magazines. It also lists over fifty-five different types of trade, technical, and professional journals. Within each of these types you will find a large assortment of individual magazines, each vying for position to attract the most readers within their specified potential audience.

What types of magazines are being published? One popular type of consumer magazine is the hobby and craft publication. Examples include *Antique Review, Beckett Football Card Monthly, Ceramics Monthly, Decorative Artist's Workbook, Fine Woodworking, Lapidary Journal, Popular Woodworking, Sports Collectors Digest, Toy Shop,* and the list could go on and on. The types of trade, technical, and professional journals are just as varied. For example, *Culinary Trends* is published for chefs and restaurant owners. *Professional Mariner* is aimed at, as you can guess, professional mariners. A study of such directories as *Literary Market Place* will provide you with many such sources.

The point is that magazines, whether consumer or trade, consist of essays (usually sandwiched between advertising layouts). Magazines need essays. Lots of essays. But not just any essays. They need tightly focused, well-written essays that exhibit effective use of those same literary elements that you are studying to prepare for the SAT II: Literature test.

The essay written for publication in a magazine is generally called a magazine article. Its length may vary from very short (a few hundred words) to more lengthy articles of a few thousand words.

SOME OF THE MOST COMMON KINDS OF MAGAZINE ARTICLES (Alphabetically listed)

Exposé	Personal Experience
Historical	Product
How-to	Seasonal
Humorous	Service
Informational	Spot-news
Inspirational	Think articles
Interview	Travel
Nostalgia	

Despite the opportunities available, having your essay (article) published, however, is not guaranteed. Many professional writers submit articles to magazines routinely. As a result, some magazines have established policies that they will not accept unsolicited manuscripts (articles that the editors have not requested to be written) and prefer to assign their main articles either to staff writers or to freelance professionals in the field.

Recognizing the need for opportunities for writers to "break into the field" and establish a relationship with publishers, magazines sometimes have columns that are open to submissions from the general readership. They may pay only a few dollars, or even nothing at all, but the experience they offer is tremendous and they do provide a chance to see your writing in print.

SAMPLE LIST OF MAGAZINE COLUMNS

Magazine:	Column Title:	Words:
Dog Magazine	Waggin' Tales	500
Plane and Pilot	Flight to Remember	1,000–1,500
Self Employed Professional	Up at Night	1,000
Career Focus	Profiles	500–1,000
Christian Parenting Today	The Lighter Side	600–700
Opportunity Magazine	Success Stories	750–900
Hearing Health	People	300–400
Italian America	Community Notebook	500
Home Cooking	Last Bite	250
Reader's Digest	Tales Out of School	300
The Walking Magazine	Ramblings	300–1,200
American Woodworker	Offcuts	1,000
Country Journal	Sentinel	300–600
Girl's Life	It Happened to Me	1,200
Field & Stream	"Finally..."	750–800
Better Homes and Gardens	Family Network	100

This also provides an opportunity for you to incorporate writing an essay for magazine publication into your test preparation study plan. Working in conjunction with your teachers and study group, you can take advantage of these opportunities by:

1. Reading selected articles, then identifying and discussing each writer's use of the literary elements
2. Writing a series of reading comprehension questions based on those articles
3. Identifying a list of possible topics for writing an article

As you read through magazines, begin looking for columns that include "invitations" for you to submit an article. Also, directories such as *Writer's Digest* include descriptions and tips concerning these types of columns on a magazine-by-magazine basis.

Browse through the magazines at your local store and you will find that the short essay is used extensively by many magazines.

Once you have selected the magazine column for which you would like to write or submit an article, you can begin your background preparation.

Step 1. Write to the magazine and request a copy of their writer's guidelines. Most magazines will send you a list of guidelines describing their aims, what they need from writers, and details concerning how many words, format for submissions, deadline dates, and so forth. When you request the guidelines, be sure that you include a #10 self-addressed, stamped envelope for the magazine staff to use to send the guidelines to you.

Step 2. While waiting for the guidelines, study at your library at least six to twelve back issues of the magazines to see what articles have already been printed in the column. Using your Active Learning notebook, list topics and count words. Analyze the writing of each essay, first to learn what has been done successfully already (to the extent that the essay was selected for publication) and then to gain practice in recognizing the use of the literary elements in the writing of others (direct preparation for taking the SAT II: Literature test).

To prepare for the test and to write your own article, analyze the essays/articles for:

1. MEANING
   - What is the essay about?
   - What is your impression of the writing?
   - What do you think the writer is trying to do with this essay?
2. FORM
   - Outline the article.
   - What organizational patterns have been used?

- Do you think that in relation to subject and writer's intent, this structural pattern is the most effective?
3. NARRATIVE VOICE
   - First person? Third person?
   - Would a change in point of view improve the article or lessen its impact?
4. TONE
   - What is the writer's attitude toward
     A. the subject?
     B. the reader?
   - The writer of this article "sounds" _____ (happy? angry? concerned?).
5. CHARACTER
   Most column articles do not include characters in the strictest sense (i.e., people); however, you still can deal with character from a different perspective. Essays can be *characterized,* meaning that you can examine the article to determine what are its distinguishing features. Actually, when "character" refers to a person, we generally think of the person's name, physical description, and finally personality traits. All these things are distinguishing features that help us to set that person—that character—apart from others.
   Characterize the article in one sentence: This essay can be characterized as _____ . (For example, this essay can be characterized as an attempt to raise awareness concerning water safety by using humor in a nonthreatening tone.)
6. USE OF LANGUAGE
   - What imagery is used?
   - Its effectiveness in achieving the writer's purpose?
   - What figures of speech are used?
   - Effectiveness?
7. MEANING(S) IN CONTEXT
   - Examine use of connotative word choices. Effects?
   - Any problems with syntax?
   - What implications are made? (The writer implies that _____.)
   After analyzing the writer's use of the literary elements, can you identify some questions that might be asked on a reading comprehension test? See if you can compose at least one question for each literary element.

Step 3. After the writer's guidelines arrive, read them carefully, then follow them in a precise way. If the publisher wants 1,500 words, do not give him or her 2,000; a maximum 1,500 words means just that—no more than 1,500 words. Learning how to follow directions is an important part of your academic career, particularly in test taking. You may have discovered a certain amount of latitude allowed when following homework assignments and classroom activities because you are in an interactive atmosphere. There are some areas, however, in which you will find that being able to understand directions and to have a willingness to focus on following those directions as carefully as possible can mean the difference between success and a less desirable performance. When you take standardized tests, you need to be alert to directions. Listen closely. Read carefully. Pay attention to detail.

Remember: Every test score, to a certain extent, reflects your ability to follow directions.

ACTIVE LEARNING NOTES FOR MOTIVATOR #3

Begin writing your article and consider the following:

As previously noted, the magazine essay can serve many different purposes. For the sake of illustration, the following Active Learning Notes are aimed at humorous articles, so often popular in magazine columns that are open to reader submissions.

There is nothing more disenchanting to man than to be shown the springs and mechanism of any art. All our arts and occupations lie wholly on the surface; it is on the surface that we perceive their beauty, fitness, and significance; and to pry below is to be appalled by their emptiness and shocked by the coarseness of the strings and pulleys.

**On Some Technical Elements
of Style in Literature,
by Robert Louis Stevenson, circa 1885**

Humorous writing, unlike the typically structured essay, is a delicate blending of structured silliness with serious fun. In other words, it is a study in paradox.

As a result, tearing apart the nuts and bolts of a comic essay that is already written may be useful, but to pin down, box in, and analyze a comic article *before* it is written may defeat the very free flow of thought necessary, frankly, to be funny. To write in a funny style requires structure, without question, and your Active Learning Notes should deal with the article's structure; but to have a humorous style to your writing also requires a certain spontaneity—or at least appearance of spontaneity—that is both relaxed and conversational.

Hugh Blair's *Lectures on Rhetoric and Belles Lettres,* published in 1783, is aimed at writing style in the larger picture; however, his following points are especially germane to a discussion of writing humorous articles:

It is not easy to give a precise idea of what is meant by Style. The best definition I can give of it, is, the peculiar manner in which a man expresses his conceptions, by means of Language. It is different from mere Language or words. The words, which an author employs, may be proper and faultless; and his Style may, nevertheless, have great faults: it may be dry, or stiff, or feeble, or affected.

Consequently, the following Active Learning Notes are presented in a different, less formal format. This change in approach also demonstrates the flexibility that you can utilize when you develop your own Active Learning Notes. The literary elements that are so crucial to your understanding in preparation for the SAT II: Literature test are at the core of this activity; however, this approach is more holistic (emphasizing the functional relationships at work within the comic essay) than analytical.

Begin your prewriting with a study of what has already been done. As previously suggested, dig deeply into the published columns of at least six to twelve issues of the magazines for which you want to write a humorous essay. By this point you should have a grasp of what types of things you are looking for: figurative language, structure, and so forth.

Next, select some well-known comic writers that you enjoy reading—the late Erma Bombeck, Dave Barry perhaps—and read several of their essays. Begin making notes concerning how they use the literary elements and at the same time come across to the reader with humor and wit.

Can you make any generalizations concerning what these writers' works have in common?

Here are a few literary element-based points to look for:

1. Generally, at the root of humor is a serious point. The humor writer tends to point out to us the problems that we refuse to address, the hypocrisies that are glossed over, the excesses that surround us. The writer's intent may be to use humor as a tool to help us to get his or her point, and the result may be the readers laughing at themselves.

2. Effective writers present their humor as a continuous flow of thought without artificial devices such as "corny jokes" that seem to be inserted as afterthoughts or the use of profanity and so-called "shock talk."

3. Wit can create humor. Some people find these two terms (*wit* and *humor*) indistinguishable; however, historically they have been defined in a cause-and-effect relationship. Wit involves clever plays on words and the skillful use of literary devices. These tools that collectively are referred to as witty sayings are used to point out the inconsistencies in human nature, thus producing humor.

4. Wordplay is not enough. The writer's attitude toward the subject must project a humorous tone that is sustained throughout the work.

5. The subject and theme need to grab the reader because he or she can identify with it. Universal subjects and themes are generally at the root of humor, e.g., food, clothing, shelter, money, love, family. Also, the humorist uses details that people can relate to, such as "the doorbell always rings *after* I get in the shower."

6. Effective humorous writing drives home the point by letting people draw their own conclusions rather than telling them what to think. For example, a serious essay may give an effective argument about the dangers to hearing health caused by rock music played at high sound levels. A comic essay about teenagers with glazed looks on their faces and car sound systems that cause glass to shatter may make the same point, but in a humorous, nonjudgmental way.

7. The voice of the humorist needs to ring with confidence and yet often will also identify himor herself as a victim or as someone who is helpless. The voice may be his or her own or that of a persona who is submerged in the situation.

8. The humorist uses satire to point out the differences between what society pretends and what is the reality of the situation. In other words, the humor essay often targets hypocrisy.

9. Humorists use many different literary tools, such as understatement, overstatement, irony (e.g., mock sympathy, such as illustrated in the paradoxical phrase "poor little rich kid"), free association, nonsense, parody, surprise, and so forth.

10. The form of the essay can create or add to the humor, e.g., mock letters or silly lists.

11. Every line does not have to be funny. Effective humorists pace the writing with "breather" space for the reader to recover enough composure to appreciate the next peak of humor.

12. Not all attempts at humor work for everyone. Can you see any of the preceding observations at work in the articles you have read? Can you add any other points to this list?

Now that you have investigated humorous essays and their relationship to the literary elements, you may want to decide upon how writing the magazine article will fit into your study plan goals and timelines. One possible plan follows. These steps could be used for planning to write most types of articles that editors welcome as submissions from readers.

Step 1. Select your subject; define your point; write the essay.

Step 2. Revise the essay to conform to restrictions, such as minimum/maximum word counts.

Step 3. Read the essay aloud. Check for rhythm and flow, effective thought pauses.

Step 4. Rewrite.

Step 5. Have your study group read the essay and offer general suggestions.

Step 6. Rewrite.

Step 7. Have your study group analyze your use of the literary elements. Discuss the effectiveness of the use of humor and write reading comprehension questions based on your article.

Step 8. Rewrite.

Step 9. Check your article against the writer's guidelines from the publisher. Make all the necessary changes.

Step 10. Check your spelling.

Step 11. Check your grammar and punctuation.

Step 12. Submit a clean, error-free copy of the article to the publisher. Be sure to include a self-addressed, stamped envelope for the publisher's response.

Training Exercise Series B

WRITING TO LEARN NONFICTION: THE AUTOBIOGRAPHY

Prewriting Review: What is autobiography?

Step 1. Reread page 72 of this book.

Step 2. Although your activity will focus on autobiography, ask your librarian to help you locate both biographies and autobiographies of various types so that you can read them to compare and contrast what forms the biography/autobiography can take. Also, you should be able to locate collections of essays in textbooks on writing and reading biographies and autobiographies.

Step 3. Investigate the major points.

Step 3a. To gain a foundation of background knowledge, consider the following points concerning *biography*:

Point #1. Biography is the written account of a person's life. Generally, the account ranges from birth to death; however, it can also focus on a particular period of his or her life.

Point #2. A biography is either:

a. Authorized, meaning that (1) the person is living and has consented in writing to cooperate with the biographer, granting interviews, providing letters, diaries, documents, and other materials and instructing friends and relatives to speak candidly with the biographer, or (2) the person is dead but his or her living relatives, heirs and assigns have agreed in writing to provide information and documents to the biographer.

b. Unauthorized, meaning that (1) the person is dead without known living relatives, heirs and assigns, with documents, papers and records being a part of the public domain, or (2) the person is living and has refused cooperation with the biographer. This last type of unauthorized biography is often avoided because of legal concerns.

Point #3. Readers' expectations of *effective* modern biography include:

a. An interesting, lively writing style
b. Elements of drama without sensationalism
c. Accuracy, accuracy, accuracy

Point #4. The biography can be of almost any length from a full-length, cradle-to-grave book to the biographical essay in which the biographer does not focus on just reciting facts, but tries to make a more concise point.

Point #5. When the subject of the biographer is a publicly known figure, you (the reader) may come to the book with preconceived notions and ideas, some of which may be inaccurate.

Psychologically, people cling to the known and view with suspicion the unknown and those ideas that contradict the known. Have you ever had the experience of knowing two people engaged in an argument? One comes to you and explains his point of view. You listen intently and feel that his argument sounds reasonable. Do you think that you may have, when the second person comes to you with her side of the story, any leaning toward the first person's position because you heard and understood his side first? What if you later learned that the first person had misrepresented the situation?

When reading a biography about a person who has certain things generally believed about him or her, the reader needs to be very careful to see if the biographer who is challenging these notions provides concrete, indisputable evidence (documented proof—references to records that authenticate the information being used). The foundation of biographical writing should be accuracy.

As you read a biography, you might ask these types of questions about the subject:

1. When you look at motives, is there any evidence to indicate *why* the person did what he or she did?

2. What circumstances surrounded the subject's life? Can you see any cause-and-effect relationships? (Use caution here—are these relationships valid?)

3. What was his or her philosophy of life? Can you cite any supporting evidence?

4. Are there any narrative episodes in the person's life that especially reveal character? (Making him or her seem endearing, more withdrawn, having high principles, and so forth?)

5. Did the person have any physical features that were distinctive, that affected his or her life? Perhaps he or she was average and even that had a relationship to some element in his or her life?

Your study of biography and autobiography should also reveal that history is filled with interesting characters whose lives have been untouched by the biographer's pen. Libraries (on university campuses, in metropolitan cities, and in small-town libraries run by historical societies, government agencies, businesses, and even small groups of interested citizens) sometimes contain the old books, letters, journals, and papers of the famous, the infamous, and the everyday people of America's past. These can provide the research materials that you need to learn about people in America's history. You may enjoy reading some of these primary sources as part of your test preparation study plan. They will provide an opportunity for you to gain experience in developing comprehension skills in reading period literature—the diction, meanings, and even rhythms that are representative of the professional and non-professional writers of past generations. Because the SAT II: Literature test can include excerpts from works written since the sixteenth century, such practice may help you gain confidence in preparing to take the test.

Another biographical form to look at is that exercised by Henry Mayhew in the mid-1800s—occupational biography. A blend of informational writing and biography, this form takes a biographical-style look at an occupation. The occupation acts as a type of person or character and then the writer develops the life of a person or character in that occupation as he or she relates to and interacts with society. To illustrate, here is an excerpt from Mayhew's occupational biography on "Coster-Lads":

> The life of a coster-boy is a very hard one. In summer he will have to be up by four o'clock in the morning, and in winter he is never in bed after six. When he has returned from market, it is generally his duty to wash the goods and help dress the barrow. About nine he begins his day's work, shouting whilst his father pushes; and as very often the man has lost his voice, this share of the labour is left entirely to him. When a coster has regular customers, the vegetables or fish are all sold by twelve o'clock, and in many coster families the lad is then packed off with fruit to hawk in the streets. . . .
>
> One lad that I spoke to gave me as much of his history as he could remember. He was a tall stout boy, about sixteen years old, with a face utterly vacant. His two heavy lead-coloured eyes stared unmeaningly at me, and, beyond a constant anxiety to keep his front lock curled on his cheek, he did not exhibit the slightest trace of feeling. He sank into his seat heavily and of a heap, and when once settled down he remained motionless, with his mouth open and his hands on his knees—almost as if paralyzed. He was dressed in all the slang beauty of his class, with a bright red handkerchief and unexceptionable boots.
>
> "My father," he told me in a thick unimpassioned voice, "was a waggoner, and worked the country roads. There was two on us at home with mother, and we used to play along with the boys of our court, in Golding-lane, at buttons and marbles. I recollects nothing more than this—only the big boys used to cheat like bricks and thump us if we grumbled—that's all I recollects of my infancy, as you calls it. Father I've heard tell died when I was three and brother only a year old. It was worse luck for us!—Mother was so easy with us. I once went to school for a couple of weeks, but the cove used to fetch me a wipe over the knuckles with his stick, and as I wasn't going to stand that there, why you see I ain't no great schollard. We did as we liked with mother, she was so precious easy, and I never learned anything but playing buttons and making leaden 'bonces,' that's all," (here the youth laughed slightly). "Mother used to be up and out very early washing in families—anything for a living. She was a good mother to us. We was left at home with the key of the room and some bread and butter for dinner. Afore she got into work—and it was a goodish long time—was shocking hard up, and she pawned nigh everything. Sometimes, when we hadn't no grub at all, the other lads, perhaps, would give us some of their bread and butter, but often our stomachs used to ache with the hunger, and we would cry when we was

werry far gone. She used to be at work from six in the morning till ten o'clock at night, which was a long time for a child's belly to hold out again, and when it was dark we would go and lie down on the bed and try and sleep until she came home with the food. I was eight year old then.

> "A man as know'd mother, said to her, 'Your boy's got nothing to do, let him come along with me and yarn a few ha'pence,' and so I became a coster. He gave me 4d. a morning and my breakfast. I worked with him about three year, until I learnt the markets, and then I and brother got baskets of our own, and used to keep mother. One day with another, the two on us together could make 2s.6d. by selling greens of a morning, and going round to the publics with nuts of a evening, till about ten o'clock at night. Mother used to have a bit of fried meat or a stew ready for us when we got home, and by using up the stock as we couldn't sell, we used to manage pretty tidy. . . ."

Some Practice Test Questions:

1. What is the subject of the first paragraph?

   (A) The relationship of a coster-boy to his father
   (B) The number of hours a coster-boy works
   (C) The duties and routine of a coster-boy
   (D) The main service of a coster-boy
   (E) The customers of a coster-boy

(The correct answer is C.)

In your study group: Write a practice test question concerning the meaning in the fourth paragraph. Also, write questions for the second and third paragraphs.

2. The progression of thought in the third paragraph can NOT be summarized as

   (A) from a two-parent to single-parent family
   (B) from lack of emotional expression to emotional expression
   (C) from the mother unemployed to the mother employed
   (D) from infancy to childhood
   (E) from hunger to plenty of food

(The correct answer is E.)

In your study group: Write a practice test question concerning the use(s) of form in this passage.

3. In the fourth paragraph, the speaker's attitude toward becoming a coster-boy seems

(A) resentful
(B) satisfied
(C) disappointed
(D) imperceptible
(E) erratic

(The correct answer is *B*.)

In your study group: Write a practice test question concerning the narrative voice as shown by the speaker's attitude toward his mother in the third paragraph.

4. The tone of the first sentence of the selection indicates to the reader that

(A) the writer has little regard for coster-boys
(B) the writer is judgmental
(C) the description that follows is surprising
(D) the description that follows is serious and perhaps sad
(E) coster-boys no longer exist

(The correct answer is *D*.)

In your study group: Write a practice test question concerning the tone of the parenthetical sentence ("here the youth laughed slightly") in the third paragraph.

5. As a character, the writer of the first two paragraphs is probably

(A) a former coster-boy himself
(B) unobservant of those around him
(C) of a different social class than the coster-boy
(D) a woman who has married a former coster-boy
(E) afraid of the coster-boy

(The correct answer is *C*.)

In your study group: Write a practice test question concerning the character of the speaker (the coster-boy) in the final two paragraphs.

6. The language of the selection in the first paragraph is expressed in

(A) imprecise diction
(B) a businesslike tone
(C) highly symbolic language
(D) an informal tone
(E) Nonstandard English

(The correct answer is *B*.)

In your study group: Write a practice test question concerning the use of language in the second paragraph. (Notice "lead-coloured eyes" and "the slang beauty of his class.")

7. In the first paragraph, "to hawk in the streets" expresses which of these concepts?

I.   Clearing the throat
II. Peddling
III. Shouting

(A) I only
(B) II only
(C) III only
(D) II and III only
(E) I, II, and III

(The correct answer is *D*.)

In your study group: Write a practice test question concerning the meaning(s) in context for this selection, such as for the following list.

• "packed off" in paragraph one
• "unexceptional boots" in paragraph two
• "the cove" in paragraph three
• "the publics" in paragraph four

Step 3b. Consider the following points concerning *autobiography,* the focus of the writing exercise:

Point #1. Autobiography is the written account of a person's own life, generally written in first person, narrative form.

Point #2. The writer's own personal diaries, journals, memories, papers, letters, and discussions with friends and family are primary sources for writing autobiography.

Point #3. Episodes and reflections concerning feelings, events, and people are frequently used as tools in autobiography.

Point #4. The autobiography can be structured in the wide variety of ways any story can be told, such as chronological order or beginning with an exciting event followed by flashbacks.

Point #5. Autobiographies are a major contribution to the cultural records of a people. Do not think that autobiography is only for the rich or famous. Although fame may attract the publicity that makes such autobiographies popular, the autobiographies of men and women in regular works leading what may seem to them to be uneventful lives join together to give historians a picture of our society and culture that would otherwise be lost or unattainable. If the only records we have are of the unusual, the most exciting, the superlatives of life, then our pictures of the past will not be valid representations of life as it really was for most people. Also, people sometimes are not good judges of what is interesting in their own lives. Every detail of what was an everyday, mundane existence to a colonial soldier could be of riveting interest to today's historian specializing in early America. The past fascinates us— especially when we can find some personal connection with it. An interesting exercise in this is to spend some time in an antique shop listening to the customers as they excitedly point to articles that remind them of what Great-grandmother Thelma used in the early 1900s.

So perhaps the autobiography can be seen as an important contribution to both the person's family, allowing children and children's children to gain insight into what events went together to make families who they are, and to the future generations who will be seeking to understand us as a society of people living in a changing world.

As you read autobiographies, however, you need to keep in mind that when people write about themselves and their own lives they may, or may not, be presenting an accurate picture. Everyone has formed opinions and biases that tend to flavor what they write, particularly in regard to personal events. Remember, in autobiography you are getting only one side of the story. Consequently, no one autobiographical account should be viewed in isolation from the larger body of whatever historical documents are available that together give us a more complete understanding of people and events.

Step 4. Make the autobiography your own.

"Make the autobiography your own" sounds like a redundancy. Yet there are structural elements that you can use to ensure that your autobiographical writing will be an accurate reflection of your life as you see it rather than an exercise in aimless remembrances.

1. A preliminary outline, of course, is a beneficial tool. The outline in the prewriting stage is a method to collect your thoughts and to bring to mind some areas you want to cover. If you find that a formal outline is cumbersome, you may find that a simple timeline will be more useful for you.
2. Gather resources—your diaries, letters, old papers, photographs, home movies—anything that will stimulate memories.
3. Talk to family and friends. Make notes concerning their reminiscences, such as stories about your birth, special holidays, and other events.

4. Make lists:
   - family members
   - places you have lived
   - schools attended
   - favorites (subjects, music, foods, people, and movies)
   - activities
   - best/worst events
   - friends
   - hobbies
   - happiest/saddest times
5. Record descriptions. Be as elaborate as you want to be in your descriptions during these preliminary stages.

FRONTIER OPTIONS

J. Hector St Jean de Crevecoeur, calling himself "Farmer James," was an eighteenth-century American settler who wrote a collection of twelve essays on how wonderful his life was as an American farmer. By his final essay, he decided to leave the farm and join the frontier Indians.

Step 5. Examine your options.

Do not limit yourself to the full novel-style autobiography. You may find that flexible incorporation of other autobiographical techniques into your study plan will be more manageable for you. Here are a few options:

1. Make your autobiography a series of letters to your future grandchildren, with each letter dealing with a different time of your life, revealing different things about yourself and the life you are leading and have led.
2. Use a diary-style format, as if you are sitting down at the end of the day reflecting on its events and disclosing your thoughts to yourself, selecting key events from throughout your life.
3. Write a directed journal of current events, such as a journal that covers just your senior year in high school or first year in college. In journal-style writing (like the diary-style format), your arrangement would be chronological; but with the journal you could, during the year, indulge in reflections on past events and speculations on future hopes and fears.

   Hint: If you decide to use the novel-style autobiographical approach, make it more manageable by dividing your outline/timeline into large sections, then into chapters. Using a separate file folder for each chapter, gather your notes and other resources and group them by chapter.
4. Write your memoirs for your family. Select a single event or series of events (for example, times you spent with your grandmother), and tell them about it.

5. Personal illustration is a fundamental tool of writing. Instructors routinely, in their class presentations and in their writing, draw upon their personal experiences to illustrate principles, concepts, and methods that they are teaching. In written form, autobiographical sketches can be used to illustrate a wide variety of information. In the following autobiographical sketch, Lillian E. Myers shares with readers her own experience of being attacked by a swarm of bees. As you read her personal account, make a list of the basic information about bees that she is conveying by means of her personal illustration.

AN ENCOUNTER WITH HONEY BEES

The area where we live has received national attention because Africanized "killer" honey bees have been found here. A local man was stung severely after the sound of his lawn mower disturbed the bees. In another incident, a swarm of bees stung two dogs to death and trapped the dogs' owners in the bathroom of their home until emergency workers could come to rescue them from the angry bees.

Reading in the newspaper about these bee attacks causes me to remember when I, too, had a frightening and painful encounter with honey bees.

When my four brothers and I were children, our parents encouraged us to pursue personal projects. My brothers had acquired a skep of honey bees as one of our wonderful ventures. Honey bees are known as *social* bees and are considered very beneficial because they pollinate vegetable gardens, fruit trees, flowers, and many farm crops, such as clover. Some amateur beekeepers call their standard wooden hives *bee skeps,* although a "skep" is a special dome-shaped hive made of interwoven straw instead of wood. My brothers were busy with many things, and I found that I became fascinated with this new project. I was a teenager at the time, and this new interest delighted me. I was very happy that I had made friends with the bees.

One of my projects was bringing ferns and violets from the woods and planting them in the area beneath the front window of the house. The skep of bees had been conveniently located across the driveway beside my favorite flower bed. By the end of summer, I had removed several delicious combs of honey; and on an especially beautiful morning, I was about to remove another tempting honeycomb.

The beehive was a square box with a small hole at the lower front edge for the bees to gain entrance. The combs hung down into the box and were removed through the top. My beekeeping downfall was the result of the covering that prevented rain from entering the hive. This was a single sheet of roofing tin about one foot longer on each side than the size of the box. In the center on the top had been placed a large rock sufficient in weight to hold the tin in place. I had to remove the rock; the resulting sound was a shot-like blast that must have reverberated through the beehive with such a force that it startled the bees. Before I could realize what had happened, the entire colony of bees attacked me. They settled right on my head, stinging fiercely. When a bee attacks, its muscles force a stinger into the flesh to pump poison into the victim. Barbs on the stinger hold it tightly in the flesh; the stinger is pulled from the bee's body and the bee soon dies. Of course, I began to scream.

My mother heard my screams and was shocked to see the seething balloon of bees my head had become. My life was saved when God gave her the presence of mind to know what to do in this critical moment. My mother had been watering flowers nearby and quickly doused my head with a bucket of water. She continued to throw water on me with as much force as possible to dislodge the bees and managed to pull me into the house. She received a number of stings herself and cried in sympathy as she picked the stingers out of my face, neck, ears, and head. She lost count in the seventies.

I remained in shock for hours, unable to lay my head on a pillow. My eyes, nose, ears, and mouth swelled into a grotesque mask. I looked and felt terrible even weeks later with a blotchy, itchy head, face, and neck and with two black eyes.

Having miraculously survived this ordeal and the following weeks of unbelievable agony, the fact that for a long time I was nervous when I heard a buzzing sound is understandable. For many years even the buzz of an ordinary housefly would make me ill and trembling with fear.

The last of the honey was never removed from that skep of bees. The entire bee hive was hauled away. Many professional beekeepers wear hoods and gloves and, if necessary, use smoke to control angry bees.

My experience demonstrates that when sufficiently frightened, even domesticated honey bees will attack. In fact, according to recent field guide publications, the stings of domesticated bees are just as poisonous as those of Africanized bees. Experts tell us, however, that Africanized bees are "wild" honey bees. They avoid humans when possible, but will aggressively defend their hive if they are disturbed.

Honey bees are essential; we need honey bees for our agricultural crops and honey production. My experience illustrates, however, that we also need to learn how to live in harmony with bees and that care should be taken not to startle or disturb bees, whether domesticated or wild.

AN INDIVIDUAL OR GROUP ACTIVITY TO PREPARE FOR THE SAT II: LITERATURE TEST

In the following activity, you will be examining each of the seven literary elements individually on three different levels:

Level 1. Practicing answering test questions

First, you will be asked three reading comprehension questions based on the selection that you just read, "An Encounter with Honey Bees." Select the most appropriate answer choices and record your answers 1–21 on separate paper. You will find the answer key to these practice test questions at the end of this activity.

Level 2. Writing your own reading comprehension questions

Select a short autobiographical selection or excerpt upon which to base writing your own reading comprehension questions. Anthologies of autobiographical sketches are available. Also, you might consider working with two- to three-page passages selected from longer autobiographical works. A few autobiographies that you might find include *The Autobiography of . . .*

> *Benjamin Franklin*
> *Bertrand Russell* (Welsh mathematician and
> philosopher)
> *Calvin Coolidge*
> *Cecil B. DeMille*
> *David Crockett*
> *Edward Gibbon* (eighteenth-century English
> historian)
> *Eleanor Roosevelt*
> *Harry S. Truman*
> *James L. Smith*
> *John Milton*
> *John Stuart Mill* (nineteenth-century English
> philosopher)
> *Mark Twain*
> *Martin Van Buren*
> *Robert A. Millikan* (twentieth-century Ameri-
> can physicist)
> *Sam Houston*
> *Theodore Roosevelt*
> *Will Rogers*
> *William Carlos Williams*

This very brief list illustrates that autobiographical works can be found written by people in a wide variety of cultural and historical roles. If you conduct this activity in your study group, you might want to select several excerpts from autobiographical works representing different centuries and/or fields of interest. Individually write at least three questions for each literary element.

Each question should include five answer choices. Turn to the diagnostic tests (pages 29–53 and 277–297), practice sets (pages 298–319), and practice tests (pages 325–411) in this book for examples.

Suggestions and guidelines for writing these questions will be given for each of the seven literary elements.

Level 3. Developing a writer's perspective

Returning to the Writing to Learn focus, examine the autobiography from a writer's perspective in working with and using each of the seven literary elements. The Level 3 suggestions that follow should help you to view the literary elements as they would relate to your own writing, as well as to the writing of others.

MEANING (Review pages 61–68.)
Practice test questions:
(Based on "An Encounter with Honey Bees")

1. What is the main idea of the selection?

(A) Children should be encouraged to have projects.
(B) The country is being threatened by "killer" bees.
(C) Honey bees can be dangerous if not handled properly.
(D) Multiple bee stings cause massive swelling.
(E) Honey bees are essential to American agriculture.

2. The writer's message in the selection is primarily a

(A) description
(B) sensible approach
(C) reminder
(D) play on words
(E) statement on nature

3. Of the ideas listed, which one defines the subject of the selection?

(A) Nature as a friend
(B) Nature as an enemy
(C) Childhood endeavors
(D) Living in harmony with nature
(E) Quick responses

Your own comprehension questions:

Using the autobiographical selection that you made at Level 2 of this activity, write two or more questions that test the writer's use of MEANING.

You could ask questions about:
a. The overall or central subject
b. The main idea of a paragraph or sentence
c. The main subject of a paragraph or sentence
d. The central concern of the writer in a paragraph or sentence
e. What the writer deals with in a specified sentence
f. The speaker's message in a paragraph or sentence
g. The main point of the speaker in the selection, paragraph, or sentence
h. The purpose of the selection
i. How the subject of the selection, paragraph, or sentence can be stated
j. Which of a list of ideas defines the subject in a specified sentence or paragraph

A writer's perspective:

Make a list of five major events in your life. Looking at each event individually, what would be your purpose or intent in writing down an account of what happened?

FORM. (Review pages 69–76, 106–109)
Practice test questions:
(Based on "An Encounter with Honey Bees")

4. The "shock" in the seventh paragraph is the result of

(A) betrayal
(B) disappointment
(C) poison
(D) water
(E) screaming

5. The effect of the account of "killer" bees in the first paragraph is to

(A) introduce the subject
(B) minimize other accounts
(C) establish a change in topic
(D) present an alternative view of bees
(E) develop a contrast to the narrator's experience

6. The progression of thought in this selection can NOT be summarized as

(A) from joy to suffering
(B) from trust to fear
(C) from contentment to shock
(D) from interest to aversion
(E) from love to hatred

Your own comprehension questions:

Using the autobiographical selection you made at Level 2 of this activity, write two or more questions that test the writer's use of FORM.

Look for these types of form-related ideas for writing questions that test reading comprehension:
a. Progressions of thought (e.g., from joy to sorrow)
b. Contrasts, such as in feelings or interests
c. Effects of certain comments on the reader
d. The writer's intent in a specific comment
e. Structural elements, such as cause-and-effect relationships, chronological sequence, spatial sequence

A writer's perspective:

Think of the most dangerous or memorable event of your life. Using the list of five concepts just listed, how would you structure an autobiographical essay describing that event?

NARRATIVE VOICE. (Review pages 110–119, 124–125)
Practice test questions:
(Based on "An Encounter with Honey Bees")

7. In order for the writer to describe honey bees as "essential" in the last paragraph, her attitude toward bees would have to be

(A) incredulous
(B) deludable
(C) thoughtless
(D) capricious
(E) pragmatic

8. In the third paragraph, the attitude of the parents toward their children's activities was

(A) propitious
(B) malicious
(C) ominous
(D) incapacious
(E) intolerant

9. The attitude of the writer in the fourth paragraph can be considered

(A) equivocal
(B) enthusiastic
(C) exasperated
(D) elusive
(E) ecumenical

Your own comprehension questions:

Using the autobiographical selection you made at Level 2 of this activity, write two or more questions that test the writer's use of Narrative Voice.

First, you need to establish the speaker's point of view. Are the speaker and the writer the same in autobiography? In developing questions about narrative voice, you will want to examine attitudes:

a. The general attitudes of each character
b. Changes in attitudes
c. Attitudes that are directed toward specific people or events
d. Contrasts and similarities in attitudes
e. The writer's attitude as a character living through the situation in contrast to the writer's attitude as a narrator recalling these events and his or her role in them

A discussion question: In examining attitudes, why must we consider the cultures and historical period of the people involved?

A writer's perspective:

Select an event that you would like to share with readers in an informational autobiographical sketch. Develop a list of your attitudes toward the people, things, and circumstances involved in that event, as well as your overall attitude toward the event itself. Be sure to include any changes in attitude you may have experienced during or as a result of the event. How, in your proposed autobiographical sketch, might you convey each of these attitudes without directly stating them?

TONE. (Review pages 126–139)
Practice test questions:
  (Based on "An Encounter with Honey Bees")

10. The tone of "conveniently located" in paragraph four makes the writer's involvement with the bees seem

(A) naive
(B) penitent
(C) impersonal
(D) inevitable
(E) complacent

11. The tone of the writer's last paragraph has qualities that are

(A) infuriated and retributive
(B) mature and practical
(C) bitter and suspicious
(D) complacent and nonchalant
(E) defensive and unrelenting

12. The following statements are accurate of the selection EXCEPT that it cannot be said that its tone

(A) toward bees is respectful and somewhat defensive
(B) toward bees is antagonistic and very angry
(C) is informational
(D) is realistic toward the dangers in beekeeping
(E) is supportive toward the value of bees

Your own comprehension questions:

Using the autobiographical selection you made at Level 2 of this activity, write two or more questions that test the writer's use of TONE.

A shift in perspective, tone questions deal with the writer's or speaker's attitudes toward the material, subject, theme, and reader. When you examine the selection for questions to ask about the tone, however, you want to think about how the speaker sounds to the reader in regard to these attitudes. Other clues to tone include historical and cultural perspectives and settings (time of day, place).

For questions about a tone that results from attitudes (tone of voice), your answer choices might include such character-related descriptive adjectives as noble or defensive. Do you remember the old horror movies in which the setting is a castle on a rainy night with thunder sounding in the background? When the tone is the result of the setting, the descriptive adjectives might relate more to a general mood (mysterious, ominous).

A writer's perspective:

Once again, consider a memorable event in your life as a potential autobiographical topic. Develop an outline and ask yourself the question, "What is my attitude toward the readers of this proposed essay?" Also, what is your attitude toward the subject of the essay? For example, if your essay is to recount an automobile accident in which your car was hit by a car driven by an intoxicated driver, you might ask, "What is my attitude toward drinking and driving?" Once you have established your attitudes toward your readers and toward the subject, develop a list of ways that you can present the characters (actions and dialogue), events, and setting of your biographical essay to set a tone that will reflect these attitudes.

A discussion question: Can the element of tone be overused or misused? What is the result?

CHARACTER. (Review pages 145–148)
Practice test questions:
(Based on "An Encounter with Honey Bees")

13. In the third paragraph, bees are characterized as

  (A) innocent victims
  (B) fascinated obsessions
  (C) productive companions
  (D) mysterious friends
  (E) charismatic enemies

14. The bee attack is characterized as

  (A) a personal vendetta
  (B) a frivolous exchange
  (C) resistance to authority
  (D) an agonizing accident
  (E) defiant resistance

15. By the end of the selection, the writer implies that she prioritizes

  (A) complacency over struggle
  (B) lenient attitudes over restrictive responses
  (C) bravery over caution
  (D) a personal vendetta over national interests
  (E) education over reactionary measures

Your own comprehension questions:

Using the autobiographical selection you made at Level 2 of this activity, write two or more questions that test the writer's use of CHARACTER.

Have your group develop a personality profile of the writer. List and describe the author's:

  a. Attitudes (as already discussed)
  b. Emotions
  c. Response mechanisms
  d. Intrinsic values

(In writing this profile, why do you need to keep historical perspective?)

Next, examine how the writer reveals his or her character (pages 149–157 of this book). Give examples, if any, of the writer's use of each of the following:

  a. Stereotyping
  b. Exposition
  c. Actions
  d. Words
  e. Thoughts
  f. The words of others about the writer (or their actions toward him or her)
  g. The setting

Based on the personality profile and character examination, you can now ask a wide range of character questions.

A writer's perspective:

Autobiographical writing is very revealing of the character of the writer. How would you characterize yourself?

USE OF LANGUAGE. (Review pages 165–192)
Practice test questions:
(Based on "An Encounter with Honey Bees")

16. In the first paragraph, "killer" symbolizes

  (A) efforts to exterminate wild honey bees
  (B) the bees' courage
  (C) the higher-than-normal toxicity of the bees' poison
  (D) the bees' vicious nature
  (E) the degree of pain inflicted by the bees

17. In the sixth paragraph, the literary device used in "the seething balloon of bees" is a

(A) metaphor
(B) simile
(C) metonymy
(D) personification
(E) symbol

18. In the fifth paragraph, the "shot-like blast" performs which of these roles?

 I. Descriptive simile
 II. Alliterative illustration
 III. Onomatopoeic description

(A) I only
(B) II only
(C) I and II only
(D) II and III only
(E) I, II, and III

Your own comprehension questions:

Using the autobiographical selection you made at Level 2 of this activity, write two or more questions that test the writer's USE OF LANGUAGE.

Examine each line of the selection and make a list of the uses of language, especially: (Use the index to find the meanings of these terms.)

Analogy	Personification
Simile	Allusion
Metaphor	Symbols
Hyperbole	Irony
Meiosis	Paradox

Also, examine the writer's use of diction. As you write the questions, do not limit them to identifying what types of figurative language are being used. Include questions about the effects of their use.

A writer's perspective:

We routinely hear comparisons made all around us: The friend who is "stubborn as a mule"; the child who is "gentle as a dove"; the "acid-tongued" co-worker; the person who is "rock-solid" in a crisis. In preparation to write an autobiographical essay about some important event in your life, what simile/metaphor can you think of that would best describe you in that situation? If you were to use that figurative language in your essay, what impression about you as a person do you think its use might give the reader?

MEANING(S) IN CONTEXT. (Review pages 193–206.)
Practice test questions:
   (Based on "An Encounter with Honey Bees")

19. "I remained in shock for hours" (paragraph seven) is connotative of all the following EXCEPT

(A) a concussion from a violent blow
(B) great surprise
(C) the effects of the poison
(D) extreme pain
(E) the violent nature of the attack

20. In its context, "smoke" in paragraph nine means which of these three definitions?

 I. A cigarette
 II. Fumes
 III. Something without value

(A) I only
(B) II only
(C) III only
(D) I and II only
(E) I, II, and III

21. "Presence of mind" in the sixth paragraph can also be paraphrased as

(A) daydreaming
(B) mental dignity
(C) an anticipatory response
(D) a flashback
(E) quick thinking

Your own comprehension questions:

Using the autobiographical selection you made at Level 2 of this activity, write two or more questions that test the writer's use of MEANING(S) IN CONTEXT.

Context is very important to determining the meaning of a word, phrase, or line, especially when the selection was written in another historical period.

Going through the account line-by-line, examine the words, phrases, and lines for their obvious meanings and then see if any implied meanings are carried with them. When you write your questions, be sure to include questions in which:

   a.   Answer choices are paraphrases of the selected word(s).

b. Answer choices require selection of the correct implication(s).

c. The uses of a given statement are examined (such as, [the phrase or line] was used as a summary, or it was used as a generalization).

d. The multiple meanings of the word(s) are given, requiring selection of the one correct meaning in context (or perhaps the one incorrect meaning, given the context).

e. The connotative meaning is required.

A writer's perspective:

A clear understanding of the writer's intended meanings of the words he or she uses is vital to effective communication. Therefore, a writer is faced with two possibilities:

1. Select words that he or she is certain can be understood by the intended readers, and/or

2. Provide contextual clues that will help the reader to discover what unfamiliar words mean. What guidelines can you use, as a writer, to determine which option is better when writing an essay?

Follow-up Activities

LEVEL 1. PRACTICING ANSWERING TEST QUESTIONS

Answer Key to Questions based on "An Encounter with Honey Bees"

1. C	8. A	15. E
2. B	9. B	16. D
3. D	10. D	17. A
4. C	11. B	18. E
5. A	12. B	19. A
6. E	13. C	20. B
7. E	14. D	21. E

LEVEL 2. WRITING YOUR OWN READING COMPREHENSION QUESTIONS

In group discussion, select the best three practice questions for each of the seven literary elements that you have written individually for the autobiographical selection that you have chosen. Present your 21-question practice test to your literature teacher for evaluation and comment.

LEVEL 3. DEVELOPING A WRITER'S PERSPECTIVE

Finally, you may want to consult an elementary teacher in your community to see if he or she is teaching a subject for which you could write a teaching-style autobiographical sketch to share with the students. For example, if the subject is basketball, you might write your sketch about how you learned to play basketball; and you might include some exciting or interesting incidents that have happened to you in connection with playing the game.

By working with the teacher and gaining feedback from the students, you could gain experience in applying autobiographical writing to a specified purpose. More to the point, the process of autobiographical writing from a teaching perspective should motivate you to research the subject of your experience so that you can incorporate ("teach") facts and concepts in your writing. The process of this research and subsequent writing will give you experience in developing reading comprehension skills in preparation for taking the SAT II: Literature test.

WRITING TO LEARN— YOUR TURN

The purpose of this book is to help you develop a study program that will improve your performance on the SAT II: Literature test.

The purpose of the Writing to Learn Training Exercises of this section is to impress upon you that improving your writing skills by making highly motivating writing exercises a part of your individual study plan can be an effective way to improve your reading comprehension skills as measured by the SAT II: Literature test.

The scope of this book is not large enough to contain examples of all the different ways a Writing to Learn Exercise can be done. By this point, however, you should be able to see a pattern in the Writing to Learn Exercises. By following this pattern as a guideline and by individualizing it to suit your personal study plan, you should be able to develop your own Writing to Learn Exercises that will be the most effective for you.

Sample Writing to Learn Pattern

Writing to Learn___(major genre)_____:

___(literary form)_____.

    Example: Writing to Learn Nonfiction: the essay.

I. PREWRITING REVIEW

What is___(literary form,_____

e.g. an essay)_____?

A. *Reread* the appropriate section of this book and any other resources available to you, including the dictionary, to establish a basic definition of the literary form.

B. *Ask your librarian* to help you find a wide range of literary examples for you to read. At the prewriting stage, read just for pleasure, allowing yourself the luxury of enjoying the literary form.

C. *Develop a list of major points* concerning the literary form. Using reference books and books on writing, develop a list of five or more significant points dealing with your literary form. For example, look for "how-to-write" books to give you tips concerning what to avoid or what to emphasize. What formats are used in this particular literary form? Has it changed over the years? How?

D. *Make the literary form your own.* How can you relate to your proposed writing project on an individual basis? Is there any way you can identify with the writing so that it will speak to you as a person? Make a list of questions that you need to answer for yourself as you do your prewriting research. What is your favorite type of reading? How do you relate to what you read? How might that influence how you write?

E. *Examine your options.* A man was interviewed on a major television program recently. He had use of only one arm and could not walk, yet he played the guitar beautifully and could play golf. Asked his philosophy of life, he said that when faced with difficulties, he does not say "I can't." Instead he asks himself, "If I can't do it this way, how else CAN I do it?" He looked for options, alternatives, the individual way.

Tip: No where will you find any more options than in writing. The secret is to discover them.

II. MOTIVATORS

Ask your study group, teachers, and librarians to help you develop a list of Motivators that will increase your personal involvement in studying to take the SAT II: Literature test. These Motivators should stimulate you to utilize the seven literary elements and higher-level reading comprehension skills by giving you opportunities to view them from a writer's perspective.

Examples:
- Writing contests
- Special classroom assignments
- Articles to submit for publication
- Family journals
- Children's stories/plays for school, library, and classes
- Letters to the editor
- School newspaper articles
- Poetry for special purposes, greeting cards, public readings

Decide upon a Motivator and select a subject that interests you (within the guidelines of the Motivator). Choose one you already know something about and are able to research adequately. Look around for those opportunities that are available to you.

III. ACTIVE LEARNING NOTES

When do you actually write your manuscript? You might want to write without restriction, then develop the Active Learning Notes during revision. You could write your manuscript and Active Learning Notes as a simultaneous process. Another option is to use your Active Learning Notes as a writing plan.

Regardless, in your Active Learning Notes, you should determine how the seven literary elements function in the type of writing that you have proposed to do. You might address each literary element individually, posing and answering for yourself questions that are relevant to the work. You might decide to take a less structured approach; however, keep in mind that you need to develop a consciousness of the literary elements as they are tested by the SAT II: Literature test.

From this point, the sample Writing to Learn Training Exercises will be in the form of suggestions and ideas for you to individualize to your own study plan.

Motivator #1. Write a family history to give as a gift to your parents.

Motivator #2. Write your life story for your future grandchildren.

Motivator #3. Write a real-life personal adventure narrative to submit to a publisher.

Tip: There are many books available today specifically written about writing one's own life story. Check in the current issue of *Books in Print* for new titles and ask your librarian to help you locate books that are considered helpful on the subject.

Active Learning Notes
Begin writing your article and consider the following:
Learn to recognize the uses of the seven literary elements in your own writing so that you can identify them in the writing of others.

Suggestions and tips:
1. Be sure that you do have a purpose statement.
2. Identify your audience so that you know what style of writing is most effective, what tone to use, and so forth.
3. You have great flexibility in form, but be consistent. Work closely with and expand your outline as needed.
4. The voice in autobiography is obvious; to what degree do you want your readers to recognize your voice?
5. Describe your attitudes and anticipated tone.
6. Anticipate ways to project and reveal character. Decide what life incidents best suit the purpose. Do not forget the secondary characters.

For Group Discussion: Have you ever said something and had your listener read more into it than you meant? Do you think we ever credit writers with figurative meanings that they did not consciously intend? What about connotative word choices? Are writers sometimes unaware that what they are writing is emotionally charged for some readers?

Training Exercise Series C

WRITING TO LEARN FICTION: THE SHORT STORY

Prewriting Review
Suggestions and tips:
1. Begin with a definition.
2. Because writing is a process, look for clues in short stories themselves as to how the writers developed their stories. Learning to identify organizational patterns in the writing of others will help you to develop cognitive skills that are tested by the SAT II: Literature test and that are important to your own writing ability.
3. Look for books that analyze short stories, but also look for books on how to write short stories.
4. Make a list of what elements go together to make a short story, such as powerful characters and so forth.
5. Short stories—what does this length restriction mean and what effect will it have on the short story's elements?

For Group Discussion: How do you know when a short story should end?

Motivators
Suggestions and tips:
1. Enter a short story contest.
2. Get permission to write a children's short story to share with the first graders in your neighborhood school.
3. Find a magazine that accepts short story submissions.
4. Write a seasonal short story to submit to your church or favorite organization's newsletter.

For Group Discussion: Add to this list of motivators.

Active Learning Notes
Suggestions and tips:
1. Think carefully about tense (past, present) and what person (first, third—or, extremely rare, second person) to write in.
2. Think carefully about intent: what do you want your reader to come away with after reading this story and what literary elements can best help you achieve this effect?
3. Do not forget the role of conflict.
4. Plot has structural parts. What about unity? How can you achieve cohesiveness in your story?
5. Focus on motivation as your character develops.
6. Can you use implication effectively within the short story that you are writing? Are there any benefits to its use?
7. Can contrasts (in characters, people, places, and so forth) be used to further your purpose?
8. Does the story "feel" complete at the end?
9. What does each of your characters want? (Make a list.) How can events and circumstances interplay with the ideas on this list?

10. Work on dialogue—does it flow? Make a point? Move the action along?
11. Can you outline your story?

For Group Discussion: Does an awareness of the symbolic uses of language as the writer writes heighten or hinder his or her expression?

Training Exercise Series D

WRITING TO LEARN FICTION: THE NOVEL

The novel is a broad category. As you do your prewriting review, first study the elements of the novel in general, then focus on the elements of the type of novel (suspense, romance, mystery) that interests you the most.

Prewriting Review
Suggestions and tips:
1. Begin with a definition.
2. Compare and contrast potential plot structures of the short story with that of the novel.
3. Again, look for books that analyze and for books that instruct ("how to write").
4. Discover book plus analysis sets, for example, you might read the novels of Charles Dickens, then read Doris Alexander's *Creating Characters with Charles Dickens,* a book that deals with how Charles Dickens pulled ideas for his characters from real life in *Bleak House, David Copperfield,* and other works.
5. Look in your local and school libraries for critical editions of books. Critical editions contain the actual literary work, then often include such helpful information concerning that work and its author as letters and commentaries written by the author. Also, they may include criticism and commentaries written by scholars and critics concerning the work and the author in relation to the work.

   Reading the reviews, letters, and so forth, that are part of critical editions can help you gain insight into the elements that work together to make a work of literature, whether in your own writings or in the works of others. Critical editions can be helpful in developing the higher level comprehension skills that are tested by the SAT II: Literature test. These books help you to compare your own understanding of literature with that of experts in the field of literary criticism and with the authors themselves.

6. Review methods to deal with long periods of time and expanses of space, as well as setting transitions.
7. Look into novels of one hundred years ago. How do they differ from those written today?
8. Search for articles written by your favorite authors in which they discuss their craft. Look for their autobiographies, also.
9. How does a narrator construct a story-line? Here are a few hints:
   a. Look into events and how they are related to one another.
   b. Look into scenes and how logical transitions are achieved.
   c. Look into characters and their relationships to
      (1) one another,
      (2) their environment, and
      (3) themselves.
10. Look into cause-and-effect relationships.

Motivators
Suggestions and tips:
1. Investigate novel contests, such as the Ernest Hemingway First Novel contest. (See *Writer's Market* for more information about contests.)
2. Develop a plot for a genre novel, such as a mystery or historical romance.
3. Write a novel for children or teenagers. Submit it to your school faculty for evaluation and/or enter it in a related contest, such as the Milkweed Prize for Children's Literature.

THE ELEMENT OF TIME
In Writing to Learn, writing is a study tool used to increase performance on the SAT II: Literature test. Consequently, when Writing to Learn the novel, a time-efficient approach might be to develop a Prewriting Review and the Active Learning Notes down to and including the outline for your novel. Write perhaps only one or two initial chapters to gain experience in recognizing and establishing setting, characters, dialogue, and other essential components of the literary elements.

If you choose to write an outline and sample chapters for your own novel, keep them in your portfolio and do not throw them away. These developmental writing stages are useful for comparison in self-evaluation of your progress in later works.

Active Learning Notes
Suggestions and tips:
1. Can you sum up your story idea in one sentence?

2. Organize your outline/plot line:

   a. Can you divide the plot into meaningful scenes?

   b. Which scenes would you consider to be major?

   c. Does your main character reach a point at which he or she comes to discover some hidden truth?

   d. Does your main character suffer a misfortune or enjoy an unexpected upturn?

   e. What is your climax?

3. You may not want your story to be continuous conflict or excitement; give your readers some down time to create emotional contrasts.

4. Can you effectively incorporate flashback?

5. Do you use summary (panoramic) techniques? See page 114 and check for effectiveness.

   Review: The scenic method contains actions/dialogue that speaks for itself; the narrator tells the reader *about* scenes in summary techniques.

6. How are you telling the story—what person (first or third)? Why are you using that person? Is your narrator omniscient in your story? Why or why not?

7. List your major and minor characters and identify goals, motivations, plot twists, and changes.

EXAMPLE:

   CHARACTER: John

   CHARACTER'S MAIN GOAL: To be company president

   CHARACTER'S MOTIVATION: Motivated by greed

   WHAT HAPPENS?   Becomes president,

   PLOT TWISTS?   but loses family

   CHANGES IN CHARACTER: Realizes mistake and gives up job to regain family

For Group Discussion: The above example is very stereotypical. How could you change John's motivational chart to be more interesting/unexpected?

Develop charts such as the one suggested to help you spot stereotypes, stale plot lines, unbelievable situations, and other problems in your story.

8. Can you write a sociological profile of your main character? The major supporting characters?

9. List and define the cause-and-effect relationships in your story.

10. Examine your setting:

   a. Describe its effect on the tone and atmosphere of the story.

   b. Describe its role in the plot development.

   c. Determine if and how it affects character development.

11. How are you going to reveal the setting to your readers? How can you engage sensory impressions to heighten the effects of the setting on your story line, character development, and (ultimately) on your reader?

12. How do your characters react to the setting?

13. Examine dialogue—isolate and check it against:

   a. Character (educational background, attitudes, and so forth)

   b. Plot line (e.g., Is the dialogue logical for the events happening?)

   c. Setting (Regional dialects)

14. For each portion of dialogue, can you establish the purpose it serves in the story? Does it reveal character, build suspense, give the reader information, establish relationships?

15. Is a subplot workable in your story?

16. What is the biography of your main character? (date and place of birth, education, parents, major relatives, job, hobbies)

17. Look at your first (or sample) chapter that you have written. What details have you included? (specific model car, description of office clutter, and so forth) Can each be justified?

POETRY AND DRAMA

The Training Exercises for prose were designed to help you gain experience in the Writing to Learn method. These same principles and procedures can also be utilized to develop training exercises for the other two major genres that are the focus of the SAT II: Literature test: poetry and drama.

The following is a very brief discussion of some of the major considerations that are involved when you develop Prewriting Reviews, Motivators, and Active Learning Notes—first in poetry, then drama.

You might find that the most difficult aspect of developing your study program is narrowing your Writing to Learn Exercise down to a realistic focus. You want to learn as much as possible about the genre and those literary elements that work together within it; however, you have a busy schedule that means you do not have time to take diversionary side-trips down roads that do not lead to accomplishing your goals (improving your skills in preparation for taking the SAT II: Literature test). As a result, you might find the discussions under Writing to Learn Poetry and Writing to Learn Drama helpful in focusing your exercises on preparing to take the SAT II: Literature test, making them a manageable part of your study plan.

Writing to Learn Poetry

PREWRITING REVIEW

One purpose of the Prewriting Review of poetry is to help you establish an understanding of poetry from an overview perspective. Consequently, you may want to begin with a study of poetry in general, both with reading the poetry of others and with surveying the "how-to-write poetry" books that are available.

As you are reading and taking notes to gain greater insight into poetry as a literary form, you should be constantly alert to the types of poetry that stir your emotions and intellect on a personal level. Perhaps you are drawn to the serious nature of some poetic forms. Do you see poetry as a means to express sentiment? You may enjoy light verse that has a more general appeal. Do you enjoy the structure of regular rhythm and rhyme patterns, or do you prefer free verse (see pages 76–84)? To what purposes can you envision your own poetry being used?

You can be making these types of decisions and observations as you are developing your Prewriting Review. First, the review will be very general in nature, then will become more focused and specific to that form of poetry that interests you most.

In developing reading comprehension skills for taking the SAT II: Literature test, some would argue that poetry presents the student with the greatest challenges. This observation may be true. Because of its diversity of forms and heavy reliance on figurative language, poetry is much like art. Some art is traditional with defined lines and recognizable shapes, a reflection of reality, or at least what most people perceive as reality. Traditional poetry, with its regular rhymes and rhythms, has a certain comfortable sense about it. For the most part, we understand. Abstract art, in contrast, utilizes non-traditional forms that are subjective. An abstract painting, for example, might mean something different to each of five people viewing it—and none of their perceptions would accurately capture what was in the mind and feelings of the artist. This is the problem that readers encounter when trying to understand some forms of poetry. The expanded use of imagery and

form, with even the position of a single letter on the line carrying with it significant meaning, makes poetry challenging for those who develop test questions and for those who are faced with answering them. The question becomes "How can a student develop skills in understanding poetry?"

First, you need to gain as much experience as possible in reading and analyzing poetry. You may want to consider checking with your local poetry club. Consider making reading and discussing poetry a regular part of your study group's activities.

Secondly, develop your skills in writing poetry. Writing your own poetry will help you to expand your thinking, giving you a different perspective. In other words, one way to gain insight into what a poet means is to share the poet's writing experience. Gaining experience in actually using figurative language, different levels of meaning, can help you recognize those uses and levels in the writings of others.

Finally, become a language collector. Some people collect stamps, coins, or baseball cards. As you are preparing to take the SAT II: Literature test, you could collect language. Using your notebook, make a list of the language uses that you encounter as you read and listen on a daily basis. Listen and watch for symbols, metaphors, similes, personification—any uses of language that carry with them multiple levels of meaning. Make note of the words/phrases and all levels of meaning that occur to you. Pay attention to the circumstances in which the language is being used. Remember: words can change in meaning, both literally and figuratively, because of time, space, and usage.

1. Begin with definitions (blank verse, free verse, poetry vs. prose)
2. Examine poetic form. Include rhythm, rhyme, and physical form.
3. Examine poetic language. Include figurative language, diction, and effects.
4. Examine poetic meaning. Include voice, tone, and character.
5. Ask your librarian to help you select poetry collections from several different periods. Read and make observations.
6. Read poetry selections aloud, then make notes concerning the relationships of sound to meaning.
7. Perhaps not surprisingly, there is a large assortment of how-to books available aimed at the would-be poet. Compare the advice of these writers to the works of poets you enjoy.
8. Read biographies and "How I was moved to write"-type books by well-known poets. Do

they have any points in common? Diversities? How are these reflected in their works?

For Group Discussion: Investigate poetry as the expression of the writer's perceptions of life experiences. For example, Sidney had opportunity to, but did not, marry Penelope Devereux (the Earl of Essex's daughter) in 1575. After she became engaged to and married Lord Rich (thus becoming the Lady Rich) in 1581, Sidney decided she was his true love after all and wrote his Sonnet 24 ("Rich fooles there be"). How can modern poets find the means for such expression in their work?

Did I my lines intend for public view,
How many censures would their faults pursue,
Some would, because such words they do affect,
Cry they're insipid, empty, uncorrect.
And many have attained, dull and untaught,
The name of wit only by finding fault.
True judges might condemn their want of wit,
And all might say they're by a woman writ.
Alas! a woman that attempts the pen
Such an intruder on the rights of men,
Such a presumptuous creature is esteemed,
The fault can by no virtue be redeemed.
They tell us we mistake our sex and way;
Good breeding, fashion, dancing, dressing, play
Are the accomplishments we should desire;
To write, or read, or think, or to enquire
Would cloud our beauty, and exhaust our time,
And interrupt the conquests of our prime;
Whilst the dull manage of a servile house
Is held by some our utmost art, and use.

Sure 'twas not ever thus, nor are we told
Fables, of women that excelled of old;
To whom, by the diffusive hand of Heaven
Some share of wit and poetry was given....

from *Introduction*
by Anne Finch, Countess of Winchilsea, 1713

For a fascinating insight into one woman's view of the world of literary women in the early eighteenth century, look into the life of Anne Finch. Also, you might find the problems encountered by Anne Bradstreet, who found that critics claimed that she either stole her poetry or its quality was the product of chance (because she was a woman), interesting. Anne Killigrew, too, dealt with similar problems, as her "Upon the Saying That My Verses Were Made by Another" implies.

MOTIVATORS

As previously mentioned, you need to identify to what purposes your poetry is suited. Most poetry is written to be shared: in poetry collections, greeting cards, love letters, special magazine columns, posters, poetry readings, and so forth. Some poetry, however, is meant as a means of expression for the poet alone. The poem that is written as a private expression of one's own feelings can be a form of catharsis (emotional release) that is very motivating.

1. Enter a poetry contest.
2. Look into writing poems and concepts for greeting cards for friends and family.
3. Check into the latest edition of *Poet's Market* (Writer's Digest Books) for writing poems for publication in poetry collections and magazines.
4. Write poems for a special birthday presentation to parents, grandparents, siblings, close friends, or to share with shut-ins.

POETRY—COWBOY STYLE

The poetry readings of the twenty-first century have diversified considerably from those of yesterday. Although coffee-house readings are still probably featured in some areas, poetry readings now appeal to a much wider audience. Poetry clubs, local universities, or colleges have scheduled appearances by guest poets or have programs that feature local or student poets performing their works. Bookstores also sometimes invite published poets for book signings and readings. The public library may have poetry readings by poets reciting their own works or the works of others. Local poets are sometimes asked to read their poems to different civic groups or at community celebrations, such as Founders Day, if the event organizers are aware of the poet's availability and are familiar with his or her work.

One of the most interesting types of poetry readings is the cowboy poetry gathering. These readings are held throughout the West and Southwest. Sponsored usually by universities and civic groups or literary organizations, they feature "cowboys" who read for their appreciative audiences poetry about life on the range. These poets are people interested in the clothing styles, language, and mystique of the American West. For example, traditionally each year in late February, Sul Ross State University in Alpine, Texas, holds its "Texas Cowboy Poetry Gathering" in which "real working cowboys" perform their works. Such events also may include story-telling, symposiums on the cowboy lifestyle, and (perhaps the most motivating of all) a cowboy-style barbecue.

Occasionally, cowboy poets will travel upon invitation to readings held at universities and cities across the United States. However, cowboy poets also have published collections of their poetry available so that you can include their works in your study plan. Adding cowboy poetry collections to your reading will provide you with a unique American perspective, as well as an opportunity to explore the vocabulary and rhythms of the West. Check with your librarian for a current list of titles.

ACTIVE LEARNING NOTES

After your poem is written, examine how you have used the literary elements. Analyze them individually, but also try to determine how the literary elements work together within and throughout the poem to convey your meaning. Are you able to state this relationship in words? Do you see any cause-and-effect relationships of one literary element on another?

1. Establish subject and form (type of poem).
2. Do not overlook the dramatic monologue, letter poems, poems containing dialogue, and other such challenging forms as possible choices.
3. Examine your diction choices: concrete/abstract, word levels, and so forth. Do they achieve the effects on both meaning and sound that you are seeking?
4. How is inflection (changes in word form to make meaning changes, such as the changes of *I* to *me* or from *walk* to *walks*) at work in your poem? Would changes in inflection affect its meaning and tone?
5. Watch for the cliche, hackneyed expressions, and trite words in your poem. This is especially difficult in greeting card verse. FOR DISCUSSION: Is there a place for such overused expressions in poetry?
6. Examine the functions of your major word choices (nouns, verbs, adjectives, and adverbs). Think about their connotative meanings. Are you satisfied?
7. How have you incorporated imagery? Have you appealed to the readers'/listeners' senses?
8. Is your grammar and punctuation appropriate to the form? If you depart from standard conventions, can you justify the need to do so?
9. Is there an idea, level of meaning, association, or tone that you want to emphasize? How can you use figures of speech to attain this emphasis?
10. Decide upon rhyme scheme and meter, if applicable.

ABOUT RHYTHM

An alternative method to using accent marks (/X) when scanning poetry is to write the accented syllables in all caps:

There LIVED a WIFE at USHer's WELL.

You will often find this method in poetry textbooks and may want to use it when writing your own poetry. When scanning poetry that is already written on worksheets, however, you may find it to be less convenient to rewrite the poetry using caps than simply to mark the syllables. (See pages 77–78 of this book.)

Writing to Learn Drama

PREWRITING REVIEW

Television, movies, the stage, radio. Drama and its intended mode of expression are almost inseparable elements to the writer. With each mode of expression comes a separate set of considerations, a different legacy of time-honored guidelines mixed with the rigors of new technology, that must be addressed by the dramatic writer at the onset of the writing process. Without question, the Prewriting Review could include not just the expected overview of drama in general, but also could individually examine drama in all its phases (from idea conception to the post-production party) for each of its possible modes of expression. However, if your schedule is too busy, you may opt to forgo at this time the in-depth study of the major dramatic modes of expression.

A more convenient approach for you might be to scan the information available to you in your library, then move directly to the elements of drama that are examined by the SAT II: Literature test. You will want to focus on meaning, of course, and you will need to gain an understanding of how the dramatic form affects the meaning.

Suggestions and tips:

1. Scan how-to-write books about drama written for
   a. Television
   b. Movies
   c. The stage
   d. Radio
2. Just to increase interest, collect vocabulary, such as:
   a. cinema verité (a type of documentary film)
   b. documentary films
   c. script
   d. screenplay

e. cross-plot (a means to figure budget and schedule)

f. master scene

g. storyboard (part of preproduction)

3. Select one dramatic form, then research the behind-the-scenes activities that go into its production, especially how a drama begins with the writer and ends with performance.

4. What does a professional script look like? What is a synopsis and how does a dramatic writer use one?

5. What is an adaptation? (To gain experience, you might want to adapt your favorite children's story into a short screenplay.)

6. Describe the role and features of dialogue as it relates to drama.

7. Look into dramas written in the 1600s, 1700s, 1800s, 1900s, and today for comparison/contrast purposes. How has drama changed as time progressed?

For Discussion: What is the role of computer technology in today's drama? What are the consequences of this technology on drama as an art form? Examine each mode of expression individually (television, movies, and the stage).

Go to see a play/movie/television drama or listen to a radio scripted program and take notes identifying the use of the literary elements. Note the effectiveness of their uses.

MOTIVATORS

Writing drama is a far more diverse field than many people realize. In addition to the obvious field of television, movies, radio, and the stage, are the important areas of educational scripts written for multimedia classroom materials (including videotapes, cassettes, and even to a certain degree the dramatic elements of scripts written to accompany slide presentations) and business scripts written for training films, advertising, promotional films, and so forth. You can find markets for selling scripts in *Writer's Market* and other such publications.

Suggestions and tips:

1. Look for contests calling for drama.

2. Write a play for the children in your local elementary school and then, if permitted, work with the school in producing and videotaping it.

3. Write reviews of local dramatic productions for submission to your school or local newspaper.

4. Write an educational script for one of your classes.

ACTIVE LEARNING NOTES

By this point you should have accomplished a rather wide-ranging Prewriting Review and determined which type of script you will be writing and for what purpose(s). In no other form of writing is the relationship of focus to purpose any more significant than in scriptwriting.

Consider the following examples.

Script Purpose	Script focus
Cinematic screenplay	Heightened visual effects
	Action in scene form
Theatrical play	Character development
	Dialogue over graphics
	Theme balanced with conflict
Educational video	Balance of entertainment with teaching technique

Perhaps making a script-writing checklist for yourself will prove beneficial as you develop your Active Learning Notes. Using the key elements that you discovered to be significant to the particular type of script that you are writing, you might add to the checklist any factors of the literary elements that relate directly to the script.

Suggestions and tips:

1. Do you have a "hook"? See page 67.

2. Have you structured your plot to suit the medium?

3. Have you written an overview?

4. Write brief character sketches of each character in your play. Examine each character.

5. Develop a conflict chart that identifies premise, points of conflict, time elements, character reaction and interaction in relation to conflict, and conflict resolution.

6. Have you structured your scenes in relation to plot development as well as dramatic form?

7. What elements are you using to sustain unity within the drama?

8. How are you conveying time and place to the audience?

SECTION FOUR. WRITING TO LEARN TO PREPARE FOR THE SAT II: LITERATURE TEST

The SAT II: Literature test measures your skills in understanding British and American literature. One way to improve your skills is to learn to appreciate and understand the writing of others by experiencing firsthand some of the challenges that other writers have encountered. As previously discussed, this book is directly aimed at helping you to improve your reading skills in preparation to take the SAT II: Literature test. Incorporating Writing to Learn Exercises into your on-going study plan can be an effective way to make your preparation time more motivating and interesting. You will gain experience in using the literary elements in your own writing and learn to understand their uses in the written works of others.

THE SEVEN MAJOR STEPS OF A WRITING TO LEARN ACTIVITY

Step I

Organize an Active Learning notebook, containing:
1. Notepaper for the Prewriting Review and Active Learning Notes.
2. Loose paper holders for clippings, notecards, and photocopies.
3. Sectional dividers to enable you to separate and group activities.
4. Charts listing activities, timeframes, responses, and other bookkeeping/organizational purposes.
5. A portfolio section to contain clean copies of all writing in its final form. If it has been submitted to contests, editors, and so forth, be sure to include a cover page with each submission copy that you file in your portfolio. The cover page should note the name of the contest/editor/publication/teacher/school, date manuscript was submitted, the number of words, a brief synopsis of its contents, and any other relevant information.

Step II

Select a genre and the literary form within that genre that you would like to write.

Step III

PREWRITING REVIEW

Define: What is   (a narrative poem, for example) ?
Research and Review
1. The appropriate section of this book
2. Books about the literary form and about how to write the literary form
3. Books containing examples of the literary form
4. Autobiographical books and articles written by authors noted for writing literary works in your chosen form
5. Books and articles written about those noted authors

Make Notes
1. List the major features of the literary form.
2. Brainstorm ways you can establish a sense of ownership or a way to personally connect with the literary form.
3. Make a list of questions for yourself that need to be answered. Then do the research and conduct interviews with your teachers, librarians, and writers in your community (if available) in order to answer your questions.
4. Develop a list of options.
5. Analyze how each literary element is best used in that literary form.

Step IV

MOTIVATORS

Make a list of performance-based, high-impact potential Motivators that require you to write, using the literary elements as needed for the literary form that you are studying.

Step V

ACTIVE LEARNING NOTES

Develop your writing from preliminary outline or brainstorming notes to the final stage. Systematically establish, in note form, how each literary element should, can, and/or does function in your work. Developing your Active Learning Notes is a learning process.

Some professional writers argue that to analyze a work as it is written suppresses the writing process. To avoid this, consider doing your Prewriting Review and selecting your Motivator(s), then giving free expression to your writing before you develop your Active Learning Notes. Remember: The essence of your Active Learning Notes is experiencing how writers use the seven literary elements.

Step VI

Utilize Active Learning Notes, Stage One.

Using your Active Learning Notes and selections from your own writing or the writings of others, write a multiple-choice reading comprehension test based on the use of the seven literary elements that are tested by the SAT II: Literature test. Administer your test in your study group.

Step VII

Utilize Active Learning Notes, Stage Two.

Make final revisions in your work and apply it to your selected Motivator(s).

A few suggestions to consider before you submit a manuscript:

1. Secure and follow all rules.
2. Be sure that your work is original and complies with all rules and laws.
3. If the work is to be performed, secure permission and cooperation of teachers, parents, administrators, and authorities involved.
4. Be professional in your manuscript presentation: *Accuracy* counts. Pay attention to details. *Neatness* counts. Sloppy presentation detracts from the impression made by the work. *Communication* counts. Keep revising until you have achieved the communication that you intend.

Accomplish the Goal

By this point, you should have some ideas of your own concerning how you can incorporate Writing to Learn Exercises in your personal study plan. These types of activities are flexible, requiring as much or as little as you decide to invest in them; and they are versatile, allowing you to concentrate on those areas that interest you the most.

An added benefit to the program is the opportunity to:

1. Attend to detail
2. Learn to organize your own thinking
3. Develop research skills
4. Exercise self-motivation by selecting your own motivators
5. Translate theoretical study into real-life performance

The skills (organization, time management, self-motivation, dealing with pressure, research skills) that are a direct product of Writing to Learn are useful both in your academic career and in preparing to take standardized tests. More specifically, Writing to Learn provides a personally challenging and productive way to learn the seven literary elements that are tested by the SAT II: Literature test.

INTERPRETIVE SKILLS AND CRITICAL READING IN CONCLUSION

When you develop your study plan, keep the following in mind: the SAT II: Literature test is a skills test. Consequently, you need to prepare from two different, but related perspectives.

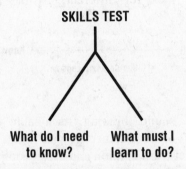

SKILLS TEST

What do I need to know?   **What must I learn to do?**

First, your study plan should clearly identify what information you need to know.

a. For the SAT II: Literature test, this foundation knowledge includes seven literary elements that are found individually and in combination within a written work.

b. Also, you should know the basic literary terms (listed on page 10) used by readers and writers when discussing literature. The reason for including terms (literary vocabulary) in your list of foundation knowledge is practical. Suppose, for example, you own an antique truck and plan to work on it so that you can enter it in an antique vehicle show. You begin working under the hood on its engine and find some parts are not working properly. You pick up the telephone and call or send an e-mail to someone knowledgeable for advice about truck engines. *If you do not know the names of the parts, how will you be able to ask questions and understand the answers?* Likewise, the basic literary terms allow critics, readers, and writers to discuss works of literature (for many different purposes) with some degree of common knowledge and understanding.

c. In conjunction with literary terms, obviously you need to have an extensive general vocabulary.

Second, your study plan should clearly identify what you need to learn to do (what skills you need to develop).

a. For the SAT II: Literature test, you need to learn to understand what you read. Specifically, you should be able to *recognize and explain* in a given British or American work of literature *what* is being communicated or said (the meaning) and *how* the meaning is being communicated.

b. Skill in identifying who is speaking, levels of meaning, tone, as well as the other literary devices is essential to your test performance.

c. As with any skill, once you have a fundamental concept of what is expected, you need to gain experience. Practice in a variety of forms, then, needs to be an important part of your study plan.

Part III (Interpretive Skills and Critical Reading) of this book provides tangible tools for you to use to develop the skills you need to improve your reading comprehension. The extensive definitions, discussions, and illustrations given on pages 57–206 for each of the seven literary elements will help you to *establish foundation knowledge* of many literary terms/concepts and their uses. Also, these pages can be used for reference in your future classes and activities. Putting the Seven Literary Elements to Work (pages 207–227) builds upon this foundation by guiding you in *practical application,* modeling three different ways to analyze the uses of the literary elements in works of literature. Writing to Learn (pages 228-268) provides the opportunity for you to learn to recognize and understand how the literary elements function in writing by *experiencing the role of writer* yourself. Combined, the three approaches given in Part III can be a major guide in your study plan. Finally, you can *gain experience in answering reading comprehension test questions* by working with the Practice Sets and Practice Tests that follow.

Your study plan should be a reflection of who you are as an individual; however, it should also include the recognized learning practices that work together to empower students to do their best, such as establishing a foundation knowledge of the subject, developing skills through practical application, gaining experience through working with different perspectives, and taking practice reading comprehension tests.

Some people view reading as a skill that requires a body of background knowledge. This is a logical view. To understand what you read requires a basis of background information and practice. In order to *excel* at understanding works of literature, however, you may want to add a new perspective to this idea: Reading is also an art that requires wisdom on the part of the reader. In other words, in addition to knowledge and practice, advanced readers learn how to make the best use of their skills and background information.

Your knowledge and experience are important to your understanding of anything you read, but knowing how to use them wisely can make a great difference in the degree of your comprehension. Here are a few suggestions to help you *aim for wisdom* in your approach to reading.

Wisdom ◄——————————◄◄ Knowledge
Make the first reading just for fun.

The first time you read a selection should be for enjoyment. Like the survey stage of a study program, reading the selection without interrupting the flow of your thinking with analyzing literary elements will help your mind adjust to the writer's style and the overall approach.

Knowledge ►►——————————► Wisdom
Read for meaning several times.

You can view a complex literary selection several ways in determining its meaning(s). Each time you read, look for different possible levels of meaning.

Wisdom ◄——————————◄◄ Knowledge
Use common sense.

Logic, sound thinking, reasonable thinking: regardless of the name, a wise reader distinguishes fact from opinion and uses good judgment in discerning the meaning and intent of what is written.

Knowledge ►►——————————► Wisdom
Be intuitive.

Sometimes an instinctive feeling can be a valid way to draw conclusions concerning what is being read. If the evidence to believe otherwise is not compelling or not there, maintain an open mind; but also consider your own intuitive feelings concerning the element.

Wisdom ◄——————————◄◄ Knowledge
Finally, remember reading really is fun.

Why are you pursuing literature as an area of interest? As you study literature, keep in mind the roles reading can take in our lives:

- companionship
- entertainment
- relaxation
- new ideas
- instruction
- mental challenges

Reading really can be an art based on wisdom, and being wise in developing your reading skills can help you to excel on the SAT II: Literature test. Also, you may discover that the more advanced your skills develop, the more fun reading will become.

PART IV

INTERPRETIVE SKILL PRACTICE

Diagnostic Test II:
Literature

Interpretive Skill
Practice Sets

ANSWER SHEET FOR DIAGNOSTIC TEST II

1. Ⓐ Ⓑ Ⓒ Ⓓ Ⓔ
2. Ⓐ Ⓑ Ⓒ Ⓓ Ⓔ
3. Ⓐ Ⓑ Ⓒ Ⓓ Ⓔ
4. Ⓐ Ⓑ Ⓒ Ⓓ Ⓔ
5. Ⓐ Ⓑ Ⓒ Ⓓ Ⓔ
6. Ⓐ Ⓑ Ⓒ Ⓓ Ⓔ
7. Ⓐ Ⓑ Ⓒ Ⓓ Ⓔ
8. Ⓐ Ⓑ Ⓒ Ⓓ Ⓔ
9. Ⓐ Ⓑ Ⓒ Ⓓ Ⓔ
10. Ⓐ Ⓑ Ⓒ Ⓓ Ⓔ
11. Ⓐ Ⓑ Ⓒ Ⓓ Ⓔ
12. Ⓐ Ⓑ Ⓒ Ⓓ Ⓔ
13. Ⓐ Ⓑ Ⓒ Ⓓ Ⓔ
14. Ⓐ Ⓑ Ⓒ Ⓓ Ⓔ
15. Ⓐ Ⓑ Ⓒ Ⓓ Ⓔ
16. Ⓐ Ⓑ Ⓒ Ⓓ Ⓔ
17. Ⓐ Ⓑ Ⓒ Ⓓ Ⓔ
18. Ⓐ Ⓑ Ⓒ Ⓓ Ⓔ
19. Ⓐ Ⓑ Ⓒ Ⓓ Ⓔ
20. Ⓐ Ⓑ Ⓒ Ⓓ Ⓔ

21. Ⓐ Ⓑ Ⓒ Ⓓ Ⓔ
22. Ⓐ Ⓑ Ⓒ Ⓓ Ⓔ
23. Ⓐ Ⓑ Ⓒ Ⓓ Ⓔ
24. Ⓐ Ⓑ Ⓒ Ⓓ Ⓔ
25. Ⓐ Ⓑ Ⓒ Ⓓ Ⓔ
26. Ⓐ Ⓑ Ⓒ Ⓓ Ⓔ
27. Ⓐ Ⓑ Ⓒ Ⓓ Ⓔ
28. Ⓐ Ⓑ Ⓒ Ⓓ Ⓔ
29. Ⓐ Ⓑ Ⓒ Ⓓ Ⓔ
30. Ⓐ Ⓑ Ⓒ Ⓓ Ⓔ
31. Ⓐ Ⓑ Ⓒ Ⓓ Ⓔ
32. Ⓐ Ⓑ Ⓒ Ⓓ Ⓔ
33. Ⓐ Ⓑ Ⓒ Ⓓ Ⓔ
34. Ⓐ Ⓑ Ⓒ Ⓓ Ⓔ
35. Ⓐ Ⓑ Ⓒ Ⓓ Ⓔ
36. Ⓐ Ⓑ Ⓒ Ⓓ Ⓔ
37. Ⓐ Ⓑ Ⓒ Ⓓ Ⓔ
38. Ⓐ Ⓑ Ⓒ Ⓓ Ⓔ
39. Ⓐ Ⓑ Ⓒ Ⓓ Ⓔ
40. Ⓐ Ⓑ Ⓒ Ⓓ Ⓔ

41. Ⓐ Ⓑ Ⓒ Ⓓ Ⓔ
42. Ⓐ Ⓑ Ⓒ Ⓓ Ⓔ
43. Ⓐ Ⓑ Ⓒ Ⓓ Ⓔ
44. Ⓐ Ⓑ Ⓒ Ⓓ Ⓔ
45. Ⓐ Ⓑ Ⓒ Ⓓ Ⓔ
46. Ⓐ Ⓑ Ⓒ Ⓓ Ⓔ
47. Ⓐ Ⓑ Ⓒ Ⓓ Ⓔ
48. Ⓐ Ⓑ Ⓒ Ⓓ Ⓔ
49. Ⓐ Ⓑ Ⓒ Ⓓ Ⓔ
50. Ⓐ Ⓑ Ⓒ Ⓓ Ⓔ
51. Ⓐ Ⓑ Ⓒ Ⓓ Ⓔ
52. Ⓐ Ⓑ Ⓒ Ⓓ Ⓔ
53. Ⓐ Ⓑ Ⓒ Ⓓ Ⓔ
54. Ⓐ Ⓑ Ⓒ Ⓓ Ⓔ
55. Ⓐ Ⓑ Ⓒ Ⓓ Ⓔ
56. Ⓐ Ⓑ Ⓒ Ⓓ Ⓔ
57. Ⓐ Ⓑ Ⓒ Ⓓ Ⓔ
58. Ⓐ Ⓑ Ⓒ Ⓓ Ⓔ
59. Ⓐ Ⓑ Ⓒ Ⓓ Ⓔ
60. Ⓐ Ⓑ Ⓒ Ⓓ Ⓔ

DIAGNOSTIC TEST II: LITERATURE

The purpose of this second 60-question diagnostic test is to:

1. Help you identify which critical reading skills based on the seven major literary elements need additional attention
2. Give you additional practice in working with the structure and format of the test
3. Enable you to understand the rationale behind "correct" vs. "incorrect" answer choices

As with Diagnostic Test I, use the provided answer sheet to record your answers. Allow yourself one hour to complete the test.

Be sure to read all directions carefully and do not use reference materials of any kind.

After you complete the test, use the Answer Key (see page 288) to check your answers and to determine your raw score. Then use the Analysis: Diagnostic Test II (see page 292) to help you evaluate your answer choices. Remember: This diagnostic test is intended both as a measurement instrument and as a teaching tool.

You will find immediately following the Analysis: Diagnostic Test II selections with accompanying questions. These practice set questions are grouped by literary elements and are intended to give you intensive practice in working with questions aimed at each of the seven major literary elements.

DIAGNOSTIC TEST II

<u>Directions</u>: The following questions test your understanding of several literary selections. Read each passage or poem and the questions that follow it. Select the best answer choice for each question by blackening the matching oval on your answer sheet. **Special attention should be given to questions containing the following words: EXCEPT, LEAST, NOT.**

<u>Questions 1–10</u> are based on the following poem.

> Art Thou Poor, Yet Hast Thou
> Golden Slumbers?
>
> Art thou poor, yet hast thou golden slumbers?
>   O sweet content!
> Art thou rich, yet is thy mind perplexed?
> _line_   O punishment!
> _(5)_ Dost thou laugh to see how fools are vexed
> To add to golden numbers, golden numbers?
> O sweet content! O sweet, O sweet content!
>   Work apace, apace, apace, apace;
>   Honest labour bears a lovely face;
> _(10)_ Then hey nonny nonny, hey nonny nonny!
>
> Canst drink the waters of the crispèd spring?
>   O sweet content!
> Swimm'st thou in wealth, yet sink'st in thine
>   own tears?
>   O punishment!
> _(15)_ Then he that patiently want's burden bears
> No burden bears, but is a king, a king!
> O sweet content! O sweet, O sweet content!
>   Work apace, apace, apace, apace;
>   Honest labour bears a lovely face;
> _(20)_ Then hey nonny nonny, hey nonny nonny!
>
>   by Thomas Dekker

1. The speaker views poverty as

    (A) an unlikely source of happiness
    (B) the only way to find happiness
    (C) not a deterrent to happiness
    (D) an unavoidable condition
    (E) an inspiration to wealth

2. Of the devices listed, the metaphor in line 16 has the effect of

    (A) hyperbole
    (B) meiosis
    (C) fallacy
    (D) oxymoron
    (E) onomatopoeia

3. The repetition of lines 7–10 in lines 17–20 suggests that this poem may be

    (A) a folk ballad
    (B) a hymn
    (C) a nonsense verse
    (D) an aubade
    (E) a song

4. For spring waters to be "crispèd" (line 11), they would be

    (A) very cold
    (B) undulating
    (C) unpolluted
    (D) stagnant
    (E) very calm

5. Line 13 is an example of which of the following?

    I.   Antithesis
    II. Paradox
    III. Antonomasia

    (A) I only
    (B) II only
    (C) III only
    (D) I and II only
    (E) I, II, and III

6. Structurally, what change occurs in line 15?

(A) Line 15 concedes the negative aspects of his premise.
(B) The speaker departs from the rhetorical question to summarize his point.
(C) It reverses the poem's theme.
(D) The speaker provides an answer to the questions posed in the first and second stanzas.
(E) Line 15 is a restatement of lines 5–6.

7. This poem is best seen as

(A) a condemnation of wealth
(B) encouragement to be poor
(C) an opinion concerning attitudes
(D) a nonsense verse lacking deep meaning
(E) a reproach against modern life

8. What is the TONE of lines 10 and 20?

(A) Dynamic
(B) Endearing
(C) Frenetic
(D) Learned
(E) Derisive

9. Lines 9 and 19 would indicate that the speaker is

(A) a happy, trustworthy worker
(B) an anxious person
(C) naive concerning work
(D) unrealistic in expectations
(E) unwilling to take work seriously

10. The contrasts presented in this poem do NOT include

(A) "poor" (line 1) and "rich" (line 3)
(B) "slumbers" (line 1) and "perplexed" (line 3)
(C) "labour" (line 9) and "lovely" (line 9)
(D) "laugh" (line 5) and "vexed" (line 5)
(E) "content" (line 2) and "punishment" (line 4)

Questions 11–16 are based on the following passage.

[a letter from an indentured female servant to her father]

Maryland, September 22nd, 1756.

Honored Father:

My being forever banished from your sight will, I hope, pardon the boldness I now take of troubling you with this. My long silence has
line been purely owing to my undutifullness to
(5) you, and well knowing I had offended in the highest degree, put a tie to my tongue and pen, for fear I should be extinct from your good graces and add a further trouble to you. But too well knowing your care and
(10) tenderness for me, so long as I retained my duty to you, induced me once again to endeavor, if possible, to kindle up that flame again. O dear father, believe what I am going to relate, the words of truth and sincerity, and
(15) balance my former bad conduct [to] my sufferings here, and then I am sure you'll pity your distressed daughter. What we unfortunate English people suffer here is beyond the probability of you in England to conceive. Let
(20) it suffice that I, one of the unhappy number, am toiling almost day and night, and very often in horse's drudgery, with only this comfort, that "You bitch, you do not half enough!" and then tied up and whipped to that
(25) degree that you'd not serve an animal. Scarce anything but Indian corn and salt to eat, and that even begrudged…Almost naked, no shoes nor stockings to wear, and the comfort after slaving during master's pleasure, what rest we
(30) can get is to wrap ourselves up in a blanket and lie upon the ground. This is the deplorable condition your poor Betty endures, and now I beg, if you have any bowels of compassion left, show it by sending me some relief.
(35) Clothing is the principal thing wanting, which if you should condescend to, may easily send them to me by any of the ships bound to Baltimore Town, Patapsco River, Maryland. Give me leave to conclude in duty to you and
(40) uncles and aunts, and respect to all friends.

Honored Father,
your undutifull and disobedient child,
Elizabeth Sprigs

11. The speaker's attitude toward her father is one of

   (A) evasiveness
   (B) contrition
   (C) contention
   (D) arrogance
   (E) aspiration

12. The speaker's words for her father to "believe what I am going to relate" (lines 13–14) reveal her

   (A) manipulative nature
   (B) complacency toward her father's feelings
   (C) resistance to her father's advice
   (D) naturally obedient character
   (E) change in character due to her hardships

13. What is the speaker's TONE?

   (A) Imposing
   (B) Impartial
   (C) Imploring
   (D) Impregnable
   (E) Impressionable

14. The main topic of the letter is

   (A) a cry for help
   (B) repentance for past sins
   (C) informing family of the situation
   (D) the unwillingness of the girl to come home
   (E) possibility of future communication

15. The "flame" (line 12) Elizabeth hopes to rekindle is

   (A) her "dutifullness"
   (B) her father's care
   (C) her father's anger
   (D) truth and sincerity
   (E) her own anger

16. Elizabeth "put a tie to my tongue and pen" (lines 6–7). What does this phrase mean?

   I.   Silence due to lack of writing materials
   II. Silence due to emotion
   III. Silence due to guilt
   IV. Silence due to illiteracy

   (A) I only
   (B) II only
   (C) III only
   (D) II and III only
   (E) III and IV only

Questions 17–26 are based on the following poem.

When I Consider How My Light Is Spent[1]

When I consider how my light is spent
Ere half my days, in this dark world and wide,
And that one talent which is death to hide
Lodged with me useless, though my soul more
bent
(5) To serve therewith my Maker, and present
My true account, lest He returning chide.
"Doth God exact day-labor, light denied?"
I fondly[2] ask. But Patience, to prevent
That murmur, soon replies, "God doth not need
(10) Either man's work or his own gifts; who best
Bear His mild yoke, they serve Him best. His
state
Is kingly. Thousands at His bidding speed
And post o'er land and ocean without rest;
They also serve who only stand and wait."

1. The poet was totally blind at about forty.
2. Imprudently

by John Milton

17. Line 9 contains a change in which of the elements?

   (A) Meter
   (B) Consonance
   (C) End rhyme
   (D) Mode
   (E) Imagery

18. The content of lines 1–8 contrasts with lines 9–14, but of the following, which is NOT a contrast?

    (A) Question and answer
    (B) Accountability and unaccountability
    (C) Resistance and acceptance
    (D) Self-interest and obedience
    (E) Impatience and patience

19. The phrase "my light is spent" (line 1), as used by the speaker, means which of these concepts?

    I.   Lack of understanding
    II. The poet's blindness
    III. Personal tragedy

    (A) I only
    (B) II only
    (C) III only
    (D) I and II only
    (E) I, II, and III

20. The rhythm and number of lines in this poem make it a

    (A) couplet
    (B) ballad
    (C) limerick
    (D) sonnet
    (E) haiku

21. Patience has an attitude toward "I" (line 8) that can be described as

    (A) indifferent
    (B) edifying
    (C) angry
    (D) resentful
    (E) patronizing

22. The central theme of the poem is that

    (A) to serve God is to be obedient in all circumstances
    (B) physical handicaps can limit service to God
    (C) the best service to God is to stand and wait
    (D) blindness has robbed the speaker of being able to serve God
    (E) the speaker is among thousands who serve God

23. What does "that one talent" (line 3) represent?

    I.   The natural abilities the speaker would use for God's service if the speaker were sighted
    II. The speaker's sight
    III. Hidden abilities that function despite the speaker's blindness

    (A) I only
    (B) II only
    (C) III only
    (D) I and II only
    (E) I, II, and III

24. "Light" (line 1) is in opposition to "dark" (line 2). This implies all the following opposing concepts EXCEPT

    (A) life and death
    (B) sightedness and blindness
    (C) good and evil
    (D) heaven and earth
    (E) knowledge and ignorance

25. "Day-labor" (line 7) can be paraphrased as

    (A) sighted service
    (B) work during the day
    (C) nine-to-five employment
    (D) physical work
    (E) work-for-hire

26. The indirect reference in line 3 to the "Parable of the Talents" in the Bible, in which the servant who buries his talent is cast into "outer darkness," is an example of

    (A) ambiguity
    (B) archaism
    (C) stock response
    (D) paratactic style
    (E) allusion

Questions 27–34 are based on the following passage.

"You have a tight boat, Mr. Barnstable," he said, "and a gallant-looking crew. You promise good service, sir, in time of need, and that

line hour may not be far distant."

(5) "The sooner the better," returned the reckless sailor; "I have not had an opportunity

of scaling my guns since we quitted Brest, though we passed several of the enemy's cutters coming up the Channel, with whom
(10) our bulldogs longed for a conversation. Mr. Griffith will tell you, pilot, that my little sixes can speak, on occasions, with a voice nearly as loud as the frigate's eighteens."

"But not to as much purpose," observed
(15) Griffith; "'vox et præterea nihil,' as we said at the school."

"I know nothing of your Greek and Latin, Mr. Griffith," retorted the commander of the Ariel; "but if you mean that those seven brass
(20) playthings won't throw a round shot as far as any gun of their size and height above the water, or won't scatter grape and cannister with any blunderbuss in your ship, you may possibly find an opportunity that will convince
(25) you to the contrary before we part company."

"They promise well," said the pilot, who was evidently ignorant of the good understanding that existed between the two officers, and wished to conciliate all under his
(30) directions; "and I doubt not they will argue the leading points of a combat with good discretion. I see that you have christened them—I suppose for their respective merits! They are indeed expressive names!"

(35) "'Tis the freak of an idle moment," said Barnstable, laughing, as he glanced his eyes to the cannon, above which were painted the several quaint names of "boxer," "plumper," "grinder," "scatterer," "exterminator," and
(40) "nail-driver."

"Why have you thrown the mid-ship gun without the pale of your baptism?" asked the pilot; "or do you know it by the usual title of the 'old woman'?"
(45) "No, no, I have no such petticoat terms on board me," cried the other; "but move more to starboard, and you will see its style painted on the cheeks of the carriage; it's a name that need not cause them to blush either."

The Pilot
by James Fenimore Cooper

27. Within the confines of the excerpt, the narrator is

(A) intrusive
(B) limited omniscient
(C) naive
(D) unreliable
(E) a participant

28. What type of language is used by Mr. Barnstable?

(A) Dialectal response
(B) A high level of diction
(C) Subordinating syntax
(D) Poetic diction
(E) Professional jargon

29. What is the subject of the conversation?

(A) An argument between Griffith and Barnstable
(B) The relative merits of ship armaments
(C) Strategies for the upcoming battle
(D) The intricacies of naming guns
(E) The major components of a war vessel

30. The relationship of Barnstable and Griffith is

(A) competitive
(B) antagonistic
(C) amiable
(D) discourteous
(E) ambivalent

31. The names of the cannons (lines 38–40) are

(A) euphemisms
(B) personifications
(C) anthropomorphisms
(D) epithets
(E) antonomasias

32. "Our bulldogs longed for a conversation" in the second paragraph is a vehicle in a metaphor describing

(A) hand-to-hand combat
(B) a gun battle
(C) a pit-bulldog fight
(D) a pre-war conference
(E) peace negotiations

33. Below are listed several definitions of "freaks." Which defines the use of the word in the phrase "the freak of an idle moment" in line 35?

   I. An abnormal thought
   II. Devoted to the thought
   III. A whim

   (A) I only
   (B) II only
   (C) III only
   (D) II and III only
   (E) I, II, and III

34. Based on his reaction to the exchange of words between Barnstable and Griffith, the pilot's style of leadership is based on

   (A) authoritative control
   (B) laissez-faire
   (C) group dynamics
   (D) chain of command
   (E) constant evaluation

Questions 35–42 are based on the following passage.

The lighthouse keeper said that when the wind blowed strong on to the shore, the waves ate fast into the bank, but when it blowed off
line they took no sand away; for in the former case
(5) the wind heaped up the surface of the water next to the beach, and to preserve in equilibrium a strong undertow immediately set back again into the sea which carried with it the sand and whatever else was in the way, and left the
(10) beach hard to walk on; but in the latter case the undertow set on, and carried the sand with it, so that it was particularly difficult for shipwrecked men to get to land when the wind blowed on to the shore, but easier when it blowed off. This
(15) undertow, meeting the next surface wave on the bar which itself has made, forms part of the dam over which the latter breaks, as over an upright wall. The sea thus plays with the land holding a sandbar in its mouth awhile before it
(20) swallows it, as a cat plays with a mouse; but the fatal gripe is sure to come at last. The sea sends its rapacious east wind to rob the land, but before the former has got far with its prey, the land sends its honest

(25) west wind to recover some of its own. But, according to Lieutenant Davis, the forms, extent, and distribution of sandbars and banks are principally determined, not by winds and waves, but by tides.

. . .

(30)   I heard of a party who went off fishing back of Wellfleet some years ago, in two boats, in calm weather, who, when they had laden their boats with fish, and approached the land again, found such a swell breaking on it, though there
(35) was no wind, that they were afraid to enter it. At first they thought to pull for Provincetown, but night was coming on, and that was many miles distant. Their case seemed a desperate one. As often as they approached the shore and
(40) saw the terrible breakers that intervened, they were deterred; in short, they were thoroughly frightened. Finally, having thrown their fish overboard, those in one boat chose a favorable opportunity, and succeeded, by skill and good
(45) luck, in reaching the land, but they were unwilling to take the responsibility of telling the others when to come in and as the other helmsman was inexperienced, their boat was swamped at once, yet all managed to save themselves.

. . .

(50)   The annals of this voracious beach! who could write them, unless it were a shipwrecked sailor? How many who have seen it have seen it only in the midst of danger and distress, the last strip of earth which their mortal eyes
(55) beheld. Think of the amount of suffering which a single strand has witnessed! The ancients would have represented it as a sea-monster with open jaws, more terrible than Scylla and Charybdis.

"Cape Cod"
by Henry David Thoreau

35. The imagery in the first paragraph makes the sea seem like a playful animal and the east wind like

   (A) driven sand
   (B) shipwrecked men
   (C) a thief
   (D) the undertow
   (E) a friend to the land

36. The first paragraph, in its entirety,

   (A) explains how beaches are formed
   (B) hypothesizes the causes of shipwrecks
   (C) relates the notion that wind and waves cause sandbars
   (D) reinforces the important role of wind to beach formation
   (E) describes the cyclical interplay of wind and wave

37. A significant factor presented in the first paragraph is that

   (A) the east wind blows onto the shore
   (B) the west wind blows onto the shore
   (C) sandbar formation is unrelated to winds and waves
   (D) winds blowing offshore carry sand away
   (E) surface water is heaped up by the west wind

38. "Scylla and Charybdis" in the last paragraph is a reference to

   (A) a special nautical term
   (B) sharks
   (C) mythology
   (D) marine vessels
   (E) anthropology

39. What is the purpose of the anecdotal episode in the second paragraph?

   (A) To illustrate the dangers of fishing
   (B) To entertain the reader without a significant point
   (C) To indicate the need for experience when boating
   (D) To illustrate the force of the water when it hits the sandbars
   (E) To sentimentalize the plight of people stranded at sea

40. The personification in the last paragraph indicates the speaker is

   (A) excited about the beautiful beach
   (B) contemplative of suffering
   (C) disgruntled toward the shipwrecked sailors
   (D) contemptuous of change
   (E) high pressured in changing the reader's attitudes

41. What do the words "voracious," "danger," and "terrible" contribute to the TONE of the last paragraph?

   (A) Scorn
   (B) Seriousness
   (C) Fear
   (D) Disdain
   (E) Outrage

42. As used in the first paragraph, "rapacious" means

   (A) forceful and greedy
   (B) tearing and destructive
   (C) cold and unrelenting
   (D) hot and gusting
   (E) vile and odious

Questions 43–49 are based on the following passage.

   A shrill sound of laughter and of amused voices—voices of men, women, and children—resounded in the street while this
line wine game lasted. There was little roughness
(5) in the sport, and much playfulness. There was a special companionship in it, an observable inclination on the part of every one to join some other one, which led, especially among the luckier or lighter-hearted, to frolicsome
(10) embraces, drinking of healths, shaking of hands, and even joining of hands and dancing, a dozen together. When the wine was gone, and the places where it had been most abundant were raked into a gridiron-pattern by
(15) fingers, these demonstrations ceased, as suddenly as they had broken out. The man who had left his saw sticking in the firewood he was cutting, set it in motion again; the woman who had left on a door-step the little pot of hot
(20) ashes, at which she had been trying to soften the pain in her own starved fingers and toes, or in those of her child, returned to it; men with bare arms, matted locks, and cadaverous faces, who had emerged into the winter light from
(25) cellars, moved away, to descend again; and a gloom gathered on the scene that appeared more natural to it than sunshine.

   The wine was red wine, and had stained the ground of the narrow street in the suburb of

(30) Saint Antoine, in Paris, where it was spilled. It
had stained many hands, too, and many faces,
and many naked feet, and many wooden
shoes. The hands of the man who sawed the
wood, left red marks on the billets; and the
(35) forehead of the woman who nursed her baby,
was stained with the stain of the old rag she
wound about her head again. Those who had
been greedy with the staves of the cask, had
acquired a tigerish smear about the mouth;
(40) and one tall joker so besmirched, his head
more out of a long squalid bag of a nightcap
than in it, scrawled upon a wall with his finger
dipped in muddy wine-lees—BLOOD.

The time was to come, when that wine too
(45) would be spilled on the street-stones, and when
the stain of it would be red upon many there.

A Tale of Two Cities
by Charles Dickens

43. What does this passage describe?

(A) A street riot
(B) An accident
(C) A political demonstration
(D) A protest
(E) A party

44. The last paragraph foreshadows that

(A) another wine game would occur
(B) wine will stain
(C) some people there would kill or be killed
(D) the people would be stained with wine
again
(E) blood stains more than wine

45. All the following characterizations can be used
to describe the people on the street EXCEPT

(A) destitute
(B) impulsive
(C) respited
(D) harrowed
(E) predictable

46. As a literary device, the man writing
"BLOOD" in wine on the wall is which of the
following?

I. Foreshadowing
II. A symbolic act
III. Dramatic understatement

(A) I only
(B) II only
(C) III only
(D) I and II only
(E) I, II, and III

47. Why does the speaker use the word
"cadaverous" (line 23) when he could have
used "pale" or "emaciated"?

(A) It connotes that these men are like the
living dead.
(B) It identifies that this is science fiction.
(C) It shows that they needed a break from
life's drudgery.
(D) It exaggerates the extent of the lack of
color of their faces.
(E) It emphasizes a sense of prose rhythm in
the line.

48. The genre of this passage can be identified as

(A) a character study
(B) descriptive narrative
(C) prose poetry
(D) an epic drama
(E) an epistolary novel

49. Of the list that follows, all can be used to
describe the TONE of lines 40–43 EXCEPT

(A) ironic
(B) comic
(C) deferential
(D) ominous
(E) expectant

Questions 50–55 are based on the following poem.

On This Day I Complete My Thirty-sixth Year

'Tis time this heart should be unmoved,
  Since others it hath ceased to move:
Yet, though I cannot be beloved,
  Still let me love!

line
(5) My days are in the yellow leaf;
  The flowers and fruits of love are gone;
The worm, the canker, and the grief
  Are mine alone!

The fire that on my bosom preys
(10) Is lone as some volcanic isle;
No torch is kindled at its blaze—
  A funeral pile.

The hope, the fear, the jealous care,
  The exalted portion of the pain
(15) And power of love, I cannot share,
  But wear the chain.

But 'tis not *thus*—and 'tis not *here*—
  Such thoughts should shake my soul, nor
    now,
Where glory decks the hero's bier,
(20) Or binds his brow.

by Lord Byron

50. Who is the speaker?

  (A) An impassioned lover
  (B) An aging paramour
  (C) A social outcast
  (D) A hermit
  (E) An unrequited lover

51. Love is characterized in the third stanza as

  (A) hostile to his needs
  (B) a fire out of control
  (C) an animal
  (D) unsatisfying
  (E) killing him

52. "The fire that on my bosom preys" is an example of

  (A) mixed metaphor
  (B) simile
  (C) caricature
  (D) *carpe diem*
  (E) apostrophe

53. The fourth stanza tells the reader that

  (A) the speaker is presently in love
  (B) love is more pain than pleasure
  (C) love is an escaped prisoner
  (D) love symbolizes unhappy emotions
  (E) the speaker plans to break free of love

54. What is the TONE of the first stanza?

  (A) Demoralizing
  (B) Defiant
  (C) Temerarious
  (D) Irresolute
  (E) Exacerbated

55. Of the definitions listed, all apply to "exalted" (line 14) EXCEPT

  (A) spiritually high
  (B) magnified
  (C) dignified
  (D) physically high
  (E) extolled

Questions 56–60 are based on the following poem.

What Sugared Terms

What sugared terms, what all-persuading art,
What sweet mellifluous words, what
  wounding looks
Love used for his admittance to my heart!
line Such eloquence was never read in books.
(5) He promised pleasure, rest, and endless joy,
Fruition of the fairest she alive.
His pleasure, pain; rest, trouble; joy, annoy,
Have I since found, which me of bliss deprive.
The Trojan horse thus have I now let in,
(10) Wherein enclosed these arméd men were
  placed—

Bright eyes, fair cheeks, sweet lips, and milk-
    white skin;
These foes my life have overthrown and razed.
Fair outward shows prove inwardly the worst:
Love looketh fair, but lovers are accurst.

                by R. Lynche

56. What does "she," as used in line 6, symbolize?

  (A) The woman he loves
  (B) Love
  (C) All women
  (D) Joy
  (E) His heart

57. What relationship do lines 13–14 have to the
rest of the poem?

  (A) They contain a reversal in thought.
  (B) They introduce a fourth element of love's
treachery.
  (C) They summarize the speaker's sense of
disillusionment.
  (D) They intensify the promises of love.
  (E) They identify the object of the speaker's
love.

58. "The Trojan horse" in the CONTEXT of line 9
is a

  (A) magnificent animal
  (B) means of deception
  (C) military maneuver
  (D) famous beast
  (E) symbol of true love

59. "Sugared terms" (line 1) can be defined by
which of these paraphrases?

  (A) Beguiling enticements
  (B) Beautiful language
  (C) Sweet negotiations
  (D) Coated stipulations
  (E) Kind words

60. Which of the descriptions that follow is the
attitude of "I" toward "Love"?

  (A) Hostile antagonism
  (B) Humble contrition
  (C) Resistant pride
  (D) Optimistic anticipation
  (E) Vanquished resignation

ANSWER KEY: DIAGNOSTIC TEST II

Step 1. Score Your Test

- Use the following table to score your test.
- *Compare* your answers to the correct answers in the table:
- ✓ Place a check in the "Right" column for those questions you answered correctly.
- ✓ Place a check in the "Wrong" column for those questions you answered incorrectly. (For quick reference later, you may also want to circle the number of each question you missed.)
- If you omitted answering a question, leave both columns blank.

Step 2. Analyze Your Test Results

- *Read* the portions of the "Analysis: Diagnostic Test II" (analysis follows the scoring table) that apply first to those questions you missed.
- *Scan* the rest of the analysis for those questions you answered correctly. This analysis identifies the correct answer, the literary element tested by each question, and briefly discusses the answer choice(s).

Step 3. Learn from Your Test Results

- *Circle* the question number on the Answer Key Table (if you have not already done so)

for each of the questions you answered incorrectly. Which literary elements were these questions testing?

Obviously, due to the interrelated scope and definitions of the seven literary elements, many of the questions are actually testing more than one literary element. Consequently, these identifications serve only as a guide to areas to *begin* your study—to pinpoint "problem" areas and to make your study plan more effective.

- *Review* the seven literary elements.

For Further Help in Literary Elements:	See Page:
1. MEANING	61
2. FORM	69
3. NARRATIVE VOICE	110
4. TONE	126
5. CHARACTER	145
6. USE OF LANGUAGE	165
7. MEANING(S) IN CONTEXT	193

You may want to plan your study program by first working through the study materials provided in this book for those literary elements you missed on the test. You should, however, eventually *review all seven literary elements* as part of your complete study program.

ANSWER KEY: DIAGNOSTIC TEST II

Scoring			Literary Element Tested						
Right	Wrong	Answer	1	2	3	4	5	6	7
		1. C			*				
		2. A						*	
		3. E		*					
		4. B							*
		5. D						*	
		6. B		*					

ANSWER KEY: DIAGNOSTIC TEST II

Scoring			Literary Element Tested						
Right	Wrong	Answer	1	2	3	4	5	6	7
		7. C	*						
		8. E				*			
		9. A					*		
		10. C						*	
		11. B			*				
		12. E					*		
		13. C					*		
		14. A	*						
		15. B						*	
		16. D						*	
		17. C		*					
		18. B		*					
		19. E							*
		20. D		*					
		21. B			*				
		22. A	*						
		23. D						*	
		24. D							*
		25. A							*
		26. E						*	
		27. B			*				
		28. E						*	
		29. B	*						
		30. C					*		
		31. D						*	

ANSWER KEY: DIAGNOSTIC TEST II

| Scoring | | Answer | Literary Element Tested | | | | | | |
Right	Wrong		1	2	3	4	5	6	7
		32. B						*	
		33. C							*
		34. C					*		
		35. C						*	
		36. E	*						
		37. A	*						
		38. C						*	
		39. D		*					
		40. B			*				
		41. B				*			
		42. A							*
		43. B	*						
		44. C							*
		45. E					*		
		46. D						*	
		47. A						*	
		48. B		*					
		49. C				*			
		50. E			*				
		51. E							*
		52. A						*	
		53. A							*
		54. B				*			
		55. D							*
		56. C					*		

ANSWER KEY: DIAGNOSTIC TEST II

Scoring			Literary Element Tested						
Right	Wrong	Answer	1	2	3	4	5	6	7
		57. C		*					
		58. B							*
		59. A							*
		60. E			*				

TO OBTAIN YOUR RAW SCORE:

_____ divided by 4 = _____
Total wrong   Score W

_____ minus _____ = _____
Total right   Score W   Score R

Round Score R to the nearest whole number for the raw score.

HOW DID YOU DO?

55–60 = Excellent
44–54 = Very Good
35–43 = Above Average
23–34 = Average
15–22 = Below Average

ANALYSIS: DIAGNOSTIC TEST II

NOTE: The scope and definition of each of the literary elements sometimes can differ among the literary critics (see discussion in Part II). As a result, the rationale behind what constitutes a correct or an incorrect answer also may differ. Many of the questions in Diagnostic Test II are testing your skills in more than one literary element. Also, each answer analysis might be viewed from more than one perspective. Consequently, this analysis should be used as only a part of your study program.

1. **C** Element 3 (NARRATIVE VOICE) Upon first reading, the best description of the speaker's view of poverty would seem to be answer B, the only way to find happiness. But does the speaker really assert poverty to be "the only way"—or even "an unlikely source" (A) of happiness? Why are the rich "perplexed" (line 3), "vexed" (line 5), and "in…tears" (line 13) while the poor have "golden slumbers" (line 1)? The state of poverty is not the source of happiness because the speaker admits in line 15 that the poor "want's burden bears." Nevertheless, despite this "burden" placed upon him by want, the poor has contentment (lines 1–2), patience (line 15), and "Honest labour" (line 9) making the burden "No burden." The attitude of the rich who are "vexed/To add to golden numbers" makes wealth a deterrent to happiness, but the contented attitude of those who are poor makes poverty not a deterrent to happiness (C).

2. **A** Element 6 (USE OF LANGUAGE) The speaker compares the poor to a king (a metaphor) in line 16. Although the poor may be in a happier emotional state than the rich, the comparison to a king is exaggerated—hyperbole (A).

3. **E** Element 2 (FORM) The poem cannot be a ballad because it is not narrative; a hymn because it is not religious; a nonsense verse because it has rhythm, logic, and does not have coined words; or an aubade because it is not about early morning. The repetitive lines do, however, suggest a lyric poem meant to be sung (E).

4. **B** Element 7 (MEANINGS IN CONTEXT) In the context, "crispèd" is the adjective form of the verb "crisp" that means the twisting movement associated with water that is swirling forth from a spring—undulating (B).

5. **D** Element 6 (USE OF LANGUAGE) Line 13 is a balanced sentence in which the conjunction "yet" establishes a contrast of ideas between two clauses of like grammatical construction (I). This antithesis is paradoxical (II) in that the person is swimming and sinking. Antonomasia is using a proper name for an associated idea—a figure of speech not applicable to line 13.

6. **B** Element 2 (FORM)

Stanza 1
Line 1 Rhetorical question
Line 3 Rhetorical question
Lines 5–6 Rhetorical question

Stanza 2
Line 11 Rhetorical question
Line 13 Rhetorical question
Line 15 "Then he…!"

Line 15 departs from the speaker's established structure of rhetorical questions, each of which is aimed at making the point summarized in line 15: The contented ("patiently want's burden bears") poor worker is without the vexation of the rich ("No burden bears").

7. **C** Element 1 (MEANING) This poem deals with attitudes. The rich are "vexed/To add to golden numbers, golden numbers" whereas the poor are contented and patient. It is this contrast in attitudes that establishes the MEANING of the poem, rather than a condemnation of wealth itself or than an encouragement to be poor. The speaker has implied a generalization, however, that the named attitudes are seen in the states or conditions of wealth and poverty.

8. **E** Element 4 (TONE) "Nonny" is a dialectal word that is used to call someone a simpleton—producing a derisive TONE.

9. **A** Element 5 (CHARACTER) This line has two possible perspectives: (1) the speaker may be personifying "Honest labour" as someone with a "lovely face" and (2) the

speaker may feel that someone engaged in "Honest Labour" will have ("bear") a "lovely face"—one that is smiling and happy. Either perspective or attitude is one of a happy, trustworthy worker (A).

10. **C** Element 6 (USE OF LANGUAGE) The poor: characterized as able to slumber, laugh, and be content. This is in contrast to the rich: characterized as being perplexed, vexed, and in punishment. The speaker characterizes "Honest labour" as "lovely."

11. **B** Element 3 (NARRATIVE VOICE) The attitude of this poor young woman is sorrow and penitence—one of contrition. She admits the wrongful nature of her actions several times (referring to her "undutifullness" and to her "former bad conduct"). She is by no means evasive either about her situation or about the hardships she must endure. Her letter shows no hint of contention or arrogance, and her only aspiration seems to be that her father will send her some clothing—a small thing in light of her deplorable situation. (Be sure to note the nonstandard spelling in this selection.)

12. **E** Element 5 (CHARACTER) Elizabeth, by her own admission, was undutiful and disobedient, a trouble to her father, and engaged in "bad conduct." Being beaten and starved has changed her CHARACTER in the sense that she admits the wrongful nature of her former conduct toward the person she is now imploring for help (E). Although some may think she is manipulating the situation (A), the deplorable nature of her current living conditions were too harsh to justify such suspicions; this girl is really in trouble—trouble, perhaps, of her own making—but trouble nonetheless.

13. **C** Element 5 (TONE) Answers B, D, and E are obviously incorrect; however, answers A and C are an opportunity for you to see how connotation can work in determining an answer choice. The reader can point to several lines in which Elizabeth implores her father for forgiveness, mercy, help; but does she not also impose upon him to send her clothes? In one sense this is true—she does place a burden upon her father to help her; however, the word impose carries with it the connotations of its other meanings, including cheating, taking advantage of others,

forcing others to do what one wants—all of which this young woman is in no position to accomplish. As a result, imploring (C) is the better answer choice of the two.

14. **A** Element 1 (MEANING) Considering her situation, Elizabeth would probably come home in a heartbeat if she could, making answer D improbable (and not supported by the passage). Answers A, B, C, and E are all possible; however, based on CONTEXT, how can you tell which answer is best? Look at the writer's purpose: why did she write this letter? She wants her family to know that she is in trouble, that she is sorry for what she did, and that they can "easily" communicate with her. She is providing them knowledge, emotional motivation, and the means to do something—she is crying for help.

15. **B** Element 6 (USE OF LANGUAGE) "Flame" is used metaphorically in this CONTEXT and is identified ("Your care and tenderness for me").

16. **D** Element 6 (USE OF LANGUAGE) The "tie to my tongue and pen" is the result of emotion ("fear") and guilt ("well knowing I had offended in the highest degree").

17. **C** Element 2 (FORM)
Line 9 marks a change in end-rhyme:

Line 1…spent	a	Line 9…need	c
Line 2…wide	b	Line 10…best	d
Line 3…hide	b	Line 11…state	e
Line 4…bent	a	Line 12…speed	c
Line 5…present	a	Line 13…rest	d
Line 6…chide	b	Line 14…wait	e
Line 7…denied	b		
Line 8…prevent	a		

18. **B** Element 2 (FORM) This two-part structure establishes several contrasts: (A) question ("Doth God exact day-labor, light denied?"—line 7) and answer ("God doth not need/Either man's work or his own gifts"—lines 9–10); (C) resistance ("my soul more bent"—line 4) and acceptance ("They also serve who only stand and wait"—line 14); (D) self-interest ("and present/My true account, lest He returning chide"—lines 5–6) and obedience ("who best/Bear His mild yoke, they serve Him best"—lines 10–11); (E) impatience ("When I consider how my light is spent/Ere half my days"—

lines 1–2) and patience ("They also serve who only stand and wait" —line 14).

Answer B, however, does not establish an accurate contrast. Although the first part includes the concept of accountability, the second part states that "who best/Bear His mild yoke, they serve Him best" (lines 10–11)—another view of being accountable, NOT unaccountable.

19. **E** Element 7 (MEANINGS IN CONTEXT) "Spent," as it is used here, can mean something being used up, worn out, tired out, or gone. "Light" can be symbolic of understanding (I), of vision (II), or of happiness (III).

20. **D** Element 2 (FORM) Sonnets are 14-line poems written in iambic pentameter.

21. **B.** Element 3 (NARRATIVE VOICE) Patience answers Milton's question to instruct him spiritually—edifying (B).

22. **A** Element 1 (MEANING) The central idea—the theme—of the poem is a statement that summarizes the main point of the poem. What is the main point Milton is making? Whether speeding "O'er land and ocean" (line 13) or standing and waiting (line 14), whether blind or sighted, the best way to serve God is to obey Him in all circumstances (lines 10–11).

23. **D** Element 6 (USE OF LANGUAGE) "And that one talent" (line 3) represents both natural gifts and abilities and sight itself that he would use in service, but both his sight and those abilities he would accomplish with and by means of his sight are "Lodged with me useless" (line 4).

24. **D** Element 7 (MEANINGS IN CONTEXT) In the CONTEXT of this poem, light comes to represent Milton's life ("Ere half my days"—line 2) as contrasted to a "dark world" of death, his sight itself as contrasted to the "dark world" of blindness, good (the means "to serve therewith my Maker"—line 5) as contrasted to a dark work of evil (that does not serve), and knowledge (understanding) as contrasted to the "dark world" of ignorance. Heaven and earth, however, are not suggested in this CONTEXT.

25. **A** Element 7 (MEANINGS IN CONTEXT) "Day-labor" is figurative, representing work or service (labor) that requires sight (day—the time when the sighted can see with the light).

26. **E** Element 6 (USE OF LANGUAGE) This is an allusion—mentioning either directly or indirectly some well-known (literary) work, event, place, or person.

27. **B** Element 3 (NARRATIVE VOICE) The passage is obviously taken from a larger work; however, in this excerpt the narrator is seen as limited omniscient because the narrator gives the reader insight into the pilot's mind, but not into the thinking of any of the other CHARACTERS.

28. **E** Element 6 (USE OF LANGUAGE) Barnstable uses the professional jargon (A) of a seaman: "scaling my guns," "the frigate's eighteens"—expressions indicative of a sailor who is used to high-sea battles.

29. **B** Element 1 (MEANING) Barnstable, Griffith, and the man identified as "the pilot" are discussing, in terms of performance, the various types of guns used on warships. Although the pilot does divert the conversation to the names of Barnstable's cannon, the focus is upon the relative merits of ship armaments (B).

30. **C.** Element 5 (CHARACTER) Their conversation might support the idea that these two men are competitive (A) or even antagonistic (B), but the narrator reveals that they have a "good understanding" between them, indicating that the banter between them is good-natured and that their relationship is amiable.

31. **D** Element 6 (USE OF LANGUAGE) These "expressive names" that describe "their respective merits" are epithets (D), nouns (in this case) that emphasize the predominant characteristics of something.

32. **B** Element 6 (USE OF LANGUAGE) "Bulldogs" is an epithet-type name for guns. The "conversation" that they long for is the exchange of fire with the guns of the other ship. This metaphor comparing a gun battle (the tenor) with a dog fight (the vehicle) also contains personification of the bulldogs/guns, thus making this also an example of mixed imagery.

33. **C** Element 7 (MEANINGS IN CONTEXT) The phrase "the freak of an idle moment" contains the contextual clue to the meaning of freak. Freak can mean all three of the listed definitions. It can refer to the abnormal (I) in a variety of circumstances. It can

also be a name used to refer to someone devoted to something (II), especially a hobby or a movie star. In this CONTEXT, however, the use of "idle moment," i.e., leisure time, indicates that these names are just whims (III).

34. **C** Element 5 (CHARACTER) Although he has misread the implications of the exchange of words between Barnstable and Griffith (he does not recognize their "good understanding"), the pilot does not command the men with authoritative control (A), refrain from interference as one would who subscribes to a laissez-faire philosophy (B), refer them to one higher in command (D), or point out their errors in thinking (E). Instead he attempts to "conciliate" the two men—using human relations within group dynamics (C).

35. **C** Element 6 (USE OF LANGUAGE) The speaker presents the east wind as "rapacious," sent by the sea "to rob the land" like a thief (C).

36. **E** Element 1 (MEANING) Note that the question specifies "in its entirety":

Wind blows on shore and waves eat into bank →
Wind blows off shore and no sand taken away →
Wind heaps up surface water at beach and undertow carries away sand →
Undertow meets own surface wave and forms dam →
Wave breaks over dam → a cyclical interplay of wind and wave (E).

37. **A** Element 1 (MEANING) Based on the opinion of Lieutenant Davis, the correct answer would be C if it were not for the word "unrelated" in that answer choice. Davis says that sandbar formation is "principally determined, not by winds and waves, but by tides"; he does NOT say it is unrelated. This type of question can be readily answered by using deductive reasoning. Answer A is supported by the following:

1. "…when the wind blowed strong on to the shore, the waves ate fast into the bank," and
2. "The sea sends its rapacious east wind to rob the land"; therefore,
3. the east wind blows on to shore.

38. **C** Element 6 (USE OF LANGUAGE) According to mythology, Scylla was a monster off the Italian coast and Charybdis was a monster in a Sicilian whirlpool. CONTEXT is essential to correctly answering this question: "ancients…sea-monster" (lines 56–57).

First, establish the context. The writer describes a beach (strand) where many shipwrecked sailors have died. He speculates that ancients would have called it "a sea-monster with open jaws, more terrible than Scylla and Charybdis."

The context does not support Scylla and Charybdis meaning "a special nautical term" because the comparison to a sea-monster makes them a reference to something alive. Sharks are alive and have open jaws, but the use of capitalization indicates that these are proper names. "Marine vessels" can immediately be eliminated because they are not alive and generally are not considered monsters. "Anthropology"—the study of mankind—is an obviously incorrect answer choice. The context and process of elimination leaves "mythology" as the correct answer: mythology includes ancient stories about monsters with proper names.

39. **D** Element 2 (FORM) The narrator is using an anecdotal episode to illustrate a point. The short narrative, itself, demonstrates a danger people encounter when fishing (A) and by means of contrast within the story demonstrates the need for experience (C); however, in the CONTEXT of the entire selection in which he is discussing winds, waves, and sandbars, he uses the short narrative to illustrate just how powerful the water hitting the shore can be—answer D.

40. **B** Element 3 (NARRATIVE VOICE) The speaker personifies the beach as both "voracious" and as the witness of suffering—both indicative of someone whose attitude is contemplative concerning the suffering caused by this particular strand.

41. **B** Element 4 (TONE) In isolation these words are indicative of elements that might cause fear (C) and perhaps outrage (E); however, in CONTEXT, they project the speaker's contemplative attitude when used within rhetorical questions and figures of speech to intensify the gravity of the subject and to establish a serious TONE (B).

42. **A** Element 7 (MEANINGS IN CONTEXT) "Rapacious" is an adjective used to describe the act of forceful seizure and the condition of being very greedy (A).

43. **B** Element 1 (MEANING) That this event is called a "wine game" eliminates answers A and D. Once the wine is gone, the people leave, conflicting with what might have been a demonstration (C). Is it a party (supported by the dancing) or is this event an accident—an unplanned happening because something has happened? The contextual clues support this latter view, especially because "these demonstrations ceased, as suddenly as they had broken out."

44. **C** Element 7 (MEANINGS IN CONTEXT) The speaker states in the last paragraph that "that wine"—blood—would stain "many there." How can the stain of blood "be red" upon someone? Either by being wounded oneself or by wounding (killing) someone else. Keeping in mind that for blood to "be spilled" refers to physical conflict/bloodshed/killing: the speaker is implying that some of the very people who had engaged in the "wine game" would eventually kill others or would perhaps be killed themselves.

45. **E** Element 5 (CHARACTER) These poor people are clearly destitute (A), underfed and in rags. That they are impulsive (B) is evidenced by "these demonstrations ceased, as suddenly as they had broken out." In their miserable condition, however, they are respited (C) by this brief episode with the wine somehow spilled in the street. The harrowing (acutely distressing) nature of their situation is readily apparent, but the one thing these people are not is predictable (E).

46. **D** Element 6 (USE OF LANGUAGE) The action of the man writing "BLOOD" in wine on the wall functions as foreshadowing of coming events, as evidenced by the final paragraph of this passage, and functions as a symbolic act on several different levels, such as:

1. A symbol of the emotional intensity that the spilled wine caused—mirrored in the spilling of blood
2. A symbol of the impulsiveness with which people can react to spilled wine or to spilled blood
3. A symbol of underlying bitterness of these poor wretched people, bitterness that could be given temporary respite by a moment of abandon when wine is spilled—or by a moment of abandon when blood is spilled

47. **A** Element 6 (USE OF LANGUAGE) Several of these answer choices are applicable; therefore, you need to evaluate the <u>best</u> answer choice. Where do you look to make this determination? CONTEXT. Where do these men with "cadaverous" faces come from and return to? They descend again into cellars—below ground—like corpses. They are alive, but their appearance is as the dead.

48. **B** Element 2 (FORM) The passage consists of a narrative episode (a crowd of people on the street rejoice over wine that has been spilled, then retreat to their previous activities) that uses very descriptive language, with special attention paid to diction.

49. **C** Element 4 (TONE) A man, slightly drunk with a baggy nightcap almost on his head would be a comic sight (B)—very ironic (A) in its contrast to the ominous (D) nature of the message he wrote—a message that leads the reader to expect (E) that a bloody conflict may well be ahead. The idea of yielding or submitting (C) is not an element of this act.

50. **E** Element 3 (NARRATIVE VOICE) The speaker's identity is revealed in the first two lines.

51. **E** Element 7 (MEANINGS IN CONTEXT) Because the fire (a vehicle for love) "Is lone" and "No torch is kindled at its blaze" (lines 10–11)—no one is caught by the sparks of his love—the love has become a self-consuming "funeral pile" (lines 12)—in other words, love is killing him (E).

52. **A** Element 6 (USE OF LANGUAGE) "Fire" is a vehicle for "love"; "preys" compares fire/love to a predator, hence a mixed metaphor (two or more vehicles for the same tenor).

53. **A.** Element 7 (MEANINGS IN CONTEXT) The speaker laments that he or she "cannot share" love, "But wear the chain" (lines 15–16). This implies that the speaker does have an object of affection—someone with whom he or she wants to "share" love.

54. **B** Element 4 (TONE) Despite the conclusion made in the first two lines, the speaker challenges the notion by defiantly proclaiming that although love is not returned, "Still let me love!" (line 4).

55. **D** Element 7 (MEANINGS IN CONTEXT) Hope, fear, jealousy, pain, power—these are all emotions, not physical attributes in this CONTEXT.

56. **C** Element 6 (USE OF LANGUAGE) "She" does indeed refer to the woman the speaker loves on a *literal level,* but the key to the symbolic use is in the <u>syntax</u>: "Fruition of the fairest she alive" (line 6)—"the fairest she alive" acts as the object of the preposition "of" with "the," "fairest," and "alive" modifying "she." In normal syntactical structure, this object would require a noun, not a pronoun. What noun could be the symbolic antecedent of the pronoun in this context? The superlative "fairest...alive" points to all women: the fairest woman alive.

57. **C** Element 2 (FORM) In traditional sonnet FORM, the rhyme scheme groups this poem's thoughts:

Lines 1–4   Love tricked the speaker.
Lines 5–8   Personified Love broke his promises.
Lines 9–12   The object of his love was a Trojan horse.
Lines 13–14 Love looks fine on the outside, but is not on the inside.

The speaker is disillusioned by love—the deceptive nature of love's appearance (C).

58. **B** Element 7 (MEANINGS IN CONTEXT) "Trojan horse" is a literary allusion (a USE OF LANGUAGE) to the battle over Helen of Troy in which a large wooden horse, filled with soldiers, was left as a "gift" before the enemy's gates. After the enemy brought in the horse, had a party, and fell asleep, the soldiers emerged from the horse and killed them. A "Trojan horse," in the CONTEXT of this poem then, refers to such deceptions that look fine on the outside but contain an enemy within. Even without being familiar with the story of Helen of Troy, you can determine the MEANING IN CONTEXT: The speaker has allowed in armed men (lines 9–11) that were placed in a beautiful body but who have overthrown and razed his life (line 12). The Trojan horse is a means of deception —answer B.

59. **A** Element 7 (MEANINGS IN CONTEXT) "To sugar" is a process by which something that is otherwise unpleasant is covered with sugar to make it more pleasant to consume. Love, to gain "admittance to my heart" "sugared," or covered with sweetness, "terms"—referring to conditions of agreement and also referring to words. Such "sugared terms" (line 1) are beguiling enticements, answer A.

60. **E** Element 3 (NARRATIVE VOICE) The speaker feels betrayed by "Love," but how does he react? You might expect him to be hostile (A), particularly after reading the description of what "Love" did to him, yet nowhere does he convey feelings of hostility. In contrast, he admits defeat (vanquishment) in line 12 and summarizes that "lovers" (among whom he counts himself) "are accurst" in line 14, giving voice to his resignation to the position in which "Love" has placed him.

INTERPRETIVE SKILL PRACTICE SETS

So far, this book has provided:

1. An introduction to the SAT II: Literature Subject Test
2. Some approaches and suggestions for developing a study plan
3. A diagnostic test and analysis aimed at introducing you to the test's format and aimed at helping you to identify your personal strengths and weaknesses
4. An item-by-item discussion and examination of the seven literary elements upon which the SAT II: Literature Subject Test is based, including some sample questions
5. A seven-step independent-study approach to practicing identifying the seven literary elements and their effects as used in literary selections
6. Models of analysis for an essay, a short story, a narrative poem, and a lyric poem to use to facilitate your practice
7. A second diagnostic test and analysis aimed at further isolating those skills that need practice

You may find that intensive practice in answering questions on each of the seven literary elements in an isolated format would be beneficial. The Interpretive Skill Practice Sets aim to give you that opportunity.

There are three Interpretive Skill Practice Sets (A, B, and C). Each set contains five literary excerpts or selections (two prose, two poetry, and one drama).

The questions are grouped in sets of five questions per literary element. You can use this intensive practice as an opportunity to practice all seven literary elements, or you may elect to practice just those literary elements that you find the most challenging.

As previously stated, the seven literary elements are very interdependent. As a result, labeling a particular test question as testing MEANING or as testing any other single literary element should not be construed to mean that the test question is testing only one literary element. In some cases a single question might actually have at its basis perspectives from several literary elements. Also, you will find that opinions may vary greatly among literary critics and analysts concerning interpretation and assignment of the literary elements, as to their effects and uses.

PRACTICE SET A

Selection One

"What have you there, Sam?"

"Called at the Post-office just now, and found this here letter, as has laid there for two
line days," replied Mr. Weller. "It's sealed vith a
(5) vafer, and directed in round hand."

"I don't know this hand," said Mr. Pickwick, opening the letter. "Mercy on us! what's this? It must be a jest; it—it— can't be true."

"What's the matter?" was the general inquiry.
(10) "Nobody dead, is there?" said Wardle, alarmed at the horror in Mr. Pickwick's countenance.

Mr. Pickwick made no reply, but, pushing the letter across the table, and desiring Mr.
(15) Tupman to read it aloud, fell back in his chair with a look of vacant astonishment quite alarming to behold.

Mr. Tupman, with a trembling voice, read the letter, of which the following is a copy:—

(20) Freeman's Court, Cornhill, August 28th, 1827.
Bardell against Pickwick

Sir,
Having been instructed by Mrs. Martha
Bardell, to commence an action against you,
(25) for a breach of promise of marriage, for which
the plaintiff lays her damages at fifteen
hundred pounds, we beg to inform you that a
writ has been issued against you in this suit,
in the Court of Common Pleas; and request to
(30) know, by return of post, the name of your
attorney in London, who will accept service
thereof.

We are, Sir,
Your obedient servants,
(35) Dodson and Fogg.

Mr. Samuel Pickwick.

There was something so impressive in the mute astonishment with which each man regarded his neighbour, and every man
(40) regarded Mr. Pickwick, that all seemed afraid to speak. The silence was at length broken by Mr. Tupman.

"Dodson and Fogg," he repeated mechanically.

(45) "Bardell and Pickwick," said Mr. Snodgrass, musing.

"Peace of mind and happiness of confiding females," murmured Mr. Winkle, with an air of abstraction.

The Posthumous Papers of the Pickwick Club
by Charles Dickens

Selection Two

Lusus animo debent aliquando dari,
Ad cogitandum melior ut redeat sibi.
—Phædrus "Fables," xiv. 5.

line The mind ought sometimes to be diverted,
(5) that it may return the better to thinking.

I do not know whether to call the following letter a satire upon coquettes, or a representation of their several fantastical accomplishments, or what other title to give it; but, as it is, I
(10) shall communicate it to the public. It will sufficiently explain its own intentions, so that I shall give it my reader at length, without either preface or postscript:

"MR. SPECTATOR:
(15) "Women are armed with fans as men with swords, and sometimes do more execution with them. To the end therefore that ladies may be entire mistresses of the weapons which they bear, I have erected an academy for the
(20) training up of young women in the exercise of the fan, according to the most fashionable airs and motions that are now practised at court. The ladies who carry fans under me are drawn up twice a day in my great hall, where they
(25) are instructed in the use of their arms, and exercised by the following words of command:—Handle your fans, Unfurl your fans, Discharge your fans, Ground your fans, Recover your fans, Flutter your fans. By the
(30) right observation of these few plain words of command, a woman of a tolerable genius, who will apply herself diligently to her exercise for the space of but one half-year, shall be able to give her fan all the graces that can possibly
(35) enter into that little modish machine.

"But to the end that my readers may form to themselves a right notion of this exercise, I

beg leave to explain it to them in all its parts.
When my female regiment is drawn up in
(40) array, with everyone her weapon in her hand,
upon my giving the word to handle their fans,
each of them shakes her fan at me with a
smile, then gives her right-hand woman a tap
upon the shoulder, then presses her lips with
(45) the extremity of her fan, then lets her arms fall
in an easy motion, and stands in readiness to
receive the next word of command. All this is
done with a close fan, and is generally learned
in the first week…."

"Fans"
by Joseph Addison

Selection Three

Irreparableness

I have been in the meadows all the day,
And gathered there the nosegay that you see,
Singing within myself as bird or bee
line   When such do field-work on a morn of May.
(5)   But now I look upon my flowers, decay
Has met them in my hands, more fatally
Because more warmly clasped,—and sobs are
    free
To come instead of songs. What you say,
Sweet counsellors, dear friends? that I should
    go
(10) Back straightway to the fields and gather
    more?
Another, sooth, may do it, but not I.
My heart is very tired, my strength is low,
My hands are full of blossoms plucked before,
Held dead within them till myself shall die.

by Elizabeth Barrett Browning

Selection Four

On the Grasshopper and the Cricket

The poetry of earth is never dead:
When all the birds are faint with the hot sun,
And hide in cooling trees, a voice will run
From hedge to hedge about the new-mown
line   mead;
(5)   That is the grasshopper's—he takes the lead
In summer luxury—he has never done
With his delights; for when tired out with fun
He rests at ease beneath some pleasant weed.
The poetry of earth is ceasing never:

(10) On a lone winter evening, when the frost
Has wrought a silence, from the stove there
    shrills
The cricket's song, in warmth increasing ever,
And seems to one in drowsiness half lost,
The grasshopper's among some grassy hills.

by John Keats

Selection Five

The Tragedy of
Julius Caesar

(from Scene II.)

THIRD CITIZEN.
The noble Brutus is ascended: silence!

MARCUS BRUTUS.
line   Be patient till the last.
(5)   Romans, countrymen, and lovers! hear me for
my cause; and be silent, that you may hear:
believe me for mine honour; and have respect
to mine honour, that you may believe: censure
me in your wisdom; and awake your senses,
(10) that you may the better judge. If there be any
in this assembly, any dear friend of Cæsar's,
to him I say, that Brutus' love to Cæsar was
no less than his. If, then, that friend demand
why Brutus rose against Cæsar, this is my
(15) answer,—Not that I loved Cæsar less, but that
I loved Rome more. Had you rather Cæsar
were living, and die all slaves, than that Cæsar
were dead, to live all free men? As Cæsar
loved me, I weep for him; as he was fortunate,
(20) I rejoice at it; as he was valiant, I honour him:
but, as he was ambitious, I slew him. There is
tears for his love; joy for his fortune; honour
for his valour; and death for his ambition.
Who is here so base that would be a
(25) bondman? If any, speak; for him have I
offended. Who is here so rude that would not
be a Roman? If any, speak; for him have I
offended. Who is here so vile that will not
love his country? If any, speak; for him have I
(30) offended. I pause for a reply.

CITIZENS.
None, Brutus, none.

MARCUS BRUTUS.
Then none have I offended. I have done no
(35) more to Cæsar than you shall do to Brutus.
The question of his death is enroll'd in the

Capitol; his glory not extenuated, wherein he was worthy; nor his offences enforced, for which he suffer'd death. Here comes his body,
(40) mourn'd by Mark Antony:

Enter Antony *with* Cæsar's *body.*

who, though he had no hand in his death, shall receive the benefit of his dying, a place in the commonwealth; as which of you shall not?
(45) With this I depart,—that, as I slew my best lover for the good of Rome, I have the same dagger for myself, when it shall please my country to need my death.

CITIZENS.
(50) Live, Brutus! live, live!

FIRST CITIZEN.
Bring him with triumph home unto his house.

SECOND CITIZEN.
Give him a statue with his ancestors.

(55) THIRD CITIZEN.
Let him be Cæsar.

FOURTH CITIZEN.
Cæsar's better parts
Shall be crown'd in Brutus.

(60) FIRST CITIZEN.
We'll bring him to his house with shouts and clamours.

MARCUS BRUTUS.
My countrymen,—

(65) SECOND CITIZEN.
Peace, silence! Brutus speaks.

FIRST CITIZEN.
Peace, ho!

MARCUS BRUTUS.
(70) Good countrymen, let me depart alone,
And, for my sake, stay here with Antony:
Do grace to Cæsar's corpse, and grace his speech
Tending to Cæsar's glories; which Mark Antony,
(75) By our permission, is allow'd to make.
I do entreat you, not a man depart,
Save I alone, till Antony have spoke. [*Exit*]

FIRST CITIZEN.
Stay, ho! and let us hear Mark Antony.

by William Shakespeare

Questions about MEANING

1. What is the subject of the letter in Selection One?

   (A) A breach of promise suit against Dodson and Fogg
   (B) A breach of promise suit against Samuel Pickwick
   (C) A writ of damages by Pickwick against Mrs. Martha Bardell
   (D) A writ of damages by the Court of Common Pleas against Pickwick
   (E) A breach of promise suit against Martha Bardell

2. What is the main idea of Selection Two?

   (A) Ladies should never use fans without training.
   (B) Fans are deadly weapons in the hands of ladies.
   (C) Letters to *The Spectator* are highly edited.
   (D) Ladies can be trained to use fans just as men are trained to use swords.
   (E) Fans are beautiful when used properly.

3. The main subject of the poem in Selection Three is

   (A) picking flowers
   (B) an awareness of life
   (C) dying flowers
   (D) an awareness of death
   (E) singing in the fields

4. The central concern of the poem in Selection Four is

   (A) insects
   (B) seasons of the year
   (C) nature's meaning (sounds and rhythms)
   (D) sounds of seasons
   (E) nature's cycles

5. Marcus Brutus's speech to the citizens in lines 4–30 of Selection Five deals with

   (A) justification for killing Cæsar
   (B) resistance to enemies
   (C) acquiring power and privilege
   (D) contending for the empire
   (E) political success

Questions About FORM

1. The "Mute astonishment" (line 38) of the men in Selection One is the result of

   (A) the sealed secrecy of the letter
   (B) their total trust in Pickwick's innocence
   (C) their disappointment in Pickwick's behavior
   (D) the untimely nature of the letter
   (E) the unexpected import of the letter

2. The effect of the narrator's comments about the letter in the second selection (lines 6–13) is to

   (A) prepare the readers for a shock
   (B) reveal the absurdity of the notion of training ladies to use fans
   (C) communicate that the letter is self-explanatory
   (D) present an alternative view from that of the letter
   (E) change the topic in contrast to that of the letter

3. The progression of thought in Selection Three can NOT be summarized as

   (A) from joy to sorrow to resignation
   (B) from singing to crying to silence
   (C) from work to play to death
   (D) from life to decay to death
   (E) from abandon to contemplation to conclusion

4. Lines 1–8 contrast with lines 9–14 in the fourth selection in which of the following ways?

   (A) Summer and winter
   (B) Grasshopper's voice and cricket's song
   (C) Hot and cold
   (D) Reality and unreality
   (E) Activity and inactivity

5. The dramatist in Selection Five reveals a departure in structure in line 70 by changing from

   (A) direct address to indirect statement
   (B) Brutus taking responsibility to fleeing the scene
   (C) active to passive resistance in Marcus Brutus's speech to the citizens
   (D) prose to blank verse in Marcus Brutus's speech to the citizens
   (E) the imperative to the interrogative

Questions About NARRATIVE VOICE

1. Dodson and Fogg's attitude in Selection One toward Mr. Pickwick is set forth as

   (A) impersonal and pragmatic
   (B) antagonistic and decisive
   (C) complacent and verbose
   (D) pedantic and morbid
   (E) indecisive and hypocritical

2. In order for the letter in the second selection to be "a satire upon coquettes" (line 7), the writer's attitude toward ladies and their uses of fans would have to be

   (A) ironic sadness
   (B) a blend of hate and revenge
   (C) a blend of humor and censor
   (D) inspired sarcasm
   (E) a blend of defiance and resistance

3. What major change is initiated in line 11 of Selection Three?

   (A) The speaker changes attitude.
   (B) Death becomes a greater enemy than the transient nature of flowers.
   (C) A greater emphasis is placed on flowers.
   (D) The speaker becomes like the "bird or bee" of line 3.
   (E) The speaker resists a change in attitude.

4. In Selection Four, the narrator's attitude toward summer is set forth as

(A) bitter
(B) longing
(C) ambivalent
(D) curiously indifferent
(E) antagonistic

5. In Selection Five, the attitude of the speaker toward Cæsar can be considered

(A) contrite
(B) complacent
(C) melancholic
(D) self-justifying
(E) redoubtable

Questions About TONE

1. The speaker's tone sets forth that the three men regard the letter in Selection One as

(A) an entertaining surprise
(B) a curious setback
(C) an embarrassing communication
(D) a dangerous threat
(E) an unexpected shock

2. The tone of the narrator's comment in Selection Two concerning the letter's form as related to purpose in line 9 ("or what other title to give it") is best mirrored by which of these paraphrases?

(A) Who cares?
(B) Who knows?
(C) Is this necessary?
(D) How rude!
(E) Help!

3. The speaker's tone in the third selection in the last line is

(A) resigned
(B) parenthetical
(C) mawkish
(D) indignant
(E) resentful

4. The speaker's tone in the last two lines of the fourth selection is set forth as

(A) cavalier
(B) calculating
(C) dreamlike
(D) self-demeaning
(E) pious

5. In Selection Five, the citizens use a tone toward Marcus Brutus that is

(A) defensive
(B) combative
(C) jocular
(D) reverential
(E) quarrelsome

Questions About CHARACTER

1. In the first selection, "alarmed at the horror in Mr. Pickwick's countenance" (lines 11–12) emphasizes Mr. Pickwick's state of

(A) surprise
(B) anticipation
(C) disappointment
(D) resentment
(E) expectancy

2. As a character, the writer of the letter in the second selection is probably

(A) inexperienced
(B) unlettered
(C) imperceptible
(D) frivolous
(E) imaginative

3. The speaker's friends in the third selection could be characterized as

(A) perceptive
(B) impertinent
(C) obtuse
(D) erratic
(E) obsequious

4. According to the speaker in Selection Four, grasshoppers are personified as

(A) hypocritical
(B) self-delusional
(C) fun loving
(D) exaggerative
(E) misdirected

5. In the fifth selection, Marcus Brutus wants the citizens to believe that he is

(A) compassionate
(B) patriotic
(C) perseverant
(D) capricious
(E) sententious

Questions About USE OF LANGUAGE

1. The language of the letter in the first selection is expressed in

(A) imprecise diction
(B) a businesslike tone
(C) highly symbolic language
(D) an informal tone
(E) Nonstandard English

2. The figurative use of "men with swords" (lines 15–16) in the second selection reinforces a sense that

(A) men should use swords like women use fans
(B) the writer is unknowledgeable about war
(C) women should be able to use both fans and swords
(D) fans are weapons, too, and require training for use
(E) men should be able to use both fans and swords

3. In the third selection, line 3 contains

(A) an understatement
(B) an overstatement
(C) a simile
(D) a metaphor
(E) personification

4. In the fourth selection, lines 3–8 present the grasshopper as if it were a

(A) worthless lifeform
(B) renewable energy
(C) playing person
(D) mysterious thing
(E) destructive insect

5. In the fifth selection, the question "Who is here so rude that would not be a Roman?" is

(A) rhetorical
(B) sarcastic
(C) paradoxical
(D) an overstatement
(E) an understatement

Questions About MEANING(S) IN CONTEXT

1. As can be presumed from the letter in Selection One, Mr. Pickwick had

(A) never met Mrs. Martha Bardell
(B) married Mrs. Bardell
(C) stolen from Mrs. Bardell
(D) a relationship with Mrs. Bardell
(E) worked for Mrs. Bardell

2. In the second selection, the introductory quote (lines 1–5) implies that

(A) the letter is too frivolous for use
(B) the letter is presented as a diversion for readers
(C) minds are wasted with useless reading
(D) minds can be trained by diversionary thinking
(E) the letter is presented as a work meriting serious contemplation

3. In the third selection, "more warmly clasped" (line 7) expresses which of these concepts?

   I.   Cherished firmly
   II. Body heat
   III. Destructive actions

   (A) I only
   (B) II only
   (C) III only
   (D) I and II only
   (E) I, II, and III

4. In line 13 of the fourth selection, "drowsiness half lost" can be paraphrased as

   (A) a sleepless night
   (B) insomnia
   (C) dreams
   (D) incoherence
   (E) going to sleep

5. The statement in lines 18–23 of the fifth selection is set forth as

   (A) a summary of the personal actions of Marcus Brutus concerning Cæsar
   (B) a generalization regarding Cæsar's character
   (C) a series of excuses for Cæsar's murder
   (D) a response to ungrounded charges
   (E) the emotional ramblings of a man over the death of his friend

PRACTICE SET B

Selection One

"Goodwives," said a hard-featured dame of fifty, "I'll tell ye a piece of my mind. It would be greatly for the public behoof, if we women,
line being of mature age and church-members in
(5) good repute, should have the handling of such malefactresses as this Hester Prynne. What think ye, gossips? If the hussy stood up for judgment before us five, that are now here in a knot together, would she come off with such a
(10) sentence as the worshipful magistrates have awarded? Marry, I trow not!"

"People say," said another, "that the Reverend Master Dimmesdale, her godly pastor, takes it very grievously to heart that
(15) such a scandal should have come upon his congregation."

"The magistrates are God-fearing gentlemen, but merciful overmuch,—that is a truth," added a third autumnal matron. "At the very least,
(20) they should have put the brand of a hot iron on Hester Prynne's forehead. Madam Hester would have winced at that, I warrant me. But she,—the naughty baggage,—little will she care what they put upon the bodice of her
(25) gown! Why, look you, she may cover it with a brooch, or such like heathenish adornment, and so walk the streets as brave as ever!"

"Ah, but," interposed, more softly, a young wife, holding a child by the hand, "let her
(30) cover the mark as she will, the pang of it will be always in her heart."

The Scarlet Letter
by Nathaniel Hawthorne

Selection Two

The rational intercourse kept up by conversation is one of our principal distinctions from brutes. We should therefore endeavor to turn this
line peculiar talent to our advantage, and consider
(5) the organs of speech as the instruments of understanding: we should be very careful not to use them as the weapons of vice, or tools of folly, and do our utmost to unlearn any trivial or ridiculous habits, which tend to lessen the
(10) value of such an inestimable perogative. It is, indeed, imagined by some philosophers, that even birds and beasts (though without the power of articulation) perfectly understand one another by the sounds they utter; and that
(15) dogs, cats, etc., have each a particular language to themselves, like different nations. Thus it may be supposed that the nightingales of Italy have as fine an ear for their own native woodnotes as any signor or signora for
(20) an Italian air; that the boars of Westphalia gruntle as expressively through the nose as the inhabitants in High German: and that the frogs in the dykes of Holland croak as intelligibly as the natives jabber their Low Dutch. However
(25) this may be, we may consider those whose tongues hardly seem to be under the influence of reason, and do not keep up the proper conversation of human creatures, as imitating the language of different animals. Thus, for
(30) instance, the affinity between Chatterers and Monkeys, and Praters and Parrots, is too obvious not to occur at once; Grunters and Growlers may be justly compared to Hogs; Snarlers are Curs that continually show their
(35) teeth, but never bite; and the Spitfire passionate are a sort of wild cats that will not bear stroking, but will purr when they are pleased. Complainers are Screech-Owls; and Story-tellers, always repeating the same dull
(40) note, are Cuckoos. Poets that prick up their ears at their own hideous braying are no better than Asses. Critics in general are venomous Serpents that delight in hissing, and some of them who have got by heart a few technical
(45) terms without knowing their meaning are no other than Magpies. I myself, who have crowed to the whole town for near three years past, may perhaps put my readers in mind of a Barnyard Cock; but as I must acquaint them
(50) that they will hear the last of me on this day fortnight, I hope they will then consider me as a Swan, who is supposed to sing sweetly at his dying moments.

On Conversation
by William Cowper

Selection Three

To His Son

Three things there be that prosper all apace
And flourish, while they are asunder far;
But on a day they meet all in a place,
line And when they meet, they one another mar.
(5) And they be these: the wood, the weed, the wag.
The wood is that that makes the gallows tree;
The weed is that that strings the hangman's bag;
The wag, my pretty knave, betokens thee.
Now mark, dear boy: while these assemble not,
(10) Green springs the tree, hemp grows, the wag
    is wild;
But when they meet, it makes the timber rot,
It frets the halter, and it chokes the child.
God bless the child!

by William Wordsworth

Selection Four

Worldly Place

Even in a palace, life may be led well!
So spake the imperial sage, purest of men.
Marcus Aurelius. But the stifling den
line Of common life, where, crowded up pell-mell,
(5) Our freedom for a little bread we sell,
And drudge under some foolish master's ken
Who rates us if we peer outside our pen—
Match'd with a palace, is not this a hell?
Even in a palace! On his truth sincere,
(10) Who spoke these words, no shadow ever came;
And when my ill-school'd spirit is aflame
Some nobler, ampler stage of life to win,
I'll stop, and say: 'There were no succour here!
The aids to noble life are all within.'

by Matthew Arnold

Selection Five

Act I. Scene 1

A hall in the DUKE'S *palace*

Enter the DUKE *of Ephesus,* ÆGEON, *the
Merchant of Syracuse,* GAOLER, OFFICERS,
and other ATTENDANTS

ÆGEON.   Proceed, Solinus, to procure my
    fall,
    And by the doom of death end woes and all.

DUKE.   Merchant of Syracusa, plead no more;
line   I am not partial to infringe our laws.
(5)   The enmity and discord which of late
    Sprung from the rancorous outrage of your
      duke
    To merchants, our well-dealing countrymen,
    Who, wanting guilders to redeem their lives,
    Have seal'd his rigorous statutes with their
      bloods,
(10)   Excludes all pity from our threat'ning looks.
    For, since the mortal and intestine jars
    'Twixt thy seditious countrymen and us,
    It hath in solemn synods been decreed,
    Both by the Syracusians and ourselves,
(15)   To admit no traffic to our adverse towns;
    Nay, more: if any born at Ephesus
    Be seen at any Syracusian marts and fairs;
    Again, if any Syracusian born
    Come to the bay of Ephesus—he dies,
(20)   His goods confiscate to the Duke's dispose,
    Unless a thousand marks be levied,
    To quit the penalty and to ransom him.
    Thy substance, valued at the highest rate,
    Cannot amount unto a hundred marks;
(25)   Therefore by law thou art condemn'd to die.

ÆGEON.   Yet this my comfort: when your
      words are done,
    My woes end likewise with the evening sun.

The Comedy of Errors
by William Shakespeare

Questions About MEANING

1. The central subject of the first selection mostly concerns

(A) sacrifice
(B) honor
(C) punishments
(D) destiny
(E) women

2. The main idea in Selection Two is that

(A) people who do not use proper conversation are like animals
(B) animals can talk
(C) insults can be effective forms of communication
(D) philosophers believe that animals communicate
(E) animals have nationalities

3. The speaker's message in Selection Three is primarily a

(A) description
(B) warning
(C) reminder
(D) play on words
(E) statement on nature

4. The main point of the speaker in Selection Four is that

(A) living in a palace is the means to a well-led life
(B) a well-led life does not depend on external conditions
(C) working for a living is slavery
(D) the sage was a wise man
(E) life is lived in stages

5. What is the dramatic situation of the scene in Selection Five?

(A) The Duke of Ephesus is afraid of the Duke of Syracuse.
(B) A merchant has been unjustly seized and condemned to death in Syracuse.
(C) A merchant of Syracuse wants to die.
(D) A Syracuse merchant is to be executed because of a trade war with Ephesus.
(E) An escaped convict is posing as a merchant from Syracuse.

Questions About FORM

1. The persuasive speech of the "hard-featured dame" in the first paragraph of Selection One is intended to

(A) further intimidate Hester Prynne
(B) begin a discussion among the townswomen that reveals their attitudes
(C) summarize Hester's problem
(D) introduce Dimmesdale's role in helping Hester
(E) simply narrate the episode

2. Selection Two is structured in part on

(A) cause and effect
(B) analogy
(C) chronological sequence
(D) spatial sequence
(E) induction

3. There are three parts of the poem (lines 1–4, lines 5–8, and lines 9–13) in Selection Three. Which of these sets of words most clearly reflect those parts?

(A) Generalization; application; threat
(B) Definition; application; warning
(C) Generalization; explanation; warning
(D) Warning; explanation; threat
(E) Application; warning; threat

4. The last two lines in the poem in Selection Four provide an effect that is

(A) an ironic twist to line one
(B) to intensify the argument of the first stanza
(C) to deny line one
(D) a simplification of the argument
(E) a resistance to the argument

5. Selection Five is structured as

(A) couplets
(B) a chorus
(C) a ballad
(D) caricature
(E) blank verse

Questions About NARRATIVE VOICE

1. The attitude of the young wife in Selection One toward Hester, in contrast to the others, is slightly

(A) ambivalent
(B) sympathetic
(C) devitalized
(D) satirical
(E) conciliatory

2. In Selection Two, the speaker's attitude concerning those who "do not keep up the proper conversation" (lines 27–28) is revealed as one of

(A) admiration
(B) complacency
(C) intolerance
(D) amusement
(E) hypocrisy

3. The change in line 8 of Selection Three from the third person "they" (line 5) to the first person "my" and second person "thee" indicates that the speaker's attitude in the poem is

(A) didactic
(B) hostile
(C) impersonal
(D) mocking
(E) cruel

4. What is the attitude of "I" (line 13) toward Marcus Aurelius in the fourth selection?

(A) Receptive
(B) Ambitiously antagonistic
(C) Blameworthy
(D) Bravado
(E) Bitterly disapproving

5. The attitude of the Duke toward Ægeon in Selection Five can be considered

(A) naive
(B) disingenuous
(C) disillusional
(D) stern
(E) penitent

Questions About TONE

1. The tone of "the naughty baggage," in Selection One, makes the speaker sound

(A) flamboyant
(B) laconic
(C) ostentatious
(D) spiteful
(E) flattering

2. When the speaker calls critics "Serpents" and "Magpies" (lines 43 and 46) in the second selection, the tone can be seen as

(A) sarcastic
(B) laudatory
(C) defiant
(D) concordant
(E) circumspect

3. The speaker's tone in the third selection might lead the hearer to regard the boy as

(A) gallant
(B) a thief
(C) mischievous
(D) supine
(E) incorrigible

4. The speaker's tone implies, in Selection Four, that the words of the "imperial sage" are

(A) serious
(B) noble
(C) pious
(D) pedantic
(E) pithy

5. Ægeon's tone, in Selection Five, can be recognized as

(A) reticent
(B) resigned
(C) defensive
(D) disparaging
(E) boisterous

Questions About CHARACTER

1. The character of the third matron in Selection One can be thought of as

(A) insincere
(B) autocratic
(C) inclement
(D) charismatic
(E) sophisticated

2. In Selection Two, the speaker wants his readers to think of him as

(A) severe
(B) restrictive
(C) lenient
(D) profound
(E) self-determined

3. In Selection Three, the direct address "dear boy" (line 9) emphasizes which of the following in the speaker's character?

(A) Heartlessness
(B) Arrogance
(C) Brazenness
(D) Austerity
(E) Bemusement

4. In Selection Four, the speaker reveals that he or she prioritizes

(A) complacency over struggle
(B) intrinsic values over physical wealth
(C) intellectual over physical strength
(D) sincerity over insincerity
(E) freedom over wealth

5. As presented in Selection Five, the Duke's decision is based on what he puts forth as

(A) a personal vendetta
(B) his position of authority
(C) a keen dislike of Ægeon
(D) resistance to authority
(E) national interests

Questions About USE OF LANGUAGE

1. As used in the last paragraph of the first selection, "mark" symbolizes

(A) her freedom
(B) bravery
(C) shame
(D) high fashion
(E) courage

2. In the second selection, the literary device used in lines 51–53 is a

(A) metonymy
(B) simile
(C) punch line
(D) digression
(E) metaphor

3. In the third selection, "the wood, the weed, the wag" (line 5) perform which of these roles?

I.   Symbols of warning
II. An alliterative device
III. Dead metaphors

(A) I only
(B) II only
(C) I and II only
(D) II and III only
(E) I, II, and III

4. In the fourth selection, "bread" (line 5) symbolizes

(A) the necessities of life
(B) free enterprise
(C) entrepreneurship
(D) money
(E) resourcefulness

5. As used in line 9 of the fifth selection, "with their bloods" is

(A) a metaphor for dying for one's country
(B) confirming that they will be spared
(C) referring to medical use of blood
(D) a ritual to belong to the guilders
(E) figurative language for people's lives

Questions About MEANING(S) IN CONTEXT

1. In line 19 of Selection One, "autumnal" is used to mean

(A) fall-like
(B) colorful
(C) elderly
(D) cool
(E) bitter

2. As used in the second selection, the word "instruments" (line 5) is used to mean all these concepts EXCEPT

    (A) the means to do something
    (B) tools
    (C) sound devices
    (D) formal documents
    (E) implements

3. "Frets the halter" in line 12 of the third selection can also be paraphrased as

    (A) worries the timid
    (B) wears the noose
    (C) ruffles the garment
    (D) irritates the hesitant
    (E) gnaws the animal

4. In its context, "rates" in line 7 of the fourth selection means which of these three definitions?

    I.   Scolds
    II. Appraises
    III. Esteems

    (A) I only
    (B) II only
    (C) III only
    (D) I and II only
    (E) I, II, and III

5. In the fifth selection, lines 11–12 are connotative of all the following EXCEPT that

    (A) body parts are being procured
    (B) the argument is on both physical and emotional levels
    (C) hostility in this case has a sense of abruptness
    (D) the stirring up of trouble began with Syracuse
    (E) Ægeon is guilty due to nationality

PRACTICE SET C

Selection One

A stern smile curled the Prince's lip as he
spoke. Waldemar Fitzurse hastened to reply
that Ivanhoe was already removed from the
line lists, and in the custody of his friends.
(5)   'I was somewhat afflicted,' he said, 'to see
the grief of the Queen of Love and Beauty,
whose sovereignty of a day this event has
changed into mourning. I am not a man to be
moved by a woman's lament for her lover, but
(10) this same Lady Rowena suppressed her sorrow
with such dignity of manner that it could only
be discovered by her folded hands and her
tearless eye, which trembled as it remained
fixed on the lifeless form before her.'
(15)   'Who is this Lady Rowena,' said Prince
John, 'of whom we have heard so much?'
'A Saxon heiress of large possessions,'
replied the Prior Aymer; 'a rose of loveliness,
and a jewel of wealth; the fairest among a
(20) thousand, a bundle of myrrh, and a cluster of
camphire.'
'We shall cheer her sorrows,' said Prince
John, 'and amend her blood, by wedding her
to a Norman. She seems a minor, and must
(25) therefore be at our royal disposal in marriage.
How sayst thou, De Bracy? What thinkst thou
of gaining fair lands and livings, by wedding a
Saxon, after the fashion of the followers of the
Conqueror?'
(30)   'If the lands are to my liking, my lord,'
answered De Bracy, 'it will be hard to
displease me with a bride; and deeply will I
hold myself bound to your Highness for a
good deed, which will fulfil all promises made
(35) in favour of your servant and vassal.'
'We will not forget it,' said Prince John;
'and that we may instantly go to work,
command our seneschal presently to order the
attendance of the Lady Rowena and her
(40) company—that is, the rude churl her guardian,
and the Saxon ox whom the Black Knight
struck down in the tournament—upon this
evening's banquet. De Bigot,' he added to his
seneschal, 'thou wilt word this our second
(45) summons so courteously as to gratify the pride
of these Saxons, and make it impossible for
them again to refuse; although, by the bones

of Becket, courtesy to them is casting pearls
before swine.'

Ivanhoe
by Sir Walter Scott

Selection Two

That the machine has dealt art in the grand
old sense a death-blow, none will deny—the
evidence is too substantial: art in the grand old
line sense, meaning art in the sense of structural
(5)   tradition, whose craft is fashioned upon the
handicraft ideal, ancient or modern; an art
wherein this form and that form as structural
parts were laboriously joined in such a way as
to beautifully emphasize the manner of the
(10) joining…craft that will not see that human
thought is stripping off one form and donning
another, and artists are everywhere, whether
catering to the leisure class of old England or
ground beneath the heel of commercial abuse
(15) here in the great West, the unwilling
symptoms of the inevitable, organic nature of
the machine they combat, the hell-smoke of
the factories they scorn to understand.
And, invincible, triumphant, the machine
(20) goes on, gathering force and knitting the
material necessities of mankind ever closer
into a universal automatic fabric; the engine,
the motor, and the battleship, the works of art
of the century!
(25)   The machine is intellect mastering the
drudgery of earth that the plastic art may live;
that the margin of leisure and strength by
which man's life upon the earth can be made
beautiful, may immeasurably widen, its
(30) function ultimately to emancipate human
expression!
It is a universal educator, surely raising the
level of human intelligence, so carrying within
itself the power to destroy, by its own
(35) momentum, the greed which in [William]
Morris's time and still in our own time turns it
to a deadly engine of enslavement. The only
comfort left the poor artist, sidetracked as he
is, seemingly is a mean one: the thought that
(40) the very selfishness which man's early art
idealized, now reduced to its lowest terms, is

swiftly and surely destroying itself through the
medium of the machine.

(45) The artist's present plight is a sad one, but
may he truthfully say that society is less well
off because architecture, or even art, as it was,
is dead, and printing, or the machine, lives?
Every age has done its work, produced its art
with the best tools or contrivances it knew, the
(50) tools most successful in saving the most
precious thing in the world—human effort…

> "The Art and Craft of the
> Machine: Democracy and
> New Forms in Architecture"
> Speech
> by Frank Lloyd Wright

Selection Three

The Parting

Since there's no help, come let us kiss and
    part—
Nay, I have done, you get no more of me;
And I am glad, yea, glad with all my heart,
line That thus so cleanly I myself can free.
(5) Shake hands for ever, cancel all our vows,
And when we meet at any time again,
Be it not seen in either of our brows
That we one jot of former love retain.
Now at the last gasp of Love's latest breath,
(10) When, his pulse failing, Passion speechless lies,
When Faith is kneeling by his bed of death,
And Innocence is closing up his eyes,
Now if thou would'st, when all have given
    him over,
From death to life thou might'st him yet recover.

> by Michael Drayton

Selection Four

On Time

Fly envious Time, till thou run out thy race,
Call on the lazy leaden-stepping hours,
Whose speed is but the heavy plummet's pace;
line And glut thy self with what thy womb devours,
(5) Which is no more than what is false and vain,
And merely mortal dross;
So little is our loss,
So little is thy gain.
For when as each thing bad thou hast entombed,
(10) And last of all, thy greedy self consumed,

Then long Eternity shall greet our bliss
With an individual kiss;
And Joy shall overtake us as a flood,
When every thing that is sincerely good
(15) And perfectly divine,
With Truth, and Peace, and Love shall ever
  shine
About the supreme Throne
Of him, t' whose happy-making sight alone,
When once our heav'nly-guided soul shall
  climb,
(20) Then all this earthy grossness quit,
Attired with stars, we shall for ever sit,
Triumphing over Death, and Chance, and thee,
O Time.

> by John Milton

Selection Five

ACT II. Scene I.

Enter ANGELO, ESCALUS, *a* JUSTICE,
PROVOST, OFFICERS *and other*
ATTENDANTS

ANGELO. We must not make a scarecrow
  of the law,
Setting it up to fear the birds of prey,
And let it keep one shape till custom make it
Their perch, and not their terror.
line
(5) ESCALUS. Ay, but yet
Let us be keen, and rather cut a little
Than fall and bruise to death. Alas! this
  gentleman,
Whom I would save, had a most noble father.
Let but your honour know,
(10) Whom I believe to be most strait in virtue,
That, in the working of your own affections,
Had time coher'd with place, or place with
  wishing,
Or that the resolute acting of our blood
Could have attain'd th'effect of your own
  purpose
(15) Whether you had not sometime in your life
Err'd in this point which now you censure
  him,
And pull'd the law upon you.

ANGELO. 'Tis one thing to be tempted,
  Escalus,
Another thing to fall. I not deny
(20) The jury, passing on the prisoner's life,

May in the sworn twelve have a thief or two
Guiltier than him they try. What's open
   made to justice,
That justice seizes. What knows the laws
That thieves do pass on thieves? 'Tis very
   pregnant,
(25) The jewel that we find, we stoop and take't,
Because we see it; but what we do not see
We tread upon, and never think of it.
You may not so extenuate his offence
For I have had such faults; but rather tell me,
(30) When I, that censure him, do so offend,
Let mine own judgment pattern out my death,
And nothing come in partial. Sir, he must die.

    ESCALUS.   Be it as your wisdom will.

Measure for Measure
by William Shakespeare

Questions About MEANING

1. In Selection One, the purpose of the passage is
   to describe a situation in which

   (A) Lady Rowena is a beautiful Norman
       woman
   (B) Prince John has no control over the
       Saxons
   (C) Lady Rowena refuses to see Prince John
   (D) a Saxon heiress is given to a Norman for
       marriage as a favor from Prince John
   (E) the Saxons and Normans are at war

2. The main idea of the first paragraph in
   Selection Two is that

   (A) art is dead
   (B) artists cater to social classes while
       succumbing to commercial abuse
   (C) the machine will inevitably give way to
       hand-crafted art
   (D) hell-smoke of factories proves the nature
       of the machine
   (E) the machine represents change that is
       resisted by artists

3. Selection Three's subject can be stated as

   (A) an angry departure
   (B) dying love
   (C) a reversal of fortunes
   (D) resisting change
   (E) love and hate

4. Of the ideas listed, which one defines the
   subject of Selection Four?

   (A) Time's destroying power
   (B) Eternal happiness
   (C) Eternity over Time
   (D) Time as a race
   (E) Time as a friend

5. The drama of the fifth selection can be
   summarized as

   (A) two brothers discussing legal theories
   (B) the Deputy defending an accused man
   (C) Escalus defending himself against false
       charges
   (D) an argument in which a Justice accuses
       the Deputy of a crime
   (E) a Justice defending an accused man to the
       Deputy

Questions About FORM

1. In Selection One, how does Fitzurse know that
   Lady Rowena was upset?

   (A) Inductive reasoning
   (B) Deductive reasoning
   (C) Process analysis
   (D) Analogy
   (E) Cause-and-effect

2. The speech in Selection Two includes elements
   of

   (A) chronology, problem-solving, and climax
   (B) chronology, persuasion, and spatial
       sequence
   (C) persuasion, criticism, and definition
   (D) deduction, climax, and narration
   (E) narration, definition, and persuasion

*3. In the Selection Three poem, what is the role of lines 13–14 to the poem as a whole?

(A) They summarize that the speaker really no longer is in love.
(B) They imply that the speaker is still in love.
(C) They mourn the death of love.
(D) They establish that death and love are synonymous.
(E) They reinforce the speaker's determination to end the relationship.

4. In the fourth selection, line 11 contains a change in the poem's

(A) voice
(B) tone
(C) subject
(D) rhyme scheme
(E) imagery

5. What happens as a result of the change of rhythm of "Ay, but yet" in line 5 of the fifth selection?

(A) It breaks the monotony of the passage.
(B) It echoes the rhythm of line 9.
(C) It threatens the unity of the dialogue.
(D) It emphasizes the speaker's contrasting attitude.
(E) It reinforces Angelo's point.

* Note concerning Set C, Selection Three, question 3 on FORM:

Your knowledge of FORM is tremendously valuable in these types of questions. This sonnet has an abab cdcd efef gg pattern. As previously discussed, the rhyme scheme alone is a clue: the poem is divided into four parts. Probably each part will be a progression of thought with the last couplet being perhaps a summary or perhaps a reversal. In lines 1–4 a paraphrase reveals that the speaker has been in a love relationship that is ending. The speaker's attitude? Defiant? Angry? Perhaps resentful? Lines 5–8 indicate that he does not want to let on that they were ever in love. In lines 9–12 he very dramatically personifies love, passion, faith, and innocence as they die. The reader can anticipate in the final couplet a significant point—either confirmation of the attitude he has projected so far or a reversal.

Now if thou would'st, when all have given him over,
From death to life thou might'st him yet recover.

Who is "him"? Personified love—the same love that is dying in lines 9–12. The speaker, however, says (in paraphrase), you (the person ending the relationship) can make love "recover." Now look at the answer choices. Obviously this is a reversal rather than a summary, so answer A is not correct. Answers C, D, and E also do not reflect the MEANING of the couplet. But answer B—the lines imply that the speaker is still in love—can be justified, because he has given the object of his love the power to bring love back into being.

How else might the ways FORM contributes to MEANING be questioned in this poem?

• Central contrasts, such as "death" (lines 9–12) and "life" (line 14), "cancel" (line 5) and "recover" (line 14), and so forth.
• Sequence, such as "part" (line 1) to "cancel" (line 5) to "death" (line 11) to "recover" (line 14) emphasize a progression from hopelessness to hope.

Questions About NARRATIVE VOICE

1. Prince John's view of Lady Rowena and the Saxons in Selection One can be described as the attitude of one who is

(A) easily offended
(B) deeply sentimental
(C) used to a position of authority
(D) on the defensive
(E) willing to accommodate for the needs of others

2. The speaker views "the poor artist" (line 38 in Selection Two) with an attitude that is

(A) directly disapproving
(B) gently satirical
(C) exaggerated in its criticism
(D) unconventional in its intensity
(E) sentimental

3. The context of the Selection Three poem reveals that the speaker ("I") is

(A) a social outcast
(B) an unfaithful lover
(C) an indifferent friend
(D) a close, personal friend
(E) a rejected lover

4. In the Selection Four poem, the speaker's attitude toward "the supreme Throne" (line 17) is expressed in terms that are

(A) worshipful
(B) unrelenting
(C) fearful
(D) defensive
(E) reluctant

5. In Selection Five, Angelo's attitude has qualities that make him seem

(A) irresponsible
(B) unyielding
(C) ambitious
(D) contemptuous
(E) sentimental

Questions About TONE

1. In the first selection, De Bracy perceives Prince John's tone when offering him a Saxon bride as

(A) congenial
(B) condescending
(C) facetious
(D) amusing
(E) defensive

2. The following statements are accurate of Selection Two EXCEPT that it cannot be said that its tone

(A) toward artists is critical
(B) toward artists is somewhat mocking
(C) toward machines is antagonistic
(D) is optimistic about machines
(E) is defensive of machines

3. The speaker's tone in lines 1–8 of the third selection can be seen as

(A) outraged indignation
(B) incredulous
(C) fascinated obsession
(D) courteous
(E) defensive pride

4. The speaker's tone in lines 1–2 of the fourth selection has a sound that is

(A) bitter
(B) lackluster
(C) futile
(D) cajoling
(E) defiant

5. The tone of Angelo's conclusion in line 32 of the fifth selection has qualities that are

(A) bitter and suspicious
(B) infuriated and retributive
(C) determined and authoritative
(D) retaliatory and jaundiced
(E) jealous and hostile

Questions About CHARACTER

1. In the second paragraph of the first selection, Lady Rowena's character is revealed as

(A) scared and cowering in her grief
(B) indecisive in her grief
(C) having decorum in her grief
(D) being complacent in her grief
(E) being immature in her grief

2. In the second selection, artists are characterized as

(A) complacent
(B) unwilling to change
(C) self-indulgent
(D) innocent victims
(E) nonchalant

3. "…you get no more of me" (line 2 of the third selection) makes the speaker's character seem ruled by

(A) hurt pride
(B) hate
(C) hardness
(D) an obliging nature
(E) leniency

4. How does the speaker in the fourth selection characterize "Time"?

(A) As gluttonous
(B) As hypocritical
(C) As bluffing
(D) As mysterious
(E) As secretive

5. In Selection Five, Escalus's words show him to be someone who

(A) is given to flights of fancy
(B) does not understand logical reasoning
(C) has not fully considered the ramifications of his position
(D) uses logical reasoning to present his case
(E) resists authority and defies the law

Questions About USE OF LANGUAGE

1. The literary device used to refer to Lady Rowena in Selection One ("the Queen of Love and Beauty"—line 6) is called a(n)

(A) epitaph
(B) euphemism
(C) synecdoche
(D) epithet
(E) metonymy

2. In the second selection, lines 3–10 produce an effect that serves to

(A) exaggerate the speaker's position
(B) amplify "art in the grand old sense" (lines 3–4)
(C) understate the speaker's position
(D) point out paradoxes in art
(E) rhetorically question the "handicraft ideal" (line 6)

3. With personified Faith kneeling as Love, Passion, and Innocence die (lines 9–12 in the third selection), the effect is to

(A) render no hope for Love's survival
(B) emphasize the speaker's anger
(C) mark a shift in TONE
(D) assert the power of Love
(E) imply that the speaker still holds hope of reconciliation

4. In the fourth selection, the direct address in lines 1–10 to personified Time is an example of

(A) irony
(B) parody
(C) apostrophe
(D) cacophony
(E) understatement

5. In Selection Five, Angelo makes his point in lines 1–4 by using a(n)

(A) analogy
(B) mixed metaphor
(C) simile
(D) allusion
(E) allegory

Questions About MEANING(S) IN CONTEXT

1. From the context of the first selection, a "seneschal" (line 38) probably is a(n)

(A) member of royalty
(B) vassel
(C) captured enemy
(D) agent in charge of the estate
(E) court jester

2. The "universal educator" in line 32 of the second selection is

(A) art
(B) human expression
(C) idealized art
(D) greed
(E) the machine

*3. In the context of the third selection, how can "cleanly" (line 4) be defined?

   I.   Completely
   II. In a sportsmanlike manner
   III. Morally pure

  (A) I only
  (B) II only
  (C) III only
  (D) I and II only
  (E) I, II, and III

4. In the fourth selection, "mortal dross" (line 6) probably is a reference to

  (A) spiritual life
  (B) carnal life
  (C) waste matter
  (D) time itself
  (E) worthless character

5. In the fifth selection (lines 22–23), justice seizing on someone occurs because of

  (A) opportunity
  (B) vengeance
  (C) the law only
  (D) a sense of fairness
  (E) equal rights

* Note concerning Set C, Selection Three, question 3 on Meanings of Words, Phrases, and Lines in Context:

Not only does "cleanly" refer to (I) completely, it also connotatively means in a sportsmanlike manner (II) because line 5 refers to shaking hands—an act of two opponents after a contest—and means "morally pure" (III) because, again in line 5, the speaker cancels vows.

ANSWER KEY: INTERPRETIVE SKILL PRACTICE SETS

Practice Set A

Questions About MEANING

1. **B**   2. **D**   3. **D**   4. **C**   5. **A**

Questions About FORM

1. **E**   2. **C**   3. **C**   4. **B**   5. **D**

Questions About NARRATIVE VOICE

1. **A**   2. **C**   3. **E**   4. **B**   5. **D**

Questions About TONE

1. **E**   2. **B**   3. **A**   4. **C**   5. **D**

Questions About CHARACTER

1. **A**   2. **E**   3. **C**   4. **C**   5. **B**

Questions About USE OF LANGUAGE

1. **B**   2. **D**   3. **C**   4. **C**   5. **A**

Questions About MEANINGS OF WORDS, PHRASES, AND LINES IN CONTEXT

1. **D**   2. **B**   3. **D**   4. **E**   5. **A**

Practice Set B

Questions About MEANING

1. **C**   2. **A**   3. **B**   4. **B**   5. **D**

Questions About FORM

1. **B**   2. **B**   3. **C**   4. **A**   5. **E**

Questions About NARRATIVE VOICE

1. **B**   2. **C**   3. **A**   4. **E**   5. **D**

Questions About TONE

1. **D**   2. **A**   3. **C**   4. **D**   5. **B**

Questions About CHARACTER

1. **C**   2. **D**   3. **D**   4. **B**   5. **E**

Questions About USE OF LANGUAGE

1. **C**   2. **B**   3. **C**   4. **A**   5. **E**

Questions About MEANINGS OF WORDS, PHRASES, AND LINES IN CONTEXT

1. **C**   2. **D**   3. **B**   4. **D**   5. **A**

Practice Set C

Questions About MEANING

1. **D**   2. **E**   3. **B**   4. **C**   5. **E**

Questions About FORM

1. **A**   2. **C**   3. **B**   4. **B**   5. **D**

Questions About NARRATIVE VOICE

1. **C**   2. **B**   3. **E**   4. **A**   5. **B**

Questions About TONE

1. **A**   2. **C**   3. **E**   4. **E**   5. **C**

Questions About CHARACTER

1. **C**   2. **B**   3. **A**   4. **A**   5. **D**

Questions About USE OF LANGUAGE

1. **D**   2. **B**   3. **E**   4. **C**   5. **A**

Questions About MEANING(S) IN CONTEXT

1. **D**   2. **E**   3. **E**   4. **B**   5. **A**

PART V

PRACTICE TESTS

ANSWER SHEET FOR PRACTICE TEST ONE

1. Ⓐ Ⓑ Ⓒ Ⓓ Ⓔ
2. Ⓐ Ⓑ Ⓒ Ⓓ Ⓔ
3. Ⓐ Ⓑ Ⓒ Ⓓ Ⓔ
4. Ⓐ Ⓑ Ⓒ Ⓓ Ⓔ
5. Ⓐ Ⓑ Ⓒ Ⓓ Ⓔ
6. Ⓐ Ⓑ Ⓒ Ⓓ Ⓔ
7. Ⓐ Ⓑ Ⓒ Ⓓ Ⓔ
8. Ⓐ Ⓑ Ⓒ Ⓓ Ⓔ
9. Ⓐ Ⓑ Ⓒ Ⓓ Ⓔ
10. Ⓐ Ⓑ Ⓒ Ⓓ Ⓔ
11. Ⓐ Ⓑ Ⓒ Ⓓ Ⓔ
12. Ⓐ Ⓑ Ⓒ Ⓓ Ⓔ
13. Ⓐ Ⓑ Ⓒ Ⓓ Ⓔ
14. Ⓐ Ⓑ Ⓒ Ⓓ Ⓔ
15. Ⓐ Ⓑ Ⓒ Ⓓ Ⓔ
16. Ⓐ Ⓑ Ⓒ Ⓓ Ⓔ
17. Ⓐ Ⓑ Ⓒ Ⓓ Ⓔ
18. Ⓐ Ⓑ Ⓒ Ⓓ Ⓔ
19. Ⓐ Ⓑ Ⓒ Ⓓ Ⓔ
20. Ⓐ Ⓑ Ⓒ Ⓓ Ⓔ

21. Ⓐ Ⓑ Ⓒ Ⓓ Ⓔ
22. Ⓐ Ⓑ Ⓒ Ⓓ Ⓔ
23. Ⓐ Ⓑ Ⓒ Ⓓ Ⓔ
24. Ⓐ Ⓑ Ⓒ Ⓓ Ⓔ
25. Ⓐ Ⓑ Ⓒ Ⓓ Ⓔ
26. Ⓐ Ⓑ Ⓒ Ⓓ Ⓔ
27. Ⓐ Ⓑ Ⓒ Ⓓ Ⓔ
28. Ⓐ Ⓑ Ⓒ Ⓓ Ⓔ
29. Ⓐ Ⓑ Ⓒ Ⓓ Ⓔ
30. Ⓐ Ⓑ Ⓒ Ⓓ Ⓔ
31. Ⓐ Ⓑ Ⓒ Ⓓ Ⓔ
32. Ⓐ Ⓑ Ⓒ Ⓓ Ⓔ
33. Ⓐ Ⓑ Ⓒ Ⓓ Ⓔ
34. Ⓐ Ⓑ Ⓒ Ⓓ Ⓔ
35. Ⓐ Ⓑ Ⓒ Ⓓ Ⓔ
36. Ⓐ Ⓑ Ⓒ Ⓓ Ⓔ
37. Ⓐ Ⓑ Ⓒ Ⓓ Ⓔ
38. Ⓐ Ⓑ Ⓒ Ⓓ Ⓔ
39. Ⓐ Ⓑ Ⓒ Ⓓ Ⓔ
40. Ⓐ Ⓑ Ⓒ Ⓓ Ⓔ

41. Ⓐ Ⓑ Ⓒ Ⓓ Ⓔ
42. Ⓐ Ⓑ Ⓒ Ⓓ Ⓔ
43. Ⓐ Ⓑ Ⓒ Ⓓ Ⓔ
44. Ⓐ Ⓑ Ⓒ Ⓓ Ⓔ
45. Ⓐ Ⓑ Ⓒ Ⓓ Ⓔ
46. Ⓐ Ⓑ Ⓒ Ⓓ Ⓔ
47. Ⓐ Ⓑ Ⓒ Ⓓ Ⓔ
48. Ⓐ Ⓑ Ⓒ Ⓓ Ⓔ
49. Ⓐ Ⓑ Ⓒ Ⓓ Ⓔ
50. Ⓐ Ⓑ Ⓒ Ⓓ Ⓔ
51. Ⓐ Ⓑ Ⓒ Ⓓ Ⓔ
52. Ⓐ Ⓑ Ⓒ Ⓓ Ⓔ
53. Ⓐ Ⓑ Ⓒ Ⓓ Ⓔ
54. Ⓐ Ⓑ Ⓒ Ⓓ Ⓔ
55. Ⓐ Ⓑ Ⓒ Ⓓ Ⓔ
56. Ⓐ Ⓑ Ⓒ Ⓓ Ⓔ
57. Ⓐ Ⓑ Ⓒ Ⓓ Ⓔ
58. Ⓐ Ⓑ Ⓒ Ⓓ Ⓔ
59. Ⓐ Ⓑ Ⓒ Ⓓ Ⓔ
60. Ⓐ Ⓑ Ⓒ Ⓓ Ⓔ

PRACTICE TEST ONE

Time allowed: One hour

<u>Directions</u>: The following questions test your understanding of several literary selections. Read each passage or poem and the questions that follow it. Select the best answer choice for each question by blackening the matching oval on your answer sheet. **Special attention should be given to questions containing the following words: EXCEPT, LEAST, NOT.**

<u>Questions 1–8</u> are based on the following passage.

No doubt it was having a strong effect on him as he walked to Lowick. Fred's light hopeful nature had perhaps never had so much
line of a bruise as from this suggestion that if he
(5) had been out of the way Mary might have made a thoroughly good match. Also he was piqued that he had been what he called such a stupid lout as to ask that intervention from Mr Farebrother. But it was not in a lover's
(10) nature—it was not in Fred's—that the new anxiety raised about Mary's feeling should not surmount every other. Notwithstanding his trust in Mr Farebrother's generosity, notwithstanding what Mary had said to him,
(15) Fred could not help feeling he had a rival: it was a new consciousness, and he objected to it extremely, not being in the least ready to give up Mary for her good, being ready rather to fight for her with any man whatsoever. But the
(20) fighting with Mr Farebrother must be of a metaphorical kind, which was much more difficult to Fred than the muscular. Certainly this experience was a discipline for Fred hardly less sharp than his disappointment
(25) about his uncle's will. The iron had not entered his soul, but he had begun to imagine what the sharp edge would be. It did not once occur to Fred that Mrs Garth might be mistaken about Mr Farebrother, but he
(30) suspected that she might be wrong about Mary. Mary had been staying at the parsonage lately, and her mother might know very little of what had been passing in her mind.

Middlemarch
by George Eliot

1. Lines 28–31 imply that

   (A) Fred dislikes Mary
   (B) Fred does not trust Mr. Farebrother
   (C) Fred disliked his late uncle
   (D) Mrs. Garth gossiped about Mary and Mr. Farebrother
   (E) Mary is Mr. Farebrother's sister

2. The narrator's comments in lines 15–19 make Fred seem to be

   (A) unsympathetic and jubilant
   (B) jealous and selfish
   (C) jealous and enraptured
   (D) comfortless and irritating
   (E) indulgent and forbearant

3. The phrase "metaphorical kind" (line 21) conveys the idea that the fight is

   (A) illusionary
   (B) allegorical
   (C) undisciplined
   (D) physical
   (E) mental

4. The statement in lines 24–25 that Fred was disappointed about his uncle's will is intended as

   (A) an observation concerning Fred's character
   (B) an allusion to a large cash settlement
   (C) an implication concerning Fred's financial status
   (D) an inference concerning the value of discipline
   (E) a conclusion concerning his uncle's character

5. The "bruise" in line 4 contextually denotes

   (A) injured flesh
   (B) a beating
   (C) injured feelings
   (D) verbal abuse
   (E) physical abuse

6. Lines 25–27 contain a figure of speech known as

   (A) a simile
   (B) a metaphor
   (C) alliteration
   (D) literary allusion
   (E) personification

7. As the words "light hopeful nature" (lines 2–3), "a stupid lout" (line 8), "a lover's nature" (lines 9–10), and "a new consciousness" (line 16) are used, they

   (A) imply that Fred's character is being challenged
   (B) suggest that Fred is deceitful
   (C) are bitterly ironic in tone
   (D) reinforce the metaphorical aspects of Fred's nature
   (E) indicate that Fred is not really in love

8. An accurate inference from the passage would be that Fred is

   (A) self-sacrificial
   (B) a stupid lout
   (C) a conscientious lover
   (D) a fortune seeker
   (E) somewhat egotistical

Questions 9–21 are based on the following poem.

A Bed of Forget-Me-Nots

Is love so prone to change and rot
We are fain to rear Forget-me-not
By measure in a garden-plot?—

line I love its growth at large and free
(5) By untrod path and unlopped tree,
Or nodding by the unpruned hedge,
Or on the water's dangerous edge
Where flags and meadowsweet blow rank
With rushes on the quaking bank.

(10) Love is not taught in learning's school,
Love is not parcelled out by rule:
Hath curb or call an answer got?—
So free must be Forget-me-not.
Give me the flame no dampness dulls,
(15) The passion of the instinctive pulse,
Love steadfast as a fixèd star,
Tender as doves with nestlings are,
More large than time, more strong than death:
This all creation travails of—
(20) She groans not for a passing breath—
This is Forget-me-not and Love.

by Christina Rossetti

9. The poem's main subject is concerned with the

   (A) brevity of love
   (B) nature of love
   (C) growing of Forget-me-nots
   (D) death of love
   (E) freedom of flower gardens

10. Contextually, "flags" in line 8 are

   (A) weeds
   (B) national symbols
   (C) flowers
   (D) stones
   (E) shaped gardens

11. "Rank" can have several connotative and denotative meanings. How can it be understood as used in line 8?

    I.   Bad taste
    II. Bad smell
    III. Growing vigorously
    IV. In rows

    (A) I only
    (B) II only
    (C) III only
    (D) I and II only
    (E) I, II, and IV only

12. "Blow" in line 8 means which of these definitions?

    I.   Bloom
    II. Move in the wind
    III. Carried in the wind

    (A) I only
    (B) II only
    (C) III only
    (D) II and III only
    (E) I, II, and III

13. What is the purpose of lines 1–3 as they relate to the rest of the poem?

    (A) They set a mocking tone for the poem.
    (B) They reveal the speaker's sense of insecurity.
    (C) They emphasize the poem's dismal tone.
    (D) They introduce the analogy that is the basis of the poem.
    (E) They reinforce the passionate nature of love.

14. The speaker compares Forget-me-nots and

    (A) flags
    (B) garden-plots
    (C) death
    (D) school
    (E) love

15. In what way do lines 4–9 relate to lines 10–21?

    (A) They are allusional.
    (B) They are metaphorical.
    (C) They reflect extreme pessimism.
    (D) They reinforce a sense of dispassionate sympathy.
    (E) They are allegorical.

16. The speaker's feeling toward love is that

    (A) love is short-lived
    (B) love can be learned
    (C) love should be unrestrained
    (D) love is weak and fragile
    (E) love is disciplined

17. The questions asked in lines 1–3 and line 12 can be considered

    (A) insolent
    (B) hostile
    (C) ambivalent
    (D) indifferent
    (E) rhetorical

18. In the context of the poem, the opposition of "untrod," "unlopped," and "unpruned" (lines 5–6) to "school," "rule," and "curb" (lines 10–12) emphasizes that

    (A) gardens can be unkempt
    (B) love is eternal
    (C) flowers are wild
    (D) love is free
    (E) love can be controlled

19. In line 16, which of these literary devices is used?

    (A) Metaphor
    (B) Simile
    (C) Personification
    (D) Understatement
    (E) Synaesthesia

20. In the first stanza, "garden-plot" (line 3) becomes for the speaker which of the representations listed below?

(A) A figure for confinement
(B) A symbol of beauty
(C) A place to raise Forget-me-nots
(D) A place of change
(E) An imaginative place for love to exist

21. The speaker implies in lines 1–3 that we attempt to structure love to

(A) prevent its destruction
(B) capture its joy
(C) measure its impact
(D) control its effects
(E) forget its measure

Questions 22–28 are based on the following passage.

"See! Master Coffin," cried the lieutenant, pointing out the object to his cockswain as they glided by it, "the shovel-nosed gentlemen
line are regaling daintily; you have neglected the
(5) Christian's duty of burying your dead."
The old seaman cast a melancholy look at the dead whale, and replied:
"If I had the creature in Boston Bay, or on the Sandy Point of Munny Moy, 'twould be
(10) the making of me! But riches and honor are for the great and the larned, and there's nothing left for poor Tom Coffin to do, but to veer and haul on his own rolling tackle, that he may ride out the rest of the gale of life
(15) without springing any of his old spars."
"How now, Long Tom!" cried the officer; "these rocks and cliffs will shipwreck you on the shoals of poetry yet; you grow sentimental!"
"Them rocks might wrack any vessel that
(20) struck them," said the literal cockswain; "and as for poetry, I wants none better than the good old song of Captain Kidd; but it's enough to raise solemn thoughts in a Cape Poge Indian, to see an eighty-barrel whale
(25) devoured by sharks—'tis an awful waste of property! I've seen the death of two hundred of the creaters, though it seems to keep the rations of poor old Tom as short as ever."

The cockswain walked aft, while the vessel
(30) was passing the whale, and seating himself on the taffrail, with his face resting gloomily on his bony hand, he fastened his eyes on the object of his solicitude, and continued to gaze at it with melancholy regret, while it was to be
(35) seen glistening in the sunbeams, as it rolled its glittering side of white into the air, or the rays fell unreflected on the black and rougher coat of the back of the monster. In the meantime, the navigators diligently pursued their way for
(40) the haven we have mentioned, into which they steered with every appearance of the fearlessness of friends, and the exultation of conquerors.
A few eager and gratified spectators lined
(45) the edges of the small bay, and Barnstable concluded his arrangement for deceiving the enemy, by admonishing his crew that they were now about to enter on a service that would require their utmost intrepidity and sagacity.

The Pilot
by James Fenimore Cooper

22. Tom Coffin does not get rich from this whale because

(A) he is too depressed
(B) he lacks sufficient line and tackle
(C) he is not interested in wealth
(D) he is misled by the lieutenant
(E) he is too far from a trading center

23. Tom blames his situation in part on

(A) the shovel-nosed gentleman
(B) his lack of position and education
(C) the lieutenant
(D) the whale
(E) Captain Kidd

24. Tom compares himself in lines 12–15 to

(A) fishing tackle
(B) a ship in a storm
(C) the whale
(D) a whaling ship at work
(E) Boston Bay

25. When the officer refers to "these rocks and cliffs" (line 16–18), he means that

   (A) dangerous land formations lie ahead
   (B) the ship is about to wreck
   (C) there are setbacks in Tom's life
   (D) they are going to hit a whale
   (E) the ship is sinking

26. The "shovel-nosed gentlemen" in line 3 are

   (A) the ship's crew
   (B) Tom's friends
   (C) sharks
   (D) visiting royalty
   (E) the ship's officers

27. In what tone of voice does the lieutenant say "you have neglected the Christian's duty of burying your dead" (lines 4–5)?

   (A) Patronizing mockery
   (B) Sarcastic teasing
   (C) Accusatory wrath
   (D) Kind insistence
   (E) Aggressive hostility

28. Tom's misunderstanding (lines 19–20) of the officer's remark (lines 16–18) is ironic because

   (A) Tom did not get to salvage the whale
   (B) the boat was already shipwrecked
   (C) Tom was not really sentimental
   (D) the officer lacked insight into Tom's meaning
   (E) Tom, himself, had been speaking metaphorically

Questions 29–37 are based on the following poem.

Come Down, O Maid

"Come down, O maid, from yonder mountain
   height.
What pleasure lives in height (the shepherd
   sang),
In height and cold, the splendor of the hills?
But cease to move so near the heavens and
line   cease
(5) To glide a sunbeam by the blasted pine,
To sit a star upon the sparkling spire;

And come, for Love is of the valley, come,
For Love is of the valley, come thou down
And find him; by the happy threshold, he,
(10) Or hand in hand with Plenty in the maize,
Or red with spirted purple of the vats,
Or foxlike in the vine; nor cares to walk
With Death and Morning on the Silver Horns,
Nor wilt thou snare him in the white ravine,
(15) Nor find him dropped upon the firths of ice,
That huddling slant in furrow-cloven falls
To roll the torrent out of dusky doors.
But follow; let the torrent dance thee down
To find him in the valley; let the wild
(20) Lean-headed eagles yelp alone, and leave
The monstrous ledges there to slope, and spill
Their thousand wreaths of dangling water-smoke,
That like a broken purpose waste in air.
So waste not thou, but come; for all the vales
(25) Await thee; azure pillars of the hearth
Arise to thee; the children call, and I
Thy shepherd pipe, and sweet is every sound,
Sweeter thy voice, but every sound is sweet;
Myriads of rivulets hurrying thro' the lawn,
(30) The moan of doves in immemorial elms,
And murmuring of innumerable bees."

                              by Alfred, Lord Tennyson

29. The genre of this poem is called

   (A) a pastoral love lyric
   (B) a pastoral love epic
   (C) a didactic narrative
   (D) a dramatic monologue
   (E) a pastoral elegy

30. The poem is written in

   (A) ballad stanza
   (B) blank verse
   (C) couplets
   (D) forced rhyme
   (E) sonnet form

31. The speaker in the poem can be identified through context as

   (A) a young girl
   (B) the mountain
   (C) a shepherd
   (D) the hills
   (E) Love

32. The literary devices used in lines 7–8 include

    (A) paradox and internal rhyme
    (B) simile and echo
    (C) echo and internal rhyme
    (D) simile and alliteration
    (E) metaphor and paradox

33. The tone of the speaker's question in lines 2–3 in the context of the poem is

    (A) condemning
    (B) didactic
    (C) impetuous
    (D) explosive
    (E) conciliatory

34. Lines 7–19 refer to love figuratively, making it appear as

    (A) a friend of death
    (B) only a visitor to the mountain
    (C) an angry force in the mountain
    (D) someone living happily in the valley
    (E) the victim of the mountain

35. The speaker sees the "mountain height" (line 1) and the "valley" (line 7) as symbolic of all the following concepts EXCEPT

    (A) lack of love and love
    (B) unhappiness and happiness
    (C) death and life
    (D) day and night
    (E) cold and warmth

36. In this poem, what is the role of the mountain?

    I.   A symbol of aloofness
    II. A metaphor of snowy climates
    III. The abstract image of the maid

    (A) I only
    (B) II only
    (C) III only
    (D) I and III only
    (E) I, II, and III

37. The poem's meaning is discerned through several elements of opposition; however, which of the following pairs of words does NOT correctly reflect these elements?

    (A) "height" (line 1) and "down" (line 8)
    (B) "maid" (line 1) and "Morning" (line 13)
    (C) "blasted" (line 5) and "Plenty" (line 10)
    (D) "white" (line 14) and "red" (line 11)
    (E) "eagles" (line 20) and "children" (line 26)

Questions 38–42 are based on the following passage.

    Dream delivers us to dream, and there is no
end to illusion. Life is a train of moods like a
string of beads, and as we pass through them
line they prove to be many-colored lenses which
(5) paint the world their own hue, and each shows
only what lies in its focus. From the mountain
you see the mountain. We animate what we
can, and we see only what we animate. Nature
and books belong to the eyes that see them. It
(10) depends on the mood of the man whether he
shall see the sunset or the fine poem. There
are always sunsets, and there is always genius;
but only a few hours so serene that we can
relish nature or criticism. The more or less
(15) depends on structure or temperament.
Temperament is the iron wire on which the
beads are strung. Of what use is fortune or
talent to a cold and defective nature? Who
cares what sensibility or discrimination a man
(20) has at some time shown, if he falls asleep in
his chair? or if he laugh and giggle? or if he
apologize? or is infected with egotism? or
thinks of his dollar?

               "Experience"
               by Ralph Waldo Emerson

38. The speaker's use of language in this passage projects a tone that is

    (A) hostile
    (B) placating
    (C) contemplative
    (D) antagonistic
    (E) arrogant

39. In this passage, a string of beads is a figuratively used

   (A) symbol of illusions
   (B) vehicle to explain the relationship of temperament to moods
   (C) vehicle to illustrate temperament's role in dreams
   (D) literary allusion
   (E) reference to the events of life

40. According to the passage, how we see the world is determined by

   (A) our dreams
   (B) nature
   (C) books
   (D) criticism
   (E) our moods

41. According to the passage, which of the following gives value to fortunes or talent?

   (A) Dreams
   (B) Moods
   (C) Nature
   (D) Animations
   (E) Temperament

42. The speaker's use of rhetorical questions emphasizes

   (A) the importance of a defective nature
   (B) his own sense of disillusionment
   (C) the importance of temperament
   (D) the dreamlike quality of life
   (E) his argumentative tone

Questions 43–53 are based on the following poem.

Devoid of Reason

Devoid of reason, thrall to foolish ire,
I walk and chase a savage fairy still,
Now near the flood, straight on the mounting hill,
Now midst the woods of youth, and vain desire.
line
(5) For leash I bear a cord of careful grief;
For brach I lead an overforward mind;

My hounds are thoughts, and rage despairing blind,
Pain, cruelty, and care without relief.
But they, perceiving that my swift pursuit
(10) My flying fairy cannot overtake,
With open mouths their prey on me do make,
Like hungry hounds that lately lost their suit,
And full of fury on their master feed,
To hasten on my hapless death with speed.

by Thomas Lodge

43. Using the more specific word "hounds" (line 7) rather than the more general word "dogs" has which of these effects?

   (A) Emphasizes that they hunt prey
   (B) Illustrates the speaker's sense of drama
   (C) Varies the tone of the poem
   (D) Symbolizes all predators
   (E) Reinforces a sense of grief

44. The hounds in the poem are best set forth as

   (A) a savage fairy
   (B) the speaker's angry thoughts
   (C) the speaker's troubled thoughts
   (D) death
   (E) reason

45. The meaning of "an overforward mind" (line 6) can be seen in the paraphrase

   (A) mentally unstable
   (B) a mind ahead of its time
   (C) precocious
   (D) too mentally advanced
   (E) politically active

46. The phrase "walk and chase" (line 2), as used in the poem, structurally is mirrored by which of these phrases?

   (A) Slow down and speed up
   (B) Stroll and pursue
   (C) Pursue and overtake
   (D) Behold and despise
   (E) Lead and follow

47. The central situation of the poem is that

    (A) the speaker is insane
    (B) the speaker is a sportsman
    (C) an angry enemy is killing the speaker
    (D) anger is self-destructive
    (E) anger is therapeutic

48. By considering the poem in its entirety, the reader should view the speaker's attitude toward the fairy as

    (A) frenzied
    (B) insolent
    (C) reverential
    (D) derisive
    (E) laudable

49. The role of lines 13–14 in terms of the rest of the poem can be summarized by which of these statements?

    (A) They intensify the speaker's sense of justice.
    (B) They summarize the irony of the speaker's situation.
    (C) They signal a departure from the subject.
    (D) They intensify the falsity of the speaker's words.
    (E) They threaten the position of the fairy established in lines 2 and 10.

50. Lines 13–14 contain which of the following phonic devices?

    (A) Echo rhyme
    (B) Eye rhyme
    (C) Imperfect rhyme
    (D) Onomatopoeia
    (E) Alliteration

51. Line 9 is pivotal to the meaning of the poem because which of the following happens?

    (A) Anger is made more intense.
    (B) The speaker's position changes from attacker to victim.
    (C) The hounds become real.
    (D) The speaker's position changes from fear to anger.
    (E) The fairy is caught.

52. The meaning of the poem is structurally contrasted between lines 1–8 and lines 9–14. This contrast is NOT seen in the words

    (A) "chase" (line 2) and "cannot overtake" (line 10)
    (B) "I lead" (line 6) and "they, perceiving" (line 9)
    (C) "foolish ire" (line 1) and "hapless death" (line 14)
    (D) "savage fairy" (line 2) and "hungry hounds" (line 12)
    (E) "flood" (line 3) and "speed" (line 14)

53. The hounds' attack in lines 9–14 is symbolically ironic because

    (A) the hounds are not really dogs
    (B) dogs do not really chase fairies
    (C) hunting dogs seldom turn on their masters
    (D) the speaker has already confessed to his lack of reason
    (E) the speaker's own angry thoughts are destroying him

Questions 54–60 are based on the following passage.

Mrs Moorland was a very good woman, and wished to see her children every thing they ought to be; but her time was so much
line occupied in lying-in and teaching the little
(5) ones, that her elder daughters were inevitably left to shift for themselves; and it was not very wonderful that Catherine, who had by nature nothing heroic about her, should prefer cricket, base ball, riding on horseback, and running
(10) about the country at the age of fourteen, to books—or at least books of information—for, provided that nothing like useful knowledge could be gained from them, provided they were all story and no reflection, she had never
(15) any objection to books at all. But from fifteen to seventeen she was in training for a heroine; she read all such works as heroines must read to supply their memories with those quotations which are so serviceable and so soothing in
(20) the vicissitudes of their eventful lives.

From Pope, she learnt to censure those who
'bear about the mockery of woe.'

From Gray, that
> '*Many a flower is born to blush unseen.*
(25) > '*And waste its fragrance on the desert air.*'

From Thompson, that
> —'*It is a delightful task*
> '*To teach the young idea how to shoot.*'

And from Shakespeare she gained a great
(30) store of information—amongst the rest, that
> —'*Trifles light as air,*
> '*Are, to the jealous, confirmation strong,*
> '*As proofs of Holy Writ.*'

That
(35)
> '*The poor beetle, which we tread upon,*
> '*In corporal sufferance feels a pang as great*
> '*As when a giant dies.*'

And that a young woman in love always looks
(40) > —'*like Patience on a monument*
> '*Smiling at Grief.*'

> *Northanger Abbey*
> Jane Austen

54. That Mrs. Moorland's time "was so much occupied in lying-in and teaching the little ones" (lines 3–5) supports the idea that

(A) education was reserved for male children
(B) she bore many children
(C) she was reclusive
(D) she avoided adult company
(E) that children were seen and not heard

55. As used in lines 6–7, "not very wonderful" is a litote meaning

(A) awesome
(B) to be wondered at
(C) to be expected
(D) terrible
(E) the object of wonder

56. A conclusion that can be drawn from the passage is that

(A) Catherine sought heroism despite her background
(B) Catherine is not the heroic type
(C) the poets say much about heroism
(D) Mrs. Moorland was inadequate as a parent
(E) Catherine disliked reading

57. As described in this passage in lines 1–15, Catherine is

(A) a scholar
(B) morose
(C) perfunctory
(D) a tomboy
(E) quarrelsome

58. According to the passage, before the age of fifteen, Catherine chose books that were

(A) "how-to" books
(B) shallow stories
(C) self-help
(D) romances
(E) heroic

59. In its context, who are "those who 'bear about the mockery of woe'" (line 22)?

I.   People who insult those in grief
II. People who pretend to be suffering misfortune
III. People who express grief through laughter

(A) I only
(B) II only
(C) III only
(D) I and III only
(E) I, II, and III

60. Shakespeare's simile in lines 35–38 is a use of language called the

(A) symbol
(B) rhetorical question
(C) parody
(D) meiosis
(E) hyperbole

ANSWER KEY: PRACTICE TEST ONE

1. D	7. A	13. D	19. B	25. C	31. C	37. B	43. A	49. B	55. C
2. B	8. E	14. E	20. A	26. C	32. C	38. C	44. B	50. E	56. A
3. E	9. B	15. B	21. A	27. B	33. E	39. B	45. D	51. B	57. D
4. A	10. C	16. C	22. E	28. E	34. D	40. E	46. B	52. E	58. B
5. C	11. C	17. E	23. B	29. A	35. D	41. E	47. D	53. E	59. B
6. B	12. A	18. D	24. B	30. B	36. A	42. C	48. A	54. B	60. E

TO OBTAIN YOUR RAW SCORE:

_____ divided by 4 = _____
Total wrong   Score W

_____ minus _____ = _____
Total right   Score W   Score R

Round Score R to the nearest whole number for
the raw score.

HOW DID YOU DO?

55–60 = Excellent
44–54 = Very Good
35–43 = Above Average
23–34 = Average
15–22 = Below Average

ANSWER SHEET FOR PRACTICE TEST TWO

1. Ⓐ Ⓑ Ⓒ Ⓓ Ⓔ
2. Ⓐ Ⓑ Ⓒ Ⓓ Ⓔ
3. Ⓐ Ⓑ Ⓒ Ⓓ Ⓔ
4. Ⓐ Ⓑ Ⓒ Ⓓ Ⓔ
5. Ⓐ Ⓑ Ⓒ Ⓓ Ⓔ
6. Ⓐ Ⓑ Ⓒ Ⓓ Ⓔ
7. Ⓐ Ⓑ Ⓒ Ⓓ Ⓔ
8. Ⓐ Ⓑ Ⓒ Ⓓ Ⓔ
9. Ⓐ Ⓑ Ⓒ Ⓓ Ⓔ
10. Ⓐ Ⓑ Ⓒ Ⓓ Ⓔ
11. Ⓐ Ⓑ Ⓒ Ⓓ Ⓔ
12. Ⓐ Ⓑ Ⓒ Ⓓ Ⓔ
13. Ⓐ Ⓑ Ⓒ Ⓓ Ⓔ
14. Ⓐ Ⓑ Ⓒ Ⓓ Ⓔ
15. Ⓐ Ⓑ Ⓒ Ⓓ Ⓔ
16. Ⓐ Ⓑ Ⓒ Ⓓ Ⓔ
17. Ⓐ Ⓑ Ⓒ Ⓓ Ⓔ
18. Ⓐ Ⓑ Ⓒ Ⓓ Ⓔ
19. Ⓐ Ⓑ Ⓒ Ⓓ Ⓔ
20. Ⓐ Ⓑ Ⓒ Ⓓ Ⓔ

21. Ⓐ Ⓑ Ⓒ Ⓓ Ⓔ
22. Ⓐ Ⓑ Ⓒ Ⓓ Ⓔ
23. Ⓐ Ⓑ Ⓒ Ⓓ Ⓔ
24. Ⓐ Ⓑ Ⓒ Ⓓ Ⓔ
25. Ⓐ Ⓑ Ⓒ Ⓓ Ⓔ
26. Ⓐ Ⓑ Ⓒ Ⓓ Ⓔ
27. Ⓐ Ⓑ Ⓒ Ⓓ Ⓔ
28. Ⓐ Ⓑ Ⓒ Ⓓ Ⓔ
29. Ⓐ Ⓑ Ⓒ Ⓓ Ⓔ
30. Ⓐ Ⓑ Ⓒ Ⓓ Ⓔ
31. Ⓐ Ⓑ Ⓒ Ⓓ Ⓔ
32. Ⓐ Ⓑ Ⓒ Ⓓ Ⓔ
33. Ⓐ Ⓑ Ⓒ Ⓓ Ⓔ
34. Ⓐ Ⓑ Ⓒ Ⓓ Ⓔ
35. Ⓐ Ⓑ Ⓒ Ⓓ Ⓔ
36. Ⓐ Ⓑ Ⓒ Ⓓ Ⓔ
37. Ⓐ Ⓑ Ⓒ Ⓓ Ⓔ
38. Ⓐ Ⓑ Ⓒ Ⓓ Ⓔ
39. Ⓐ Ⓑ Ⓒ Ⓓ Ⓔ
40. Ⓐ Ⓑ Ⓒ Ⓓ Ⓔ

41. Ⓐ Ⓑ Ⓒ Ⓓ Ⓔ
42. Ⓐ Ⓑ Ⓒ Ⓓ Ⓔ
43. Ⓐ Ⓑ Ⓒ Ⓓ Ⓔ
44. Ⓐ Ⓑ Ⓒ Ⓓ Ⓔ
45. Ⓐ Ⓑ Ⓒ Ⓓ Ⓔ
46. Ⓐ Ⓑ Ⓒ Ⓓ Ⓔ
47. Ⓐ Ⓑ Ⓒ Ⓓ Ⓔ
48. Ⓐ Ⓑ Ⓒ Ⓓ Ⓔ
49. Ⓐ Ⓑ Ⓒ Ⓓ Ⓔ
50. Ⓐ Ⓑ Ⓒ Ⓓ Ⓔ
51. Ⓐ Ⓑ Ⓒ Ⓓ Ⓔ
52. Ⓐ Ⓑ Ⓒ Ⓓ Ⓔ
53. Ⓐ Ⓑ Ⓒ Ⓓ Ⓔ
54. Ⓐ Ⓑ Ⓒ Ⓓ Ⓔ
55. Ⓐ Ⓑ Ⓒ Ⓓ Ⓔ
56. Ⓐ Ⓑ Ⓒ Ⓓ Ⓔ
57. Ⓐ Ⓑ Ⓒ Ⓓ Ⓔ
58. Ⓐ Ⓑ Ⓒ Ⓓ Ⓔ
59. Ⓐ Ⓑ Ⓒ Ⓓ Ⓔ
60. Ⓐ Ⓑ Ⓒ Ⓓ Ⓔ

PRACTICE TEST TWO

Time allowed: One hour

Directions: The following questions test your understanding of several literary selections. Read each passage or poem and the questions that follow it. Select the best answer choice for each question by blackening the matching oval on your answer sheet. **Special attention should be given to questions containing the following words: EXCEPT, LEAST, NOT.**

Questions 1–12 are based on the following poem.

The Spring

Now that the winter's gone, the earth hath lost
Her snow-white robes, and now no more the frost
Candies the grass, or casts an icy cream
line   Upon the silver lake or crystal stream;
(5)   But the warm sun thaws the benumbèd earth,
And makes it tender; gives a sacred birth
To the dead swallow; wakes in hollow tree
The drowsy cuckoo and the humble-bee.
Now do a choir of chirping minstrels bring
(10) In triumph to the world the youthful spring.
The valleys, hills, and woods in rich array
Welcome the coming of the longed-for May.
Now all things smile, only my love doth lour;
Nor hath the scalding noonday sun the power
(15) To melt that marble ice, which still doth hold
Her heart congealed, and makes her pity cold.
The ox, which lately did for shelter fly
Into the stall, doth now securely lie
In open fields; and love no more is made
(20) By the fireside, but in the cooler shade
Amyntas now doth with his Chloris sleep
Under a sycamore, and all things keep
Time with the season; only she doth carry
June in her eyes, in her heart January.

by Thomas Carew

1. The relationship between "my love" in line 13 and the "earth" in line 1 can be seen in the relationship of

(A) "grass" (line 3) and "fields" (line 19)
(B) "ice" (line 15) and "congealed" (line 16)
(C) "May" (line 12) and "June" (line 24)
(D) "hollow tree" (line 7) and "shelter" (line 17)
(E) "cold" (line 16) and "warm" (line 5)

2. Given the context of the poem, the ox most likely went to shelter in lines 17–19 because it

(A) was startled by the bee in line 8
(B) was avoiding the "scalding noonday sun" (line 14)
(C) was fleeing winter storms
(D) was seeking "cooler shade" (line 20)
(E) was afraid of the cold-hearted lover

3. In the final line, the incongruity that "she doth carry June in her eyes, in her heart January" implies that

(A) her looks are deceptive
(B) she suffers from poor vision
(C) she really does enjoy spring
(D) her actions cover a warm personality
(E) she dislikes cold weather

4. In its context, "smile" (line 13) makes nature seem

   (A) repugnant and loathsome
   (B) jubilant and responsive
   (C) aesthetic and unrestrained
   (D) wary and deliberate
   (E) impetuous and audacious

5. In the context of the poem as a whole, the speaker has an attitude toward "my love" (line 13) that is projecting

   (A) critical discrimination
   (B) cautious prudence
   (C) undaunted daring
   (D) angry impatience
   (E) apprehensive trepidation

6. In lines 14–16, what literary device is used to describe the coldness of her heart?

   (A) Allegory
   (B) Hyperbole
   (C) Caricature
   (D) Simile
   (E) Interior monologue

7. The synaesthesia of "melt that marble ice" appeals to which of the following senses?

   (A) Thermal, tactile, and visual
   (B) Thermal, aural, and kinesthetic
   (C) Gustatory, thermal, and tactile
   (D) Kinesthetic, olfactory, and visual
   (E) Tactile, visual, and gustatory

8. The poem contains a contrast that can be seen in all the following pairs EXCEPT

   (A) "snow-white robes"…"no more the frost" (line 2)
   (B) "the warm sun"…"the benumbèd earth" (line 5)
   (C) "makes"…"gives" (line 6)
   (D) "dead"…"wakes" (line 7)
   (E) "smile"…"lour" (line 13)

9. The poem can be called

   (A) a pastoral sonnet
   (B) a celebration of spring
   (C) an ode to spring
   (D) a comparison and contrast of the seasons
   (E) an expression of frustration by a daunted lover

10. "Dead" (line 7) contextually means all the following EXCEPT

    (A) barren
    (B) unproductive
    (C) cold
    (D) unfruitful
    (E) unerring

11. As used in this poem, June and January (line 24) figuratively represent all the following EXCEPT

    (A) elements of personality
    (B) months of the year
    (C) warmth and coldness
    (D) change and resistance to change
    (E) new growth and dormancy

12. "Candies" in line 3 is a play on words meaning

    (A) to preserve
    (B) to sweeten
    (C) to cover
    (D) to crystallize
    (E) to congeal

Questions 13–23 are based on the following passage.

    "Are you mad, old man?" demanded Sir
Edmund Andros, in loud and harsh tones.
"How dare you stay the march of King
line James's Governor?"
(5)   "I have stayed the march of a King himself,
ere now," replied the gray figure, with stern
composure. "I am here, Sir Governor, because
the cry of an oppressed people hath disturbed
me in my secret place; and beseeching this
(10) favor earnestly of the Lord, it was vouchsafed
me to appear once again on earth, in the good
old cause of his saints. And what speak ye of

James? There is no longer a Popish tyrant on the throne of England, and by tomorrow noon,
(15) his name shall be a byword in this very street, where ye would make it a word of terror. Back, thou that wast a Governor, back! With this night thy power is ended—to–morrow, the prison!—back, lest I foretell the scaffold!"
(20)   The people had been drawing nearer and nearer, and drinking in the words of their champion, who spoke in accents long disused, like one unaccustomed to converse, except with the dead of many years ago. But his
(25) voice stirred their souls. They confronted the soldiers, not wholly without arms, and ready to convert the very stones of the street into deadly weapons. Sir Edmund Andros looked at the old man; then he cast his hard and cruel
(30) eye over the multitude, and beheld them burning that lurid wrath, so difficult to kindle or to quench; and again he fixed his gaze on the aged form, which stood obscurely in an open space, where neither friend nor foe had
(35) thrust himself. What were his thoughts, he uttered no word which might discover. But whether the oppressor were overawed by the Gray Champion's look, or perceived his peril in the threatening attitude of the people, it is
(40) certain that he gave back, and ordered his soldiers to commence a slow and guarded retreat. Before another sunset, the Governor, and all that rode so proudly with him, were prisoners, and long ere it was known that
(45) James had abdicated, King William was proclaimed throughout New England.

> "The Gray Champion"
> by Nathaniel Hawthorne

13. The tone of " 'I have stayed the march of a King himself, ere now' " (lines 5–6) makes the Gray Champion seem

(A) audacious and in rapport
(B) unyielding and conniving
(C) propitious and conducive
(D) challenging and defiant
(E) indulgent and acquiescent

14. Contextually, "stay" in line 3 is a way of saying

(A) to hinder
(B) to wait
(C) to quell
(D) to await
(E) to endure

15. Another way of saying "drinking in" (line 21) is

(A) imbibing liquid
(B) absorbing mentally
(C) swallowing hard
(D) swallowing liquor
(E) toasting

16. Sir Edmund Andros's character in this passage seems as one who is

(A) a cynic
(B) a benefactor
(C) unmercifully cruel
(D) compassionately natured
(E) sympathetic

17. The identity of the Gray Champion can be surmised from this passage to be

(A) a respected townsman
(B) well known in the area
(C) used to public speaking
(D) too old to fight in the battle
(E) a mysterious figure

18. Below is a list of statements concerning the passage. All are supported by the context EXCEPT that the

(A) narrative is at a point of climax
(B) main character is the Gray Champion
(C) villain is Sir Edmund Andros
(D) tone is comical
(E) tone is patriotic

19. Which of these literary devices is used in lines 13–19?

    (A) Rhetorical question
    (B) Sarcasm
    (C) Foreshadowing
    (D) Satire
    (E) Paradox

20. In lines 11–19, the Gray Champion implies that

    (A) the Governor will escape
    (B) the current king should be respected
    (C) he is afraid
    (D) he can influence future events
    (E) retreat is his only option

21. The Gray Champion's tone in lines 11–19 is

    (A) stolid
    (B) placid
    (C) nonchalant
    (D) indulgent
    (E) threatening

22. Of what significance are the words "ere" (line 6), "ye" (lines 12, 16), "thou" (line 17), and "wast" (line 17)?

    (A) They indicate the time and place of the origin of the speaker.
    (B) They satirize the usual language of the period.
    (C) They imply that the speaker is unbalanced.
    (D) They are the same diction used by the townspeople.
    (E) They suggest that the Gray Champion is German.

23. In line 30, "so difficult to kindle" implies that

    (A) the people do not really care
    (B) the people were incited against their natures
    (C) the people have endured much cruelty
    (D) the people will not continue to be angry
    (E) the people are really on Sir Edmund's side

Questions 24–32 are based on the following poem.

Poems from the Passionate Pilgrim

Fair is my love, but not so fair as fickle;
Mild as a dove, but neither true nor trusty;
Brighter than glass, and yet, as glass is, brittle;
line Softer than wax, and yet, as iron, rusty:
(5)   A lily pale, with damask dye to grace her,
    None fairer, nor none falser to deface her.

Her lips to mine how often hath she joined,
Between each kiss her oaths of true love
    swearing!
How many tales to please me hath she coined,
(10) Dreading my love, the loss thereof still fearing!
    Yet in the midst of all her pure protestings,
    Her faith, her oaths, her tears, and all were
    jestings.

She burnt with love, as straw with fire flameth,
She burnt out love, as soon as straw out-burneth;
(15) She framed the love, and yet she foiled the
    framing,
She bade love last, and yet she fell a-turning.
Was this a lover, or a lecher whether?
Bad in the best, though excellent in neither.

                    by William Shakespeare

24. Lines 15 and 18 are structured as elements

    (A) that understate the case
    (B) in antithesis
    (C) that overstate the case
    (D) of a narrative poem
    (E) of a riddle

25. Which of the following literary devices is used in line 1?

    (A) Alliteration
    (B) Apostrophe
    (C) Catastrophe
    (D) Forced rhyme
    (E) Metaphor

26. This poem's meaning includes a central contrast that is reinforced by all the following pairs EXCEPT

    (A) "Fair"…"fickle" (line 1)
    (B) "fairer"…"falser" (line 6)
    (C) "lips"…"joined" (line 7)
    (D) "burnt with love"…"burnt out love" (lines 13–14)
    (E) "lover"…"lecher" (line 17)

27. "She foiled the framing" (line 15) deals with

    (A) the speaker's falsifying of love's evidence
    (B) destruction of property
    (C) painted picture frames
    (D) allegorical figures of fine art
    (E) her thwarting of the very love she devised

28. The relationship of her dread of the speaker's love to her fear of losing it in line 10 is an example of a(n)

    (A) litote
    (B) paradox
    (C) oxymoron
    (D) malapropism
    (E) induction

29. Which of the following is the best description of the overall structural development of the theme in this poem?

    (A) The poem is a narrative epic.
    (B) The speaker compares, then contrasts, and finally praises his lover.
    (C) The speaker develops a series of compliments and criticisms.
    (D) The poem is a trilogy of love lyrics.
    (E) The speaker and his lover engage in dialogue.

30. In line 12, "all were jestings" projects an attitude of

    (A) disillusionment
    (B) congeniality
    (C) intimacy
    (D) devotion
    (E) isolation

31. Which of the answers listed identifies the literary device used to describe the speaker's lover in lines 2–4 and 13?

    (A) Simile
    (B) Metaphor
    (C) Personification
    (D) Synecdoche
    (E) Metonymy

32. The literary device used in lines 10 and 15–16 is

    (A) cacophony
    (B) dissonance
    (C) symbolism
    (D) mock heroism
    (E) irony

Questions 33–42 are based on the following passage.

'…Your sister is an amiable creature; but *yours* is the character of decision and firmness, I see. If you value her conduct or happiness,
line infuse as much of your own spirit into her, as
(5) you can. But this, no doubt, you have been always doing. It is the worst evil of too yielding and indecisive a character, that no influence over it can be depended on.—You are never sure of a good impression being durable. Every
(10) body may sway it; let those who would be happy be firm.—Here is a nut,' said he, catching one down from an upper bough. 'To exemplify,—a beautiful glossy nut, which, blessed with original strength, has outlived all the
(15) storms of autumn. Not a puncture, not a weak spot any where.—This nut,' he continued, with playful solemnity,—'while so many of its brethren have fallen and been trodden under foot, is still in possession of all the happiness
(20) that a hazel-nut can be supposed capable of.' Then, returning to his former earnest tone: 'My first wish for all, whom I am interested in, is that they should be firm. If Louisa Musgrove would be beautiful and happy in her November
(25) of life, she will cherish all her present powers of mind.'

Persuasion
by Jane Austen

33. The speaker's tone can be considered

    (A) outraged
    (B) inhibited
    (C) inquisitive
    (D) didactic
    (E) masterful

34. As used in the passage, November

    (A) is simply a month of the year
    (B) renders the speaker's point moot
    (C) refers to an appointment to be made
    (D) symbolizes old age
    (E) is a vehicle for firmness

35. The speaker uses a nut as

    (A) a simile
    (B) an example of a weak character
    (C) a midday snack
    (D) a vehicle to explain a firm character
    (E) an expression of insult

36. Based on contextual clues, the reader can conclude that the auditor's sister

    (A) resists change
    (B) is a younger sister
    (C) lacks resolve
    (D) is unbalanced
    (E) is much older than the auditor

37. The speaker dislikes a "too yielding and indecisive" character (lines 6–7) because

    (A) he was once betrayed
    (B) such a person is not reliable
    (C) such a character does not leave a good impression
    (D) such a person grows old early
    (E) he is too judgmental

38. Why does the speaker use the phrase "its brethren" (lines 17–18) rather than "the other nuts"?

    (A) It implies that nuts are part of a family.
    (B) It conveys that nuts provide a serious analogy.
    (C) It echoes his point concerning the auditor's sister.
    (D) It symbolizes the hazel-nut family.
    (E) It establishes personification within the analogy.

39. What is the subject of the speaker's advice?

    (A) Character building
    (B) Horticulture
    (C) Raising hazel-nuts
    (D) Sibling relationships
    (E) Respect

40. The second sentence (lines 3–5) indicates that

    (A) the sister is unhappy
    (B) the auditor has influence over her sister
    (C) the sister misbehaves
    (D) the auditor is weak-natured
    (E) the speaker has never met the sister

41. What is the result of the speaker addressing the auditor in the third person in the last sentence?

    (A) It is insulting in tone.
    (B) It emphasizes an overbearing attitude.
    (C) It renders his advice less presumptuous.
    (D) It indicates a lack of communicative skills.
    (E) It recalls the perspective of his initial advice.

42. In what type of language is the speaker's advice given?

    (A) Poetic diction
    (B) Prose rhythms
    (C) Comparison and contrast structure
    (D) Unusual syntax
    (E) Highly personalized and metaphoric language

Questions 43–51 are based on the following poem.

Somewhere or Other

Somewhere or other there must surely be
    The face not seen, the voice not heard,
The heart that not yet—never yet—ah me!
    Made answer to my word.
line
(5) Somewhere or other, may be near or far;
    Past land and sea, clean out of sight;
Beyond the wandering moon, beyond the star
    That tracks her night by night.

Somewhere or other, may be far or near;
(10)   With just a wall, a hedge, between;
With just the last leaves of the dying year
    Fallen on a turf grown green.

             by Christina Rossetti

43. The use of "—never yet—ah me!" in line 3

    (A) renders the speaker's emotion more intense
    (B) illustrates the speaker's lack of communicative skills
    (C) suggests that someone is listening
    (D) implies that no one is really there
    (E) introduces a new thought

44. The speaker's feelings toward "The face" in line 2 project a sense of

    (A) hostility
    (B) longing
    (C) incredulity
    (D) anxiety
    (E) authority

45. As used in this poem, the "heart" (line 3) serves as

    (A) the main point of an argument
    (B) the center of emotions
    (C) an organ that pumps blood
    (D) courage
    (E) memorization

46. Of the following representative pairs of words, which mirrors the contrast between the second and third stanzas?

    (A) "night"…"year"
    (B) "moon"…"turf"
    (C) "night"…"green"
    (D) "sea"…"hedge"
    (E) "tracks"…"Fallen"

47. In its context, "tracks" (line 8) implies that the star

    (A) marks the sky at night
    (B) is a sportsman
    (C) is hunting
    (D) is seeking the speaker's love
    (E) leads the way

48. What is the result of the use of "grown green" in line 12?

    (A) It contrasts life against the death in line ll.
    (B) It summarizes the meaning of the poem.
    (C) It emphasizes the speaker's hopelessness.
    (D) It suggests that the turf lacks proper care.
    (E) It combines a sense of freedom with care.

49. In the poem, the "face…voice…heart" (lines 2–3) is

    I.   a synecdoche representing an unknown person
    II. a metaphor for lost people
    III. a symbol of being alone

    (A) I only
    (B) II only
    (C) III only
    (D) II and III only
    (E) I, II, and III

50. The poem's theme deals with

    (A) roaming to far places
    (B) the importance of a home
    (C) strangers in strange places
    (D) reconciliation with an estranged person
    (E) the existence of a person that the speaker has never met

51. What is the consequence of "near or far" (line 5) and "far or near" (line 9)?

    (A) The reversal interrupts the rhyme scheme.
    (B) The diction places emphasis on the metrical patterns.
    (C) The reversal implies confusion of the speaker.
    (D) The syntactical arrangement places emphasis on "far" in the second stanza and on "near" in the third stanza.
    (E) The syntactical arrangement places emphasis on "near" in the second stanza and on "far" in the third stanza.

Questions 52–60 are based on the following passage.

    …Our day of dependence, our long apprenticeship to the learning of other lands, draws to a close. The millions that around us
line are rushing into life cannot always be fed on
(5) the sere remains of foreign harvest. Events, actions arise that must be sung, that will sing themselves. Who can doubt that poetry will revive and lead in a new age, as the star in the constellation Harp, which now flames in our
(10) zenith, astronomers announce, shall one day be the pole star for a thousand years?
    In this hope I accept the topic which not only usage but the nature of our association seem to prescribe to this day—the American
(15) Scholar. Year by year we come up hither to read one more chapter of his biography. Let us inquire what light new days and events have thrown on his character and his hopes…. The state of society is one in which the members
(20) have suffered amputation from the trunk and strut about so many walking monsters—a good finger, a neck, a stomach, an elbow, but never a man.
    Man is thus metamorphosed into a thing,
(25) into many things. The planter, who is man sent out into the field to gather food, is seldom cheered by any idea of the true dignity of his ministry. He sees his bushel and his cart, and nothing beyond, and sinks into the farmer,
(30) instead of man on the farm. The tradesman scarcely ever gives an ideal worth to his work but is ridden by the routine of his craft, and the soul is subject to dollars. The priest

becomes a form; the attorney a statute-book;
(35) the mechanic a machine; the sailor a rope of the ship.
    In this distribution of functions the scholar is the delegated intellect. In the right state he is *Man Thinking*. In the degenerate state, when
(40) the victim of society, he tends to become a mere thinker, or still worse, the parrot of other men's thinking.

                  "The American Scholar"
              by Ralph Waldo Emerson

52. The focus of the first paragraph is that

    (A) America is dependent on foreign scholarship
    (B) poetry is like a star
    (C) there is a population explosion
    (D) Harp will be the next pole star
    (E) America must engage in intellectual pursuits

53. By figuratively using "metamorphosed" in line 24, the speaker

    (A) renders the argument a philosophically macabre issue
    (B) emphasizes the mundane aspects of the issue
    (C) suggests that the change is an element of science fiction
    (D) shows a lack of respect for society
    (E) puts aside the previous discussion of amputation

54. "Poetry will revive" (lines 8–9) indirectly reveals that in the speaker's opinion

    (A) poetry is a person
    (B) poetry is universally dead
    (C) poetry is like a star
    (D) American poetry is loved by millions
    (E) American poetry is not being written or read

55. The metaphor used in the last paragraph is found in the phrase

    (A) "the degenerate state"
    (B) "the parrot of other men's thinking"
    (C) "when the victim of society"
    (D) "distribution of functions"
    (E) "to become a mere thinker"

56. A significant effect of the phrase "man sent out into the field to gather food" (lines 25–26) over the word "planter" is that

(A) thing rather than man is emphasized
(B) he becomes more like the farmer
(C) man rather than thing is emphasized
(D) true dignity is lost through a cause-and-effect relationship
(E) planting becomes a philosophical experience

57. In the second paragraph, the speaker would have the reader believe that Americans have become

(A) too specialized and labeled
(B) American Scholars
(C) representatives of the association
(D) characterized and hopeful
(E) eager to encounter "new days and events"

58. In the context of line 5, "sere" can be seen as

(A) withered
(B) sparse
(C) unhealthy
(D) contaminated
(E) rotted

59. In the context of the passage, what does the speaker identify as being the cause of the degenerated state of man?

(A) The American Scholar
(B) The trunk
(C) Society
(D) Foreign scholars
(E) Harp

60. An implication produced by the use of the word "apprenticeship" (line 2) is that

(A) American Scholars have been experiencing a period of learning from foreign men's thinking
(B) the speaker advocates sending students abroad to study
(C) the speaker advocates stopping the practice of sending students abroad to study
(D) we still have much to learn from foreign men's thinking
(E) our degree of dependence on foreign learning must expand to include the oncoming millions

ANSWER KEY: PRACTICE TEST TWO

1. **E**	7. **A**	13. **D**	19. **C**	25. **A**	31. **A**	37. **B**	43. **A**	49. **A**	55. **B**
2. **C**	8. **C**	14. **A**	20. **D**	26. **C**	32. **E**	38. **E**	44. **B**	50. **E**	56. **C**
3. **A**	9. **E**	15. **B**	21. **E**	27. **E**	33. **D**	39. **A**	45. **B**	51. **D**	57. **A**
4. **B**	10. **E**	16. **C**	22. **A**	28. **B**	34. **D**	40. **B**	46. **D**	52. **E**	58. **A**
5. **D**	11. **B**	17. **E**	23. **C**	29. **C**	35. **D**	41. **C**	47. **C**	53. **A**	59. **C**
6. **B**	12. **C**	18. **D**	24. **B**	30. **A**	36. **C**	42. **E**	48. **A**	54. **E**	60. **A**

TO OBTAIN YOUR RAW SCORE:

_____ divided by 4 = _____
Total wrong   Score W

_____ minus _____ = _____
 Total right   Score W   Score R

Round Score R to the nearest whole number for
the raw score.

HOW DID YOU DO?

55–60 = Excellent
44–54 = Very Good
35–43 = Above Average
23–34 = Average
15–22 = Below Average

ANSWER SHEET FOR PRACTICE TEST THREE

1. Ⓐ Ⓑ Ⓒ Ⓓ Ⓔ
2. Ⓐ Ⓑ Ⓒ Ⓓ Ⓔ
3. Ⓐ Ⓑ Ⓒ Ⓓ Ⓔ
4. Ⓐ Ⓑ Ⓒ Ⓓ Ⓔ
5. Ⓐ Ⓑ Ⓒ Ⓓ Ⓔ
6. Ⓐ Ⓑ Ⓒ Ⓓ Ⓔ
7. Ⓐ Ⓑ Ⓒ Ⓓ Ⓔ
8. Ⓐ Ⓑ Ⓒ Ⓓ Ⓔ
9. Ⓐ Ⓑ Ⓒ Ⓓ Ⓔ
10. Ⓐ Ⓑ Ⓒ Ⓓ Ⓔ
11. Ⓐ Ⓑ Ⓒ Ⓓ Ⓔ
12. Ⓐ Ⓑ Ⓒ Ⓓ Ⓔ
13. Ⓐ Ⓑ Ⓒ Ⓓ Ⓔ
14. Ⓐ Ⓑ Ⓒ Ⓓ Ⓔ
15. Ⓐ Ⓑ Ⓒ Ⓓ Ⓔ
16. Ⓐ Ⓑ Ⓒ Ⓓ Ⓔ
17. Ⓐ Ⓑ Ⓒ Ⓓ Ⓔ
18. Ⓐ Ⓑ Ⓒ Ⓓ Ⓔ
19. Ⓐ Ⓑ Ⓒ Ⓓ Ⓔ
20. Ⓐ Ⓑ Ⓒ Ⓓ Ⓔ

21. Ⓐ Ⓑ Ⓒ Ⓓ Ⓔ
22. Ⓐ Ⓑ Ⓒ Ⓓ Ⓔ
23. Ⓐ Ⓑ Ⓒ Ⓓ Ⓔ
24. Ⓐ Ⓑ Ⓒ Ⓓ Ⓔ
25. Ⓐ Ⓑ Ⓒ Ⓓ Ⓔ
26. Ⓐ Ⓑ Ⓒ Ⓓ Ⓔ
27. Ⓐ Ⓑ Ⓒ Ⓓ Ⓔ
28. Ⓐ Ⓑ Ⓒ Ⓓ Ⓔ
29. Ⓐ Ⓑ Ⓒ Ⓓ Ⓔ
30. Ⓐ Ⓑ Ⓒ Ⓓ Ⓔ
31. Ⓐ Ⓑ Ⓒ Ⓓ Ⓔ
32. Ⓐ Ⓑ Ⓒ Ⓓ Ⓔ
33. Ⓐ Ⓑ Ⓒ Ⓓ Ⓔ
34. Ⓐ Ⓑ Ⓒ Ⓓ Ⓔ
35. Ⓐ Ⓑ Ⓒ Ⓓ Ⓔ
36. Ⓐ Ⓑ Ⓒ Ⓓ Ⓔ
37. Ⓐ Ⓑ Ⓒ Ⓓ Ⓔ
38. Ⓐ Ⓑ Ⓒ Ⓓ Ⓔ
39. Ⓐ Ⓑ Ⓒ Ⓓ Ⓔ
40. Ⓐ Ⓑ Ⓒ Ⓓ Ⓔ

41. Ⓐ Ⓑ Ⓒ Ⓓ Ⓔ
42. Ⓐ Ⓑ Ⓒ Ⓓ Ⓔ
43. Ⓐ Ⓑ Ⓒ Ⓓ Ⓔ
44. Ⓐ Ⓑ Ⓒ Ⓓ Ⓔ
45. Ⓐ Ⓑ Ⓒ Ⓓ Ⓔ
46. Ⓐ Ⓑ Ⓒ Ⓓ Ⓔ
47. Ⓐ Ⓑ Ⓒ Ⓓ Ⓔ
48. Ⓐ Ⓑ Ⓒ Ⓓ Ⓔ
49. Ⓐ Ⓑ Ⓒ Ⓓ Ⓔ
50. Ⓐ Ⓑ Ⓒ Ⓓ Ⓔ
51. Ⓐ Ⓑ Ⓒ Ⓓ Ⓔ
52. Ⓐ Ⓑ Ⓒ Ⓓ Ⓔ
53. Ⓐ Ⓑ Ⓒ Ⓓ Ⓔ
54. Ⓐ Ⓑ Ⓒ Ⓓ Ⓔ
55. Ⓐ Ⓑ Ⓒ Ⓓ Ⓔ
56. Ⓐ Ⓑ Ⓒ Ⓓ Ⓔ
57. Ⓐ Ⓑ Ⓒ Ⓓ Ⓔ
58. Ⓐ Ⓑ Ⓒ Ⓓ Ⓔ
59. Ⓐ Ⓑ Ⓒ Ⓓ Ⓔ
60. Ⓐ Ⓑ Ⓒ Ⓓ Ⓔ

PRACTICE TEST THREE

Time allowed: One hour

Directions: The following questions test your understanding of several literary selections. Read each passage or poem and the questions that follow it. Select the best answer choice for each question by blackening the matching oval on your answer sheet. **Special attention should be given to questions containing the following words: EXCEPT, LEAST, NOT.**

Questions 1–10 are based on the following speech.

Speech delivered to the Women's State Temperance Society convention in Rochester, New York in 1853

We have been obliged to preach woman's rights because many, instead of listening to what we had to say on temperance, have
line questioned the right of a woman to speak on
(5) any subject. In courts of justice and legislative assemblies, if the right of the speaker to be there is questioned, all business waits until that point is settled. Now, it is not settled in the mass of minds that woman has any rights
(10) on this footstool, and much less a right to stand on an even pedestal with man, look him in the face as an equal, and rebuke the sins of her day and generation. Let it be clearly understood, then, that we are a woman's rights
(15) society; that we believe it is woman's duty to speak whenever she feels the impression to do so; that it is her right to be present in all the councils of church and state. The fact that our agents are women settles the question of our
(20) character on this point.
    Again, in discussing the question of temperance, all lecturers, from the beginning, have made mention of the drunkards' wives and children, of widows' groans and orphans'
(25) tears. Shall these classes of sufferers be introduced but as themes for rhetorical flourish, as pathetic touches of the speaker's eloquence? Shall we passively shed tears over

their condition, or by giving them their rights,
(30) bravely open to them the doors of escape from a wretched and degraded life? Is it not legitimate in this to discuss the social degradation, the legal disabilities of the drunkard's wife? If in showing her wrongs,
(35) we prove the right of all womankind to the elective franchise; to a fair representation in the government; to the right in criminal cases to be tried by peers of her own choosing— shall it be said that we transcend the bounds
(40) of our subject?…

by Elizabeth Cady Stanton

1. The phrase "passively shed tears" (line 28) is a paradox that can also be seen in which of the phrases listed below?

   (A) Excitedly exclaimed approval
   (B) Passionately cried out
   (C) Shockingly revealed the truth
   (D) Aggressively withdrew himself
   (E) Stressfully explained herself

2. In this selection, the speaker's tone includes qualities that are

   (A) frustrated and intense
   (B) genuinely hopeful
   (C) compromising and complacent
   (D) reluctantly hopeful
   (E) disdainfully reticent

3. As used in its context, "obliged to preach woman's rights" (lines 1–2) would lead the reader to believe that

   (A) the Temperance Society's primary goal was to preach "woman's rights"
   (B) the women were being forced to abandon the temperance issue
   (C) the Temperance Society was ineffective in suffrage issues
   (D) the women were turning to religion to communicate their suffrage and temperance issues
   (E) the women were forced to "woman's rights" in order to be heard on the temperance issue

4. The opposing sides of the issue are connotatively represented by all the following EXCEPT

   (A) passiveness…bravery
   (B) wrong…right
   (C) confusion…clarity
   (D) deception…sincerity
   (E) degradation…fair representation

5. Of the statements listed below, which mirrors the relationship between the first paragraph and the second paragraph?

   (A) The Temperance Society is "a woman's rights society"; it advocates women owning property.
   (B) Lack of "woman's rights" impedes the fight against drunkenness; granting "woman's rights" could be a boon to the women and children suffering from husbands and fathers who are drunkards.
   (C) Women are the agents of the Temperance Society; lecturers can participate through eloquence.
   (D) Women have a duty to speak concerning pressing social issues; drunkards' wives live wretched and degraded lives.
   (E) Most people do not believe women have rights to free speech; most people deplore drunkenness.

6. In the second paragraph, the speaker would have the reader believe that some lecturers are

   (A) imprudent
   (B) discreet
   (C) quiescent
   (D) insincere
   (E) emotional

7. The connotations of the phrase "transcend the bounds of our subject" (lines 39–40)

   (A) emphasize that the struggle for "woman's rights" is beyond the scope of the temperance issue
   (B) demonstrate that men often do hold women in subjection
   (C) contrast that, if an examination of "woman's" suffering proves the need for "woman's rights," then such discussion is germane to the subject
   (D) contrast the baseness of the subject of drunkenness to the loftiness of the subject of temperance
   (E) facilitate a shift in tone in the argument, from outrage to lofty self-confidence

8. What is the organizational pattern the speaker uses to persuade her audience?

   (A) Metaphorical reasoning
   (B) Process analysis
   (C) Inductive/deductive reasoning
   (D) Spondaic stress
   (E) Metrical scan

9. In line 30, the speaker uses the phrase "the doors of escape" as a(n)

   (A) simile for "woman's" legal rights
   (B) epithet for "woman's" legal rights
   (C) euphemism for "woman's" legal rights
   (D) anachronism for the Women's Rights Movement
   (E) hyperbole for "woman's" rights

10. "Footstool" and "pedestal" (lines 10–11), as used in this passage, represent

   (A) the aesthetic distance between man and woman
   (B) a denouement to establish a final point
   (C) synaesthesia of sound and sight
   (D) the speaker's platform
   (E) an elevation of tone to heighten the argument

Questions 11–23 are based on the following poem.

Wood-notes

Whoso walks in solitude
And inhabiteth the wood,
Choosing light, wave, rock and bird
line Before the money-loving herd,
(5) Into that forester shall pass,
From these companions, power and grace.
Clean shall he be, without, within,
From the old adhering sin;
All ill dissolving in the light
(10) Of his triumphant piercing sight:
Not vain, sour, nor frivolous;
Nor mad, athirst, nor garrulous;
Grave chaste, contented tho' retired,
And of all other men desired,
(15) On him the light of star and moon
Shall fall with pure radiance down;
All constellations of the sky
Shall shed their virtue thro' his eye.
Him Nature giveth for defence
(20) His formidable innocence;
The mountain sap, the shells, the sea,
All spheres, all stones, his helpers be;
He shall meet the speeding year
Without wailing, without fear;
(25) He shall be happy in his love,
Like to like shall joyful prove;
He shall be happy while he woos,
Muse-born, a daughter of the Muse.
But if with gold she bind her hair
(30) And deck her breast with diamond,
Take off thine eyes, thy heart forbear,
Tho' thou lie alone on the ground!

by Ralph Waldo Emerson

11. The subject of the poem deals with

   (A) the benefits of living close to nature
   (B) wilderness survivals
   (C) becoming a hermit
   (D) resisting temptations
   (E) nature watching

12. Which of the phrases listed below mirrors the paradox seen in the phrase "formidable innocence" (line 20)?

   (A) Innovative mistake
   (B) Paralyzing fearfulness
   (C) Defective fortifications
   (D) Legalized permissiveness
   (E) Innocuous dreadfulness

13. In lines 9–10, which of the following sound devices is used?

   (A) Dissonance
   (B) Onomatopoeia
   (C) Assonance
   (D) Cacophony
   (E) Caesura

14. What is the theme of lines 29–32?

   (A) A rejection of wealth
   (B) An admonition to reject natural physical beauty
   (C) A rejection of the earth's treasure
   (D) An admonition to reject a mate who has different values
   (E) An admonition to reject all love

15. Based on the context of the rhyme scheme, the writer of this poem probably intends all the following pairs of words to correspond EXCEPT

   (A) "solitude" (line 1) and "wood" (line 2)
   (B) "bird" (line 3) and "herd" (line 4)
   (C) "moon" (line 15) and "down" (line 16)
   (D) "innocence" (line 20) and "sea" (line 21)
   (E) "love" (line 25) and "prove" (line 26)

16. Line 29 contains a change in

   (A) rhythm
   (B) rhyme scheme
   (C) voice
   (D) verse form
   (E) dialect

17. "Walks in solitude" in line 1 contrasts with "money-loving herd" in line 4. This contrast

   (A) emphasizes the individualism of the forester
   (B) emphasizes the loneliness of the forester
   (C) echoes the theme of line 22
   (D) suggests points of comparison
   (E) symbolizes the problems people face with loneliness

18. In the context of the poem, the forester's character is shown to be one of

   (A) a malcontent
   (B) fearful only of death
   (C) higher moral character
   (D) unnatural qualities
   (E) irresponsible behavior

19. The consequences of the use of apocope in lines 13, 18, and 32 are

   (A) allusional
   (B) metrical
   (C) symbolic
   (D) rhetorical
   (E) metaphoric

20. The natural elements are portrayed as

   (A) hostile to the forester
   (B) ambivalent to the herd
   (C) compassionate to the daughter of the Muse
   (D) challenges to the forester
   (E) friends to the forester

21. The opposing ideas within the poem are NOT seen in

   (A) individualism...conformity
   (B) courage...fear
   (C) innocence...sinfulness
   (D) reality...unreality
   (E) happiness...unhappiness

22. In the context of the entire poem, the forester (line 5) contrasts to the herd (line 4) and projects which of these ideas?

   I.   The natural man vs. the artificial man
   II. An indictment against contrived literary forms
   III. A statement of the forester's mistake in judgment
   IV. An indictment against exchanging true values for monetary gain

   (A) I only
   (B) II only
   (C) I, III, and IV only
   (D) I, II, and IV only
   (E) I, II, III, and IV

23. In this poem, the "daughter of the Muse" (line 28) "with gold" in her hair (line 29) is which of these literary uses?

   I.   A representative of vanity
   II. A characterization of artificiality
   III. A symbol of contrived literary forms

   (A) I only
   (B) II only
   (C) III only
   (D) I and III only
   (E) I, II, and III

Questions 24–33 are based on the following passage.

   And lest some should persuade ye, Lords and Commons, that these arguments of learned men's discouragement at this your
line Order are mere flourishes, and not real, I
(5) could recount what I have seen and heard in other countries where this kind of inquisition tyrannizes; when I have sat among their learned men, for that honor I had, and been counted happy to be born in such a place of
(10) philosophic freedom as they supposed England was, while themselves did nothing but bemoan the servile condition into which learning amongst them was brought; that this was it which had damped the glory of Italian
(15) wits; that nothing had been there written now these many years but flattery and fustian. There it was that I found and visited the

famous Galileo, grown old, a prisoner to the
Inquisition for thinking in astronomy
(20) otherwise than the Franciscan and Dominican
licensers thought. And though I knew that
England then was groaning loudest under the
prelatical yoke, nevertheless I took it as a
pledge of future happiness that other nations
(25) were so persuaded of her liberty.

"Areopagitica"
by John Milton

24. What is the central topic of the passage?

(A) Intellectual freedom
(B) Animosity among countries
(C) Italy's justice system
(D) English literature
(E) Italian licensers

25. The organizational pattern used most by the
writer of this passage is best decribed as

(A) cause and effect
(B) comparison and contrast
(C) definition
(D) process analysis
(E) analysis and classification

26. What is the speaker's purpose?

(A) Persuasion
(B) Information
(C) Entertainment
(D) Description
(E) Definition

27. Contextual clues show that "Galileo" (line 18)
refers to a(n)

(A) poet and philosopher of the Order
(B) rebel against intellectual dictatorship
(C) English astronomer
(D) symbol of the Inquisition
(E) Franciscan licenser

28. The main reason for the irony in the
admiration held by other countries for the
speaker's country is that

(A) England truly had more intellectual
freedoms
(B) the other countries did not really know
England
(C) England was less philosophically free
than the other countries
(D) the other countries enjoyed hidden
freedoms
(E) both England and the other countries were
partners in the Order

29. According to the speaker, repression of
learning in Italy resulted in writing that was

(A) strong and forthright
(B) defensive and satirical
(C) insincere and pretentious
(D) shocking and cynical
(E) humble and direct

30. Lines 1–4 put forth the idea that

(A) supporters of the Order contend that the
opposition is just putting on a show
(B) the Order was not really issued
(C) there are no supporters for the Order
(D) there is real general support for the Order
(E) the opposition to the Order lacks sincerity

31. The "prelatical yoke" (line 23) contributes to
meaning as a

(A) simile for causing a loud noise
(B) gently satirical view of the Order
(C) mocking description of ecclesiastical
groups
(D) personification of the Order
(E) metaphor for ecclesiastical rules
governing intellectual matters

32. The final statement of the passage is presented for which of these intents?

    (A) A change in attitude of the speaker
    (B) A statement of the speaker's optimism
    (C) A statement of the speaker's sense of forlornness
    (D) A challenge to other countries
    (E) An example of ungrounded pessimism

33. Use of the word "servile" in line 12 is connotative that

    (A) learning had become submissive to others' dictates
    (B) all philosophic freedoms were gone
    (C) the Order was a slave to philosophy
    (D) England was not a slave-state
    (E) Italy had conquered philosophic freedom

Questions 34–44 are based on the following poem.

The Flower

Once in a gólden hour
  I cast to earth a seed.
Up there came a flower,
The people said, a weed.

line
(5) To and fro they went
  Thro' my garden-bower,
And muttering discontent
  Cursed me and my flower.

Then it grew so tall
(10) It wore a crown of light,
But thieves from o'er the wall
  Stole the seed by night.

Sow'd it far and wide
  By every town and tower,
(15) Till all the people cried,
  'Splendid is the flower.'

Read my little fable:
  He that runs may read.
Most can raise the flowers now,
(20) For all have got the seed.

And some are pretty enough,
  And some are poor indeed;
And now again the people
  Call it but a weed.

by Alfred, Lord Tennyson

34. The main theme of the "fable" (line 17) is

    (A) the problems gardeners face with thieves
    (B) a statement concerning dishonesty
    (C) the intense beauty inherent in some plant forms
    (D) how human nature affects perceptions of value
    (E) the probability that something beautiful will be stolen

35. In this poem, the word "runs" (line 18) means which of the definitions listed below?

    I.   Moves swiftly or rapidly
    II. Thinks quickly without hindrance
    III. Meditates
    IV. Melts and flows

    (A) I only
    (B) II only
    (C) IV only
    (D) I, II, and III only
    (E) II and III only

36. In its context, "read" (line 18) means which of the definitions listed below?

    I.   Utter aloud
    II. Learn true meaning
    III. Foretell
    IV. Record or show

    (A) I only
    (B) II only
    (C) IV only
    (D) I, III, and IV only
    (E) I, II, and IV only

37. In this poem, the progression of "weed" (line 4) to "flower" (line 16) to "weed" (line 24) represents the

    (A) lack of horticultural knowledge of the people
    (B) admiration with which the speaker looks at the flower
    (C) ironic nature of the people's attitude
    (D) despair with which the speaker views the people
    (E) hostility of the people toward the speaker

38. The hour was "golden" in line 1 because

   (A) the sun was shining
   (B) the seed became a splendid flower
   (C) the flower was yellow
   (D) the seed was yellow
   (E) the seed was gold

39. Contextually, "wore a crown of light" (line 10) makes the flower seem

   (A) regal and beautiful
   (B) prolific
   (C) lanky and leggy
   (D) top-heavy and weighted down
   (E) fragile and airy

40. Line 17 contains a change in

   (A) rhyme scheme
   (B) imagery
   (C) tone
   (D) speaker
   (E) voice

41. Of the pairs of words listed below, which mirrors the contrast of the development of "the flower" in this poem?

   (A) Turnips…turnip greens
   (B) Lawn…crabgrass
   (C) Queen Anne's Lace…ragweed
   (D) Roses…thorns
   (E) Grapes…vine

42. The phrase "Cursed me and my flower" (line 8) highlights the people's

   (A) limited vocabularies
   (B) judgmental natures
   (C) acceptance of the situation
   (D) deferential attitude
   (E) diabolical plan

43. The speaker wants the reader to view the fable as

   (A) just a clever story
   (B) an amusing anecdote
   (C) aimed at children
   (D) a tall tale
   (E) an important lesson in life

44. The speaker undergoes a change in attitude toward "my flower" in lines 1–4 and 9–12 in contrast to the description in lines 21–24 because

   (A) the speaker also considers the flower a weed
   (B) the flower will never be a weed to the speaker
   (C) the speaker is no longer emotionally attached to the flower
   (D) the flower really was a weed all along
   (E) the people's perception has not influenced the perception of the speaker

Questions 45–52 are based on the following passage.

'Who is it, then, Mr Kenneth?' I repeated impatiently.

'Hindley Earnshaw! Your old friend
line Hindley—' he replied. 'And my wicked
(5) gossip; though he's been too wild for me this long while. There! I said we should draw water—But cheer up! He died true to his character, drunk as a lord—Poor lad; I'm sorry, too. One can't help missing an old companion;
(10) though he had the worst tricks with him that ever man imagined, and has done me many a rascally turn—He's barely twenty-seven, it seems; that's your own age; who would have thought you were born in one year?'
(15)   I confess this blow was greater to me than the shock of Mrs Linton's death: ancient associations lingered round my heart; I sat down in the porch, and wept as for a blood relation, desiring Kenneth to get another
(20) servant to introduce him to the master.

    I could not hinder myself from pondering on the question—'Had he had fair play?' Whatever I did, that idea would bother me: it was so tiresomely pertinacious that I resolved
(25) on requesting leave to go to Wuthering Heights, and assist in the last duties to the dead. Mr Linton was extremely reluctant to consent, but I pleaded eloquently for the friendless condition in which he lay; and I
(30) said my old master and foster-brother had a claim on my services as strong as his own. Besides, I reminded him that the child, Hareton, was his wife's nephew, and, in the

absence of nearer kin, he ought to act as its
(35) guardian; and he ought to and must inquire
how the property was left, and look over the
concerns of his brother-in-law.

Wuthering Heights
by Emily Brontë

45. Which of the literary devices listed below is
used in lines 7–8 to characterize Hindley?

(A) Metaphor
(B) Personification
(C) Paradox
(D) Simile
(E) Amplification

46. The speaker implies that her request to go to
Wuthering Heights was really for the purpose
of

(A) determining the circumstances of
Hindley's death
(B) mourning the dead
(C) playing the spy for Mr. Linton
(D) establishing property rights
(E) leaving Mr. Linton's employment

47. Mr. Kenneth's relationship to Hindley
Earnshaw can be seen to include all the
following EXCEPT

(A) Kenneth and Hindley were friends
(B) Hindley deceived Kenneth
(C) Kenneth views Hindley as an alcoholic
(D) Kenneth views Hindley as very young
(E) Kenneth and Hindley hated one another

48. The last paragraph supports the idea that
Hareton is

(A) the speaker's son
(B) the speaker's half-brother
(C) Mr. Kenneth's son
(D) Mrs. Linton's nephew
(E) Hindley Earnshaw's nephew

49. Which of the following is NOT a meaning of
the phrase "tiresomely pertinacious" as it is
used in line 24?

(A) Unyielding
(B) Perverse
(C) Obstinate
(D) Determined
(E) Stubborn

50. The speaker's argument to Mr. Linton can best
be identified as

(A) a type of inductive reasoning
(B) fanciful and unfounded
(C) a type of deductive reasoning
(D) an appeal to his sense of retribution
(E) half-hearted and dutiful

51. The phrase "draw water" (lines 6–7) is
possibly a slang expression meaning to

(A) bring water from a well
(B) prepare refreshments
(C) cry
(D) prepare bath water
(E) drain a flooded area

52. The best definition of "gossip" as it is used in
line 5 is

(A) a foster-parent
(B) a close friend
(C) a person who chatters
(D) a person who repeats idle talk
(E) a person who repeats rumors about others

Questions 53–60 are based on the following poem.

My Lute, Be as Thou Wast

My lute, be as thou wast when thou didst grow
With thy green mother in some shady grove,
When immelodious winds but made thee move,
line And birds on thee their ramage did bestow.
(5) Sith that dear voice which did thy sounds
approve,
Which used in such harmonious strains to flow,
Is reft from earth to tune those spheres above,
What art thou but a harbinger of woe?
Thy pleasing notes be pleasing notes no more,

(10) But orphan wailings to the fainting ear;
Each stop a sigh, each sound draws forth a tear,
Be therefore silent as in woods before,
Or if that any hand to touch thee deign,
Like widowed turtle, still her loss complain.

by William Drummond

53. "My lute" in line 1 is an example of the poet's use of

(A) simile
(B) metaphor
(C) personification
(D) apostrophe
(E) litote

54. The poem presents

(A) the speaker's passionate love of music
(B) a contrast of the natural to the unnatural
(C) the speaker mourning the death of a loved one
(D) a youth speaking to his music teacher
(E) an individual addressing music

55. The change in rhyme scheme of lines 5–8 as contrasted to lines 1–4 is echoed in the

(A) change in tone of lines 5–8
(B) change in rhythm
(C) revelation of a reversal in tone in line 9
(D) renewed sense of optimism in line 9
(E) revelation of meaning in lines 5–8

56. The lute's "green mother" (line 2) is a figurative reference to a

(A) tree
(B) grove
(C) wind
(D) bird
(E) singer

57. By using the context of the poem, "widowed turtle" in line 14 can be viewed as

(A) a reptile, known for withdrawing into its hard shell
(B) a turtleback, known in archaeology as a stone implement
(C) a turtledove, known for devotion to its mate
(D) turtlehead herb, known for the shape of its corolla
(E) turtle peg, known for its use in harpooning sea turtles

58. The lute's music seems to represent which of the following for the speaker?

(A) A musical instrument
(B) Reflections of the speaker's mood
(C) A friend and companion
(D) Light and harmony
(E) Nature

59. The speaker views the lute with feelings that can be described as

(A) shocked
(B) condescending
(C) dispassionate
(D) fearless
(E) antagonistic

60. Of the following, which is the LEAST acccurate statement concerning the poem?

(A) It is a sonnet.
(B) Lines 9–10 contain a metaphor.
(C) Line 2 contains personification.
(D) The phrase "orphan wailings" (line 10) refers to children of the speaker.
(E) "Ramage" (line 4) contrasts with "harmonious" (line 6).

ANSWER KEY: PRACTICE TEST THREE

1. **D**	7. **C**	13. **C**	19. **B**	25. **B**	31. **E**	37. **C**	43. **E**	49. **B**	55. **E**
2. **A**	8. **C**	14. **D**	20. **E**	26. **A**	32. **B**	38. **B**	44. **C**	50. **C**	56. **A**
3. **E**	9. **B**	15. **D**	21. **D**	27. **B**	33. **A**	39. **A**	45. **D**	51. **C**	57. **C**
4. **C**	10. **D**	16. **B**	22. **D**	28. **C**	34. **D**	40. **A**	46. **A**	52. **B**	58. **B**
5. **B**	11. **A**	17. **A**	23. **E**	29. **C**	35. **E**	41. **C**	47. **E**	53. **D**	59. **E**
6. **D**	12. **E**	18. **C**	24. **A**	30. **A**	36. **B**	42. **B**	48. **D**	54. **C**	60. **D**

TO OBTAIN YOUR RAW SCORE:

_____ divided by 4 = _____
Total wrong   Score W

_____ minus _____ = _____
 Total right   Score W   Score R

Round Score R to the nearest whole number for the raw score.

HOW DID YOU DO?

55–60 = Excellent
44–54 = Very Good
35–43 = Above Average
23–34 = Average
15–22 = Below Average

ANSWER SHEET FOR PRACTICE TEST FOUR

1. Ⓐ Ⓑ Ⓒ Ⓓ Ⓔ
2. Ⓐ Ⓑ Ⓒ Ⓓ Ⓔ
3. Ⓐ Ⓑ Ⓒ Ⓓ Ⓔ
4. Ⓐ Ⓑ Ⓒ Ⓓ Ⓔ
5. Ⓐ Ⓑ Ⓒ Ⓓ Ⓔ
6. Ⓐ Ⓑ Ⓒ Ⓓ Ⓔ
7. Ⓐ Ⓑ Ⓒ Ⓓ Ⓔ
8. Ⓐ Ⓑ Ⓒ Ⓓ Ⓔ
9. Ⓐ Ⓑ Ⓒ Ⓓ Ⓔ
10. Ⓐ Ⓑ Ⓒ Ⓓ Ⓔ
11. Ⓐ Ⓑ Ⓒ Ⓓ Ⓔ
12. Ⓐ Ⓑ Ⓒ Ⓓ Ⓔ
13. Ⓐ Ⓑ Ⓒ Ⓓ Ⓔ
14. Ⓐ Ⓑ Ⓒ Ⓓ Ⓔ
15. Ⓐ Ⓑ Ⓒ Ⓓ Ⓔ
16. Ⓐ Ⓑ Ⓒ Ⓓ Ⓔ
17. Ⓐ Ⓑ Ⓒ Ⓓ Ⓔ
18. Ⓐ Ⓑ Ⓒ Ⓓ Ⓔ
19. Ⓐ Ⓑ Ⓒ Ⓓ Ⓔ
20. Ⓐ Ⓑ Ⓒ Ⓓ Ⓔ

21. Ⓐ Ⓑ Ⓒ Ⓓ Ⓔ
22. Ⓐ Ⓑ Ⓒ Ⓓ Ⓔ
23. Ⓐ Ⓑ Ⓒ Ⓓ Ⓔ
24. Ⓐ Ⓑ Ⓒ Ⓓ Ⓔ
25. Ⓐ Ⓑ Ⓒ Ⓓ Ⓔ
26. Ⓐ Ⓑ Ⓒ Ⓓ Ⓔ
27. Ⓐ Ⓑ Ⓒ Ⓓ Ⓔ
28. Ⓐ Ⓑ Ⓒ Ⓓ Ⓔ
29. Ⓐ Ⓑ Ⓒ Ⓓ Ⓔ
30. Ⓐ Ⓑ Ⓒ Ⓓ Ⓔ
31. Ⓐ Ⓑ Ⓒ Ⓓ Ⓔ
32. Ⓐ Ⓑ Ⓒ Ⓓ Ⓔ
33. Ⓐ Ⓑ Ⓒ Ⓓ Ⓔ
34. Ⓐ Ⓑ Ⓒ Ⓓ Ⓔ
35. Ⓐ Ⓑ Ⓒ Ⓓ Ⓔ
36. Ⓐ Ⓑ Ⓒ Ⓓ Ⓔ
37. Ⓐ Ⓑ Ⓒ Ⓓ Ⓔ
38. Ⓐ Ⓑ Ⓒ Ⓓ Ⓔ
39. Ⓐ Ⓑ Ⓒ Ⓓ Ⓔ
40. Ⓐ Ⓑ Ⓒ Ⓓ Ⓔ

41. Ⓐ Ⓑ Ⓒ Ⓓ Ⓔ
42. Ⓐ Ⓑ Ⓒ Ⓓ Ⓔ
43. Ⓐ Ⓑ Ⓒ Ⓓ Ⓔ
44. Ⓐ Ⓑ Ⓒ Ⓓ Ⓔ
45. Ⓐ Ⓑ Ⓒ Ⓓ Ⓔ
46. Ⓐ Ⓑ Ⓒ Ⓓ Ⓔ
47. Ⓐ Ⓑ Ⓒ Ⓓ Ⓔ
48. Ⓐ Ⓑ Ⓒ Ⓓ Ⓔ
49. Ⓐ Ⓑ Ⓒ Ⓓ Ⓔ
50. Ⓐ Ⓑ Ⓒ Ⓓ Ⓔ
51. Ⓐ Ⓑ Ⓒ Ⓓ Ⓔ
52. Ⓐ Ⓑ Ⓒ Ⓓ Ⓔ
53. Ⓐ Ⓑ Ⓒ Ⓓ Ⓔ
54. Ⓐ Ⓑ Ⓒ Ⓓ Ⓔ
55. Ⓐ Ⓑ Ⓒ Ⓓ Ⓔ
56. Ⓐ Ⓑ Ⓒ Ⓓ Ⓔ
57. Ⓐ Ⓑ Ⓒ Ⓓ Ⓔ
58. Ⓐ Ⓑ Ⓒ Ⓓ Ⓔ
59. Ⓐ Ⓑ Ⓒ Ⓓ Ⓔ
60. Ⓐ Ⓑ Ⓒ Ⓓ Ⓔ

PRACTICE TEST FOUR

Time allowed: One hour

Directions: The following questions test your understanding of several literary selections. Read each passage or poem and the questions that follow it. Select the best answer choice for each question by blackening the matching oval on your answer sheet. **Special attention should be given to questions containing the following words: EXCEPT, LEAST, NOT.**

Questions 1–7 are based on the following passage.

Bailey and Elizabeth exchanged a trapped look. It was Bailey who answered the questioning child. 'A long time ago,' he said,
line 'your mother and Mr. Ferris were once married.
(5) Before you were born—a long time ago.'
'Mr. Ferris?'
The little boy stared at Ferris, amazed and unbelieving. And Ferris's eyes, as he returned the gaze, were somehow unbelieving too. Was
(10) it indeed true that at one time he had called this stranger, Elizabeth, Little Butterduck during nights of love, that they had lived together, shared perhaps a thousand days and nights and—finally—endured in the misery of
(15) sudden solitude the fiber by fiber (jealousy, alcohol and money quarrels) destruction of the fabric of married love.
Bailey said to the children, 'It's somebody's suppertime. Come on now.'

"The Sojourner"
by Carson McCullers

1. The subject of this passage can be described as

(A) a couple's relationship with their son
(B) a boy learning of his mother's previous marriage
(C) a man learning that his former wife remarried
(D) a man meeting his wife's first husband
(E) a woman resisting the turmoil in her life

2. Lines 1–2 imply that

(A) Bailey and Elizabeth are fugitives
(B) Bailey and Elizabeth do not want Ferris to meet the child
(C) Bailey dislikes Elizabeth
(D) Bailey plans to trick Ferris and the boy
(E) Bailey and Elizabeth had not planned to tell about Ferris and Elizabeth

3. The best explanation of "Little Butterduck" is as

(A) a nickname
(B) personification
(C) amplification
(D) anthropomorphism
(E) aphorism

4. In line 17, "fabric" is used as which of the following?

(A) It is a tenor in a simile.
(B) It is a tenor in a metaphor.
(C) It is a vehicle in a simile.
(D) It is a vehicle in a metaphor.
(E) It is a symbol in a paradox.

5. The question in line 6 is the result of

(A) the introduction of Bailey as the child's father
(B) the recognition that Elizabeth is the little boy's mother
(C) the boy's confusion over what he has learned
(D) the boy's protests over going to supper
(E) the child's anger at Bailey over being told what to do

6. Ferris is "unbelieving too" (line 9) because

(A) like the boy, he does not know of Elizabeth's previous marriage
(B) he does not know the identity of the little boy
(C) time and events have distanced him from Elizabeth
(D) "Elizabeth" is not really the woman's name
(E) Bailey obviously dislikes Ferris

7. The word "stranger" (line 11) serves to

(A) imply that Ferris and Bailey have never met before
(B) intensify a sense of estrangement
(C) diminish the sense of foreboding
(D) suggest that Ferris and Elizabeth have just met
(E) dispel any implications that Ferris and Elizabeth know one another

Questions 8–21 are based on the following poem.

The Art of Poetry

A poem, where we all perfections find,
Is not the work of a fantastic mind;
There must be care, and time, and skill, and pains;
line Not the first heat of inexperienced brains.
(5) Yet sometimes artless poets, when the rage
Of a warm fancy does their minds engage,
Puffed with vain pride, presume they understand,
And boldly take the trumpet in their hand:
Their fustian muse each accident confounds;
(10) Nor can she fly, but rise by leaps and bounds,
Till, their small stock of learning quickly spent,
Their poem dies for want of nourishment.

In vain mankind the hot-brained fool decries,
No branding censures can unveil his eyes;
(15) With impudence the laurel they invade,
Resolved to like the monsters they have made.
Virgil, compared to them, is flat and dry;
And Homer understood not poetry:
Against their merit if this age rebel,
(20) To future times for justice they appeal.
But waiting till mankind shall do them right,
And bring their works triumphantly to light,
Neglected heaps we in bye-corners lay,
Where they become to worms and moths a prey.

by John Dryden

8. The topic of this poem is

(A) writers of artless poetry
(B) inspired monsters
(C) writers of artful poetry
(D) how to compose artful poetry
(E) the works of Homer and Virgil

9. Concerning "artless poets" (line 5), the speaker conveys an attitude that is

(A) exultant
(B) convivial
(C) beguilingly larkish
(D) tediously practical
(E) bitterly disapproving

10. A "fantastic mind" (line 2), in contrast to line 3, is in reference to

(A) capricious thinking
(B) wonderfully talented thinking
(C) genius
(D) creativity
(E) imagination

11. "And Homer understood not poetry" (line 18) is an expression that reveals the artless poets'

(A) submissive humility
(B) chagrined countenance
(C) pompous arrogance
(D) groveling servility
(E) dignified venerability

12. Which of these statements best conveys a reaction of artless poets to criticism of their poetry?

    (A) They look to Virgil and Homer to prove them correct.
    (B) They accept criticism and use it to improve.
    (C) They refuse any unjustly received rewards.
    (D) They claim that a coming age will prove them correct.
    (E) They discontinue writing and leave their poems in neglected heaps.

13. That the works of artless poets become "neglected" and moth-eaten (lines 23–24) in the future can be seen as

    (A) tragic
    (B) ironic
    (C) surprising
    (D) sentimental
    (E) melodramatic

14. The poem is described in lines 11–12 in terms of a

    (A) bird in flight
    (B) depository of learning
    (C) starving, living thing
    (D) monster to be killed
    (E) proud overseer

15. The speaker's tone in lines 17–18 can be considered

    (A) sarcastic
    (B) uncensorious
    (C) magnanimous
    (D) roguish
    (E) reverential

16. Which of the following phrases identifies the meaning of "laurel" as used in line 15?

    I.   Honors and awards for poetry
    II. Fame as artful poets
    III. Plants about which poems are written

    (A) I only
    (B) II only
    (C) III only
    (D) I and II only
    (E) I, II, and III

17. The main contrast of the poem is best reflected by which of these pairs of phrases?

    (A) "the work of a fantastic mind" (line 2) and "a warm fancy" (line 6)
    (B) "Puffed with vain pride" (line 7) and "dies for want" (line 12)
    (C) "care, and time, and skill, and pains" (line 3) and "small stock of learning" (line 11)
    (D) "With impudence" (line 15) and "to worms and moths a prey" (line 24)
    (E) "this age rebel" (line 19) and "to worms and moths a prey" (line 24)

18. The "fustian muse" (line 9), as used in context, represents

    (A) inspired thinking
    (B) beautiful poetry
    (C) a monster
    (D) pompous thoughts
    (E) skill in writing

19. "Nor can she fly, but rise by leaps and bounds" (line 10) serves to emphasize

    (A) that writing requires a muse
    (B) the inconsistent quality of artless poetry
    (C) the experiences gained in writing poetry
    (D) that writing poetry requires time
    (E) that poems lift the reader's thoughts

20. Which of the following statements best reflects the speaker's attitude toward writing poetry?

    (A) Writing poetry takes work.
    (B) Many different styles are necessary.
    (C) Artless poets can learn and grow.
    (D) Poems outlive their writers.
    (E) Even artless poets can contribute to the art of poetry.

21. The speaker implies that artless poets are

    (A) hardworking but untalented
    (B) careful and humble
    (C) disrespectful but talented
    (D) cautious and resolved
    (E) lazy and proud

Questions 22–28 are based on the following passage.

The sea, vast and wild as it is, bears thus the waste and wrecks of human art to its remotest shore. There is no telling what it may
line not vomit up. It lets nothing lie; not even the
(5) giant clams which cling to its bottom. It is still heaving up the tow-cloth of the *Franklin*, and perhaps a piece of some old pirate's ship, wrecked more than a hundred years ago, comes ashore today. Some years since, when a
(10) vessel was wrecked here which had nutmegs in her cargo, they were strewn all along the beach, and for a considerable time were not spoiled by the salt water. Soon afterward, a fisherman caught a cod which was full of
(15) them. Why, then, might not the Spice Islanders shake their nutmeg trees into the ocean, and let all nations who stand in need of them pick them up? However, after a year, I found that the nutmegs from the *Franklin* had
(20) become soft.

You might make a curious list of articles which fishes have swallowed—sailors' open clasp-knives, and bright tin snuffboxes, not knowing what was in them—and jugs, and
(25) jewels, and Jonah. The other day I came across the following scrap in a newspaper.

A RELIGIOUS FISH—A short time ago, mine host Stewart, of the Denton Hotel, purchased a rock-fish, weighing about sixty
(30) pounds. On opening it he found in it a certificate of membership of the M.E. Church, which we read as follows:

Methodist E. Church	Member
Founded A. D. 1784	
(35) Quarterly Ticket	18
	Minister

For our light affliction, which is but for a moment, worketh for us a far more exceeding *and* eternal weight of glory.
(40) —2 Cor. 4:17.

O what are all my sufferings here,
If, Lord, thou count me meet
With that enraptured host t' appear,
And worship at thy feet.

(45) The paper was, of course, in a crumpled and wet condition, but on exposing it to the sun,

and ironing the kinks out of it, it became quite legible.

Denton [Maryland] Journal
"Cape Cod"
by Henry David Thoreau

22. The "*Franklin*" probably refers to

(A) a man
(B) a fish
(C) a shore
(D) a cargo
(E) a boat

23. "Jonah," as used in line 25, is a(n)

(A) metaphor
(B) allusion
(C) simile
(D) aphorism
(E) antithesis

24. Of the literary devices listed below, which is used in lines 24–25 to describe items found in fishes?

(A) Slanted rhyme
(B) Alliteration
(C) Apostrophe
(D) Dead metaphor
(E) Eye rhyme

25. As used in line 21, "curious" can be considered as also meaning

(A) accurate
(B) fastidious
(C) strange
(D) prying
(E) desirous to know

26. A possible reason that the certificate of membership was newsworthy is that

(A) it was still legible after being eaten by a fish
(B) it was so old
(C) it was from a shipwreck
(D) it contained no names or addresses
(E) it contained a poem in the certificate

27. In line 42, "meet" can NOT be considered to mean

(A) encountered
(B) suitable
(C) qualified
(D) adapted
(E) fit

28. In lines 23–24, "not knowing what was in them" might lead one to believe that

(A) fish lack intelligence
(B) snuff attracts fish
(C) the fish were attracted by the brightness
(D) snuff is poisonous to fish
(E) the snuff harmed the fish

Questions 29–42 are based on the following poem.

The Light of Other Days

Oft in the stilly night
  Ere slumber's chain has bound me,
Fond Memory brings the light
line   Of other days around me:
(5)   The smiles, the tears
      Of boyhood's years,
  The words of love then spoken;
    The eyes that shone,
    Now dimm'd and gone,
(10) The cheerful hearts now broken!
Thus in the stilly night
  Ere slumber's chain has bound me,
Sad Memory brings the light
  Of other days around me.

(15) When I remember all
  The friends so link'd together
I've seen around me fall
  Like leaves in wintry weather,
    I feel like one
(20)   Who treads alone
Some banquet-hall deserted,
    Whose lights are fled
    Whose garlands dead,
And all but he departed!
(25) Thus in the stilly night
  Ere slumber's chain has bound me,
Sad Memory brings the light
  Of other days around me.

by Thomas Moore

29. Which of the following is the LEAST applicable definition of "stilly" as it is used in this poem?

(A) Simple
(B) Still
(C) Calm
(D) Silent
(E) Quiet

30. "Light" (line 3), in the context of this poem, is connotative of all the following EXCEPT

(A) a previous time
(B) understanding
(C) remembrances
(D) awareness
(E) radiation

31. In line 2, sleep is made to appear as a

(A) weak link
(B) towing device
(C) golden necklace
(D) captor
(E) thief

32. The speaker uses "Thus" in lines 11 and 25 rather than "Oft" as in line 1. What is the effect?

(A) It shifts the tense of the stanza.
(B) "Oft" implies frequence, whereas "Thus" implies infrequency.
(C) "Thus" establishes a cause and effect relationship.
(D) "Thus" emphasizes the tone.
(E) "Thus" signals a restatement of the theme.

33. Of the pairs of words listed below, which best reflects the contrast of lines 5–8 to lines 9–10?

(A) "eyes" (line 8) and "hearts" (line 10)
(B) "tears" (line 5) and "broken" (line 10)
(C) "night" (line 1) and "light" (line 13)
(D) "love" (line 7) and "cheerful" (line 10)
(E) "Fond Memory" (line 3) and "Sad Memory" (line 13)

34. The speaker in the poem is best described as someone who is feeling

    (A) nostalgic and happy
    (B) lonely and abandoned
    (C) warm and caring
    (D) wistful and peaceful
    (E) angry and bitter

35. The relationship between "friends" in lines 15–18 and "I" in lines 19–24 is also seen in which of the following pairs?

    (A) "fall" (line 17) and "dead" (line 23)
    (B) "wintry" (line 18) and "deserted" (line 21)
    (C) "remember" (line 15) and "feel" (line 19)
    (D) "link'd together" (line 16) and "alone" (line 20)
    (E) "leaves" (line 18) and "lights" (line 22)

36. Of the literary devices listed below, which is used to describe the friends in lines 15–18?

    (A) Simile
    (B) Illusion
    (C) Personification
    (D) Understatement
    (E) Overstatement

37. This poem can best be seen as presenting the thoughts of someone

    (A) who is becoming fearful of death
    (B) whose friends and family are gone
    (C) whose life is just beginning
    (D) who has not adjusted to feelings of guilt
    (E) who is in love

38. Contextually, moving from "boyhood's years" (line 6) to "wintry weather" (line 18) to "departed" (line 24) reflects a change from the

    (A) abstract to the concrete
    (B) sad to the happy
    (C) past to the future
    (D) spoken to the unspoken
    (E) real to the unreal

39. The poem's overall subject is

    (A) youth
    (B) memories
    (C) old age
    (D) death
    (E) sleep

40. Line 19 is notable for introducing which of the following?

    (A) The rhyme scheme changes from that of the first stanza.
    (B) Personification is used to depict the speaker's life.
    (C) Light becomes a symbol for vision.
    (D) The speaker examines his present condition.
    (E) The speaker refuses to be comforted by Memory.

41. What is the effect of the simile as used in lines 19–24?

    (A) It highlights the events missing in the speaker's life.
    (B) It contrasts the role of "Memory" in line 27.
    (C) It introduces the element of fear into the speaker's tone.
    (D) It depicts the speaker's boyhood years.
    (E) It emphasizes the speaker's sense of loneliness.

42. The "banquet-hall" in line 21 is contextually referring to

    (A) a place to eat
    (B) a gathering place
    (C) the speaker's life
    (D) the place where the speaker once met people
    (E) the speaker's old home

Questions 43–47 are based on the following passage.

This outward mutability indicated, and did not more than fairly express, the various properties of her inner life. Her nature
line appeared to possess depth, too, as well as
(5) variety; but—or else Hester's fears deceived her—it lacked reference and adaptation to the

world into which she was born. The child
could not be made amenable to rules. In giving
her existence, a great law had been broken;
(10) and the result was a being, whose elements
were perhaps beautiful and brilliant, but all in
disorder; or with an order peculiar to
themselves, amidst which the point of variety
and arrangement was difficult or impossible to
(15) be discovered. Hester could only account for
the child's character—and even then, most
vaguely and imperfectly—by recalling what
she herself had been, during that momentous
period while Pearl was imbibing her soul from
(20) the spiritual world, and her bodily frame from
its material of earth. The mother's impassioned
state had been the medium through which
were transmitted to the unborn infant the rays
of its moral life; and, however white and clear
(25) originally, they had taken the deep stains of
crimson and gold, the fiery lustre, the black
shadow, and the untempered light, of the
intervening substance. Above all, the warfare
of Hester's spirit, at that epoch, was
(30) perpetuated in Pearl. She could recognize her
wild, desperate, defiant mood, the flightiness
of her temper, and even some of the very
cloud-shapes of gloom and despondency that
had brooded in her heart. They were now
(35) illuminated by the morning radiance of a
young child's disposition, but, later in the day
of earthly existence, might be prolific of the
storm and whirlwind.

The Scarlet Letter
by Nathaniel Hawthorne

43. The speaker presents Pearl's character as

(A) dull and insipid
(B) intelligent but willful
(C) underdeveloped but skillful
(D) temperamental but loving
(E) guilty and morose

44. The passage supports the idea that

(A) Hester and Pearl were nothing alike
(B) Pearl was much calmer in nature than
    Hester
(C) Hester felt guilt over Pearl's character
(D) Hester and Pearl hate one another
(E) Pearl is deeply attached to Hester

45. The phrase "later in the day of earthly
existence" (lines 36–37) can be thought of as

(A) childhood
(B) death
(C) old age
(D) adulthood
(E) infancy

46. In the last sentence, "storm and whirlwind" are
used as vehicles in a metaphor describing

(A) the epoch of Pearl's birth
(B) Hester's character mirrored in Pearl
(C) dispositions in general
(D) Pearl's physical appearance
(E) a radiant personality

47. The phrase "outward mutability" (line 1) can
be seen as

(A) inner change
(B) resistance to change
(C) physical growth
(D) a variety of personalities
(E) character change

Questions 48–52 are based on the following poem.

Answer

Sound, sound the clarion, fill the fife!
    To all the sensual world proclaim,
One crowded hour of glorious life
    Is worth an age without a name.

by Sir Walter Scott

48. The poem exhibits elements that are

(A) apologetic
(B) apathetic
(C) aphoristic
(D) apocalyptic
(E) aposiopetic

49. Of the devices listed below, which is used to draw the hearer's attention in line 1?

    (A) Alliteration, echoism, and spondaic foot
    (B) Triple rhyme
    (C) Echoism and pun
    (D) Alliteration, enjambement, and echoism
    (E) Imperfect rhyme

50. Of the following phrases, which best conveys the theme of the poem?

    (A) A glorious life of anonymity
    (B) Quality of life over quantity
    (C) A celebration in the sensual world
    (D) Longevity over reputation
    (E) Responsibilities

51. The contrasting theme of the poem could be expressed as

    I. "Crowded"…"worth"
    II. "Glorious"…"without a name"
    III. "Hour"…"age"

    (A) I only
    (B) II only
    (C) I and II only
    (D) II and III only
    (E) I, II, and III

52. In line 4, the "name" connotes

    (A) a royal title
    (B) a concept or denomination
    (C) a good reputation or honor
    (D) a representative
    (E) an appellation

Questions 53–60 are based on the following passage.

Act I. Scene 1

Narvarre. The King's *park*

Enter the King, Berowne, Longaville, *and* Dumain

KING. Let fame, that all hunt after in their lives,
        Live regist'red upon our brazen tombs,
        And then grace us in the disgrace of
            death;
        When, spite of cormorant devouring
            Time,

line
(5)   Th' endeavour of this present breath
            may buy
        That honour which shall bate his
            scythe's keen edge,
        And make us heirs of all eternity.
        Therefore, brave conquerors—for so
            you are
        That war against your own affections
(10)   And the huge army of the world's
            desires—
        Our late edict shall strongly stand in
            force:
        Navarre shall be the wonder of the
            world;
        Our court shall be a little Academe,
        Still and contemplative in living art.
(15)   You three, Berowne, Dumain, and
            Longaville,
        Have sworn for three years' term to
            live with me
        My fellow-scholars, and to keep those
            statutes
        That are recorded in this schedule here.
        Your oaths are pass'd; and now
            subscribe your names,
(20)   That his own hand may strike his
            honour down
        That violates the smallest branch herein.
        If you are arm'd to do as sworn to do,
        Subscribe to your deep oaths, and keep
            it too.

LONGAVILLE. I am resolv'd; 'tis but a three
            years' fast.
(25)   The mind shall banquet, though the
            body pine.
        Fat paunches have lean pates; and
            dainty bits
        Make rich the ribs, but bankrupt quite
            the wits.

                        "Love's Labour's Lost"
                        by William Shakespeare

53. The situation of this drama is that

(A) the king is planning a military battle
(B) three men request the king's help
(C) the king is about to die and plans his final hours
(D) Time has cut into the heart of Navarre
(E) the king enlists three men to three years of study

54. The king's motivation, as described in lines 1–7, is

(A) to establish his reputation beyond his death
(B) to prevent his own death
(C) to reestablish his rule in Navarre
(D) to entrap his three friends
(E) to conquer "the huge army of the world's desires" (line 10)

55. The metaphor in lines 8–10 suggests that the "statutes" in line 17

(A) are laws of Navarre
(B) are part of a peace negotiation
(C) concern physical rules
(D) are part of a military code
(E) resemble a battle plan for soldiers

56. In this scene, there is a symbolic conflict between

(A) youth and age
(B) women and men
(C) peace and war
(D) life and death
(E) learning and ignorance

57. The king's words reveal that he is

(A) a coward
(B) anticipating war
(C) a war hero
(D) new to scholarship
(E) an idealistic man

58. As used in the passage, the contrasts of "banquet...pine" (line 25), "Fat...lean" (line 26), and "rich...bankrupt" (line 27) are designed to

(A) diminish the importance of the statute
(B) mirror the king's search for immortality
(C) emphasize the incompatibility of learning and sumptuous living
(D) impact the grace found in death
(E) imply that Time does not really devour

59. As presented in the drama, the elements in line 27 ("Make rich the ribs, but bankrupt quite the wits") are in

(A) corroboration
(B) trisyllabical form
(C) antithesis
(D) a tragic flaw
(E) a cotangent

60. In the paradoxical relationship of "grace . . . in the disgrace of death" (line 3), the grace is the result of

(A) posthumous celebrity
(B) the hunt for fame
(C) human greed
(D) death itself
(E) life itself

ANSWER KEY: PRACTICE TEST FOUR

1. **B**	7. **B**	13. **B**	19. **B**	25. **C**	31. **D**	37. **B**	43. **B**	49. **A**	55. **C**
2. **E**	8. **A**	14. **C**	20. **A**	26. **A**	32. **C**	38. **C**	44. **C**	50. **B**	56. **D**
3. **A**	9. **E**	15. **A**	21. **E**	27. **A**	33. **E**	39. **B**	45. **D**	51. **D**	57. **E**
4. **D**	10. **A**	16. **D**	22. **E**	28. **C**	34. **B**	40. **D**	46. **B**	52. **C**	58. **C**
5. **C**	11. **C**	17. **C**	23. **B**	29. **A**	35. **D**	41. **E**	47. **C**	53. **E**	59. **C**
6. **C**	12. **D**	18. **D**	24. **B**	30. **E**	36. **A**	42. **C**	48. **C**	54. **A**	60. **A**

TO OBTAIN YOUR RAW SCORE:

_____ divided by 4 = _____
Total wrong   Score W

_____ minus _____ = _____
  Total right   Score W   Score R

Round Score R to the nearest whole number for the raw score.

HOW DID YOU DO?

55–60 = Excellent
44–54 = Very Good
35–43 = Above Average
23–34 = Average
15–22 = Below Average

ANSWER SHEET FOR PRACTICE TEST FIVE

1. Ⓐ Ⓑ Ⓒ Ⓓ Ⓔ
2. Ⓐ Ⓑ Ⓒ Ⓓ Ⓔ
3. Ⓐ Ⓑ Ⓒ Ⓓ Ⓔ
4. Ⓐ Ⓑ Ⓒ Ⓓ Ⓔ
5. Ⓐ Ⓑ Ⓒ Ⓓ Ⓔ
6. Ⓐ Ⓑ Ⓒ Ⓓ Ⓔ
7. Ⓐ Ⓑ Ⓒ Ⓓ Ⓔ
8. Ⓐ Ⓑ Ⓒ Ⓓ Ⓔ
9. Ⓐ Ⓑ Ⓒ Ⓓ Ⓔ
10. Ⓐ Ⓑ Ⓒ Ⓓ Ⓔ
11. Ⓐ Ⓑ Ⓒ Ⓓ Ⓔ
12. Ⓐ Ⓑ Ⓒ Ⓓ Ⓔ
13. Ⓐ Ⓑ Ⓒ Ⓓ Ⓔ
14. Ⓐ Ⓑ Ⓒ Ⓓ Ⓔ
15. Ⓐ Ⓑ Ⓒ Ⓓ Ⓔ
16. Ⓐ Ⓑ Ⓒ Ⓓ Ⓔ
17. Ⓐ Ⓑ Ⓒ Ⓓ Ⓔ
18. Ⓐ Ⓑ Ⓒ Ⓓ Ⓔ
19. Ⓐ Ⓑ Ⓒ Ⓓ Ⓔ
20. Ⓐ Ⓑ Ⓒ Ⓓ Ⓔ

21. Ⓐ Ⓑ Ⓒ Ⓓ Ⓔ
22. Ⓐ Ⓑ Ⓒ Ⓓ Ⓔ
23. Ⓐ Ⓑ Ⓒ Ⓓ Ⓔ
24. Ⓐ Ⓑ Ⓒ Ⓓ Ⓔ
25. Ⓐ Ⓑ Ⓒ Ⓓ Ⓔ
26. Ⓐ Ⓑ Ⓒ Ⓓ Ⓔ
27. Ⓐ Ⓑ Ⓒ Ⓓ Ⓔ
28. Ⓐ Ⓑ Ⓒ Ⓓ Ⓔ
29. Ⓐ Ⓑ Ⓒ Ⓓ Ⓔ
30. Ⓐ Ⓑ Ⓒ Ⓓ Ⓔ
31. Ⓐ Ⓑ Ⓒ Ⓓ Ⓔ
32. Ⓐ Ⓑ Ⓒ Ⓓ Ⓔ
33. Ⓐ Ⓑ Ⓒ Ⓓ Ⓔ
34. Ⓐ Ⓑ Ⓒ Ⓓ Ⓔ
35. Ⓐ Ⓑ Ⓒ Ⓓ Ⓔ
36. Ⓐ Ⓑ Ⓒ Ⓓ Ⓔ
37. Ⓐ Ⓑ Ⓒ Ⓓ Ⓔ
38. Ⓐ Ⓑ Ⓒ Ⓓ Ⓔ
39. Ⓐ Ⓑ Ⓒ Ⓓ Ⓔ
40. Ⓐ Ⓑ Ⓒ Ⓓ Ⓔ

41. Ⓐ Ⓑ Ⓒ Ⓓ Ⓔ
42. Ⓐ Ⓑ Ⓒ Ⓓ Ⓔ
43. Ⓐ Ⓑ Ⓒ Ⓓ Ⓔ
44. Ⓐ Ⓑ Ⓒ Ⓓ Ⓔ
45. Ⓐ Ⓑ Ⓒ Ⓓ Ⓔ
46. Ⓐ Ⓑ Ⓒ Ⓓ Ⓔ
47. Ⓐ Ⓑ Ⓒ Ⓓ Ⓔ
48. Ⓐ Ⓑ Ⓒ Ⓓ Ⓔ
49. Ⓐ Ⓑ Ⓒ Ⓓ Ⓔ
50. Ⓐ Ⓑ Ⓒ Ⓓ Ⓔ
51. Ⓐ Ⓑ Ⓒ Ⓓ Ⓔ
52. Ⓐ Ⓑ Ⓒ Ⓓ Ⓔ
53. Ⓐ Ⓑ Ⓒ Ⓓ Ⓔ
54. Ⓐ Ⓑ Ⓒ Ⓓ Ⓔ
55. Ⓐ Ⓑ Ⓒ Ⓓ Ⓔ
56. Ⓐ Ⓑ Ⓒ Ⓓ Ⓔ
57. Ⓐ Ⓑ Ⓒ Ⓓ Ⓔ
58. Ⓐ Ⓑ Ⓒ Ⓓ Ⓔ
59. Ⓐ Ⓑ Ⓒ Ⓓ Ⓔ
60. Ⓐ Ⓑ Ⓒ Ⓓ Ⓔ

PRACTICE TEST FIVE

Time allowed: One hour

<u>Directions</u>: The following questions test your understanding of several literary selections. Read each passage or poem and the questions that follow it. Select the best answer choice for each question by blackening the matching oval on your answer sheet. **Special attention should be given to questions containing the following words: EXCEPT, LEAST, NOT.**

<u>Questions 1–8</u> are based on the following passage.

'Could Colonel Forster repeat the particulars of Lydia's note to his wife?'
'He brought it with him for us to see.'
line Jane then took it from her pocket-book, and
(5) gave it to Elizabeth. There were the contents:

MY DEAR HARRIET,

You will laugh when you know where I am gone,
and I cannot help laughing myself at your
surprise tomorrow morning, as soon as I am
(10) *missed. I am going to Gretna Green, and if*
you cannot guess with who, I shall think you a
simpleton, for there is but one man in the world
I love, so think it no harm to be off. You need
not send them word at Longbourn of my going,
(15) *if you do not like it, for it will make the surprise*
the greater, when I write to them, and sign my
name Lydia Wickham. What a good joke it will
be! I can hardly write for laughing. Pray make
my excuses to Pratt, for not keeping my engage-
(20) *ment, and dancing with him to night. Tell him*
I hope he will excuse me when he knows all, and
tell him I will dance with him at the next ball
we meet, with great pleasure. I shall send for
my clothes when I get to Longbourn; but I wish
(25) *you would tell Sally to mend a great slit in my*
working muslin gown, before they are packed
up. Good bye. Give my love to Colonel Forster,
I hope you will drink to our good journey.

Your affectionate friend,
(30) LYDIA BENNET.

'Oh! thoughtless, thoughtless Lydia!' cried Elizabeth when she had finished it. 'What a letter is this, to be written at such a moment. But at least it shews, that *she* was serious in
(35) the object of her journey. Whatever he might afterwards persuade her to, it was not on her side a *scheme* of infamy. My poor father! how he must have felt it!'
'I never saw any one so shocked. He could
(40) not speak a word for full ten minutes. My mother was taken ill immediately, and the whole house in such confusion!'
'Oh! Jane,' cried Elizabeth, 'was there a servant belonging to it, who did not know the
(45) whole story before the end of the day?'

Pride and Prejudice
by Jane Austen

1. Lydia Bennet's letter indicates that she

(A) is priggish and pedantry in her attitude toward her family
(B) is going on vacation to Gretna Green
(C) is eloping with Pratt
(D) is in love with Pratt
(E) is eloping with Wickham

2. Of the following, all are correct concerning the letter EXCEPT that

 (A) it reveals that Lydia has planned the trip well in advance
 (B) its tone is giddy and excited
 (C) it reveals that Lydia's plans were not generally known
 (D) its purpose is to announce a surprise
 (E) it was addressed to Mrs. Forster

3. Elizabeth's remarks concerning the letter's contents indicate that

 (A) Lydia is not really in love
 (B) Wickham does love Lydia
 (C) Wickham may not intend to marry Lydia
 (D) the family will take the news well
 (E) Wickham's intentions are sincere

4. Elizabeth's response to the letter shows that she

 (A) disapproves of Lydia's conduct
 (B) is jealous of Lydia's happiness
 (C) does not understand what has happened
 (D) is very happy for Lydia
 (E) wishes that she, too, could elope

5. The expression "a scheme of infamy" (line 37) means

 (A) a respectable idea
 (B) a shameful plan of action
 (C) a well-planned course of action
 (D) an ill-advised idea
 (E) a concise statement of intents and purposes

6. Under the circumstances of the letter, for Lydia to promise Pratt a dance at the next ball reveals that her feelings are

 (A) shy and coy
 (B) embarrassed and resentful
 (C) humble and introspective
 (D) flippant and insolent
 (E) direct and pragmatic

7. The words "simpleton" (line 12), "joke" (line 17), and "laughing" (line 18) show that Lydia

 (A) is a congenial person
 (B) has an inappropriate attitude
 (C) regards her family as emotionally unstable
 (D) has a keen sense of perception
 (E) suspects that the family knew of her plan

8. Elizabeth's question in lines 43–45 reveals that

 (A) she wants to find someone who can tell her more
 (B) such a servant should be dismissed
 (C) she wishes Lydia's action could be kept secret
 (D) the servants are generally unaware of such happenings
 (E) Lydia took care that no servants would learn of her plan

Questions 9–15 are based on the following poem.

Epilogue to Asolando

At the midnight, in the silence of the sleep-time,
    When you set your fancies free,
Will they pass to where—by death, fools
        think, imprison'd—
Low he lies who once so loved you, whom
line   you loved so,
(5)   —Pity me?

Oh to love so, be so loved, yet so mistaken!
    What had I on earth to do
With the slothful, with the mawkish, the
        unmanly?
Like the aimless, helpless, hopeless, did I drivel,
(10)   —Being—who?

One who never turn'd his back but march'd
        breast forward,
    Never doubted clouds would break,
Never dream'd, though right were worsted,
        wrong would triumph,
    Held we fall to rise, are baffled to fight better,
(15)   Sleep to wake.

No, at noonday in the bustle of man's work-time
    Greet the unseen with a cheer!
Bid him forward, breast and back as either
        should be,

'Strive and thrive!' cry 'Speed,—fight on, fare
    ever,
(20)   There as here!'

by Robert Browning

9. "Sleep to wake" in line 15 has the effect that

(A) it emphasizes the tragedy of death
(B) it enlarges the speaker's sense of loss
(C) it symbolizes mourning
(D) it indicates that the auditor might not
    wake
(E) it implies a sense of optimistic
    anticipation

10. The main topic of this poem is

(A) developing character
(B) the need to mourn
(C) attitudes toward death
(D) resisting temptations
(E) bravery in battle

11. The title "Epilogue" in relation to the poem's
    meaning can be considered as

(A) an ironic situation
(B) a play on words
(C) a reference to the auditor
(D) an element in opposition
(E) personification

12. The sentence "Greet the unseen with a cheer!"
    (line 17) is given as which of the following?

(A) As a statement of an optimistic attitude
(B) As an unrealistic approach to grief
(C) As a sarcastic remark
(D) As a hypocritical statement of advice
(E) As an indictment of all disagreeing
    opinions

13. "There as here!" (line 20) can be thought of as

(A) in the poem as out of the poem
(B) at work as at play
(C) in death as in life
(D) at night as in day
(E) for the auditor as for the speaker

14. The effect of the words "slothful…mawkish…
    unmanly" (line 8) and "aimless, helpless,
    hopeless" (line 9) is summarized by which of
    the following answers?

(A) They connote that the speaker's character
    is flawed.
(B) They reinforce the speaker's sense of dread.
(C) They suggest that the auditor's character
    is flawed.
(D) They contrast with the character traits
    presented in lines 11–15.
(E) They strongly defend the auditor's
    position of intolerance.

15. Of the literary devices listed below, which is
    used in lines 11–15 to establish character?

(A) Apostrophe
(B) Consonance
(C) Personification
(D) Antonomasia
(E) Amplification

Questions 16–24 are based on the following passage.

In the very olden time, there lived a semi-
barbaric king, whose ideas, though somewhat
polished and sharpened by the progressiveness
line of distant Latin neighbors, were still large,
(5) florid, and untrammelled, as became the half
of him which was barbaric. He was a man of
exuberant fancy, and, withal, of an authority
so irresistible that, at his will, he turned his
varied fancies into facts. He was greatly given
(10) to self-communing, and when he and himself
agreed upon anything, the thing was done.
When every member of his domestic and
political systems moved smoothly in its
appointed course, his nature was bland and
(15) genial; but whenever there was a little hitch,
and some of his orbs got out of their orbits, he
was blander and more genial still, for nothing
pleased him so much as to make the crooked
straight, and crush down uneven places.
(20)   Among the borrowed notions by which his
barbarism had become semified was that of
the public arena, in which, by exhibitions of
manly and beastly valor; the minds of his
subjects were refined and cultured.

(25)   But even here the exuberant and barbaric fancy asserted itself. The arena of the king was built, not to give the people an opportunity of hearing the rhapsodies of dying gladiators, nor to enable them to view the inevitable *(30)* conclusion of a conflict between religious opinions and hungry jaws, but for purposes far better adapted to widen and develop the mental energies of the people. This vast amphitheatre, with its encircling galleries, its mysterious *(35)* vaults, and its unseen passages, was an agent of poetic justice, in which crime was punished, or virtue rewarded, by the decrees of an impartial and incorruptible chance.

   When a subject was accused of a crime of *(40)* sufficient importance to interest the king, public notice was given that on an appointed day the fate of the accused person would be decided in the king's arena—a structure which well deserved its name; for, although its form *(45)* and plan were borrowed from afar, its purpose emanated solely from the brain of this man, who, every barleycorn a king, knew no tradition to which he owed more allegiance than pleased his fancy, and who ingrafted on *(50)* every adopted form of human thought and action the rich growth of his barbaric idealism.

The Lady or the Tiger?
by Frank Stockton

16. The words "large, florid, and untrammelled" (lines 4–5) are characteristic of which of the following personality traits?

   I.   Boastful
   II. Traitorous
   III. Restrained
   IV. Abstruse

   (A) I only
   (B) II only
   (C) III only
   (D) I and IV only
   (E) II and IV only

17. As used in the passage, "self-communing" (line 10) can be recognized as

   (A) schizophrenia
   (B) consulting with counselors
   (C) relying on the thinking of others
   (D) counterintelligence
   (E) introspection

18. Which of the answers below can be considered the vehicle used to describe problems in the king's life?

   (A) Pinballs
   (B) Electrons
   (C) Solar system
   (D) Molecules
   (E) Eyes

19. From where did the king get the idea of the public arena?

   (A) Self-communing
   (B) Distant Latin neighbors
   (C) Nature
   (D) Planetary signs
   (E) Domestic and political systems

20. Within the last paragraph, the king is characterized by the speaker as

   (A) lonely
   (B) dull
   (C) reliable
   (D) morally motivated
   (E) self-confident

21. The words "barbaric idealism" (line 51), as seen as a paradox, compares with which of the following?

   (A) Savage beasts
   (B) Gentle children
   (C) Respectful dignitaries
   (D) Honor among thieves
   (E) Life among enemies

22. Historically, "a conflict between religious opinions and hungry jaws" (lines 30–31) can be exemplified by

    (A) theological debates
    (B) throwing Christians to the lions
    (C) theological criticisms
    (D) the Salem witch trials
    (E) resistance to civil authority

23. As used in line 36, "poetic justice" is used ironically because

    (A) although impartial, chance is in antithesis to true justice
    (B) justice requires no agent
    (C) justice was the subject of the king's poetry
    (D) the amphitheatre is being personified
    (E) crime usually is rewarded and virtue punished

24. As given in line 47, the phrase "every barleycorn a king" can best be thought of as

    (A) a king over an agricultural society
    (B) a king in every respect
    (C) commoners given royal status
    (D) a society that worships grain
    (E) a humorous personification for a drunken king

Questions 25–30 are based on the following poem.

Ah! Sun-flower

Ah, sun-flower! weary of time,
Who countest the steps of the Sun;
Seeking after that sweet golden clime,
Where the traveller's journey is done;

line

(5) Where the Youth pined away with desire,
And the pale Virgin shrouded in snow,
Arise from their graves, and aspire
Where my sun-flower wishes to go.

                              by William Blake

25. In the poem, "snow" (line 6) is which of the following?

    I.   A symbol of purity
    II. A personified dress
    III. The agent of cold and preservation

    (A) I only
    (B) II only
    (C) III only
    (D) I and III
    (E) I, II, and III

26. Which of the following best expresses the theme developed throughout the poem?

    (A) "Seeking" (line 3) and "arise" (line 7)
    (B) "countest" (line 2) and "pined" (line 5)
    (C) "journey" (line 4) and "sun-flower" (line 8)
    (D) "traveller's" (line 4) and "Youth" (line 5)
    (E) "golden" (line 3) and "pale" (line 6)

27. The word "aspire" (line 7), in context, means which of the following?

    I.   Exhale
    II. Desire
    III. Ascend
    IV. Seek

    (A) I only
    (B) II only
    (C) III only
    (D) IV only
    (E) I, II, and III only

28. The sun-flower is described in lines 1–4 in terms of

    (A) a devitalized life form
    (B) ambitious for fame and glory
    (C) able to fulfill its wishes
    (D) bound to the earth
    (E) seeking warmer weather

29. The sun-flower, as defined in the poem, is best seen as

    (A) a symbol of warmth
    (B) a vigorous winter flower
    (C) representing man's journey through life
    (D) a metaphor for beauty
    (E) a weed

30. A conclusion supported by the poem's context is that when the "journey is done"

    (A) the sun-flower's travels will begin
    (B) the sun will find the "sweet golden clime" (line 3)
    (C) counting the sun's steps will cause the sun-flower to die
    (D) wishing will turn to desire
    (E) time will no longer be a factor

Questions 31–40 are based on the following passage.

Whether heroic verse ought to be admitted into serious plays is not now to be disputed: it is already in possession of the stage; and, I dare
line confidently affirm that very few tragedies, in
(5) this age, shall be received without it. All the arguments which are formed against it can amount to no more than this—that it is not so near conversation as prose; and therefore not so natural. But it is very clear to all who under-
(10) stand poetry that serious plays ought not to imitate conversation too nearly. If nothing were to be raised above that level the foundation of poetry would be destroyed. And if you once admit of a latitude, that thoughts may be exalted,
(15) and that images and actions may be raised above the life, and described in measure without rhyme, that leads you insensibly from your own principles to mine: you are already so far onward of your way that you have forsaken the
(20) imitation of ordinary converse; you are gone beyond it; and to continue where you are is to lodge in the open field, betwixt two inns. You have lost that which you call natural, and have not acquired the last perfection of art. But it
(25) was only custom which cozened us so long: we thought, because Shakespeare and Fletcher went no farther, that there the pillars of poetry were to be erected; that, because they excellently described passion without rhyme,
(30) therefore rhyme was not capable of describing it. But time has now convinced most men of that error. It is indeed so difficult to write verse that the adversaries of it have a good plea against many who undertake that task without
(35) being formed by art or nature for it.

"Of Heroic Plays"
by John Dryden

31. Heroic verse is described in lines 1–3 in terms of

    (A) an orphan art form
    (B) a conquering force
    (C) something incapable of sustaining interest
    (D) someone greedy of dramatic presentation
    (E) something resistant to change

32. Lines 3–5 suggest that

    (A) heroic verse is infrequently used
    (B) tragedies do not contain heroic verse
    (C) people do not want heroic verse in tragedy
    (D) audiences and critics expect tragedies to have heroic verse
    (E) most tragedies without heroic verse are received

33. Heroic verse is defined as

    (A) 14-line poems in iambic pentameter
    (B) unrhymed lines in iambic pentameter
    (C) a form of parody
    (D) an iambic pentameter quatrain with an abab rhyme scheme
    (E) rhymed couplets in iambic pentameter

34. As revealed in the passage, the speaker considers prose

    (A) more natural than heroic verse
    (B) more desirable than heroic verse
    (C) the mainstay of tragedy
    (D) too imitative of conversation
    (E) too exalted

35. The speaker's attitude implies that

    (A) not all tragedies are tragic
    (B) poetry is a higher level of communication than prose
    (C) prose is a higher level of communication than poetry
    (D) unrhymed prose of exalted images is best
    (E) tragedy should imitate natural conversation

36. Lines 28–31 might be called an error in reasoning because the statement is

 (A) based on the false assumption that Shakespeare and Fletcher "excellently described passion without rhyme"
 (B) an overstatement
 (C) a faulty generalization
 (D) an understatement
 (E) describing a construct that is structurally impossible

37. As presented by the speaker, a conclusion might be reached that the tragedies of Shakespeare and Fletcher

 (A) are in heroic verse
 (B) are rhymed
 (C) used no poetic images
 (D) used the exalted language of poetry, but without rhyme
 (E) do not use the exalted language of poetry

38. According to the speaker (line 24), "the last perfection of art" is acquired through

 (A) rhyme
 (B) rhythm
 (C) prose
 (D) drama
 (E) tragedy

39. The inference of the last sentence is that the speaker

 (A) will entertain no arguments against verse in drama
 (B) views verse as a simple matter to include in drama
 (C) highly respects prose writers
 (D) believes writing verse is a universal skill
 (E) would prefer no verse to poorly written verse

40. Being lodged "in the open field, betwixt two inns" (line 22) metaphorically describes

 (A) conversational prose without rhyme
 (B) conversational prose with rhythm
 (C) images too exalted for conversation, but without the rhyme of poetry
 (D) no rhyme or poetic images
 (E) no poetic images, but rhymed lines

Questions 41–46 are based on the following poem.

Popular

Popular, Popular, Unpopular!
'You're no Poet'—the critics cried!
'Why?' said the Poet. 'You're unpopular!'
line Then they cried at the turn of the tide—
(5) 'You're no Poet!' 'Why?'—'You're popular!'
Pop-gun, Popular and Unpopular!

by Alfred, Lord Tennyson

41. Of the literary devices listed below, which is used to set the tone of the speaker's message in the poem as a whole?

 (A) Simile
 (B) Metaphor
 (C) Personification
 (D) Alliteration
 (E) Apostrophe

42. In the last line, the speaker's meaning is accentuated by the use of

 (A) rhyme
 (B) onomatopoeia
 (C) mixed figures
 (D) genteel comedy
 (E) elision

43. Which of the following maxims best summarizes the speaker's meaning?

 (A) What turns around comes around.
 (B) A bird in hand is worth two in the bush.
 (C) A stitch in time saves nine.
 (D) Pride goes before a fall.
 (E) He cannot win for losing.

44. The main situation in the poem can be described as that of

 (A) an unpopular poet
 (B) a popular poet
 (C) a problem of perceptions
 (D) poor poetry
 (E) a problem of talent

45. The label "critics" (line 2) refers to people who

   (A) analyze and review literary works
   (B) hate poetry
   (C) love poetry
   (D) deliberately avoid reading popular poetry
   (E) personally dislike poets

46. The effect of "Pop-gun" in the last line serves to

   (A) imply danger from critics
   (B) emphasize the erratic nature of popularity
   (C) vilify critics
   (D) threaten those who criticize the work
   (E) change the tone of the poem

Questions 47–54 are based on the following passage.

   I need not speak of the voyage home but
may add a few remarks as to arctic work, on
points not generally understood. The incentive
line of the earliest northern voyages was
(5) commercial, the desire of the northern
European nations to find a navigable northern
route to the fabled wealth of the East. When
the impracticability of such a route was
proven, the adventurous spirit of Anglo-Saxon
(10) and Teuton found in the mystery, the danger,
the excitement, which crystalized under the
name North Pole, a worthy antagonist for their
fearless blood. The result of their efforts has
been to add millions to the world's wealth, to
(15) demonstrate some of the most important
scientific propositions, and to develop some of
the most splendid examples of manly courage
and heroism that adorn the human record.
   Let me call your attention to that flag, that
(20) tattered and torn and patched flag you see
hanging over the mantel there. That is the flag
from which I have taken pieces for deposit in
the cairns I built. You will notice that three
pieces are gone. One is in the cairn at the
(25) "farthest north," 87.6 degrees; a second piece
I placed in a cairn I built on one of the twin
peaks of Columbia, Cape Columbia; and the
third in the cairn on the northern point of
Jesup Land....

(30)   In view of the fact that the work has defined
the most northern land in the world, and has
fixed the northern limit of the world's largest
island, was that work a useless expenditure of
time, effort, and money? Neither the club nor
(35) I think so. The money was theirs, the time and
effort mine.

> "Arctic Exploration"
> by Robert E. Peary

47. The speaker's purpose is best described as

   (A) persuasive
   (B) argumentative
   (C) prescriptive
   (D) informative
   (E) descriptive

48. As used by the speaker, the LEAST accurate understanding of "blood" (line 13) is

   (A) parental heritage
   (B) temperament
   (C) life fluid
   (D) race
   (E) disposition

49. The North Pole is described in lines 11–13 in terms of

   (A) a suitable opponent
   (B) a villain
   (C) a friend to man
   (D) the personification of an Anglo-Saxon or Teuton
   (E) a coward

50. By stating "The money was theirs, the time and effort mine" in the last line, the speaker is

   (A) suggesting that he is dissatisfied with the arrangement
   (B) referring to the inequitable aspects of the journey
   (C) indicating that the money was inadequate for the journey
   (D) stressing the more romantic elements of an expedition
   (E) suggesting that he views the responsibility for expenditures as an equitable dichotomy

51. The speaker does NOT credit the Anglo-Saxon and Teuton explorers with advances in

  (A) bloodline research
  (B) economics
  (C) science
  (D) humanity
  (E) exploration

52. A "cairn" (lines 23–28) is

  (A) a cavern or cave
  (B) an ice cave
  (C) a cliff
  (D) a landmark
  (E) a flag holder

53. Probably, the flag

  (A) was desecrated by the explorers
  (B) is an antique from the Anglo-Saxons
  (C) is worn and torn from the hardships of the expedition
  (D) represents the speaker's family crest
  (E) is no longer of any value due to its condition

54. Of the following definitions, "crystalized" (as it is used in line 11) means

  (A) coated with sugar
  (B) coated with something else to give a false appearance
  (C) caused to form crystals
  (D) was given a definite form
  (E) assumed a crystalline form

Questions 55–60 are based on the following poem.

The Scholar

My days among the Dead are past;
Around me I behold,
Where'er these casual eyes are cast,
line The mighty minds of old:
(5) My never-failing friends are they,
With whom I converse day by day.

With them I take delight in weal
And seek relief in woe;
And while I understand and feel
(10) How much to them I owe,

My cheeks have often been bedew'd
With tears of thoughtful gratitude.

My thoughts are with the Dead; with them
I live in long-past years,
(15) Their virtues love, their faults condemn,
Partake their hopes and fears,
And from their lessons seek and find
Instruction with an humble mind.

My hopes are with the Dead; anon
(20) My place with them will be,
And I with them shall travel on
Through all Futurity;
Yet leaving here a name, I trust,
That will not perish in the dust.

by Robert Southey

55. The subject of this poem is

  (A) dying young
  (B) perspectives on learning from past scholars
  (C) resisting death through being a scholar
  (D) famous past scholars
  (E) the overemphasis placed on education

56. The speaker can best be labeled as someone who

  (A) is dead
  (B) is a past student
  (C) is a scholar
  (D) is unlearned
  (E) is a future scholar

57. What is the speaker's attitude toward "the Dead" (line 1) as revealed in the central theme of the poem?

  (A) Deferential, but not worshipful
  (B) Ungrateful
  (C) Antagonistic
  (D) Humble, but not responsive
  (E) Shortsighted

58. What effect is produced by the last two lines of the poem?

 (A) They make the speaker seem vain.
 (B) They intensify the pessimistic tone.
 (C) They reinforce the continuous nature of scholarship.
 (D) They indicate that scholarship is rare.
 (E) They stress the sincere nature of scholars.

59. The third and fourth stanzas establish a contrast that is reflected in which of these pairs of words?

 (A) Dead...alive
 (B) Seek...travel
 (C) Humble...hope
 (D) Past and present...future
 (E) Instruction...name

60. Based upon its contextual use, the word "live" (line 14) conveys which of these statements summarizing the speaker's position?

 I. The speaker has forgotten the lives of the Dead.
 II. The speaker intellectually feeds on past knowledge.
 III. The speaker's mind dwells on the past.

 (A) I only
 (B) II only
 (C) III only
 (D) II and III only
 (E) I, II, and III

ANSWER KEY: PRACTICE TEST FIVE

1. E	7. B	13. C	19. B	25. A	31. B	37. D	43. E	49. A	55. B
2. A	8. C	14. D	20. E	26. A	32. D	38. A	44. C	50. E	56. C
3. C	9. E	15. E	21. D	27. C	33. E	39. E	45. A	51. A	57. A
4. A	10. C	16. A	22. B	28. D	34. A	40. C	46. B	52. D	58. C
5. B	11. B	17. E	23. A	29. C	35. B	41. D	47. D	53. C	59. D
6. D	12. A	18. C	24. B	30. E	36. C	42. B	48. C	54. D	60. D

TO OBTAIN YOUR RAW SCORE:

_____ divided by 4 = _____
Total wrong   Score W

_____ minus _____ = _____
Total right   Score W   Score R

Round Score R to the nearest whole number for the raw score.

HOW DID YOU DO?

55–60 = Excellent
44–54 = Very Good
35–43 = Above Average
23–34 = Average
15–22 = Below Average

ANSWER SHEET FOR PRACTICE TEST SIX

1. Ⓐ Ⓑ Ⓒ Ⓓ Ⓔ
2. Ⓐ Ⓑ Ⓒ Ⓓ Ⓔ
3. Ⓐ Ⓑ Ⓒ Ⓓ Ⓔ
4. Ⓐ Ⓑ Ⓒ Ⓓ Ⓔ
5. Ⓐ Ⓑ Ⓒ Ⓓ Ⓔ
6. Ⓐ Ⓑ Ⓒ Ⓓ Ⓔ
7. Ⓐ Ⓑ Ⓒ Ⓓ Ⓔ
8. Ⓐ Ⓑ Ⓒ Ⓓ Ⓔ
9. Ⓐ Ⓑ Ⓒ Ⓓ Ⓔ
10. Ⓐ Ⓑ Ⓒ Ⓓ Ⓔ
11. Ⓐ Ⓑ Ⓒ Ⓓ Ⓔ
12. Ⓐ Ⓑ Ⓒ Ⓓ Ⓔ
13. Ⓐ Ⓑ Ⓒ Ⓓ Ⓔ
14. Ⓐ Ⓑ Ⓒ Ⓓ Ⓔ
15. Ⓐ Ⓑ Ⓒ Ⓓ Ⓔ
16. Ⓐ Ⓑ Ⓒ Ⓓ Ⓔ
17. Ⓐ Ⓑ Ⓒ Ⓓ Ⓔ
18. Ⓐ Ⓑ Ⓒ Ⓓ Ⓔ
19. Ⓐ Ⓑ Ⓒ Ⓓ Ⓔ
20. Ⓐ Ⓑ Ⓒ Ⓓ Ⓔ

21. Ⓐ Ⓑ Ⓒ Ⓓ Ⓔ
22. Ⓐ Ⓑ Ⓒ Ⓓ Ⓔ
23. Ⓐ Ⓑ Ⓒ Ⓓ Ⓔ
24. Ⓐ Ⓑ Ⓒ Ⓓ Ⓔ
25. Ⓐ Ⓑ Ⓒ Ⓓ Ⓔ
26. Ⓐ Ⓑ Ⓒ Ⓓ Ⓔ
27. Ⓐ Ⓑ Ⓒ Ⓓ Ⓔ
28. Ⓐ Ⓑ Ⓒ Ⓓ Ⓔ
29. Ⓐ Ⓑ Ⓒ Ⓓ Ⓔ
30. Ⓐ Ⓑ Ⓒ Ⓓ Ⓔ
31. Ⓐ Ⓑ Ⓒ Ⓓ Ⓔ
32. Ⓐ Ⓑ Ⓒ Ⓓ Ⓔ
33. Ⓐ Ⓑ Ⓒ Ⓓ Ⓔ
34. Ⓐ Ⓑ Ⓒ Ⓓ Ⓔ
35. Ⓐ Ⓑ Ⓒ Ⓓ Ⓔ
36. Ⓐ Ⓑ Ⓒ Ⓓ Ⓔ
37. Ⓐ Ⓑ Ⓒ Ⓓ Ⓔ
38. Ⓐ Ⓑ Ⓒ Ⓓ Ⓔ
39. Ⓐ Ⓑ Ⓒ Ⓓ Ⓔ
40. Ⓐ Ⓑ Ⓒ Ⓓ Ⓔ

41. Ⓐ Ⓑ Ⓒ Ⓓ Ⓔ
42. Ⓐ Ⓑ Ⓒ Ⓓ Ⓔ
43. Ⓐ Ⓑ Ⓒ Ⓓ Ⓔ
44. Ⓐ Ⓑ Ⓒ Ⓓ Ⓔ
45. Ⓐ Ⓑ Ⓒ Ⓓ Ⓔ
46. Ⓐ Ⓑ Ⓒ Ⓓ Ⓔ
47. Ⓐ Ⓑ Ⓒ Ⓓ Ⓔ
48. Ⓐ Ⓑ Ⓒ Ⓓ Ⓔ
49. Ⓐ Ⓑ Ⓒ Ⓓ Ⓔ
50. Ⓐ Ⓑ Ⓒ Ⓓ Ⓔ
51. Ⓐ Ⓑ Ⓒ Ⓓ Ⓔ
52. Ⓐ Ⓑ Ⓒ Ⓓ Ⓔ
53. Ⓐ Ⓑ Ⓒ Ⓓ Ⓔ
54. Ⓐ Ⓑ Ⓒ Ⓓ Ⓔ
55. Ⓐ Ⓑ Ⓒ Ⓓ Ⓔ
56. Ⓐ Ⓑ Ⓒ Ⓓ Ⓔ
57. Ⓐ Ⓑ Ⓒ Ⓓ Ⓔ
58. Ⓐ Ⓑ Ⓒ Ⓓ Ⓔ
59. Ⓐ Ⓑ Ⓒ Ⓓ Ⓔ
60. Ⓐ Ⓑ Ⓒ Ⓓ Ⓔ

PRACTICE TEST SIX

Time allowed: One hour

Directions: The following questions test your understanding of several literary selections. Read each passage or poem and the questions that follow it. Select the best answer choice for each questions by blackening the matching oval on your answer sheet. **Special attention should be given to questions containing the following words: EXCEPT, LEAST, NOT.**

Questions 1–11 are based on the following passage.

'Talking of scandal,' returned Mr Fellowes, 'have you heard the last story about Barton? Nisbett was telling me the other day that he
line dines alone with the Countess at six, while
(5)   Mrs Barton is in the kitchen acting as cook.'

'Rather an apocryphal authority, Nisbett,' said Mr Ely.

'Ah,' said Mr Cleves, with good-natured humour twinkling in his eyes, 'depend upon it,
(10) that is a corrupt version. The original text is, that they all dined together with *six*—meaning six children—and that Mrs Barton is an excellent cook.'

'I wish dining alone together may be the
(15) worst of that sad business,' said the Rev. Archibald Duke, in a tone implying that his wish was a strong figure of speech.

'Well,' said Mr Fellowes, filling his glass and looking jocose, 'Barton is certainly either
(20) the greatest gull in existence, or he has some cunning secret,—some philtre or other to make himself charming in the eyes of a fair lady. It isn't all of us that can make conquests when our ugliness is past its bloom.'

(25) 'The lady seemed to have made a conquest of him at the very outset,' said Mr Ely. 'I was immensely amused one night at Granby's when he was telling us her story about her husband's adventures. He said, "When she
(30) told me the tale, I felt I don't know how,—I felt it from the crown of my head to the sole of my feet".'

Mr Ely gave these words dramatically, imitating the Rev. Amos's fervour and
(35) symbolic action, and every one laughed except Mr Duke, whose after-dinner view of things was not apt to be jovial. He said,—

'I think some of us ought to remonstrate with Mr Barton on the scandal he is causing.
(40) He is not only imperilling his own soul, but the souls of his flock.'

'Depend upon it,' said Mr Cleves, 'there is some simple explanation of the whole affair, if we only happened to know it. Barton has
(45) always impressed me as a right-minded man, who has the knack of doing himself injustice by his manner.'

'Now *I* never liked Barton,' said Mr Fellowes. 'He's not a gentleman....'

Amos Barton
by George Eliot

1. In lines 1–3, Mr. Fellowes's choice of words

   (A) suggests that Barton was the subject of previous scandals
   (B) introduces gossip to their conversation
   (C) marks the beginning of a joke
   (D) renders what he says as unbelievable
   (E) weakens his credibility

2. Mr. Ely characterizes Nisbett as

   (A) a credible witness
   (B) pyschologically unbalanced
   (C) someone not to be believed
   (D) learned and authoritative
   (E) a lawyer

3. Which of the following could be considered synonymous with "corrupt" as used in line 10?

   (A) Rotten
   (B) Evil
   (C) Taking bribes
   (D) Foreign admixtures
   (E) Containing alterations

4. The main difference in meaning between the two versions of the story concerning Barton centers on

   (A) Mrs. Barton's cooking
   (B) whether the Countess was actually there
   (C) greed and corruption
   (D) the prepositions "at" and "with"
   (E) dining in the kitchen

5. "Six," as used in line 4, refers to

   (A) children
   (B) time
   (C) a date
   (D) dinner guests
   (E) age

6. The "figure of speech" (line 17) implied by Duke's tone can be seen as which of these uses?

   (A) Personification of dining
   (B) "Sad business" representing Duke
   (C) "Dining alone together" representing many other bad circumstances
   (D) Apostrophe to Barton
   (E) Rhetorical question for Barton

7. Mr. Fellowes's tone in lines 18–20 can be considered

   (A) humorous
   (B) sad
   (C) angry
   (D) unrelenting
   (E) suspicious

8. Fellowes characterizes Barton in lines 20–21 as either

   (A) guilty or innocent
   (B) naive or clever
   (C) easily deceived or a deviser of a secret plan
   (D) a fraud or possessor of a love charm
   (E) athletic or witty

9. Lines 40–41 contain inferences that Mr. Barton

   (A) is a shepherd
   (B) is a sheep farmer
   (C) does not care about scandal
   (D) resists constructive criticism
   (E) is in a position of leadership

10. The tone of "Now I never liked Barton" (line 48) conveys an attitude that is

    (A) overbearing and judgmental
    (B) humorous and charming
    (C) expectant and excited
    (D) respectful and placating
    (E) suspicious and resentful

11. The expression used in lines 31–32 is an example of which of the following?

    (A) Cliche
    (B) Pun
    (C) Satire
    (D) Contradiction
    (E) Witticism

Questions 12–30 are based on the following poem.

The Hurricane

Happy the man who, safe on shore,
   Now trims, at home, his evening fire;
Unmov'd he hears the tempests roar,
line   That on the tufted groves expire:
(5) Alas! on us they doubly fall,
Our feeble barque must bear them all.

Now to their haunts the birds retreat,
   The squirrel seeks his hollow tree,
Wolves in their shaded caverns meet,
(10)   All, all are blest but wretched we—
Foredoomed a stranger to repose,
No rest the unsettled ocean knows

While o'er the dark abyss we roam,
   Perhaps, with last departing gleam,
(15) We saw the sun descend in gloom,
   No more to see his morning beam;
But buried low, by far too deep,
On coral beds, unpitied, sleep!

But what a strange, uncoasted strand
(20)   Is that, where fate permits no day—
No charts have we to mark that land,
   No compass to direct that way—
What Pilot shall explore that realm,
What new Columbus take the helm!

         * * *

(25) The barque, accustomed to obey,
   No more the trembling pilots guide:
Alone she gropes her trackless way,
   While mountains burst on either side—
Thus, skill and science both must fall;
(30) And ruin is the lot of all.

              by Philip Freneau

12. The effect of the use of caesura in line 10 is

(A) to emphasize a sense of contrast
(B) to imply that animals are of major importance
(C) to echo the "all" in line 6
(D) to continue the established meter
(E) to resume the stress begun in line 5

13. The attitude of the speaker toward the man on shore (line 1) reflects the speaker's

(A) good humor
(B) anger
(C) respect
(D) sympathy
(E) fear

14. Why do "Wolves in their shaded caverns meet" (line 9)?

(A) They are escaping the man on shore.
(B) They are haunted by the birds and squirrels.
(C) They are strangers to the land.
(D) They are seeking shelter from the storm.
(E) They are being tracked by the barque.

15. The most appropriate descriptive adjective to convey the speaker's tone and meaning concerning the "strange, uncoasted strand" (line 19) is

(A) exotic
(B) unfamiliar
(C) mysterious
(D) beautiful
(E) friendly

16. The relationship established in the paradoxical phrase "uncoasted strand" (line 19) is reflected in which of the following phrases?

(A) Childless mother
(B) Rainless desert
(C) Frosted cake
(D) Mirrored wall
(E) Uncontrolled anger

17. As used in line 24, "Columbus" is a literary device known as

(A) antonomasia
(B) antithesis
(C) aphaeresis
(D) aphorism
(E) apocope

18. Of the following statements, which one best summarizes the effect of "Unmov'd" in line 3?

   (A) It stresses the man on shore's sense of safety.
   (B) It emphasizes the speaker's stubborn attitude.
   (C) It projects the turbulent nature of the storm.
   (D) It echoes the violence of the hurricane.
   (E) It contrasts with the evening fire in line 2.

19. Of the following pairs of words, which pair LEAST effectively illustrates the contrast in content developed within the first two stanzas of the poem?

   (A) "Safe" (line 1)…"Foredoomed" (line 11)
   (B) "hears" (line 3)…"bear" (line 6)
   (C) "barque" (line 6)…"ocean" (line 12)
   (D) "repose" (line 11)…"unsettled" (line 12)
   (E) "happy" (line 1)…"wretched" (line 10)

20. In line 4, the phrase "on the tufted groves expire" reveals the man on shore's

   (A) position of danger
   (B) impending death
   (C) need to escape
   (D) sheltered position
   (E) resistance to escape

21. In line 11, "a stranger" would probably be identified as

   (A) one who is unfamiliar to the speaker
   (B) one who is unaccustomed to rest
   (C) one who is a guest of the speaker
   (D) one who is a visitor on the ship
   (E) one who is a foreigner on the shore

22. An implication of "Foredoomed" (line 11) most likely is that the speaker

   (A) is antagonistic toward strangers
   (B) wants strangers to remain in repose
   (C) believes that repose is only for strangers
   (D) is resistant concerning accepting the outcome of the storm
   (E) believes that his turbulent end is inevitable

23. In line 15, which of the following changes occurs?

   (A) The sun is obscured by fog.
   (B) A shift to personification enlivens the scene.
   (C) A change to past tense of the verb introduces the concept of death.
   (D) Use of first person plural emphasizes the reader's sense of danger.
   (E) Introduction of imperfect rhyme emphasizes danger.

24. What is a "barque" (line 6)?

   (A) A sailor
   (B) A man on shore
   (C) A pilot
   (D) A storm
   (E) A sailing vessel

25. Of the following statements, which one best summarizes the main idea of the concluding couplet (lines 29–30)?

   (A) Skill and science could prevent their loss.
   (B) The ship is a product of science.
   (C) Skill and science caused the ship's destruction.
   (D) Man cannot overcome nature.
   (E) Some may escape the ruin of the storm.

26. The "mountains" in line 28 can be thought of as all the following EXCEPT

   (A) the destruction of safety and security as they burst
   (B) symbols of stability in an explosive situation
   (C) a vehicle in a metaphor describing the water
   (D) ironic representations of places of safe haven
   (E) a vehicle in a simile describing the distant land

27. The word "Perhaps" (line 14) creates an effect that serves to

   (A) suggest that the storm may pass soon
   (B) stress the uncertainty that many will die
   (C) symbolize the hope of the storm's passing
   (D) establish a pattern of alliteration
   (E) suggest some may not have seen the sunset

28. From a contextual perspective, "abyss" (line 13) can mean all the following EXCEPT

(A) the center of an escutcheon
(B) a great gulf of water
(C) immeasurable amounts
(D) the immensity of depth
(E) the ocean depths

29. Line 27 refers to the barque figuratively as a

(A) ship out of control
(B) vagrant caught in a storm
(C) social outcast
(D) pilot lost at sea
(E) lost, blind woman feeling her way

30. In line 21, "that land" might be seen as which of the concepts listed below?

I. A distant safe haven
II. Death
III. The bottom of the sea

(A) I only
(B) II only
(C) III only
(D) II and III only
(E) I, II, and III

Questions 31–38 are based on the following passage.

Hasty Pudding
[corn meal mush] A Poem, in Three Cantos

Omne tulit punctum qui miscuit utile dulci ["He has gained all approval who has mixed the useful with the sweet"—HORACE]
He makes a good breakfast who mixes pudding with molasses.

PREFACE

A simplicity in diet, whether it be considered with reference to the happiness of individuals or the prosperity of a nation, is of more
(line) consequence than we are apt to imagine. In
(5) recommending so important an object to the rational part of mankind, I wish it were in my power to do it in such a manner as would be likely to gain their attention. I am sensible that it is one of those subjects in which example
(10) has infinitely more power than the most

convincing arguments or the highest charms of poetry. Goldsmith's *Deserted Village,* though possessing these two advantages in a greater degree than any other work of the kind, has
(15) not prevented villages in England from being deserted. The apparent interest of the rich individuals, who form the taste as well as the laws in that country, has been against him; and with that interest it has been vain to contend.
(20)   The vicious habits which in this little piece I endeavor to combat, seem to me not so difficult to cure. No class of people has any *interest* in supporting them; unless it be the interest which certain families may feel in vying with each
(25) other in sumptuous entertainments. There may indeed be some instances of depraved appetites, which no arguments will conquer; but these must be rare. There are very few persons but what would always prefer a plain dish for
(30) themselves, and would prefer it likewise for their guests, if there were no risk of reputation in the case. This difficulty can only be removed by example; and the example should proceed from those whose situation enables
(35) them to take the lead in forming the manners of a nation. Persons of this description in America, I should hope, are neither above nor below the influence of truth and reason, when conveyed in language suited to the subject.
(40)   Whether the manner I have chosen to address my arguments to them be such as to promise any success is what I cannot decide. But I certainly had hopes of doing some good, or I should not have taken the pains of putting
(45) so many rimes together. The example of domestic virtues has doubtless a great effect. I only wish to rank *simplicity of diet* among the virtues. In that case I should hope it will be cherished and more esteemed by others than it
(50) is at present.

by Joel Barlow

31. The speaker probably intends "diet" (line 1) to convey which of the following meanings?

    I.   A regulated manner of living
    II. Eating habits
    III. Daily fare

    (A) I only
    (B) II only
    (C) II and III only
    (D) I and III only
    (E) I, II, and III

32. The speaker's purpose includes

    (A) informing
    (B) persuading
    (C) hypothesizing
    (D) instructing
    (E) describing

33. According to the speaker, Goldsmith's *Deserted Village* (line 12)

    (A) prevented England's villages from being deserted
    (B) is the best poem ever written
    (C) is a convincing argument and charming poetry
    (D) overcame English laws
    (E) provides a powerful example of his premise

34. In the context of line 19, "vain" means

    (A) having no genuine value
    (B) conceited
    (C) lacking in sense
    (D) trivial
    (E) ineffective

35. The second paragraph puts forth that

    (A) most people prefer simplicity in diet
    (B) the argument will be difficult to execute
    (C) not enough people are willing to take the lead
    (D) truth and reason have been abandoned
    (E) the language is not suitable to the subject

36. The speaker considers simplicity of diet to be

    (A) unattainable
    (B) without interest
    (C) a virtue
    (D) a risk to reputation
    (E) below the influence of truth and reason

37. The speaker's view includes that

    (A) vicious habits cannot be broken
    (B) depraved appetites prevent the general assimilation of virtue
    (C) most people prefer elegant dishes
    (D) leaders set a good example
    (E) "rimes" (line 45) are of best influence in this case

38. In line 41, "them" should be identified as

    (A) people of depraved appetites
    (B) American social leaders
    (C) families competing in sumptuous entertainments
    (D) English landed gentry
    (E) lawyers

Questions 39–46 are based on the following poem.

CANTO I

Ye Alps audacious, through the heavens that rise,
To cramp the day and hide me from the skies;
Ye Gallic flags, that o'er their heights unfurled,
line Bear death to kings, and freedom to the world.
(5) I sing not you. A softer theme I choose,
A virgin theme, unconscious of the muse,
But fruitful, rich, well suited to inspire
The purest frenzy of poetic fire.
  Despise it not, ye bards to terror steeled,
(10) Who hurl your thunders round the epic field;
Nor ye who strain your midnight throats to sing
Joys that the vineyard and the stillhouse bring;
Or on some distant fair your notes employ,
And speak of raptures that you ne'er enjoy.
(15) I sing the sweets I know, the charms I feel,
My morning incense, and my evening meal,
The sweets of Hasty Pudding. Come, dear bowl,
Glide o'er my palate, and inspire my soul.
The milk beside thee, smoking from the kine,

(20) Its substance mingled, married in with thine,
Shall cool and temper thy superior heat,
And save the pains of blowing while I eat.
  Oh! could the smooth, the emblematic song
Flow like thy genial juices o'er my tongue,
(25) Could those mild morsels in my numbers chime,
And, as they roll in substance, roll in rime,
No more thy awkward unpoetic name
Should shun the muse, or prejudice thy fame:
But rising grateful to the accustomed ear,
(30)(All bards should catch it, and all realms revere!

"Hasty Pudding"
by Joel Barlow

39. The subject of the poem is based upon

  (A) the importance of writing poetry
  (B) a patriotic theme
  (C) extolling the virtues of eating a hot cereal
  (D) advice to other poets to write about mundane subjects
  (E) writing epic poetry

40. As used in line 22, "pains" can be thought of as

  (A) great care or effort
  (B) torture
  (C) a hurting sensation
  (D) penalty
  (E) hunger pains

41. Which of the definitions below is the definition of "the kine" as used in line 19?

  (A) A friendly person
  (B) Sugar maple trees
  (C) Cows
  (D) The cookstove
  (E) Lanterns

42. The speaker claims to eat Hasty Pudding

  (A) for breakfast and dinner
  (B) only on special days
  (C) within the confines of poetic verse
  (D) at a "distant fair" (line 13)
  (E) only with "sweets" (line 15)

43. In the first stanza, the speaker contends that Hasty Pudding is

  (A) a well-known patriotic subject
  (B) loftier than the Alps
  (C) a theme akin to odes, mountains, and flags
  (D) not as inspiring as patriotic themes
  (E) a subject that is new to poetry

44. Of the following devices listed, which is used in lines 17–18?

  (A) Apostrophe
  (B) Alliteration
  (C) Simile
  (D) Metaphor
  (E) Aposiopesis

45. In lines 23–26, the speaker uses elements of syntactical parallelism to

  (A) establish a pattern of onomatopoeia
  (B) reinforce the alliterative pattern of the previous stanza
  (C) enhance the simile comparing the writing process and eating
  (D) negate anticipated antagonism toward the simplicity of the subject
  (E) point out his sense of urgency in the matter

46. The song is "emblematic" (line 23) in that the poet wants the poem

  (A) to be filled with moralistic mottoes
  (B) and the process of writing it to represent the Hasty Pudding experience
  (C) to reflect a lofty theme and patriotic tone
  (D) and the process of writing it to incorporate elements of established symbols
  (E) to become accepted as part of the main body of symbolic literature

Questions 47–53 are based on the following passage.

  I had been now thirteen days on shore, and had been eleven times on board the ship; in which time I had brought away all that one
line pair of hands could well be supposed capable
(5) to bring, though I believe verily, had the calm

weather held, I should have brought away the whole ship, piece by piece. But preparing the twelfth time to go on board, I found the wind began to rise; however, at low water I went on
(10) board, and though I thought I had rummaged the cabin so effectually, as that nothing more could be found, yet I discovered a locker with drawers in it, in one of which I found two or three razors and one pair of large scissors, with
(15) some ten or a dozen of good knives and forks; in another I found about thirty-six pounds value in money, some European coin, some Brazil, some pieces of eight, some gold, some silver.

I smiled to myself at the sight of this money.
(20) "O drug!" said I aloud, "what art thou good for? Thou art not worth to me, no, not the taking off of the ground; one of those knives is worth all this heap; I have no manner of use for thee; e'en remain where thou art and go to the bottom as
(25) a creature whose life is not worth saving." However, upon second thoughts, I took it away, and wrapping all this in a piece of canvas, I began to think of making another raft; but while I was preparing this, I found the sky overcast,
(30) and the wind began to rise, and in a quarter of an hour it blew a fresh gale from the shore; it presently occurred to me that it was in vain to pretend to make a raft with the wind off shore, and that it was my business to be gone before
(35) the tide of flood began, otherwise I might not be able to reach the shore at all. Accordingly I let myself down into the water and swam across the channel, which lay between the ship and the sands, and even that with difficulty
(40) enough, partly with the weight of the things I had about me, and partly the roughness of the water, for the wind rose very hastily, and before it was quite high water, it blew a storm.

But I was gotten home to my little tent,
(45) where I lay with all my wealth about me very secure. It blew very hard all that night, and in the morning, when I looked out, behold, no more ship was to be seen; I was a little surprised, but recovered myself with this
(50) satisfactory reflection, viz., that I had lost no time, nor abated no diligence to get everything out of her that could be useful to me, and that indeed there was little left in her that I was able to bring away if I had had more time.

Robinson Crusoe
by Daniel Defoe

47. The circumstances described in the passage support the idea that the speaker has

(A) the nature of a petty thief
(B) an ineptitude toward his circumstances
(C) been part of a salvage crew
(D) innate survival skills
(E) a plan for an immediate rescue

48. The use of figurative language in the second paragraph (lines 19–25) includes all the following EXCEPT

(A) elements of mixed figures
(B) metaphor
(C) simile
(D) personification
(E) meiosis

49. The phrase "vain to pretend" (lines 32–33) might also be worded as

(A) conceited actions to take
(B) trivial to allege
(C) useless to plan
(D) lacking in sense to put in a claim
(E) unimportant to feign

50. In line 34, "my business" refers to the speaker's

(A) salvaging operation
(B) anxiety or concerns
(C) power of interference over the ship
(D) matter or affair
(E) policy

51. "Viz" (line 50) means

(A) in other words
(B) for example
(C) namely
(D) about
(E) equal to

52. Which of the following attitudes does the narrator exhibit toward the storm?

(A) Shock and despair
(B) Gripping fear
(C) Unsubmissive resistance
(D) Calm composure
(E) Self-satisfied defiance

53. The speaker's "second thoughts" in line 26 serve to indicate his

(A) anticipation of a change in circumstances
(B) indecisive character
(C) deeply insightful nature
(D) overwhelming sense of greed
(E) tendency toward elements of a split personality

Questions 54–60 are based on the following poem.

My Life—to Discontent a Prey

My life—to Discontent a prey—
    Is in the sere and yellow leaf.
'Tis vain for happiness to pray:
line   No solace brings my heart relief.
(5) My pulse is weak, my spirit low;
    I cannot think, I cannot write.
I strive to spin a verse—but lo!
    My rhymes are very rarely right.

I sit within my lowly cell,
(10)   And strive to court the comic Muse;
But how can Poesy excel,
    With such a row from yonder mews?
In accents passionately high
    The carter chides the stubborn horse;
(15) And shouts a 'Gee!' or yells a 'Hi!'
    In tones objectionably hoarse.

In vain for Poesy I wait;
    No comic Muse my call obeys.
My brains are loaded with a weight
(20)   That mocks the laurels and the bays.
I wish my brains could only be
    Inspired with industry anew;
And labour like the busy bee,
    In strains no Genius ever knew.

(25) Although I strive with all my might,
    Alas, my efforts all are vain!
I've no *afflatus*—not a mite;
    I cannot work the comic vein.
The Tragic Muse may hear my pleas,
(30)   And waft me to a purer clime.
Melpomene! assist me, please,
    To somewhat higher heights to climb.

            by Henry S. Leigh

54. The rhyme, as used in lines 1 and 3 and in lines 6 and 8, conforms to the definition of

(A) forced rhyme
(B) masculine rhyme
(C) imperfect rhyme
(D) internal rhyme
(E) feminine rhyme

55. In line 27, the speaker characterizes himself as NOT

(A) moody
(B) troubled
(C) conceited
(D) argumentative
(E) inspired

56. Of the pairs of words listed below, which pair demonstrates *rime riche*?

(A) "Gee" and "Hi" (line 15)
(B) "horse" (line 14) and "hoarse" (line 16)
(C) "court" and "comic" (line 10)
(D) "strive" (line 25) and "mite" (line 27)
(E) "higher" and "heights" (line 32)

57. The poem is about

(A) the isolation of the poet
(B) the poet's genius
(C) mythology
(D) the poet's reliance on the Muses for his verse
(E) the quietness needed for writing poetry

58. In relation to the rest of the poem, the last four lines include

(A) a change of rhythm
(B) the speaker's discontent replaced by tragedy
(C) a mood shift from futile to hopeful
(D) change of rhyme scheme
(E) a mood shift from despairing to self-reliant

59. Personified "Discontent" in line 1

    (A) shows the speaker's anger
    (B) serves as a friend
    (C) emphasizes a desire to change
    (D) serves to victimize the speaker
    (E) comforts the speaker

60. The speaker can be described as all the following EXCEPT

    (A) discouraged
    (B) self-reliant
    (C) wanting to write comic poetry
    (D) dependent
    (E) wanting the Muses to get to work

ANSWER KEY: PRACTICE TEST SIX

1. A	7. A	13. E	19. C	25. D	31. E	37. D	43. E	49. C	55. E
2. C	8. D	14. D	20. D	26. E	32. B	38. B	44. A	50. B	56. B
3. E	9. E	15. B	21. B	27. E	33. C	39. C	45. C	51. C	57. D
4. D	10. A	16. A	22. E	28. A	34. E	40. A	46. B	52. D	58. C
5. B	11. A	17. A	23. C	29. E	35. A	41. C	47. D	53. A	59. D
6. C	12. A	18. A	24. E	30. D	36. C	42. A	48. E	54. B	60. B

TO OBTAIN YOUR RAW SCORE:

_____ divided by 4 = _____
Total wrong   Score W

_____ minus _____ = _____
Total right   Score W   Score R

Round Score R to the nearest whole number for the raw score.

HOW DID YOU DO?

55–60 = Excellent
44–54 = Very Good
35–43 = Above Average
23–34 = Average
15–22 = Below Average

ANSWER SHEET FOR PRACTICE TEST SEVEN

1. Ⓐ Ⓑ Ⓒ Ⓓ Ⓔ
2. Ⓐ Ⓑ Ⓒ Ⓓ Ⓔ
3. Ⓐ Ⓑ Ⓒ Ⓓ Ⓔ
4. Ⓐ Ⓑ Ⓒ Ⓓ Ⓔ
5. Ⓐ Ⓑ Ⓒ Ⓓ Ⓔ
6. Ⓐ Ⓑ Ⓒ Ⓓ Ⓔ
7. Ⓐ Ⓑ Ⓒ Ⓓ Ⓔ
8. Ⓐ Ⓑ Ⓒ Ⓓ Ⓔ
9. Ⓐ Ⓑ Ⓒ Ⓓ Ⓔ
10. Ⓐ Ⓑ Ⓒ Ⓓ Ⓔ
11. Ⓐ Ⓑ Ⓒ Ⓓ Ⓔ
12. Ⓐ Ⓑ Ⓒ Ⓓ Ⓔ
13. Ⓐ Ⓑ Ⓒ Ⓓ Ⓔ
14. Ⓐ Ⓑ Ⓒ Ⓓ Ⓔ
15. Ⓐ Ⓑ Ⓒ Ⓓ Ⓔ
16. Ⓐ Ⓑ Ⓒ Ⓓ Ⓔ
17. Ⓐ Ⓑ Ⓒ Ⓓ Ⓔ
18. Ⓐ Ⓑ Ⓒ Ⓓ Ⓔ
19. Ⓐ Ⓑ Ⓒ Ⓓ Ⓔ
20. Ⓐ Ⓑ Ⓒ Ⓓ Ⓔ
21. Ⓐ Ⓑ Ⓒ Ⓓ Ⓔ
22. Ⓐ Ⓑ Ⓒ Ⓓ Ⓔ
23. Ⓐ Ⓑ Ⓒ Ⓓ Ⓔ
24. Ⓐ Ⓑ Ⓒ Ⓓ Ⓔ
25. Ⓐ Ⓑ Ⓒ Ⓓ Ⓔ
26. Ⓐ Ⓑ Ⓒ Ⓓ Ⓔ
27. Ⓐ Ⓑ Ⓒ Ⓓ Ⓔ
28. Ⓐ Ⓑ Ⓒ Ⓓ Ⓔ
29. Ⓐ Ⓑ Ⓒ Ⓓ Ⓔ
30. Ⓐ Ⓑ Ⓒ Ⓓ Ⓔ
31. Ⓐ Ⓑ Ⓒ Ⓓ Ⓔ
32. Ⓐ Ⓑ Ⓒ Ⓓ Ⓔ
33. Ⓐ Ⓑ Ⓒ Ⓓ Ⓔ
34. Ⓐ Ⓑ Ⓒ Ⓓ Ⓔ
35. Ⓐ Ⓑ Ⓒ Ⓓ Ⓔ
36. Ⓐ Ⓑ Ⓒ Ⓓ Ⓔ
37. Ⓐ Ⓑ Ⓒ Ⓓ Ⓔ
38. Ⓐ Ⓑ Ⓒ Ⓓ Ⓔ
39. Ⓐ Ⓑ Ⓒ Ⓓ Ⓔ
40. Ⓐ Ⓑ Ⓒ Ⓓ Ⓔ
41. Ⓐ Ⓑ Ⓒ Ⓓ Ⓔ
42. Ⓐ Ⓑ Ⓒ Ⓓ Ⓔ
43. Ⓐ Ⓑ Ⓒ Ⓓ Ⓔ
44. Ⓐ Ⓑ Ⓒ Ⓓ Ⓔ
45. Ⓐ Ⓑ Ⓒ Ⓓ Ⓔ
46. Ⓐ Ⓑ Ⓒ Ⓓ Ⓔ
47. Ⓐ Ⓑ Ⓒ Ⓓ Ⓔ
48. Ⓐ Ⓑ Ⓒ Ⓓ Ⓔ
49. Ⓐ Ⓑ Ⓒ Ⓓ Ⓔ
50. Ⓐ Ⓑ Ⓒ Ⓓ Ⓔ
51. Ⓐ Ⓑ Ⓒ Ⓓ Ⓔ
52. Ⓐ Ⓑ Ⓒ Ⓓ Ⓔ
53. Ⓐ Ⓑ Ⓒ Ⓓ Ⓔ
54. Ⓐ Ⓑ Ⓒ Ⓓ Ⓔ
55. Ⓐ Ⓑ Ⓒ Ⓓ Ⓔ
56. Ⓐ Ⓑ Ⓒ Ⓓ Ⓔ
57. Ⓐ Ⓑ Ⓒ Ⓓ Ⓔ
58. Ⓐ Ⓑ Ⓒ Ⓓ Ⓔ
59. Ⓐ Ⓑ Ⓒ Ⓓ Ⓔ
60. Ⓐ Ⓑ Ⓒ Ⓓ Ⓔ

PRACTICE TEST SEVEN

Time allowed: One hour

Directions: The following questions test your understanding of several literary selections. Read each passage or poem and the questions that follow it. Select the best answer choice for each question by blackening the matching oval on your answer sheet. **Special attention should be given to questions containing the following words: EXCEPT, LEAST, NOT.**

Questions 1–6 are based on the following passage.

I do not think that we ever knew his real name. Our ignorance of it certainly never gave us any social inconvenience, for at Sandy Bar
line in 1854 most men were christened anew.
(5) Sometimes these appellatives were derived from some distinctiveness of dress, as in the case of "Dungaree Jack"; or from some peculiarity of habit, as shown in "Saleratus Bill," so called from an undue proportion of
(10) that chemical in his daily bread; or from some unlucky slip, as exhibited in "The Iron Pirate," a mild, inoffensive man, who earned that baleful title by his unfortunate mispronunciation of the term "iron pyrites."
(15) Perhaps this may have been the beginning of a rude heraldry; but I am constrained to think that it was because a man's real name in that day rested solely upon his own unsupported statement. "Call yourself Clifford, do you?"
(20) said Boston, addressing a timid new-comer with infinite scorn; "hell is full of such Cliffords!" He then introduced the unfortunate man, whose name happened to be really Clifford, as "Jay-bird Charley,"—an
(25) unhallowed inspiration of the moment, that clung to him ever after.

"Tennessee's Partner"
by Bret Harte

1. The narrator's comments concerning "Saleratus Bill" reveal that he

(A) especially enjoyed bread
(B) used large amounts of yeast
(C) earned a high salary
(D) made bread that was sour
(E) used large amounts of baking soda

2. Lines 5–10 contain elements of all the following EXCEPT

(A) cause and effect
(B) amplification
(C) example
(D) metonymy
(E) personification

3. The LEAST accurate description of "a rude heraldry," as used in line 16, is

(A) a barbarous devising of family lineage
(B) a discourteous announcement
(C) a robust harbinger of official status
(D) a vulgar granting of nomenclature
(E) an inaccurate genealogical lineage

4. That "The Iron Pirate" was named mispronouncing "iron pyrites" might indicate that

(A) Sandy Bar was a shipping port
(B) Sandy Bar was a mining town
(C) the man really was a pirate
(D) the man was known as a thief
(E) the man was born in Sandy Bar

5. In line 21, "of infinite scorn" emphasizes Boston's

   (A) sense of indignation
   (B) anger at injustice
   (C) insolence
   (D) resistance of authority
   (E) quiescence

6. The statement made in lines 1–4 can be described as

   (A) a statement of reality regarding the situation
   (B) an opinion held by the narrator only
   (C) a controversial premise to an argument
   (D) a contention in a debate
   (E) a feeble excuse for inexcusable conduct

Questions 7–16 are based on the following poem.

The Sonnet
II

Scorn not the sonnet; Critic, you have frown'd,
Mindless of its just honours; with this key
　Shakespeare unlock'd his heart; the melody
line Of this small lute gave ease to Petrarch's wound;
(5) A thousand times this pipe did Tasso sound;
　With it Camöens sooth'd an exile's grief;
　The Sonnet glitter'd a gay myrtle leaf
Amid the cypress with which Dante crown'd
His visionary brow: a glow-worm lamp,
(10) 　It cheer'd mild Spenser, call'd from Faery-land
To struggle through dark ways; and, when a damp
　Fell round the path of Milton, in his hand
The Thing became a trumpet; whence he blew
Soul-animating strains—alas, too few!

　　　　　by William Wordsworth

7. In the poem in its entirety, the speaker reveals an attitude toward "Critic" (line 1) that can be considered

   (A) angry and belligerent
   (B) reproachful and retaliatory
   (C) censorious and didactic
   (D) provocative and probing
   (E) class-conscious and authoritative

8. From the context, "Camöens" (line 6) probably refers to a

   (A) political prisoner
   (B) poet
   (C) revolutionary
   (D) critic
   (E) sonnet

9. The speaker's use of "alas, too few!" in the last line produces which of the effects listed below?

   (A) It summarizes that not enough poets write sonnets.
   (B) It contends that more critics should appreciate the sonnet.
   (C) It sets forth an element of quantity over quality.
   (D) It heightens the sense of nostalgia and melancholy of the sonnet.
   (E) It shifts emphasis to a yearning for Milton to have written more sonnets.

10. The phrase "a gay myrtle leaf/Amid the cypress" (lines 7–8) figuratively means that

   (A) Dante wrote sonnets about nature
   (B) myrtle leaves are pretty in cypress arrangements
   (C) the sonnet provided a contrast among Dante's works about death
   (D) myrtle leaves and cypress were used to foretell the future
   (E) Dante favored sonnets over more serious poetic forms

11. In this poem, the vehicles "key" (line 2), "lute" (line 4), and "trumpet" (line 13) emphasize

   (A) the weaknesses of Shakespeare, Petrarch, and Milton
   (B) the means by which poets achieve their ends
   (C) the ways sonnets can be used musically
   (D) the emotional release, solace, and stimulus that the sonnet provides
   (E) the contrast to Tasso, Camöens, and Dante

12. Of the literary devices listed below, which is used in lines 3–4 to influence the metrical movement?

 (A) Feminine ending of "key"
 (B) Enjambement
 (C) Metric lines of trimeter
 (D) Extensive use of the spondee
 (E) Alternating anapests and trochees

13. The effect of the syntactical placement of "in his hand" in line 12 is to

 (A) emphasize Milton's skill
 (B) make "The Thing" (line 13) of greater importance
 (C) put aside the theme of the poem
 (D) recognize the balance of subject and execution
 (E) attract greater attention to the poem over the poet

14. In the last line, "alas, too few!" is said in a tone that is

 (A) nonchalant
 (B) zealous
 (C) wistful
 (D) ambitious
 (E) incendiary

15. In line 9, "a glow-worm lamp" is a metaphoric reference to

 (A) a critic
 (B) Spenser
 (C) a sonnet
 (D) Faery-land
 (E) Dante

16. In line 14, the speaker uses the word "Soul-animating" for the purpose of

 (A) making the sonnet into a higher literary form
 (B) varying the rhythm
 (C) suggesting that Milton had died
 (D) establishing an alliterative relationship with "strains"
 (E) symbolizing death

Questions 17–26 are based on the following passage.

So much for Industry, my Friends, and Attention to one's own Business; but to these we must add *Frugality,* if we would make our
line Industry more certainly successful. A Man
(5) may, if he knows not how to save as he gets, *keep his Nose all his life to the Grindstone,* and die not worth a *Groat* at last. A *fat Kitchen makes a lean Will,* as Poor Richard says; and,

  Many Estates are spent in the Getting,
(10) *Since Women for Tea forsook Spinning and
    Knitting,*
  *And Men for Punch forsook Hewing and
    Splitting.*

If you would be wealthy, says he, in another Almanack, *think of Saving as well as of Getting: The Indies have not make Spain rich,*
(15) *because her* Outgoes *are greater than her* Incomes. Away then with your expensive Follies, and you will not have so much Cause to complain of hard Times, heavy Taxes, and chargeable Families; for, as Poor Dick says,

(20) *Women and Wine, Game and Deceit,
    Make the Wealth small, and Wants great.*

And farther, *What maintains one Vice, would bring up two Children.* You may think perhaps, That a *little* Tea, or a *little* Punch
(25) now and then, Diet a *little* more costly, Clothes a *little* finer, and a *little* Entertainment now and then, can be no *great* Matter; but remember what Poor Richard says, *Many* a Little *makes a Mickle;* and farther, *Beware of*
(30) little *Expences; a small Leak will sink a great Ship;* and again, *Who Dainties love, shall Beggars prove;* and moreover, *Fools make Feasts, and wise Men eat them.*

"Poor Richard Improved"
by Benjamin Franklin

17. The speaker is most concerned with which of the following topics?

 (A) Economy and temperance
 (B) Occupation and commerce
 (C) Socials and hospitality
 (D) Taxes and wages
 (E) Food and drink

18. Which of the following pieces of advice can be best understood literally but not figuratively?

   (A) "A fat Kitchen makes a lean Will." (lines 7–8)
   (B) "If you would be wealthy…think of Saving as well as of Getting." (lines 12–14)
   (C) "What maintains one Vice, would bring up two Children." (lines 22–23)
   (D) "A small Leak will sink a great Ship." (lines 30–31)
   (E) "Who Dainties love, shall Beggars prove." (lines 31–32)

19. A "Groat" (line 7) can be thought of as

   (A) a small farm animal
   (B) a portion of fabric
   (C) a portion of rum cut with water
   (D) a trivial amount
   (E) a painful cry

20. Which of the following adjectives can be used to describe Poor Richard's advice?

   (A) Dialectal
   (B) Episodic
   (C) Aphoristic
   (D) Epistolary
   (E) Satiric

21. Use of the term "Poor Dick" (line 19) contributes to the sense that

   (A) the speaker feels sorry for Dick
   (B) Dick is actually not wealthy
   (C) Dick did not follow his own advice
   (D) the speaker is being sarcastic
   (E) the speaker feels comfortable in quoting him

22. In the selection, "Nose…to the Grindstone" (line 6) is a saying that expresses which of the following ideas?

   I.   Working at close range to a millstone
   II. Staying at hard, steady labor
   III. Unremitting self-requirement in work and duty

   (A) I only
   (B) III only
   (C) I and II only
   (D) II and III only
   (E) I and III only

23. The personified "fat Kitchen" (line 7) is actually

   (A) a heavyset cook
   (B) an oversized kitchen
   (C) extravagance in the food budget
   (D) a diet too rich in animal fat
   (E) a greasy kitchen

24. As supported by the context of the passage, "lean Will" (line 8) alludes to

   (A) undernourishment
   (B) poor diet
   (C) a dwindling estate to inherit
   (D) a life-threatening illness
   (E) hard labor

25. "Many a Little makes a Mickle" (lines 28–29) might be restated as which of the following expressions?

   (A) Gain a little, lose a little
   (B) Sew on the bottom what you took off the top
   (C) It all adds up to trouble
   (D) One step forward and two steps back
   (E) Pennies add up to dollars

26. "Away then" in line 16 has a tone that is

   (A) bombastic
   (B) desiderative
   (C) obsequious
   (D) authoritative
   (E) disparaging

Questions 27–32 are based on the following passage.

I used to see packs of half-wild dogs
haunting the lonely beach on the south shore
of Staten Island, in New York Bay, for the
line sake of the carrion there cast up; and I
(5) remember that once, when for a long time I
had heard a furious barking in the tall grass of
the marsh, a pack of half a dozen large dogs
burst forth on to the beach, pursuing a little
one which ran straight to me for protection,
(10) and I afforded it with some stones, though at
some risk to myself; but the next day the little
one was the first to bark at me. Under these
circumstances I could not but remember the
words of the poet:

(15)   Blow, blow, thou winter wind
Thou art not so unkind
   As *his* ingratitude;
Thy tooth is not so keen,
Because thou art not seen,
(20)   Although thy breath be rude.

Freeze, freeze, thou bitter sky,
Thou dost not bite so nigh
   As benefits forgot;
Though thou the waters warp,
(25) Thy sting is not so sharp
   As friend remembered not.

Cape Cod
by Henry David Thoreau

27. The overall theme of this passage is

(A) a defense for an unwise action
(B) a musing upon an ironic situation
(C) an angry accusation against disloyalty
(D) a revelation of poor judgment
(E) an attempt at appearing confident

28. In the passage, what is the literary role of the little dog?

I.   A vehicle in an analogy
II. A symbol of ingratitude
III. A character representing a type of person

(A) I only
(B) II only
(C) I and III only
(D) II and III only
(E) I, II, and III

29. Because of the events and circumstances of the episode, the speaker's attitude toward the little dog becomes

(A) betrayed and hurt
(B) hostile and angry
(C) confused and ambivalent
(D) sympathetic and concerned
(E) determined and aggressive

30. The incident at New York Bay brings the poem to the speaker's mind because

(A) the speaker is feeling sentimental and lonely
(B) the poem describes the weather at the bay
(C) the speaker is reminiscing about a former friend
(D) the poem describes the cruelty of an unrequited friendship
(E) the speaker was stimulated intellectually by the fear of the event

31. In the poem, the speaker seems to view the natural elements as

(A) dangerous threats
(B) symbols of deception
(C) understandable harshness
(D) unexplainable phenomena
(E) unrelenting challengers

32. In the second stanza of the poem, the "bitter sky" is an example of

(A) alliteration
(B) paradox
(C) irony
(D) synaesthesia
(E) digression

Questions 33–38 are based on the following passage.

She heeded nothing of what I said; but
when she had tasted the water and drawn
breath, she went on thus—
line 'I tell you I could not forget it; and I took
(5) my revenge: for you to be adopted by your
uncle, and placed in a state of ease and
comfort, was what I could not endure. I wrote
to him; I said I was sorry for his
disappointment, but Jane Eyre was dead: she
(10) had died of typhus fever at Lowood. Now act
as you please: write and contradict my
assertion—expose my falsehood as soon as
you like. You were born, I think, to be my
torment: my last hour is racked by the
(15) recollection of a deed which, but for you, I
should never have been tempted to commit.'
'If you could be persuaded to think no more
of it, aunt, and to regard me with kindness and
forgiveness—'
(20) 'You have a very bad disposition,' said she,
'and one to this day I feel it impossible to
understand: how for nine years you could be
patient and quiescent under any treatment, and
in the tenth break out all fire and violence, I
(25) can never comprehend.'
'My disposition is not so bad as you think. I
am passionate, but not vindictive. Many a
time, as a little child, I should have been glad
to love you if you would have let me: and I
(30) long earnestly to be reconciled to you now:
kiss me, aunt.'
I approached my cheek to her lips: she
would not touch it. She said I oppressed her
by leaning over the bed, and again demanded
(35) water. As I laid her down—for I raised her and
supported her on my arm while she drank—I
covered her ice-cold and clammy hand with
mine: the feeble fingers shrank from my
touch—the glazing eyes shunned my gaze.
(40) 'Love me, then, or hate me, as you will,' I
said at last, 'you have my full and free
forgiveness: ask now for God's and be at
peace.'

Jane Eyre
by Charlotte Brontë

33. The element of conflict in this passage
revolves around

(A) two women angry over past wrongs
(B) a woman struggling against death
(C) two people both wanting child custody
(D) a woman and her conscience
(E) a mother and her daughter

34. The woman probably complained that Jane
"oppressed her by leaning over the bed" (lines
33–34) because she

(A) really felt ill
(B) was communicating her continued hatred
(C) was protecting Jane from contagion
(D) needed fresh air and space
(E) wanted to intensify Jane's sense of guilt

35. After the woman's admission concerning the
adoption, why would Jane behave as she does?

(A) She never really wanted to be adopted.
(B) She is anticipating developing a new
relationship.
(C) She is building on the bond of their old
relationship.
(D) The woman is very ill and Jane truly
forgives her.
(E) Jane is pretending forgiveness to achieve
family status.

36. The tone of lines 10–13 can be considered

(A) reconcilable
(B) propitious
(C) audacious
(D) collaborative
(E) synergetic

37. As evidenced in the second paragraph, the
woman's attitude is best summarized by which
of these statements?

(A) She blames the uncle for abandoning
Jane.
(B) She blames Jane for the wrong she did to
Jane.
(C) She is truly sorry and accepts full
responsibility.
(D) She is released from her tormented guilt.
(E) She assumes that Jane will forgive her.

38. Of the following list of literary devices, which one is used in line 24 to describe Jane's personality?

(A) Simile
(B) Personification
(C) Synecdoche
(D) Metonymy
(E) Metaphor

Questions 39–45 are based on the following poem.

A Winter Piece

From frozen climes, and endless tracts of snow,
From streams which northern winds forbid to
    flow,
What present shall the muse to *Dorset* bring,
line Or how, so near the pole, attempt to sing.
(5) The hoary winter here conceals from sight
All pleasing objects which to verse invite.
The hills and dales, and the delightful woods,
The flow'ry plains, and silver-streaming floods,
By snow disguis'd, in bright confusion ly,
(10) And with one dazzling waste fatigue the eye.
    No gentle breathing breez prepares the spring,
No birds within the desert region sing,
The ships, unmov'd, the boist'rous winds defy,
While rattling chariots o'er the ocean fly.
(15) The vast *Leviathan* wants room to play,
And spout his waters in the face of day.
The starving wolves along the main sea prowl,
And to the moon in icy valleys howl.
O'er many a shining league the level main
(20) Here spreads itself into a glassy plain:
There solid billows of enormous size,
Alps of green ice, in wild disorder rise.

                            by Ambrose Philips

39. The speaker alludes to which of the following as the occasion for this poem?

(A) A letter home from a boy to Dorset
(B) A poet speaking to "the muse" (line 3)
(C) A poet examining the winter landscape for inspiration
(D) Dorset inviting a writer to describe a blizzard
(E) An individual learning to sing about nature

40. The speaker presumes in lines 3–7 that

(A) the speaker is inspired by the "frozen climes" (line 1)
(B) Copenhagen is a center for poetic activity
(C) the speaker is expecting a gift to be sent
(D) ideas for writing poetry are influenced by geographic location
(E) the speaker is seeking a gift to purchase

41. All the pairs listed below reflect the main contrast developed in the poem EXCEPT

(A) "frozen" (line 1)…"flow" (line 2)
(B) "winds" (line 2)…"sing" (line 4)
(C) "conceals"…"sight" (line 5)
(D) "forbid" (line 2)…"invite" (line 6)
(E) "delightful" (line 7)…"confusion" (line 9)

42. As used in line 10, the literary role of "waste" is as a(n)

(A) allusion to well-lit areas
(B) ironic allusion
(C) symbol of man's problems
(D) hyperbole
(E) play on words

43. Why is there a lack of "room to play" (line 15)?

(A) Frozen water
(B) Severe wind
(C) Encroaching civilization
(D) Severe drought
(E) Snowdrifts

44. The "glassy plain" (line 20) is an example of which of these literary devices?

(A) Antithesis
(B) Personification
(C) Metaphor
(D) Synecdoche
(E) Metonymy

45. The use of "rattling" in line 14 is a phonic device known as

    (A) oxymoron
    (B) onomatopoeia
    (C) alliteration
    (D) euphony
    (E) low style

Questions 46–52 are based on the following passage.

    In order to gain a clear and just idea of the design and end of government, let us suppose a small number of persons settled in some

line sequestered part of the earth, unconnected
(5) with the rest; they will then represent the first peopling of any country, or of the world. In this state of natural liberty, society will be their first thought. A thousand motives will excite them thereto; the strength of one man is
(10) so unequal to his wants, and his mind so unfitted for perpetual solitude, that he is soon obliged to seek assistance and relief of another, who in his turn requires the same. Four or five united would be able to raise a
(15) tolerable dwelling in the midst of a wilderness, but one man might labor out the common period of life without accomplishing any thing; when he had felled his timber he could not remove it, nor erect it after it was
(20) removed; hunger in the mean time would urge him to quit his work, and every different want would call him a different way. Disease, nay even misfortune, would be death; for though neither might be mortal, yet either would
(25) disable him from living, and reduce him to a state in which he might rather be said to perish than to die.
    Thus necessity, like a gravitating power, would soon form our newly arrived emigrants
(30) into society, the reciprocal blessings of which would supersede, and render the obligations of law and government unnecessary while they remained perfectly just to each other; but as nothing but Heaven is impregnable to vice, it
(35) will unavoidably happen that in proportion as they surmount the first difficulties of emigration, which bound them together in a common cause, they will begin to relax in their duty and attachment to each other: and
(40) this remissness will point out the necessity of establishing some form of government to supply the defect of moral virtue.

Common Sense
by Thomas Paine

46. The first sentence is presumably

    (A) an opinion asserted through lack of experience
    (B) establishing a cause-and-effect relationship
    (C) a statement of fantasy
    (D) the speaker's summary statement
    (E) establishing structure of an analogous model

47. According to the speaker, society is mostly a result of

    (A) disease
    (B) hunger
    (C) necessity
    (D) vice
    (E) duty

48. In the last paragraph, the speaker wants the reader to believe that

    (A) laws are reciprocal blessings
    (B) law and government are products of virtue
    (C) government is based on common causes
    (D) overcoming difficulties gives place to vice
    (E) establishing government binds people together

49. The speaker distinguishes "to perish" from "to die" (lines 26–27) to emphasize

    (A) the inevitability of death for men who are alone
    (B) the disabilities that result from living alone
    (C) the demoralizing effects of loneliness
    (D) the destructiveness of disease and accident
    (E) the ironic situation misfortune places upon a man who is alone

50. In the final paragraph, gravity is used as a vehicle in a simile to explain

(A) why men form societies
(B) the reciprocal blessings of societies
(C) the obligations of law and government
(D) why laws are necessary
(E) defects of moral virtue

51. The "assistance and relief" discussed in line 12 are the result of

(A) a need for structure
(B) excitement over change
(C) natural liberty
(D) law and government
(E) wants and loneliness

52. As used in line 24, "mortal" indicates

(A) fatal or causing death
(B) of this world
(C) causing death of the soul
(D) affecting with fear of death
(E) implacable

Questions 53–60 are based on the following passage.

Act I
Scene, an Apartment at Charlotte's
CHARLOTTE and LETITIA discovered

LETITIA.   And so, Charlotte, you really think the pocket-hoop unbecoming.

CHARLOTTE.   No, I don't say so. It may be
line   very becoming to saunter round the house of
(5)   a rainy day; to visit my grand-mamma, or to
go to Quakers' meeting: but to swim in a
minuet, with the eyes of fifty well-dressed
beaux upon me, to trip it in the Mall, or
walk on the battery, give me the luxurious,
(10)   jaunty, flowing, bell-hoop. It would have
delighted you to have seen me the last
evening, my charming girl! I was dangling
o'er the battery with Billy Dimple; a knot of
young fellows were upon the platform; as I
(15)   passed them I faltered with one of the most
bewitching false steps you ever saw, and
then recovered myself with such a pretty
confusion, flirting my hoop to discover a jet

black shoe and brilliant buckle...how my
(20)   little heart thrilled to hear the confused
raptures of—"Demme, Jack, what a delicate
foot!" "Ha! General, what a well-turned—"

LETITIA. Fie! fie! Charlotte [stopping her mouth], I protest you are quite a libertine.

(25) CHARLOTTE.   Why, my dear little prude,
are we not all such libertines? Do you think,
when I sat tortured two hours under the
hands of my friseur, and an hour more at my
toilet, that I had any thoughts of my Aunt
(30)   Susan, or my cousin Betsey? though they are
both allowed to be critical judges of dress.

LETITIA.   Why, who should we dress to please, but those who are judges of its merit?

CHARLOTTE.   Why, a creature who does
(35)   not know Buffon from Soufflé—Man!—my
Letitia—Man! for whom we dress, walk,
dance, talk, lisp, languish, and smile. Does
not the grave Spectator assure us that even
our much bepraised diffidence, modesty,
(40)   and blushes are all directed to make
ourselves good wives and mothers as fast as
we can? Why, I'll undertake with one flirt
of this hoop to bring more beaux to my feet
in one week than the grave Maria, and her
(45)   sentimental circle, can do, by sighing
sentiment till their hairs are grey.

LETITIA.   Well, I won't argue with you;
you always out-talk me: let us change the
subject. I hear that Mr. Dimple and Maria
(50)   are soon to be married.

CHARLOTTE.   You hear true. I was
consulted in the choice of the wedding
clothes. She is to be married in a delicate
white satin, and has a monstrous pretty
(55)   brocaded lutestring for the second day....

The Contrast
by Royall Tyler

53. The girls' conversation has

(A) a didactic tone
(B) metaphoric constructions
(C) an abundance of slang
(D) poetic diction
(E) highly structured syntax

54. In line 54, "monstrous pretty" is an example of which of the following literary devices?

   (A) Hyperbole
   (B) Apostrophe
   (C) Simile
   (D) Oxymoron
   (E) Alliteration

55. The context reveals that seemingly the "Spectator" (line 38) refers to a(n)

   (A) bodyguard
   (B) accepted authority on conduct
   (C) nanny
   (D) religious leader
   (E) overseer

56. Charlotte (lines 12–18) probably

   (A) accidentally fell
   (B) was at a wild, drunken party
   (C) was surprised by the boys' admiration
   (D) is defensive of her conduct
   (E) deliberately tripped

57. The word "swim" (line 6) connotatively suggests

   (A) too large clothing
   (B) moving through water
   (C) to be in a flood
   (D) smooth motions
   (E) covered with liquid

58. A "libertine" (line 24), as used in this context, is someone who is

   (A) morally unrestrained
   (B) a freedman
   (C) a skeptic
   (D) politically involved
   (E) a member of a sect

59. Maria is characterized by Charlotte as

   (A) headstrong
   (B) lacking in social skills
   (C) emotional
   (D) older
   (E) argumentative

60. From her comments, Charlotte indicates that she

   (A) has a fiance
   (B) is as sentimental as Maria
   (C) resents Letitia's attitude
   (D) concurs with the "Spectator"
   (E) was insulted by Letitia's protest

ANSWER KEY: PRACTICE TEST SEVEN

1. E	7. C	13. A	19. D	25. E	31. C	37. B	43. A	49. E	55. B
2. E	8. B	14. C	20. C	26. D	32. D	38. E	44. C	50. A	56. E
3. E	9. E	15. C	21. E	27. B	33. D	39. C	45. B	51. E	57. D
4. B	10. C	16. D	22. D	28. E	34. B	40. D	46. E	52. A	58. A
5. C	11. D	17. A	23. C	29. A	35. D	41. B	47. C	53. C	59. C
6. A	12. B	18. B	24. C	30. D	36. C	42. E	48. D	54. D	60. D

TO OBTAIN YOUR RAW SCORE:

_____ divided by 4 = _____
Total wrong   Score W

_____ minus _____ = _____
Total right   Score W   Score R

Round Score R to the nearest whole number for the raw score.

HOW DID YOU DO?

55–60 = Excellent
44–54 = Very Good
35–43 = Above Average
23–34 = Average
15–22 = Below Average

INDEX

NOTES

NOTES

NOTES

NOTES

NOTES